Anthropology

The Study of People

HARPER'S COLLEGE PRESS

A DEPARTMENT OF HARPER & ROW, PUBLISHERS

New York | Hagerstown | San Francisco | London

ANTHROPOLOGY

The Study of People

John Friedl

THE OHIO STATE UNIVERSITY

John E. Pfeiffer

A Leogryph Book

Project Editor / Ken Friedman
Assistant Editor / Sharon Rule
Design and Chapter Opening Art / Jane Byers Bierhorst
Production Manager / Eileen Max
Composition / Baskerville, by Typographic Services, Inc.

Cover design and photograph by Jane Byers Bierhorst (textile from the San Blas Islands, Panama)

Line art on pages 90–91, 268, 269, 305 by Jane Byers Bierhorst

LC no. / 76-56667
ISBN no. / 06-167412-5

Contents

IV/ANTHROPOLOGICAL LINGUISTICS

V/CULTURAL ANTHROPOLOGY

sixteen   Religion, Magic, and Witchcraft   425

seventeen   Economics, Politics, and Social Control   455

VI/CONCLUSION

Preface

In the pages that follow, you will be introduced to the field of anthropology—first the scope and method of the discipline, then some of the basic areas of study within it, and finally some of the ways in which it can be meaningful to us in understanding and solving the problems of living in the twentieth century. One of the goals of the book is to help us see ourselves from a new perspective. The sections dealing with physical anthropology and archeology help place modern humankind in the framework of biological and cultural change. The success of efforts to promote social change depends on a fuller understanding of tensions and modes of thinking and acting which were established millions of years ago. The fact that much contemporary behavior has deep and ancient roots is not a cause for pessimism. It does not imply that change is impossible. But it does imply that changes should be based on knowledge, on observation and analysis, rather than on preconceived notions about human nature.

The sections dealing with cultural anthropology help place our society in the context of other societies of the world. They also stress the diversity of our own society. The anthropologist James Spradley has pointed out that as kids brought up in America we learn the myth of the melting pot—that groups with cultural differences come together and work out their differences, becoming truly "American," in a way of life best for everyone. This myth leads us to the goal of *preserving* our institutions to restore bygone days, with a sense of commitment to old values. What we learn in anthropology should lead us to question this goal as we expose the myth of *one* American culture shared by all Americans. We should be aware of differences and seek to change institutions or create new ones to deal with differences.

Throughout the book we have tried to avoid the use of jargon. As practically everyone knows, jargon doesn't always make very much sense. We have all learned, for example, to follow the news reports by wading through official government language which frequently bears no relation to reality. When we hear of "differential affluence" we immediately think "poverty." "Famine" becomes "distribution of hunger," while our polluted environment is spoken of in terms of "ecological variability." Many other social problems are likewise masked in official jargon which does not really cover them up, but somehow seems to make them more palatable.

Social scientists, including anthropologists, are as guilty as anyone of the gamesmanship involved in the use of jargon. Sociologists have all but defined away the problems of drug addiction, prostitution, gambling, etc., by calling them "victimless crimes." Anthropologists, in an attempt to describe the life of the slum dweller in terms that do not convey middle-class values and judge by middle-class standards, have invented the term "culture of poverty." We can thus set out to describe this life style in purely objective terms, immune from the criticism that we are taking slum dwellers to task for not living like suburban middle-class families, but we never really solve the problem we are describing. We simply make a word game out of it.

A few terms are obviously necessary, because anthropologists deal with concepts that are not commonly used by others. Where they are necessary we have tried to define them in context, and have also included them in an end-of-chapter glossary.

Another goal of the book has been to present the most up-to-date information, especially in the rapidly changing field of physical anthropology. Examples of new and exciting discoveries covered in the text are: the fossil evidence for the australopithecine precursors of the genus *Homo*; new developments in the study of primate behavior, including the studies of orangutan, gorilla, and macaque social organization, and chimpanzee learning ability; the evolution of language, including the studies of brain anatomy and physiology, and child language acquisition; and the intensive studies of fast-disappearing hunting and gathering groups in the Arctic region, the Kalahari desert, and Australia.

The book contains a number of pedagogical features we hope will be useful to students. At the end of each chapter, there is first a summary and a glossary. Then there is an article that serves as an illustration of the material in the chapter. Also at the end of the chapter is a listing of references to other anthropological works that bear upon the material discussed, so that the reader can follow up on any topic that may have stimulated interest. Within the chapter itself are two other features. Short biographical sketches, accompanied by photos, focus on the anthropologists whose work is central to the field being discussed. The two-page features called "Controversy" take an in-depth look at the discipline of anthropology in process, presenting both sides of issues of fact and interpretation that are still under debate.

The final judgment on any textbook must come from the students and instructors who use it. The experience of many teachers, and the responses of many students, have aided the authors in shaping this present book. But we should be sorry to see the feedback process stop here. No book is perfect, and there is always room for improvement in later editions. Therefore, we would be grateful for any comments from students or instructors who use this book, and who feel strongly enough about its strengths and/or weaknesses to take the time to drop us a note. For convenience, please send all such comments to John Friedl at the Department of Anthropology, The Ohio State University, Columbus, Ohio 43210.

Acknowledgments

It would be impossible to name all the people who in one way or another contributed to the making of this book. Many of the investigators whose work is discussed in the text have been generous in supplying photographs, information, and on occasion hospitality at the sites of their research. Others have helped in numerous ways. Special appreciation is due to Lewis Binford, University of New Mexico; François Bordes, University of Bordeaux; Desmond Clark, University of California, Berkeley; Irven DeVore, Harvard University; Clark Howell, University of California, Berkeley; Mary Leakey and the late Louis S. B. Leakey, The National Museums of Kenya; Hallam Movius, Harvard University; George Schaller, New York Zoological Society; and Sherwood Washburn, University of California, Berkeley.

Another kind of help is equally important in its own way, for in the preparation of such a wide-ranging work as this, financial assistance becomes essential, and appreciation is due to the foundations and other organizations that help to finance the necessary research, travel, and "thinking time." In this regard, John Pfeiffer wishes to acknowledge especially the assistance of the Wenner-Gren Foundation for Anthropological Research, the National Institute of Mental Health, and the Carnegie Corporation of New York; John Friedl wishes to acknowledge a grant from the National Institutes of Health (Training Grant GM-1224) for supporting his research.

John Friedl would also like to acknowledge particular intellectual debts: to Robert Carola, who played an important role in the development of the cultural anthropology sections of this book; to Gerald Berreman, whose influence will be evident in Chapter 19; and to Jack Potter and George Foster, both of whom contributed much to the thinking that underlies Chapter 18. Finally, there are all those past students to whose interest and questions formal gratitude is offered in so many prefaces. In this case the gratitude is not merely formal, but very real.

Anthropology

The Study of People

chapter one

Anthropology is the most scientific of the humanities, the most humanist of the sciences.

ERIC WOLF

Introduction/WHAT IS ANTHROPOLOGY?

Most people have never heard of anthropology, or if they have it was in the context of an exotic foreign tribe or the "missing link" between monkeys and humans. So we will begin by defining the subject of this book.

We used to say that anthropology was simply the study of man. Then women's liberation came along and quite rightly pointed out that we studied women as well, and so now we might say, tongue in cheek, that anthropology is the study of man—embracing woman. But that leaves us with much too broad a range for a single discipline. After all, don't all of the social sciences, including sociology, psychology, eco-

nomics, political science, and even some aspects of geography, study people? Yet anthropology is different from these other approaches to the study of the human species. In this chapter we will see exactly what the differences are, and how anthropology fits in with the total picture of social science. We will also look at the various sub-disciplines within the field of anthropology, to see what different kinds of anthropologists are interested in, and how these interests fit together and build upon one another to give us an overall perspective for understanding all of human behavior.

The actual word "anthropology" is derived

Early European encounters with peoples such as this Amahuaca Indian from Peru, produced bizarre tales of their "savage" ways of life.

from two Greek words, *anthropos* (man) and *logos* (study or science). Anthropologists are interested in all aspects of the human species and human behavior, in all places and at all times, from the origin and evolution of the species through its prehistoric civilizations, down to the present. And remember too that understanding behavior is the ultimate aim of anthropology—not just economic behavior, the focus for the economist, or political behavior, the central concern of the political scientist—but all behavior.

Anthropology is as old as humanity. The term might be a relatively recent innovation, and the acceptance of anthropology as a discipline worthy of a separate department within the university hierarchy is less than a century old. But people have always been curious about themselves, and have always asked anthropological kinds of questions and sought the answers to them in the spirit in which anthropologists conduct research today. Of course, we have no written records to take us back to the dawn of the human species, but for as far back as we do have records they indicate that people had an interest in human nature and the diversity of people in the world around them. Herodotus, the Greek historian who is sometimes referred to as the Father of History, might also be called an anthropologist. In writing of the events of his time, he raised a number of questions concerning the differences between the Greeks and other peoples in surrounding areas. He theorized that the peoples encountered in the Persian Wars must represent an earlier stage of Greek society. Later, Thucydides, in his accounts of the Peloponnesian War, made an even stronger statement of the evolutionary notion that these barbarians represented a stage through which Athenian culture had already passed in its rise to civilization. Thus he was not only comparing different groups, but also actually engaging in analysis of the differences, trying to understand

Masked dancers of the Kwakiutl Indians illustrate the importance of ritual within every human society.

what caused them and what could explain the current state of his own society.

In Western Europe the age of exploration and discovery that followed the decline of the Middle Ages saw an increased interest in the varieties of peoples and customs around the world. As Europe broke out of its isolationist shell, explorers, adventurers, missionaries and travelers came into contact with curious societies. These people lived in ways the Europeans found so strange that they felt compelled to describe these practices in utmost detail. The more contact they had with different cultures around the world, the more information was collected and published, creating greater and

greater interest in the study of such people. Although some of the early attempts at scientific analysis of foreign customs and peoples of radically different appearance were quite unsophisticated—almost comical in retrospect—still they represented the beginning of a movement that was to lead to the development of anthropology as a science. Are these strange peoples in the far corners of the earth related to each other, and to us? How do their customs compare to ours? And how can we explain such a wide range of behavior? These were the kinds of questions for which early anthropologists sought answers. Never mind that today such questions seem a bit simplistic. If they hadn't been posed and their answers sought, we wouldn't be any farther along today than our fifteenth-century forerunners were.

It wasn't until the nineteenth century that anthropology really began to gel as a separate discipline. The roots of anthropology as a science can be found in the natural sciences of that period, including biology, botany, and zoology. There had been a long tradition in these fields of recording all of the diverse species of animals and plants discovered in different parts of the world and trying to figure out the relationship between them, as well as how they had grown apart and changed in different directions—in other words, their evolution. Charles Darwin's early research is typical of this era. During his five-year voyage around the world in 1831–1836, he gathered the information about animal and plant varieties that ultimately enabled him to put together his ideas about evolution. But Darwin was only one of many naturalists who were piecing together the story of evolution, and while he was concentrating upon plants and animals, others were concerned specifically with the human species. Anthropologists were asking the same kinds of questions about similarities and differences in human behavior that biologists and zoologists were posing about animals. Thus the early scientific interest in different cultures paralleled the natural sciences, and might even be seen as an extension of them.

Today anthropology has become a broad-based study, much more than any other scientific discipline. This is perhaps its greatest value, for it provides insights into a wider variety of problems than any other field. Anthropology includes a broad range of approaches derived from both the natural sciences (biology, zoology, anatomy and physiology) and the social sciences (sociology, psychology, human geog-

Culver Pictures, Inc.

Charles Darwin *(1809–1882) is the man most often linked with the discovery of evolution. Actually, his major contribution to evolutionary theory was the concept of* natural selection. *He saw organisms in competition against the forces of nature, and those best able to cope with the pressures survived at the highest rate and passed on their advantageous characteristics. Although Darwin did not mean for his theory of evolution to be applied to human social and cultural change, it was proposed by many social scientists that cultures evolved in a struggle for survival, just as animals did. This doctrine, inappropriately called "Social Darwinism," was ultimately used to justify white supremacist policies of western nations in their domination of Third World peoples.*

raphy, economics, political science and history). Anthropology is able to relate all of these disciplines to its quest for an understanding of human behavior, and draws upon all of them to interpret the way in which biological and social factors enter into the picture.

THE BRANCHES OF ANTHROPOLOGY

In the sense that anthropology is interested in human behavior, it is no different from any other social science. The main distinctions are found in the method by which anthropology pursues that interest, and in the number of different perspectives—corresponding to the different branches of anthropology—that contribute to the overall understanding. Each branch of anthropology studies one special aspect of behavior, and although each works separately with its own methods and its own subject matter, together they form a whole that is distinct from all other social sciences.

Physical Anthropology

Physical anthropology is that branch concerned with our relationship to other animals, our derivation and evolution, and our special physical characteristics such as mental capacity, shape of the hand, and erect posture. In other words, *physical anthropology studies human evolution and human variation.* It is closely related to several of the natural sciences: zoology, in terms of the relationship to other animals and the overall place of the human species in the process of evolution; biology, in terms of the evolution of humans from early pre-human forms; anatomy and physiology, in its concern with the structure of the human body, the relationship of the various parts, and the operation or function of these different parts; genetics, in its concern with human variation in the world today; and even psychology, in the investigation of our mental makeup and its relationship to behavior.

Physical anthropology considers the human species as a biological entity, as well as a social animal. Some physical anthropologists are concerned primarily with the past forms of pre-

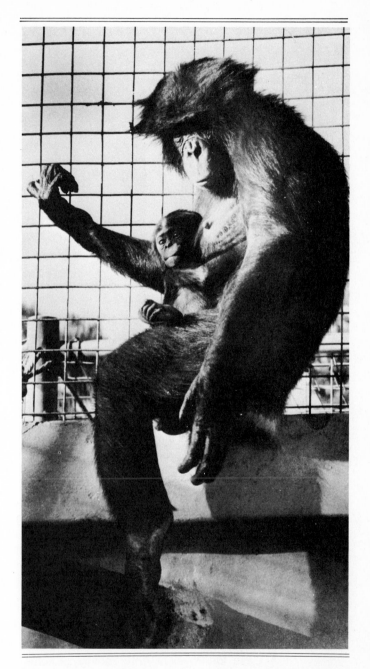

Primatology is the branch of physical anthropology which studies our near relatives, such as this pigmy chimp and her infant. Early hominids may have looked something like this.

A calf is being bled by these cattle-raising nomads. The physiological inability to produce lactase is rarely found among these tribesmen.

human and early human species, an area of study known as *fossil man*. Others concentrate on the similarities and differences between the various primate species, which include not only humans, but apes and monkeys as well. This area of study is called *primatology*. A third area, known as the study of human variation, or *anthropological genetics,* deals with contemporary as well as historical variations among populations of humans. It is concerned with questions such as the adaptation of a group of people to a specific climate, the natural immunity of some peoples to certain diseases, and the all-important question of racial difference.

A Case for Physical Anthropology: Lactase Deficiency / Whether studying fossils, primates, or human genetics, physical anthropologists are especially concerned with the in-

teraction between the biological and cultural aspects of humans, as the following example illustrates. In much of the world, a physiological condition renders a large proportion of the adult population unable to digest milk properly. An enzyme called *lactase* is necessary for the successful assimilation of milk by the body; without it milk causes the bowels to become distended, and cramps, gas and diarrhea ensue. All infants have the capacity to produce this enzyme, but in only two population groups do most adults have it. If this seems odd to us, it is because the United States contains one of these two populations: white Euro-Americans. (The other is comprised of the Nilotic Negroes of East Africa.) Significantly enough, these populations are the two main groups who practice dairying in which raw milk is consumed. Of course, other groups also raise cattle. Typically, however, they do not drink milk as such, but rather consume it in other forms that can be digested more readily. The Chinese, for example, engage in dairying, but adult Chinese generally do not consume raw milk. Even though inability to produce lactase is not universal among Chinese people, cultural values and taste preferences in China lead even those who can digest raw milk to shun its use.

The conclusion we can draw from this study is that there has been a parallel development in cultural and biological evolution. Cultural values in the form of a taste preference for milk changed, and were associated with genetic change leading to the lack of ability to drink milk. Which came first is not clear, although it seems probable that the taste for milk did not change until the capacity to assimilate it was lost genetically. At any rate, the study leads us to an understanding of the interplay between genetic change and cultural change, and between biology and culture. It also teaches us the interesting lesson that our American habit of drinking milk throughout our adult lives is not only shown to be unnecessary by the experience of other peoples, but also it is undesirable in most cultures. The common advertising slogan "you never outgrow your need for milk" would certainly not be effective in most of the rest of the world!

By studying human nature, the variety of peoples in the world today and in the past, and the relationship of the human species to others, we are better able to understand why we behave the way we do. The physical anthropologist gives us valuable information about the uniqueness and limitations of our physical structure. Why are we different from apes, for example? It is important to know the ramifications of being able to walk with erect posture on two feet, rather than having to use our hands to steady ourselves.

By providing answers to the question of what makes human beings unique among animals, physical anthropology gives us the first clues in understanding human behavior. It tells us what the basis for that behavior is, and what the limitations upon it are. It tells us why we should expect others to behave within those limitations, and what variations are possible. In other words, physical anthropology spells out the limits of human behavior. Perhaps most important of all, physical anthropology teaches us that no matter how much diversity we might find in the world around us, the most remarkable fact is not how different people are but how similar they are, and this is a crucial lesson in getting along in the world today.

Archeology

A second branch of anthropology is *archeology*, sometimes called *prehistory* because it is concerned primarily with the period of human

Archeology focuses on the physical remains of early societies, such as these pre-Aztec structures near Mexico City.

existence prior to written records or historical accounts. The aim of this branch is to reconstruct the origin, spread and evolution of culture. It does this by examining the remains that we are fortunate enough to find of past societies. Archeology differs from physical anthropology in that it is concerned with culture, while physical anthropology focuses on the biological aspects of the human species.

Archeologists assume the same task as other kinds of anthropologists, in that they also are concerned with understanding as much as possible about human behavior. The difference is that their materials are the unwritten records of past societies. They do not have the opportunity to sit down with living members of those societies and go over the various interpretations of what is found. They cannot observe living people, but must abstract from the remains of the past whatever they can about how the people once lived.

Furthermore, what remains is not necessarily what the people might have left had they wanted to give archeologists a clear picture of what was important to them. Prehistoric people did not have the historians of the future in mind when they emptied their garbage or buried their dead; they did not provide a time capsule containing records of their total life. Thus archeologists must not only interpret the materials left behind within the limited context in which they are found, such as a burial site or a refuse pit, but must attempt to paint a picture of an entire way of life without hope of ever recovering physical evidence for much of it. They can make an inventory of the kinds of tools or

Ruins are being excavated at Pergamum, an ancient Greek site located in what is now western Turkey.

Artifacts such as this stone axe provide us with more information about technology than any other aspect of culture.

weapons early humans used at a particular site, and can note which ones are found most frequently, how they are made, and so forth. But archeologists can never know what a tool meant to the individual who used it. They can only make guesses based upon personal involvement with the items of their own material culture.

Archeology offers an opportunity to look into the distant past of the human species and try to reconstruct the picture. But it is like doing a jigsaw puzzle with most of the pieces missing, and without the picture of the finished puzzle on the box to work from. Archeologists have a few things that fit together, they can guess about many others, but they really don't have enough to put it all together with complete confidence. Every new piece found fits somewhere, though, and they never know when the next piece will give the key to interpreting a

whole new section of the puzzle of life in prehistoric times. That is the challenge and the excitement of archeology.

A Case for Archeology: The Domestication of Corn

/ One of the great puzzles of prehistory, on which archeologists all over the world are hard at work, is the evolution of agriculture. Fifteen thousand years ago all people hunted wild game and gathered wild plants to provide themselves with food. Then changes took place that led to the development of agriculture. Over a period of thousands of years, wheat, barley, corn, rice and other crops were *domesticated* in different regions. Humans had begun to take greater control of their own destiny, planting instead of depending on nature. The problem for archeologists is what, when, how, and why all this took place. Richard S. MacNeish, an archeologist at the Peabody Museum in Andover, Massachusetts, has spent the last thirty years investigating the origins of the domestication of corn.

Before 1945, it was believed that corn developed from a wild grass in either Mesoamerica, South America or southeast Asia. In 1948, tiny corn cobs were uncovered in the American Southwest and in the following year in Mexico. With the help of Paul Mangelsdorf, a botanist at Harvard University, MacNeish identified and classified each sample of early corn. They all proved to be primitive, but clearly domesticated, varieties of corn. MacNeish continued his search for the source of domesticated corn over the next ten years, excavating first in northern Mexico then further south in Honduras and Guatemala. Some sites yielded early corn but not the wild ancestor.

Since similar types were being uncovered in northern and southern Mesoamerica, MacNeish concluded that corn was probably domesticated somewhere in the middle, in central Mexico. He also knew that dry regions held

Agricultural themes are prominent in the religious rituals of many societies, reflecting the importance of agriculture in human development. Here, an Indian corn dance.

the best possibilities for preservation of plant remains and that the ancestor of corn was probably a highland grass. Thus the search narrowed to dry, highland valleys in the region south of Mexico City. Three areas fit this description, one of which was the Tehuacan Valley. MacNeish's first trip there turned up little of interest. With the help of students who knew most of the caves in the area, his second attempt proved more successful. Working with two guides, he examined one promising rock shelter at which he decided to dig.

From January 21 to January 27 (1960) the three of us, Pablo, Hector and I, tested the cave. Behind a large rock roughly in the center of the shelter we dug a two-meter square to a depth of about two meters, using trowels. We took out everything, including loose dirt, by bucket loads and put it through a mesh screen to be sure that we missed nothing. Slowly we peeled out the successive *strata*. . . . On January 27 after lunch, Pablo, working well down in the preceramic stratum, recovered a tiny corn cob no more than an inch long. Only half believing, I took his place in the bottom of the pit. After a short period of troweling and cleaning away dirt with a paint brush, I uncovered two more tiny cobs. We held in our hands possible ancestors to modern domesticated corn.

This impression was confirmed a month or two later by Mangelsdorf when he examined the cobs at Harvard University. . . . These were the oldest corn cobs that had ever been found.[1]

1. Richard S. MacNeish, Introduction. In Douglas S. Byers (Ed.), *The Prehistory of the Tehuacan Valley*. Austin: University of Texas Press, 1967, Volume I, p. 5.

MacNeish had uncovered the beginnings of modern corn but the search for a complete understanding of the process of domestication is still going on today.

Anthropological Linguistics

The study of language from an anthropological perspective forms a third branch of the discipline. Of course, linguistics also exists as a separate discipline, but anthropologists who specialize in this area are particularly concerned with the relationship between language and cultural behavior. They ask questions about language from the point of view of the human species, rather than trying to describe the language or its structure. The central focus is still people, and they regard language as a part of our social world.

One area of interest in anthropological linguistics deals with the origin of language. This could just as well be a question for physical anthropologists. There is presently an important controversy over what form of fossil hominid was the first to have the capacity for speech. Another area of concentration deals with the role of language in the context of social behavior. This is a relatively new field known as *sociolinguistics,* and it is concerned with the way we use the language we speak (or the different forms of it, for we all know different variations of the English language that we use in different contexts).

A third area of interest in anthropological linguistics is the study of *folk categories,* that is, the units of meaning into which a language breaks up the universe. Every language conveys much of the content of a culture in the items it labels with separate words. For instance, in one

To these Eskimo children, variations in the texture of snow are extremely important, a fact reflected in their language.

Eskimo language there are 12 separate and un-related words for wind and 22 words for snow. That is, 22 different kinds of snow are recognized and given names that are not simply different forms of the same root word, but different words altogether. It is apparently not significant to us who speak English that there are minute variations in snow types, and so we use adjectives to describe these variations—wet snow, powder snow, etc. Occasionally we use different words, such as sleet or hail, but that is about all the elaboration we have in our language. On the other hand, we have an extremely large vocabulary to deal with complex technological aspects of our culture, which are more significant to us. Let's look at the automobile, for example: we have sedans, convertibles, coupes, fastbacks, wagons, buses, vans, trucks, and so on down the line. Obviously we would not expect a member of a society where automobiles are not found to understand our distinctions—to him, a car is a car, period. But then to us, snow is snow, period.

A Case for Anthropological Linguistics: Color Categories / One of the most intriguing examples of folk categories is the colors different languages recognize. We all know that there is an extremely wide range of colors in nature. In fact, if you have ever tried to decide what color to paint your house, and have pondered over dozens of color charts at the paint store, you know just how many variations of the same color there can be. We can look at ten different shades of green, and even though we recognize that they are different, we will still call them all "green," thus lumping them into the same category. An interesting experiment is to take finely graded colored samples (such as come on a custom-mixed paint color chart) ranging from green to blue, containing perhaps thirty different shades. If you look at both extremes, you will say with ease that one is green, and the other blue. The hard part comes in drawing the line somewhere in the middle between one shade and another, saying that one belongs to the category "green" and the other to the category "blue." In fact, sometimes we get around this problem by inventing another category, "blue-green."

In our language we know that this category "blue-green" is really not a separate category but merely a convenient designation for the transition between two categories. We know this because we do not have a separate word for it. This indicates to us that while blue and green are significant, the transition from one to the other is less significant. But in another language, spoken by people of another culture, there could easily be a word which designates "blue-green" as a separate category. Certainly there is no reason why this could not be done—after all, isn't green a transition between blue and yellow?

Here we begin to see how language can affect the way we order the universe, by establishing artificial categories into which we plug all of our perceptions. The point is that they *are* artificial; our culture, through our language, determines the way we order our perceptions. Now if one language can set up more categories for color than we have, certainly another can set up fewer such categories. The Navaho term for green includes blue and purple. Zuñi Indian language uses a single term for both yellow and orange. Some Indian languages have words for only two or three colors, and everything with color that the individual sees is placed in one of these two or three categories—for example, gray, blue, or red. What about yellow, orange, green, etc.? Are these people color blind? Of course not, only the distinction between, say, green and blue is not significant. It doesn't mean that they can't tell the difference between a cardinal and a robin. It simply means that they don't classify them as different in terms of color, although they certainly perceive color

Body adornment differs widely among different cultures. This New Hebrides Islander would probably consider traditional Japanese dress and cosmetics very strange and unattractive.

differences. In contrast, English has as many as 3,000 words to refer to different shades of color—scarlet, vermillion, crimson, maroon, murrey, magenta, cerise. Where we divide the spectrum and establish arbitrary boundaries around colors is a purely subjective cultural factor, and it is important to know that it can vary from one culture to another. The expression of such differences is found in the language spoken by each group.

Cultural Anthropology

We come now to cultural anthropology. Actually, in a strict sense, we could also include archeology and anthropological linguistics under this heading, for they are both concerned with culture—the archeologist with the cultures of prehistoric peoples, and the linguist with a specific aspect of culture in both the past and the present. But since these sub-disciplines are generally acknowledged to be separate from the major focus of cultural anthropology, it is better to accept this distinction.

Cultural anthropology, as the term is commonly used today, generally refers to the study of existing peoples. Further, it is based upon a comparative approach, that is, its aim is to understand and appreciate the diversity in human behavior, and ultimately to develop a science of human behavior, through the comparison of different peoples throughout the world. In the United States we frequently make a distinction between two areas of cultural anthropology: *ethnology* and *ethnography*. Ethnology is the comparative study of culture and the investigation of theoretical problems using information about different groups. Ethnography is simply the description of one culture, and is not a comparative study. In other words, an ethnological study is based on two or more ethnographies; the latter form the raw material for the former. To avoid confusion we will use the term *cultural anthropology* to cover both of these, but you should know what the terms mean since you will certainly come across them in other anthropological readings.

Thus there are two main tasks involved in the work of the cultural anthropologist, to describe the cultures of other peoples and to compare them. As we saw in the example of color categories, such description is not an easy task, since putting something from another cultural context into the concepts and words available in the English language is not always possible. In fact, we might consider an anthropologist's description of a foreign culture somewhat of a cultural translation—the aim of the description is to make it clear to the reader just what it is like

American Anthropological Association

Alfred Louis Kroeber *(1876–1960) was for many years considered the dean of American anthropology. His early work centered on the study of American Indians. Kroeber was also interested in the process of culture change, and relied heavily upon history to support his studies of the growth of civilization. In* Configurations of Culture Growth *(1944) he compared six major civilizations of the world through historical records in an attempt to find a regular pattern of change. He was inclined to see history and anthropology as much more closely related disciplines than many of his colleagues, as reflected in* An Anthropologist Looks at History, *published after his death.*

to live as an individual of the other culture lives. Accurate descriptive work, cultural translation, is the essential basis for comparative studies, which after all are crucial to understanding human behavior.

Since, as we have admitted above, other social

If there are obvious similarities between these women of two different cultures, there are also obvious differences. Early anthropologists tended to stress the differences.

sciences have the same goal as anthropology, what makes cultural anthropology different? Perhaps the most obvious difference is that the scope of anthropology is much broader than that of any other social science. Economics deals only with economic behavior, political science only with political behavior, and so on. Cultural anthropology, on the other hand, is concerned with all of those areas, from a comparative perspective, and especially with the interrelationships between these areas of behavior in any particular society. It overlaps with every other social science in at least some areas of interest, yet it still retains its individuality.

The distinction between history and anthropology was a subject of intense debate for many years. Is anthropology, after all, merely the study of human history in all its various forms? Although this debate has subsided, one cannot truthfully say that it has been com-

Here the similarities between this modern American woman and the Cree Indian woman are very obvious. Modern anthropology studies the common traits shared by all cultures as well as those peculiar to each group.

pletely resolved. No anthropologist can work without an awareness of the past, of what the particular sequence of events was that led to the situation under study. In describing another culture, or in comparing aspects of two cultures, the anthropologist dares not ignore the historical background.

Yet there is no doubt that history and anthropology are distinct disciplines. For one thing, historians focus on past events, and their investigation of values, motivations, and behavior is directed toward the explanation of why things occurred the way they did in one particular sequence of events. Anthropology seeks to generalize from such historical explanations. It is not enough to say that history is more of an art, while anthropology is more of a science, or that anthropologists use history more than historians use anthropology. Indeed it is difficult to distinguish history from anthropology in many respects, except to point out the historian's retrospective approach to past events, in contrast to the cultural anthropologist's emphasis upon understanding contemporary events as they are happening.

Perhaps the most difficult distinction to make between disciplines in the social sciences is between cultural anthropology and sociology. One important difference is that sociology is concerned more with the study of our own society, while anthropology is a comparative discipline which focuses on all societies at all times. Sociology is primarily interested in the present; anthropology deals just as much with the past. These distinctions, however, are growing less valid every day, as anthropologists begin to adopt sociological methods and sociologists adopt the comparative approach of anthropology.

Another way of looking at the difference between the two disciplines is to note that sociology tends to be more quantitative, while anthropology tends to be more qualitative. What this means is that sociology generalizes from

Contact between different cultures can result in an exchange of ideas. What advantages or disadvantages might arise from bottle-feeding among the Eskimos?

broad surveys of large numbers of people. The anthropologist relies upon a close and intimate knowledge of just a few members of the total group to form impressions, and although they might not be valid for the society as a whole (i.e., quantitative), they are certainly valid in greater depth for the small sample studied (i.e., qualitative). The anthropologist will spend weeks tracing a lead to the answer to a particu-

lar question, mainly because of an intense personal involvement in the study. The sociologist, on the other hand, cannot afford to become so deeply involved in the surveying of a larger sample of the society. This is not to condemn either discipline, but rather to point out a basic difference between them. Perhaps it is best illustrated by the comment of one anthropologist, who, in poking fun at the expensive studies of inner-city social problems conducted at a great social distance, described a sociologist as someone who spends $50,000 to find a whorehouse. (One wonders if after all this expense, the sociologist might not be led into the parlor only to find an anthropologist playing the piano.)

Thus probably the major difference between anthropology and sociology lies in the methods used in each discipline. Anthropology uses the intensive method of study, while sociology is more inclined to employ a survey approach, less intensive but more inclusive.

A Case for Cultural Anthropology: Culture and Psychology / Recently John Friedl, anthropologist and co-author of this text, was asked to serve as a consultant to the child psychology division of the medical school at Ohio State University where he teaches. As Friedl describes it: a case had been referred to them, and the director of this particular program thought it would be of interest to see whether there were other cultures in which the behavior under question was acceptable. The case concerned a foster mother who was discovered to be practicing strict toilet training upon an infant placed in her care. The infant was only a few weeks old, and training at such an early age is certainly an unacceptable practice in American culture. As the story unfolded, it became apparent that the woman took good care of the child, showed it warmth and affection, and in all other ways was an ideal foster parent. However, the fact that she had trained the infant to defecate while she

Toilet-training practices vary greatly among different cultures, as this scene from a European nursery school indicates.

held it over newspaper alarmed the officials assigned to the case.

I was asked, as consulting anthropologist, to cite references to early toilet training in other cultures. Apparently the medical personnel in charge of the program thought that if an anthropologist could show that such a pattern was practiced elsewhere, it would make it more acceptable to the local officials. I was able to cite a few examples of early training, although none so early as the case under consideration. But the main thrust of my presentation to the group called together to hear the case was that in order to understand the practices of the mother, we had to know something about her own culture and her background. If in fact this was a common practice within the subculture of American society in which she was raised, and if it was successful (that is, if people raised this way turned out to be healthy, normal individuals in American society), then we should not

question its validity. I was even able to get the case worker to admit that the mother herself had been trained this way, and that several other members of her family had also been raised with similar practices.

The difference between psychology and anthropology comes through strongly in this example. My approach as a cultural anthropologist was to see if what was considered deviant in our own middle-class American culture was in fact acceptable in another cultural setting. However, I am sorry to say that I was overruled by the psychologists (and Freudian psychiatrists). Their main concern was whether the child was being raised according to the norm in American society, and they took that norm to be the way they, as white, middle-class Americans, were raised. Deviation from that norm was strictly forbidden, no matter whether it might be perfectly acceptable and common practice in another culture, or in another American subculture. They spoke of the "harm" that would come to the child, as if the absence of a strict middle-class upbringing were the kiss of death. There was discussion among the Freudians in the room about the problem of the child mixing up his sexual identity, and the failure of the mother to relate to anything but an "empty" baby. But no sense of relativity was evidenced; no mention was made of other deviant practices in other cultures, which ultimately produced healthy, normal adults.

HOLISM: THE TRADEMARK OF ANTHROPOLOGY

We conclude this chapter on the definition and scope of anthropology by pointing out again that anthropology, as distinct from all other social sciences, is an integrated approach including the study of the physical nature of the human species, our past, our unique capabilities as well as our limitations, and the tremendous variety as well as the startling similarities across cultural boundaries. The anthropological approach is sometimes called *holistic*, because it integrates so many different areas of concern. It is not just the study of economic behavior, or the structural relations between social groups. It is the attempt to understand all of human behavior in all contexts, in all places, and at all times. And it does this by drawing from many different disciplines. The anthropologist is a person who brings to a study a wide background from many different fields. Biology and physiology are frequently required for graduate students in physical anthropology; geology, geography, ancient history, and sometimes even architecture are necessities for the archeologist; and cultural anthropologists have come from all walks of life. To study peasant society cross-culturally we should know something about agriculture; to study personality cross-culturally we must have a background in psychology; and so on for every possible area of concentration within cultural anthropology.

Let us point this up by using an example. Suppose we want to make a comparison of the way in which children learn their culture in two different groups. Because the primary topic of concern is culture, we would logically assume that cultural anthropology would be the place to start. But when we look deeper, we find that the cultural anthropologist must rely upon training in any one of a number of different fields to insure the success of such a study. For example, we must know something about psychology, to understand the processes of the formation of personality and character in the early years of infancy. We must have expertise in at least some areas of elementary education to comprehend the process of training in the early years. It would help if we had some knowledge about the physical nature of the infant, which could be obtained through studies in physical anthropology, to enable us to tell what the physical process of child training was all about. Linguistics could provide a better understanding of the ways in which a child learns a language and the kinds of patterns that are instilled upon the infant's brain at that early age. And in addition to all of these outside factors, we must be knowledgable in the culture of each group, to understand the attitudes of parents toward children in the societies (e.g., do they favor males over females? do they expect males to accept different roles than females at an early age? do parents treat their children with much care and personal attention or do they leave them relatively unattended?)

As this example illustrates, holism in anthropology is the attempt to get the whole picture, to put it all together and to apply knowledge from many different spheres to the understanding of any aspect of behavior. It is this holistic approach, more than anything else, that distinguishes anthropology from other social sciences. And it is this holistic approach that makes an anthropological study so difficult to carry out and at the same time so rewarding when it all fits together.

Summary

The study of anthropology is commonly divided into four major subfields. *Physical anthropology* deals with the evolution of the human species, the relationship between humans and other primate species, and the variety of human forms in the world today. From the physical anthropologist we learn of the capabilities for bearing culture that distinguish humans from all other animals. *Archeology* is the branch that takes up where physical anthropology leaves off, reconstructing the evolution of culture (rather than the evolution of the capacity for culture). The archeologist is necessarily limited by the kinds of information that remain thousands of years after the people have lived. *Anthropological linguistics* is a third field within anthropology that treats the relationship between language and culture, and the functions of language and communication for human behavior. *Cultural anthropology* is the study of human societies, both present and past. It seeks to describe the wide variety of cultural forms throughout the world, and to compare and analyze them, with the ultimate goal of understanding human behavior.

Anthropology is related to other social sciences in that all share a common interest in understanding human behavior. It differs, however, in that it is a broader approach, whereas economics focuses upon economic behavior, political science upon political behavior, etc. This multifaceted approach, called *holism*, is the trademark of anthropology. Holism is the ability to consider a wide variety of viewpoints in understanding human behavior—for example, the physical anthropologist's knowledge of the human capacity for culture, the archeologist's information about past examples of human behavior, the anthropological linguist's assumptions about the role of language and communication in social relations, and the cultural anthropologist's understanding about the variety of culturally accepted behavior in the world today. All of these approaches contribute to the breadth of anthropology as a discipline.

Glossary

adaptation The result of a group of animals or plants being molded by the environmental forces or pressures (climate, altitude, etc.) in a specific region.

anthropological genetics The area of physical anthropology that studies the contemporary and historical variations among human populations.

anthropological linguistics The sub-discipline of anthropology that is concerned with the relationship between language and cultural behavior.

anthropology The discipline that utilizes the holistic approach to investigate all aspects of human behavior, in all places and at all times.

archeological site Any location that demonstrates disturbance from human activity or that provides material and physical evidence of human activity.

archeology The sub-discipline of anthropology whose aim is the reconstruction of the origin, spread and evolution of culture.

cultural anthropology The sub-discipline of anthropology that is based upon a comparative approach to the study of existing peoples.

domestication The process of breeding wild plants and animals, selecting for specific traits appropriate to food sources for humans.

ethnography A branch of cultural anthropology that is concerned with the description of a single culture.

ethnology A branch of cultural anthropology that is concerned with the comparative study of culture and the investigation of theoretical problems using information about different groups.

evolution The natural process in which forces from the environment (climate, altitude, etc.) mold the characteristics of groups of plants and animals.

folk categories The units of meaning into which a language breaks up the universe.

fossil man The area of physical anthropology that studies the past forms of pre-human and early human species.

holistic approach The approach utilized in anthropology that integrates a wide variety of disciplines in the study of human behavior.

lactase deficiency A physiological condition found in much of the world in which a large proportion of the adult population is unable to digest milk properly.

physical anthropology The sub-discipline of anthropology concerned with the study of human evolution and human variation.

primate The order of mammals that includes monkeys, apes and humans.

primatology The area of physical anthropology that investigates the physiological and behavioral similarities and differences among the various primate species—monkeys, apes and humans.

sociolinguistics A branch of anthropological linguistics that studies the way that people use language or communicate in different situations (e.g. lecturing to a class, speaking to one's parents, talking to friends).

Additional Reading

Physical anthropology

Poirier, Frank E.

1974 In Search of Ourselves. An Introduction to Physical Anthropology. Minneapolis: Burgess Publishing Company.

A complete basic introduction to contemporary physical anthropology.

Archeology

Deetz, James

1967 Invitation to Archeology. Garden City, N.Y.: The Natural History Press.

A brief and very readable book covering archeology.

Hole, Frank, and Robert F. Heizer

1973 An Introduction to Prehistoric Archeology. Third Edition. New York: Holt, Rinehart and Winston.

A thorough textbook surveying the field of prehistory.

Anthropological linguistics

Carroll, John B.

1964 Language and Thought. Englewood Cliffs, N.J.: Prentice-Hall.

A short analysis of language as it functions in a cultural context. Although it leans toward a psychological approach to the study of language, this book is useful in understanding some of the basic questions of anthropological linguistics as well.

Hymes, Dell (editor)

1964 Language in Culture and Society. New York: Harper & Row.

A collection of articles on topics in anthropological linguistics, including a survey of classical approaches and modern methods.

Cultural anthropology

Downs, James F.

1971 Cultures in Crisis. Beverly Hills: Glencoe Press.

A short, entertaining and extremely well-written book, although necessarily superficial because of its short length.

Keesing, Roger M., and Felix M. Keesing

1971 New Perspectives in Cultural Anthropology. New York: Holt, Rinehart and Winston.

One of many cultural anthropology textbooks which benefits from the use of lengthy ethnographic examples to illustrate the major points raised in the text.

Practical information on anthropology as a career

Bernard, H. Russell, and Willis E. Sibley

1975 Anthropology and Jobs: A Guide for Undergraduates. Washington, D.C.: American Anthropological Association.

A survey of career opportunities outside college teaching open to those with degrees in anthropology.

Fried, Morton H.

1972 The Study of Anthropology. New York: T. Y. Crowell.

A practical guide to some of the most common questions concerning the study and practice of anthropology.

chapter two

Physical Anthropology/ EVOLUTION, GENETICS, AND THE PRIMATES

The human story is known in broad outline. The *hominids* of some 15 million years ago were small, hairy, apelike creatures—considerably less than humans, but something more than *apes*. They probably used tools such as digging sticks and clubs, and walked upright a good deal of the time as they carried their tools. Furthermore, although the odds are that monkeys and apes lived almost exclusively on plant foods in those days as they do now, the tool users depended increasingly on meat.

But they did not specialize in meat eating as did lions and other carnivores. They could not afford to. They became omnivores, exploiting practically every available source of food. Their earliest campsites date back two to three million years ago and contain animal bones, the only direct traces of their diets which have endured through the ages—mainly the remains of rodents and other small animals, with an occasional big-game kill. Like most present day hunter-gatherers, however, they probably lived mainly on plant foods.

Survival demanded intimate knowledge of a wide variety of natural resources. Our ancestors learned early when fruits and nuts would be ready for eating, and they also learned to be there at the right time to obtain their share, and preferably more, in competing with other plant eaters. They also became more efficient predators. Such developments put a premium on planning and cooperation, on a steadily increasing ability to observe, remember and analyze. Adult males, generally the least sociable members of groups, had to share their kills with one another and with those back at the home base. One result was a notable expansion of the brain. The hominids of a million to half a million years ago had brains about twice as large as their predecessors, brains in the modern size range.

The rise of *Homo sapiens* is intimately connected to the rise of increasingly complex social organizations and methods of obtaining food. We began to dominate the scene more than a hundred thousand years ago, and ever since then cultural evolution has been moving at an accelerating rate. The final phase of prehistory, the last twentieth or so of the long journey from the pre-humans who were newcomers on the savanna to modern humans, includes the oldest traces of religion and art. It also includes the high point in the development of the hunt, mass killing of herd animals on a many-band or tribal basis—and then the decline of the hunt as an activity essential to the community, a decline that began some ten thousand years ago with the invention of agriculture. The invention of writing about four or five millennia later may be taken as the official end of prehistory.

Something unprecedented happened during the course of these and subsequent events, something that acquires special meaning in the light of all that happened before the appearance of *Homo sapiens*. Our position with respect to other animals involves two apparently contradictory truths, namely, that we have much in common with them (far more than is generally realized) and, at the same time, that we represent another order of being. *Homo sapiens* is not merely a new *species* but the pioneer of a very recent and entirely new kind of evolution.

MENDELIAN INHERITANCE AND GENETICS

All previous species, some 500 million of them including extinct as well as surviving forms, evolved by *mutation* and *natural selection*. And all species, from whales and giant redwood trees to tadpole-shaped viruses so small that several billion of them would fit comfortably into a sphere no bigger across than the period at the end of this sentence, share certain basic similarities at the molecular level. They transmit their characteristics from generation to generation in the form of *genes*, discrete and highly organized molecules of hereditary materials.

Gregor Mendel, an Austrian monk, was the first to provide evidence for the existence of discrete particles of hereditary material. Curiously, his work was completed in 1865 but was not noticed by the scientific world until 1900. Mendel experimented in his monastery garden with pure strains of common peas that differed from each other in a single observable characteristic—height, color, skin texture. With the care and patience possible only in special environments, he hand-fertilized the egg-containing flowers of each plant with the selected pollen. In one experiment pure tall plants were crossbred with pure short plants. The resulting second generation offspring were all tall. Next, these hybrids were self-fertilized, that is, the eggs of the plant were fertilized only with the pollen of the same plant. To his surprise, Mendel found that the third generation offspring included both tall and short plants. Here was proof that hereditary characteristics must be determined by particulate factors, what we call genes today. While we now know the situation to be somewhat more complex—some traits are controlled by combinations of genes and some genes control more than one trait—the simplicity of Mendel's experiments stands as a monument to scientific method.

Gregor Mendel (1822–1884) *received his first botanical training grafting trees in the small family orchard. Upon entering the Augustinian monastery at Brünn, Austria in 1843, Mendel began experimenting with crosses of flowers. By 1865 he had discovered the constant ratios of reproduction of different types of pea plants—short and tall, yellow-seeded and green-seeded, and so on—which gave him the foundation for his laws of inheritance. He reported his findings to the Brünn Society for the Study of Natural Science, but the learned gentlemen were unimpressed by the work of this unknown amateur. However, they did agree to publish the report. Two years later Mendel was made abbot of his monastery. He now had little time for scientific work, and his findings dropped out of sight. A generation later they were rediscovered independently by three different scientists working in the field of genetic research, and their value was finally recognized.*

Just as all species are subject to the Mendelian Laws of Inheritance, the molecular basis of inheritance, *nucleic acid,* is also the same. *DNA* (short for deoxyribonucleic acid), the most common form of nucleic acid, generally exists as a double helix, two long atomic chains interconnected and tightly coiled into a spiral-staircase structure, and including large numbers of the same four nitrogen-containing units or "bases": adenine (A), thymine (T), cytosine (C) and guanine (G). The order in which these units occur in the DNA of a particular species determines the nature of that species. The bases may be thought of as a kind of genetic alphabet, letters which spell out the specifications for organisms and control the manufacture of proteins that form living tissue. Imagine a series of DNA molecules, genes, uncoiled to produce long strings of bases attached to one another. A string starting "C-A-G-T-T-A . . ." might represent the instructions for the shaping of an amoeba, and strings starting "C-G-A-C-T-G . . ." and "A-C-C-T-A-G . . ." might represent a monkey and an elephant respectively.

A complete collection would consist of some 10 million such strings, one for each existing species. Furthermore, although there are some exceptions, the general rule is that the more complicated an organism, the longer the genetic message it transmits to its offspring, that is, the more instructions required for the building of future generations. The total length of all the DNA chains in some viruses is less than 1/25,000 of an inch, while it takes about five feet of DNA to make a human.

Living things are designed to maintain the integrity of the hereditary material. DNA molecules with their bases in proper order are duplicated over and over again in generations of sperm and egg cells, and the duplicating mechanisms may work with wonderful accuracy. They may turn out a million or more highly organized molecules in succession, each one made up of large numbers of atoms and each one a faithful copy of the one before it, within close biological tolerances.

This process reflects a massive conservatism, a way developed over the ages to preserve things as they are, to maintain distinct and unchanging species. Powerful biological forces resist change. No other process is so nearly flawless; certainly no man-made machine can approach it. But sooner or later a slip-up or mutation occurs on the genetic assembly line. It may be a very small change, perhaps a missing base or two, or a "misspelling" in the form of a change of base order, say, from "A-T-C-G" to "A-G-C-T."

A DNA molecule departs in a small way from inherited genetic blueprints, and that makes all the difference. If there were no slipups, no mutations, the highest form of life today, assuming life could exist at all, might be a single-celled organism. *Evolution,* the "force like a hundred thousand wedges" which so impressed Darwin, exists simply because nothing is perfect, not even the chemical operations of heredity which represent the closest thing to perfection, to infallible reproduction, that we know of.

EVOLUTION

Darwin didn't comprehend the sources of variation in the natural world but he carefully noted that in species after species, the general rule is that each individual differs from all others. The second point of his evolutionary scheme was that sooner or later, either through population growth or change in the environment or both, the resources necessary for survival will grow scarce. When this happens, there will be a competition for available resources and those that are better adapted to the environment because of their minor variations will tend to survive at a higher rate. Third, the survivors pass on the advantageous characteristics to their offspring, so that the next generation reflects

their makeup to a greater extent. In this way evolution proceeds slowly, over many generations, reflecting minor variations in the adaptation of a population to a changing environment.

New species are formed in isolation, under conditions which permit a measure of independent evolution. In the vast majority of cases the first steps take place when geographic barriers, anything from a stream that cannot be crossed to an ocean or a range of mountains, divide parts of the ancestral species from one another. The separated subpopulations begin to undergo distinctive changes. Mutations which would formerly have spread throughout the ancestral population now accumulate on either side of the barrier. Furthermore, since no two environments are exactly alike, the adaptations called for on either side of the barrier will differ in certain respects.

After a sufficient number of generations, the net effect is two genetically incompatible subpopulations. The differences between them have become so great that even if the barrier is removed or crossed they can no longer interbreed to reproduce generations of viable offspring. At this point a new species is said to have arisen. Darwin studied such a case on the Galapagos Islands which lie in the Pacific Ocean about 600 miles from the nearest mainland, the coast of Ecuador. The islands included more than a dozen species of finches, all of them the descendants of a colony of finches presumably blown to the islands by high winds, and all of them sufficiently isolated from one another to develop different adapations and species status.

The Galapagos finches provide a good model for the origin of species throughout the course of evolution, and new species are still being formed. For example, the Grand Canyon in northern Arizona separates two kinds of squirrel, one on the northern side of the canyon and the other on the southern side, which had a common ancestor centuries ago and have been

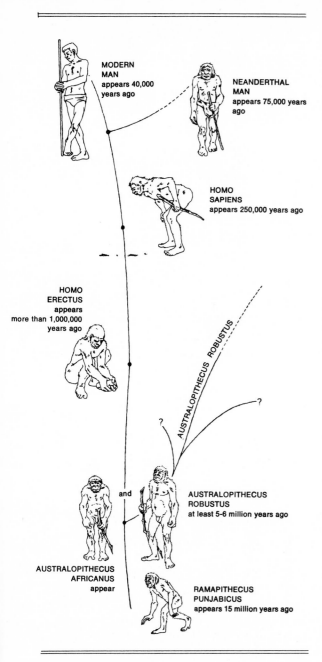

diverging genetically ever since. It is a question whether the squirrels have yet become sufficiently different to be classified as different species, but they seem to be heading in that direction.

HUMAN VARIATION

Humans have also developed subspecies variations, or *races,* in response to geographic barriers and variations in the environment. The modern study of race began with the attempt of nineteenth century scientists to isolate pure races of man. Implicit in this concept of racial purity was the assumed superiority of one race over another. Johann Friedrich Blumenbach, a German anatomist, was among those who believed that modern populations were the degenerated offspring of crosses among pure racial types. For Blumenbach and many of his followers, the study of human variation became a quest for criteria that would allow mankind to be sorted into discrete categories.

Readily visible biological characteristics were first used in these researches. Skin color retained its popularity as a sorting criterion from ancient times, despite the difficulty in objectively measuring differences in shade. And the German biologist Ernst Haeckel suggested that hair form—straight, wavy, curly and so forth—might be used. It was however, found that the hair of an individual can change during his lifetime. Paul Topinard, a French anthropologist, proposed the use of the nasal index; human populations could be divided into wide-nosed, medium-nosed and narrow-nosed categories.

Regardless of their ability to differentiate living populations, none of these features was applicable to the analysis of human fossils. Measurements of the skull provided a solution. The skull is preserved more often than any other part of the body and was believed by

MODERN MAN
appears 40,000 years ago

NEANDERTHAL MAN
appears 75,000 years ago

HOMO SAPIENS
appears 250,000 years ago

HOMO ERECTUS
appears more than 1,000,000 years ago

AUSTRALOPITHECUS ROBUSTUS

and

AUSTRALOPITHECUS ROBUSTUS
at least 5-6 million years ago

AUSTRALOPITHECUS AFRICANUS
appear

RAMAPITHECUS PUNJABICUS
appears 15 million years ago

One possible path of human evolution in Europe, Asia, and Africa from about 70 million years ago to the present.

Controversy

The Inheritance of Acquired Characteristics: Science vs. Politics

Darwin was not the only naturalist to attempt to explain the origin of species. Years before the publication of Darwin's work, a Frenchman named Jean-Baptiste Lamarck proposed a theory to account for speciation which differed radically from Darwin's idea of natural selection. For Darwin, the environment was a force which eliminated from the breeding population those individuals not adapted for survival. Lamarck assigned to the environment a very different role. He thought that environmental factors changed the structural characteristics of organisms, and that these changes were then passed down to succeeding generations. For example, Lamarck would have explained the long neck of the giraffe as the result of generations of giraffes stretching to eat the leaves of tall trees. Each giraffe passes a slight gain in height to its offspring which then begins its career a little taller. Lamarck's theory is very attractive because it allows each individual to contribute its share to the adaptation of the species. No individual is denied the brass ring of evolutionary success—provided, of course, that it is willing to stretch for it.

Emotionally satisfying though it may be, Lamarck's theory has one serious drawback—it is totally unsupported by any verifiable evidence. We know today that organisms pass on their characteristics through their genes, and that the genetic material is unaffected by any alteration in the organism's gross anatomy. Even without this knowledge, however, one can easily demonstrate the fallacy of Lamarck's theory. Boxer dogs, for example, have their ears bobbed and their tails cropped as puppies. Yet each generation of boxers is born with long tails and floppy ears. For hundreds of generations, Jewish males have been circumcised. Nevertheless, the male infants have foreskins which differ not in the least from those of groups that do not practice circumcision. That such surgery must be repeated generation after generation surely casts doubt on the possibility that alterations to the body can be transmitted to offspring.

With such evidence against it, Lamarck's theory would appear to have little chance of being accepted. Yet, during relatively recent times, scientists in one of the world's major industrial powers not only embraced Lamarck's ideas, but elevated them to the status of official doctrine.

Trofim Denisovich Lysenko, a Soviet agronomist, was the man responsible for this curious turnabout. Lysenko had developed his own genetic theory which he called "Michurinism," after I.V. Michurin, a self-educated plant breeder. "Michurinism," or, as it later came to be called, "Lysenkoism," was a rejection of everything that had been learned about genetics since the experiments of Gregor Mendel. Lysenko insisted that all parts of an organism played a significant part in the hereditary process and that the chromosomes had no special importance. He defined the basic principle of his thought as "the unity of the organism with its environment." Yet his ideas remained vague, of little scientific value.

Whatever its shortcomings as science, Lysenko's work had the advantage of appearing in the right place at the right time. The agricultural crisis which nearly crippled the Soviet Union during the 1930s caused government officials to become unusually receptive to innovative techniques. On the basis of some poorly performed, largely inconclusive experiments, Lysenko convinced the Party chiefs that his methods would lead to richer harvests. Under the dictatorship of Joseph Stalin, Lysenko became the most powerful figure in Soviet agriculture and the inheritance of acquired characteristics became official dogma. Those who disagreed were relieved of their positions. Lysenko's influence began to wane after the death of Stalin in 1953. In 1965 he lost his post as director of the Institute of Genetics. The era of Lysenkoism was at an end.

How was Lysenko able to become so influential? How was it possible that ideas which blatantly contradicted orthodox genetic theory came to be accepted as gospel within the Soviet Union? These are difficult questions to answer, and yet two factors seem clear. First, Lysenko's ideas were appealing to Soviet leaders, not because of their experimental basis, but because they coincided with the philosophy of Marx and Engels, two avowed Lamarckians. Second, the rise of Lysenko took place in a society in which free scientific inquiry had become impossible. Conformity with official political doctrine had replaced the rigorous testing of hypotheses as a criterion for determining the validity of a theory. Under these conditions, a man such as Lysenko, a man willing to tell the power structure exactly what it wanted to hear, became virtually unstoppable. Nevertheless, it is significant that, even in such circumstances, scientific fact eventually overcame political dogma.

many anthropologists to be immune to environmental and developmental influences. Under the direction of Blumenbach and others, the *cephalic index*, head width divided by head length multiplied by 100, was developed as the most useful skull measurement. Anthropologists travelled throughout the world measuring skulls. In Europe the information was correlated with data on fossil populations and on the distribution of skin color and other physical features.

As with other measures of racial affiliation, however, the cephalic index was eventually shown to be subject to the effects of the environment. In a series of classic studies the American anthropologist, Franz Boas, showed that cephalic index could change from one generation to the next in unmixed populations that had just moved from one geographic area to another. The changes were presumably due in part to the effects of climate and diet on development of the offspring of the migrants.

The search for environmentally inert traits continued. During the first decade of the twentieth century an Austrian doctor, Karl Landsteiner, discovered that although all normal human red blood cells always looked the same under a microscope, they could be divided into several discrete categories on the basis of their chemical reactions with serum, the fluid part of the blood. His work demonstrated that the outer surface of the red blood cell was coated with substances called *antigens*. These antigens came in two varieties, which Landsteiner labeled A and B. Any one individual could have either of these, in which case he would have type A or type B blood; both of them, type AB; or none of them, type O. The presence of these different antigens proved to be under the control of a single gene. Discovery of other human blood differences controlled by other genes followed in rapid succession.

As with cephalic index, blood type data were collected throughout the world to determine

The New York Public Library

Franz Boas (*1858–1942*) *received his early training in mathematics and physics, but became interested in anthropology after a trip to Baffinland, in the Northwest Territories of Canada. In 1899 Boas became Professor of Anthropology at Columbia University. Boas was a leading figure in the attack against the theory of cultural evolution prominent in the nineteeth century. Most evolutionary scales ranked non-Western societies lower than Europeans because they did not have a pattern of monogamous marriage or a fully developed concept of private property or a complex bureaucratic system. Instead, Boas argued strongly for a position of cultural relativism, in which one culture may not be judged or ranked according to the standards of another.*

racial categories. Sometimes the data yielded patterns similar to those obtained for more traditional characteristics such as head and nose form, or skin color; many times they did not.

There are obvious physical differences between these young Masai women and a group of typical American white women. What other variations might an anthropologist also seek to determine?

Some blood characteristics changed from north to south and others changed from east to west. To deal with these variations a new system of terminology was devised. Systematic variation in gene frequency from place to place came to be known as a *cline*.

The investigation into human variation shifted from a search for immutable races to a search for principles of change. It became obvious that the different human subspecies were products of the adaptive responses of populations to different environments. No pure races exist today nor ever existed in the past. Like all living forms, we are subject to the evolutionary pressures that create variations within a species. Sickle-cell anemia, for instance, is associated with regions in which malaria is common. Two features that vary consistently with each other

may be responses to the same environmental component, just as skin color and nose form are in some way associated with the strength of solar radiation. Modern students of human variation define race as any population that differs from other populations of the same species in the frequency of one or more genes. The physical anthropologist is more interested in discovering the relationship between a physical trait and the environment than in defining a fixed number of human races. The aim is to discover why people differ from each other as well as how they differ.

The human species is subject to the same evolutionary forces that shaped and are shaping our fellow species. The geography of our speciation and subspecies formation, the specific barriers that isolated hominid populations at various times in the past, are unknown. But there were barriers, and we are the result of them. Like all other creatures humans arose by the process of mutation and natural selection, and we continue to depend on our genes. The big difference is that in them genetic evolution plays the major role, while in humans cultural evolution has developed to an unprecedented degree.

The things other species need to survive, to escape and kill and adapt, are generally built in as part of their bodies. Their genes determine the growth of fur, horns, scales, claws, wings, and so on. People learn and pass accumulated knowledge as well as genes from generation to generation; we make a wide variety of shelters and weapons and, to an increasing extent, our own environments. It is culture that permits us, a single species, to spread throughout the world, to live and reproduce in high mountain valleys, semideserts, tropical rain forests, and subzero Arctic regions. Of course, genes continue to operate in us, just as learning may play an important role among other species. After all, we inherit our brain, and it, more than anything else, makes us human.

THE PRIMATE ORDER

The development of our world of learning and tradition begins with the physical evolution of the primates, the order that includes monkeys and apes and humans. The earliest primates, small rodent-like creatures known as *prosimians* or premonkeys, quickly took to the trees. It was a time of rising temperatures and extensive forests. Today's dwindling forests, stretches or patches of woodland among cities and deserts and eroded regions and farms, are mere remnants of what used to be. A belt of almost continuous tropical and subtropical forests

thousands of miles wide extended from Seattle and Vancouver to southern Argentina and Chile, from London to Cape Town, from Japan to southern Australia. In the Sahara, woodlands and savannas and lakes existed where desert is now. There were crocodiles, palm trees, and swamps in England, France, and the northwestern United States.

Prosimians had to adapt to a strange new world, a new dimension, among the dense foliage and branches and canopies of the forests, and how they did it is of direct concern to us. Humans are forest creatures to the extent that their basic structures, brain, sense organs, limbs, and reproductive system, evolved in the forests. Later developments generally called for modifications and elaborations of those structures rather than for totally new ones. *Preadaptation*, the evolution of features in one environment which also happen to be as appropriate or even more so in a future environment, has been important in the shaping of all species including *Homo sapiens*.

Life in the trees offered interesting evolutionary possibilities, largely because it was not a complete exploitation of the third dimension like the flight of birds. Flying, which puts a premium on lightness, produced small and highly specialized species. As in man-made flying machines, every fraction of an ounce of weight that could be dispensed with was. One result has been a brain incorporating within a small space circuitry far more compact than anything yet designed by engineers concerned with transistors and solid-state physics. It coordinates elaborate nesting and mating behavior, communications, keen eyesight, and swift maneuvers in space. It gained compactness at the price of some flexibility—bird behavior tends to have a set, stereotyped quality.

Life on the ground provided another range of opportunities. Proceeding at a different pace, it did not need to be as automatic. It permitted the development of big bodies and big

The Fayum Depression in Egypt, shown above, is rich in primate fossils. In the lower photo a fossil is being prepared for removal.

brains and offered the possibility of flexible, adjustable behavior based to a greater degree on learning. There was time on the ground for watching, pausing, and a measure of preparation. Species could prowl about and lie in wait. Lying in wait demands control and the delay of reflexes and, at the same time, a readiness for swift responses. Inhibition achieved through regulatory centers in the nervous system serves

the survival of animals that can bide their time. On the other hand, the challenge and complexity of general navigation, of hunting and escaping, was less on the ground than in free flight.

Life in the trees combined certain features of the earthbound and aerial modes of existence. Species could evolve with brains large enough for considerable learning as well as for the built-in circuitry to subserve advanced visual powers and sensory and muscular coordination. Even more significant, life in the trees introduced a unique feature, a new and chronic psychological insecurity or uncertainty. Air and ground do not suddenly change their properties. As a rule, the ground is reasonably broad and solid, and makes a dependable platform; the air is consistently insubstantial and must be coped with accordingly. The uncertainty in the trees amounts almost to unpredictable changes of state. The environment is full of discontinuities, surprises. Regarded from a ground dweller's point of view, it is roughly equivalent to moving too rapidly to stop through tall dense grasses without being able to see more than a few feet ahead. At any moment, one may suddenly come upon a deep hole directly in the path, too wide to step across. Such hazards may be numerous and scattered at random over the terrain. Frequent swift decisions are required about how far to jump and in what direction. To live in trees is to be confronted continually with analogous emergencies, analogous "holes" in the form of gaps between branches.

Prosimians that took up life in the trees some 70 million years ago had only recently evolved from ground-dwelling insect eaters and were not yet thoroughly adapted to their new environments. They must have lost their footing and fallen rather more frequently than existing species. That meant a high death rate not only as a direct outcome of the accidents themselves but also from predators which are always ready to kill off handicapped individuals. The weeding-out process of natural selection had

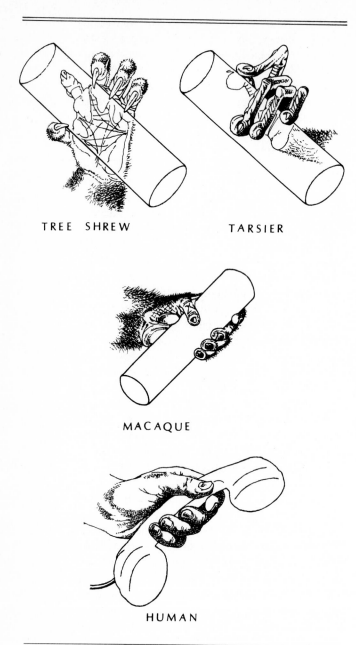

TREE SHREW

TARSIER

MACAQUE

HUMAN

Shrew and primate grips: from claws to human grip with fully opposed thumb. The refinement of the human hand into its present form was an extremely important phase of human evolution.

begun again. Individuals that had fewer accidents than their less fortunate contemporaries lived longer, produced more offspring, and eventually superseded them.

The most fundamental way of preventing falls is to hold on. It is no surprise, therefore, that the most highly evolved characteristic among prosimians, the characteristic that distinguishes them most sharply from their ancestors, was a refined grasping mechanism.

The odds are that primates had fingers practically from the beginning, rather than claws which are characteristic of such primitive species as the present-day long-tailed tree shrews of Southeast Asia. Tree shrews, incidentally, are sufficiently like both rodents and primates so that paleontologists have shifted them from one order to the other several times. (The latest, and probably final, decision is that they are not primates.) Some tree shrews go abroad only at night, and all of them are vicious fighters and voracious eaters, consuming their own weight or more of food each day.

The ancestors of tree shrews, like many other early *mammals* and reptiles, traveled through dense tropical forests mainly along branches too big around for grasping, and held on with claws adapted for digging into bark. The earliest primates, on the other hand, took advantage of a new niche. They moved along narrower motorways that had not been fully exploited, smaller and finer branches which could be grasped by fingers equipped with flattened nails and a thumb capable of moving opposite the other four digits to form a locking grip.

Other changes came with increasing exploitation of forest environments. In preprimate mammals the eyes tended to be small and were located on the sides of an extended and tapering snout. In prosimians the eyes became larger, perhaps as an adaptation to let in more light and improve nighttime vision. Furthermore, they moved forward like twin headlights as the snout retreated, which results in better depth perception, an enormous advantage related to the use of the hands and fingers and to close manipulative work. Although three-dimensional vision is limited to about ten feet, it helps improve accuracy and sure-footedness in leaping from bough to bough. These and other developments were intimately connected with the development of more elaborate brains. In particular, moving about in a rich three-dimensional arboreal environment favored the expansion of the *cerebral cortex* or outer bark of the brain. This structure arose in response to an earlier adventure in evolution, appearing as a rudimentary pinhead-sized patch of cells on the brain surfaces of the first creatures that came out of the sea and took up life on land. But the cortex really began coming into its own with the rise of mammals, as an organ to coordinate highly complex behavior, to analyze messages flowing in from the sense organs, and to send messages of its own to the muscles.

The prosimian brain was still small, the size of a pea in a two-inch skull, but by this stage of evolution its cortex had spread like a gray tide over the brain's surface and consisted of a thin sheet of millions of nerve cells. One cortical area was located toward the front of the head. The most important part of the so-called smell brain, it had a long and respectable history dating back to creatures which guided themselves primarily with the sense of smell. The newer part of the cortex, located at the back of the brain, had expanded to deal with the increasing amount of visual information involved in the successful performance of arboreal acrobatics.

Improved grasping preceded improved "thinking," in line with an ancient evolutionary tradition. Muscle and the special senses such as sight and smell, movement and sensation, are primary—and nerves evolved to serve them. The predominance of the brain, of intelligence and language and discovery, is a very recent development.

The First Monkeys

A major turning point in the history of primates occurred about 35 million years ago. Prosimians had been highly successful for millions of years, multiplying and spreading widely and dominating the vast forests of the times. Then they began declining rapidly, probably because of intense competition from their own kind, from monkeys and apes. Geological changes that had begun long ago, and had helped accelerate the passing of the dinosaurs, were approaching a climax.

The weight of sediments accumulating on the floor of the great sea that stretched from Spain to Malaya caused a sagging in some places, an upward buckling in others, and the appearance of island ridges which were to become the Alps. Mountain-building processes elsewhere gave rise to precursors of the Himalayas, Rockies and Andes.

The tarsier, a small prosimian, has large, frontally-located eyes which provide it with a three-dimensional view of its environment.

An abundant region of this period lay on the Egyptian coast of the Mediterranean, part of the Spain-to-Malaya sea, extending some hundred miles farther inland to cover areas where Cairo and the Pyramids stand today. Coastal plains and savannas merged with thick and humid tropical forests, through which sluggish swamp-lined rivers moved to the shallow sea. The rivers carried the bodies of many animals, and their sands buried the bodies. In relatively recent times lava from the depths of the earth forced its way to the surface, and cracks in the crust formed steep cliffs and ridges.

The region called the Fayum Depression is a wasteland on the eastern edge of the Sahara, one of the world's richest fossil-primate sites. Between the turn of the century and 1960, collectors had found only seven pieces of primate remains in the Fayum, but since 1960 more than two hundred have been found in expeditions headed by Elwyn Simons of Yale University. Among the finds is part of a lower jaw which may represent the earliest-known ancestor of living monkeys, a diagnosis based largely on tooth studies. It had thirty-two teeth, like most present-day monkeys, as compared with thirty-four teeth for most prosimians, and a special four-*cusp* pattern also typical of monkeys. It was probably about the size of a small cat, which is large enough for a prosimian (although not for a monkey) and accords with the general trend toward increasing size among primates.

Within 5 million years monkeys had spread throughout the forests and developed the basis for an entirely different kind of viewing and dealing with the world. Every change was part of a complex of interrelated changes, part of an emerging evolutionary pattern. The sense of smell declined in importance. A generation or two ago, investigators attributed this decline to the notion that it is impossible to make or to follow clear-cut scent trails in the trees, that arboreal primates could not use the sense of smell

to detect sharply defined, coherent and directional patterns in the broken-up context of leaves and branches and gaps between them.

This turns out not to be the case. Primates and other arboreal species mark out clearly defined territories and trails by urinating at strategic spots; they can distinguish friend from foe by odors. But the sense of smell assumed a secondary position in comparison with sight. The olfactory nerve, which carries signals from nose to brain, decreased in diameter, a development indicated by comparative measurements of the holes in the nasal part of the skull through which the nerve passes. The decline is *recapitulated* in human growth: some olfactory-nerve cells begin dying off even before birth, and about half of them have died by middle age.

The hands acquired a considerably richer supply of nerve cells and fibers concerned with the sense of touch. Hands and sense organs evolved together, each development accelerating the other in an involved feedback relationship. Fingers became more and more mobile, capable not only of moving faster but also of assuming a far greater variety of positions. Devices designed originally for grasping and holding on were used increasingly to get food and, even more important, to pick up objects, bring them closer, and turn them around to examine from all angles. The ability to manipulate in this way was new in the history of terrestrial life, and reached a high point in the monkey family.

In fact, from one point of view the monkey's universe was the first to contain full-fledged objects. The very notion of objects, of an environment made up of separate and distinct things some of which could be moved for one's own purposes, came with the simian way of life, with a superbly developed visual sense and advanced manipulative powers. The world was "objectified," fragmented into things which stood out from the background, as it had never been before. Eyes placed at the sides of the head see landscapes as two-dimensional flat sheets and respond to motion across the sheets; they are poorly designed to detect what does not move or what moves slowly and directly toward rather than across the field of vision, such as a stalking tiger.

A more and more complete picture of reality, a revelation, came with the movement of the eyes from a side to an up-front position and, at least as important, with the coming of color vision, which developed to an advanced stage among monkeys. Imagine that you can see things in two dimensions only. You are standing on a plain looking toward a place where animals move among tall grasses and shrubs, and everything has a flat stage-set quality, some of the animals merging in part with the landscape and others well camouflaged and entirely invisible.

Then as you watch you acquire stereoscopic and color vision and the scene changes. The scene begins to take on depth, slowly at first and more rapidly later, as shapes and shadows seem to move forward and backward and assume their natural places. The animals and objects which were visible but not in full perspective begin to stand out more completely as distinct entities. The animals and objects which were invisible in two-dimensional black-and-white viewing become increasingly visible with the appearance of a richer and richer variety of colors, so that even at a distance you get the feeling of almost being among them.

Something like this happened gradually during primate evolution. Color vision helped in detecting predators and later, when primates themselves became increasingly predatory, potential prey. Also, Marcel Hladik and Georges Pariente at the National Museum of Natural History in Brunoy, France, are investigating the possibility that color vision played and plays a role in selecting food. Preliminary studies of monkeys sharing the same forest areas in Ceylon and Panama indicate that they tend to

TREE SHREW

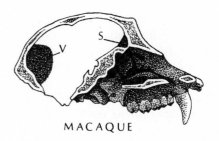

MACAQUE

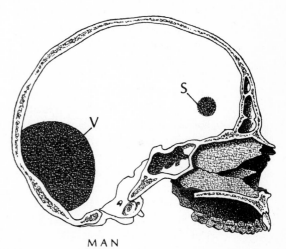

MAN

V - VISION
S - SMELL

As primates evolved, the visual centers of the brain expanded and the olfactory centers became proportionally smaller. The shrew brain is included for comparison.

exploit foods of different colors, and that different species may be sensitive to these preferred colors.

Our visual apparatus is a direct heritage from life in the trees. It has changed little since the days when monkeys were the earth's highest primates. The structure of the monkey brain reflected the increasing emphasis on vision. The cortex expanded considerably, perhaps about two to three times, burying most of the old smell-brain centers. Although a large part of the expansion involved the visual cortex at the back of the brain, other areas were affected; for example, certain areas concerned with the control of finger movements—a tiny strip of cortex on the right side of the brain controlling the fingers of the left hand, a corresponding left-side strip the right hand.

Generally speaking, the finer the detail, the larger mapping area required, a principle which applies to the wrist, arm, foot, toes and other parts that became more mobile among monkeys. Furthermore, as the skin incorporated a richer supply of nerve cells registering the sense of touch, "touch" maps also became larger and more detailed. The expansion of the cortex was the net effect of the expansions of many kinds of maps. It also included larger association areas, areas devoted to the swift analysis of information flowing from many sense organs, those recording the state of affairs within as well as outside the body, and from noncortical brain structures such as the *cerebellum*, attached to the brain stem at the back of the head, which coordinates balance and the tensions of more than 150 pairs of opposing muscles.

The brain, in short, was modified to serve the needs of a new kind of animal. It included structures designed to coordinate at extremely rapid rates the movements of muscles and sets of muscles involved in complex manipulations, climbing, leaping, chasing and being chased. These structures could take orders from the cortex. But they also had to be capable of automatic operations on their own, because monkeys are restless and agile and lightweight, and often move so fast that there is no time for deliberation. Their entire behavior pattern represented and represents a special and highly dynamic adaptation to the forests.

The First Apes

There were other kinds of primates in the trees. The pressure is always on in evolution. Life does not stay put but tends always to become more diverse, to develop new forms adapted to new and varied conditions. Sometimes it is a matter of occupying new places, filling hitherto empty living zones—as, for example, when fish invaded the land more than 350 million years ago, or when prosimians and some rodents took to the trees. In other cases it may involve a new time zone, as when certain species of early mammals exploited the possibilities of nocturnal feeding. Another type of adaptation, another major variation of the primate theme, arose at about the same time monkeys appeared on the scene or perhaps somewhat later. The Fayum Depression has also yielded remains of the earliest-known members of the ape family, *Aegyptopithecus*, which developed a different approach to the forest world and a different type of biological organization.

A large part of the difference involved ways of using branches to obtain food. Most of the food in trees hangs at the ends of branches where it is beyond the reach of many animals and has the best chances of not being eaten. (This is its evolution for survival.) But apes have an ingenious way of getting at such places. A characteristic posture of an ape in a tree is very roughly that of a monkey which has slipped and managed to save itself by hanging on with its hands.

But what represents an emergency for the monkey has become an important form of behavior for the ape. In the structure of their wrists, arms, elbows and shoulders they are adapted for hanging suspended full length under branches as well as for walking on top of them as monkeys generally do. In fact, feeding far out on slender branches is easier for apes than it is for monkeys; monkeys are lighter, but they must go on four feet. Sherwood Washburn of the University of California in Berkeley, a leading investigator of primate evolution and behavior, points out that an ape can distribute its weight strategically among three branches by holding fast with two feet and a hand and reaching out for a succulent piece of fruit with its free hand: "This is a distinctive behavior pattern of apes which can hang comfortably with one arm and do things with the other arm. Only an ape could have any possible reason for designing a bus or a subway train with straps."

But no ape is as good at swinging along through the trees as the gibbon. Using its powerful arm and shoulder muscles, it can propel itself thirty feet or more in one fluid movement, one of the most spectacular aerial maneuvers among nonflying animals. But in the course of evolving such talents, it had to stay small for the same reason that birds are small, to assure lightness and maximum mobility. (Gibbons are lighter than many monkeys, weighing only about ten to fifteen pounds.)

If all apes had gone the way of the gibbon, today's most advanced primates would be master aerialists rather than intellectuals. Some species followed another line of development, involving an evolutionary compromise between body weight and acrobatic skill. The most obvious advantage of being big was to discourage predators. The smallest prosimians and monkeys are fair game for the most abundant carnivores, small carnivores like snakes and eagles and jackals. (If they have any choice, large carnivores do not bother to eat such small game.) But only leopards, lions and other big cats take on orangutans and chimpanzees or the largest monkeys such as baboons. And nothing goes

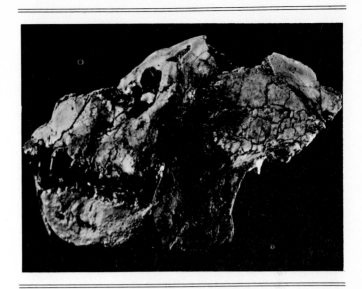

Aegyptopithecus is one of the earliest known apes.

after gorillas but man, who goes after everything.

There may have been another reason for becoming bigger. Another possibility, suggested by Robert Martin of University College, London, is based on observations of present-day species. Monkeys generally use food more efficiently than apes, grinding plant materials more thoroughly and thus permitting more complete digestion. Some species have compartments in their stomachs which are specialized to break down leafy foods; others, like the baboon, aid processes of digestion by softening food in cheek pouches before swallowing it. When competition for food is intense, as it might well have been 15 million years ago, any advantage in obtaining energy from food pays off handsomely in terms of survival.

So apes may have become bigger in self-defense, a point reinforced by the fact that in Asia, where arboreal monkeys are few, apes have remained relatively small. In Africa *gorillas* and their ancestors may have specialized in

Larger body size is an important evolutionary adaptation. This baboon is more than a match for most predators.

highland-mountain living, while *chimpanzees* foraged mainly in lower woodland-orchard regions. Big primates roamed more widely and spent more time on the ground as well as in the trees, partly because they had less to fear and partly because they needed more food and had to travel farther for it. In other words, they encountered a wider and more varied environment.

Their evolving anatomy permitted a greater variety of movements. New nerve pathways developed in consequence—the cerebral expression of new possibilities. New cortical pathways appeared. The possible routes along which nerve signals may pass from sense organs to muscles increased enormously. The cortex is in part an organ of analysis, a dense feltwork of billions of nerve cells which lies between stimulus mechanisms and response mechanisms, between experience and action. Its complexity reflected the new complexity of the apes' world.

The ape brain responded to a new way of life and expanded with increased body size. As usual, the cortex expanded most. In early prosimians, as in most present-day prosimians, it tended to be a smooth gray sheet, since it lay almost entirely on the surface of the brain. But among apes it became wrinkled and folded primarily because the increasing variety of movement, the increasing role of hand-eye coordination, demanded more nerve pathways for the transmission and analysis of information. To meet this demand, natural selection favored the maximum cerebral tissue within the confines of a given skull capacity, so that the cortex spread down into crevices in the underlying white matter, a process already evident among monkeys. Perhaps 25 to 30 per cent of the ape cortex is buried in the crevices as compared with 7 per cent for monkeys.

Many forces shaped primates during the period from 70 to 25 million years ago. Important parts of the record are still missing; for example, we do not know what happened during the transition time when prosimians evolved into monkeys and apes. The earliest-known species, represented by fossils in deposits of the Fayum, had obviously done considerable evolving before that.

But the record is clear on one point. Primates are evolution's most promising way of adapting mammals, inheritors of the earth after the decline of the dinosaurs, to the uncertainties and challenges of life in the trees. Something more happened in the process of adaptation. Some species were equipped not only for forest dwelling but also for a new and bold adventure, the invasion of open country which foreshadowed the coming of *Homo sapiens.*

SCIENCE ON RACE

Patricia McBroom

The following article by Patricia McBroom is a report on a conference called for scientists of diverse backgrounds to discuss the concept of race. While race has been the center of social controversy in the United States for the last fifteen or twenty years, it is curious to find the same controversy invading the halls of science. At least one of the lessons contained in this article is that science does not exist apart from a social environment. It is part of a culture, and the issues it grapples with are often related to events in the society at large. Paralleling the opposing views in the general population, are scientists with opposing analyses. Certainly this does not justify both sides of the argument, but we will leave it to the reader to compare the two perspectives.

For eight hours last week, 20 scientists alternately denied and upheld the concept of human races. When all had been said, Dr. Theodosius Dobzhansky, professor of genetics at Rockefeller University, took the podium and in measured tones offered his opinion of the symposium: "I am known as a compromiser," he said, "but the conflicting opinions tonight are beyond my ability to compromise."

"To deny the existence of racial differences is futile," he told the American Association for the Advancement of Science panel on "The Utility of the Construct of Race."

If races did not exist they would have to be

invented in order to deal with the "wild variety" of three billion people, said Dr. Dobzhansky.

At the same time, he noted, there is "no careful, objective definition" of race that permits grouping people into discrete categories. If such separation existed, mankind would be composed of distinct species, not different races.

Dr. Dobzhansky said the number of races the human species can be divided into is a completely arbitary matter. It could be three, four, five or 35.

Brazil, in fact, recognizes 40. A current textbook lists five while another acknowledges 65.

Herein lies the scientific controversy: Because the races overlap, creating a continuum, and because that continuum can be broken into as many parts as one wishes, some scholars are maintaining that races do not exist at all.

Mankind is a single continuous species, said Dr. Morton H. Fried, an anthropologist from Columbia University. So loose are the divisions below the species level, that it is impossible, he said, to sensibly relate race to any other variable. Studies which attempt links between race and such things as intelligence and adaptability are "destructive and antisocial," he charged. They cannot even define accurately what they wish to study, he said.

Dr. Fried called for an end to the "pseudoscientific investigation of race."

Dr. Fried's comments served to point out the miasma that often distorts racial studies in the United States. Several speakers acknowledged that the American concept of race is a product of "hyper-conflict." It is so loaded with emotional connotations that many scientists have shied away from the subject altogether, fearing that their work, particularly work on genetics, would be misinterpreted and misused.

Also any attempt to study races in the United States encounters environmental inequality which makes basic racial distinctions virtually impossible.

To some scientists such distinctions are mythical in any case. Heredity and environment interact so completely that the two are forever inseparable: "Any work that tries to separate them is scientifically worthless," said Dr. Herbert G. Birch of the Albert Einstein College of Medicine.

In this view, a concept of race that rests on genes alone is invalid as a basis for study.

Dr. Birch recalled an experiment in which rats were supposedly bred for brightness and dullness. The trouble was they were selectively bred according to how well they ran a particular maze. When the maze—the rat's environment—was changed to highlight visual cues, the dull rats became bright and the bright ones, dull. Applied to humans, the rat test simply means that many tests of intelligence do not ask the right questions. Nor do human environments always ask the right questions; change the conditions and very subtle differences, perhaps even racial differences, in sight, hearing and touch, make large differences in the ability to learn and achieve.

Two symposium members, however, did venture out on a racial limb. Substituting the word "populations" for "races," Drs. Benson E. Ginsberg of the University of Chicago and William S. Laughlin of the University of Wisconsin said that the differences between human groups are more than skin deep.

The human species is not genetically uniform, either in physical appearance, physiology or behavior and was probably less so in the past than it is today, said geneticist Ginsberg.

Human populations have been separated by distance, geography, language, religion and other cultural factors—all of which helped to determine which human traits were valued and therefore which genes were multiplied.

"It would be nothing short of remarkable if we were to find that the Ainu (Japan) and the Zulu (Africa) were alike in genetic capacities and therefore in behavioral characteristics."

Dr. Ginsberg and Laughlin contended that the different populations of the earth are not in fact equal genetically, but all have equal potential. Every reasonably large human group possesses the full spectrum of human genes, in so far as talent and behavior are concerned, they said.

The two men estimated that any group of 30,000 people on earth is genetically capable of recreating every accomplishment of mankind, without genetic crossing from any other group.

The number, 30,000, is a guess based on the achievements of past civilizations such as the Mayan which, while isolated from outside genes, generated mathematics, astronomy, writing, architecture and the concept of zero—all from a base of primitive hunters.

Genetic potential was probably pulled out by population density, said Dr. Laughlin. Density allowed the gifted to seek each other out, marry selectively, and thus accentuate the genes responsible for memory, intellect and talent.

While "positive" selection took place, "negative" selection did not. There was no attempt to breed out talent, simply a failure to exploit potential. And genetic potential does not atrophy from disuse, said Dr. Ginsberg, "The deuces remain in the deck."

Recognizing these genetic differences between populations "offers the major scientific hope for upgrading our biological condition," Dr. Ginsberg told the symposium. He estimated that the full human potential can be pulled out of any population within seven to ten generations. This will occur naturally, through the tendency of gifted people to marry each other, once society offers full educational opportunity.

Since the Ginsberg-Laughlin thesis was treated with near total silence throughout, it is questionable whether other panelists considered this construct of race to be a "major scientific hope" for upgrading the human species.

But some areas of agreement emerged, the most important one being that no superiority or inferiority can be attributed to race and that the word "race," no longer useful, should be replaced with "population."

Summary

Humans are a product of evolution as is every other living form on earth. Evolution is based on the transmission of traits from one generation to the next by discrete particles called genes. The existence of these hereditary particles was first discovered in 1865 by Gregor Mendel, an Austrian monk. Heredity does not produce a blending of traits in a population; it produces a group of distinctive individuals. Today we know that the hereditary material is a chemical, usually deoxyribonucleic acid, DNA. But the chemical writing is never perfect: alterations in this genetic blueprint appear as mutations in the offspring. Most mutations are lethal. Some are advantageous: they increase the ability of the organism to survive, to reproduce, to contribute to future generations. Over time, with a changing environment, the accumulation of distinctive variations in a population can yield a new species, a population incapable of interbreeding with its ancestral form to produce viable offspring. This is Darwin's theory of natural selection.

Subspecies variation in humans is also a product of interaction with the environment. The source of many racial characteristics is not presently known but physical anthropologists are working hard to uncover as many as possible. It is no longer assumed that there were ever pure races of humans. A race is any population that differs from any other population of the same species in the frequency of at least one gene.

What distinguishes us from other creatures is our culture, the ability to alter our relationship to the environment independent of the slow process of physical evolution. The preconditions for human culture arose with the development and elaboration of arboreal life in the evolution of prosimians, apes and monkeys. Many of the attributes now associated with man—sharp eyesight, swift, coordinated movement, the ability to grasp, an elaborated brain—were necessary for survival in the precarious environment of the forest.

Apes and monkeys separated into specialized forms exploiting different food sources approximately 35 million years ago. Monkeys remained four-legged animals, apes developed the ability to stand on two hindlimbs, grasping higher branches with their forelimbs. While monkeys were limited to the fruit hanging near the trunks of trees, apes could reach out to the choice fruit at the tips of branches.

Some ape forms developed greater hindlimb specialization, evolving a pattern of limited bipedalism and partial ground foraging for subsistence. Without the inherent weight limitations of arboreal life, the ground-oriented apes evolved into larger organisms with larger brains. Increasingly terrestrial apes, already capable of bipedalism for short spurts and probably developing a curiosity about their environment, were the precursors of the first hominids.

Glossary

Antigen Any foreign substance in the body that stimulates the production of antibodies by the agents of immunity in the blood.

Ape The family of hominoids—the chimpanzee, the gorilla, the gibbon and the orangutan—most closely related to humans.

Baboon A savanna and semidesert-dwelling African primate, an Old World monkey, known for its elaborate social structure based on dominance.

Blood serum The fluid portion of the blood that contains the agents of immunity.

Cephalic index Head width divided by head length multiplied by 100.

Cerebellum The portion of the brain which regulates the skeletal muscles.

Cerebral cortex The outer layer of the brain which controls and integrates thought and the senses.

Chimpanzee A woodland-dwelling African primate, an ape, bearing the closest evolutionary relationship to *Homo sapiens* of all the apes.

Cline Gradually increasing and decreasing frequencies of physical traits over distance.

Cusps The bumps on the grinding surfaces of teeth. Different species of primates have different cusp patterns.

DNA Deoxyribonucleic acid—the chemical in most organisms that carries the genetic code.

Evolution The continuous modification of the genetic makeup of a population of organisms over generations by natural selection.

Fossil The imprint of the remains of a living form.

Gene A segment of the genetic material, DNA, that controls a single trait in an organism.

Gibbon A forest-dwelling Asian ape known for its ability to swing through the trees, hand over hand from branch to branch.

Gorilla A highland forest-dwelling African primate, an ape, the largest of the primates.

Hominid The family of humans including modern *Homo sapiens* and its earlier fossil forms.

Hominoid The superfamily that includes modern *Homo sapiens*, its ancestral forms, and the apes.

Homo sapiens The genus and species of modern humans.

Mammals The class of vertebrates to which primates belong.

Mutation A change in the genetic composition of the DNA of an organism.

Natural selection The principal mechanism of evolutionary change as described by Darwin. Those best suited to the environment contribute more offspring to future generations, changing the genetic characteristics of the population over time.

Nucleic acids The components of the genetic code in DNA.

Orangutan A forest dwelling Asian primate, an ape.

Preadaptation The evolution of features in one environment that are adaptive in future environments.

Primate The order which includes the prosimians, humans, apes and monkeys.

Prosimian The pre-monkey from which the other primates evolved.

Race Any population that differs from other populations of the same species in the frequency of one or more genes.

Recapitulation The repetition of the evolution of any trait of a species in the development of the individual organism.

Sickle-cell anemia A hereditary disease which affects the red blood cells, and which originated in areas of the world where there is a high incidence of malaria.

Species A population of naturally or potentially interbreeding organisms.

Additional Reading

Alland, Alexander
1967 Evolution and Human Behavior. Garden City, New York: Natural History Press.

An excellent survey of evolution from Darwinian theory through the interaction of culture and evolution.

Eimerl, Sarel and Irven DeVore
1965 The Primates. New York: Time-Life Books.

A survey of primate studies well adapted for the introductory level.

Garn, Stanley M.
1961 Human Races. Springfield, Illinois: Charles C. Thomas.

An interesting theoretical and factual discussion of race.

Howell, F. Clark
1971 Early Man. New York: Time-Life Books, 2nd edition.

A basic elementary discussion of the evolution of humans.

chapter three

In 1654 Archbishop Ussher of Armagh, Ireland, . . . calculated from biblical genealogies that the earth had been created in 4004 B.C. In fact, one of Ussher's contemporaries determined the precise time—the twenty-third day of October at nine o'clock in the morning.

E.L. SIMONS

THE FIRST MEMBERS OF THE HUMAN FAMILY

Our ancestors arose 15 million years ago in the slowly changing subtropics of the Old World. The restlessness in the earth, a heritage from earlier periods, continued as the crust buckled and pushed up sediments thousands of feet thick that had accumulated on the floors of ancient seas. The buckling produced great mountain chains and intermontane valleys, including the great ranges of the Alps and Himalayas. Gases, ash and lava poured out of volcanic craters and increased rains produced intense erosion along the slopes of mountains and foothills. Worldwide annual temperatures fell, perhaps by as much as an average of five degrees Fahrenheit or so.

A broad forest extended from the west coast of Africa to the East Indies, but not the solid unbroken forest of former times. The savanna was on the move. Grasses spread in a slow tide among the trees, and there were dry plains wide as oceans, particularly on the lee side of newly formed highlands. Penetrating into the plains were dark peninsular stretches of gallery forest. In a sense nature was more natural then, the wilderness was wilder, than it has ever been since. It might have been an Eden of a sort except for, or perhaps because of, the fact that *Homo sapiens* had not yet put in an appearance. But his coming, the shift into savanna lands, was imminent.

49

Most primates spent most of their lives in the shade, leading enclosed lives inside "green caves" of leaves and vines. They found pathways high in the forests, trails for leaping and swinging in the canopies of trees, familiar branches and footholds among dense foliage. They avoided more exposed places like open woodlands where trees were somewhat fewer and farther between. Most of all, they avoided the wide-open, bright, uneasy places where savanna grasses rustled at the very edges of the woodlands.

Of course, then as now a few individuals were always ready to push their luck and investigate alien terrain.

So restless young prehominids, like their counterparts among many other species, probably spent considerable time playing I-dare-you games and trying out environments which primates had not exploited. But it took more than that to bring about full-scale, permanent changes. Something had to happen to make small groups move out of relatively safe forests into the favorite hunting grounds of the big cats and other predators, and judging by the sort of forces generally at work in evolution, it probably involved the problem of getting enough food.

It could have been a matter of warmer and drier climates, less rainfall and dwindling forests; or perhaps the forests were not shrinking but primate populations were on the increase. Both possibilities have been suggested, and the evidence is insufficient to make out a solid case for either one of them. At any event, the effect was the same—too many individuals for the available food supply. The hominid story from this stage on seems to be an increasing exploitation of increasingly open terrain.

Chimpanzees offer a model of the social organization of the early hominids that moved into open terrain. The most striking single fact about chimpanzees is the flexibility of their social life, the lack of any rigid form of organization. It represents about as much of a departure from a rigid type of organization characteristic of baboons, for example, as can be found among the higher primates, and serves to emphasize the great variety of primate adaptations. Chimpanzees are more human than baboons, or rather they jibe better with the way we like to picture ourselves, as freewheeling, unpredictable individuals who do not take readily to regimentation, and who are frequently charming. (Charm is relatively rare among baboons.) On the basis of recent studies, they can now be described as lively, easygoing and relatively independent creatures with a social system sufficiently flexible to allow considerable freedom of movement and individual action. Similarly, the advanced primates of 15 million years ago moved almost entirely in and out of shadows and along old ancestral trails. But some bands began to invade territory in which no ape had yet established a foothold, venturing away from the safe depths of forests and out into less dense woodlands toward the wide-open spaces of the savanna.

THE EARLY HOMINIDS

Our earliest ancestors were probably creatures like this who spent a good deal of time in trees and slept in trees at night. But during the day they came down to the ground increasingly, foraging for the most part for plant foods. That means they naturally moved away from denser parts of the forests, where plants were scarce because little sunlight penetrated the trees, to opener forest territory where sunlight and plants were more abundant, to woodlands and grassy areas near seasonally flooded lakes and rivers within the forests. At times they may have ventured away from the last stands of trees at forest fringes out into wide grassy savannas, foraged there for a while, and scampered back into the forests.

Scale of Geological Time

Era	Period	Epoch	Some Important Events in Life of the Times	Began (Millions of Years Ago)	Duration (in Millions of Years)
CENOZOIC	Quaternary	Recent	Modern species of animals; human civilization	.01	.01
		Pleistocene	First members of the genus *Homo*	3	3
	Tertiary	Pliocene	Anthropoid radiation and culmination	10	7
		Miocene	of mammalian specialization.	25	15
		Oligocene	Mammals, birds and insects	40	15
		Eocene	dominant on land.	60	20
		Paleocene		70	10
MESOZOIC	Cretaceous		Dinosaurs; marsupial and placental mammals; the first flowering plants.	135	65
	Jurassic		Dinosaurs; first mammals and birds.	180	45
	Triassic		First dinosaurs.	230	50
PALEOZOIC	Permian		Mammal-like reptiles; insects; widespread glaciation.	280	50
	Carboniferous		First reptiles; dense coal forest.	350	70
	Devonian		Fishes dominant; first amphibians.	400	50
	Silurian		Primitive fish; invasion of land by plants.	425	25
	Ordovician		First verebrates; invertebrates dominate oceans.	500	75
	Cambrian		Invertebrates; marine algae.	600	100
PRE-CAMBRIAN			Multicellular invertebrates. Earliest known fossils, 3.3 billion years ago.	Origins of Earth?	

Like these desert baboons, early hominids must have had to keep a constant lookout over the dangerous savanna.

One result was a wider-ranging type of primate—since food tends to be more widely dispersed in open country—and significant changes in posture and walking. Apes used their feet not only as supports but also as grasping devices, for example, while eating fruit at the ends of slender branches. Furthermore, they naturally assumed a bent-forward posture, were capable of two-footed walking (but rarely and not for long periods), and usually moved along on their hands as well as on the soles of their feet. Their feet and hands were not fully specialized for support and grasping respectively.

A more complete division of labor was taking place among the first hominids. It was the beginning of the process which eventually resulted among other things in the human stride, a unique primate development involving a series of precisely controlled and timed operations. The stride starts with arch and toe acting as a lever, lifting the body gradually until it rises several inches above its standing height. Measurements show that at this point the average person remains in a delicate balance for about two-tenths of a second as his entire weight rests on the foot. Then a final push, which lasts less than half that time, propels him forward so that his other foot "glides" in for a smooth rather than a jarring landing.

The search continues for direct fossil evidence to document the evolution of the human stride and other hominid features. The ideal situation would be to have a record as ample as that which exists for the evolution of the horse, a series of fossils which shows the gradual change from a collie-sized creature with short chunky teeth and fourteen toes each with its own hoof to the modern long-toothed, four-hooved species. Unfortunately, the hominid record is still far less detailed, although recent years have seen some important new finds and new interpretations of old finds.

One development involves an incredibly churned-up part of East Africa, the region around Fort Ternan in Kenya about forty miles east of Lake Victoria, where violent movements in the earth have formed a complex and heavily eroded system of hills and valleys.

In 1961 the late Louis Leakey, director of the National Museums' Center for Prehistory and Paleontology in Nairobi and perhaps the most successful searcher for hominid remains, started digging on the slope of one of the hills, at a site discovered by a local orange grower who was looking for mineral deposits and found fossils instead. The site is rich, having already yielded more than 10,000 bones in an area about the size of a large living room. Leakey believed that it may once have been a place where waters, and occasionally poisonous gases, rose up from fissures deep in the earth, and that the gases killed animals coming to drink. (He knew of several such places in the Congo.) During his first season of digging he found the remains of a pygmy giraffe, a pygmy

Louis S.B. Leakey
(1903–1972)
*was born to missionary parents in
Kabete, Kenya, a Kikuyu settlement overlooking the Rift Valley.
His first sixteen years were spent
acquiring a Western education
from his governess and a Kikuyu
education from his playmates. The
intimate knowledge of culture,
language and natural habitat
gained from early life in Africa
served Leakey well in his later
fieldwork. During the 1920s and
30s he led four major expeditions
to East Africa that laid the foundations for the late prehistory of the
region. While active in the study of
animal behavior and Kikuyu
ethnography, Leakey is best known
for excavations at Olduvai Gorge.
He began digging there in 1931,
producing a number of significant
publications. The expedition was
near financial collapse in 1959,
however, when Mary Leakey made
the famous Australopithecus find
that reorganized our knowledge of
early hominids. In the next twelve
years the Leakey family uncovered
48 hominid fossils, at Olduvai
Gorge.*

elephant, numerous antelopes, and an unusual variety of primate.

Geologists at the University of California in Berkeley have dated the group of extinct species by dating samples of volcanic rock found with them. Atoms of radioactive potassium in the rock break down spontaneously into the inert gas argon. The gas is trapped in rock crystals after the lava cools (there is no gas to start with) and accumulates at a steady rate which can be measured with the aid of devices capable of detecting fractions of a billionth of an ounce of material. According to this "radioactive clock" technique—which, incidentally, has also been used to date crystalline rocks brought back from the moon—the Fort Ternan fossils are about 14 million years old, give or take a few hundred thousand years.

Examination of the primate specimen, which includes part of an upper jawbone and several associated teeth, reveals certain distinctively human features. The proportions of the reconstructed jaw indicate a shortened face with a very much reduced snout; the curvature of the jaw suggests a widely arched dental arc rather than the narrow U-shaped arc typical of recent apes. These and other characteristics, such as the smallness of the teeth, can be interpreted in two ways. They are human characteristics in themselves, but that does not necessarily mean that this particular primate was a member of the human family.

Many types of apes existed 14 million years ago, and this diversity implies a wide diversity and range of physical characteristics—long faces and intermediate-sized faces as well as shortened faces, differently shaped dental arcs, different-sized teeth, and so on. Thus certain primate species may have had a few hominid traits without being hominids in many other respects and thus, of course, without belonging to the human line. On the other hand, Leakey announced that the Fort Ternan specimen exhibits enough hominid features to qualify as an entirely new variety of primate, which helps fill "an enormous gap in the panorama of man's development," the gap between apes and creatures like ourselves.

Ramapithecus

The announcement proved of special interest to Elwyn Simons, whose digging in the Fayum region of Egypt is only part of a long and continuing investigation of primate evolution. He had spent considerable time studying hundreds of fossils from sites throughout the world in an effort to avoid the bad habit which affects paleontologists as well as others—overestimating the importance of one's own work. Since it is generally more satisfying to discover something new than to confirm someone else's discovery, paleontologists often make too much of their finds. The tendency is to interpret small differences in tooth size and other factors, differences that fall within the normal range of individual variation, as signs of a new genus or at least a new species. In an extreme case, North American grizzly bears, now recognized as members of a single species which also includes Old World varieties, were once divided into more than twenty species.

The upper jaw of Ramapithecus, one of our earliest known ancestors.

Aware of a similar tendency in primate studies, Simons recognized the Fort Ternan specimen as a hominid, a member of the family of man, but not as a new genus or even a new species. He pointed out that the collection at Yale's Peabody Museum included an upper-jaw fragment and four teeth of the same sort of creature which a native worker had found about three decades earlier in foothills of the Himalayas, in the Siwalik Hills of the Punjab Province of northern India. Furthermore, he had already reconstructed the jaw and estimated the size of a missing *canine tooth* by the size of the empty socket. This hypothetical tooth turned out to be an almost perfect match with a real canine found at the Kenya site.

Not long after the Fort Ternan announcement, Simons launched a more intensive survey of previously found material stored in museums, and gained as much fresh information as had been obtained during the previous search for new evidence in the field. For one thing, he "discovered" still another specimen of the same hominid species. That is, he reclassified an upper-jaw fragment which had also been found in the Punjab hills about half a century ago, kept in the collection of the Geological Survey of India ever since, and identified mistakenly as belonging to an extinct ape.

At this point the reexamination of old finds took a new turn. The Yale investigator noted that the three specimens, one from East Africa and two from India, were all parts of upper jawbones, a curious observation because collectors generally find more lower jawbones, which are denser and more compact and hence more resistant to decomposition. He began to wonder whether some lower jawbones had actually been found and duly tucked away on museum shelves, but not recognized for what they were. As frequently happens in research, asking the right question is more than half the battle. No sooner had Simons decided on what to look for than he found it, and in his own museum.

The Yale collection included three specimens, all lower-jaw fragments with *molar teeth*, all found in India years ago, and all classified as remains of a special genus of fossil ape. But the fragments fitted neatly with corresponding upper-jaw fragments already identified tentatively as those of a creature on the direct line of human descent. If future studies confirm such conclusions, this phase of the work will eliminate an entire genus and several species from fossil records, a fitting climax to a survey which has helped clear away some of the debris of primate nomenclature and furnished for the first time a plausible reconstruction of the remote stages of human evolution.

One of our earliest-known ancestors consisted of a single species with the official title *Ramapithecus punjabicus.* ("Rama" is the name of a hero in Hindu mythology, the incarnation of the deity Vishnu; "pithecus" is Greek for "ape"; and "punjabicus" signifies the part of India where typical material was first discovered.) Not many *Ramapithecus* specimens have been recovered so far, a total of some fifteen jaw fragments and more than forty teeth, representing perhaps twelve to twenty individuals. But that is enough to serve as the basis for a number of interesting speculations. For example, fossil traces occur not only in Africa and India but also in the coal beds of Hunan Province in China, the Jura Mountains of southern Germany, and perhaps in north central Spain— and it is possible that members of this species moved about freely in the world's savannas and forests. If this assumption is correct, if widespread distribution is any criterion, they must have been highly adaptable and quite capable of dealing with a variety of circumstances.

LIFE ON THE SAVANNA

Current thinking about the way *Ramapithecus* lived is based on studies of their fossil teeth, in-cluding the small canines, which have been used to support different theories. According to the oldest theory, small hominid canines are a sign of habitual tool use. Many primates have large canines and put them to good use for purposes indicated, for example, by the behavior of the type of baboon in the savannas of Kenya in Africa, another primate whose ancestors turned from tree dwelling to life on the ground. Under conditions of tension a male baboon in his prime will stop, face an opponent, open his mouth wide in a prodigious yawn, and flash a set of four huge and sharp canines. There is nothing particularly subtle about this gesture. It is a direct threat and warning. It says more clearly than words that the opponent is likely to be ripped if he does not get out of the way.

The flashing of canines serves as an effective symbol. More often than not trouble is avoided and the opponent does indeed get out of the way. When threats and warnings fail, however, these teeth may go into action. They are a baboon's most formidable weapons, and in the last analysis his position in the social order of the troop depends on how well he can fight. Apes as well as baboons, and for that matter carnivores such as lions and tigers, also use them in dismembering prey and shredding plant food. Gorillas have been seen ripping the tough outer layers off bamboo shoots to get at the pith inside, in a kind of banana-peeling operation.

But *Ramapithecus* was not equipped with such large, deep-rooted slashing and puncturing devices. The canines were small like ours and had smaller and more shallow roots, all of which has certain fundamental implications in the light of evolutionary theory. Since the survival of a species depends on vigorous offensive and defensive action, on eating and not being eaten, the body can include no superfluous structures, and generations of development ensure that every part of every individual is shaped for maximum efficiency. There must be a reason

Controversy

Ramapithecus: Hominid or Pongid?

In 1934 a Yale graduate student named G. Edward Lewis described a new fossil primate found in the hills of northern India. Despite his observation of some apparently hominid characteristics, Lewis considered the specimen a pongid, naming it *Ramapithecus punjabicus.* Since that time, other specimens have been discovered in many different areas of the world and have been classified as belonging to the genus *Ramapithecus.* Whether the specimens labeled *Ramapithecus* are actually pongid or hominid remains a controversy to this day.

Paleontologists distinguish between hominids and pongids on the basis of skull features, teeth, and skeletons. In the case of *Ramapithecus,* only a few jawbones and teeth have been available for analysis to date. The question, then, is whether enough can be learned from these dental and jaw remains to identify the hominid family to which *Ramapithecus* belongs.

The major trends in the development of hominid teeth include the decrease in size of the back molars and the shortening of the canines to a height level with that of the rest of the teeth. The complete lack of the third molar, the wisdom tooth, in many people today is part of the same evolutionary tendency towards smaller back teeth. A third characteristic important in the analysis of fossil teeth is the wear pattern which is used to determine the diet of the animal. The controversy over the status of *Ramapithecus* centers on the analysis of these traits.

The body size of *Ramapithecus* has been estimated at around forty to eighty pounds, roughly that of a pygmy chimpanzee. For a primate of this size, he had a face which was long and flat and relatively small upper incisors. Simons and Pilbeam interpret these as hominid characteristics and suggest the possibility that *Ramapithecus* had tools to perform the functions which the large incisors perform in other primates. So far, however, there is no material evidence that he used tools to any greater extent than does the modern chimpanzee.

Some physical anthropologists suggest that *Ramapithecus* was evolving into a ground feeder, thus differentiating himself from the pongids. The small size of the back molars and the wear patterns of the teeth are interpreted as evidence of movement away from an entirely arboreal life. He may have spent most of his time in the trees, coming to the forest floor a few times a day to feed on seeds and other small, tough morsels. A shift to the forest floor might also have been associated with bipedalism, or perhaps knuckle-walking. However, this cannot be established with certainty in the absence of fossil limb bones.

Was *Ramapithecus* a hominid, then? Pilbeam believes that the facial and dental characteristics of the fossil foreshadowed those of later hominids in both form and function. On this basis, he placed *Ramapithecus* on the path to *Australopithecus* and *Homo*. While he considers that the boundary between hominid and pongid is ultimately arbitrary, he prefers a hominid status for *Ramapithecus*. Whatever the particular classification, Pilbeam believes that *Ramapithecus* is definitely in the line of human descent.

Some investigators, however, see serious flaws in Pilbeam's analysis. According to L.O. Greenfield, several of the features used to argue for hominid status for *Ramapithecus* are shared by various modern and extinct pongids. Greenfield discredits the use of tooth wear as a criterion for hominid status since the *Ramapithecus* wear patterns are within the range of variation of hominids and of modern and fossil pongids. Additionally, a valid comparison of tooth wear can be made only between animals of equal maturity. Otherwise, the wear patterns of an older primate on a soft plant diet could be confused with the wear patterns of a younger primate on a hard seed diet. Until such factors as age can be taken into account, the validity of our conclusions is questionable, according to Greenfield.

Greenfield also discounts conclusions drawn from the study of the size of *Ramapithecus'* molars. He points out that these molars generally do not display the size differences which characterize the molars of early hominids. Indeed, *Ramapithecus'* molar specimens display a range of variation more pongid-like than hominid-like. Even those which show a moderately large decrease in size from front to back can be easily matched by living apes of equivalent age. According to Greenfield, the same holds true for other presumably distinguishing criteria such as molar width, enamel thickness, and the relative thickness of the jaw. Undoubtedly, the controversy over *Ramapithecus'* place in evolutionary history will not be resolved until more fossil evidence is discovered and carefully compared.

This baboon's display of sharp canine teeth serves as an unmistakable warning. Compare its canines with those of Ramapithecus in figure 3-4.

for every significant change. Bony armor does not become thinner or movement slower unless compensating factors come into play.

In this context the reduction of the canine teeth was interpreted to mean that *Ramapithecus* had other ways of taking care of himself. In other words, canines became smaller, because they were no longer needed for attack and defense.

Recent studies suggest a more plausible theory, which depends neither on the assumption of early and extensive hominid tool use nor on the notion of a tooth-and-claw struggle for existence. The theory involves original research by Clifford Jolly of New York University on fossil baboons, extinct relatives of so-called gelada baboons which today live on the high treeless plateaus of central Ethiopia. He notes, among other things, that the canines of males tended to become somewhat smaller and shorter in the course of their evolution than the canines of males belonging to a species of savanna-dwelling baboon.

Since these primates do not use weapons, some factor other than fighting must be at work, and Jolly believes the difference is primarily a matter of diet. Gelada baboons eat an unusually high proportion of grass seeds, stems and other tough plant tissues, and their extinct relatives probably consumed similar foods. Such material must be ground up and calls for a powerful chewing action. And that, in turn, poses a mechanical problem, since large canine teeth tend to interlock, making side-to-side jaw movements less efficient. This problem has put an evolutionary premium on those males with smaller and smaller canines, which reduce chances of interlocking and permit more complete grinding—and the same changes occurred in times past among early hominids who also had to cope with increasing quantities of tough plant foods as they foraged increasingly on the ground.

This argument does not rule out the possibility that early hominids used weapons. Indeed, if we can judge by the behavior of chimpanzees today, the odds are that they did—and that may have had an indirect bearing on canine reduction. The fact that our ancestors were quite capable of wielding weapons probably permitted the evolution of considerably smaller canine teeth without a great disadvantage in fighting and defense.

The main point about Jolly's theory is that it focuses on diet rather than fighting as the major factor in reducing canines. The theory is considerably broader than that, however, and helps account for a whole complex of further changes, dental and otherwise. For example, efficient grinding of tough foods also requires very large and closely packed cheek teeth, molars and premolars, a feature found in both gelada baboons and *Ramapithecus*.

Bipedalism

Another feature of hominid behavior, and another major problem, concerns the development of an upright posture and walking in the human line. Many theories have been offered to explain why a two-footed gait should have developed in the first place. The value of this new form of primate locomotion is not at all self-evident. It is certainly not an inevitable consequence of coming down to earth from the trees, and the example of the baboon, among other species, shows that primates can live on the ground without walking upright. As a matter of fact, an upright posture has several important disadvantages. Animals balancing themselves on two feet are easier to knock over, more conspicuous, and less agile when it comes to dodging and feinting and other escape tactics.

So there must have been advantages. Furthermore, they must have been enormous advantages to overcome all the drawbacks, the illogic and awkwardness, of *bipedalism*. Certain

theories turn out to be quite inadequate to account for so drastic a change in locomotion. For example, primates often stand erect for a time when circumstances demand it, say, when they want a better view of the surrounding terrain. This is a familiar sight in the Amboseli Game Reserve, where baboons, including infants no more than two or three months old, often stand up on their hind legs at the sound of a passing car or to keep track of the rest of the troop.

Such conduct is common among baboons and other ground-dwelling primates. In fact it has been cited in support of the "reconnaissance" theory of human bipedalism. The idea is that savanna-exploring hominids were frequently killed by lions and other predators lurking in tall grasses, that evolution put a premium on standing erect as a way of spotting predators at a distance and avoiding them—and that a by-product of standing erect was the release of the hands for use in coping with the environment. But this advantage is not big enough. The theory does not clarify the main problem. It presents a convincing argument for the benefits of occasional but not habitual bipedalism, without indicating what type of living conditions could have made reconnaissance so important that it brought about a radical departure from conventional patterns of primate locomotion.

There are better arguments for the notion that walking on two feet evolved as a way of carrying food more efficiently. There is plenty of evidence for such behavior among primates of all ages. Jane van Lawick-Goodall of the Gombe Stream Research Center on the shores of Lake Tanganyika, Africa, has spent more than ten years observing chimpanzees in the forests of northwest Tanzania, and has seen the apes "loading their arms with choice wild fruits, then walking erect for several yards to a spot of shade before sitting down to eat." Macaque monkeys on Kyushu Island, Japan, may walk more than sixty feet from forest to beach to wash dirt off handfuls of sweet potatoes (pro-

Japanese macaques routinely remove dirt from sweet potatoes by washing them. They will often walk upright when carrying potatoes back and forth to the water.

vided by scientists to entice the animals into open country where they can be observed).

These and many similar examples are sufficient to show that apes and monkeys can walk upright upon occasion just as we can go on all fours when the demand arises, as in clambering up a steep bank or moving along under low branches or crawling through low passages in caves. But food carrying is simply not a big enough advantage for them. They can do it perfectly well without full-time bipedalism and in environmental settings little different from those prevailing during the earliest days of hominid evolution.

The problem is to figure out what special forces and circumstances might have favored the major shift from part-time to full-time bipedalism. In this connection meat eating and sharing may be significant. (Individual plants are rarely big enough to share, and plant eaters are generally neither sharers nor carriers.) Killing even a small animal may provide a hunter with ten or fifteen pounds of meat, more than he can eat, and may be worth carrying back to a camp or home base. The record certainly indicates that meat eating inevitably led to greater sharing, and that meant carrying food over long distances—a development which could have contributed to the selection of populations made up of individuals who could walk several miles while carrying one or more small animals.

Hunting and sharing seem to go together, among chimpanzees as well as among people. In fact, the chimpanzee is the only nonhuman primate known to share meat in the wild, and van Lawick-Goodall has often seen a successful hunter tear a piece of meat off a carcass and give it to a fellow troop member begging with outstretched hand. Sometimes the sharing is reluctant. One young female found that the only way she could get a banana from her mother (who usually had a boxful to herself) was to go into a full-fledged temper tantrum, hurling herself to the ground and flailing her arms and screaming, and even that did not work all the time. In general sharing is not practiced regularly, but the feeling is that it soon would be if hunting itself became a regular thing.

The very fact that hominids foraged increasingly on the ground where food tends to be dispersed may have encouraged new forms of locomotion. Bipedalism happens to be a comfortable and convenient way of covering large areas, once it has been developed. It would also be promoted by the use of tools, a theory that differs from most other theories, which assume that erect posture came first and that the release of the hands was a secondary "bonus" effect. The notion that things also worked the other way around was originally suggested by

Jane van Lawick-Goodall *(1934–)*
began her famous research on wild chimpanzees in 1960. Three years before she had paid her own way to Africa, driven by an interest in wildlife that dated back to her childhood. In Nairobi, Kenya she was introduced to Louis Leakey, the famous prehistorian, who hired her as secretary and field assistant, Leakey became convinced of van Lawick-Goodall's commitment to animal studies and suggested she return to England for courses in primatology. He also directed her to the Gombe Stream Reserve near Lake Tanganyika because the area was relatively untouched by modern contact and the environment was similar to Olduvai Gorge during australopithecine times. It took van Lawick-Goodall most of the first fourteen months just to gain acceptance by the chimpanzees, but time and patience paid off in information of incalculable value to the study of human prehistory.

Darwin, and has been reemphasized by Washburn.

Tool Use

Washburn points out that the factor which provided the primary selective pressure for the shift to full-time bipedalism was the enormous advantage of another highly developed human characteristic, the use of tools. Tools opened up many possibilities, not only in defense against predators but also in digging up and preparing food. So bands composed of individuals which could stand and walk upright more easily and for longer and longer periods, and hence had their hands free increasingly for tool use, flourished rapidly at the expense of bands less fitted to survive in the savanna.

Assuming that this is what happened, the problem is how tool use itself evolved. There are clues to a possible answer. Imagine an adventurous hominid or prehominid, a primitive *Ramapithecus* perhaps, looking for food in the savanna and wandering too far and suddenly being confronted by a predator directly in the escape route to the nearest trees. Such encounters could have been frequent in the beginning. They are by no means rare nowadays. One hardly ever observes actual attacks, which are generally carried out at night, but a leftover leg or some other fresh piece of primate carcass lying in the savanna dust the next morning indicates the failure of escape tactics. Also, examinations of the droppings of leopards and other big cats indicate that monkeys are well preyed on.

At one time our ancestors had no effective way of fighting back when brought to bay by large predators. But they may well have developed special forms of display, bluffing behavior, which helped them to delay attacks and even to get away in some cases. The trick among all animals in all such emergencies is to make themselves look more frightening, often by increasing apparent stature. Puffer fish double or triple their body size by inflating themselves into globes; birds may ruffle their feathers and puff out their chests and spread their wings wide; cats arch their backs and their fur stands on end.

All such reactions are "natural" in the sense that they tend to be automatic, hereditary, and that they consist essentially of mechanical and physiological changes in body structure. But it is possible that a new principle may have been at work in the displays of prehominids and that they began to reach out for something external, something not built in and not part of the body which would help them to appear bigger and more formidable. In other words, they may have put up a bluff by artificial means, using branches or clumps of tall grass or perhaps long bones to enlarge their body images.

The general tendency to pick up and wave things is common among contemporary apes. When chimpanzees and gorillas are aroused, they often grab a nearby stick or branch and swing it about in a vigorous, random flailing motion. Van Lawick-Goodall reports that on rare occasions playing with branches may take on a strange, ritualistic quality. A big male chimpanzee may become tremendously excited, break a branch off a tree, brandish it about, and rush down a mountain slope (often on two feet) dragging it behind him. Then he rushes up the slope and repeats the action several times. The significance of this behavior is not known, but sometimes other males will join the fun in a mass "branch-waving display . . . calling, tearing off and waving large branches, hurling themselves to the ground from the trees."

Branch-waving plays a less mysterious role when chimpanzees are frustrated or angry with one another, in which case shaking branches is part of displays that may include slapping or stamping on the ground and high-pitched screaming. They have been seen charging at one another with sticks in their hands, and although in general they simply threaten and do not strike, they sometimes use sticks to attack one another. The apes also show a special concern with branches when they climb into a tree where they expect to spend some time, either to build a nest for the night or to play with another chimpanzee. They move from limb to limb, breaking off dead branches and dropping them to the ground below, as if they were clearing away deadwood so that the tree would be a safe place for maneuvering.

Apes have an ample repertoire of basic branch-handling activities and manipulations which they use in different combinations and sequences under different circumstances. Although no one has ever reported seeing a real-life encounter between an armed ape and a predator, a Dutch zoologist produced an analogous situation experimentally about eight years ago in the Congo. Adriaan Kortlandt of the University of Amsterdam arranged things so that a stuffed dummy leopard could be pulled out of some shrubbery and into a meadow when a troop of wild chimpanzees was being observed.

Here is how he describes one such confrontation when the stuffed leopard appeared with a chimpanzee-doll "victim" in its claws: "There was a moment of silence first. Then hell broke loose. There was an uproar of yelling and barking, and most of the apes came forward and began to charge at the leopard. . . . Some charges were made bare-handed; in others the assailants broke off a small tree while they ran toward or past the leopard, or brandished a big stick or broken tree in their charge, or threw such a primitive weapon in the general direction of the enemy. . . . Both when attacking and when looking at the leopard, the apes again and again uttered a special blood-curdling type of barking yell."

For all the sound and fury, however, it was more of a mobbing-type display calculated to harass the leopard and make it go away than a practiced and skillfully directed use of weapons. Clubs were brandished and hurled, but there were no actual hits. The interesting thing about all this is that the chimpanzees were forest dwellers, and attacks from leopards and other predators tend to be infrequent in forests.

In later studies Kortlandt reports far more direct action among wild chimpanzees living in the sort of open savanna country in Guinea, where predators are more common. There was no doubt about the chimpanzees' objectives under these conditions. They beat up the dummy leopard with repeated and well-aimed heavy blows using clubs up to six feet long. Van Lawick-Goodall has seen chimpanzees throwing stones at baboons, and although they seldom hit their targets, some individuals are more accurate than others. The implication is that early hominids may also have used clubs and missiles from time to time.

Some investigators have another explanation for the origins of tool use, an explanation which accents the search for food rather than defense. According to Leakey, evidence for the food hypothesis may already have been uncovered in the form of the broken shinbone of an oxlike animal found at Fort Ternan. The break is the depressed or indented kind which might have been produced by a rock, and suggests that perhaps a hungry *Ramapithecus* wielded the rock to make a meal of the bone marrow, although similar breaks have been found among bones in leopard lairs. The effort to check such possibilities indicates why analyzing fractured fossil bones is an important phase of present-day research.

Tools could have been used in gathering foods. The observations of van Lawick-Goodall in Tanzania do much to weaken a notion supported over the years by many investigators from Benjamin Franklin and Friedrich Engels to modern anthropologists, namely, that although other animals may upon occasion use

Chimpanzees often make and use simple tools. Here they probe a termite hill with long grass stems, licking off the termites that cling to the stems.

tools, we are the only regular maker of tools. Chimpanzees also make tools to obtain one of their favorite foods, termites. During most of the year termite hills are covered with a thick concretelike shell to protect them from birds, monkeys and other termite eaters. But in late October or early November, just before the onset of the rainy season, worker termites drill holes through the shell, destroying all but the outermost fraction of an inch—so that they can emerge quickly when the rains come, begin their nuptial flights, and found new colonies.

While the termite operates by instinct, the chimpanzee operates by insight. He has learned when a termite hill is ripe for exploitation and where the thinly covered holes are. Then he takes a bit of vine or a slender stick, trims it neatly and carefully by pulling off leaves and side shoots, breaks it off to a length of six to twelve inches, and approaches the hill. After licking the probe he pokes it through the shell and into one of the holes, and waits a moment or two. When he draws the probe out, termites are clinging to it and he licks them off as gleefully as a child with a lollipop. (Incidentally, van Lawick-Goodall has eaten termites and finds them "rather flavorless.")

In such foraging, chimpanzees may plan ahead. For example, they do not always find a promising termite hill and then proceed to make a probe. They may make the probe first, anticipating a meal of termites, although neither termites nor termite hills are in sight. One chimpanzee carried a suitably prepared stick in its mouth for half a mile, inspected eight hills without finding a good one, and then dropped the tool. So these apes seem to have the basic concept of a tool as something to be shaped for a situation that has not yet materialized, and there is reason to believe that *Ramapithecus* was at least as ingenious.

The full range of tool using among wild apes is yet to be understood. Junichiro Itani of the University of Kyoto, Japan, reports that chimpanzees in western Tanzania, occupying territories up to a hundred miles south of the Gombe Reserve, crack hard fruits with stone "hammers," scoop honey out of honeycombs with twigs and sometimes use sticks to attack one another. This is definitely cultural behavior. Different practices are observed in different areas. Gombe chimpanzees employ the sponge method of getting at water in a tree crotch, presumably because the trick was discovered at some time in the past and has been transmitted from generation to generation ever since. But Budongo chimpanzees have another method which happens to be less efficient, simply dipping their hands into the natural bowls and licking the water off their fingers. Such knowledge is passed along by imitation. A juvenile may see its mother probing for termites and immediately try to prepare and use probes of its own, an activity that may go on for hours.

CONCLUSION

In any case, notice that the use of implements as accessories or extensions of the body bears a direct relationship to developments that had taken place beforehand in the trees. Part of the story, of course, concerns the sort of dexterity required to grasp and pull branches and to swing along from branch to branch. But the coming of stereoscopic color vision was an even more important factor. As already indicated, objects acquired a new meaning, a new reality, with the appearance of highly advanced visual mechanisms. They were viewed in full perspective and tended to "leap out" of the background more completely and vividly for primates than for other visually inferior animals. To put it another way, primates acquired richer and more detailed perceptions—and it is precisely this faculty which more than anything else created a heightened awareness of objects as distinct and clear-cut entities capable of serving as display elements and ultimately as tools.

It follows from Washburn's theory that once the new way of life caught on, once its advantages were proved in the field as it were, it achieved a new kind of momentum of its own. The relationship between tool use and bipedalism acquired a two-way self-reinforcing quality. It was not only that increased tool use brought about the selection of changes in body structure which made for more efficient bipedalism. More efficient bipedalism, in turn, freed the hands more and more for increased tool use and provided more time for acquiring new manipulative skills. In such a developing process it becomes increasingly difficult to distinguish cause and effect.

The process yielded further advantages as by-products. Walking erect resulted in a continuous and more panoramic view of the savanna, an increased ability to see things coming and to detect and anticipate danger. Looking ahead from an elevated position may also have

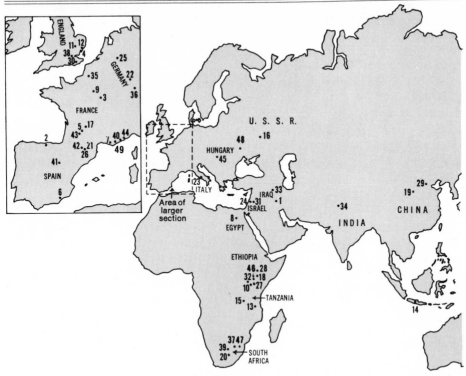

MAJOR PREHISTORIC SITES: EUROPE, AFRICA, AND ASIA

Time Code:

[1] 60,000,000 to 4,000,000 years ago
[2] 4,000,000 to 1,000,000 years ago
[3] 1,000,000 to 200,000 years ago
[4] 200,000 years ago to the present

Things Found:

A art
B bones of primates
F fire
L living floors
T tools

Key to sites on map

1 Ali Kosh [4] L,T
2 Altamira [4] A,T
3 Arcy [4] B,F,L,T
4 Clacton-on-Sea [3] T
5 Combe Grenal [4] F,L,T
6 Cueva de Ambrosio [4] B,F,T
7 Escale cave [3] B,F,L,T
8 Fayum Depression [1] B
9 Pincevent [4] A,F,L,T
10 Fort Ternan [1] B
11 High Lodge [4] T
12 Hoxne [4] T
13 Isimila [4] F,L,T
14 Java site [3] B
15 Kalambo Falls [4] B,F,L,T
16 Kostenki [4] A,B,F,L,T

17 LaChapelle-aux-Saints [4] B,T
18 Lake Rudolf site [3] B,T
19 Lantian site [3] B
20 Makapan [3] B
21 Mas D'Azil [4] A,T
22 Mauer site [3] B
23 Monte Circeo [4] B,T
24 Mt. Carmel [4] B,F,T
25 Neanderthal [4] B
26 Niaux [4] A,T
27 Olduvai Gorge [3] B,L,T
28 Omo [3] B,T
29 Peking Man [3] B,F,T
30 Piltdown (discredited)
31 Qafzeh [4] B,F,T
32 Rusinga Island [1] B
33 Shanidar cave [4] B,F,L,T

34 Siwalik Hills [1] B
35 St. Acheul [3] T
36 Steinheim [4] B
37 Sterkfontein [3] B,T
38 Swanscombe [4] B,T
39 Taung [3] B
40 Terra Amata [4] F,L,T
41 Torralba-Ambrona [3] B,F,L,T
42 Tuc d'Audoubert [4] A,T
43 "Valley of Caves" [4]
44 Vallonet cave [3] B,T
45 Vérteszöllös [3] B,F,L,T
46 Lothagam [1] B
47 Swartkrans [3] B
48 Molodova [4] B,T,L,F
49 Lazaret

extended the sense of the future. So there is something to the reconnaissance theory. There is also something to the food-carrying theory, although it may have been more important to carry infants than food, which is generally eaten on the spot. If bipedalism produced a foot designed above all for support and with greatly reduced grasping capacities, infants could no longer have clung as effectively to their mothers and would have had to be carried. In fact, one case of upright walking among baboons involved a mother who from time to time was forced to move a few steps on two feet so that she could support her infant.

Another indirect benefit of bipedalism may have been that it helped to discourage the most dangerous predators, the big cats. A predator knows its prey from repeated encounters, repeated successes and failures in the hunt, and part of that knowledge in early hominid times must have been a firmly ingrained image of its prey as a four-footed animal. George Schaller of the New York Zoological Society, who has observed tigers in India and lions in Tanzania as well as gorillas in the Congo, comments on this possibility: "Some big cats turn into man-eaters, a fact interesting chiefly because it is so rare. They hunt by lying in wait or approaching stealthily and bounding on the victim's back, and they bite at the neck. Man is bipedal and thus does not furnish a good target, a good horizontal plane for the cats to jump on. Perhaps that is one thing that deters them today, and deterred them in the past."

These and other ideas lean heavily on speculation; they are neither proved nor universally accepted. We have no pelvis, leg, or foot remains providing direct evidence of bipedalism. Nor do we have any identifiable tool remains from this period. On the other hand, these speculations fit in with much of what we have learned to date from fossils, primate behavior and related studies. The inference is strong that *Ramapithecus* was among the first hominids, that they represent a widespread and successful breed. The most recent *Ramapithecus* finds, from Hungary, Greece and Turkey, also show distinct hominid features mixed with some pongid features. Also, theoretical considerations indicate that he probably used tools and perhaps was somewhat better than present-day apes at walking about on two feet.

There is much to learn about the forerunners of *Ramapithecus*. Efforts have been made to trace the hominid line back further than the 14-million-year-old date at Fort Ternan. A date of 20 million years has been estimated for certain fossil primate specimens, including some found on Rusinga Island in Lake Victoria, long a favorite hunting ground of Leakey and his wife Mary, an accomplished investigator in her own right. But most qualified specialists feel that the specimens are the remains of an ape rather than a hominid.

Some doubt also exists about evidence from Egypt's Fayum which Simons has suggested may indicate that the first representatives of the human line appeared 25 million years ago. Other investigators favor a more recent date. Washburn, for example, cites biochemical studies of primate blood proteins conducted by Vincent Sarich at the University of California as part of his argument that hominids and apes did not emerge as separate lines until 5 million to 10 million years ago. As of now, the tendency is to stick with *Ramapithecus* and an estimate of about 15 million years. Even if he is not considered a full hominid, *Ramapithecus* is certainly the best existing candidate from which to trace the hominid line.

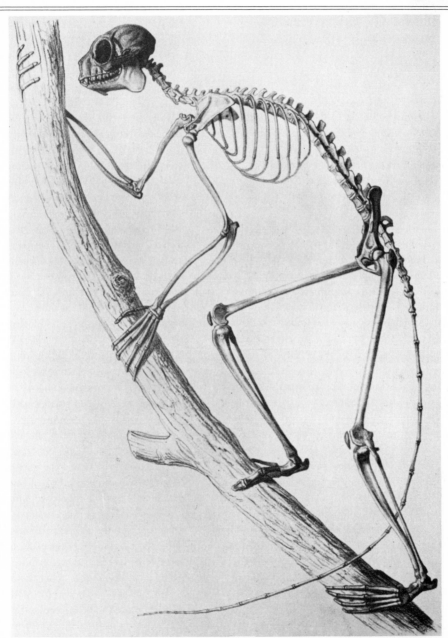

Hunting the "Dawn Apes" of Africa

by E. L. Simons

Elwyn Simons, the author of the article that follows, "Hunting the 'Dawn Apes' of Africa," is one of the foremost experts on the evolution of the first hominids and pongids. This article describes one of his expeditions to the Fayum desert in Egypt.

Almost all of the existing knowledge of the Old World ancestors of apes, men and monkeys is based on 28 to 35-million-year-old fossils from the Fayum desert of Egypt. Marine mammals were reported from these beds in 1879, but the varied and exotic series of land mammals was not found until about 1900. The six recent Yale University expeditions have uncovered fossilized fragments which shed new light on the origin and evolution of African mammals, including man's forerunners. Among the latter are bones of the oldest undoubted great ape and the first relatively complete upper jaws of Oligocene (25 to 35 million years ago) apes, together with fossils of monkey relatives. Until now, the oldest known upper jaws of any higher primates specially related to man dated back to 19 million years ago.

The first light on the early age of mammals in the "dark continent" was shed by reports resulting from several paleontological collecting expeditions sent to the area mainly in the decade after 1900. During this period fossils of four genera and species of ancient Egyptian "apes" were found and named: *Parapithecus, Propliopithecus, Apidium* and

© *Discovery* (Peabody Mus. Nat. Hist., Yale Univ.), **4**(1), 1968.

Moeripithecus. Species of the first two of these primates were established on relatively complete mandibles. These were widely figured in books on paleontology and human evolution, and came to serve as the basis for almost all discussions of the origin of the higher primates, or "Anthropoidea." The type species of *Moeripithecus* and *Apidium,* on the other hand, were based on jaw fragments with few teeth. The scantiness of the remains of the latter two limited scientific discussion of their affinities.

Curiously enough, however, no further productive field research on this early African primate fauna was undertaken until the Yale University expedition began in 1960. Perhaps this inactivity was due to the relative lack of success of earlier expeditions in finding smaller vertebrate remains. Small fossils are seldom preserved in coarse river-deposited sands and gravels; before 1960 only about 20 pieces of mammals of cat size or smaller had been found in the Fayum. As a result, for more than half a century virtually all consideration of the initial stages of man's ancestry, and that of apes, was based on the fragmentary evidence of the parts of four different lower jaws from Egypt. Two of these dentally resembled apes, the other two, monkeys.

With such fragmentary material to work on as existed before the Yale expeditions, scientists varied in the interpretations of the evolutionary meaning of these remains of early higher primates. Certain partly misleading ideas about these earliest-known close relatives of man were proposed initially and then continued to be quoted and requoted in textbooks. Thus discussions of *hominoid* origins departed farther and farther from the facts. Apparently only a few persons ever bothered to study the original dawn ape fossils at Stuttgart, Germany, and consequently *Parapithecus* was often said to fore-shadow Hominidae (the taxonomic family of man), *Propliopithecus* thought to be an early gibbon, and *Moeripithecus* was taken as a possible monkey forerunner. Actually, none of these suppositions has subsequently proven correct.

To clarify the status of some of these important fossils the author organized and directed the six recent paleontological Yale expeditions to Egypt. Apart from recovery of more or better primate remains another major objective of the Fayum expeditions was to study the environment in which these ancient apes lived. Comparison of fossil plants and animals with their living relatives often helps paleontologists determine the broad environmental conditions within which prehistoric species flour-ished. To understand how our ancient forerunners lived it is particularly important to understand their ecological setting.

By combining information on the Fayum fossil primates with interpretation of their environment, questions such as the following can receive at least partial answers. How recently were the ancestors of both men and apes still tree dwellers? When did the latest common ancestors of man and apes, particu-larly the African apes, exist? What are the relation-ships of Oligocene apes and monkeys to later forms?

ANCIENT MAN IN THE FAYUM

The Fayum "bone fields" (which have revealed all we know of the Oligocene life of the African continent) are situated in an arid desert about 65 miles southwest of Cairo and along the northern margin of the Fayum Depression at the eastern edge of the Sahara. Not only is this area of importance in the study of the history of African land mammals but the region is of considerable interest to archaeologists as well. The interaction of man and environment along the shores of brackish Lake Qarun has long been in progress. In fact, the region itself takes its name from an ancient Egyptian word for lake, *phiom.*

After the Fayum depression had been formed, probably by wind erosion in the Pliocene or early Pleistocene, a large lake developed in the area, fed by occasional Nile floods spilling in from the east. This great tamarisk-lined lake abounded in wild fowl and fish. Hippopotamus and gazelle grazed along its reedy shores and ostrich stalked the uplands. Today the dry margins of this former lake are littered with the bones of these animals and of the stone tools of several successive levels of habitation by Stone Age hunters. About 4,000 years ago the Fayum region achieved great importance due to the irrigation projects of Amenemhat I and his successors of the XII Dynasty. These ancient Egyptians temporarily stabilized the diminishing lake level by regulating the natural canal from the Nile at Lahún. A network of canals branching from this main source watered the southern margin of the depression and early estab-lished the Fayum province as the richest agricultural region of Egypt after the Nile delta.

In Ptolemaic times irrigation projects and further exposure of arable clays of the lake temporarily allowed establishment of agricultural cities on the north shore. Now the long abandoned ruins of these cities project raggedly from the horizons of the Fayum bone fields. In this desert modern paleon-tologists occasionally come across Graeco-Roman coins and even the bones and teeth of these classical Egyptian agriculturists.

A roadway largely made of petrified wood is another relic of the ancient Egyptians. This appar-ently was used to transport blocks of basalt on sleds from the lava flow at the top of the cliffs to a point near the north shore of the lake where the quarried materials could have been removed by boat. Al-though untrodden for almost 4,000 years, parts of it look as if they had been completed yesterday. This road has more than historical significance. If the approximate time of its construction could be determined, much could be learned about the rate and manner of recent desert erosion by wind and water through study of the effects of flash flooding and sandblasting of the petrified wood pavement of this roadway.

A TROPICAL FOREST

The plant and animal fossils contained in these ancient riverlain deposits show that the Oligocene environment of the northern coast of Africa contrasted sharply with conditions in the region today. The richest fossil beds contain numerous trunks of trees often as long as 30 meters (98 feet). Although some early geologists speculated that "removal" of branches from these trunks indicated that these trees had been brought down flooded rivers from forest lands many hundreds of miles to the south, there is considerable evidence against this conjecture. Tropical forest trees typically have straight boles with few branches except at the crown in the canopy. Such trees after waterlogging in stream channels soon lose roots and branches, and so reach the condition seen in the Fayum logs without much transport. Moreover, many of the small vertebrate remains are too delicate to have been moved far among gravels. Many of these also belonged to animals whose present-day relatives dwell in forested regions, so it seems unlikely that the fossil logs and the vertebrate bones were derived from different areas. Although impressions of leaves from these trees have not been preserved in the Fayum sands, a number of seed pods have. Studies of the seed pods and of the types of wood represented have helped determine the forest flora. Altogether the picture indicated by these plant remains is of a tropical gallery forest which flourished in or very near the Fayum region in Oligocene times. Since the region adjoined the shore there were probably also areas of open savannah or coastal plains.

Thus in picturing the environment of the dawn apes one can imagine that they lived in the forest canopy, as most generalized primates, such as lemurs, bush-babies, marmosets, etc., do today. A misjudged leap between branches overhanging a stream or an incautious visit to the waterside could have resulted in fatal attacks from aquatic enemies. An indication of the inexperience of these ancient primates is that the degree of tooth eruption in their jaws shows that most were not adult. In fact only one of the many dozens of jaws now known is of an old individual with an advanced stage of tooth wear.

One further ecological deduction about the environment of the dawn apes may be indicated by the rarity of members of the small mammal fauna other than primates and rodents. This may mean that the undergrowth near the Oligocene streams was too dense or too wet to maintain an abundance of small mammals. However, the primates and rodents which are the common faunal elements might have reached such relatively inaccessible river banks through the forest canopy.

LOCATING FOSSIL CONCENTRATIONS

Each main type of fossil occurrence presents problems to the vertebrate paleontologist. The process of locating bone concentrations and extracting the fossils from the rock varies greatly from one country to another. In the Fayum there is no problem of seeing a maximum of rock exposure, as there is no cover of vegetation. Even so, spots where there are concentrations of small vertebrate remains rich enough to warrant extensive excavation are extremely rare. An added complication is that the main rock type is a loose sand or "sandstone" which is only occasionally consolidated. In excavations the sand tends to slump back into the quarry or be blown into the "bone pits" by the wind. Thus, digging for fossils is not too practical.

Strong winds blowing across the desert are common and were a perpetual annoyance to earlier collectors and to our first expeditions. We found, however, that even the winds could be put to use in collecting—an unusual method of recovering fossils. It is only necessary for us to remove the "desert pavement" (a gravel cover consisting mainly of larger fragments of chert, lava and quartz which have resisted wind and water erosion). When this crust is gone the wind scours along the surface and a constant swirl of blowing sand gradually erodes the quarry face. In general, the fossils are not moved by the wind so that after a storm, collectors can harvest the quarry face.

Cementing with one of the newer types of plastic resins is particularly important for fossil mammal jaws from these sediments for, unlike most vertebrate bones of equal antiquity, there has been little mineralization, or penetration of the bone by hardening minerals carried in by ground water. Since these fossils have not thus been "hardened" they are exceedingly fragile. The light buff and whitish colors of the fossil bones are very close to those of the surrounding sands and gravels. It takes a practiced eye to locate the smaller fossils even on well blown-off surfaces.

THE FAYUM PRIMATES

In addition to numerous jaws now recovered indicating the existence in the African Oligocene of at least nine primate species, a collection of several isolated skull and limb bone fragments has been made, culminated by the recovery of a partial skull of *Aegyptopithecus.* In general terms these show what Oligocene Anthropoidea were like but, except on grounds of size it is not possible to associate particular skeletal fragments with one or another of the known species.

What does the known anatomy of the Fayum primates tell us? Four parts of frontal (forehead) bones of different sizes all show that the dawn apes had comparatively narrow snouts between the eyes, some forebrain expansion and relative reduction of olfactory lobes. These correlate with predominance of the visual sense over the olfactory in higher primates. Moreover, in all four specimens, the left and right frontals are fused into one bone along the mid-line, as is also true in the newly reported skull of *Aegyptopithecus.* These two bones remain separate in nearly all lower primates or prosimians at least until old age. But frontal fusion at an early individual age is characteristic of higher primates or Anthropoidea. One of the new Fayum primate frontals appears to belong to a sub-adult, as indicated by the striated texture of the bone. Nevertheless the specimen has completely fused frontals.

The limb skeleton is poorly known but some of the toe bones and ankle bones have been recovered as well as the humerus and ulna of the forelimb. Taken together these postcranial remains indicate a structural grade intermediate between lemurs and Old World higher primates. This grade is best seen today in various South American monkeys.

One additional find of interest in the main primate quarry were the tail bones of primates. Because of their size these might belong with one of the larger Oligocene primate species which on dental grounds are clearly hominoids. Previously living and fossil apes were characterized as tailless, but in tracing back their evolution, they must ultimately, of course, have had tailed ancestors. Perhaps these large tail bones from the Fayum indicate that this was so for Oligocene apes. Moreover, it has recently been shown from the size of the spinal canal in sacral vertebrae of the Miocene gibbon *Pliopithecus* that this early ape also had a long tail. Thus as we gain better knowledge of early apes the old distinction between tailless apes and the tailed monkeys breaks down.

CONCLUSION

Considered as a group, much about the probable course of primate evolution can be learned from the many specimens of the dawn apes now known. Various of these Egyptian Oligocene species can be interpreted as showing relationships to earlier and later Old World primates.

In closing it is perhaps well to bear in mind that none of the dawn apes and monkeys needs necessarily be close to the ancestry of any living primates— African or otherwise. Scientists even today know almost nothing of the first half of the Age of Mammals in Africa and have only scanty faunal samples from this continent during Oligocene and Miocene times. Many African Early Tertiary primate species must have existed about which we know nothing and some of which may have been more directly related to living man and his relatives than any we now know. The search for these is one of the exciting challenges to geobiologists of the future.

Summary

The development of hominids from forest-dwelling apes some 15 million years ago coincides with the shrinkage of the forest cover stretching across much of Africa and Asia. The prehominids, experiencing population pressure from various competitive species, expanded into newly formed grasslands.

The earliest fossil hominid remains were discovered by Louis Leakey near Fort Ternan, Kenya in 1961. The reduced snout, the U-shaped jaw, the small teeth—all hominid characteristics, led Leakey to classify the specimen as a hominid despite its great age, 15 million years. This fossil caught the attention of another leading physical anthropologist, Elwyn Simons, owing to its similarity to a jawbone he had recently reconstructed. A search of previously uncovered fossils in museum collections around the world led Simons to discover a series of specimens mislabeled as early apes. He concluded that all these remains belonged to the same genus as Leakey's Fort Ternan find. The genus was named *Ramapithecus* after one of the specimens from India.

The *Ramapithecus* form raises two intriguing questions. First, why are his teeth, especially his canines, so small: second, how did he develop bipedalism? Most apes have large, protruding canines utilized in threats of aggression, fighting, and in the consumption of foods requiring tearing and dismemberment. The reduced canines of *Ramapithecus* might imply the possession of some functional equivalent, perhaps tools and weapons. However, the evidence for tool use by *Ramapithecus* is almost negligible. A more plausible explanation is suggested by the study of the contemporary species of gelada baboons. The gelada baboon consumes grass seeds and tough plant foods which require heavy grinding with the molar teeth. Its canines have undergone reduction in size as an evolutionary adaptation to the mechanics of side to side grinding with which large canines interfere. By analogy, the reduced canines of *Ramapithecus* may have been an adaptation to a similar diet.

The most reliable, but indirect, evidence of the origin of bipedalism comes from the study of living primates. Baboons are capable of occasional bipedalism, often standing on two legs to survey an area. Chimpanzees are known to walk several yards with armfuls of fruit; macaque monkeys of Japan walk up to sixty yards carrying food. This suggests food conveyance was a stimulus to bipedalism. Yet, carrying is a restricted activity among non-human primates and cannot fully explain the origins of bipedalism. An alternative hypothesis is to link food transport with sharing behavior, particularly of meat, as a stimulus to bipedalism. Plants can easily be consumed by the gatherer as they are collected, while a hunter is often left with more than he can eat. The social advantages of sharing a kill at a home base may have resulted in more and more bipedal locomotion. Interestingly, the only recorded incidents of sharing among non-human primates involved fresh-killed prey.

It is also possible that habitual bipedalism led to more elaborate forms of tool use. While chimpanzees and gorillas throw rocks and wave branches when threatened, actions more akin to display than tool use, chimpanzees are known to employ small sticks to eat termites and leaf sponges to drink water. Tool use is well within the behavioral repertoire of apes and monkeys but is limited by the use of the forelimbs for locomotion. A bipedal *Ramapithecus*, with free hands, may have employed more complex patterns of tool use than modern primates. While direct evidence is limited, speculation based on knowledge of living primates indicates that carrying, sharing, meat consumption, tool use and bipedalism combined to reinforce each other in a circle of cause and effect.

Glossary

Bipedalism   The act of walking, running or in some other way moving about on two legs; characteristic of hominids.

Canine teeth   The pointed eyeteeth that lie between the incisors and the premolars in primates. In humans, they are used in tearing or ripping food: in other species, canines are also used in threats of aggression.

Molar teeth   The large grinding teeth found in the back of the mouth in all hominoids.

Additional Reading

Eckhardt, Robert B.

1972   Population Genetics and Human Origins. Scientific American, volume 226, no. 1, pp. 94–103.

   A controversial, nevertheless fascinating interpretation of the position of the primate fossil Gigantopithecus.

Lawick-Goodall, Jane van

1971   In the Shadow of Man. Boston: Houghton Mifflin.

   Lawick-Goodall's popularized book on her research among chimpanzees.

Pilbeam, David

1972   The Ascent of Man. New York: Macmillan.

   A good introduction to human evolution. Covers many of the theoretical problems facing anthropologists in dating and analyzing fossils.

Simons, Elwyn L.

1964   The Early Relatives of Man. Scientific American, volume 211, no. 1, pp. 60–77.

   A brief, in depth discussion of early primate evolution.

Simons, Elwyn L. and Peter C. Ettel

1970   Gigantopithecus. Scientific American, volume 222, no. 1, pp. 77–85.

   This is an excellent discussion of Gigantopithecus from the first teeth found though the analysis of its place in primate evolution.

chapter four

We shall never be able
to point to a specific time
and a specific creature and
say here man began.
LOUIS LEAKEY

SOUTHERN APES— LINKS IN HUMAN EVOLUTION

Ramapithecus stands alone, isolated in time, a face or the shadow of a face seen in the distance. Its successors, like its predecessors, are still elusive. Practically nothing is known about developments from about 8 or 9 million years ago, which represents roughly the most recent date for *Ramapithecus* as identified by Pilbeam and Simons, to about 5 million years ago, the biggest gap in the story of human evolution. We can expect to obtain new knowledge in the years ahead as expeditions get under way in East Africa, the Siwalik Hills, Saudi Arabia and other regions. But we cannot expect too much,

for conditions widely prevalent during that period could hardly have been less favorable for the preservation of fossils.

Although the fossil record for the 5 million years after *Ramapithecus* is still unclear, the geological record suggests a great deal about the probable course of human evolution. During the Pliocene, a gradual drying out of the forests occurred. The reduction of available living space for tree-dwelling apes was certainly not rapid enough to drive the apes out of the trees. For the most part, they simply moved to other trees. As the tropical forests slowly de-

75

clined, however, some apes took advantage of ground life on the forest edge. While an arboreal way of life guaranteed an abundant supply of figs and other fruit, the savanna offered grasses, roots, seeds, and tender shoots as well. An animal which adapted to life on the forest edge could enjoy the best of both worlds.

Over the course of many millennia, a population of pre-hominids may have begun to break their ancestral ties to the forest. Increasing bipedalism, the use of tools, and the evolution of a larger and more complex brain would have been extremely valuable in competing for food and other resources on the savanna. Modification of the hands and teeth would serve as additional advantages to a creature which could then pick up and grind seeds as a source of food. Moreover, each of these changes appears to have played a role in the evolution of the others, although it is not yet clear exactly what

A water hole at Amboseli: our early ancestors lived on such savannas.

caused them. Did the use of tools initiate anatomical changes or did anatomical changes lead to the use of tools? Was the shift to the consumption of open-territory vegetation the key element?

As the early hominids underwent physical changes in response to their new ecological niche, certain changes in social organization may have occurred as well. It would not take the hominids long to discover that hunting small animals was a useful occupation on the savanna. A division of labor arose when females specialized in gathering available fruits and nuts and caring for the young while the males traveled in pursuit of their prey. Each member of the group became familiar with a region covering hundreds of square miles. Hunting is always a chancy business, however, and the males could not always be relied upon to return with meat. It would be the job of the females to gather the wild-growing vegetation which made up the bulk of the day-to-day diet. Exactly when and how this division of labor first occurred will probably never be known, but it is clear that the hunting and gathering way of life may be traced to the early hominids' advance into the savanna.

Meanwhile, other changes were taking place besides the general increase in the extent of arid lands. Africa was about to experience one of the most spectacular series of upheavals in the history of the earth. Pressures building under the earth's crust fractured mountains, pushed up volcanoes, ripped open the bottoms of lakes and punched holes in broad plains to create new bodies of water. The result was a far-flung fracturing, the Great Rift Valley, extending about 4,000 miles from the Zambezi River area of Mozambique in the south, up through East Africa and Ethiopia, and north as far as the Valley of the Jordan in Israel. The Jordan River, the Dead and Red seas, Lakes Edward and Albert and Tanganyika and Malawi are some of the places where water has filled steep, parallel-sided valleys along the fracture lines of the Rift.

The effects of rifting in Africa on human evolution are more difficult to specify than the effects of the increase of deserts and semi-deserts. Certainly the movements of hominids were altered as traditional migration routes were abandoned and new ones established. Before the rifting, Africa was essentially a broad plain created by the erosion of ancient mountain ranges, a plain rising gradually to heights of more than a mile. The top of the rise formed a continental divide running north and south, with the waters of the Congo Basin draining west off the slopes into the Atlantic Ocean and other waters draining east into the Indian Ocean. Rivers separated hominid populations from one another and restricted their movements to zones running east and west.

Rifting changed that pattern. Instead of flowing in a west-to-east direction from the divide to the Indian Ocean, rivers tended to flow north and south along Rift lines and drained internally in Rift valleys. Hominid bands could also move more freely along new north-south migration routes, although the problem of timing remains to be solved. Did populations of advanced hominids evolve on the plains of southern Africa and spread to the north when the rivers shifted, or evolve in East Africa and spread south, or in both regions and mingle? Some investigators suspect that post-Rift migrations were from south to north, but the evidence is so sparse that no one really knows.

THE NEW HOMINID

Almost 5 million years of geological change passed during the time between *Ramapithecus* and the next phase of the fossil record. Then the story picks up again, and it is a new story based on evidence discovered in increasing quantities during the past few years. Imagine

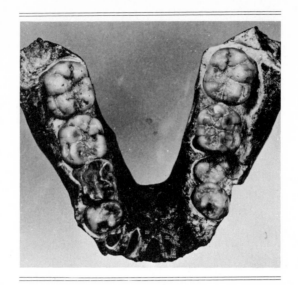

The *lower jawbone and teeth of* Australopithecus robustus. *Notice the unusually large molars.*

that you are in a helicopter flying high over an African savanna late one hot prehistoric afternoon. From that perspective things appear very much as they do today. You can look down on a dry grassy plain, straw-colored except for scattered bushes and trees, dark green clumps near swamps and water holes, and the lone winding ribbon of green that marks the course of a large river where it empties into a lake.

Coming down for a closer view, hovering at the edge of the trees along a stretch of the river, you might at first sight see nothing to suggest that you are not in the twentieth century. There are many familiar-looking birds, monkeys, hyenas, antelopes, giraffes, and even a hippopotamus wallowing in the mud—all of them very much like today's varieties. Then you notice some strange animals: little three-toed horses grazing near the trees, and a herd of elephants with two tusks in their lower jaws and two in their upper jaws.

But the most surprising sight lies in another

An artist's conception of the head of A. robustus.

The earliest known trace of these creatures exists in the form of an age-blackened bit of lower jawbone from Africa, announced in 1971 by Bryan Patterson of Harvard's Museum of Comparative Zoology. The specimen had been studied on and off for nearly four years, ever since it was found one August afternoon lying on a sun-baked clay slope of Lothagam Hill in the Kenya badlands near the southwestern end of Lake Turkana, formerly Lake Rudolf which is part of the African Rift Valley.

Part of Patterson's job was to identify the

The fossil below is a fragment of Australopithecus *jawbone more than 5 million years old. Above is a modern human jawbone, showing location of fragment.*

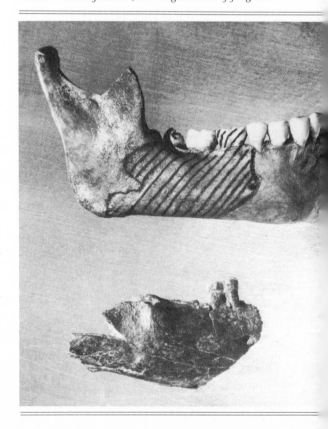

direction. With the trees at your back, you look out over the wide savanna, and see a troop of creatures heading for the forest. Even at a distance there is something familiar about them. They move like people. They walk fully upright, arms swinging freely at their sides. A mother runs over to a group of scuffling children and scolds as she snatches her child away. The leader strides forward confidently with the alert no-nonsense attitude of a Western sheriff making sure the coast is clear.

Now you have a shock as he approaches and you see him clearly for the first time. Judging by his gait and posture and by the general feeling of humanness about the troop, you expect to confront a fellow human being. Instead, he is four feet tall, about the size of a modern child of seven or eight. Even more surprising is his face. His jaw and mouth are thrust forward with the trace of a muzzle. He has a low forehead and flattish nose and a remote half-wild look which is somehow not quite human. As the sun sets, the troop reaches the water hole and begins climbing into the trees to prepare for the night.

specimen as definitely as possible. He went mainly by the shape of the jawbone, and the shape and wear patterns of the single tooth remaining in place, a molar. For example, the tooth's grinding surface was worn unevenly, included a number of deep pits, and showed extensive wear on the sides where the tooth had fitted against neighboring teeth. These characteristics and others are rare among apes, but typical of creatures far more like a human than any other previous primate—members of the genus *Australopithecus* or "southern ape." The same characteristics also indicated that Patterson's find belonged to the more advanced *africanus* species of the genus *Australopithecus*.

Australopithecus remains were first discovered in the southern part of Africa by Raymond Dart, professor of anatomy at the Medical School of the University of the Witwatersrand in Johannesburg. One afternoon in 1924 he received two crates filled with fossil-bearing rocks collected by a miner at a limestone quarry in the village of Taung ("place of the lion" in Bantu) near the edge of the Kalahari Desert about two hundred miles away. The quarry had already yielded the skull of a baboon, among other things, and there was always the possibility of finding remains of a more advanced primate. This is precisely what happened. Dart came across a large block which had been blasted out of a tunnel-like cave in a limestone cliff and which contained the cast of a large brain case and major parts of a skull and jaw. He speculated that "the face might be somewhere there in the block." He went to work with hammer and chisel and, for the most delicate work, one of his wife's knitting needles.

In a subsequent report he recalls the long process of separating the fossil bones from their matrix of sand and lime: "No diamond cutter ever worked more lovingly or with such care on a priceless jewel—nor, I am sure, with such inadequate tools. But on the seventy-third day, December 23, the rock parted. I could view the

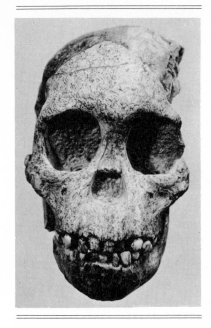

The *"Taung baby,"* the *Australopithecus* child whose skull was discovered by Dart.

face from the front, although the right side was still imbedded. (The complete extraction process took more than four years.) The creature which had contained this massive brain was no giant anthropoid such as a gorilla. What emerged was a baby's face, an infant with a full set of milk teeth and its permanent molars just in the process of erupting. I doubt if there was any parent prouder of his offspring than I was of my Taung baby on that Christmas."

About five weeks later the South African anatomist announced his find in a paper published in the British journal *Nature*. The report noted that the canine teeth of the Taung specimen were small, and that this implied an upright posture and increasing use of the hands and the probable use of tools and weapons. It also noted the significance of the fact that the specimen had been found in a near-desert site where life must have been difficult and required "enhanced cerebral pow-

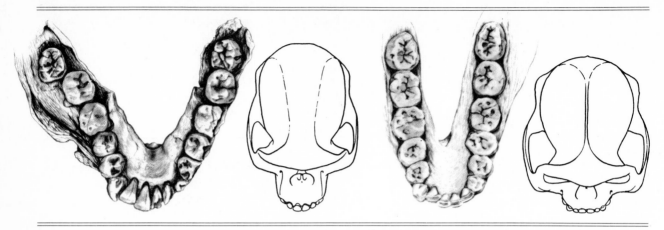

The jaws and skulls of Australopithecus robustus *(left)*
and africanus *(right).*

ers" for survival. Dart described the specimen as that of an "ultra-simian and prehuman stock, . . . a manlike ape," and officially christened it *Australopithecus africanus,* the first representative of a new species.

His report also made a strong case for Africa as the continent where humans first appeared, a point first made by Darwin. Specifically, it suggested that *Homo sapiens* must have arisen in dry and grassy savannas and not in dense tropical forests as many anthropologists believed. Food was so abundant in the forests and life so easy that apes faced no major challenges, and remained apes. "For the production of man a different apprenticeship was needed to sharpen the wits and quicken the higher manifestations of intellect—a more open veldt country where competition was keener between swiftness and stealth, and where adroitness of thinking and movement played a preponderating role in the preservation of the species."

Although Dart's general conclusions were correct, they came at the wrong time. *Ramapithecus* had not yet been identified, and it was widely assumed that walking on two feet and

tool use could not be expected, even among humanlike apes. Most investigators regarded the "Taung baby" as an ape not on the line that led to humans but more like the chimpanzee or gorilla. They were less interested in discussing its nature than in the fact that it had been discovered so far south and in a near-desert region.

Furthermore, all eyes then were on Asia, where the earliest known traces of humans had been found. One of the major scientific projects of the time was a large-scale American expedition organized to look for human remains in Mongolia and the Gobi Desert, an expedition which in the words of one caustic commentator "promised man but delivered eggs," dinosaur eggs uncovered in the Gobi Desert.

So far as most anthropologists were concerned, Dart was working in the wrong part of the world. They also felt that he had found the wrong kind of human ancestor. *Australopithecus* had a small brain, weighing perhaps a pound, or about a third as much as the brain of modern people, and that did not fit in with prevailing theory. According to Dart's former teacher Elliot Smith and most of his colleagues, the brain was a kind of pacemaker in human evolution. We had arisen from apelike species which had big brains to start with and then proceeded to take advantage of this favorable beginning by evolving to human status.

There was some evidence for this theory. In 1913, a British lawyer and part-time antiquarian, Charles Dawson, reported that he had discovered the remains of an individual with a human skull and an apelike jaw in a gravel pit in the village of Piltdown near the eastern coast of England. This material, together with skull fragments and apelike teeth which Dawson found later in a field two miles away, puzzled many investigators because the contrast between the humanness of the skull and the apishness of the jaw was so great. But since the remains tended to confirm the brain-as-pacemaker theory, they were more readily accepted at face value.

Dart had to wait until the weight of accumulating evidence and the exposure of Piltdown man as a fraud forced other workers to recognize that his "southern apes" were actually full-fledged hominids. The first confirmation came a dozen years later from a site nearer home, thirty miles west of Johannesburg. It lies in the Transvaal with its wide, dry rolling plains, waist-high golden grasses, clumps of trees, and a dryness so prevalent that there is a joke about what to do when you fall into a South African river. You get up and brush yourself off. One of the few wet waterways of the region, the Klip River, winds through a broad valley and rises from a swamp. Not far from the swamp, on a farm known as Sterkfontein, is a *kopje* or little hill with a long history.

The hill is a block of limestone formed some two billion years ago when Africa was submerged beneath a shallow sea, covered by more than six miles of sediments and lava, and then exposed by erosion. Waters seeped down through cracks in the rock and dissolved away calcium-containing deposits, producing small cavities at first and later a system of deep caves. One of the caves still exists; the others have crumbled away. Limestone quarrymen moved into its several hundred yards of underground passages more than sixty years ago. There they found fossils, many of which were sold to tourists on Sundays when the mine was open to the public. Also on sale was a guidebook which included an invitation: "Come to Sterkfontein and find the missing link."

One Sunday visitor took the invitation literally. Robert Broom, a Scottish-born physician and paleontologist who lived in South Africa, had immediately recognized the significance of Dart's specimen. In 1936 he dropped in to have a look at Sterkfontein, where, as at Taung, baboon fossils had recently been discovered. (As fellow ground dwellers, the ancestors of humans and baboons shared life on the savanna.) It was the start of a second career for the sixty-nine-year-old investigator. Within two weeks he found pieces of the skull of an adult *Australopithecus,* and he decided to concentrate on the search for early humans.

During the succeeding years Broom and his young assistant John Robinson, now professor

The "Piltdown man" skull which was one of anthropology's most famous hoaxes. An artist's conception of Piltdown man.

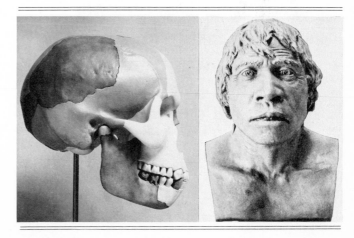

Controversy

The Australopithecines: How many species?

As physical anthropologists continue to investigate the nature and number of hominid lineages, many questions remain unresolved. One ongoing controversy concerns the *Australopithecus robustus* and *Australopithecus africanus* hominid lineages of 3 to 5 million years ago. Do these australopithecine forms, commonly referred to as robust and gracile, respectively, account for one, two or three distinct genera? The graciles are distinguished from the robusts by their smaller, lighter build and their rounded face and skull, unmarked by large brow ridges or crests on top of the skull.

Many investigators maintain that the gracile and robust forms represent two species of a single genus, *Australopithecus,* the gracile being an earlier, more generalized relative of the robust. Others believe the two represent distinct genera, and classify them as *Australopithecus africanus* and *Paranthropus robustus.* From his study of skull and tooth structure, J. T. Robinson concluded that the graciles were omnivores while the robusts were vegetarians. This dietary hypothesis was based in part on the larger canine teeth of the graciles and the large molars and reduced canines of the robusts. Thus, according to

Robinson, *Australopithecus africanus* was a superior walker and tool-maker who evolved into *Homo erectus,* while *Paranthropus robustus* remained in the forest and became extinct.

Recent statistical studies, however, suggest that the differences in molar tooth size between the graciles and the robusts are largely insignificant. Contrary to Robinson's hypothesis, it appears that graciles and robusts ate similar foods. Milford Wolpoff has indicated that the crest on top of the skull and the heavy bones associated with the robust are merely features related to the size of the individual. Another researcher used computer analysis to determine that the robust and gracile forms overlap greatly in stature, tending to corroborate the single species theory. Wolpoff and others have concluded that if there are two separate species of australopithecines, they overlap so greatly in physical form that complete specimens cannot be distinguished on the basis of any consistent physical criteria.

Some physical anthropologists have suggested that some or all of the differences between gracile and robust forms are functions of sexual dimorphism— that graciles and robusts are merely female and male members of the same species. At this point, however, there is little evidence available to substantiate this hypothesis.

A theory proposed by Louis Leakey holds that the australopithecines lived side by side with another species known as *Homo habilis. Homo habilis* is characterized by a larger brain, erect posture, and greater manual dexterity, according to Leakey. While the australopithecines were evolutionary dead ends, he believes *habilis* to be the predecessor of modern humans. New evidence is constantly being examined and evaluated as many new finds turn up in East Africa. Some investigators now consider *Homo habilis* to be an advanced member of the gracile aus- tralopithecine group. If this hypothesis is correct, the gracile form could be the ancestor of both the extinct robust form and modern humans. Others take the extreme view that none of the presently known fossil hominids lie directly in the human ancestry since there were many hominid species alive at the same time, most of which became extinct. They consider it highly unlikely that we would find the remains of the one hominid species that evolved into modern humans.

of anthropology at the University of Wisconsin, conducted excavations at Sterkfontein and two nearby sites. It was slow work. The fossil-containing deposits of sand, earth, bone and shattered rock were cemented together by lime salts and as hard as concrete. The only practical way to get at the material was to drill holes in it, blast it into chunks with sticks of dynamite, and, later in the laboratory, pick away at the chunks or treat them with mild acid.

In 1938, Broom discovered some startling fossil evidence. With the help of a boy from a farm at Kromdraii, Broom pieced together most of a third *Australopithecus* skull. Although the skull was clearly related to previous *Australopithecus* fossils, it differed markedly from these earlier finds. The skull was more massive with a heavier jaw and larger teeth, and its owner was estimated to weigh some 100 pounds and to stand only four feet tall. Broom claimed that he had discovered a new animal to be named *Paranthropus robustus,* or robust near-human. Most scientists rejected this claim but eventually recognized his find as a new species to be called *Australopithecus robustus.* The discovery of a seemingly later but, in many ways, even less humanlike species of *Australopithecus* raised many new questions about human evolution.

Meanwhile, Dart sent students to another rich site he had heard about during the 1920s, located about 150 miles away in the Makapan Valley. At one end were red cliffs and a waterfall, a "Lost World" valley as wild in appearance today as it was when our ancestors wandered there more than 20,000 centuries ago. Makapan included a network of caves under a domed roof larger than a football field and some ten stories high.

A familiar pattern led Dart to the ruins of this huge cave system in 1945: a limestone quarry, abandoned long ago, and the finding of a fossil baboon. Two years later one of his students recovered the back part of an *Aus-*

Robert Broom *(1866–1951) was born in Scotland and received his early training in anatomy at Glasgow University. After moving to South Africa in 1903, he devoted himself to teaching zoology and geology at Victoria College and to searching for fossil species of mammal-like reptiles. Shortly after Raymond Dart announced his find at Taung, he was visited by Broom. Together they examined the startling new find, eventually agreeing that it was, in fact, the "connecting link" between humans and early apes. Broom's interest in hominid fossils soared; it wasn't until eleven years later, in 1936, however, that he found the time to take up a new career hunting for pre-human remains. That same year, at the age of sixty-nine, Broom uncovered the first mature* Australopithecus.

tralopithecus skull from the quarry dump. A year after that it was a lower jaw, and within another four months part of a face and several other pieces, parts of a skullcap and upper jaw and pelvis. The evidence was piling up, and none of it checked with the notion that people had big brains from the beginning, or with the increasingly puzzling Piltdown remains.

It was Joseph Weiner, now at the London School of Hygiene and Tropical Medicine and then at Oxford University, who, mulling over the peculiar Piltdown remains one day in 1953, suddenly considered deception as a serious possibility. Special studies conducted at Oxford and the British Museum of Natural History removed all doubts. The Piltdown skull fragments belonged to a modern human, the jawbone and teeth to a modern ape. The material had been filed down, chemically treated and otherwise tampered with to make it appear ancient and authentic. Then someone had planted the doctored specimens in the gravel pit.

The job was done quite skillfully, but that is not what fooled the experts. They were taken in mainly because they had no reason to suspect a deliberate fraud. The truth became evident as soon as the possibility of fraud was seriously considered. The culprit has not been publicly identified, and his motive is a mystery. Exposure of the skulduggery alerted anthropologists to the possibility of deception, and the odds against their succumbing to another major hoax are enormous. Furthermore, it helped discredit once and for all the theory that we were created big-brained and fully human, and cleared the way for a more plausible theory based on evidence from South Africa and elsewhere.

OLDUVAI GORGE

New evidence has been accumulating ever since. Besides the Lothagam Hill specimen, Patterson found part of a 4-million-year-old upper arm bone of *Australopithecus* at another site about forty miles away; its status, *robustus* or *africanus,* is still uncertain. The Rift Valley region around Lake Turkana, the source of this upper arm bone, is located about 350 miles from Nairobi—past Mount Kilimanjaro; past an extinct Rift Valley volcano, and down the other side into the Serengeti Plain, one of Africa's great game reserves.

Buried deep beneath the Serengeti is another plain. It lies under some three hundred feet of volcanic ash and sand and lake sediments, except for one area in which nature has carried out a large-scale excavation. About fifty thousand years ago, rifting produced a series of cliffs over which swift rivers cascaded, gouging down through accumulated deposits and exposing part of the old plain. The torrents created a miniature Grand Canyon, the twenty-five-mile-long Olduvai Gorge, the world's richest source of information about the beginnings of humans.

A view of Olduvai Gorge, where many fossils of early hominids have been discovered.

The information buried at Olduvai Gorge has been uncovered largely through the efforts of Louis Leakey, who was born in Kenya and grew up with his two sisters and brothers as the only white children in a Kikuyu village (his parents were English missionaries). Leakey devoted his life to the discovery and excavation of African sites. From the beginning he felt there was something special about Olduvai, even before it yielded anything extraordinary. Within a few hours after arriving there for the first time, he found stone tools on the slope of a side gully less than a hundred yards from his tent and determined to start a search for remains of the toolmakers.

That was in 1931, a generation after a German entomologist discovered Olduvai. Leakey returned again and again over the years, accompanied by his wife Mary. Season after season, they camped not far from the edge of the gorge, walked down into canyons to explore areas as much as ten miles away and shared a water hole with rhinoceroses and other big game. ("We could never get rid of the taste of rhino urine," Leakey recalled, "even after filtering the water through charcoal and boiling it and using it in tea with lemon.")

They found many concentrations of tools and animal bones, sites to be excavated in the future if sufficient funds and help became available, but few hominid fossils until one July morning in 1959. Prehistorians in the field never stop looking, and Mary happened to be walking along the same slope where her husband had first found tools nearly three decades before. This time a recent rock slide had exposed previously buried deposits. Mary noticed a bit of skull and, stuck in the face of a nearby cliff, two very large and shining brown-black pre-molar teeth whose size and cusp pattern indicated a parimate more advanced than a monkey or ape.

It took the Leakeys nineteen days to free the teeth and parts of a fossil palate from the soft rock, sift tons of rubble and dirt, and gather a total of more than four hundred bone fragments. Some months later at a scientific meeting, Leakey invited a few privileged colleagues to an advance preview of a new find. He opened a black box and removed the beautifully reconstructed skull of an eighteen-year-old *Australopithecus*.

Until July of 1959, only two species of *Australopithecus* were believed to exist. The Leakeys' discovery, however, suggested an individual different from either of the known species. This new specimen shared the large teeth and face of *A. robustus* but had a deeper and more arched palate resembling that of modern humans. Potassium-argon dating revealed the fossil to be about 1.75 million years old. Leakey proposed that his find be recognized as a new genus, but it was instead classified as a new species to be called *Australopithecus boisei* in honor of Charles Boise. Many physical anthropologists, however, considered *boisei* to be a variation of *robustus*.

Not long after the discovery in East Africa, the National Geographic Society began supporting the Leakeys' work, providing funds for workers and equipment. During the next thirteen months about 7,000 tons of dirt and rock were moved, more than twice as much as had been moved during all the previous digging seasons. Since then Olduvai has yielded a number of important and surprising discoveries, including the first absolute date for such early sites. The South African sites have not been dated because the only sufficiently accurate "radioactive clock" currently available, the potassium-argon technique, depends on the analysis of volcanic minerals, and volcanoes were not erupting in South Africa during hominid times. But there are such minerals at Olduvai, and the deposits containing the 1959 skull turned out to be about 1,750,000 years old, nearly twice as old as had previously been estimated on the basis of geological studies. The new date has done much to increase respect for the hominids of the times: their relatively advanced development appears more striking the earlier they lived.

THE LIFE OF *AUSTRALOPITHECUS*

So far, remains representing more than twenty individuals have been found in older and more recent deposits, including a number of rarely preserved foot and hand bones. The feet of the Olduvai hominids are remarkable because they are so much like ours. They are smaller, the foot of one adult being about seven inches long, or about the foot size of an eight-year-old child today, and show a few other minor differences. But they show that *Australopithecus* and his contemporaries walked upright, a conclusion supported by studies of his pelvis, particularly the upper part of the hipbone blade, which is shortened and tilted toward the vertical position. As a rule, apes bend forward when they walk on two feet, because their hipbone blade is long and bent forward. Nor can they stride as we do, as their main thigh and buttock muscles tend to flex the leg so that walking must be done in a weak, bent-knee fashion.

Whether *Australopithecus* walked as well as we do is another question. Adrienne Zihlman of the University of California in Santa Cruz has conducted extensive studies of walking patterns in nonhuman primates and modern humans as well as the relevant fossil material, and concludes: "*Australopithecus* would have required more muscle energy than modern man to perform the same actions. He probably walked with toes turned out and might have carried his weight more on the outside of the foot."

He was, then, a creature in transition. Achieving an upright stance was only one part of the story. Yet to come were refinements of "internal rotation," more efficient hip-joint action which

A pebble tool (left) and a chopper (right), representative of the first stone tools made by our ancestors.

would reduce fatigue during long trips in search of food and new places to live. Zihlman emphasizes that these and related developments also favored the coordination and balance required to aim and throw accurately, and to stand still for long periods during the stalking of game. However, Zihlman's is not the only interpretation. Scientists at the Biomechanics Laboratory at Western Reserve University analyzed *Australopithecus* pelvis and femur samples, concluding that there is nothing to distinguish his walk from ours.

Stone tools discovered in recent excavations reveal as much as fossil remains. Findings indicate that they were not as backward or primitive as was once believed. For a long time no stone tools were announced from any of the South African sites, which was no surprise. Most investigators assumed that toolmaking was beyond the capacities of such small-brained hominids, although tool use involving "ready-made" unworked objects was considered a definite possibility. In fact, this notion was so taken for granted that when incontrovertibly shaped tools were found at Sterkfontein in 1956, they were immediately and widely attributed to more-advanced creatures.

Louis and Mary Leakey examining an early living floor in Olduvai Gorge.

This position had to be abandoned four years later with the finding of the first skull at Olduvai and the Leakeys' increased pace of excavation. The evidence was clear: shaped tools were found in the same layers that contained hominid remains. Nevertheless, granted that the hominids actually made tools, the general expectation seemed to be that they must have been extremely crude tools, and at first only extremely crude tools were recognized and reported. Indeed, the tools found were so crude that it would be impossible to identify anything much cruder as an artifact. Scientists often see what they believe, and their findings and interpretations tend to confirm their expectations.

The older sites of Olduvai, those located in deposits not far from the bottom of the gorge, have yielded interesting collections of stone materials. The great majority of pieces look like nothing in particular and would be gathered by specialists only. They may not be tools at all but simply rubble, natural chunks of rock which have not been shaped or altered in any way. Yet even unworked material has something to tell us about prehistoric activities. The stones consist mainly of lava and quartz which do not come from the immediate vicinity of the site itself. They were carried in from places at least three miles away, perhaps to hurl at marauding animals or to hold down animal skins. If the hominids slept on the ground, as Leakey believed, stones could have been placed on damp surfaces under straw and grasses to make a dry bedding, or above the straw and grasses to keep the material from blowing away during the day.

One of the most common worked tools found among the rubble is the *chopper*. If such pieces make up an appreciable proportion of the total stone assemblage, one can be reasonably sure that they were made by human hands. But the finding of a few flaked stones that could be tools means nothing at all, because they could also have been produced by nature rather than by humans.

Desmond Clark has walked along English beaches examining stones chipped and broken by pounding surf. Many stones showed the removal of a single flake from one side, and some had flakes removed from both sides or both ends. Revil Mason of the University of the Witwatersrand in Johannesburg once examined 20,000 stones collected at Makapan. A number of them looked as if they were worked tools, but after considering the assemblage as a whole he realized that there was no solid evidence for the presence of artifacts. Nature had done the shaping. One tell-tale characteristic is that natural flakes tend to have striking angles over 90° while man-made flakes are removed with angles under 90°. But there is also crossover; natural flakes can be found with low angles of detachment and vice versa. At the most rudimentary level it is not easy to distinguish accidents from artifacts. As Abbé Henri Breuil, one of France's foremost prehistorians, observed: "Man made one, God made ten thousand—God help the man who tries to see the one in ten thousand."

Most of the choppers among the earliest Olduvai collections are slightly smaller than a tennis ball. But there is another kind of chopper which John Napier of the Royal Free Hospital in London shows to visitors to his London office. He has two walnut-sized choppers made of greenish lava, and although the hand of an *Australopithecus* was smaller than ours, it was not so small that such miniature tools would fit it comfortably. They must have been held with the thumb and ring and index fingers and used for some purpose such as preparing small pieces of plant or animal food. Olduvai sites also include bone tools such as a flattened and highly polished rib of a zebra or some other horselike species, which was possibly rubbed against hides to make them smooth and pliable.

Recent discoveries suggest that these hominids were not only versatile toolmakers but that they engaged in fairly complex activities. For example, a site at the bottom of the gorge contains eleven different kinds of stone implements, such as engraving-gouging tools, quadrilateral "chisels," large and small scrapers, and other special-purpose tools generally made of difficult-to-work lavas and quartz.

These tools seem highly individualistic in that they cannot be classified readily and are not shaped according to a few standardized traditional patterns, but they are not crude. In fact, they represent a complete surprise to prehistorians who had previously found related tools only in sites a million years more recent. In this sense the tools come a million years too soon, and it is almost as if one opened up a musty vault in the Great Pyramid of Egypt and found vacuum cleaners and television sets. "At first the tools were a great shock to us," Mary Leakey comments, "and we had a hard time believing it. After this, it should be easy to believe anything."

AUSTRALOPITHECUS REINTERPRETED

Another element of shock associated with the discovery of tools at Olduvai Gorge was that they were first found in association with the more robust *Australopithecus boisei*. Previous to the Leakeys' discovery, anthropologists had assumed that the more human *africanus* was the ancestor of modern humans.

The new evidence seemed to suggest the unlikely possibility that the more apelike *Australopithecus boisei* was the first user of tools. A few years later, the Leakeys discovered some new specimens which differed significantly from all of the previous *Australopithecus* finds. Even more humanlike than *africanus,* this creature was dubbed *Homo habilis,* or "handy man," by its discoverers. Apparently it was *habilis* that had created the tools originally credited to *Australopithecus boisei.* Not all anthropologists, however, were willing to accept the Leakeys' claim that *habilis* was the first true member of the genus *Homo.*

There was little room for doubt that *africanus* and *robustus* existed at the same time. The evidence from Olduvai revealed that the highly robust *boisei* and the highly gracile *habilis* coexisted on the same living floor also. Was *boisei* the ancestor of *robustus*? Was *habilis* a descendent of *africanus*? Did *habilis* evolve directly into *Homo sapiens,* or did he do so only after evolving into *Homo erectus* or, perhaps, *Homo sapiens neanderthalensis*? Obviously there were a great many answers yet to be found.

Subsequent finds in Omo and in East Rudolf helped to fill in more of the picture. There could no longer be any doubt that *boisei* coexisted with a gracile hominid species for about a million years. The robust *Australopithecus boisei,* however, seemed to be largely unchanged over the course of two million years while his gracile contemporary gradually became more

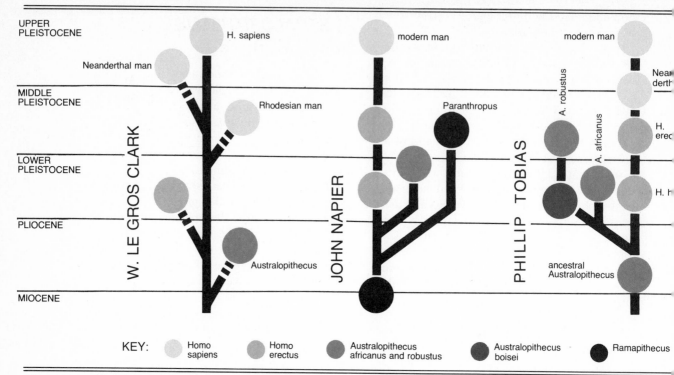

Alternative interpretations of the human family tree.

brainy. Eventually, the robust species was driven to extinction.

In 1974, at a place called Hadar in northern Ethiopia, Donald C. Johanson of Case-Western Reserve University discovered a well-preserved gracile *Australopithecus* skeleton believed to be nearly three million years old. In addition, he found jawbones which seemed to be of the same age and to be human in nature. Here at last was evidence of evolution in action. Did Johanson's find represent the birth of humankind? The focus of attention in studying human evolution was rapidly shifting northward from southern Africa where the early hominids were first discovered.

In late October of 1975, Mary Leakey announced a new and startling discovery made in Tanzania. The new fossils were found in

Laetolil, an area some 25 miles south of Olduvai which the Leakeys had first visited in 1935. Leakey's new find included two almost complete lower jaws with most of their teeth as well as other jaw fragments and teeth. All the fossils, found between layers of volcanic ash, came from a single species. Radioactive dating revealed them to be some 3.75 million years old—nearly a million years older than the oldest fossils found by Richard Leakey in Kenya in 1972 or those found by Johanson in Ethiopia.

Mary Leakey concluded that *Australopithecus* was not the ancestor of modern humans. Rather, she proposed that *Australopithecus* was an offshoot of the hominid line which coexisted with the genus *Homo* at some point but gradually died out. If these conclusions, supported by Clark Howell of the University of California at

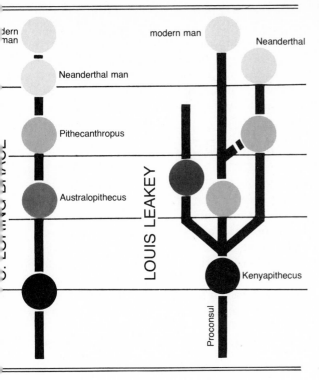

Berkeley and others, are correct, then the human lineage is much older than was suspected, and the date at which human and ape lineages became separated must be pushed back.

A great deal more is known today than was known twenty years ago about the origins of the human species. We know that the earliest hominids slowly emerged from the forests under relatively stable ecological conditions, and we know that modern humans did not evolve from these early hominids in a direct linear manner as was once supposed. The relationship among the various species of *Australopithecus,* the status of *habilis,* and the identity of the first true members of the genus *Homo* are issues which remain shrouded in mystery. A great deal of research has yet to be done before these questions can be answered.

HOMINID LIVING SITES

There are, however, other sources of information in addition to the fossil remains. At some sites, tools and other objects exist in practically the same positions they occupied when hominids lived near the ancient lake and streams. It is nothing new that evidence of this sort may be preserved at more recent sites representing the days of early civilizations with elaborate palaces and courtyards and battlements. The ashes of Vesuvius which buried Pompeii in A.D. 79 left houses and floors and furniture and bodies in place, but few investigators suspected that there were living patterns of any sort two million years before Pompeii, much less that they could possibly have survived ancient eruptions and subsequent geological changes.

Yet such patterns do exist. Objects covered gently by volcanic ash or fine lake sediments may be moved little or not at all, and such *living floors* survive almost in mint condition like intricate three-dimensional mosaics. Reading a living-floor is something like trying to decipher a code or translate a manuscript in a strange language, the symbols being patterns in the positions of the objects. For example, the site at the bottom of the Olduvai Gorge which yielded surprisingly varied tools also included another unexpected feature. The work called for the marking of many chunks of unworked and individually undistinguished stone. Only gradually did it become apparent that the stones were arranged in a definite pattern. The pattern shows up clearly in a map prepared by Mary Leakey, who learned precise digging techniques at a hill-fort site in Devon, England. It consists of piles of rock placed in a rough semicircle around a saucer-shaped area, perhaps a crude windbreaker.

Incidentally, this site has been dated by the potassium-argon method and also by a new radioactive-clock method which depends on the analysis of bits of volcanic glass scattered over the area. The glass contains traces of U-238, the radioactive form of uranium used in early atomic weapons, whose atoms split at a regular rate and leave "fission tracks" in the glass. The tracks look like tiny grooves under the microscope, and can be counted to provide a measure of the time elapsed since the glass cooled. According to results reported by General Electric investigators, the stone semicircle is 2,030,000 years old, plus or minus 280,000 years, which makes it the oldest man-made structure known.

Mary Leakey has also drawn a large map of the 3,400-square-foot living floor where she and her husband found the *Australopithecus* skull in 1959. The map shows the precise positions of more than four thousand artifacts and fossils, and includes an area about fifteen feet in diameter which is thick with shattered pieces of rock and bone and choppers. Outside this area the concentration of material drops off sharply until one comes to another area, a few feet from the main concentration, containing larger bone fragments and unshattered bones.

This pattern has been interpreted as a "dining room" complex. The tools, chips, flakes and bone splinters mark a part of the site set aside for the job of smashing bones to get at the marrow. Almost every bone that could yield marrow has been smashed. The nearby concentration of bones, including jaws and skulls which do not contain marrow, is believed to be a kind of garbage heap. Between the heap and the main concentration is an almost bare arc-shaped area, which may have been a windbreak of branches because it lies directly in the path of prevailing winds in the region today. Another possibility is that the barrier helped protect hominids from predators, a strategy still used today not only by native tribes but in the Leakeys' camp itself to discourage wandering leopards, lions and rhinoceroses. The site is definitely a home base. Although we cannot tell how long it was occupied, the bones and other material must have accumulated over a period of years during which hominid bands left their lakeside camp and returned many times. They achieved a new kind of stability, a source of experiences and associations centered about one relatively small region where traditions and techniques and taboos could be developed.

PRIMATE BEHAVIOR

Studies of existing primates supplement deductions based on material recovered from the earth. At first, monkeys and apes were studied in laboratories and zoos instead of in savannas and forests. Instead of venturing into the great outdoors where they could observe primates living freely, investigators went indoors to observe primates locked in cages. Captive primates engaged in numerous and bloody fights, often to the death, killed their infants and indulged in bizarre sexual activity, all of which might have been predicted by analogy with the actions of people subjected to prison conditions. Biologists had mistaken social pathology for normal behavior. Arguing from caged to free-ranging primates, they assumed violence to be an innate primate characteristic, part of the basic heritage of monkeys and apes, and unfortunately of humans.

The first systematic study of wild primates came in 1931, when Ray Carpenter of Pennsylvania State University began observing howler monkeys in Panama, but extensive research did not start until the decades following World War II. Early work created a certain amount of confusion as primates failed to behave as expected. Anthropologists and zoologists entered wildernesses expecting mayhem and found peace. Indeed, fighting was so rare that in the beginning each observer made a special point of reexamining his own results. Perhaps the species he was studying represented an exception to the rule of violence or the animals were

INCREASING SOCIAL COMPLEXITY

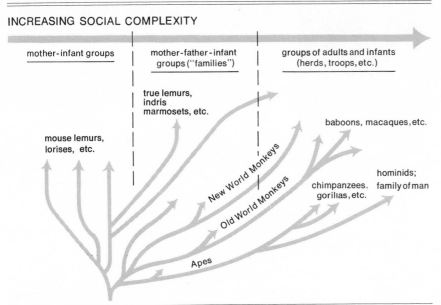

mother-infant groups

mother-father-infant
groups ("families")

groups of adults and infants
(herds, troops, etc.)

true lemurs,
indris
marmosets, etc.

baboons, macaques, etc.

mouse lemurs,
lorises, etc.

hominids;
family of man

chimpanzees,
gorillas, etc.

New World Monkeys

Old World Monkeys

Apes

Social evolution among primates.

members of unusually amicable troops. Later the observers realized that they had been dealing with the normal state of affairs. Their findings have since been confirmed by continuing field studies involving some hundred investigators in a dozen countries, including Japan, India, Kenya, Uganda and Borneo. Wild primates and most wild animals tend to avoid fighting with one another. Survival is too serious for the luxury of violent dissension. If primates behaved as aggressively in the wild as they do in cages, they would have become extinct long ago.

The striking point about primates is not the existence of aggression but its uses and control. The members of a troop of primates depend on one another as intimately and directly as if they were physically connected by tough nerve fibers. The group is the adaptive unit, and the more that is learned about groups, the more notions about individualism will have to be revised. The evolutionary trend among mammals has been toward increasingly complex and close-knit groups.

The baboons of Nairobi Park and the Amboseli Game Reserve, in Kenya, exemplify the importance of groups in the primate way of life. The baboons move in diurnal cycles, locked into the clockwork rhythm of sunrises and sunsets. They sleep in the trees, halfway out on the branches, and begin to stir with the first light of day in a groggy half-trance state somewhat reminiscent of more advanced primates like ourselves. "They tend to awaken very sluggishly," according to Irven DeVore of Harvard, "and you get the impression that what they need most is a cup of coffee." The next two hours are spent in waking up and grooming one another, always near the sleeping tree or trees.

When time comes for leaving the trees, one begins to feel the difference between forest and savanna. The forest offers many hiding places and escape routes and refuges in the trees, and

(Top) This troop of baboons stays within easy reach of the protective trees that border the savanna. (Below) Baboons move in a carefully structured defense formation, guarding the nucleus of mothers and infants. Early humans may have travelled in similar formations.

life can be relatively relaxed. But there is more fear and danger in the open savanna. Tourists today are forbidden to get out of their cars, and investigators do so at their own risk and generally make a practice of coughing softly so that any predators in the vicinity may hear and not be surprised.

The boldest troop members leave the trees first, adult males who are not at the top of the social hierarchy and juveniles corresponding roughly to older teen-agers in a human group. They move rapidly in a beeline and do not look back. Other older juveniles and adult females follow. Next comes the central nucleus of the troop—mothers with their infants and the

youngest juveniles and the most dominant and, generally, the biggest and oldest males. The back part of the troop is a mirror image of the front with more juveniles and adult females following the nucleus group and more adult males bringing up the rear.

Females with young at the center of the troop enjoy a very special status. In a sense the troop exists for them. DeVore points out that by far the most important force in binding the troop together, in a close-knit social unit, is the infant: "It is scarcely possible to over-emphasize the significance of the newborn baboon. It becomes the center of interest, absorbing the attention of the entire troop. From the moment the birth is discovered, the mother is continuously surrounded by the other baboons, who walk beside her and sit as close as possible when she rests." About four out of every five offspring are born between October and December, at the onset of the rainy season in Kenya, when the food supply is about to reach a peak.

One of the important features about the primate way of life is that child rearing is essentially a group activity. Mothers aggregate at the center of the troop, and other baboons, drawn by the enormous attraction of the infants, join the cluster. Juveniles and adult females come near and smack their lips and try to touch one of the infants, although the mother prevents any outside contact for the first week or two. Adolescent females also approach, and learn how to care for the infants they will bear by carrying and fondling the infants of others. The central nucleus is ideally designed for the learning process, and infants born into complex primate societies have a great deal to learn.

A baboon troop on the move makes a formidable array and is attacked only rarely and only by lions. Its early-morning trek takes it a few hundred yards or a few miles to the day's main feeding place, where intensive eating may go on for as much as two or three hours after the area has been surveyed for possible predators. Often you come across a troop feeding together with a herd of impalas in a natural and effective association, since baboons have fine eyesight and impalas have a fine sense of smell. Between them they can detect practically any predator and give the alarm in the form of warning barks. Baboons seem to recognize and respond to the alarm cries of many other species.

It is amazing how much food baboons can obtain from apparently barren areas. They pull up everything in plain sight and then scan the ground for withered stalks and other signs of succulent plant runners, detecting almost invisible, hairlike filaments which mark the location of deeper-lying tubers, bulbs, and roots. At midday they rest, usually not far from the feeding place in a shady spot where grooming clus-

Infant baboons play or nurse while one mother grooms another.

ters form, juveniles and infants play, and adults take a siesta or sit quietly and keep watch.

The periods of feeding and relaxation are never completely devoid of tension. A day in the life of a baboon troop is characterized by swells of rising and receding tensions. Every baboon receives a more or less continuous flow of information about the state of mind of other baboons and transmits information to them about its own feelings. The air is alive with signals: lip-smacking and soft grunts, which are most frequent and indicate peaceful intentions; hard direct stares (the most powerful gestures of all); and threatening yawns revealing large canine teeth, individuals standing stiff with shoulders hunched and neck hair raised. Every now and then there is a chase accompanied by loud grunting and screeches of fear.

Little harm comes of the commotion. Most threats do not lead to a chase, for the threatened individual makes some sort of submissive gesture such as moving away slowly or screeching loudly with lips curled in an "appeasement grin." When chases do occur, they generally end with the fugitive pressing his body to the ground and the pursuer holding him there for a moment and then walking off. Bloodshed is rare, serious injury even rarer. As a rule, quarrels last less than half a minute. They can be interpreted as letting off steam or maintaining a certain level of excitement and alertness among individuals who really have little else to do. The net effect is to achieve stability through a sort of regulated turbulence.

The tense alertness of the males is counterbalanced by the affection other members of the troop show for each other. The locus of this affection is in the central group, among the aggregated females and infants. Of all expressions of affection grooming is by far the most frequent. One baboon sits or lies on its back as another baboon parts and searches through its fur, picking or licking off every speck of alien material. The picture is one of rapt concentra-

(Left) A grooming group, with an infant holding the leg of a dominant male. (Right) Baboons at a water hole. Notice the large male in a "guard" position at far right while females and juveniles drink.

tion. The groomer scans the fur intently, section by section, while the individual being groomed closes his eyes or looks to the side and wallows in contentment, always avoiding a direct look at the groomer which is a sign of aggression.

Grooming almost certainly serves a hygienic function. Africa is a paradise for all forms of life, including an assortment of insects and parasites. Among the Kalahari Bushmen, boys delouse one another beginning early in the morning. Among baboons, mothers groom newborn infants every few minutes, and morning grooming groups of two to eight individuals form as soon as troops come down from their sleeping trees. The licking and picking of wounds may also have a cleansing effect and help account for the fact that healing often proceeds very quickly.

Above all, however, grooming brings individuals together. Sensual pleasure is involved, and the effect seems to be far more intensive when an individual is being groomed than when he grooms himself. The most common grooming cluster consists of two females, at least one with an infant. The next most common cluster is two females with infants and, in addition, an adult male. Although females participate in the activity more often than males and devote more time to it, it has a special significance for the male. The grooming of one individual by another tends to be more frequent among baboons and other primates with rigid hierarchies, as if the very rigidity demanded a compensating increase of affection.

The baboon troop serves to create an equilibrium between individual aggression and cooperation. For all the tensions and chases, most of the day consists of peaceful feeding and resting and grooming. Affection represents the pervading force, and the power of affection is indicated by its durability and continuity.

After resting, the troop does not go any farther from the trees where it will spend the night. The second feeding place generally lies on the way back, for tensions rise as the afternoon wears on. Several years ago DeVore observed an encounter between predators and a troop which was already within sight of its sleeping place in a shallow valley. One baboon stopped eating and turned to look in the direction of a clump of trees about a hundred yards away. Suddenly an old male baboon grunted twice and walked toward the trees. Almost immediately he was joined by about half a dozen other males, big adults and juveniles that advanced with him side by side in a tight line. At this point DeVore saw the heads of two cheetahs sticking up out of the grass near the trees only a hundred feet or so ahead of the line. The line advanced until it was about sixty feet away, when several of the baboons broke out of formation and made a lunging charge directly at the cheetahs. The big cats turned and ran off, and the baboons behind the line started eating again.

Defensive tactics are not always so successful; lions do not run under similar circumstances. Baboons are safe or comparatively safe only when they have reached sleeping trees near rivers and permanent water holes, and even there they may occasionally fall prey to leopards. Shortly after sunset they are dozing off and the day has come full circle. The troop moves about three miles a day on the average, often returning to the same trees which it left early in the morning. Normally every member of this tightly organized cluster of monkeys is constantly in sight of the other members. Many baboons spend their entire lives within a few miles of the places where they were born.

Our ancestors may have lived comparable lives on similar savannas millions of years ago. They had to face the same dangers, and they had to evolve some type of social hierarchy. A high degree of organization is essential on the savanna. Life is a continual emergency and the odds in favor of survival are greater if each individual knows what to do in case of trouble. Our ancestors also took cues from the alarm cries of other creatures and moved across open areas with rear guards and vanguards and "side riders" in the same basic formation used more recently in covered-wagon trains and naval convoys.

Of course, emphasizing the similarities between baboons and hominids can take us just so far. There were also great differences just on the verge of making their impact and, more significant, a potential for even greater differ-

ences. *Australopithecus* was hunting and gathering. Furthermore, he was already beginning to change nature in a new way, to "fight back" by refusing to take things as he found them and modifying things, however slightly, and evolving toward an increasing measure of independence. Signs of the trend may be seen in the existence of home bases and a crude wall-like structure which shows that, although he lived in the open, he may have been learning to protect himself from savanna winds.

His surprisingly advanced tools imply a variety of activities and purposes, a brain already capable of some sort of language, and the possibility of social organizations far more elaborate than those of lesser primates. Bernard Campbell of Cambridge University in England has suggested that the human family originated during early *Australopithecus* times, on the theory that troops and bands tend to break into small groups when rainfall declines and the land turns to semidesert, and dwindling sources of food and water are few and widely dispersed.

Such conditions demand the dispersal of populations. Many individuals coming en masse upon one of these sources would soon exhaust it without satisfying their needs, and some might perish before reaching the next source perhaps miles away. Limited resources are best exploited by small groups consisting of a single male and one or more females and their children. Similar behavior occurs during dry seasons among primates today, among the Bushmen of the Kalahari as well as baboons. Campbell believes that the human family may have developed as an established institution during year-long periods of grave and extensive food and water shortages. Whatever the data eventually reveal about the *Australopithecus* origins of the genus *Homo,* the information collected so far clearly demonstrates the developing adaptation of human culture to life on the savanna.

Focus

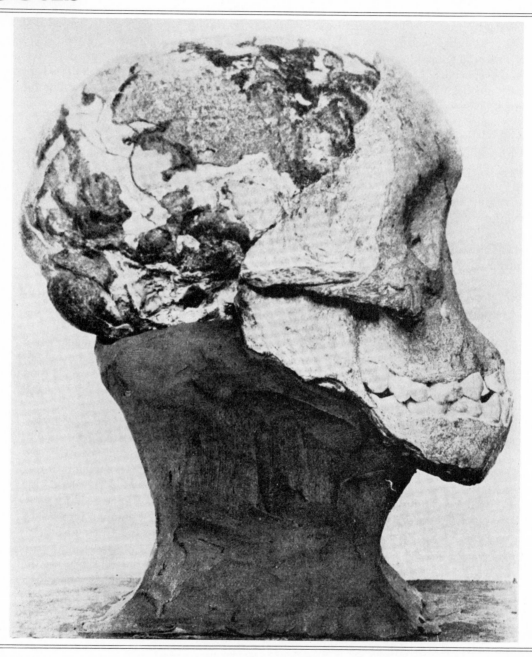

Phillip V. Tobias   The Taung Skull Revisited

Southern Africa has always presented problems to physical anthropologists because of the lack of dating methods applicable to the region. Without the accurate placement of a fossil in time, the value of a find is severely diminished. While East Africa has had a series of volcanic eruptions that can be dated with the potassium-argon technique, South Africa has remained geologically dormant. The following article by Phillip Tobias demonstrates the value of the application of recent advances in geology to the sorting of the fossil record.

When a rock containing a small fossil skull came into the hands of Raymond Dart, a young Australian anatomist, half a century ago, man's ideas about his own evolution were destined to change. Excavated by a miner from a lime works at Taung, a village about 400 miles southwest of Johannesburg, South Africa, the skull was embedded in calcified cave earth, or breccia.

Nothing like it had ever before been discovered. Scientists had dreamed of finding a "missing link," a fossil that might show features intermediate between those of apes and men. To Dart, the Taung skull showed just such features. It was a hitherto unprecedented amalgam of apelike and manlike features. He called the species to which the creature had belonged *Australopithecus africanus: austral,* meaning "southern"; *-pithecus* from the Greek *-pithekos,* meaning "monkey" or "ape."

His claims for the discovery were relatively modest as the wisdom of hindsight now shows. The fossil's

Excerpted, with permission, from *Natural History* Magazine, December, 1974. Copyright © The American Museum of Natural History, 1974.

structural features led Dart to claim that the creature was a higher primate belonging to an extinct ape species that had a number of features similar to those of man. The environment of Taung, the treeless verge of the Kalahari Desert, and the associated animal remains led Dart to ascribe to *Australopithecus* a way of life different from that of any extant forest-dwelling ape and approaching more closely that of early man.

A storm of controversy greeted the announcement, and his claims evoked arguments that were not settled until the lapse of twenty-five years and the discovery of many new australopithecine fossils in South and East Africa had produced a most compelling body of evidence.

Today there are hundreds of specimens of early hominids that have been wrested from the earth at five locations in South Africa, three in Tanzania, six in Kenya, and two in Ethiopia. The total number of individuals represented by the growing stockpile of fossils now runs to several hundred. Fossil teeth alone number well over 1,000. Vertebrae, pelves, and limb bones have supplemented skulls and teeth. Our ideas about these early hominids become more complete every year.

The australopithecines had small brains and large premolars and molars. But even within this genus of the Hominidae, there are two or three species. One species had a light frame, slender muscles, a small jaw, and, in contrast, fairly large incisors and canines. This gracile species is usually called *Australopithecus africanus.*

Another australopithecine species, although probably not taller, was sturdier. Its front teeth were on the small side, but its molars and premolars were very large indeed; also its jaws were much heavier, its muscles more beefy, and its body weight almost certainly greater. To this robust kind of ape-man scientists have given the name *Australopithecus robustus*. In East Africa, the robust form reached such hefty and Herculean proportions that some regard it as representing another species called *Australopithecus boisei*. The two robust australopithecines, however, are fairly closely related to each other.

Specimens of another early hominid have features that distinguish them from *Australopithecus*. More particularly, their brain cases are enlarged (both absolutely and in relation to their medium-sized bodies) 50 to 70 percent above those of *Australopithecus africanus* and they may have been even better adapted to standing upright and walking on two legs. There is evidence that although australopithecines began to use tools, this other early hominid was the first to make stone tools systematically and with a consistent pattern. Paleontologists have thus classified it as belonging to *Homo*. One kind of early *Homo* is named *Homo habilis,* another is the extinct *Homo erectus,* and the third, the extant *Homo sapiens.*

With six possible species of hominids—three of *Australopithecus* and three of *Homo*—and with five of these six species extinct, which of them were our ancestors? A study of the anatomy may provide answers to this question, although it is essential to know the time periods in which each fossil group existed to gain a clearer picture of man's evolution.

The evidence suggests that by three million years ago, the ancestral *Australopithecus* had given rise to the first members of *Homo*. About the same time or soon after, the ancestral hominid gave rise to another line of development. An increasing dependence on larger and larger premolars and molars with accompanying hypertrophy of the jaws and the chewing muscles marked this species. In South Africa, this trend attained modest proportions in *Australopithecus robustus;* in East Africa it reached a crescendo in the aggrandized *Australopithecus boisei*. Both of these closely related robust lineages seem to have died out about one million years ago and apparently made no contribution to modern man.

Australopithecus africanus, in this view, spawned two major offshoots—*Homo* and the robust lineages. Did the gracile australopithecine itself persist alongside these two sets of possible competitors? There is little or no trace of such persistence—except perhaps for the Taung child.

Until recently, there was little real information about the age of any of the South African australopithecine caves. None of the five sites in the Transvaal and Cape Province contained undisturbed materials suitable for radioisotope dating; however, the faunal remains discovered with the australopithecine remains at each site could indicate the relative ages—the oldest and the youngest—of the hominid fossils. In East Africa, paleontologists have correlated the faunal remains with potassium-argon dates enabling them to describe the kinds of pigs and elephants living at each stage during the past five million years. By comparing fossils of similar species found in South African sites with those of East Africa, they have been able to infer that the fauna of Makapansgat and Sterkfontein in the Transvaal corresponded to that living in Kenya two and a half to three million years ago. Similarly, the fauna accompanying the Swartkrans australopithecines matches the East African fauna of about two million years ago. Such comparisons have not yet proved possible for Taung because the fauna there, save for baboons, is relatively sparse.

For many years paleontologists regarded Taung as the oldest of the five South African sites. Yet the evidence for this view was slender, based mainly on sketchy samples of small mammals. Lawrence Wells of Cape Town has questioned the traditional view.

Two new lines of evidence within the past year have strongly confirmed Wells's view. Timothy C. Partridge, a young South African geomorphologist, has attempted to determine the approximate date that the *Australopithecus*-bearing limestone caves opened to the exterior. By gradual extension of underground cavities in the limestone formations, hastened by roof collapses and erosion of the land surface, subterranean caves acquire an external opening. Only after this occurs can surface-derived materials, including animal bones and soil, fall to the bottom of the cave and begin the process of breccia formation.

Partridge has found that the Makapansgat cave opened 3.7 million years ago; Sterkfontein, 3.3 million; and Swartkrans, 2.6 million. Partridge's dates are all somewhat older than the dates placed on the fauna in the same sites.

Taung provided Partridge with his greatest surprise; he found that the cave had opened within the past 900,000 years. In another recent study, Karl Butzer of the University of Chicago has meticulously restudied the sequence of geologic events at Taung and, by comparing them with sequences elsewhere, has concluded that the Taung deposit may be younger than that of Swartkrans and Kromdraai.

If these claims prove correct and the date of the opening of the Taung cave is indeed more recent than 900,000 years ago, the age of the Taung australopithecine skull could well be less than 800,000 years.

In East Africa, the most recent australopithecine deposits are those of Peninj in northern Tanzania and Chesowanja in central Kenya. Both have been dated to just over one million years old. Both, incidentally, have yielded fossilized bones of robust australopithecines, evidence that the robust hominid lineage survived long after the gracile australopithecines gave way to *Homo*.

Does the recent age of Taung change its status? Most paleontologists have classified the gracile hominids of Sterkfontein and Makapansgat as belonging to the same species as Taung— *Australopithecus africanus*. Yet the new evidence of the recency of the Taung skull places two million years between it and the earlier gracile ape-men of Sterkfontein and Makapansgat.

There are several possibilities to explain this wide interval. While *Australopithecus africanus* was evolving into *Homo* in East Africa, a southerly branch of the species may have persisted in South Africa for another couple of million years as a relict population of living fossils. Or perhaps, by chance, the later hominid finds dated to the two-million-year interval just do not include any gracile australopithecines.

For a number of years I have questioned whether it is correct to assign the juvenile Taung and the gracile hominids of Makapansgat and Sterkfontein to the same species. The prepubertal status of Taung makes comparison with the adult and adolescent specimens of those other sites difficult. The only permanent teeth that can be compared are the upper and lower first molars, while there are not many milk teeth from either the gracile or the robust australopithecines that can be compared with the Taung teeth. So I worried about whether Taung was or was not the same kind of creature.

The young date of Taung has justified my worries. If a gap of two million years really exists between the Taung skull and the others and if they are in the same lineage, how are we to account for this lengthy survival of the species when all around were hominizing into *Homo* or specializing into *robustus*?

At the chronological level to which Taung has now been provisionally assigned, the only other hominids known are the last of the robust australopithecines and *Homo erectus*. Was Taung a third surviving hominid contemporary with these others, as our existing views maintain? I suggest rather that it could represent one or the other of the two well-known groups of hominids that were its contemporaries. Clearly, brain size and facial and dental morphology would rule out Taung's being *Homo erectus*. There remains the last of the robust hominids. The hypothesis that Taung represents a juvenile robust australopithecine would recognize what the fossil record suggests—the early extinction of the gracile australopithecines, not long after some of their populations had evolved into early *Homo*.

The suggestion that Taung may belong to the robust line is the subject of a new heated controversy, just as it was half a century ago. But argument, rhetoric, and vituperation will not solve the problem. Only a new and meticulous study of the Taung skull, in comparison with the other early hominid juveniles now available from both South and East Africa, will permit Dart's child of 1924 to show itself in its true colors.

Summary

The discovery of *Australopithecus* by Raymond Dart in 1924 marked the beginning of a new era in the search for our ancestry. Dart's discovery of the "Taung baby" in southern Africa aroused a great deal of skepticism but also initiated much interest in additional search and study. In 1936, Robert Broom helped to confirm Dart's claim that *Australopithecus* represented a new species by assembling fragments of an adult skull found at Sterkfontein. Two years later, Broom discovered a new species known as *Australopithecus robustus*. *Australopithecus robustus* outweighed Dart's *africanus* by some 25 pounds and stood nearly a foot taller. Evidence indicated that the more apelike species co-existed in time and space with the earlier discovered gracile form of *Australopithecus*.

Africanus and *robustus* were believed to be the only species of their genus until 1959. At that time, Louis and Mary Leakey discovered *Australopithecus boisei* at the Olduvai Gorge in East Africa. *Australopithecus boisei* proved to be 1.75 million years old. On the living floor inhabited by this new species were found pebble choppers flaked on one or two sides to make a sharp cutting edge. It appeared that *Australopithecus* not only manufactured and used tools but that he was an animal with culture.

New theories followed quickly in the years to come. In 1964, the Leakeys announced that the tools which had been attributed to *boisei* were actually used by a creature they called *Homo habilis*, the first true human. The status of *habilis* remains unresolved to this day. Later finds in East Africa by Richard Leakey and by Donald C. Johanson pushed back the date of human ancestry still further. In late 1975, Mary Leakey revealed the discovery of hominid fossils believed to be some 3.75 million years old.

The study of living primates augments the reconstruction of hominid life from fossils. Savanna-dwelling baboons have been the focus of much attention because they occupy an environmental zone similar to that of early hominids. Baboon troops are organized into a social hierarchy with dominant males at the pinnacle and various levels of subordinates below them. While individual positions in the hierarchy are established through threats of aggression which sometimes lead to fighting, the dominance hierarchy generally functions to maintain internal peace and defense against external attack. When moving across open spaces, mothers and infants are sheltered in the center of the troop with dominant males nearby, prepared to face predators from any direction. Subordinate males form a protective periphery around the entire group. Alone, no baboon could survive the predatory cats of the savanna.

Infants and mothers are as much the centers of social attention as they are the focus of defense. When engaged in grooming activities, picking parasites and insects from hair, cleaning wounds and socializing through touching, mothers with newborn infants and dominant males are the central figures. Generally, baboon society is oriented toward the protectors and the reproducers of the troop. The most striking element is that aggression is a controlled, adaptive force that assures the survival of the group as a whole.

The analogy between *Australopithecus* and baboon society is not total: *Australopithecus* had tools, a terrestrial home base and a bipedal gait. But the study of primate society provides insights into the basic cooperative, social orientation *Australopithecus* must have had in order to survive in the savanna.

Glossary

Choppers   Stone tools made from rounded pebbles flaked on one or two sides to form a cutting edge.

Living floor   The remains of an area where prehistoric people lived, preserved in the context in which it was used.

Potassium-argon dating   A method of dating fossil remains indirectly by measuring the decay of radioactive potassium into argon in volcanic material above the fossil.

Additional reading

Cole, Sonia
1963   The Prehistory of East Africa. New York: Macmillan.

A complete discussion of East African prehistory, geography, and geology for the advanced student.

Howells, William
1959   Mankind in the Making. New York: Doubleday.

Howells' book, although somewhat dated, still serves as a good introduction to human evolution.

Kortlandt, Adriaan
1962   Chimpanzees in the Wild. *Scientific American*, volume 206, no. 5, pp. 128–138

One of the early discussions of the behavior of chimpanzees in the wild with some interesting insights.

Lawick-Goodall, Jane van
1967   My Friends the Wild Chimpanzees. Washington, D.C.: National Geographic Society.

As usual, van Lawick-Goodall does an excellent job of describing behavior of the chimpanzees.

Leakey, Mary D.
1966   A Review of the Oldowan Culture from Olduvai Gorge, Tanzania. *Nature*, volume 210, pp. 462–466.

The classic overall discussion of the Oldowan culture. An excellent examination of the characteristics of this tool industry for the advanced student.

Napier, John
1962   The Evolution of the Hand. *Scientific American*, volume 207, no. 6, pp. 56–75.

Napier presents a clear exposition of the functional anatomy of the human hand as a machine for manipulating the environment.

chapter five

*To walk behind anyone along a lane is a
thing that, properly speaking, touches the
oldest nerve of awe.*
G.K. CHESTERTON

THE EARLY MIGRATIONS OF OUR ANCESTORS

A major surprise of the 1963 digging season at the Olduvai Gorge occurred one January morning when an African worker announced he was going to find a fossil hominid, and did precisely that—turning up some time later with a matchbox containing a few badly broken hominid teeth. He had picked them up in the middle of a track made by cattle belonging to local Masai tribesmen, which meant that a valuable specimen had probably been trampled to bits. In fact, hundreds of further fragments were recovered after some two months of scraping, sweeping and sifting mud.

One result of this episode was a specimen known unofficially as "Poor George" (or, at the suggestion of an anonymous punster, "Olduvai George"). John Pfeiffer saw the specimen one Sunday at the Leakeys' home outside Nairobi. Mary removed it from a safe in her office and placed it, as carefully as an antique dealer with a fragile vase, on a folded blanket. It was a skull about the size of a softball, with prominent brow ridges, representing some two hundred fragments glued and plastered together by Mary "on odd Sundays" over a period of more than eight months.

Poor George in his prime was more of a human than *Australopithecus*. Among other

Mary Leakey *(1913–)*
*is best known as the wife of Louis
Leakey, the famous prehistorian.
She is, however, an archeologist of
repute in her own right. Before
marrying Leakey in 1936, she
excavated a number of important
sites in England and in Africa.
After 1936, the couple worked as a
team in most undertakings. While
Louis specialized in paleontological analysis, Mary pioneered techniques for the excavation of early
occupation sites. She was responsible for the preservation of the*
Australopithecus *living floor at
Olduvai Gorge and for the
analysis of the Oldowan tools.
Since the death of Louis Leakey in
1972, Mary has continued the
excavations at Olduvai Gorge on
her own.*

things, his brain was bigger; his teeth were
smaller, more like ours. His remains were
found just below the sterile wind-blown deposits, which indicates that he lived more than a
million years ago. He or individuals very much
like him may have made tools at one of Olduvai's most unusual sites, which was located
near a deposit of flintlike stone, has vast

amounts of waste flakes and chips, and is probably the oldest known quarry-workshop. And
records dating back as much as a million or
more years before that include traces of some
of his probable ancestors, the advanced hominids reported from older Olduvai sites and
from Lake Rudolf and Swartkrans.

The status of most of these specimens has not
yet been settled once and for all. Identifications
tend to be, or should be, tentative, and some
doubt still exists whether certain specimens currently classified as *Australopithecus* are or are not
men. This state of affairs is to be expected. Investigators are dealing with creatures in transition. Furthermore, the investigators themselves
are in transition as far as their thinking goes.
The more specimens they find, the more they
take into account in attempting to put together
a consistent picture, and they are finding more
specimens all the time.

HOMO ERECTUS

But there is little doubt about the evolutionary
status of Poor George and his descendants.
They represent true people, and belong to the
widespread species known as *Homo erectus*. The
species includes a number of highly publicized
representatives which stirred up some debate
during the early days of research in human
evolution, and whose significance is just beginning to be appreciated in light of recent studies.
A notable story, according to one anthropologist "the greatest story of serene confidence I
have ever heard," concerns the first *erectus* remains to be discovered.

About seventy-five years ago Eugène Dubois,
a young Dutch anatomist, performed the
highly unlikely feat of deducing where hominid
remains should be found, and then going out
and finding them. His argument was that one
should look in the tropics, specifically in the
East Indies, where apes still lived and where no

glaciers had come to disturb possible sites. By 1892 he had extracted part of the jaw, skull and other fossil bones of a "missing link" from the bank of a river in central Java, a creature which he regarded as more advanced than an ape and not quite a man.

Dubois found a reasonably respectful audience for his ideas, especially considering the tradition of heated disbelief which still prevails among prehistorians. (For some reason, when investigators in this field disagree, they disagree rather more violently and bitterly than investigators in other branches of science.) Certainly the Java remains received far more support than Dart's Taung baby was to receive three decades or so later. But some anthropologists were skeptical and suggested that the remains might be those of a small-brained relatively modern man, perhaps a microcephalic idiot. Others believed it was a giant gibbon; still others refused to commit themselves.

The situation became clearer following excavations in China which started during the 1920s as the result of a strange series of events. For centuries expeditions had gone out into the remote mountain gorges and caves of Mongolia, China and Indonesia and brought back tons of fossils annually, but not in the name of science. The expeditions were led by traders supplying the enormous demand for "dragons' teeth" which, according to Far Eastern folklore, had potent medical effects. Chemists and apothecaries ground the bones into a fine sour-tasting powder and used it in a variety of elixirs and tonics probably no more ineffective than many over-the-counter preparations currently for sale in the drugstores of the western world.

Paleontologists aware of these practices had long been shopping for fossils at local apothecary stores and inquiring about the locations of promising sites. One such inquiry led from a human tooth purchased at a Peking store to a large debris-filled limestone cave in Dragon's

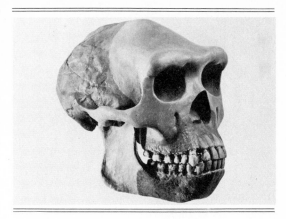

Reconstructed skull of Homo erectus, *the first truly human primate. The darker portions are the original skull.*

Hill about thirty miles from the city, where excavations were carried out between 1923 and 1936. By the time digging stopped, workers had reached a depth of some 160 feet without hitting bedrock and had unearthed fourteen "Peking man" skulls, about 150 teeth and other remains representing more than forty individuals who resembled the Java individual.

Hearths and tools were found in the deposits, and also signs of a long struggle between Peking man and other cave dwellers. Some of the deepest and oldest layers contained animal bones only, large carnivores like sabertooth tigers and giant hyenas together with their prey. Other layers sandwiched between the animal layers contained only human remains, indicating that the carnivores had been driven out of the caves for a time. There were no animal layers in the uppermost deposits. Peking man seems eventually to have won in the struggle.

These discoveries more than vindicated Dubois. In fact, they showed that he had been too conservative and that his Java find was not a pre-human but a full-fledged human. But by that time Dubois had become a secretive, conservative and eccentric old man. He went into

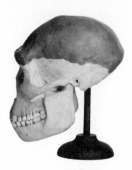

Java man, *discovered by Eugène Dubois (1858–1940). Dubois was one of the few paleontologists to deduce where hominid fossils should be found and, then, with an ease that has astounded twentieth-century anthropologists, simply go out and find them. Dubois reasoned that the remains of our early ancestors should exist in Africa or Malaya where modern apes survive. While serving as a Dutch army surgeon in Java in 1891, he began digging along a river edge rich with the remains of many species of extinct animals. In 1892, just two years after making a prediction as to where the remains of early humans should be located, he uncovered Java man, the first* Homo erectus *fossil.*

virtual hiding, belittled the significance of the Chinese excavations, felt his colleagues were plotting against him, and buried his fossils in a chest in the ground. (The rumor that he retracted his ideas and decided that after all he had found only a big gibbon, a myth incorporated into practically all textbooks, was deliberately circulated by another paleontologist whose own finds had been challenged by Dubois.)

It happens that all the Peking man material, which had taken so long to find, was lost without trace during World War II. According to a recent version of what occurred, the remains had been packed in crates and were en route to the United States for the duration as part of the personal luggage of a young Marine doctor heading for home in 1941. Intercepted by the Japanese, he managed to leave the crates with Chinese friends and Swiss and French officials before being imprisoned until the end of the war. Now there is a chance the material may be traced, and perhaps recovered.

Fortunately, the record remains, and it includes fine plaster casts of the skulls, although the original specimens would be much more useful in continuing studies. During the past decade digging has resumed on Dragon's Hill. Workers have found tools, animal bones, and some further Peking man fragments in deeper levels of the large cave as well as in nearby caves. Digging has also resumed in Java, and two other skulls and skull fragments have recently been found in the central part of the island not far from the site where Dubois made his original discovery.

Java and Peking man may be more than 750,000 years old, and most other *Homo erectus* remains date back at least 400,000 to 500,000 years. The earliest specimen in Europe is a lower jawbone uncovered in 1907 in a sandpit near Heidelberg, Germany. In 1963, the year when Poor George was found, an expedition led by Woo Ju-kang of the Chinese Academy of Sciences discovered the lower jawbone of an individual named Lantian man after Lantian County in northwest China. The specimen was embedded deep in a hundred-foot deposit of red clay and, judging by its size, Lantian man was probably a woman. The following year Ju-kang and his associates unearthed the skull of another Lantian specimen, again, probably a woman more than thirty years old.

Other *erectus* traces have been found during

the past decade, among other places near a Mohammedan cemetery on top of a sand dune in Algeria and on an ancient shoreline of Lake Chad in the Sahara. Further remains come from a Hungarian limestone quarry in the village of Vertesszöllös about thirty miles from Budapest. In a valley where a tributary of the Danube once flowed, investigators are excavating an important sealed-in site with hearths, burned bones and charcoal, many tools, and several teeth and part of a skull representing what is probably an advanced *erectus* individual.

So evidence accumulates to give a fuller picture of the rise and spread of the family of humans throughout the Old World. Africa is our homeland, the place where our oldest known remains and sites are located. It was in Africa that we established ourselves as toolmakers and hunters and advanced social animals learning to live in millions of square miles of open country with no winters, among ocean-wide grasslands and herds among the grasses. But as time passed, our future involved the rest of the

An artist's conception of Homo erectus *as he might have looked half a million years ago, foraging in the wilderness of Java.*

Controversy

Fossils: Why are there different interpretations?

Nearly all of the advances in unraveling the knots of evolutionary history derive from the comparison of newly discovered fossils with earlier finds. By observing and analyzing the differences and similarities between specimens, physical anthropologists attempt to arrive at a better understanding of the evolution of modern humans.

However, just as all people differ in some way, every fossil is unique. Even specimens taken from the same geological deposit will differ in some respect from all previously known fossils. Many elements contribute to variation in fossils, and the interpretation of these elements has been the source of many controversies in physical anthropology.

Individual variation is perhaps the simplest source of difference among fossils. Every individual is unique. Even the skeletons of identical twins will reveal some subtle differences between the two. A more complex factor is the age of the individual at the time of his death. Every primate grows larger and heavier as it matures. Different parts of the body, however, grow at different rates. In humans, for example, the face is very small and tucked beneath the cranium at birth. Gradually, the brain and cranium grow, but the face grows even faster. In adults, the nose and lips project beyond the forehead.

The relative rate of growth and the end point of development differ from species to species. A baby chimp and a human infant both have large crania and small faces, but the chimp's cranium grows much more slowly, eventually reaching a volume roughly one-third that of a human's at maturity. The ape's face, on the other hand, spreads forward to become larger than that of a human in order to accommodate the ape's larger teeth.

Evidence indicates that the relative growth rates of different parts of the body have changed over the span of evolutionary history. This provides a valuable clue in the search for our first truly human ancestor. Presumably, as we evolved over millions of years, our teeth grew smaller, facial projection reduced, our brain expanded, and so forth. These changes resulted from adjustments in relative growth rates. However, the effects of aging suggest the possibility that a fossil trait might be the result of the maturity of the specimen, not its evolutionary position. Does a skull with a face that is small relative to the brain belong to an evolutionarily advanced early human, or does it belong to a member of a less evolved species who died young, before such distinguishing features as projecting jaws could develop? The answer is often indeterminable in the absence of other evidence.

The factor of age in fossil analysis arises in the controversy over *Ramapithecus'* status as a hominid. Some researchers believe that *Ramapithecus'* tooth wear pattern is indicative of the more abrasive diet and powerful chewing characteristic of hominids. Critics of this position, however, point out that the tooth wear patterns observed in these specimens are closely matched by those of very mature apes. The teeth of an old pongid could be mistaken for those of a young hominid. Comparisons of tooth wear patterns are meaningless unless they are made between individuals of similar age.

Sex is another major source of fossil variation. Adult males tend to be larger and heavier than females. Generally, their bones are thicker and display larger areas of roughness where major muscles were attached. In many cases, the male is also characterized by a larger skull with protruding brow ridges. This sexual dimorphism appears to have declined significantly over the course of human evolution. Today, it is much more pronounced among the apes than among humans.

Sexual dimorphism has often been involved in the analysis of controversial fossils. Generally, larger specimens are assumed to belong to the male of the species. The trend toward reduced dimorphism, however, indicates that females from an earlier population could be confused with males from a later, evolved group. The factor of sexual dimorphism comes up in the effort to classify the robust and gracile forms of *Australopithecus.* Do these two forms represent two distinct genera or species, or are they actually no more than male and female representatives of the same species? Again, resolution of the controversy awaits the accumulation of additional evidence.

Geography is yet another factor in fossil variation. Variation in human populations around the world is often reminiscent of those differences which are due to the influences of age and sex. Europeans, for example, tend to have small teeth and jaws in comparison to Australian aborigines with their massive molars and projecting jaws. The Australian is also characterized by a sloping forehead and relatively heavy brow ridges. Paralleling this variation, males in any population tend to have heavier brow ridges than females. Clearly, the underlying element of evolutionary change influences all factors involved in fossil variation. Only larger samples of fossils defined by age, sex and geographic distribution will help clarify many of the controversies in the study of hominid evolution.

world to a greater and greater extent.

The oldest and only *Australopithecus* specimen yet recovered outside Africa may be a lower-jawbone fragment which comes from Java and dates back some two million years. But the earliest known works of hominids, traces of camping sites and tools, do not turn up until about a million years later, more than 3,500 miles from the Olduvai Gorge, in southeastern France. They were collected in Vallonet cave, found some time ago by a young schoolgirl, among frost-shattered rocks and deposits sealed in by stalagmites.

The oldest known human campsite in Europe was discovered at Vallonet cave, near Monte Carlo

According to estimates based on animal remains and the geology of the site, this material may be more than a million years old.

Another site, the Escale cave, contains traces of about the same age or perhaps somewhat younger. In 1960, workers dynamiting a road through the valley of the Durance River not far from Marseilles exposed the back chambers of the buried cave and noted old bones among the limestone debris. Excavations conducted since then have furnished the earliest conclusive evidence for the use of fire, traces of charcoal and ash, fire-cracked stones, and five reddened hearth areas up to a yard in diameter. Escale is believed to include relatively undisturbed living floors; it promises to be one of the most important sites ever discovered in Europe.

MIGRATION

An important question, and we have no answer for it, is why our ancestors left Africa at all and, given that fact, why specifically during this period—say, two million to one million years ago—and not sooner. After all, they had been around for at least four to five million years before that without, as far as currently available evidence goes, entering the vast Eurasian continent. A complete theory would take account of such problems, and might have a bearing on the sort of restlessness that moves people today.

Geological changes certainly affected the movements of hominids and other animals, and the last two million years or so mark not only the rise of humans but also one of the most unstable climatic periods in the earth's history. Large-scale northward migrations may have become possible for the first time after the formation of the African Rift Valley removed water barriers by shifting the courses of major rivers from a general east-west to a north-south direction.

The coming of glaciers also had at least an

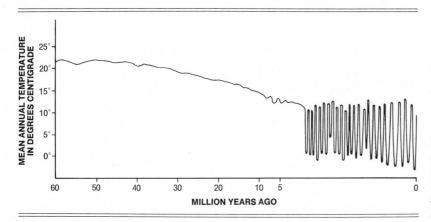

This schematic curve shows a slow temperature decline and recent fluctuations in Central Europe during the past 60 million years. The time scale is greatly exaggerated for the last 5 million years

indirect effect on the timing and course of migrations from Africa into other continents. Prehistory features what Karl Butzer of the University of Chicago calls "one of the rare spasms of extensive and recurrent glaciation affecting the planet." Indeed, no human being has yet lived under conditions which, considering the prevailing climates of the past, can be regarded as normal. The previous spasm had come and gone more than 200 million years ago. The latest one was preceded by a relatively quiet period, a long calm before the storm.

More than 60 million years ago, in prosimian times long before the appearance of modern monkeys and apes, the earth consisted mainly of tropics. Vast forests and grasslands were widespread; alligators and other reptiles splashed about in steamy swamps as far north as Montana and Wyoming. The average year-round temperature of Central Europe was about 70 degrees Fahrenheit. Temperatures held fairly steady for about 30 million years and then started falling, probably as a result of mountain-building upheavals which created the Alps, Himalayas and Rockies and altered wind flows and general weather conditions over oceans and continents. Gradually the world became much cooler, average temperatures in Europe dropping some twenty degrees.

The stage was set for a spectacular phenomenon. About 10 million years ago climates started to "oscillate," temperatures falling to subfreezing levels and rising and falling again in a series of cold spasms. Snows in the north and on the highest mountains no longer melted away during summer thaws, but piled up layer by layer season after season to form great ice masses or glaciers. During cold periods ocean levels fell as more and more water was locked up in the glaciers which advanced from the poles and covered large portions of the earth. The process reversed during warmer periods, ocean levels rising again as the glaciers melted and retreated.

We do not know why these oscillations occurred, but one plausible theory associates them with events in regions around the South Pole. The enormous pressure of growing glaciers on the Antarctic continent caused the ice at the bottom of the glaciers to melt, creating layers of water; melting may also have been produced by heat rising from radioactive minerals in the earth. The net effect was that the Antarctic glaciers tended to float on the layers of water, which acted as a kind of hydraulic jack, lifting the ice masses until parts broke off and slid into the sea. These segments were more than a mile high and hundreds of

The lone baboon is fair game for any nearby predator. Many primates, like early humans, realize that there is safety in numbers.

thousands of square miles in area, enough to cool the oceans and produce ice ages in the Northern Hemisphere. According to the theory, this is a cyclical process.

Certainly some such process was at work in times past to bring about a series of glacial stages and warmer interglacial periods. Incidentally, the question of how many glacial stages there were is still wide open. The traditional number based on older observations is four, and is still cited in widely read books. But new research, most of it conducted within the past decade, points toward many major advances and retreats of great ice sheets, more than twenty and perhaps as many as forty.

Africa was far from the steep fronts of mile-high ice masses that moved like giant bulldozers down from polar regions. But its highest mountains felt the cold, and during glacial times the snow line on the slopes of Mount Kenya extended some five thousand feet lower than it does today. More widespread effects are suggested by pollen studies which indicate that the Ice Age influenced climates all over the world, conditions being cooler and wetter in Africa when glaciation was most extensive in polar regions.

The new work draws attention to possible relationships between such changes and barriers to free migration. For example, increased rainfall during the first glacial stage may have created steppes and savannas and lakes in the Sahara and opened up routes across previously impassable desert. On the other hand, the Kalahari to the south may have advanced as the glaciers retreated in drier times during the subsequent interglacial stage, while at Olduvai layers containing early hominid remains and traces of a broad lake with deep waters are covered by deposits of wind-blown sand and ash.

Social forces, critical changes in evolving human behavior patterns, may have been at least as important as geological forces in early migrations from Africa. For example, there was the establishment of home bases where members of prehistoric bands could rest if necessary in comparative safety. Such bases are unknown among lesser primates. All members of a baboon troop, for example, leave sleeping trees together in the morning and return together at night. Weak or sick or injured members must try to keep up, and if they cannot they are left behind. Within hours after the troop has gone and probably before its heart stops beating, the deserted baboon is devoured by a predator. (Lions and other carnivores prey primarily on incapacitated animals.)

Washburn emphasizes the importance of the home base: "The whole evolutionary impact of disease and accident on the human species was changed when it became possible for an individual to stay in one place and not have to take part in the daily round of the troop. Certainly one of the reasons why it has been possible for man to migrate without building immunity to local diseases is that his way of life allows him to be far sicker than a baboon and still recover. Injuries to the legs are common and are far more serious, of course, for a biped than for a quadruped. It is the home base that changes sprained ankles and fevers from fatal diseases to minor ailments."

If home bases helped make migrations possible, however, they do not explain why—or when—migrations actually occurred. Perhaps crowding or, since crowding can be a relative thing, as we are learning today, the feeling of being crowded has remote prehistoric origins. Perhaps groups of younger individuals felt an urge to live well away from the old folks at home, and moved on to the next valley. Or it could have been an urge to wander and explore, to go somewhere simply for the sake of going, and preferably to a place where no one had been before.

But why during a particular period, and not before or after? There is no shortage of possibilities or bright ideas; there rarely is. The problem remains to figure out what sort of evidence could prove or disprove a particular theory, and then to go out and find the evidence. In general, such work has not been done. So we continue to speculate about the forces which sent our ancestors across the Sahara and out of Africa. The *Australopithecus* wanderers who reached Java two million years ago presumably came by way of northeastern Africa, Israel, Iran and southern India and found tropical climates in the Far East.

But later emigrants who settled in places like the Vallonet and Escale caves had to deal with harsher conditions in glacial lands. Their probable route into Europe was also through northeastern Africa and Israel, and then perhaps across the Dardanelles in Turkey where there was either a land bridge or else very narrow straits with slow tides. The most direct route, across Gibraltar, had tremendous tides associated with a deep submarine canyon, and was a formidable barrier to early hominids. Based on estimates of prehistoric migration rates in more recent times, and the estimates are very rough, it might have taken them about

three to four thousand years to spread from Olduvai to southeastern France, moving and settling down and moving again generation after generation at an average rate of about a mile a year.

THE HOMINID BRAIN

Who made the crossing is not known for certain, since no hominid remains have been found in the earliest living sites such as those at Vallonet and Escale. It might have been *Australopithecus*, although the odds favor *Homo erectus*, who had an appreciably larger brain and presumably an enhanced ability to adapt to new environments. In fact, the expansion of the brain is one of the most spectacular developments in human prehistory.

It is a good example of what George Gaylord Simpson of Harvard calls "quantum evolution," an explosive burst of new adaptations. Of course, "explosive" is a relative term. Simpson warns that "considerable imagination must be used to conceive of an explosion that makes no noise and goes on for several million years," and a process which lasts that long is fast only on a time scale involving many hundreds of millions of years.

Rapid changes took place among early hominids. There are a number of ways of looking at the phenomenon. According to one study, the average cranial capacity of *Australopithecus africanus,* dating back more than five million years, is 442 cubic centimeters. The cranial capacity of *Homo erectus,* which includes Java man and Peking man together with specimens discovered more recently and dating back less than half a million years ago, varied from 775 to nearly 1,300 cubic centimeters, with an average of 937.7 cubic centimeters. The upper part of that range overlaps the range for modern man, less than 1,000 to about 2,000 cubic

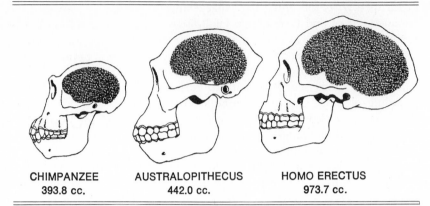

These average cranial capacities indicate that brain size was more than doubled from Australopithecus *to* Homo erectus. *The chimpanzee brain has been included for comparison.*

CHIMPANZEE	AUSTRALOPITHECUS	HOMO ERECTUS
393.8 cc.	442.0 cc.	973.7 cc.

centimeters. In other words, some members of *Homo erectus* had brains larger than many people living today. The brain had more than doubled in some five million years.

Another, somewhat broader, way of looking at the development involves body as well as brain changes. Although the following figures are averages and rough estimates, and different figures could be selected, the general trend can be regarded as a process in three stages:

1. From *Ramapithecus* (15,000,000 years ago) to the first *Australopithecus* (5,000,000 years ago), a 10,000,000-year span during which body weight increased from perhaps 50 to 75 pounds and cranial capacity increased from 300 to 450 cubic centimeters.
2. From the first *Australopithecus* (5,000,000 years ago) to more advanced forms as found at Olduvai and elsewhere (2,000,000 years ago), a time span of 3,000,000 years, during which body weight increased from 75 to 100 pounds and cranial capacity increased from 450 to 700 cubic centimeters.
3. From advanced forms (2,000,000 years ago) to full-fledged *Homo erectus* (500,000 to 400,000 years ago), a time span of about 1,500,000 years during

which body weight increased from 100 to 125 pounds and cranial capacity increased from 700 to a maximum of 1,200 cubic centimeters.

The picture is one of accelerating increase. Something had happened to step up the pace of change, or to put it another way, something had interrupted the naturally slow course of evolution—and a shift in dietary habits was one significant factor. The period which saw an increase in brain size from 700 to 1,200 cubic centimeters also saw the rise of hunting, although the beginnings of hunting probably go back much further than two million years.

The remains of animals found at Taung in South Africa and the oldest Olduvai sites suggest that our ancestors were hardly impressive hunters to start with. They undoubtedly killed and ate large species very early in the game, the earliest record so far being the presumed hippopotamus-butchering site found in the east Lake Rudolf area. But there is a predominance of small-game remains, the bones of ducks and geese and many other birds as well as lizards, rats, hares, tortoises and the young of various antelopes.

The pattern changes in more recent times. Moving upward from sites in the lowest levels of Olduvai to those below and above the wind-blown deposits, a number of things seem to be on the increase together. There were changes in species other than hominids. Apparently many previous species were scattered and wiped out during arid desert times, and replaced by new forms, including an assortment of unusually large breeds, particularly among the plant eaters.

Human beings were among the predators of such species, and of species outside Africa. At Vertesszöllös the bones of large animals such as bears, bison and deer (broken and split, presumably for the marrow) tend to be concentrated in those deposits which also contain tools and other traces of humans, while Peking man showed a marked preference for venison, nearly three-quarters of the remains found at the Dragon's Hill cave being those of two species of wild deer.

The basic problem is why humans turned increasingly from small to big game and, before that, why they turned to meat eating in the first place. Most primates are vegetarians in the sense that they live chiefly on fruits, grasses, leaves and other plant foods. But probably many primates, and many mammals, for that matter, may become meat eaters under certain circumstances. For example, if a baboon happens to come across a nest of fledgling birds it may on rare occasions scoop up the contents casually, without breaking stride. In other words, meat eating may be incidental.

It may also be considerably more than that, however. A male baboon has been observed pursuing a hare in a zigzag dodging course for about seventy yards. The chase lasted more than a minute. It ended when the hare jumped over a log and "froze" motionless on the other side, only to be picked up and devoured by its pursuer. This tactic fools many predators with poor color vision, and baboons may use it themselves, but in general it plays into the hands of primates whose highly developed color vision helps them to detect motionless objects.

A more complex event took place a few years ago, when John Pfeiffer, one of the authors of this text, spent several weeks in Kenya with Irven DeVore. One July afternoon they were driving through the Royal Nairobi National Park, looking for baboons as usual and heading for a ford across a shallow stream. Suddenly they saw directly ahead a large male baboon with a freshly killed hare in its mouth, a noteworthy event in itself since meat eating is rarely observed. But there was more to come. A whole troop was crossing the stream, and a few seconds later another large male passed with another hare, and not long after that a third male carrying the remains of a small antelope.

This was an unusual observation, the only recorded example of multiple killings among primates in the wild. But they had missed seeing, probably by only a few minutes, something even more unusual—how the killings had been carried out. Although further knowledge about predatory behavior is required to account for what happened, DeVore suggests a possible explanation: "The whole troop seemed excited, jittery. Since baboons eat small animals in a matter of minutes these animals must all have been killed recently and almost simultaneously. Perhaps one baboon came upon a hare lying in the grass and picked it up casually, and the sight of the act aroused other baboons to go after hares and other small game in the vicinity. In other words, it might have been a spontaneous flurry of activity, a kind of brief blood-lust episode."

The episode, of course, represented only one incident in the experience of one troop. It might never occur again in just that way. A casual killing in the future might arouse troop members as before, but the excitement could peter out quickly if other small animals did not happen to be nearby. On the other hand, if a similar experience did recur, the practice of killing could catch on and be passed along from generation to generation within the troop, and

Many ordinarily vegetarian primates will eat meat if the opportunity arises. This baboon is devouring the remains of a young gazelle.

also to other troops occupying the same region. The practice might never become established in another region, either because favorable circumstances do not occur frequently enough or because there is ample plant food. DeVore emphasizes that meat eating among baboons may be a matter of group tradition, like the washing off and eating of sweet potatoes among Japanese monkeys.

Similar influences may have been at work in determining the evolutionary adaptations of early hominids. We bear the marks of vegetarian origins in teeth not specialized for ripping and tearing like those of true carnivores and in the sort of long gut generally associated with a diet of plant food. Furthermore, we still seem to digest vegetable fats better than animal fats. Medical research indicates that an important factor in hardening of the arteries may be the formation of deposits of poorly digested fatty products on inner blood-vessel walls.

CONCLUSION

According to current thinking, *Australopithecus* adapted to life on the savanna and acquired a taste for red meat. In the beginning it may be that its ancestors ventured out of the forests mainly during times of temporary and relatively mild shortages of fruits and other preferred foods.

Later on during prolonged dry periods when *Australopithecus* and its forerunners came to stay, they had to find an evolutionary zone for themselves and exploit the natural resources of the savanna to the fullest possible extent. They began competing in earnest with other species—with herbivores and their fellow primates for plant foods and perhaps with other primates, including giant baboons, for sleeping trees. And perhaps the conflicts and occasional killings that resulted from competitive encounters had something to do with promoting an increased awareness of other species as potential prey.

Certainly meat might have been especially important in providing a well-balanced diet. As far as plant foods are concerned, grassy savanna lands may offer less protein to vegetarian primates than a forest or woodland environment, and in addition the work of foraging over wider areas in a less abundant environment could have contributed to an increased need for protein. Furthermore, there may have been an expanding need for more protein to nourish an expanding brain.

Running down small game was probably one of the early methods of obtaining meat. Many animals are swift runners, in relatively short spurts. But then they tend to slow down and stop as if they were going on the assumption that the spurts would be enough to shake off or discourage pursuers. Even larger animals like kangaroos and zebras and wildebeests can be run down by species that do not give up after the first dash but follow persistently, species like wolves and wild dogs and humans.

One archeologist observed a chase of this sort a few years ago while he was looking for artifacts on a rock-covered hill in Zambia. An African was running at top speed over and around the rocks, chasing a young antelope about the size of a collie dog and losing ground as the antelope darted over a slope and disappeared. But the African kept running and came back a while later with the live animal in his arms. (He took it home to feed and kill later.)

Leakey studied primitive hunting techniques and tried many of them himself in an effort to understand better and perhaps reconstruct prehistoric strategies. He actually learned an effective way of running down hares: "When you see a hare, it runs straight away and you run straight after it. It has its ears back as it goes, but not all the way back. The ears move all the way back when it's about to dodge, a sharp right or a sharp left.

An excavation at Ambrona has uncovered elephant bones and tusks, the remains of a feast of meat by early humans.

"Now if you're right-handed you always dash to the right anticipating a dodge to the right. That means the odds are fifty-fifty, and you should catch half the hares you chase right off. If you've guessed correctly, the hare runs by instinct directly at you and you can scoop it up like fielding a fast grounder. Even if it happens to get past you, you haven't necessarily lost it. Stop and watch. It will probably dart under a bush and freeze there, assuming it has gotten rid of you. Then you can go over and simply pick it up."

Hares are among the animals that can be killed and dismembered in a few moments with teeth and bare hands. But this direct method will not work for other small game. The skins of young antelopes, which must have been a significant source of meat, are so tough that they can be penetrated only with sharp cutting tools, and efforts to get at the meat may well have led to the regular use of such tools. *Australopithecus* probably first turned to naturally sharp rocks or rocks split as a consequence of bashing bones, or rocks that were hurled at escaping prey and missed and broke as they ricocheted off cliff walls.

The increasingly frequent use of deliberately shaped stone tools in preference to the ready-made variety, the imitation of accidental chipping and flaking, could have come about in a relatively straightforward manner. It could have been "discovered" several times before being accepted as a tradition to be passed along from generation to generation like meat eating itself. Certainly the result was a new and efficient pattern of behavior, as Leakey demonstrated on a number of occasions. One Christmas Eve at his Olduvai camp an audience of attentive Masai tribesmen watched him spend half a minute making a chopper out of a handy rock, and twenty minutes skinning and cutting up the carcass of a freshly killed antelope.

A widespread tendency among certain primates, the casual and episodic eating of meat, had been transformed into something habitual and part of a way of life. The transformation involved a complex combination of circumstances in the continuing transition from primitive ape-man forms to human beings—the use and shaping of stone tools, migrations out of Africa, the spread of savannas, the availability of prey and undoubtedly other factors. Going after small game represents an important early stage. It leads at an accelerating rate to full-scale hunting, which involves increased division of labor between the sexes, and to the full-scale development of evolution by culture and tradition.

A Hominid Skull's Revealing Holes

C. K. Brain

While the significance of the predatory activities of australopithecines and Homo erectus *has been discussed, little mention has been made of the evidence that humans were also the prey. In this article, C.K. Brain describes the evidence for predation on early hominids by the carnivores of a few million years ago. He assigns a major role in the evolution of* Homo erectus *from* Australopithecus africanus *to this predation.*

The valley was already in shadow when the band of ape-men crossed the grassy hillside to the shelter of the trees fringing the river. A young male lingered behind, unaware of the leopard crouched among the rocks of a nearby dolomite cliff. With a single leap the predator landed on the youth's back and sank its canines into his throat. After a brief struggle the leopard picked up its prey, dragged it to the base of a large *Celtis* tree growing beside the cliff, and carried the body up the vertical trunk into the branches above, where it started to feed.

What role has predation of this sort played in controlling populations of early hominids? As hunters and gatherers evolved in Africa, they formed a part of a natural predator-prey community: hunters in their own right, but also potential prey for the larger carnivores. The degree to which predation affected early human life can only be discovered by examining preserved remains; such remains are

Reprinted, with permission, from *Natural History* Magazine, December, 1974. Copyright © The American Museum of Natural History, 1974.

rare, but they do occur at a few sites. One is Swartkrans, an ancient cave within a mile of the Sterkfontein fossil site in the dolomite country of South Africa's Transvaal. Not only does the Swartkrans cave deposit contain abundant remains of *Australopithecus robustus,* together with bones of associated carnivores, but it has also yielded evidence that early men lived alongside the australopithecines.

In 1949, when it appeared that the fossil deposits at Sterkfontein had been exhausted, paleontologists Robert Broom and J. T. Robinson turned their attention to a new site, Swartkrans, a mile northwest of Sterkfontein. The new site interested them because they had seen fossil bones in exposed breccia on the hillside there. The first block of rock that Broom and Robinson excavated contained part of an australopithecine jaw. Subsequently, other blocks of the fossil-bearing rock, dislodged from the breccia by dynamite charges, revealed numerous australopithecine and other faunal remains.

Unfortunately, lime miners as well as paleontologists had their eye on Swartkrans. While the paleontological team was away over the Christmas holidays, a local miner moved in with his gang. So it was that Swartkrans became a lime mine during 1950 and 1951.

In 1965, the miners having long gone, I returned to the site to investigate what was left of the fossil-bearing rock. For seven years we worked through the miners' rubble, sorting out the rock and exploring the ramifications of the cave system. Gradually a picture emerged of how the cave evolved.

The formative process began several million years ago when the dolomite below the water table was dissolved, forming a cavern. With the passage of time the water level dropped and the subterranean cavern filled with air. Then a large block of dolomite, weighing many thousands of tons, fell from the roof into the cavern below, dividing up the space and creating what we have named the outer, inner, and lower caves. Percolating solutions deposited a substantial stalagmite over the fallen floor block, while stalactites encrusted the walls and roof.

About one and a half million years ago, erosion of the dolomite above the cavern produced a shaft linking the outer cave to the surface. Soil, rocks, debris, and bones of australopithecines and other animals washed through the shaft to build up the deposit, which when calcified by dripping solutions, formed the primary breccia of the outer cave. Over a period of a million years, water passing down the shaft and through other cracks in the roof of the cave severely eroded this mass.

A second shaft developed close to the outer cave's south wall half a million years ago. Through it came another deposit, known as the secondary breccia. It contained no australopithecines, but had traces of *Homo erectus* as well as comparatively modern faunal remains. This later sediment infiltrated the eroded surface of the primary breccia, creating a complicated stratigraphic situation. It also filled the inner cave.

During the last half million years, erosion of the dolomite hillside has removed the roof of the outer cave, exposing the two breccias on the surface. Water flowing to the lower cave has carved a series of irregular channels through both breccias, further complicating an already complex situation.

We only recently discovered that the outer cave contained two breccias of very different ages. For years we assumed that this cavern contained a single deposit and that all the fossils from it were of about the same age. But I was continually nagged by the problem that the australopithecine fossils were found in only one part of the outer cave. Breccia from close to the north wall of the cave invariably contained australopithecine remains, while similar material from elsewhere in the cavern, although rich in bone,

had none. By studying the breccia faces, we concluded that there were two separate formations, probably of different ages, that had entered the cavern through different shafts.

I then separated the fossils on the basis of the type of breccia that enclosed them and was delighted to find an almost complete agreement between this division and that based on taxonomy alone. The fauna associated with the australopithecines proved to be an ancient one, including many extinct forms, while that from the secondary breccia had a decidedly modern aspect. By the time the second shaft opened at Swartkrans, the australopithecines had disappeared from the scene, although traces of true man, or *Homo*, are evident in both the older and younger breccias.

On the basis of South and East African evidence, a picture has emerged of at least two early hominid lineages. One was the gracile *Australopithecus–Homo* line leading to modern man; the other, the robust australopithecine lineage, which apparently led to extinction at some point within the last million years. For a considerable time, representatives of both lineages were living at the same time.

What could have caused the extinction of the robust australopithecines? Two possibilities come to mind: competition with more advanced hominids and predation by carnivores. The Swartkrans site can throw some light on the matter.

The primary breccia at Swartkrans has yielded remains of more than seventy australopithecine individuals ranging in age from infants to mature adults. Almost half the individuals were subadult when they died. Since the evidence is conclusive that *Homo* survived after the final disappearance of the australopithecines, it is quite probable that the advancing technology of *Homo* contributed to the extinction of any other hominids who may have competed for natural resources. But in addition to this possibility, Swartkrans provides evidence to suggest that predation by carnivores could have been an important factor.

The australopithecine fossil remains at Swartkrans are preserved in a surprisingly small volume of deposit. We have never found complete skeletons, but the preserved remains show characteristic evidence of carnivore damage. Skeletal evidence of carnivores themselves is particularly abundant in the primary breccia. Parts of thirteen individual leopards, as well as remains of four species of hyena, have been recovered.

Where leopards and hyenas share the same territory, leopards must feed in places inaccessible to the scavengers if they are to retain their prey. In a woodland habitat, leopards have little difficulty in finding suitable trees for the storage of their prey, but in open country the situation is more difficult.

Swartkrans is situated in an area of undulating grasslands almost devoid of trees except along the water-courses. The cave's fossil fauna, dominated by gregarious plains-living species, suggests that open grassland conditions have prevailed over the last one and a half million years. Leopards hunting on the grasslands have to use cliffs, caves, and the few available trees to protect the prey they kill.

In this countryside, caves are typically of the shaft or sinkhole variety, with depressions surrounding their entrances. While the hillsides themselves are devoid of trees, the cave entrances characteristically support several large stinkwood (*Celtis*) or wild fig (*Ficus*) trees, which flourish in the depressions as a result of the protection afforded them from frost and fire. Leopards are attracted to the dolomite caves as places of safe retreat, while the nearby trees are valuable for the storage of their prey. The food remains of the leopards fall into the cave entrances, and some remains, missed by the waiting hyenas, work their way far below the surface. The Swartkrans primary breccia deposit accumulated over a period of perhaps 20,000 years, during which leopards probably used the cave and its trees on innumerable occasions as a feeding place and lair.

One of the australopithecine fossils from Swartkrans appears to bear direct evidence of leopard predation. The specimen consists of the incomplete brain case of a juvenile, thought to have been about twelve years old at death. In each parietal bones is a small hole, somewhat elongated laterally.

The holes were evidently made by two pointed objects with tips slightly divergent. On the internal surface of the parietals, flakes of bone have been lifted, suggesting that the bone was fresh and pliable when the injury was inflicted.

A carnivore may have caused the damage; the spacing agrees best with that of the lower canines of a leopard. The upper canines would have fit into the eye sockets. Considering modern leopard feeding behavior one is tempted to infer that the injury was not inflicted during the kill, but rather while the child was being dragged to the final feeding site.

The evidence of the Swartkrans cave suggests that the robust ape–men, our slow-witted vegetarian relatives, were once common on the Transvaal grasslands. For some reason they disappeared, the hazards of life on the open savanna having become too much for them. Among those hazards, the leopard may have loomed large, causing many an australopithecine nightmare.

Summary

The first fossil hominid included in the human genus, *Homo erectus*, evolved approximately 1 million years ago from its *Australopithecus* predecessors. *Homo erectus* remains were first uncovered in 1892 by a Dutch anatomist, Eugène Dubois, in Java. In the 1920's, a second set of *Homo erectus* remains was discovered in China. The Chinese site also yielded evidence of the use of fire and tools by *Homo erectus*. Since then remains of our closest non-*sapiens* ancestor have been found in East Africa, Algeria, Hungary and France.

The spread of our ancestors throughout the Old World is partially explained by the cyclic oscillations in the earth's climate. In the past four million years the atmospheric temperature has alternately dropped and risen for periods of hundreds of thousands of years. The result has been the spread of glaciers throughout the cooler regions of the world followed by periods of thawing and rising ocean levels. Each oscillation opened and closed migration routes.

For hominids, migration is most feasible when the group is associated with a home base. The home base permits the sick and injured to rest and recuperate, thus enhancing the group's ability to survive contact with new diseases and increasing the potential for successful adaptation to new areas. The pattern of semipermanent campsites made migration a feasible solution to population pressure on the African savanna as long as migration routes remained open.

The most significant anatomical difference between *Australopithecus* and *Homo erectus* is the vastly increased size of the *Homo erectus* brain. In the relatively short span of 4 million years the hominid brain more than doubled in size. This is quantum evolution, an explosive burst in the rate of evolutionary change. The large *Homo erectus* brain is associated with the rise of habitual hunting and meat eating.

According to current thinking, the origin of meat eating is tied to the adaptation of *Australopithecus* to the savanna environment. Competition with other species—herbivores and other primates—during seasons of shrinking plant resources may have produced competitive encounters and occasional killing. All primates are known to be sporadic consumers of meat and killers of small prey. It is possible that *Australopithecus*, the culture-bearing animal, developed a tradition of meat eating, a tradition highly adaptive to savanna life. Most likely the game consumed was small animals, many of which tire easily after spurts of speed. As has been demonstrated by modern hunters and gatherers, small game are easy to catch and consume with a minimum of technology.

Additional Reading

Braidwood, Robert J.
1967 Prehistoric Men. Glenview, Illinois: Scott, Foresman.

> An excellent book on the prehistory of humans. Designed to attract the popular audience, yet factual enough for the introductory level.

Howells, William W.
1966 Homo Erectus. Scientific American, volume 215, no. 5, pp. 46–53.

> Howells discusses how fossils are classified as well as the specifics on Homo Erectus.

Shapiro, Harry
1971 The Strange Unfinished Saga of Peking Man. Natural History, volume 80, November, pp. 8–18, 74–83.

> An excellent historical discussion of the finding and subsequent loss of Peking Man.

Poirier, Frank E.
1973 Fossil Man, An Evolutionary Journey. C.V. Mosby Co.

> The best synthesis of the fossil record available to date.

chapter six

*Man is an exception, whatever else
he is. If it is not true that a divine
being fell, then we can only say
that one of the animals went
entirely off its head.*
G.K. CHESTERTON

There are arguments on the other side, one point being that rocks and branches could hardly have served as formidable weapons against lions and leopards and sabertoothed tigers. Such tactics may work today because big cats, having learned to associate us with weapons that make noise and do lethal damage from afar, will generally walk away from their kills when human scavengers or observers like George Schaller appear on the scene. Ever since the widespread use of guns in Africa, natural selection has been favoring predators that fear humans and retreat discreetly at our approach, since they presumably live longer and have more offspring than less-cautious predators. For the protection of tourists visiting South Africa's Kruger Park, rangers make a policy of deliberately killing off lions which do not fear people. Before the coming of guns, however, predators may have stood their ground more often than they do today, and early hominids may have had to wait for the big cats to eat their fill.

In any case, scavenging of some sort probably took place, putting early hominids in direct competition with other species. Plant food comes relatively easy in the forests where chimpanzees and gorillas live today, but it is, and was, a constant problem on the savanna. Turning to meat, *Australopithecus* would have been compelled to beat off other scavengers, including jackals and hyenas as well as vultures, and presumably to carry hunks of meat into trees or rock shelters high on the sides of rocky slopes where it could eat in peace. It clearly had many reasons to fear lions and other large predators, but, if it was indeed a scavenger, it also benefited from their prowess.

The rock in the hand of Homo erectus *may have aided him in killing small animals for food. However, there is little evidence that he used the rock against other members of the species.*

ers, that might have been a far more effective deterrent, on the theory that predators would have steered clear of the only animals capable of inflicting pain at a distance without actually making physical body-to-body contact.

THE HUNT

In time, *Australopithicus* did more of its own killing, and it probably had many opportunities.

George Schaller on the Serengeti Plain with a zebra foal "kill."

Judging by conditions on present-day African savannas, there were very likely lion kills and leopard kills (often left dangling in trees), as well as a large number of newborn, crippled and otherwise helpless individuals in great herds of wildebeests and other antelopes. Although archeological proof of such behavior is difficult to come by, there are other ways of approaching the problem. Investigators themselves have gone out into the savanna searching for meat, in an effort to learn at first hand something about the tactics of early hominids.

For one week in July, 1969, Schaller and Gordon Lowther of York University, Toronto, camped by a river bank in the woodlands of Tanzania's Serengeti Plain, about 70 miles west of the Olduvai Gorge. They covered an area of about 75 square miles around the camp, five days on foot and two days by car. The scavenging was reasonably good, yielding four freshly abandoned lion kills which were thoroughly

devoured but would have provided prehistoric hunters with brains and bone marrow. One day, guided to a thicket by circling vultures, they found a bull buffalo that had died of disease or old age; the vultures and hyenas had been at work, but more than 500 pounds of meat and skin still remained. Another source of scavanged meat would have been the prey of wild dogs, highly effective hunters which were surprisingly easy to chase away from their kills.

As far as doing their own killing was concerned, the investigators counted it a "kill" if they could run down or stalk an animal and come close enough to hold on to its tail. This happened on two occasions. Once Schaller saw a zebra foal standing alone, gave chase, and after a brief sprint, caught up with it and grasped it firmly by mane and tail. Judging by its awkward gait while trying to escape, and by the fact that it had been abandoned, the foal was suffering from some disease; it was released, but undoubtedly fell prey not long afterward to carnivores who were playing for keeps.

Later on the same day Schaller stalked a young giraffe until he was directly in front of it, looking into its eyes. It was blind, and dashed off after he grabbed its tail. During another meat-gathering experiment, this one carried out on the open grassy plains instead of in woodlands, a hare and a number of crouching gazelle fawns were encountered and could have been killed without much trouble. Dismembering any prey could readily have been accomplished with the aid of sharp-edged rocks conveniently lying about.

Notice that in all cases the animals were very young, small, sick, old or dead. Capturing a large, live, healthy individual presents an entirely different problem. On one occasion Schaller ran full speed at a group of wildebeests with a stick in his hand, and succeeded in cornering an adult male. It was a fleeting triumph. The animal promptly turned and lunged at Schaller, who wisely stopped in his tracks and decided to leave well enough alone. A hunter ready to risk his life, and perhaps working with a companion or two, might or might not have outmaneuvered and eventually killed the angry bull.

It was only a matter of time until our ancestors evolved fairly elaborate predatory techniques. Five hunters working together can obtain appreciably more than five times as much meat as a lone small-game hunter. Other animals also practice hunting strategies. Schaller reports that if a herd of gazelles is grazing on the bank of a stream, lions may attempt a "pincer" movement, one lion circling around to the left, another circling to the right and perhaps two or three others advancing at a very slow pace directly toward the stream and herd. Wolves and wild dogs also hunt in groups. Recent studies of African hunting dogs on the Serengeti Plain show that gazelles have not yet learned to flee soon enough. They start running away only when a dog can generally overtake them. A gazelle has a reasonably good chance of escaping from a single dog by zigzagging tactics, but it rarely escapes from a pack which can attack from several directions at once.

Packs have also evolved ways of hunting wildebeest calves. The objective is to separate a calf from the herd, which means first of all snarling and snapping and coming as close as possible to the edge of the herd until the bulls charge. The dogs avoid the charge of the large antelopes, and then dart in to harass the mothers and calves in the core of the herd. As long as the core group remains together, the pack can do nothing. But the instant a calf becomes panicky and breaks away, the entire pack goes after it. The mother may try to defend the calf for a while, but she soon runs off to join the stampeding herd.

Hunting is rarely reported among nonhu-man primates, although something quite like it does occur. Van Lawick-Goodall has seen a group of chimpanzees stalking a young baboon that had wandered from its troop, but it ran off before anything happened. On another occasion she saw a successful maneuver: "The prey, a red colobus monkey, was sitting in a tree when an adolescent male chimpanzee climbed a neighboring tree and remained very still as the monkey looked toward it. A second adolescent male chimpanzee then climbed the tree in which the colobus was sitting, ran quickly along the branch, leapt at the colobus, and caught it . . . presumably breaking its neck, as it did not struggle or call out." The other chimpanzee, a confederate, then jumped into the tree to share the kill.

Such cooperative activities are not seen often. But they take place often enough to indicate not only that chimpanzees like meat, but also that they have the skill and intelligence to become regular hunters should the pressure become sufficiently strong—as it did among our hominid ancestors. In more than a decade of observing, van Lawick-Goodall has recorded about a hundred cases of meat eating and some thirty examples of hunting.

She notes what seem to be meat-eating "crazes," periods when hunting and killing are notably more frequent than usual. One incident may be enough to serve as a trigger. Perhaps there is a brief and bloody encounter with a bush pig or some other small animal, and other members of the troop see and become excited and increasingly aware of meat and potential victims, in a kind of blood-lust episode inferred by DeVore among the Nairobi baboons. A chimpanzee craze may last for a month or more, during which time dominant males generally get the lion's share of the meat, and then it generally peters out until the next episode.

More recently, Geza Teleki, working as van Lawick-Goodall's assistant at Gombe National

Park in Tanzania, has reported frequent stalking, killing, eating, and even sharing of prey among chimpanzees. Sharing ranged from picking up the pieces dropped by others to grabbing bits from the hands of others, to communicating the desire for meat and receiving some in response. Clearly, hunting is not a human invention. The predatory behavior of chimpanzees suggests a pattern of cooperation perhaps not unlike that of our ancestors—that is, a system of sharing resources characterized by the sexual division of labor. The elaboration of hunting techniques developed by *Australopithecus* may reflect a difference essentially of degree and not of kind. As hominid social cooperation became more complex, hominid hunting may have become more successful.

It often appears inappropriate, however, that hunting receives more of the stress in discussions of human evolution than does gathering. On the one hand this is a product of the male-oriented society in which we live; on the other hand, it is a reasonable representation of the evolution of human society. We have always known that chimpanzees and baboons gathered and consumed the vegetation around them. Thus, it has appeared that successful hunting was the major innovation, the new piece in the system that gave rise to culture. It now seems that hunting can be found among nonhuman primates, and that the appropriate stress, the basic importance of the expansion of hunting among our early ancestors is in the cooperation it required. It was not the development of specifically male skills that altered the way of life of our ancestors, but the division of skills between men and women and the sharing that became necessary with this division. Sharing and cooperation changed the way of life of *Ramapithecus* and *Australopithecus*, not hunting. Hunting was the significant development in technology, but sharing was the basis of society. While the hunt is always a dramatic event, its proper place in human evolution should not be overstated.

Map of a living floor at Torralba, showing the location of various objects unearthed.

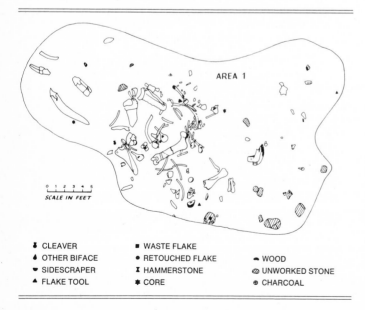

AREA 1

SCALE IN FEET
0 1 2 3 4 5

♪ CLEAVER   ■ WASTE FLAKE
◢ OTHER BIFACE   ● RETOUCHED FLAKE   ➤ WOOD
▼ SIDESCRAPER   ✗ HAMMERSTONE   ◫ UNWORKED STONE
▲ FLAKE TOOL   ✦ CORE   ⊕ CHARCOAL

THE GROWTH OF CULTURE

As our ancestors grew larger in body and brain, their way of life became increasingly complex in many respects. Large primates, requiring more plant and animal food and relative safety from predators, generally cover wider territories in search of food than do small ones. Some small plant-eating monkeys, for example, spend almost their entire lives in half a square mile of forest, while vegetarian gorillas may range over some fifteen to twenty square miles. The first people traveled over far greater distances in search of food. Like a pack of wolves or wild dogs, a band of primitive humans may have roamed over some 500 to 1500 square miles in the course of a lifetime.

Such ever widening horizons led our ancestors to many of the earliest social institutions. Hunters who traveled great distances in search of prey needed help in raising their young and in gathering the vegetation upon which daily survival was based. The sexual division of labor and the institution of a home base were created to help deal with these problems. As their environment became more complex, men and women became increasingly interdependent in developing new skills and new techniques of survival.

The evolution of culture was a multifaceted phenomenon in which positive feedback played a very significant role. Positive feedback is a process in which one variable in a system changes in such a way as to induce change in other variables which, in turn, feed back to reinforce the first change. In the case of the early hominids, it was the move from the forest into the open savanna which set off a chain of mutually interactive changes. Bipedalism, the use of tools, and the eating of meat were all highly advantageous traits in the new environment. Did our ancestors begin to stand upright in order to be more efficient tool-users and hunters, or did they become more efficient tool-users and hunters because they were able to stand upright? Whatever the exact chain of cause and effect may have been, it is clear that changes in body and life-style evolved side by side.

EVOLVING BRAIN

One of the most significant factors in the changing hominid way of life was the growth of the brain. In many ways, the brain reflects the state of the outer world. As their environment became more complex, our ancestors had to expand their capacity to learn and to think in order to survive. As our ancestors roamed more widely in search of plants and animals, followed and anticipated the natural flora and fauna, and learned sharing and caring and other rules of evolving social systems, they had more to remember and analyze—all of which

put a premium on a large brain with a larger memory capacity.

Evolution added more mnemons, or memory units and the brain grew like a benign tumor at the head end of the spinal cord. Of course, it was far more than a mere increase in gross size. Subtle changes were taking place in internal organization, especially in the nerve circuitry required to inhibit, to control the not doing of things, continuing a long-established trend in primate evolution. The mnemon with its advance fiber and retreat fiber is the anatomical expression of an elementary choice, an alternative; depending on experience, one of the two fibers will be blocked. The multiplication of mnemons is the anatomical expression of the increasing complexity of hominid society, the multiplication of alternative behavior patterns.

Restraint did not come automatically. Every choice, every course of action selected for the future benefit of the group rather than for the immediate satisfaction of the individual, had to be learned and remembered. Events weeded out those with an inferior capacity for learning and remembering. The hunt demanded patience and waiting—waiting for prey at water holes or salt licks, waiting for properly ripe fruits and nuts to appear and waiting for the others at the home base.

There was also waiting for the fulfillment of sexual urges. Younger males who could bide their time and control themselves in the presence of aggressive dominant males outlived those who could not. In anatomical terms, selection favored a "rewiring" of the brain so that increasing numbers of inhibitory, retreat fibers ran from the highest control center, the cerebral cortex, to subcortical centers which released sex hormones and aroused sexual urges. Changes in brain size necessitated other anatomical adaptations as well. The female body had to adjust to the delivery of bigger-brained individuals.

From a strictly engineering point of view, the

Controversy

Why don't women hunt? Biology or culture?

Every society exhibits a division of labor according to sex, but the nature of this division varies greatly from culture to culture. In one village, for example, pottery making is viewed as the exclusive domain of men while in another it is looked upon as "woman's work." Despite this diversity, however, certain social functions are almost invariably associated with a single sex. Outstanding among these is the hunt.

Hunting is considered to be "man's work" in nearly every known society. One possible explanation of this phenomenon is that men are better equipped biologically to be hunters. According to this argument, a woman's physical capabilities are limited by her reproductive functions. She has a wider pelvis and broader hips than a man in order to accommodate the birth process. These modifications prevent women from running as fast or as long as men. A woman's anatomy also renders her less effective in the throwing of spears and other objects. In addition, women tend to adapt less readily to changes in temperature than men. This factor could be extremely significant among hunters in tropical regions.

On the whole, according to this biological approach, men are larger, have greater muscular strength, superior lung capacity, and a hormonal-based tendency toward greater aggressiveness. They are not subject to the periodic physical and psychological stress which characterize the menstrual cycles of many women. Proponents of the biological explanation of sex roles also argue that the traditionally male specialty of hunting has been the basis of human subsistence throughout most of evolutionary history and that too few non-hunting generations have occurred for the human body to alter its fundamental structure. In other words, sex roles are viewed as an inescapable part of our biological heritage. Tampering with those roles would amount to engaging in an essentially unnatural act.

Opponents of the biological interpretation point out that sex roles are predominantly cultural phenomena. Physiological differences between the sexes need not be as significant in the assignment of social roles as they tend to be. The muscular inferiority of women is less the cause of their social position than its consequence. Even hormonal functioning has been demonstrated to be influenced by social factors. Certainly a large number of women could easily be trained to assume traditionally male roles despite their slight anatomical disadvantages.

Proponents of this sociological interpretation agree that bearing children is the lot of women in every society and that the social role of women must invariably be made compatible with their procreative function. They also argue, however, that the social role of women is extremely flexible except for the last months of pregnancy. In many cultures the men, the elderly, and the older children play a major role in caring for the children; women often nurse the offspring of others; and various taboos on sexual activity limit the amount of time a woman is pregnant. Such factors allow the females of many societies to engage in long distance trade, to wander over large areas gathering wild plants, even to carry hundred pound loads for long periods of time.

Why, then, are men so consistently the hunters and women the gatherers in semi-nomadic foraging societies? While the biological determinists point to the basic physiological differences between men and women, the sociological approach argues that the major reason is the small size and high infant mortality rate among hunters and gatherers. In order to maintain the population, all the women of child-bearing age are very often pregnant. Since the shift in body balance during the latter stages of pregnancy makes hunting extremely impractical for pregnant women, the training of female hunters is not a viable alternative. It is not pregnancy itself that limits the possibility of female hunters in foraging societies but the frequency of pregnancy and the necessity of bearing children. Ultimately, the lives of men can be risked in hunting and warfare because they are less valuable than those of women in insuring the perpetuation of the society.

obvious way of allowing for the delivery of bigger-brained infants is to enlarge the pelvic opening and widen the hips, and evolutionary pressures were at work which favored this solution. The difficulty is that individuals with wider hips and related modifications lost a measure of mobility. As far as speed is concerned, the ideal pelvis is a male pelvis. Women cannot generally run as fast as men, a disadvantage in prehistoric times when flight was called for frequently.

Another theoretical way of meeting the problem is to go to the other extreme and avoid the necessity for widening the hips. If the infant is born sufficiently early in its development so that its brain is still small, delivery difficulties can be minimized or eliminated. The limitation in this direction, however, concerns the danger of being brought into the world in an immature state; the earlier an infant is born, the smaller its chances for survival. The death rate for premature infants, infants weighing 5.5 pounds or less, is about three times higher than for full-term infants.

Confronted with these alternatives, nature settled on a not altogether happy compromise. Natural selection arrived at a solution in which the hips were widened sufficiently to permit delivery of an infant with a somewhat larger brain, a brain sufficiently developed to ensure a reasonable chance of survival. On the other hand, the brain was by no means fully developed. It was still immature and small enough so that the hip widening did not reduce the mother's mobility to a dangerous extent. So the brain had to do most of its growing after birth. A rhesus monkey is born with a brain that has already reached nearly three-quarters of its adult size, but the brain of a newborn *Homo erectus* infant had probably completed only about a third of its growth.

Delayed maturity means extending the state of infancy, and that had crucial repercussions. Most mammals are ready to fend for themselves only a few months after birth, but a

In primate evolution the tendency is towards single births, allowing a special type of mother-infant bond.

unique type of growth was established among primates. Monkeys remain helpless for about a year, apes for two to three years; *Homo erectus* was helpless for perhaps four to five years (as compared with six to eight years for modern people). Indeed, the first human infants were not only helpless longer than the infants of other primates, but they were more helpless as they could not cling to their mothers.

Another trend in primate evolution is away from large litters and toward single births, or at least litters consisting of no more than two or three offspring. This devlopment, like the development of stereoscopic vision and other features, is mainly a consequence of life in the trees, where it is considerably more difficult to care for infants than on the ground or in dens and burrows. One result is that prenatal growth can proceed at a more leisurely pace. Among species with large litters there is competition for nourishment and space within the uterus, a condition favoring relatively rapid growth and a short gestation period. Since higher primates typically give birth only to one infant, however, such competition does not exist and a slower rate of growth is possible.

MOTHER, FATHER AND CHILD

The focus has been increasingly on the infant as an individual, in a way that can never be the case among species with large litters. A single birth is more special, and can receive more care and attention. Campbell points out that in the final analysis it is a matter of quality instead of quantity: "Evolution has selected in man a reproductive process that enables him to maintain his numbers in a hostile environment, not by mass production but by prenatal protection and postnatal care."

The infant smile, studied intensively by Anthony Ambrose, director of the Behavior Development Research Unit of St. Mary's Hospital in London, promotes the development of a social relationship between mother and child that assures postnatal care.

Ambrose believes that smiling evolved from laughter, and that the social smile, which is unique to humans, evolved as a special adaptation designed to strengthen bonds among people. The first such bond is with the mother.

The smile may have evolved as a signal or communication specifically to help make up for the handicap of infant immobility. Of course,

crying could always be used to bring the prehistoric mother to the spot. But crying alone was not enough. The infants of other primate species have vocal signals of some sort which indicate at a distance the nature and intensity of their distress, and something extra was called for to deal with the human predicament, something to hold the mother's attention longer and after the nursing and burping were done. The infant represented only one of several alternative social contacts available to her. It had a high priority, to be sure. But it still had to compete for her time against other individuals and groups of individuals with demands of their own. Smiling became an essential way of meeting this competition.

The forces of natural selection come into play under such circumstances. Ambrose's research indicates that the smile is simply mild or low-intensity laughter minus chuckling and other sounds, and more relaxed. When it first appeared after nursing, mothers no doubt responded with cooing sounds or the prehistoric equivalent thereof, and other forms of affec-

Smiling is an important means of communication between mother and infant. Illustrated are medium and high intensity smiles.

tion. Infants capable of making a ready connection between such pleasant responses and their mothers, learned to smile more and received more care and attention than other infants and prospered accordingly.

It was extremely important for the infant to form a deep attachment to its mother and to form it swiftly. Conditions existing in prehistoric times favored rapid learning at an early age. Judging by the records of contemporary infants, the process may have started during the third month of life with a sudden decrease in smiling at any human face and an increase in smiling at the mother's face. If an infant had not formed a firm attachment by the age of six or seven months, it probably never would. The evidence suggests the evolution of a sensitive or critical period, when the infant is particularly ripe for learning the smiling response and associated behavior.

Prolonged infancy is only part of an evolutionary process which has brought prolonged childhood, prolonged adolescence, and prolonged life, part of the slower pacing of things in a species which relies more than any other species on learning. It is difficult to imagine the young of a rapidly maturing species learning to behave appropriately in a highly organized hunting and gathering band. A child that could run, fight, and feed itself within six months or less after birth would probably not excel at the art of learning complex and flexible social responses. It would find itself too busy being a vigorous animal. The human type of growing up demands a delay in such activities. It is well served by early immobility and dependency which permit observations and listening, contemplation of a sort, before full-time commitment to active doing. For example, although the circumstances under which language arose are unknown, it was probably evolving in important ways as our ancestors were adapting to life on the savanna, and a connection may have existed between slow maturation and the ability

to acquire new linguistic skills. A docile infant and an experienced adult must have made an effective combination for the establishment of social communications, in prehistoric times.

One effect of prolonged infant dependence was to intensify both specialization and interdependency between males and females. Their decreased mobility made women the obvious choice for staying behind and caring for the young while the men hunted. At the same time, the men could not take time off from the hunt to gather the plant material upon which their day-to-day survival depended. Each sex depended upon the other to perform the tasks for which each was best qualified. Again, a system of positive feedback was in operation. As the male role of hunter and protector strengthened and the female role of homemaker and gatherer expanded, each role further reinforced the specialization of the other. Successful male-female interdependency fostered greater and greater interpendence.

At the same time other forces were fostering new and closer and more enduring bonds among males, a point stressed by Lionel Tiger of Rutgers University. As men cooperated in going after a wider variety of game, the emphasis was more and more on planning, selecting places for hunting and appropriate hunting strategies, developing more sophisticated ways of communicating, learning and sharing skills. Men on the hunt in wildernesses went away in groups, ranged widely and stayed away perhaps all night and perhaps on occasion for several nights. They began forming the all-male associations which more recently have led to such things as clubs, lodges, athletic competition and secret initiations. Women were in the process of becoming the "other" sex, at least from the male perspective.

Of course, much of the research on contemporary hunters and gatherers has been carried out by male anthropologists talking to other men. If women were providing the information, the men might be labeled the "other" sex. Similarly, the role of hunting in these societies has been vastly overstated. As Richard Lee, who studied the Kung Bushmen of the Kalahari Desert in Africa, discovered, the men are always ready, willing, and able to relate elaborate tales of famous chases. Lee's careful examination of Bushman life, however, revealed that the women provide most of the daily caloric intake. They gather wild mongongo nuts from the desert to provide the group with staples. But the dreary work of walking, stooping and gathering is poorly adapted to the creation of myths. In contrast, hunting is an unpredictable drama, at times producing more than can be consumed, at times providing barely enough to maintain the hunters away from camp for a few days. It is a challenge of one species to another,

Young chimpanzees have much to learn. Play between mother and infant is an important part of the learning process.

a fight to the death drawing out the skills of the hunters and the hunted.

Anthropologists have mistaken the drama, the heroic tales of hunting for the reality of everyday life. The story is being corrected today but the evolutionary implications of this changing image will take years to sort out. It might eventually turn out that women, the child bearers and gatherers of subsistence, were the central elements of *Homo erectus* society while the men were superfluous, peripheral. Perhaps it is significant that one man and twenty women can reproduce to maintain a society while twenty men and one woman cannot.

In addition to male-female specialization, differences intensified within the male community itself, stresses between younger and older males. This was nothing new among primates. Van Lawick-Goodall observes that among chimpanzees the young male has hard lessons to learn. Early in adolescence, which starts between the ages of seven and eight, he becomes independent of his mother and increasingly capable of dominating females, who used to dominate him. But this is also the time when larger, dominant males become increasingly aggressive toward him, and tend to keep him

A Kalahari woman gathering food, with her young child on her shoulders.

away from females. His frustration may be expressed by charging through the troop dragging branches and throwing rocks, but even here he must learn to be careful because all the hubbub may get on the nerves of the dominant males. Or he may wander off alone into the forest.

Making it, getting into the club of dominant males, was as important to hominid as to chimpanzee adolescents, only rather more complicated. The institution of hunting probably provided new ways for an adolescent to take out his frustrations to prove himself. It was one further step in the accelerating development of symbols, as hunting and the eating of meat acquired new values and meanings.

Such changes dramatize *Homo sapiens'* special position among species. It provides an example of evolution in the process of being put to its most severe test. All species survive by adapting, but our adaptations are far more elaborate and tend to become increasingly so. The past is only in part a story of divisive forces which tended to create new and conflicting groups within groups. Society is possible because the conflicts served to accelerate the building up of powerful counterforces, in a continuing interplay of tension and relaxation.

The hunting and gathering way of life served to increase cooperation among all members of the group. Humans became the only primates to kill regularly for a living and the only primates to share regularly on a day-to-day basis involving the entire group. All other primates are supremely self-centered when it comes to feeding and forage strictly for themselves. Even more important, life on the savanna led to a division of labor between the sexes, with the males concentrating on obtaining animal foods and females concentrating on plant foods.

Intricate networks of causes and effects are involved in such major changes of life-style. One cause-effect sequence begins with the question of what favored a male-female division of labor in obtaining food. The first answer is that infants were dependent longer, so that females had less time for prolonged hunts and specialized in plant foods which could generally be gathered in the vicinity of the home base. Tracing the sequence back one more step, infant dependency was prolonged because of the expansion of the brain, because limitations in widening the female pelvis demanded infants designed for considerable brain growth after birth. Bigger brains, in turn, were necessary for an increasingly complex life-style. Increased division of labor and increased social complexity selected further for intelligence and cooperation and for increased expansion of the brain.

SEX AND ALLIANCE

So evolution worked to establish a secure, stable, social framework in a milieu of potentially disruptive forces. The new framework had to be strong and flexible enough to include male-male as well as male-female associations. The problem has not yet been solved to the complete satisfaction of either sex, but early steps toward a solution included changes in patterns of sexual behavior, changes designed to reduce other new tensions and anxieties.

The typical pattern among mammals involves regular bursts of sexual frenzy which take precedence over all other activities. At every ovulation or immediately after, all non-human females, including occasional nursing females, come into *estrus* or "heat." Sexual activity is so concentrated and intense during such periods that it tends to interrupt the care of the young and all other forms of behavior. This sort of all-inclusive *estrus* ensures effective reproduction among most mammals which have rapidly maturing offspring, but not among primates. If all the females in a primate troop were subject to three days of sexual mania every month or so, it would probably be to the detriment of their slow-maturing infants.

Natural selection brought about a modification in monkeys and apes, to the extent that *estrus* ceases during the later part of pregnancy and the early part of nursing.

A modified form of *estrus* is fully compatible with the primate way of life, that is, with the way of life of nonhuman primates. The human is the only mammal in which *estrus* has disappeared entirely. Ralph Holloway of Colombia University suggests that this development may have started with the appearance of *Australopithecus* more than five million years ago. It was certainly established among the hunting bands of *Homo erectus*. *Estrus* cycles may simply have made less and less sense in a species with single births spaced further and further apart as the period of infant dependency lengthened. A new reproductive rhythm was being established; *estrus* no longer served an evolutionary purpose and eventually disappeared.

More positive forces may have been at work to speed the departure of *estrus*. The female of the species became sexually receptive at practically any time, eliminating periods during which male competition and aggressiveness reached a peak and contributing further to the stability of life. Extended sexual receptivity on the part of females served also to extend the period of their attractiveness to males and may have helped counterbalance the appeal of male-male associations. The changing pattern of female behavior helped to tie the male more securely into the mother-offspring group, the beginnings of the family.

The extension of the possiblity of choice in timing of sexual relations led to what Campbell calls "the individualization of sexual relations." *Estrus*, even as modified among nonhuman primates, is beyond the individual's control. Its presence and absence are determined by the automatic turning on and off of sex-hormone secretions, presumably by a kind of biological clock in the brain which keeps track of the passage of time and periodically triggers the activity of centers concerned with the arousal of sexual urges. Under such conditions the sex act among early hominids, as among contemporary monkeys and apes, tended to be relatively impersonal and mechanical.

When sexual urges came under a measure of voluntary control, individuals for the first time had some degree of choice as to when and with whom to mate. Relationships between males and females tended to become more personal and enduring. The choice of sexual partners was probably influenced by social considerations more like the traditional arranged marriage rather than like the highly individualistic

The interior of a men's hut in Papua, New Guinea. Only after an elaborate initiation into adulthood are young men allowed to enter it.

and romantic choice of partners with which most of us are more familiar. Nevertheless, replacement of automatic hormonal control of sexual behavior by some measure of self-control may have laid the foundation for both heterosexual and homosexual love among humans. A system of positive feedback operated to promote both greater human freedom and closer human alliances.

Changing sexual patterns brought new orders of social complexity, new things to be learned and remembered, new inhibitions and prohibitions. Early humans might have developed *incest taboos*, for example, partly for economic reasons, as a method of population control. The fact that human males mature sexually years before they mature socially probably created as many problems in prehistoric times as it does today. Contemporary hunting and gathering groups have devised a variety of marriage customs and rituals to ensure that the production of children is delayed until the male has learned the ways of hunting and is fully prepared to provide for a family—and incest, like premarital sexual intercourse, is incompatible with these objectives.

Incest taboos may have helped to reduce conflict, jealousies and rivalries, within hunter families or protofamilies. Such restrictions might also have reduced rivalries among families, counteracting any tendency of the group to break up into competing family units—just as *exogamy* counteracted any tendency of the tribe to break up into competing bands. The effect would be to produce a more integrated group, a wider and more inclusive system of communal bonds and the basis for formal kinship relations. Gregory Bateson of the University of Hawaii has pointed out that when the objective is just the opposite, when it is desired to create an exclusive rather than an inclusive situation, incest may be permitted. Thus brother-sister marriages were the rule among the royal families of dynastic Egypt.

Mating among members of different groups, a characteristic of primitive tribes, may have arisen in prehistoric times when a number of hunting-gathering bands occupied the same region. "The exclusive control of a hunting territory can be effectively maintained only with the mutual consent of neighboring bands," Washburn notes. "Excessive fighting over territorial borders both disturbs game and dissipates the energy of the hunters. The exchange of mates between neighboring groups helps to insure friendly relations . . . because it disperses persons with close emotional ties among many groups and over a large area."

Establishing social systems based on such exchanges and alliances became a matter of survival. Variations in the available resources emerged as a force favoring new kinds of cooperation as well as conflict. There were new rules for playing the game, rules that required a greater flexibility of behavior. The control of mating within the group continued, but on appropriate occasions additional rules were followed involving the control of out-group mating, out-marriage or *exogamy*.

Natural selection also put a premium on the development of a moral sense. A hominid that at the approach of a predator cries out to warn the other members of its group may draw attention to itself and run the risk of being killed. But a mathematical analysis of such behavior shows that it may actually thereby increase its reproductive success if close relatives are aided or if the individuals it has benefited return the favor. In other words, it acts so as to preserve and pass on its genes to succeeding generations, and so do other members of the group.

This is one result of an important study by Robert Trivers of Harvard. The system of course depends on doing unto others as they did unto you, or reciprocal altruism, and Trivers shows that such behavior is likely to favor groups of relatively long-lived individuals who, like the early hominids, live together and are

These members of the Tasaday tribe are using the friction of a fire drill to start a fire. This is probably one of the fire-making methods used by early humans.

mutually interdependent for food and defense. Natural selection would favor those individuals with a strong sense of moral responsibility and would foster such qualities as gratitude, sympathy, and friendship. Ultimately, a social system would be developed which would be most effective in utilizing available natural and human resources.

FIRE

The process of human evolution was complicated and enriched by the greatest technological advance of the times, the use of fire. The first force of nature to be domesticated, fire gave early humans a new degree of independence. By bringing fire to the living places, people created zones of warmth and light in the darkness, achieved a way of keeping the night and nighttime prowlers at bay, and acquired the freedom to explore new lands with harsh climates.

Our ancestors probably first obtained fire ready-made from natural sources such as volcanoes. (The first sign of artificial firemaking, an iron-pyrites ball with a deep groove produced by repeated striking to create tinder-igniting sparks, comes from a Belgian site only about 15,000 years old.) According to Kenneth Oakley of the British Museum of Natural History, "Man could also have relied on accidental fires started by lightning in dry bush or grass-land or where there were seepages of mineral oil and gas. Occasionally in damp environments coal or shale-oil deposits might be ignited by spontaneous combustion, and during the last century one such fire burned for four years in Dorset."

Perhaps hunters camped near fire, a natural resource like game and water and shelter. They may sometimes have left otherwise favorable areas when fires began petering out. If so, they had to take it with them when they moved away. It had to be kept burning like the Olym-, pic flame, fed and nursed like a newborn infant. Each band may have had a fire bearer, who was responsible for carrying and guarding embers in a cup of clay covered with green leaves, and who breathed the embers into flame when the band found a new place to live.

Fire provided more than warmth. It soon became another factor in setting *Homo erectus* apart from other species. With it they could move more freely. Fire must have kept the predators as well as the cold at a safe distance. On icy wilderness nights big cats and other predators, attracted by the smell of meat and the light, stayed outside the protective circle of the fireside. Perhaps early humans observed that on occasion animals scrambled even further away when sparks flew at them out of the flames, and they may have learned to produce the same effect by hurling glowing pieces of wood at them. In any case, they eventually began using fire more aggressively, in a shift from defense to offense.

With fire also they could drive predators from the caves they sought for their homes. Their earliest known hearths were located in the caves, originally occupied by stronger and longer-established killers. Before fire they often had to be content with second-best sites, rock shelters, and overhangs with their less effective protection. Fire, however, could help drive other killers out. Bears and hyenas and many other cave-dwelling animals shared the Durance Valley with early humans, but they stayed out of their caves. Only after they had learned to tame fire could humans become regular cave dwellers.

Homo erectus also used fire to become a more and more effective predator himself, to stampede animals, and to produce more effective spears. The Australian aborigines charred the tips of their digging sticks lightly, a treatment which hardens the core of the wood and makes the outer part more crumbly and easier to sharpen. *Homo erectus* was acquainted with this technique at least 80,000 years ago, as indicated by a yew spear with a fire-hardened point found at a site in north Germany. Some investigators feel that equally advanced treatments had been developed as far back as the days of Peking man.

Cooking is also believed to date back to these times, mainly on the basis of indirect but convincing evidence involving teeth, sensitive indicators of evolutionary change. Regular cooking may have helped reshape the contours of the human face, in a kind of chain-reaction process. According to one theory, softer foods put less of a strain on the jaws and jaw muscles, which became smaller along with the molar teeth. This in turn had an effect on the design of the rest of the skull. Massive overhanging brow ridges and other thick bony protuberances had evolved largely as structures to which powerful jaw muscles could be attached, and they were reduced as the muscles dwindled in size. Furthermore, the skull itself became thinner, perhaps one of the changes involved in expanding the cranium to house a bigger brain.

Cooking also played a part in promoting more restraint. With the advent of cookery, humans tended to spend less time devouring freshly killed game on the spot and more time back at the cave eating with the rest of the band around a hearth. The domestication of fire was one more step in human domestication. Inhibition is as much a mark of evolutionary advance as action itself.

Above all, fire was light. It increased the length of the day, creating a new kind of day independent of the movements of the sun. Life became less routine. Humans no longer rose and slept with the rising and setting of the sun. As they had become independent of one great natural rhythm, the internal rhythm of *estrus*, so now they were independent of the external rhythm of day and night. The hours after dark were hours of relative leisure which they could use to plan more and more complex activities.

The existence of elaborate plans implies the evolution of more sophisticated ways of communicating. Language, the most human form of human behavior, must have taken a tremendous spurt when hunting was on the rise and hearths burned brightly past sunset. There was so much to share: details of past successes in the hunt, tall tales about the big ones that got away, strategies for future hunts, rules about hunting territories and the division of kills, and a growing store of myths and legends.

The fireside became an institution, a cohesive force bringing members of the band closer together, old as well as young. Other primates also had their patriarchs and matriarchs, but now old age acquired a new importance. Now individuals too old to fight or carry heavy things or hunt became important because they remembered things beyond the memories of others—particularly things that happened rarely, such as floods and other catastrophes, and things that required special knowlege, such as the settling of territorial disputes and the treatment of illnesses. The elders took their places at the fireside and were consulted and listened to.

Finally, fire presumably played a role in the earliest religious experiences. We know that prehistoric hunters carrying torches and lamps penetrated deep into the remotest chambers of caves, covered the walls with paintings and en-

The cooking fire served as a social center for our early ancestors just as it often does today. After this Kalahari woman roasts nuts over the fire, the men will gather to eat and talk.

gravings of animals, and met by firelight to practice rituals whose purposes we can only speculate about. These underground meetings took place during the past 30,000 years or so. But many investigators are convinced that humans engaged in similar activities hundreds of thousands of years before the coming of art, and that they used fire to serve a double purpose, to arouse excitement as well as provide light. Fire may be a stimulant as potent as drugs in arousing visions and previsions, and as such would have served the purposes of priests and priestesses, the cultural descendants of the early fire bearers.

Many factors went into the shaping of *Homo erectus*—hunting, gathering, cooperation, fire, selection for bigger brains, prolonged infant dependency, loss of *estrus*, the coming of the family and taboos and traditions. Each factor contributed in an important way to this development of a new and uniquely human way of life.

Focus

Robert S. O. Harding and
Shirley C. Strum

The Predatory Baboons
of Kekopey

The data presented by Harding and Strum are significant not simply as a report of primate predation but as a record of primate social evolution as well. The similarities between the development of hunting among the baboons of Kekopey and the hominid evolutionary scheme we have presented are overwhelming. Perhaps, as Harding and Strumm suggest, we are too interested in discovering the distinctive traits which set humans apart from other primates to see the basic similarities in adaptation to changing environments.

The olive baboons moved slowly across the African plain that lay deep in the shadow of the cliffs on whose ledges the troop would sleep in safety for the night. Suddenly, an adult male stopped in the foot-high grass and pounced. The sharp bleat that followed betrayed the presence of a newborn Thomson's gazelle, still too weak to outrun its captor.

The baboon held the infant to the ground and tore at its soft belly with his teeth. When the antelope stopped moving, the baboon commenced eating, but perhaps intimidated by the presence of other male baboons, which had approached and were staring at the scene, he picked up the carcass in his jaws and ran twenty yards away. The others pursued. Within an hour the male had consumed most of the flesh, but as he walked away from the remains another

Reprinted, with permission, from *Natural History* Magazine, March, 1976. Copyright © The American Museum of Natural History, 1976.

male quickly seized the last bits of flesh and skin.

Incidents of this sort have become quite common among the baboon troops that range freely through Kekopey, a cattle ranch near the village of Gilgil, 70 miles northwest of Nairobi, in the Central Rift Valley of Kenya. Although Kekopey comprises 45,000 acres, the sparse grass supports only 4,500 cattle.

Impala and Thomson's gazelle are the dominant antelope species in this part of the ranch. In 1970, when we first began our study, their exact numbers were not known, but a survey on 18,000 acres of open grassland and scrub on the ranch resulted in a count of 800 impala and 1,600 Thomson's gazelle. Baboons also inhabit this part of the ranch; our 1970 census, which covered some of this area, showed seven troops ranging in size from 35 to 135 animals and living in overlapping home ranges.

Predators had been greatly reduced but not completely eliminated. To permit the raising of domestic stock, the lion population had been systematically destroyed by shooting. And in recent years, ranch owners live-trapped some of the ranch's leopards for removal to national parks in Kenya. . . .

The ecosystem at Kekopey has thus undergone considerable modification over the years. Baboons, however, have for the most part escaped the human harassment that is their lot elsewhere in Africa, where they are trapped for medical experimentation or killed because of their fondness for human food crops. Despite the obvious alterations in the ecosystem, we decided to proceed with our research in this natural laboratory.

Although baboons subsist mostly on grasses, seeds,

roots, and other plant matter, they were known to occasionally capture and kill small animals. Sheepherders in southern Africa, for instance, have long complained of baboon troops raiding their herds and taking young lambs. And a number of scientists had described baboon predatory behavior, but in no case had they reported a troop killing more than 20 animals annually.

As a result we were not surprised to learn that the baboons at Kekopey killed and ate small animals, but we did not anticipate the extent to which they engaged in this behavior. During the first year's research, we saw members of the one troop we were studying kill and eat 47 small animals—principally baby gazelles and some hares. This was a meat-eating rate higher than any then reported for a nonhuman primate group.

Baboons spend the greater part of each day feeding and moving from one foraging site to another with other members of their troop. Movements are usually unhurried, with individuals stopping from time to time to feed on the grasses and other vegetation that cover the valley floors. Our observations disclosed that it was during such leisurely progressions that many of the killings of small prey took place. Since both hares and young antelopes attempt to conceal themselves from predators by crouching in long grass or behind bushes, some of the baboons located and killed these animals by chance in the course of normal troop movement.

Yet, as we became more accustomed to the baboons' usual movement patterns, we discovered that the troop was moving deliberately through herds of grazing Thomson's gazelle. And several times, adult males left the troop to detour through nearby gazelle herds, scanning the ground on all sides as they went. Males also explored the heavy scrub that small dik-diks frequent.

Of the fifty baboons in the troop in 1970, four were adult males and nineteen were adult females. At first, killing was predominantly a male activity. The adult females killed only three animals—infant hares. We never saw juvenile baboons even try to catch an animal. Of the three females who killed the

hares, only one succeeded in keeping any part of her prey; the other two were chased and threatened by adult males until they dropped their catch. Capturing prey was not only largely a male activity, it was a solitary one as well. Although one male baboon once successfully took up the chase of a young gazelle driven near him by another male, the baboons did not seem to cooperate in running down prey nor did a male baboon voluntarily share his catch with another troop member.

In 1970 and 1971, two-thirds of all the animals killed were newborn antelope of various species, with Thomson's gazelle the most frequent. About one-quarter of the animals consumed were Cape hare, and the balance included a button quail and several other animals that we could not identify from the scraps the baboons left. We never saw troop members eating carrion, although they had several chances to do so, nor did they try to catch every animal of the appropriate size.

Their sleeping cliffs, for instance, abounded with rock hyrax, and although baboons eat these small furry creatures elsewhere in Africa, we never saw the study troop attempt to catch them. And although an adjacent troop often caught helmeted guinea fowl, the troop we were studying ignored flocks of these birds as they walked cackling through the baboons' midst.

By late 1972, the troop had grown to sixty baboons—the result of births and emigration of adult males from nearby troops—and the animals' meat-eating tendencies had increased. In 1,200 hours of observation between 1972 and 1974, we saw them capture 100 small animals, roughly twice as many as they killed during a similar number of hours in 1970–71.

Not only were the baboons consuming more meat; their behavior toward acquiring meat had changed as well. Adult females, which had shown little interest in meat eating during the first years of our study, began to capture prey in significant numbers—hares for the most part, but some infant antelopes as well. All females were now present at some of the kills but two, in particular, were present at more kills than several of the adult males, and always waited, patiently but persistently, at the site for the male to finish eating. While some watching males might give up and leave before the carcass was abandoned, these females remained, seemingly undaunted in their determination, and in the end, had their turn at the meat.

It did not take long before the females also became bolder; rather than drop an animal when a large adult male approached, a female might try to outrun or outmaneuver him and the attempt was often successful. During the period from 1972 to 1974, adult females caught 14 percent of all prey; we also noticed that immature baboons were becoming involved in meat eating. The offspring of the two females that seemed particularly interested in meat frequently had the opportunity to investigate prey, and predictably, they were the first immature baboons to eat meat. At first their presence in the vicinity of kills simply reflected their mothers' interest. But as they grew older and became more independent, their interest continued whether or not their mothers were present at a particular episode.

It was not only maternal bonds that helped meat-eating behavior to spread among the younger baboons; long-term male bonds with infants and juveniles also created opportunities for meat eating among the young baboons even when their mothers had no special interest in meat. Many young baboons thus began their meat-eating behavior as a result of their special, close relationship with a male.

Older juveniles often began eating meat by chance—stumbling across a meat-eating episode while chasing one another in play. Such incidents seemed to make little impression on the young baboons, unless one chanced to get a scrap or two of meat. Behavior changed markedly in such a case; the young baboon would begin to join the hangers-on at kills until, through patience and persistence, it too got some meat. Juveniles then began to seek out and capture prey on their own, to the point that in the period from 1972 to 1974, they caught 16 percent of the prey.

Over the years the tactics used by adult male

baboons to obtain meat changed dramatically. They began to supplement fortuitous captures and occasional detours through grasslands rich in prey with more concerted and systematic efforts. Upon sighting a herd of gazelles as much as a quarter of a mile away, one or more males often left the troop and approached the herd. By January 1974, this was an almost daily event. At first each male acted independently, but adult males always remain constantly aware of each other's location and actions; as a result, when one male made a kill or seemed about to do so, the others often abandoned their own efforts and converged on the successful hunter.

In one such incident, three males noticed another male chasing a gazelle and ran toward him. To get to the scene of the chase, they had to ascend a small hill that concealed their approach from both predator and prey. Just as he was about to abandon the chase, the baboon in pursuit of the gazelle suddenly found the three other males blocking the prey's escape route. The closest male then took up the effort, and when he appeared to flag, another continued it. For a moment the gazelle appeared to be outrunning its pursuers, but it changed direction in response to a similar movement from the baboon chasing it, and in so doing, ran into the third of the newly arrived males. The gazelle almost escaped when the pursuing baboon momentarily hesitated, but a quick bite to the underbelly put an end to the chase.

From that point on, the male baboons gradually adopted this relay system as a regular stratagem, chasing their prey toward a nearby male instead of out on the open plain. Such joint ventures appeared to be more successful than those carried out by lone males.

Adult male baboons also began to scatter antelope herds more frequently in an apparent attempt to find young animals of suitable size. This tactic often revealed a young antelope breaking from cover in the grass to run after its mother. The baboons might then spend as much as two hours covering large amounts of ground in attempts to close in on the antelope mother and her infant. As this tactic became more successful, deliberate searching for other prey in different habitat—such as dik-dik in brushy areas—became less frequent.

The persistence of the male baboons' efforts was impressive. On several occasions the troop moved through one particular area for a number of consecutive days, and each time males unsuccessfully pursued the same young gazelle. Each venture lasted up to two hours and took the baboons as much as two miles from the rest of the troop, out of sight and, apparently, out of contact. Once, after hunting the same herd for three days, the males finally captured and consumed a young antelope.

In the beginning of 1973 the male baboons could not seem to discriminate between all-male herds and mixed or all-female herds of Thomson's gazelle. Since only those including females contained potential prey animals, the baboons at first wasted considerable time and energy in scattering male herds. Later, however, the baboons were able to assess the herds, ignoring all-male ones and pursuing only female groupings within a mixed herd.

For their part, the Thomson's gazelle began to show vigilance toward baboons, especially those herds that had been hunted several times in a row. Once a baboon of any size appeared, the gazelles became alert and moved off, the adult females herding their infants away from the baboons. This vigilance, in turn, created new difficulties for the baboons and may have offset, at least partially, the advantage they had gained through their innovations in hunting behavior.

During the first year's observations, baboons did not share meat voluntarily; indeed, the adult males who did most of the killing at that time were highly intolerant of other baboons in their vicinity. As predatory behavior spread through the troop over the years, however, we observed the animals eating simultaneously from the same piece of meat or pile of scraps and even moving aside to make room for other baboons. We saw none of the gestures that chimpanzees use in begging for meat nor did we see food items other than meat ever shared, even between a mother and her infant. Such meat-sharing relationships appear to coincide with already existing long-term bonds, such as those between mothers and infants or individual males and females.

Over the past five years, the troop appears to have developed more efficient and sophisticated methods of capturing and consuming prey. We shall never know how the predatory behavior began, for the baboons were already eating meat when we began to study the troop, but we can make some educated guesses about why predation has developed to such an extent. The most plausible has to do with the apparent antelope population explosion that resulted when the natural ecosystem of Kekopey was altered for raising cattle. Thomson's gazelle, predominantly grazing animals whose preferred habitat is open grassland, have benefited the most from these changes.

While we can only speculate about the origins of the baboons' predatory behavior at Kekopey, we know a great deal about the social dynamics underlying its spread through the troop. The behavior clearly proceeded along preexisting lines of social bonding—from mother to offspring, male to juvenile, and between male and female. We do not know whether the behavior was initiated by one or several individuals, but it seems to have become firmly established and is at this time independent of any one individual.

In a series of experiments involving the introduction of new foods to groups of macaques, Japanese anthropologists have documented the importance of individual behavior and social bonds in the diffusion of new behavior patterns involving different food items in a primate group. At Kekopey we witnessed a natural experiment in which, once again, individual behavior and social relationships played crucial roles in determining which animals acquired the new behavior.

There is no reason to think that we have seen the full development of the baboons' potential for predatory behavior, but of course there are limits to its expansion. Chief among these is probably the size of the prey animal, for nonhuman primates usually prey upon animals smaller than themselves; the anatomy typical of monkeys and apes allows for the easy capture and consumption of such prey. We would be greatly surprised if these baboons began to capture adult impala or adult Thomson's gazelle.

Just as social factors facilitated the spread of predatory behavior within the troop, they may also set limits. Most troop members are physically capable of capturing prey and eating meat, but females and immature animals will probably not become involved in the hunting behavior that takes adult males far away from the troop for long periods. Adult males are relatively mobile, often transferring from troop to troop. Females and young baboons, however, would have to abandon old behavior patterns, which have important integrative functions within the troop, and acquire new ones if they were to take part in extended hunting forays. As evidence of this behavioral difference between adult males and other baboons, females and young approached only those kills that occurred near the troop. They usually ignored those that took place at a distance, unless the prey was carried close to the troop.

Anthropologists have traditionally believed that only humans among the primates kill and eat animals as a regular part of their diets. Some have even felt that the hunting, meat-eating adaptation has been so important in human evolution that we would be better advised to turn to social carnivores—such as lions—rather than nonhuman primates as models for early human populations. Documentation of hunting and meat eating by chimpanzees at the Gombe National Park in Tanzania and elsewhere in Africa, however, has forced a modification of this position. With predatory baboons now added to the equation, we can identify a primate potential for predation, one that our earliest hominid ancestors must have shared. The baboon and chimpanzee studies demonstrate how sophisticated and successful predation can be among primates without any of the unique attributes of the human hunting adaptation, such as the ability to manufacture tools.

There are many differences, of course, between the predatory behavior of human and nonhuman primates, for while the diet of the earliest hominids may have resembled that of today's baboons or chimpanzees, archeological evidence suggests that early man took part in organized hunting forays. The killing of large animals in large numbers is unique to humans among the primates, and it is tempting to speculate that the ability to manufacture tools and the development of sophisticated communication methods may have been the key to successful hunting of this nature.

As far as primates are concerned, however, there is no doubt that the capture, killing, or consumption of even a single large animal poses problems that are of a wholly different order from those encountered in the hunting of small animals. By comparing human and nonhuman primate hunting patterns, we can learn much both about the behaviors and behavioral potentials we share and those that are unique.

Predatory behavior in primates probably did not have a single origin but may have developed at many different places and at many different times, possibly even under widely varying environmental conditions. This notion is important in considering human evolution, for it suggests that basic human adaptations may also have had multiple origins. Considering the speed with which the baboons elaborated their predatory behavior, it is also possible that after an initial adaptive shift to a new behavior in early human populations, further development of this behavior proceeded more rapidly than we think. The behavior of the baboons also shows that individual and social factors could well have had an important influence on the perpetuation of new behavioral adaptations.

The spread of predatory behavior among the Kekopey baboons prompts us to appreciate the complexity of adaptive shifts, both behavioral and anatomical, and adds to our growing realization that simple hypotheses tend to retard, rather than advance, an understanding of human evolution. The realization brings us back to the original insights of Darwin and Huxley, who theorized that all primates are linked along a single evolutionary continuum, one in which artificial barriers erected by humans to assure their own unique status have no rational grounds for existence.

Summary

Human society appears to have begun taking shape some five million years ago. Social interaction probably arose in response to the challenges presented by the new savanna environment. One advantage of savanna life was the availability of meat. Hunting was too risky to be depended upon as a steady source of nutrition, so a hunting and gathering system evolved to allow the fullest exploitation of available resources. As omnivores, the early hominids had to know a great deal more about the animals and plants in their environment than did those animals which relied exclusively on either meat or vegetation. The need to make more complex decisions and to interact in more intricate ways with other individuals contributed to the evolution of a larger and more humanlike brain.

The changes which were undergone as the hominids adapted to the savanna involved much positive feedback. The use of tools, the assumption of an upright posture, bipedal locomotion, and enlargement of the brain were all mutually interactive factors in human evolution. One consequence of brain enlargement was a shorter gestation period and a longer period of infant dependency. As the female anatomy gradually changed to allow for a larger birth canal and infants were born at an earlier stage of fetal development, the nature of male and female roles was adjusted accordingly. Males became the hunters and protectors while females became the plant gatherers and child raisers. A system of mutual cooperation and interdependency evolved and became increasingly more important as brain size expanded in response to greater social complexity.

Another interesting outgrowth of delayed maturity was the evolution of the infant's smile. In humans, the smile served to cement the social bond between mother and infant. The slow pace of child development also provided time for the acquisition of language skills and other behavioral patterns appropriate to the evolving human culture. Prolonged dependency tended to increase the specialization of and cooperation between males and females as well.

Extended childhood was accompanied by the elimination of the *estrus* cycle and the development of controlled sexual receptivity. The ability to limit and direct sexual urges promoted group stability by reducing competition among males for access to females and offered the potential for a choice of partners and long-term male-female bonding. Consistent with these developments was the evolution of the incest taboo which furthered small group stability. Controlled sexual urges also permitted the development of rules of *exogamy* which fostered alliances between neighboring groups. Marriage is a more efficient mechanism of territorial defense than warfare. With each step in social complexity, the brain increased its memory and decision-making capabilities.

Another source of change in the final stages of hominid evolution was the use of fire. Initially taken from natural sources, fire provided warmth to move into colder climates, light to enter caves and a weapon to clear the caves of predators, a tool for stampeding prey into swamps and a source of heat for cooking. Additionally, it was a source of group cohesion, bringing people together in the evening, and a stimulus to the imagination and fantasy of *Homo erectus*.

GLOSSARY

Estrus A stage in the reproductive cycle of nonhominid, female primates, around the time of ovulation, at which time they are most receptive to copulation.

Exogamy The prohibition of marriage within a group, however that group is defined. Exogamy, which requires marriage outside the group, developed among hunters and gatherers as a mechanism of forming peaceful alliances between neighboring groups.

Incest taboo　A set of rules found in some form in every society, which prohibits sexual relationships between certain relatives. The incest taboo developed among hunters and gatherers as a mechanism of limiting conflict between members of a highly interdependent familistic society.

Mnemon　A memory unit consisting of half a dozen interconnected nerve cells centered on a classifying cell, which receives impulses from the senses and sends messages to the muscles through a 'retreat' fiber or an 'advance fiber'.

Ungulates　A group of plains-dwelling hoofed mammals commonly hunted by late hominids and modern humans.

Tiger, Lionel and Robin Fox

1971　The Imperial Animal. New York: Holt, Rinehart and Winston.

While based on some controversial premises, this book contains many interesting ideas about the similarities and differences between humans and animals. Additionally, it is enjoyable reading.

Additional Readings

Eiseley, Loren C.

1954　Man the Fire-Maker. *Scientific American*, volume 191, no. 3, pp. 52–57.

An interesting discussion of the first uses of fire.

Firth, Raymond

1965　Primitive Polynesian Economy. *Ed./Auth:*

An in-depth examination of the relationship between culture and economy. The reading is intense, but well worth it.

Pfeiffer, John E.

1955　The Human Brain. New York: Harper.

A constructive examination of the mechanics of the brain.

Thomas, Elizabeth Marshall

1959　The Harmless People. New York: Knopf.

And interesting narrative on the culture of the Kalahari Bushmen of southern Africa.

chapter seven

Archaeology/
HOMO ERECTUS
CULTURE

The rise of hunting brings with it a basic change in the kinds of evidence available to anthropologists for the reconstruction of prehistory. Beginning between 750,000 and 500,000 years ago, the material remains of hominids developed to the point that they were recognizable independently of the telltale physical remains of the species. At Torralba, Spain, and Dragon's Hill near Peking, China, cultural remains—living floors, butchering sites, tools, ash from fires—have been uncovered. Prehumans had begun to alter their environments in increasingly recognizable ways. Although there are tool assemblages and living floors associated with *Australopithecus* at Olduvai Gorge, much of the reconstruction of the life of *Australopithecus* has depended on inferences drawn from the minute analysis of the fossil remains and on analogies with living primates. With *Homo erectus,* the reconstruction of living patterns depends more and more on the examination of material artifacts, the objects they left behind. The archeologist specializes in uncovering and analyzing these material remains, predominantly tools of stone, of the earliest hominids with a fully developed culture.

LOCATING A SITE

Before archeologists excavate, they must first find the location of remains that have been preserved, hidden from view for eons.

Imagine a prehistoric twilight with hunters stopping by a stream, scooping a hollow place in the earth for a hearth, sharpening old flints and shaping new ones, eating meat by the fire and coming close for warmth and curling up at the edge of the fire to sleep. After a stay of a few days or a few weeks, the hunters abandon camp and the seasons go to work. Leaves and branches fall and form new earth; winds blow in dust and sand and volcanic ash. The area is flooded and a lake appears. Sediments drift down through the waters and settle and accumulate on the bottom.

Then the lake dries up, and another cycle starts. Decades pass and centuries and millennia, and something endures. The original occupation floor may be preserved like a flower pressed between the pages of a diary, or the fossil imprint of a fern on rock. There are discarded tools, charred bones, and the remains of

Attempting to distinguish human-made artifacts from natural formations is a long and arduous task.

fires that sputtered out long ago, traces of camps where humans stayed a while and disturbed the earth and then moved on. There are sites where living patterns have persisted for as much as two to three million years.

A worldwide search is under way for new sites which will reveal more about the ways of creatures in the first throes of becoming human. Expeditions are searching in back-country bordering lakes in the African Rift Valley, on slopes rising from the flat plains of northern Thailand, among the foothills of the Rockies and Himalayas and Urals, along the Mediterranean coast, in the deserts of Australia, in valleys gouged out of the plateaus of central Spain.

Expeditions are part adventure and part sheer drudgery. Work in the field often begins with the inspection of geological maps indicating where promising deposits lie exposed or near the surface, ancient lake sediments or dunes or river banks which may include the remains of prehistoric camps and campers. The next step may involve aerial photographs of the mapped terrain, pairs of photographs placed edge to edge and looked at through a stereo viewer so that trees, cliffs, gullies, hills and other features appear sharp and in three dimensions as if one were flying over the region on a clear day.

The latest advance in the technology of site-searching involves a half-ton, remote-sensing "eye in the sky" satellite recently launched in California. Equipped with a television-type scanning device, it is viewing the world from a height of about 500 miles and taking synchronized photographs in green, red, and infrared light every twenty-five seconds, each photograph covering an area of about 10,000 square miles (100 miles on a side). Some of the photographs, specifically the ones covering the Chaco Canyon National Monument region of New Mexico, are being studied in intensive detail to learn how they can be used to identify places where people lived many thousands of years ago—extinct river beds and lakes, soils rich in organic matter and clays, hidden springs and other water sources, fine debris at the bottoms of cliffs, stream and beach gravels and wind-deposited sands which may contain ancient artifacts. The insights gained in this way, in the course of checking a region already well known archeologically, will be used to examine features of satellite photographs of less well known regions.

The real work starts after photography and other techniques have pinpointed a number of likely-looking areas for detailed on-the-ground surveying. Since most unexplored regions are located far off the beaten track in country too rugged even for Land Rovers, that means getting out and walking. On a typical day you wake at sunrise, tramp through brush and brambles, bending low to avoid the thorns, half-slide and half-fall down the steep sides of ravines, follow the courses of dried-out stream beds, and then try to find your way back before nightfall. You may walk fifteen miles or more in eight hours, with about forty minutes off to eat and rest, and that goes on day after day for as long as it takes to cover an area systematically.

Every search is a gamble, and many searches end with little or nothing to show for them. Under such conditions success, when it comes, is especially sweet. For example, an important site was discovered a number of years ago by Desmond Clark of the University of California at Berkeley just as he was on the verge of quitting. The setting is one of the wildest and most magnificent in Africa, near the southern end of Lake Tanganyika where the Kalambo River winds sluggishly through a high valley, moves faster as it nears the edge of a cliff, and plunges seven hundred feet into a dark tropical canyon. One morning Clark was walking back from the falls along the spillway gorge when, after nearly falling into a pit dug by natives to trap wild pigs, he happened to look down at a point where the river makes a sharp meander.

A family of Homo erectus *may have looked very much like this group.*

"I almost missed the place completely," he recalls. "The grass, which is normally about eight feet high and thick as your finger, had been burned off, revealing a sheer erosion cut in the river bank, and you look at practically every sheer cut. This one was touch and go, but I did look. I hung on to a couple of roots, lowered myself over the edge, and found some nice tools dating back to the Middle Stone Age of Africa about 25,000 to 30,000 years ago. Then I dropped to the bottom, where still older tools, *hand axes* and *cleavers,* were sticking out from the bank as well as pieces of carbonized wood. I could hardly believe that it was the real thing."

EXCAVATION

Once a site has been found, the work really starts, and it is slow and demanding work. It calls for the application of new digging methods, or rather methods developed chiefly during the past seventy-five years by archeologists in Germany, Denmark, England and other countries at farm and village sites of the past four or five thousand years. A site is approached with almost surgical care and precision. First the outer cover of very recent rock and soil must be removed, taking pains to expose but not cut into underlying occupation layers. Then the job is to obtain as complete a picture as possible of the patterns in the layers.

Every item, every piece of bone and rock, worked or unworked, and chips and flakes as well as tools, must be exposed but not moved. Every object is part of the pattern of objects; it means nothing by itself. Its position is all important. The digging rate varies depending on how much material lies on the living floor. But in a reasonably good spot it may take one person an entire eight-hour day squatting in the dust under a hot sun to excavate two or three inches deep in an area about the size of a bridge-table top.

Much of the time is spent doing paperwork. Using a steel rule or a yardstick, you measure the position of every single one of several hundred pieces of material, its location on the living floor, and its depth beneath the surface of the site. One may also record the direction in which the piece is pointing because, among other things, that may help you check on whether or not the site has actually been disturbed. If a large proportion of the pieces are pointing in the same general direction, it may mean that they have been moved by flowing water; while unmoved pieces tend to be oriented at random. All this information is written in a notebook together with the number of each piece and its type, that is, whether it is a tool and if so what sort of tool. Later the pieces are washed and numbered for identification, using a fine pen and India ink.

The general practice is not to excavate a site completely, because of the peculiar nature of archeological evidence. In other sciences experiments can always be repeated and results checked. Astronomers can always make new observations of the sun and planets; biologists have an ample supply of organisms for continuing laboratory studies. Once an archeologist excavates a site, however, there can be no checking or retracing of steps. That particular arrangement of buried objects is unique. There is no other arrangement like it, and it can never be fully re-created again. Clues missed because of carelessness or ignorance are gone forever.

An appalling amount of information has been lost because of bad practices in the not-too-remote past. Profit-minded diggers have destroyed many fine sites simply to obtain a few beautifully worked flint and bone tools to sell to museums, tourists or private collectors, using rush tactics to complete in a few hours excavations which should have been carried out over periods of weeks. One notorious plunderer was caught in the act of trying to remove a section of the ceiling of a French rock shelter, a section containing a sculpted fish. The organized and semisanctioned looting of archeological sites has been an international scandal for some time, and legislation is at last being considered not only to prosecute the looters but also to prevent the purchase of looted material by some museum officials and other not overly scrupulous collectors whose desire for objects of art keeps the looters in business.

Even without such hazards, excavating is sufficiently difficult to tax the ingenuity and patience of legitimate workers. Even seasoned archeologists have unwittingly destroyed evidence, simply because they did not know it was there. For example, about fifty years ago Danish investigators developed the so-called *flotation technique* which makes it possible to collect fragments of organic material from excavated deposits—and takes advantage of the fact that materials of different densities may be separated by their tendencies to float or sink in different solutions. At successive stages flotation separates plant and bone from clay and stone particles, plants from bone, and different sizes of bone and plant material from one another.

The procedure has proved of considerable value to a number of investigators. For example, Stuart Struever of Northwestern University is conducting large-scale studies of Hopewell Indian communities in Illinois, and at one of his sites the technique helped provide a far more balanced picture of human activities than did conventional methods alone. The old picture, based on the excavation of large quantities of large animal bones and flint points, was of a community living predominantly by hunting. But plant remains hitherto discarded and now extracted by flotation included thousands of tiny fish bones, seed and nutshell and wood-charcoal fragments, and indicated a far more varied hunting-gathering way of life. The technique is used more widely than it was a few years ago, but a great deal of information is still being thrown away with the dirt discarded at many prehistoric sites.

Another increasingly useful technique is the analysis of fossil pollen, grains whose tough outer coatings have been preserved in such fine detail that grasses, shrubs, oak, holly, pine, juniper, palm and dozens of other plants can be identified under the microscope. It is painstaking work. Each grain is examined at magnifications of 400 to more than 1,500 times for size, shape, types and distribution of spiny and rod-like extensions, and a wide variety of surface features. Each grain has about 40 to 50 different features which are significant and must be noted; hundreds of grains may be analyzed daily, and a project may continue for weeks. The result is a powerful aid in reconstructing past climates and environments.

Contemporary diggers, knowing of research in new techniques of excavation, generally leave one-fourth to one-half of a site undug for future workers who will come with more advanced techniques and greater knowledge.

There are exceptions, of course. Sites may be excavated completely and in a hurry when they are scheduled to be destroyed for non-ar-

The "Dragon Bone Hill" site near Choukoutien, China, where the skull of Sinanthropus—Peking man—*was discovered.*

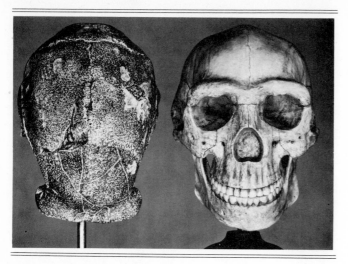

Two views of the "Peking man" skull after restoration.

cheological reasons, and that is happening more and more frequently as construction crews build new homes and highways for expanding populations. For example, work was recently halted for five months during the building of new apartments on the French Riviera, when bulldozers exposed tools and other signs of a prehistoric encampment. In this case, as in the case of the Nile Valley sites flooded by the Aswan Dam in Egypt, the objective was to recover as much evidence as possible in a limited time.

HOMO ERECTUS SITES

The 300,000 year old site near Torralba, Spain, like many prehistoric sites, was discovered by workers excavating for nonscientific reasons. In 1888 railroad workers were digging a trench for a water main and found fossil bones and stone tools. Starting in 1907, a Spanish nobleman and amateur archeologist spent about five years excavating not far from the now-abandoned railroad station. Although his findings indicated that the site was one of the

most important in Europe, no one thought of digging there again until 1960, when Clark Howell spent a day at Torralba.

Howell located the overgrown trenches and back dirt of the old excavation, collected a few tools and bone fragments in adjoining fields, and decided that further digging was called for. More than half the site had been left unexcavated, so he and his associates and crew including some thirty local farmers, worked in the region for the next three summers, thirty-four weeks in all. They spent about $75,000; excavated a total of 20,000 square feet to an average depth of about eight feet; collected more than 500 pollen samples, 2,000 stone tools and waste pieces, and uncounted fossil bones; and also mapped twenty-odd living-floor areas.

The site apparently served as a prehistoric *abattoir*, a place for butchering and meat processing. Concentrated in a relatively small area are the remains of at least thirty elephants, twenty-five horses, twenty-five red deer, ten wild oxen, and half a dozen rhinoceroses. The remains lie where they were abandoned long ago. One 270-square-foot area contains much of the left side of a large adult elephant with tusks and bones unbroken and in place as if put together for an exhibit. The pelvis is missing and so is the skull, although the lower jaw was left intact. The area also contained four flake tools that might have been used for cutting. Another somewhat larger area nearby includes some of the bones of this same elephant; most of them have been shattered. There is a broken right leg bone, some vertebrae, and fragments of ribs, upper jaw and collar bone as well as two stone cleavers and more flakes.

This evidence suggests that the two areas were used for different purposes. What seems to have happened is that the elephant was killed and dismembered in the area containing its left side and the unbroken bones, and that large pieces of meat were carried to the nearby area for further butchering and processing. Two

Raymond Dart *(1893–   )*
*was a young professor of anatomy
at the medical school in Johannesburg, South Africa when he uncovered the famous Taung child in
1924. While most of his colleagues
viewed* Australopithecus africanus, *as he named the species,
with suspicion, Dart was undaunted in his attempt to reconstruct the life of our early ancestors. He uncovered primitive stone
tools and concluded that* Australopithecus *was bipedal long
before the finds at Olduvai Gorge
led to a general acceptance of a
bipedal, tool manufacturing early
hominid. From the markings on a
number of skulls, Dart also concluded that* Australopithecus
*was a cannibal. This, however, is
doubted by most anthropologists
today.*

other areas include finer splinters and fragments, and occur together with a cleaver and a
number of heavy side scrapers. It is more
difficult to deduce what was going on here, but
hunters may have been eating their share of the
spoils—perhaps cleaning all the meat off the
bones with the aid of the scrapers and then, like
Australopithecus at Olduvai more than a million
years previously, smashing the bones for the
marrow inside.

A great deal more can be learned from this
association of remains. What is the significance
of the arrangement of the large elephant's left-
side bones? At first the theory was that the animal had been caught in a swamp, struggled to
pull itself out, and finally fallen on its left side.
According to this notion, it sank so deeply that
only its right side was exposed and accessible to
butchery, so prehistoric hunters took what they
could and did not try to get at the buried left
side.

But the theory has not survived a more detailed analysis. The elephant may indeed have
become stuck in the mud; its remains are pre-

Excavators at the Torralba hunting and butchering site.

served in clay-silt deposits, signs of a fossil swampland. The left-side bones, however, were not left in place. Leslie Freeman of the University of Chicago has prepared an extensive report on Torralba and points out, among other things, that the bones are not completely articulated, that is, they are not all fitted neatly joint in joint. Also, they have all been turned over. It seems that the animal was completely butchered, and after the butchering, someone took some of the big left bones and vertebrae and laid them down side by side to produce a partially reconstructed skeleton. Why anyone would have done this is another question. It may have been a game, joke or ritual, but there are no clues to support these or any other guesses.

The next question is how the elephant became bogged down in the first place. Torralba lies in a steep-sided little valley which includes the headwaters of a principal tributary of the Ebro River; even today, under generally dry conditions, places exist in the region where the water level rises to within a few inches of the surface and where a heavy animal would break through and sink. The terrain was wetter in the time of the elephant killers, perhaps representatives of *Homo erectus*. Fossil pollen gathered at the site indicates that there was a pine forest on the plateau, a sluggish meandering stream in the poorly drained valley, and seasonal swamplands with dense reeds and sedges.

Prehistoric humans must have stood often on high ledges and slopes, and followed the leisurely movements of herds grazing in the valley below. Perhaps now and then a young and unwary elephant wandered away from the herd and suddenly found itself sinking in thick mud. If so, hunters would hardly have missed the chance to race down and close in for the kill; indeed, a surprisingly high proportion of the elephant bones unearthed at Torralba are those of juveniles. Perhaps the large adult, the elephant whose skeleton had been partially reassembled, had also wandered into a swamp and was promptly dispatched.

On the other hand, the hunters might have played a rather more active role. The elephants may not have simply blundered into the swamp, an explanation which after all implies that they were too stupid to avoid dangerous places during the course of their everyday movements, and which fails to account for the fact that many animals seem to have been driven to disaster, as indicated by certain items found in surrounding areas and carefully mapped, items that excavators of the past would not have considered worth charting.

In the area Howell collected many bits of charcoal and carbon which were distributed in an unusual fashion. Instead of being concentrated in a few spots, which would be the case if they represented hearths where fires burned over long periods of time, the materials are thinly and very widely scattered. Perhaps the charcoal represents the remains of hearths dispersed by the wind, but Howell suggests another possibility: "Whoever lit these fires was apparently burning grass and brush over large areas and for a definite purpose. My guess is that the purpose was to drive elephants along the valley into the swamps."

So the evidence, the burned material and the concentrated remains and the fossil bogs, tells a story of human activities more than three hundred millennia ago. It suggests that meat eaters were doing far more than waiting to take advantage of occasional accidents; that they had observed herds long and carefully, knew the habits of elephants, and were capable of a high degree of planning and cooperation. Other studies indicate that they generally lived in small bands of about thirty or so individuals, and a single band could not provide sufficient manpower for a large-scale, highly organized elephant drive. Several bands probably joined forces in the hunt at Torralba.

Howell discovered another major site in the

region, or rather rediscovered a site where, according to old records, preliminary excavations had been carried out half a century ago. The records merely stated that the work was done "in Ambrona," a village in the same valley as Torralba and less than two miles away, but that was not enough information to locate the site. Then one day in 1962, when Howell asked his workers whether they knew of any places with fossil bones, a man answered: "Yes, in my field"—and it turned out to be the missing site. Subsequent investigations uncovered a kill and butchering site with deposits of about the same age as the Torralba deposits, remains of the same kinds of animals with elephants again predominant (perhaps forty to fifty individuals being represented), and a number of most important living floors.

An actual hearth at Terra Amata, shown after excavation.

One area included most of the skeleton of an enormous bull elephant, an old animal judging by his very worn molar teeth, together with a few isolated bones of an infant and a young female. The bones, left in place just as they were excavated, are now housed in a museum built on the spot. The area also contained bones of other elephants as well as horses and red deer and wild oxen, all in deposits which had once been deep swamplands; scattered clusters of charcoal and carbon, suggesting the deliberate use of fire; and cleavers and many other tools which served to dispatch and dismember the prey. The same techniques were used here as at Torralba, perhaps by the same hunters.

Some of the most intriguing and enigmatic patterns have been found on another Ambrona living floor. The main feature consists of three long elephant bones, two thigh bones and a large tusk, arranged in a line and forming a kind of boundary some twenty feet long. Other large bones lie perpendicular to the line, and one of them is the only complete elephant skull yet found during the entire excavation at Torralba and Ambrona. One of the mysteries at these sites is where the hunters took the heads

of the elephants they killed; all but one of the heads is missing. Examination of the lone, almost-perfect Ambrona specimen shows one of the things they did with the heads. The top of the cranial vault has been smashed open, exposing the brain, which weighed ten pounds or so and was probably extracted and eaten. Not far away is another puzzling feature. For some unknown reason some prehistoric worker whittled a pencil-sharp point on the tip of an elephant tusk over four feet long.

Perhaps the tusk had something to do with the aligned bones. Specifically, it might have been driven into the ground and, together with other sharpened tusks, have served to support hides as part of a shelter. The hides might have been slung over the tusk-posts in a kind of tent formation, and anchored in place where they reached the ground by the line of large bones. Even a crude shelter would have provided at least some protection during cold nights, but whether or not it actually existed can be determined only by extensive excavations of living floors at other sites representing the same period of prehistory and comparable activities.

Above, an artist's conception of the exterior of a Terra Amata hut. Below, this type of branch shelter still in use by Australian aborigines.

Clear-cut signs of more elaborate shelters, the oldest dwelling structures known, come from another site of the same general period. The hillside site is located in Nice on the French Riviera, on a dead-end street called Terra Amata overlooking the Mediterranean, and luxury apartments stand there today. But in 1966, when the apartments were being built, bulldozers uncovered some prehistoric tools, and work stopped for five months while Henry de Lumley of the University of Aix-Marseilles, his associates, other investigators, and student volunteers spent 40,000 man-hours excavating an area of about 1,100 square feet. The Mediterranean was higher several hundred thousand years ago, and eighty feet of water covered the site of today's boulevards and hotels and beaches. Surf broke high among the hills on the shores of other beaches, and people camped on one of them at Terra Amata, on a bay near the mouth of a small river where animals came to drink.

On the slopes of an ancient sand dune, de Lumley found remains of a number of oval huts twenty to fifty feet long and twelve to eighteen feet wide—postholes, hearths, a wall of stones probably to protect the hearths from prevailing northwest winds, and the bones of deer, elephants, wild boars and other animals. He believes that the huts were made of sturdy branches, bent so as to interlock at the top, with an entrance at one end and a hole at the center to let smoke escape. The branches were supported by posts and by large and small rocks placed against the posts. There are eleven fairly thin and undisturbed occupation layers near the dune, suggesting that hunters, probably the same group throughout, visited and revisited the site for perhaps only a few days during eleven consecutive seasons. We know that the hunters came in the spring because their *coprolites*, fossilized feces, contain the pollen of plants which blossom in the late spring and early summer.

The huts may have housed ten to twenty persons. The areas closest to the firesides are clear of debris, indicating that the people slept there, a practice still observed today among the Australian aborigines. A number of domestic furnishings were also found. There are flat limestone blocks which may have provided convenient surfaces for sitting or breaking bones (similar blocks have been found at Torralba and Ambrona) as well as traces of the earliest container yet discovered, a wooden bowl with a rough bottom. In a corner near the bowl excavators found lumps of the natural pigment red ocher, lumps pointed like a pencil at one end and possibly used to color the body in preparation for some sort of ceremony.

HOMO ERECTUS CULTURE

Findings at Terra Amata supplement those at Torralba-Ambrona, specifically helping to reconstruct some details of life in early shelters. The Spanish sites have also yielded a rich and varied collection of tools, implying a correspondingly rich and varied range of activities. Cleavers, wedge-shaped objects which have a straight cutting edge at one end, were generally made by knocking flakes off both sides of a flattish piece of quartzite or flint or limestone, and served for heavy-duty chopping and hacking. Similar techniques went into the making of so-called hand axes, almond- or egg-shaped implements with thick heavy butts at one end, points at the other end and cutting edges along the sides. They were widely used over a period of more than half a million years, but, despite their name, probably for skinning and slicing meat and perhaps for woodworking rather than for chopping.

In addition to these tools Howell and Freeman collected many others which, because they are smaller and often less obviously worked, tended to be discarded along with the back dirt of past excavations. There are borers, scrapers, backed blades, burins or engravers, pointed flakes, and various kinds of notched tools. The important and exciting thing about such tools is that, like the tools found by Mary Leakey in the Olduvai Gorge, they appear far earlier in the record than anyone had expected—and signify the very early appearance of relatively advanced purposes and the tools needed to carry them out.

At the same time the tools do not seem to have changed much over exceedingly long periods. Crude choppers occupied a prominent place in prehistoric tool kits for more than two million years, hand axes may have lasted a million years or more, and Neanderthal man was using notched and toothed tools nearly two million years after their first appearance in Olduvai deposits. To be sure, the passage of time brought some significant refinements, notably the use of bone, hardwood or antler to put the finishing touches on tools already roughed out with hammerstones. (The softer materials "give" more, produce thin flakes, and permit more controlled and delicate shaping.) But the basic ideas, the basic tool types, were there from the beginning. Such evidence implies a degree of stability or conservatism inconceivable to modern humans.

There are tools of bone as well as stone at Torralba. This is one of the very few sites at which an appreciable number of undoubted bone tools have been found in living-floor contexts. (Olduvai is another such site.) Some of the more than one hundred implements appear to be versions of familiar stone types— scrapers, blades, cleavers and hand axes often made from specially split elephant tusks. Others were used to finish stone tools, to trim and retouch edges; still others, including "scoops" and spatula-like objects, have no known stone counterparts and serve as-yet-undetermined purposes.

Perhaps the most unique items found at Tor-

Controversy

Prehistoric Diet: What do all the bones mean?

The mystery of the prehistoric human diet is one which will probably never be fully solved. In the past, discussions of early human life put great emphasis on *Homo sapiens* as the hunting primate. Much of the exaggerated view of humans as carnivores was based on theories derived from the study of animal bones. Today, careful investigation of prehistoric evidence suggests that bones are as significant for what they conceal as for what they reveal.

Because bones are relatively durable, a great deal more is known about prehistoric big game consumption than is known about the consumption of small game and plants. Probably, early humans were omnivores who ate anything they could get their hands on. As spears and other weapons were invented, meat began to play a greater role in the human diet. Animal bones which have been recovered from prehistoric sites reveal a great deal about the skills and techniques of early hunters, but they provide little evidence of the relative proportions of meat and plant matter in the diet.

The eating of plants contributes very little to the archeological record. Even today, the African Bushman diet consists of over 60 percent plant matter, yet recently abandoned camps show no evidence of plant remains. The earliest evidence of a herbivorous diet in human populations dates from about 10,000 years ago, comparatively recent in evolutionary terms. This is because plants are rarely preserved for longer. The evidence comes from a number of sources—the stomach contents of human bodies preserved in bogs, feces preserved in very dry regions, prehistoric farm implements, and pollen indicating those edible plants which may have been available. Sometimes charred seeds retain recognizable characteristics indefinitely or the impression of plants or seeds trapped in pottery or clay can be identified by a botanist. At present, however, most of our knowledge of prehistoric human plant consumption is inferred from geological and paleontological clues.

Generally, the absence of animal bones at a site is assumed to imply that plant material played a significant role in the diet. This is not an entirely safe assumption, however. Because human populations have always tended to set up home bases and to share food with members of their group, early man had a tendency to leave his garbage in one place. He would usually bring small animals back whole, but was unlikely to drag the carcass of a large animal back to camp. Returning with only the carved meat, he may have left the bones at the killing site, leaving no conclusive evidence to be unearthed by the archeologist. Therefore, a site with no bones of large

prey could result from a heavy reliance on plants or big-game for subsistence.

Human teeth and bones also provide valuable insights into the prehistoric diet. The rapid wearing out of teeth with little decay or tooth loss, for example, might suggest a diet dominated by coarse foods while a high rate or loss and decay might be indicative of soft foods high in carbohydrates. Human bones can reveal the nature of human subsistence activities as well. Wells, for example, found that bones in the upper arm of certain populations were modified by the frequent use of slings. The effects of technology on the human anatomy may prove to be a valuable source of additional clues to our evolutionary history.

There seems to be no safe generalization concerning the dietary habits of prehistoric people, in part because of the limited evidence available. However, the generalized nature of the human adaptation must be taken into account also. Every culture is a functional and adaptive system which adjusts its subsistence strategy according to the availability of resources. Human evolution has been characterized by an increasingly flexible system of reliance on both plant and animal foods. Hunting has played an important role in human evolution, but it must be seen as merely one aspect of a complex pattern.

ralba are pieces of waterlogged wood which have somehow survived through the ages in clayey, boggy deposits. Marks of use and working have also survived, polishing, whittling and cutting scars, and hollowed-out sections. A few of the pieces may be parts of spears, which would make them the oldest known examples of a weapon that must have been invented early in the prehistory of hunting, although the oldest definite evidence currently is a fifteen-inch yew spear point found at Clacton-on-Sea, a site located on the eastern coast of England and believed to be at least 250,000 years old. But such remains are so rare and so fragmentary that unless very rich sources of preserved wood turn up, a remote possibility, we cannot expect to learn precisely how this material was used.

Another problem is the location of the home sites of the Torralba-Ambrona hunters. The sites we know them by are temporary only, places where they gathered for perhaps a few days and nights to kill and butcher their prey. Most of the excavated bones are the debris of meals eaten on the spot, and the hunters must have carried off the biggest, meatiest chunks. They must have had established camps in the valley, home bases not very far from the swamplands and the sluggish stream and protected from the bitter cold, for these were glacial times. Howell has not found any such camps, although he and his associates explored the entire valley for tools and other traces of human occupation.

Living floors at a permanent campsite would not only add greatly to knowledge about early hunting life, but might also yield an important type of still-missing evidence, remains of the hunters themselves. As previously indicated, they may have been members of the species *Homo erectus,* relatives of Peking man. But this is only a guess, and direct evidence would be far more satisfactory.

Finally, the high proportion of elephant remains at the Spanish sites raises certain questions. Assuming that Howell's interpretation is correct and the animals were deliberately stampeded to their death, why did the hunters do it? The answer is not obvious. Land with sufficient plant foods to support elephants can generally support ample herds of other animals as well. Indeed buffaloes, horses, wild cattle and various species of antelope are likely to be several hundred times more numerous than elephants. So concentrating on elephants may have been more than a straightforward matter of getting meat. Perhaps something ritualistic was involved in the sense that hunters killed the large animals mainly to prove their courage and skill.

Whatever the motives, findings at other sites also suggest cooperative hunting. A site in the Olduvai Gorge, a clay bed once part of a swamp, contains signs of an organized drive that may have taken place more than half a million years ago—the fossilized bones of a number of large animals. Some sort of roundup or surrounding maneuver may account for the shattered remains of more than sixty giant baboons concentrated at a Rift Valley site outside Nairobi.

OLDOWAN AND ACHEULIAN TOOLS

Analysis of tools found at various early hunting sites reveals some intriguing patterns. Comparing the Torralba-Ambrona *tool assemblages* as a whole with assemblages from other sites poses some new and subtle problems. There seem to have been two broad types of tools: the "Oldowan," named after sites in the Olduvai Gorge, where it was first identified, and the "Acheulian," which also exists at Olduvai but is named after the French site of Saint-Acheul in the Somme Valley where it was originally found. The Spanish sites fit into the latter category.

Oldowan tools trace back nearly two million years ago to the earliest sites at the bottom of the gorge, for example, the living-floor site which includes what may be a crude wall or windbreak. It includes the chopper, a heavy tool generally made on a cobblestone or oblong block, as well as lighter tools such as scrapers, engravers, notched implements and so on. This basic tool kit is found at Olduvai in higher and more recent deposits up to the bottom of the thick layer of wind-blown sand and ash, a time span of about a million years.

No traces of humans and their works appear in this layer. But above the layer, after an interval of many thousands of years, the Oldowan assemblage is found again with some additions. It not only includes choppers and other familiar tools found at earlier sites but also some new or rarely found items, the most characteristic of which are rough and battered spheroidal tools, purpose unknown. Presumably people had abandoned Olduvai during arid times, and their descendants had returned, bringing with them implements invented and refined elsewhere.

But there is an intriguing complication. Another tool kit, the Acheulian, appears for the first time just above the sterile sand-ash layers at sites contemporary with those containing Oldowan assemblages. Together with some choppers and other older items, the tool kit contains the earliest unmistakable hand axes reported to date, hand axes perhaps 700,000 or more years old. It does not contain battered spheroids and other items more characteristic of the Oldowan industry.

The big question is what the two assemblages mean, what can be deduced from the fact that two different tool kits were being used at the same time in the same general region. It may have had something to do with where people settled. Olduvai Gorge camps containing Oldowan tools were located on flatlands next to lakes, at the mouths of streams fed by runoff from nearby mountains. On the other hand, African camps containing early Acheulian tools

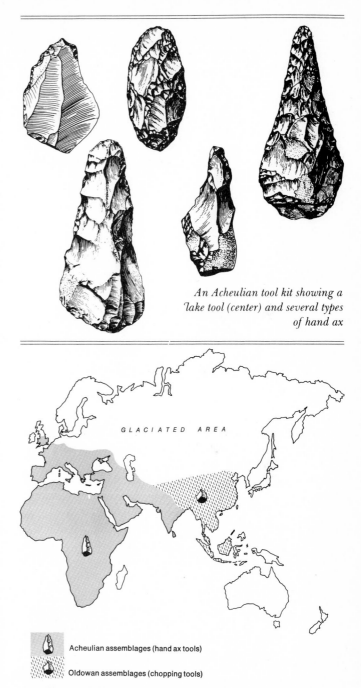

An Acheulian tool kit showing a flake tool (center) and several types of hand ax

GLACIATED AREA

Acheulian assemblages (hand ax tools)

Oldowan assemblages (chopping tools)

LOCATION OF OLDOWAN AND ACHEULIAN ASSEMBLAGES: AFRICA AND EURASIA tend to be found away from lake shores along seasonal streams.

These upstream sites have an abundance of large stones washed down from the mountainsides and tools, notably hand axes and cleavers, made from correspondingly large flakes are common in Acheulian assemblages. Such stones are rarer at lakeside sites, however, and Oldowan assemblages rarely include tools made from large flakes. In other words, people tended to use what they had in the neighborhood to do their hunting and food processing. At this level the difference between the two kinds of tool kit is to some extent a matter of different kinds of local resources.

There is certainly more to the problem. A common view is that two "traditions" are involved, two different groups of people or tribes each with their own customs and way of life, that there are Oldowan and Acheulian cultures. The problem widens when other sites are considered. Oldowan tool kits, tool kits featuring a variety of choppers and lacking cleavers as well as hand axes, predominate in the eastern part of the Old World—in northwest India, Burma, China and Southeast Asia—until about a hundred thousand years ago. On the other hand, Acheulian tool kits, including those uncovered at Torralba and Ambrona, predominate throughout the rest of the Old World, in Africa, Europe, the Near East and peninsular India. They lasted until about 75,000 years ago.

Such facts suggest a number of possible explanations. For example, *Homo erectus* may have migrated from Africa to Europe more than a million years ago, before the development of Acheulian tool kits. If so, he may not have done very well. His traces exist at only two sites, the Vertesszöllös limestone quarry in Hungary and Clacton in England, both of which have tool kits clearly derived from the Oldowan. The two oldest known European sites, the Vallonet and Escale caves of southern France, have not yet been thoroughly excavated; but if this theory is correct, they should also contain Oldowan tool assemblages. A second migration out of Africa may have come three or four hundred thousand years later when people with Acheulian tools entered Europe and took over the vast majority of available sites, including the Torralba-Ambrona sites. These people may have settled in the west and either wiped out or assimilated the descendants of earlier immigrants from Africa, or else driven them east. It could also be that the Acheulian tool kit represents a change in activities. The tool kits could have diffused into Europe with the accompanying activity changes without the actual migration of people.

The theory will stand or fall on the basis of findings yet to be made. But it does seem that the "Oldowan" people who turned up in China and Java and other parts of Southeast Asia evolved little if at all while important changes were under way among "Acheulian" peoples in the West. Hallam Movius of Harvard University has pioneered in studies of Southeast Asia, and concludes: "It seems very unlikely that this vast area could ever have played a vital and dynamic role in early human evolution, although very primitive forms of early man apparently persisted there long after types at a comparable stage of physical evolution became extinct elsewhere."

Plumbing, Philosophy, and Poetry

James E. Fitting

In "Plumbing, Philosophy, and Poetry," James E. Fitting outlines the history of the relationship of archeology to other fields of study. Whereas all professions have their identity problems in this period of specialization, archeologists are especially burdened. They must communicate with the physical scientists, such as geologists, on whom they depend for much of their data, cultural anthropologists with whom they share basic aims, and the general public who has not only been fascinated with prehistory but also pays the bills.

In spite of the strong regional traditions in North American archaeology, it is clear that there are common trends in many areas. It is not surprising that archaeological investigations began earlier in the East than in the West, and for that reason, the earliest

developmental stages are lacking in the latter area. It is also clear that with the development of even more efficient systems of communication and with the increasing mobility of archaeologists themselves, there has been a concomitant acceleration in the rates of archaeological change and the rapidity with which new analytical concepts are spread.

There has been an overwhelming increase in the number of both professional and amateur archaeologists within the past few decades. Public support of archaeology has also increased. The role of the WPA in the Southeast and the River Basin Survey in the Plains has been explained in detail in particular chapters of this volume.

Since the 1950s, the National Science Foundation has (until recently, at least) given even-handed and equitable support to archaeology around the country. As of the early 1970s, it would appear that government support for archaeology will continue, but on a diminished basis. Some archaeologists have demonstrated that the private sector is strongly interested in supporting archaeology. Only time will tell whether this type of support will be developed in other areas and what changes it will bring in archaeology. Archaeology supported by the general public conjures up the image of a scientific Disneyland, but it certainly will require archaeologists to talk to nonarchaeologists for a change—something that could not help but be beneficial.

It would be a fairly simple task to typologize North American archaeology beyond the regional level. Archaeology in the late eighteenth and early nineteenth centuries was isolated, whimsical, and certainly preparadigmatic, although its practitioners, like Thomas Jefferson, could proceed by rules that we would now call scientific. During the second half of the nineteenth century, data collecting began on a large scale throughout North America, and for the first time standardized comparative studies were undertaken. I still see no standardization of theory in this area, with geographical, direct historical and, to a much lesser extent, chronological problems being dominant.

With the appearance of formal training in anthropology around the turn of the century, archaeology became a subdivision within that discipline and participated, usually with a slight time lag, in the development of anthropology. When anthropology was descriptive and its modes of integration cultural-historical, so was archaeology. When American anthropology became analytical, archaeology, with noticeable reluctance, followed suit, but still maintained a dependent status.

Among anthropologists, archaeologists have always been viewed as an odd lot. Although they tended to follow theoretical bandwagons like dutiful puppy dogs, their other habits were less endearing. Much of their peculiar theory seemed little more than field technique, and they often talked to historians, geologists, and paleontologists and even plain folks who did not have an -ologist to their name.

After World War II there was certainly a technological revolution in archaeology. Radiocarbon dating was most significant but was only one aspect of this technological revolution. Archaeology put its plumbing in order, and although at that time

its theory must still be found in its technique, its techniques were in the process of elaboration. Individuals who worked with scientists using computers and differential equations would soon adapt these items to their own work. In the late 1950s and early 1960s, many archaeologists wondered if the complicated crafts of their field were compatible with the traditional training patterns in anthropology. At least one separate department of archaeology was formed at that time, and others were contemplated.

But plumbing does not exist by itself. To paraphrase John Gardner, the archaeology that supports its plumbers and neglects its philosophers will have neither good plumbing nor good philosophy. And neither will hold water.

After the plumbers came the philosophers. There was no question about their logic and, initially, their premises were taken from the traditional paradigms of archaeological interpretation—ones dependent on anthropology. The result was "anthropological archaeology." It was realized that the deductive potentials of archaeology are considerable and largely unrealized. Like Thomas Browne in his *Hydriotaphia* . . . , it was stated, "What songs the Syrens sang, or what name Achilles assumed when he hid himself among women, though puzzling questions are not beyond all conjecture."

The epistemology of archaeology became important, and its origins were found in positivism. Its goals, like those of anthropology, were nomothetic, but with a noble past, its relationship to anthropology changed. Its paradigm was changing, and there are some recent hints of a new independent relationship, at least symbiotic if not contributory, with general anthropology. Archaeology has moved, in Edmund Leach's . . . terms, from "butterfly collecting" to "inspired guesswork," and possibly beyond, if all things are open to the deductive potentials, the axiomatic corollaries, of its theories. It has reached a point where both its plumbing and its philosophy can hold water.

It may have also reached a point where it can do more than hold water. If its plumbing led to its philosophy, its philosophy takes it into the realm of literature. The quotation from *Hydriotaphia* was used as the introductory note for a classic deductive model, Edgar Allan Poe's "The Murders in the Rue Morgue." The subject matter of that short story is not too distant from the Sunday supplement archaeology of today. Unfortunately, too much of today's archaeology, while possessing elegant logic, lacks the style of "The Murders in the Rue Morgue." It lacks the style to live beyond the boundaries that it imposes on itself. It is, of course, a science and, as such, rapidly becomes immune from the taint of intelligibility. It has a reality, truth, and paradigm, and is accountable only to itself. However, there is another disturbing aspect of scientific truth. It is never really absolute. The King of Siam could complain of not being sure of things that he knew were absolutely certain. There are times, particularly in scientific crises, where the logically absurd becomes absurdly logical, when questions too obvious to be asked are answered in the negative, and when the only times we are really sure we are wrong are in those instances when there is no question about our being correct. General systems theory can generate its own answers, and when our interpretations take on a reality of their own, our evaluation of them passes from scientific to aesthetic. With the spiral of interpretive statements elegantly based on suspect or self-serving data, who could fail to see archaeology as more than a divine comedy, robbed of the seriousness of a Poe story by the seriousness with which it takes itself? We need to ask, "Where is the locus of archaeological reality?" Will its reliance on science, mathematics, and logic bring it closer to reality? Years ago, Leslie White . . . demonstrated that there is no contradiction in the statements, "Mathematical truths have an existence and a validity independent of the human mind" and "Mathematical truths have no existence and validity apart from the human mind." The same thing can be said for archaeology. The plumbing and the philosophy of archaeology are so perfected that their excellence exists apart from, and often in spite of, individual ignorance of them and resistance to them. The second statement is also true in a nomothetic sense, although it damns such nomothe-

tic interpretations. Truth is determined by the cultural context in which it exists. Prerevolutionary science is neither more nor less scientific than postrevolutionary science. No matter how elegant the theory or how absolute its predictions, it is still evaluated on a chessboard, a place where an infinite number of moves take place on a finite series of squares.

Archaeologists, through a series of internal developments, have learned to talk to themselves. They do not have all of the answers, but they now feel that this fault will inevitably be cured, given enough time. They still talk to other "ologists" but with a superior air that they may have lacked before, and the plain folk are left far behind.

As a science, archaeology may have matured, but as a people, archaeologists have not. The "inspired guesswork" is too certain in their minds, and it is only when, with the inspirer of the inspired guesswork, they can analyze three hundred myths and realize that they have reached no conclusion that they will again be human, inspiring, and fun. If we take the statement, "Archaeology is anthropology or it is nothing" at face value, we have two interesting alternatives. The *a priori* assumption of agreement has led to a series of logical conclusions that in turn indicate that the very statement might not be true. If archaeology is either more, or less, than anthropology, it is nothing, and if it is nothing, it is in an even better position to be yet something more.

And instead, during the brief intervals in which humanity can bear to interrupt its hive-like labors, let us grasp the essence of what our species has been and still is, beyond thought and beneath society: an essence that may be vouchsafed to us in a mineral more beautiful than any work of man; in the scent, more subtly involved than our books, that lingers in the heart of a lily; or the wink of an eye, heavy with patience, serenity and mutual forgiveness, that sometimes, through an involuntary understanding, one can exchange with a cat.[1]

Claude Levi-Strauss, *Tristes Tropiques,* New York: Atheneum, 1964, p. 398.

Summary

With the rise of hunting, cultural artifacts—tools, postholes, the bones of prey, ash from fires—begin to appear along with hominid physical remains. In many cases the artifacts are easily identifiable even in the absence of pre-human fossils. The analysis of these prehistoric material remains requires the specialized techniques of archeology.

The first task of the archeologist is to locate a site where cultural artifacts are likely to be found. Once a site is found, the careful work of excavation begins. Each layer is painstakingly removed; the position and orientation of each object is measured, recorded and the object numbered and stored. Since excavation always destroys some information, archeologists often uncover only part of a site, leaving something for future scientists.

In 1888 the earliest known evidence of big game hunting was discovered by railroad workers at Torralba, Spain. Over seventy years later a professional archeologist, Clark Howell, excavated the site, uncovering a high concentration of elephant, horse, deer, and other animal remains in association with an array of stone tools. The problem for Howell was identifying the hunting techniques employed in the slaughter of almost a hundred animals at a single site. The remains of burnt grass around the site indicate that fire was used.

Another site, Ambrona, not far from Torralba, contains the earliest known hominid shelter. Evidence of more elaborate shelters comes from Terra Amata, situated in the middle of the city of Nice, on the French Riviera.

In addition to the analysis of specific sites, archeologists employ material remains to understand worldwide patterns of change in the distribution of Oldowan and Acheulian tools over the last 700,000 years.

Glossary

Abattoir A prehistoric butchering and meat processing site.

Cleaver A wedge shaped stone tool with a straight cutting edge at one end, one of the components of Acheulian tool kits.

Coprolite The fossilized feces of prehistoric people and animals, the analysis of which provides important information on diet.

Flotation technique A technique used in the excavation of an archeological site to separate different remains from each other based on slight differences in weight.

Hand axe An almond- or egg-shaped stone implement with a thick heavy butt at one end, a point at the other end and cutting edges along the sides; a component of Acheulian tool kits.

Tool assemblage All the tools found at the same level of an archeological site presumed to have been used by members of a single prehistoric group.

Additional Reading

Bordes, François
1968 The Old Stone Age. New York: McGraw-Hill.

Bordes offers a good discussion of the tools and culture of the old stone age.

Clark, Grahame
1967 The Stone Age Hunters. New York: McGraw-Hill Co:

Excellent descriptive and illustrated discussion of prehistoric cultures.

Deetz, James
1967 Invitation to Archaeology. New York: Doubleday.

One of the best short introductions to archaeology.

chapter eight

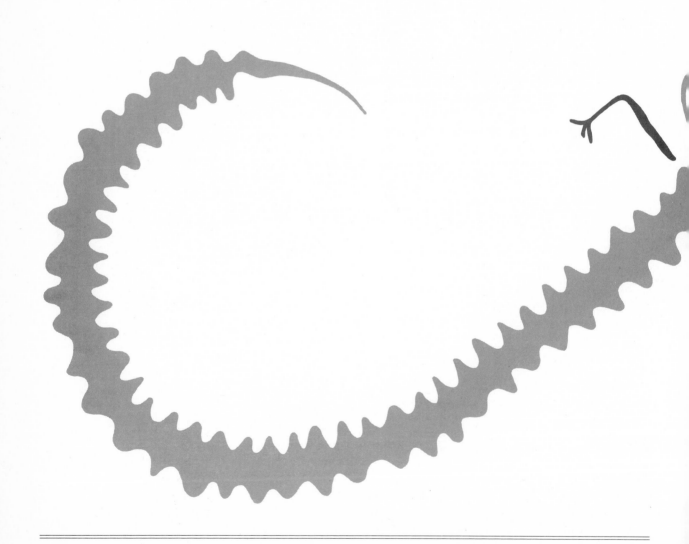

THE EARLIEST HOMO SAPIENS

The rise of hunting and other changes which came with it brought our ancestors a long way toward modern *Homo sapiens*. Now for the first time we can describe them in words which do not really apply to other animals, which make sense only in a human context. The double-edged quality of the human condition had already become evident. Practically everything which contributed to the solution of problems important to the survival of the species created new problems, new sources of tension and discord. New conflicts as well as new affections arose in the family circle.

Such complexities indicated a shift of em-

phasis in human development. It was no longer a matter of dealing only with the outside world, with climates and other species and prey and predators. An entirely new class of problems had come into being, uniquely human problems which seem to be chronically associated with cultural as contrasted to genetic or organic evolution. Dealing with the full impact of this sort of evolution demanded a new breed of humans, our immediate ancestors and the direct descendants of people like the hunters who camped at Torralba and Ambrona.

Human populations and living conditions varied widely in those days, although not as widely perhaps as they do today. According to one estimate, some 40,000 bands of hunter-gatherers occupied as many home bases scattered like outposts through the wildernesses of Africa and Asia and Europe, which averages to about a million acres per band. The earth was hardly a crowded place, but crowding can be a relative thing, and certain regions were far more densely populated than others. So then as now some environments must have been especially favorable for hunting and for the elaboration of social systems. There were also isolated "backwood" regions where the land and the living were less abundant. A band of hunter-gatherers could have wandered for years or a lifetime in these wildernesses without coming across another band.

Populations varied in many other ways. Some individuals may have had brains nearly twice as large as their smallest-brained contemporaries, as is the case today. Equally striking differences existed in the degree of sloping of the forehead, tooth size and cusp patterns, chin structure, the size of overhanging brow ridges, and so on. *Homo erectus* consisted of a number of subspecies or races. One of these, perhaps a subspecies, with a larger than average brain, living in a territory where life was neither so easy that it posed no major challenges nor so harsh as to crush initiative, evolved into modern *Homo sapiens*.

THE EARLIEST HOMO SAPIENS

We do not know where or when the transition took place, but a gravel pit in the English village of Swanscombe not far from London has yielded important fossil clues, as usual through a combination of searching and luck, in this case luck triply compounded. The Thames Valley site is a well-known collectors' paradise, possibly a place where hunters camped to kill game coming to drink from the river. Several hundred thousand stone tools must have been found there during the past century or so. But no human remains had appeared until one Saturday noon in June, 1935, when local cement workers who had stopped digging for the day noticed a piece of bone protruding from a gravel bank. It turned out to be part of the skull of a prehistoric human who had died in its early twenties.

A second lucky find occurred the following March near the original find, another bone fragment which was not only human but also happened to be part of the same skull. The two pieces fitted neatly. The last discovery represents something of an anthropological miracle. One moonlit evening during World War II a fleet of trucks came to the Swanscombe pit and removed hundreds of tons of gravel as part of the top-secret "Mulberry" harbor project to make concrete caissons or floating docks for the Allied invasion of Normandy. How many prehistoric remains were ground up for the concrete will never be known, but at least one important object was left behind and found after the war in 1955—a third skull fragment. This specimen turned up about seventy-five feet from the original find and, by remarkable coincidence, belongs to the same individual as the other two specimens; furthermore, it fits together with them to form the entire back half of a skull.

The relative age of these remains has been fairly well established. As pointed out in Chapter Five, after some 60 million years of comparatively mild and stable climates, Europe experienced a number of climatic "oscillations" when mean annual temperatures varied from 50 degrees Fahrenheit to below-freezing levels. Geological studies show that the gravels which contained the Swanscombe remains were laid down during a period of glacial retreat, a so-called interglacial stage which dates back perhaps 250,000 years.

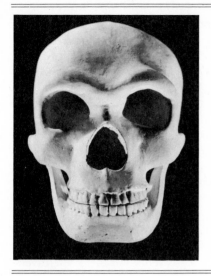

The appearance of Steinheim man was reconstructed in this way: (top) a plaster model of the skull; (center) muscles and skin built up in clay; (bottom) a completed model of the head.

Swanscombe man represents a distinct advance over its fossil predecessors, although the extent of the advance has been debated. Examination of the three fragments and reconstructions based on them indicate that it had a large brain; its cranial capacity is estimated at about 1,300 cubic centimeters, which, as pointed out in Chapter Five, lies well within the modern range. Furthermore, there is a general suggestion of rounded and expanded skull contours somewhat like a modern human's. These features have been interpreted as evidence for an apparent evolutionary leap, the sudden appearance of people who were nearly fully modern. On the other hand, the relatively low brain case and certain other characteristics suggest that the specimen may be a less advanced form intermediate between *Homo erectus* and *Homo sapiens*.

Supporting the latter viewpoint is another fossil skull found in 1933 in another gravel pit near the village of Steinheim in western Germany. This specimen includes the face and upper jaw, which are lacking in the English specimen, and it may have something to tell us about Swanscombe man, assuming, of course, that the two were contemporaries (both skulls were found in interglacial deposits) and members of the same species or subspecies. In any case, Steinheim man was modern in back but not in front. It had a sloping forehead and very large brow ridges; it was argued that Swanscombe man may have been at the same stage of development.

These impressions have been put to the test by Campbell and by Weiner, the man who exploded the Piltdown hoax. They turned to statistical techniques which depend on carefully selected measurements of corresponding areas and curvatures of different skulls. Judging by the results, Swanscombe man meets the general specifications for a transitional species, a species which is on its way but has not yet arrived. Like Steinheim man it is definitely *Homo sapiens*, but very early *Homo sapiens*, embodying certain relatively primitive as well as modern features. In short, it is just about right for its time, the product of a gradual and continuing process rather than a sudden spurt.

Statistics alone cannot solve all problems. More needs to be known about the origin of our species, for example, than the Weiner-Campbell analysis can possibly reveal. It concerns early but not earliest *Homo sapiens*. It indicates that we existed at least 250,000 years ago, but leaves open the question of when the first members of the species arose. They may have appeared fifty, a hundred, or several hundred millennia before Swanscombe-Steinheim times, depending on which current point of view strikes one as most plausible.

But the answer, if it is ever found, will come at excavations of sites yet to be discovered, and the same thing holds for the question of where our species arose. In certain respects the simplest and most direct theory is that it happened in Europe; that the men of Swanscombe and Steinheim were descendants of hunters who, judging by the remains at the Hungarian site of Vertesszöllös, may have been well on the way toward attaining *Homo sapiens* status as much as

400,000 or 500,000 years ago. According to another theory, however, they were immigrants rather than native Europeans and evolved either in the Far East, perhaps from an ancestral stock like Peking man, or else in Central Asia.

Wherever they came from, the early forerunners of modern humans probably lived pretty much as late representatives of *Homo erectus* had lived. At least, stone tools and other excavated materials suggest no obvious differences. Although its workmanship was somewhat superior, Swanscombe man was no radical innovator and made the same basic Acheulian-type tools that had been made for hundreds of thousands of years: hand axes, notched and saw-toothed implements, scrapers, engravers, and so on. There are characteristics, however, which might represent differences in behavior if we only knew enough to interpret them. Why did its tool kit include nearly twice as many hand axes as the tool kits of its Torralba-Ambrona predecessors? Why did it use an unusually high proportion of hand axes with a wide base, tapered to a point at the apex, and

Three skulls of early modern type men: (left to right) Homo erectus, Neanderthal, Cro-Magnon.

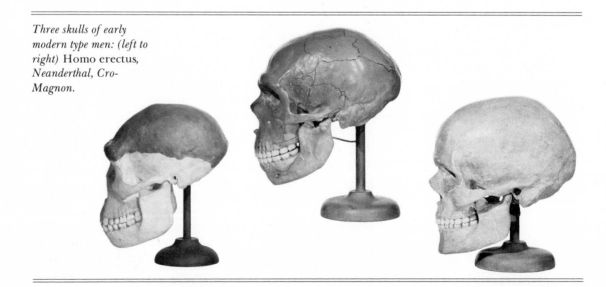

an unusually low proportion of ovate or egg-shaped hand axes? Was this a result of new activities, different ways of doing things? Or perhaps different cultures were developing with the increasing complexity of hominid society.

Another English site at Hoxne, about sixty-five miles northeast of Swanscombe, and of about the same age or slightly more recent, provides further evidence. It contains rich deposits of clay which mark the place where a huge mass of ice broke off a retreating glacier perhaps 300,000 years ago and melted slowly to form a small lake. (At another site near Birmingham, England, a block of ice about fifty feet across took more than 30,000 years to melt.) Ever since the eighteenth century the clays have been used to make bricks and terracotta pipes. In 1797 the English antiquarian John Frere visited the site and made a remarkable observation.

People do not see what they are not prepared to see; and since the notion of a remote prehistoric past simply did not exist in those days, a variety of involved theories were invented to explain away traces of this past. Flint tools, some of them beautifully shaped, were considered natural accidents like shapes seen in drifting clouds or in the gnarled branches of trees—things that had been formed either by thunder in the clouds and then fallen to earth or by lightning as it struck and shattered flint lying on the ground. Frere knew better. He found hand axes and other tools in the Hoxne clay deposits and recognized them as man-made implements dating back "to a very remote period indeed, even beyond that of the present world." (Frere, by the way, has the added distinction of being Mary Leakey's great-great-grandfather.)

Modern excavations at the site reveal a Swanscombe-type Acheulian tool kit, including the same unexplained high proportion of pointed hand axes with wide bases. Another

The advance and retreat of glaciers such as this one caused major changes in European climate during the period of human prehistory.

finding emerges from fossil-pollen studies conducted by Richard West of the University of Cambridge. Pollens recovered from gray clays and muds deposited before the coming of humans show thick oak-elm forests surrounding the lake. But signs of a different environment are found in overlying brown-green clay layers which contain tools and other human traces. A decline of oak-elm pollens and a sharp rise of grass pollens indicates that open grasslands replaced the forests.

Geological research rules out the most obvious explanation for this change, a change in climate, for the climate was generally mild throughout. Another possibility exists, however. Charcoal has been found in the occupation layers, suggesting that the deforestation was caused by fires which were originally set during a dry summer, perhaps to stampede animals as in the valley of Torralba, and then raged out of control. In any case the forests returned soon after humans left, first temperate oak-elm forests and later forests of dwarf willows and other trees found in arctic environments. Another major glaciation had begun.

NEANDERTHAL

Until recently, little evidence existed for the course of human culture during this period, which lasted more than 150,000 years. In the late 1960's, however, de Lumley published the results of an excavation at Lazaret Cave, on the outskirts of Nice. The site, dated around 150,000 years ago, contains the remains of tents some way in from the cave entrance. The tents, formed of animal skins stretched over bent branches anchored in post holes, apparently served to protect the residents from the damp cave ceiling and the strong winds coming off the Mediterranean. At the mouth of each tent is the skull of a wolf, obviously carefully positioned for some ritual or symbolic purpose. Early humans may have used the skulls to protect themselves from natural or supernatural forces. If de Lumley is correct, this is the earliest evidence of human symbolic activity. Another feature of the site is the concentrations of small marine shells found inside the tents. These have been interpreted as traces of prehistoric beds constructed of seaweed covered with animal skins. Only the shells, which attach themselves to seaweed, have been preserved for the archeological record.

Other sites also provide evidence of human activity but none as rich as Lazaret. One workshop area near Amiens, France is no larger than a living room but has yielded thousands of

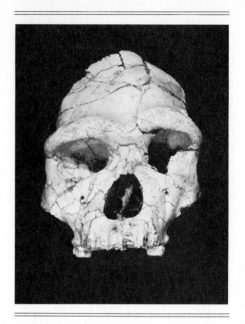

This skull was excavated by de Lumley in the Pyrenees. It is designated as pre-Neanderthal, but its relationship to Homo erectus *and* Homo sapiens *has not yet been determined.*

flint tools and associated pieces. There is another interesting site in England at High Lodge not far from Cambridge, where people camped by a lake during a time of temporary relief from arctic conditions. Many of the tools recovered from clay deposits marking the location of the lake are remarkably similar to tools found at the Somme Valley site.

Until recently, however, practically nothing was known about the evolutionary status of the people who made the tools. This was a particularly tantalizing state of affairs, since other information, such as the fact that surprising anatomical changes appeared later following the retreat of the glaciers, suggests that important developments were taking place. The only human remains recovered were a few bits of skull too fragmentary for reliable reconstructions. Now prospects are somewhat brighter because of new material from a cave in the eastern Pyrenees region of France, also excavated by de Lumley. The main find is the front half of a human face, the most complete skull specimen yet obtained for this glacial stage and the oldest-known Frenchman. Its precise relationship to *Homo erectus* and *Homo sapiens* has yet to be determined.

The next glimpse of the genus *Homo* comes from the following interglacial stage in Europe, the period from about 100,000 to 75,000 years ago. England and Ireland were part of the Continent then. Broad valleys existed where the English Channel and Irish Sea and North Sea are now.

The people living among lions, hyenas, elephants, and other European animals of the times were not what one might expect of our evolving ancestors. They were definitely *Homo sapiens,* but they belonged to a new subspecies or race, and in certain respects a strikingly more primitive subspecies. Although their brains were about as large as the brain of Swanscombe-Steinheim man, their massive receding jaws and faces seem to have been throwbacks, and were actually closer to *Homo erectus* than to *Homo sapiens.* Their remains have been found in a limestone crevice in central Germany, in deposits on the left bank of a tributary of the Tiber near Rome, and at several other sites in Europe, the Soviet Union and Palestine.

Even stranger breeds of people arose later. The bands hunting in Western Europe during most of the subsequent cold period, the next-to-last glaciation, were made up of individuals anatomically more remote from modern humans than were their predecessors who lived some six or seven thousand generations before them. They had appreciably larger brains, one of the features by which they are ranked as *Homo sapiens.* But their "primitive" features included lower cranial vaults which tended to be flat at the top and bulged at the sides, heavier

bone ridges over the eyes and at the back of the neck, and more sharply receding chins. Their bodies were stocky, short, and heavy-limbed.

These were the classic Neanderthal people, the people who come to mind whenever cave men are mentioned and who almost invariably serve as models for artists depicting early humans. They have become such symbols for good reason. As the first fossil humans to be discovered, they made a powerful impression on a world that was not ready to accept the notion of evolution or its implications. The discovery and the reaction to it mark one of the most significant and extraordinary episodes in the annals of science. This was the beginning of the study of prehistory.

In 1856, when human bones were found in a small limestone-quarry cave in the Neanderthal, a valley near Düsseldorf, Germany, practically everything discussed in this book was unknown and the rest was ignored. Some investigators recognized the importance of the re-

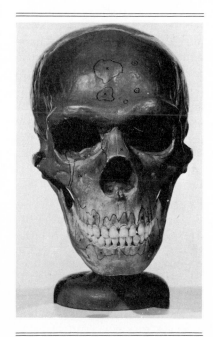

A reconstruction of the skull of Neanderthal man.

One artist's conception of Neanderthal man. Current thinking leans toward the belief that he may have had a more modern appearance.

mains from the beginning, but they were a very small minority. The predominant opinion, the opinion which people were ready to accept, was that the bones represented not an extinct breed of human but a modern, freakish and sick individual. A prominent anatomist reported that the fossils were those of an idiot who had suffered from rickets and other bone diseases and had a violent disposition. The flat forehead and heavy brows, he explained, had been caused by blows on the head. According to other authorities, the bones were those of a Cossack who had perished during Napoleon's retreat from Moscow, a victim of water on the brain, "an old Dutchman," "a member of the Celtic race." Everyone wanted to disown this human specimen.

Neanderthal man came into the world of the Victorians like a naked savage into a ladies' sewing circle. In their eyes it was a beast, which suggested not only that the past may have been less golden than the Scriptures implied but also that disturbing forces were at work in the pres-

ent. It reminded people of their Jekyll-and-Hyde qualities, of the animal side of human nature.

Attitudes began changing somewhat not long after the original 1856 discovery. The publication of Darwin's *On the Origin of Species* three years later provided a biological basis for evolution in general, and the discovery of more fossils provided new evidence for the evolution of *Homo sapiens.* Between 1866 and 1910, half a dozen sites in France and Belgium yielded Neanderthal remains associated with flint tools and the remains of woolly rhinoceroses, mammoths, cave bears, and other extinct species. There was no longer good reason to regard Neanderthal man as a mad or diseased modern. It was widely agreed that it had vanished tens of thousands of years ago.

But most investigators were slower to recognize its status as an advanced human being, much less as a fellow *Homo sapiens,* than they were recognize its fossil status. As recently as the 1920's it was considered far more remote from modern humans and far closer to the anthropoid apes than a reasonably sophisticated analysis of the evidence could possibly justify, a kind of half-monster, ungainly and ugly and brutish. This picture was based to a large extent on a highly respected and highly misleading study of a skeleton found in 1908 near the village of La Chapelle-aux-Saints in southern France.

The study is one of the most amazing phenomena in the history of our efforts to downgrade our ancestors. On the basis of casts of the inner surface of the skull, it concluded that the convolutions of the brain had been simple and "coarse" and resembled the convolutions of the "great anthropoid apes or microencephalic man" more closely than those of modern humans. Furthermore, it presented an outlandish view of Neanderthal man's posture and gait. It not only pointed to a supposed "simian arrangement" of certain spinal vertebrae and stated that it walked slumped over and with bent knees, but suggested that its feet may have been grasping organs like the feet of gorillas and chimpanzees.

As recently as 1957 this study was still being cited as a major source of information about the nature of Neanderthal man. In that year, however, the La Chapelle-aux-Saints skeleton was reexamined by William Straus of Johns Hopkins University and Alec Cave of St. Bartholomew's Hospital Medical College in London. They found that it was hardly typical, belonging to an "old" man between forty and fifty suffering from arthritis of the jaws, spine and perhaps lower limbs.

Anatomical evidence does not support the stereotype of Neanderthal man as a semihuman brute. The trouble is that myths die hard, especially myths in the area of human origins, and it may take decades before its popular image coincides with its scientific image. The latest edition of a standard text on fossil humans still presents certain major conclusions of the La Chapelle-aux-Saints study as if they had never been discredited. Apparently some anthropologists still accept these conclusions. It is little wonder that the old prejudices and clichés also persist among laymen.

Not all questions about Neanderthal man have been answered. It was one of the subspecies of *Homo sapiens* which lived in the Old World from about 70,000 to 35,000 years ago, and it should be no surprise that it and other subspecies of the times differed widely in physical characteristics, since this was the case for *Homo erectus* as it is for us and other species.

It is very probable that Neanderthal man lived in small family or tribal groups. Here is an artist's conception of Neanderthal man at his home base, the cave-like shelter in the background.

Controversy

Neanderthal Man: How smart were they?

Neanderthal man has often been depicted in films and in popular literature as a brutish lout capable of communicating only in monosyllabic grunts. Despite its out-thrust face, massive jaw, and sloping brow, however, Neanderthal man actually had a braincase larger than that of modern humans. Were the Neanderthals, with expanded brains encased in archaic skulls, more intelligent than modern humans? And, if intelligence is indeed a highly valued evolutionary adapation, why did the human brain stop growing and even shrink some in the last 100,000 years?

Anthropologists and biologists have proposed a variety of speculative theories to answer these questions. C. Loring Brace believes that the brain size of hominids grew until a point was reached at which the least brainy member of the band would be capable of mastering the traditions of its culture. At this point, Brace reasons, increased brain size would no longer represent an evolutionary advantage. Biologist Ernst Mayr proposes that, prior to the emergence of Neanderthal man, hominid bands were led by the most intelligent males. These males were permitted to have many wives and produced large numbers of brainy offspring. As hunting and gathering groups grew in size some 10,000 years ago, the genes of intelligent leaders began to account for only a small percentage of the total genetic population. Thus, the average brain size declined somewhat. Fascinating though their theories may be, neither Brace nor Mayr are supported by any hard evidence.

Today, the brain structure of fossils is studied by

means of endocranial casts, casts of the interior of the skull known as endocasts. All brains are surrounded by various fluids and tissues. In humans and apes, the brain surface itself leaves very little impression on the interior of the cranium. Nevertheless, an endocast can reveal a great deal about the general shape and proportions of the different parts of the brain. Hominid and pongid brain structures can easily be distinguished by the examination of endocasts.

One of the most immediate conclusions to be drawn from the study of endocasts is that cranial capacity does not necessarily imply the size of the brain. The human brain, for example, fills only two-thirds of the cranial space, while the brains of other primates fill even less. More significant than size, however, is the difference in structure between pongid and hominid brains. Whereas the brains of apes are characterized by relatively small temporal and parietal lobes and a large occipital cortex, the human brain features a reduced occipital cortex and large temporal and parietal lobes. Moreover, the actual surface of the human cerebral cortex is far greater than it appears. As a result of extensive folding, 64% of the surface is hidden in fissures as compared to 7% in primitive monkeys.

What is the implication of our brain structure for behavior? Our large temporal lobe is responsible for acute visual and auditory memory, while the parietal lobe allows the complex integration and association of sensory input necessary for abstract reasoning. The prefrontal area of the human brain allows us to concentrate and to sustain attention over a long period of time, while the highly evolved cerebellum allows us to exercise the precise motor control which has permitted the creation of a highly sophisticated technology. Clearly, it is the structure of the human brain, not its size, which is significant.

In modern humans, there is no necessary correlation between brain size and behavioral capability. The volume of the brain of Anatole France was less than 1000 cc while that of Jonathan Swift was more than 2000 cc. Even humans with brains smaller than those of some gorillas display patterns of behavior which are unquestionably human in nature.

Evidence suggests that a brain essentially human in character already existed some three million years ago and that the ratio of brain weight to body weight has remained constant since that time. It should not surprise us, then, to find that one of our predecessors may have had a brain larger than ours. Modern *Homo sapiens* may have smaller brains simply because they have smaller bodies.

However their brain sizes may have differed, Neanderthal and modern humans appear to have shared the same basic brain structure. Apparently, brain structure and behavioral patterns have evolved in a parallel manner, each affecting the development of the other. Neanderthal man's behavioral accomplishments would seem to be a much better indicator of its intelligence than its brain size. That it survived for so long in a hostile environment of freezing weather and a variety of would-be predators suggests a level of intelligence equal to that of modern humans.

What calls for an explanation, however, is that its distinctive set of characteristics should reappear in the sense that it was reminiscent of earlier human forms, and that it seems to have confined itself largely if not entirely to Western Europe.

One possibility is that it was cut off from its contemporaries. The longer and more completely breeding populations of a single species are separated from one another, the more widely they differ. Brief and partial isolation, such as that imposed by the institution of royal families, may produce such characteristics as the well-known protruding lower lip of the Hapsburgs which, of course, are not sufficient to create new races. Longer periods of isolation, occasioned perhaps by geographical as well as social factors, may eventually produce differences so great that the result is distinct species such as *Australopithecus africanus* and *Australopithecus robustus*.

The conditions which gave rise to the Neanderthal subspecies were somewhere between these extremes. It may have been caught in a kind of "ice trap" in Western Europe, a glacial pincers movement. During the coldest periods glaciers crept southwest from the great Scandinavian Ice Sheet into central Poland, and at the same time glaciers from the Alps moved northeast toward the Carpathians and the Danube. It was by no means a complete trap. The ice masses never met, and there was always a corridor several hundred miles wide between them. But routes through the corridor may have been few and hazardous enough during periods of severe cold to isolate many Neanderthal populations and bring about the appearance of a new subspecies.

One can only wonder at the ability of the Neanderthals to endure the intense cold of Western Europe during the next-to-last glaciation. Survival would have been impossible without reserves of food and fuel. The chief hunting grounds must have been snow meadows, wide

Le Moustier cave, where an early Neanderthal burial site was discovered.

flat areas swept by icy prevailing winds, where the snow may be only a foot deep and edible grasses grow under it. Today in Canadian sub-Arctic regions such places are a major source of food for herds of caribou and for caribou hunters, and similar regions helped feed reindeer and Neanderthal reindeer hunters some 50,000 years ago. Small game also provided meat; many traps must have been set along snow trails, the habitual routes of animals on the move.

But winter hunting could never have provided enough food by itself. According to one estimate, it takes about 800 to 900 pounds of lean meat to feed ten people for a month, and Neanderthal winters may have lasted four to five months. Such conditions demanded stockpiling, and extensive stockpiling. The people may have used underground cellars—pits hacked out of permanently frozen ground known as permafrost, as Eskimos do today—or "blue ice caves," ice-cliff formations that could serve as deep-freeze lockers.

Natural refrigerators of this sort have not yet been found, although a study of where Eskimo hunters locate their storage places today might furnish clues to archeologists in search of evidence for prehistoric practices. The record suggests that at least one family had a special larder for its winter food. A pit in a Neanderthal cave on the island of Jersey off the western coast of France apparently contained a liberal supply of large chunks of meat ready for cooking. It had been dug through deposits next to a cave wall, and included three rhinoceros skulls and the remains of at least five mammoths.

Fuel was another problem, to collect as well as to store. When wood was scarce, the Neanderthals burned bones, and they may even have learned to use fat. They and earlier people also had ways of promoting efficient burning. Soviet investigators have discovered "tailed" hearths, basins each with a narrow trench or furrow extending out from one side. Actual tests indicate the reason for the trench. Apparently it provided a kind of flue or draft through which air was drawn to produce more complete burning.

RITUAL AND EVOLUTION

Archeological excavations rarely provide direct information about the feelings of our remote ancestors; usually we are reduced to guesses, shrewd or otherwise. But now and then the past leaves patterns whose significance cannot be mistaken. During the early 1900's such evidence was uncovered at Le Moustier about thirty miles west of La Chapelle-aux-Saints; it shows that these people had developed a new way of thinking, a new attitude toward life and death.

A boy about fifteen or sixteen years old had been buried in a cave. He had been lowered into a trench, placed on his right side with knees slightly drawn and head resting on his forearm in a sleeping position. A pile of flints lay under his head to form a sort of stone pillow, and near his hand was a beautifully worked stone ax. Around the remains were wild-cattle bones, many of them charred, the remnants of roasted meat which may have been provided to serve as sustenance in the world of

the dead. (The old man of La Chapelle-aux-Saints was also buried in a trench and surrounded by stone tools.)

The record is rich in symbols which we cannot decipher. Near Monte Circeo, on the Mediterranean coast between Rome and Naples, is a deep cave whose innermost chamber contained a circle of stones, at the center of the circle a human skull with a hole bored into it. There

An artist's conception of the burial at Le Moustier. Such ritualized burial indicates that the Neanderthals had formulated some abstract beliefs about the meaning of death.

are also signs that animal rituals were practiced along with burials. A cave in a steep ravine in the mountains of Uzbek in Central Asia held the shallow grave of a young boy, and half a dozen pairs of ibex horns were stuck in the earth around the head end of the grave, indicating that an ibex cult existed here among Neanderthals more than 50,000 years ago, as it does today among people living in the same region. Other rituals involved cave bears, which often had to be driven out of caves before people could move in, and were killed by the hundreds.

One of the most revealing of recent discoveries comes from a site in the Near East, the Shanidar Cave in the Zagros Mountain highlands of Iraq about 250 miles due north of Baghdad. The site was excavated by Ralph Solecki of Columbia University. He hit bedrock at a depth of forty-five feet, which represents deposits up to 100,000 years old. Seven Neanderthal skeletons were found, three of them the remains of people crushed to death by falling rocks. One of the three was apparently recovering from a spear or knife wound in the ribs.

At least one of the individuals, a man with a badly crushed skull, was buried deep in the cave with special ceremony. One spring day about 60,000 years ago members of his family went out into the hills, picked masses of wild flowers, and made a bed of them on the ground, a resting place for the deceased. Other flowers were probably laid on top of his grave; still others seem to have been woven together with the branches of a pinelike shrub to form a wreath. Traces of that offering endure in the form of fossil pollen collected from the burial site, the remains of the ancestors of present-day grape hyacinths, bachelor's buttons, hollyhocks, and yellow-flowering groundsels.

These findings, the graves and the patterns around them, mark a great change in human evolution. Death, and presumably life, had become something special. No comparable evidence appears in earlier records, and as far as we know, humans and human ancestors had always died like other animals before Neanderthal times, being abandoned when they were too weak to keep up with the band or wandering off to wait alone for the end to come. Burial implies a new kind of concern for the individual and, according to one theory, it arose as part of a response to bitter glacial conditions when people needed one another even more than in less demanding times and formed more intimate ties and cared more intensely when death came.

From the study of contemporary hunters and gatherers we also know that ritual can bring people together: it can strengthen alliances and interdependencies. If, as we have

Ribs and pelvic region of the Neanderthal buried at Shanidar.

5 cm.

discussed, exogamy was already a feature of human society, mourning may have brought together at least two groups, the band of the deceased and that of the spouse of the deceased. Such occasions would reunite old acquaintances and provide time for considering new commitments to the exchange of women.

As cultural complexity increased, ritual may have also played a role in controlling the group's relationship to the environment. The Labrador Naskapi crack caribou shoulder blades over fire to determine the direction to take in hunting, a common form of divination. The cracks specify where the hunters are to seek prey. One anthropologist, Omar Khayyam Moore, has suggested that this ritual helps maintain the ecological balance of the region by randomizing the movement of the hunters. If the areas favored by the caribou were consistently hunted, the herds might decline in population. While we have no evidence of such ritual activities among the Neanderthal, ritualized burial might be part of a larger ritual complex.

Neanderthal man invented, or at least formalized, illusion when he invented burial. The belief in an afterlife says in effect that death is not what it seems; that it represents an apparent ending only, an ending only as far as the evidence of the senses is concerned; and that in this case, the crude evidence of the senses is wrong. Reality involves not observed and observable "facts" but an abstraction, the idea that death is actually a passage from one world to another. In this respect the burial ceremonies of prehistoric hunters expressed the kind of thinking used today to develop theories about the structure of the atomic nucleus or the expanding universe.

Another new phenomenon, another aspect of the new way of thinking, makes an appearance during Neanderthal times. Traces of violence, in the sense of person killing person, become more common. Some sort of mayhem took place in a sandstone rock shelter overlook-

The skull of the Shanidar individual, probably crushed in a rock fall.

ing a river in northern Yugoslavia, where at the turn of the century investigators recovered more than five hundred bones and bone fragments representing at least a dozen individuals. A number of the bones are charred, suggesting that cannibalism may have been practiced, while other bones show definite signs of having been cut.

Unfortunately, excavators did not work as painstakingly then as they do now, and no living-floor patterns were reported. But the mass killings hint at organized fighting among neighboring bands, a possibility strengthened by findings at other Old World sites—a flint projectile point in a rib cage, a pelvis with a spear hole in it, and skulls bashed and penetrated in various ways. Is this another sign of the *Homo sapiens* status of the Neanderthals? They not only believed in an afterlife, but they may also have taken the initiative in evolving effective ways of speeding the departure of their fellow humans to the other world. They may have invented warfare as well as religion.

Focus

Arthur Koestler

The Evolution of Man
What Went Wrong?

As we have discussed, the first evidence of an extensive ritual life in human populations appears with Neanderthal. If ritual functioned to define group membership, it also defined those who did not belong and may have laid the groundwork for the first murders. This article explores the implications of the human ability to define an "in-group" and an "out-group." It ties together many different themes.

If one looks with a cold eye at the mess man has made of his history, it is difficult to avoid the conclusion that he is afflicted by some built-in mental disorder which drives him towards self-destruction. We know that among social animals fighting is a ritual which stops short of serious injury. The prey that the

predator kills always belongs to a different species. Murder *within* the species, on an individual or collective scale, is a phenomenon unknown in the whole animal kingdom, except for man and a few varieties of ants and rats.

Evidently something must have gone wrong at some point in the evolution of *homo sapiens.* But when we ask what it is that has gone wrong, we usually get the dusty answer that all evil stems from the selfish, greedy, aggressive tendencies in human nature. That is the explanation that has been offered to us for the past 3,000 years by Hebrew prophets, Indian sages, Christian moralists and contemporary psychoanalysts; but, speaking in all humility. I find this answer unconvincing and unsupported by the historical record.

What the record indicates is that in the major disasters in our history, individual aggressiveness for selfish motives played an almost negligible part compared to unselfish loyalty and devotion to tribe, nation, religion or political ideology. Tribal wars, national wars, civil wars, religious wars, world wars are waged in the purported interest of the community, not of the individual, to decide issues that are far removed from the personal self-interest of the combatants. No doubt the lust for rape and plunder provided delightful incentives for a minority, but for the great majority the primary motive was fanatical loyalty, to the point of self-sacrifice, to king and country, leader or group.

In other words, the main trouble with man appears to be, not that he is an excessively aggressive creature, but an excessively loyal and devoted creature. He seems to have a stronger biological need than any other species to *belong,* to attach himself to a person, a group or idea, to transcend the claustrophobic confines of his self. He cannot live alone and he cannot leave alone.

One possible reason for this tendency may be the protracted helplessness and dependence of the human infant. Another reason may be the increased dependence on solidarity and cooperation of our primate ancestors when they took from the forest to the plains and turned into carnivorous hunters of prey bigger and faster than themselves. Primate societies living in the wild are also held together by strong bonds, and groups of the same primate species living in different localities may also develop different traditions and customs. But the cohesive bonds within primate families do not grow into neurotic attachments, the cohesive forces within primate groups do not attain the intensity and fervor of tribal feeling, and the differences between primate groups of the same species do not lead to violent conflicts. Only in *homo sapiens* did the cohesive forces within the group develop into fanatical loyalty to tribe, totem and its later symbolic equivalents; and only in our species did the repellent forces between groups develop into intra-specific warfare.

What I am trying to suggest is that the aggressive, self-assertive tendencies in the emotional life of the human individual are less dangerous to the species than his self-transcending or integrative tendencies.

Most civilizations throughout our history have been quite successful in taming individual aggressiveness and teaching the young how to sublimate their self-assertive impulses. But we have tragically failed to achieve a similar sublimation . . . of the self-transcending emotions.

The number of victims of individual crimes committed in any period of history is insignificant compared to the masses cheerfully sacrificed *ad majorem gloriam,* in blind devotion to the true religion, dynasty or political system. When we speak of 'blind devotion' we implicitly recognize the uncritical nature of the self-transcending urge in forming attachments to a person, group, race, flag or system of beliefs. . . .

Thus during the most of human history, the self-transcending urges of the individual could only express themselves through devotion to a narrowly defined group, with which he identified himself to the hostile exclusion of other groups; as a result, the disruptive forces have always dominated the forces of cohesion in our species as a whole. The main peril of self-transcending devotion is that it frequently acts as a vehicle for a vicarious, unselfish kind of aggression. We enter into an identificatory rapport with the hero on the movie screen, and as a result hate the perfidious villain; our anger is a vicarious emotion experienced on behalf of another person who does not even really exist, and yet we produce all the physical symptoms of a true emotion. Similarly, the emotion displayed by a crowd of demonstrators is an unselfish type of emotion derived from the identification of the individual with the group.

When alone, man is inclined to act in his own interest, regardless of others; when identified with a group, the situation is reversed. The egotism of the group feeds on the altruism of its members.

Human history is pock-marked with the scars of this infernal dialectic. As to its origins, some clues are perhaps provided by the biological factors previously mentioned—the long infantile dependence and strong social interdependence characteristic of our species. There is also the peculiar ability of the human brain to sustain belief-systems, rooted in emotion, which are incompatible and in frequent conflict with its reasoning faculties. The result is the split-minded, quasi-schizophrenic mentality, which seems to be inherent in man's condition and is reflected in his absurd and tortured history.

Let me mention briefly two further factors which seem to be equally basic to the human predicament. The first is the emergence of language as an exclusively human blessing and curse. Language promotes communication and understanding within the group; but it also accentuates the differences in tradition and beliefs between groups and erects separative barriers between tribes, nations, regions, social classes. According to Margaret Mead, among the two million Aborigines in New Guinea, 750 different languages are spoken in 750 villages, which are at permanent war with one another.

Even more dangerous, however, than the divisive effect of different vocabularies is the power of language to crystallize the implicit habits and ways of life of different communities into explicit doctrines and moral imperatives. If the citizens of Lilliput had not been blessed with language, they could not have fought a war on the question on which end to break the egg because they would not have been able to transform a habit into an ideology.

Equal in importance to the discovery of language and of the use of tools is man's discovery of death. But we should rather say: the discovery of death by the intellect and its rejection by instinct. Instinct takes existence for granted and cannot conceive of nonexistence. The refusal to accept death as a natural and final phenomenon became a dominant motive in all human cultures, and a paradigm of the split mind. It populated the atmosphere with invisible presences, most of them malevolent or at least capricious and unpredictable, who had to be propitiated and appeased at a heavy price.

The institution of human sacrifice is a phenomenon curiously neglected by anthropologists, although it is found in every part of the world at the dawn of civilization, and even at the height of pre-Columbian cultures. It is epitomized in one of the early chapters of Genesis, where Abraham prepares to cut the throat of his son out of sheer love of God. The ubiquity of human sacrifice is one of the earliest manifestations of the paranoid trend in the human psyche. The forms changed, but the trend persisted throughout the holy massacres of history, culminating in the genocidal enterprises of our time. Even the promise of eternal life was offered only to a small minority of mankind, at the price of eternal torment for the vast majority. Paradise was an exclusive country club, but the gates of Hell were open to all.

There is of course a reverse side of the medal. Devotion is not always misguided, language produced the treasures in our libraries, the discovery of death is the foundation on which pyramids and cathedrals were built. However, we are now concerned not with the glory of man but his predicament, and today that is the more urgent subject; it has achieved an urgency as never before. History is accelerating at an unprecedented rate, like molecules of a liquid coming to the boil.

The contemporary equivalent of the Writing on the Wall are the diagrammatic charts of the exponential curves representing the various explosions that surround us: population explosion, knowledge explosion, communications explosion, and the explosion of explosive power. We may have seen these curves in learned magazines, but none of us has seen a curve representing progress in theoretical and applied ethics. The reason is presumably that there is no progress to report since the days when Buddha sat under the banyan tree, waiting for his oxcart. [See *Current,* April 1968, page 58.]

In contrast to the exponential curve, which shows at first a slow, then an ever steeper rise until it seems to rocket into the sky, the missing ethical curve would show a blurred, wavy line with inconclusive ups and downs, and would never get off the ground. This contrast provides us with a simple over-all view of our history; it reflects the consequences of the split mind.

Evolution proceeds by trial and error, so we ought not to be surprised if it turned out that there is some construction fault in the circuitry that we carry inside our skulls, which would explain the unholy mess we have made of our history. The ultimate cause may be the exceptionally rapid growth of the hominid brain in the course of the last half-million years—a phenomenon which seems to be unique in evolutionary history.

The brain explosion in the second half of the Pleistocene seems also to have followed the exponential curve which has become so familiar to us—and there may be more than a superficial analogy here, as both curves reflect the phenomenon of the acceleration of history on different levels.

But explosions rarely produce harmonious results, and the evidence seems to indicate that in our case the result is insufficient coordination between the phylogenetically old areas of the brain and the new, specifically human areas of the neocortex, which were superimposed on it with such unseemly haste.

A distinguished neurophysiologist, Prof. Paul MacLean, has coined the term 'schizophysiology' for this disorderly state of affairs in our central nervous system. While our intellectual functions are carried on in the newest and most highly developed part of the brain, he says, our affective behavior continues to be dominated by a relatively crude and primitive system, by archaic structures in the brain whose fundamental pattern has undergone but little change in the whole course of evolution from mouse to man.

The consequences of this built-in schizophysiology range from so-called normal behavior, where emotional bias distorts our reasoning only within tolerable limits, through neurotic and psychotic disorder in the individual, to the collectively held beliefs in irrational causes to which we are emotionally committed in blind devotion and militant enthusiasm.

The question is, as Bertrand Russell once said, how to persuade humanity to acquiesce in its own survival. The thermonuclear reaction, once invented, cannot be disinvented, and the Pandora boxes of biological warfare are just waiting to be opened. One cannot play Russian roulette for long.

The biological evolution of man seems to have come to a standstill, at least since Cro-Magnon days; since we cannot in the foreseeable future expect a change in human nature to arise by a spontaneous mutation, our only hope seems to be to discover techniques which supplant biological evolution and provide a cure for our collective ailments. Recent advances in the sciences of life seem to indicate that once man decides to take his fate into his own hands, that possibility will be within his reach." (*The Observer* [London], Apr. 28, 1968)

SUMMARY

With the rise of the new hunting and gathering society, *Homo erectus* adapted to different environments and developed subspecies variations in brain size, cusp pattern, and brow ridge protrusion among other features. At some unknown time and location, as yet unidentified subspecies of *Homo erectus*, with a larger than average brain, evolved into a new species, *Homo sapiens*.

Two fossils, one from Swanscombe, England, the other from Steinheim, Germany, both approximately 250,000 years old, are the earliest known fully *Homo sapiens* forms. Curiously, there is no evidence of a change in tool assemblage accompanying the evolutionary shift from *Homo erectus* to *Homo sapiens*.

Between 250,000 and 100,000 years ago, the fossil record is scattered and inconclusive. At least one occupation site, however, Lazaret Cave, provides evidence of extensive cultural development. The hominid physical remains of 100,000 years ago are similar to Swanscombe in brain size but distinctly more primitive in other features—a heavier brow ridge, a receding chin and a low, flat, cranial vault. By 75,000 years ago, this constellation of traits is further accentuated in the classic Neanderthal subspecies. Neanderthal man, found throughout Europe and the Near East, is well within the range of variation of the *Homo sapiens* species despite his short, stocky, heavy limbed body and ape-like facial features.

The first Neanderthal fossil, discovered in the Neander Valley, Germany in 1856, was considered to be the remains of a victim of some rare disease, a half-crazed, wild man, or the member of some generally despised ethnic group. As Darwin's concept of evolution gained wider acceptance, so did the designation of Neanderthal as a subspecies of *Homo Sapiens*. Still, many refused to acknowledge any relationship to the fossil form until as late as the 1920's. Despite the popular conception of Neanderthal as a dull witted, brutish cave man, the archeological evidence clearly indicates that he was an intelligent, adaptable human subspecies, capable of surviving under harsh glacial conditions, inventing methods of food preservation and maintaining winter reserves of fuel.

Neanderthal man is also the first hominid known to have buried his dead. At the beginning of this century, a burial site was discovered at Le Moustier, France. Burial marks the beginning of the recognition of the individual in society and the inherent value of life.

Additional Reading

Blanc, A.C.

1961   Some evidence for the ideologies of early man. In S.L. Washburn (Ed.), Social Life of Early Man. Viking Fund Publications in Anthropology. Vol 31, pp 119–136.

An excellent examination of human ideological evolution. Some intense reading, but worthwhile.

Campbell, Bernard

1956   The Centenary of Neanderthal Man: Part I and Part II.
Man, volume 55, November–December, pp. 156–158, 171–173.

A good historical view of the Neanderthal finds.

Solecki, Ralph S.

1971   Shanidar—The First Flower People. New York: Knopf.

A fascinating, worthwhile consideration of Neanderthals.

Trevor, J. C., and D.R. Brothwell

1961   The human remains of Mesolithic and Neolithic date from Gua Chi, Kelantan. Federation Museums Journal. Vol. 7, pp 6–22.

Good discussion of Neanderthal remains.

chapter nine

THE SCIENTIFIC STUDY OF NEANDERTHAL

One of the most beautiful parts of France is the region surrounding the village of Les Eyzies more than three hundred miles southwest of Paris. Rivers have gouged the countryside out of a great limestone plateau. There are remote gorges and side valleys, wide-open valleys bounded by steep cliffs several hundred feet high, in the cliffs scooped-out places under massive overhangs—and caves, many small ones and others that extend deep into the rock.

The Les Eyzies area is primarily a center of prehistory. For all that has happened since, for all the conquests and pageantry, its richest records and deepest mysteries involve people who flourished a thousand centuries before the Romans, Neanderthal man and his ancestors and descendants. The record in this region demonstrates *Homo sapiens'* extraordinary ability to adapt, to live practically anywhere. Here we probably encountered glacial climates more rigorous and demanding than our ancestors had ever encountered before, and yet we managed to cope with icy temperatures and blizzards and accumulating snows. Certainly we could never have endured without making the most of natural resources, and the land around Les Eyzies offered a unique combination of advantages.

Les Eyzies, one of the most important centers of pre-history.

Shelter, of course, was provided by the cliffs, eroded structures formed by the lime-containing remains of tiny animals deposited and consolidated more than a hundred million years ago in the warm shallow sea that covered most of Europe. The cliffs provided raw material as well as shelter. Embedded in the limestone were large quantities of fine-grained flint in the form of nodules which, like the limestone, consist of the remains of microorganisms (in this case, colonies of single-cell animals with silica-containing shells). Water was also available, runoff from mountains in the Massif Central, where the Dordogne and Vézère rivers rose and joined a few miles below Les Eyzies and passed through on their way to the Bay of Biscay, as they do today.

Above all, there was an abundance of game during the coldest times, chiefly reindeer, which seem to have been created in large measure for the nourishment of humans and other large carnivores. Wild horses, for example, will not stay long in areas where they are being heavily hunted. But reindeer such as the caribou of the Canadian Arctic are creatures of habit, and vast herds tend to return to the same places year after year along the same well-rutted trails, across the same mountain passes, lakes, fords, rivers, and high gravel ridges. Judging by the quantities of reindeer bones found at numerous sites in the Les Eyzies region, prehistoric reindeer were equally predictable and equally vulnerable. Groups of Neanderthal hunters, working together rather like wolf packs, must have waited at strategic crossing points and stalked and killed individual animals.

Some two hundred prehistoric sites have been reported within a radius of about twenty miles of Les Eyzies, including Le Moustier and Regourdou and other burial sites mentioned in the last chapter. Many more sites are known but unreported, since every investigator familiar with the area has a private list of places he hopes to excavate some day. Most archeologists feel reasonably certain that several hundred undiscovered sites exist in the area. The great majority of reported caves, rock shelters and open-air locations with prehistoric remains have been found within a mile or two of well-traveled routes, modern roads which often follow the original courses of old carriage roads. No one really knows what lies beyond. A relatively straightforward approach would very likely lead to the discovery of further sites. Archeologists believe that a trip into these valleys would reveal that an appreciable proportion of the locations had served as the occupation sites of prehistoric people. The only difficulty is that there has been little support for such a search because enough sites are known already to keep excavators busy for four to five decades.

COMBE GRENAL

One exceptionally interesting cave site lies in the little valley of Combe Grenal, about fourteen miles from Les Eyzies, on the side of a hill not far from the Dordogne River. François Bordes, director of the Laboratory of Quaternary Geology and Prehistory of the University of Bordeaux and archeologist in charge of all investigations in the Les Eyzies region, began digging at the Combe Grenal cave in June, 1953. He expected to complete the project in short order, probably by the end of the summer, because a colleague told him that since bedrock had already been reached, only a small area remained to be exposed. But it soon turned out that the bedrock sloped sharply downhill, and he and his associates followed the dipping rock line deeper and deeper season after season without hitting bottom in the form of a level floor. When the work finally came to an end in 1964, they had made a huge hole in the ground, digging to a maximum depth of some forty feet and uncovering sixty-four layers of geological and archeological deposits.

The oldest and deepest layers can be dated approximately by geological methods. They include a clayey red soil, the clay representing muds formed during thaws of the next-to-last glaciation. These deposits are estimated to have been laid down 125,000 to 150,000 years ago, about the time when prehistoric pioneers explored the area, looked over the cave and decided to move in.

The first occupants left no fossil remains. But they may have been people rather like those represented by the skull fragments found at the Swanscombe and Steinheim sites, people clearly on the way to modern humans. They had Acheulian-type tools like some of those unearthed at Swanscombe, including hand axes designed according to the same basic pattern used by their remote Olduvai ancestors hundreds of thousands of years before. Judging by the fact that about 80 per cent of the bones found among their tools were reindeer bones, their diet included ample supplies of venison.

Combe Grenal's richest and most important deposits lie directly above the red Acheulian deposits, furnishing an almost continuous record of Neanderthal occupation from about 90,000 to 40,000 years ago. There are a few sterile layers, layers without artifacts or any traces of people, when the climate may have become too severe even for the Neanderthals, but Combe Grenal was a center of activity most of the time. Groups consisting of up to about thirty-five to forty individuals at any one time lived and died there over periods of many generations. The site includes an empty grave, extending through several of the deepest Neanderthal layers. Experienced excavators are continually observing changes in the soil, changes in color and texture and consistency, and one day Bordes noticed a small area of fine soil in a section consisting mainly of coarser material, the sort of pattern produced when earth has been loosened.

Removal of the fine material revealed a typical basin-shaped burial pit so small that it must have contained a very young child. The absence of fossil remains is difficult to explain. The grave had not been disturbed either by looters or scavenging animals. Most probably the skeleton was destroyed by the bone-dissolving action of waters seeping through layers containing sand and ashes and rock. Three smaller ceremonial pits near the grave may have held meat and clothing for the dead child, and they are also empty.

Another unusual feature was exposed in a higher, more recent layer. One of Bordes' co-workers noticed a dark circular patch of fine soil in an ashy layer; scooped out the soil, taking care to leave the ashy material intact; and ended with a hole about two inches in diameter and eight inches deep. Then he poured plaster into the hole, obtaining a cast which resembled the pointed end of a stake. This may have been one of several postholes at the mouth of the cave, where stakes were driven into the ground to support skins or woven branches and provide shelter from wind, rain and snow. Or, as will be indicated later, it may have supported a meat-drying rack.

PREHISTORIC CULTURE: STATISTICAL ANALYSIS

Combe Grenal is an especially important site for the richness of its tool assemblages and the analysis of those assemblages by a statistical approach which Bordes himself pioneered. Since excavating his first site at the age of fourteen in a valley not far from Les Eyzies, he has examined more than a million tools, most of them made by Neanderthal man. This experience is the basis for his widely used system of classifying tools. He has published a list of tool types, each type being identified clearly and objectively enough so that other investigators can make the same identifications on their own. The list includes a total of more than sixty different kinds of points, scrapers, knives, burins, and so on.

The variety of tool types itself is enough to indicate what may be deduced from other evidence such as the burial practices of the Neanderthals and their ability to live in rigorous climates, namely, that they were advanced and complicated human beings. All of the tools they used appeared in other cultures long before the rise of the Neanderthal subspecies, although in smaller proportions. But further analysis reveals another sort of variety, and more about the people. In the process of identifying and counting the tools in Neanderthal layers, Bordes discovered the existence of a number of unique and characteristic patterns. Different layers contain different proportions of

Plaster cast of a posthole discovered at Combe Grenal.

tools, different tool kits which hint at basic differences in prehistoric living.

The patterns occur among the 19,000 Neanderthal tools collected at Combe Grenal. One of them is represented in the layer where the posthole was found. The layer contained 766 tools and a great many tool types, including an assortment of scrapers and even three hand axes. But nearly 600 items in the assemblage belong to a single broad class, flints with one or more notches struck on the edges. Most of the pieces are *denticulate* or toothed tools having several notches in a row, usually three or four, forming a set of teeth and looking much like saw blades. There are also single-notch tools which might be used, among other purposes, to help scrape the bark off narrow branches in making stakes and spear shafts. The site includes nine other denticulate layers.

A second kind of tool kit is found in fourteen other layers. It also includes a variety of different tools and, again, one class of tool predominates. Nearly two out of every three pieces is a scraper, a high proportion being so-called *Quina scrapers,* named after a site where they have been found in quantity, the La Quina shelter about seventy miles northwest of Combe Grenal. The large thick tools are often delicately chipped along their curved working edges to produce a characteristic overlapping "fish scale" appearance; they may have served as heavy-duty implements to clean hides for clothing.

The discovery of these and two other tool kits has changed ways of looking at tool assemblages everywhere. Tools uncovered in Neanderthal layers generally fit into one of Bordes' four categories wherever the layers are found—not only at Combe Grenal and in the Les Eyzies region but also in Spain, Syria, Germany, Israel and other countries. The problem is what to make of such widespread and persistent patterns. Apparently they have little to do with evolution among the Neanderthals, since the tool kits do not appear in any regular sequence from the oldest to the most recent layers at various sites, and there is no conclusive evidence of simple seasonal or climatic influences.

Bordes believes that the four tool kits belong to four tribes or traditions. Different Neanderthal groups had different ways of doing things, customs handed down from much earlier times and represented by the tool kits they left behind. For example, the Quina Neanderthals may be traced to a tradition that existed nearly a hundred thousand years before them at the High Lodge site in England, where people were using similar tools, including finely worked Quina-type scrapers. Another Neanderthal tool kit may stem from Acheulian industries which first appeared more than 600,000 years ago, a line passing through intermediate stages such

as those observed in the remains at Torralba and Ambrona and, more recently, in the lowest layers at Combe Grenal itself.

The stress is on enduring elements in a world where cultural evolution proceeded very slowly compared to its current pace. Bordes believes that contacts among Neanderthal bands with different traditions were few and far between: "A man may well have lived all his life without more than a rare meeting with anyone from another tribe . . . and it is very possible that these contacts, when they did take place, were not always peaceful and fruitful." After all, it was a relatively empty world, the entire population of France probably numbering less than 20,000 persons.

Combe Grenal provides a record of successive wanderings in and out of the little Dordogne Valley by people who had developed different ways of doing things, different habits and beliefs. Groups settled in the cave, eventually died out or left in search of better living conditions or new hunting grounds or simply because they wanted a change of scene (there were always more than enough caves and shelters to go around), and were replaced by other groups in a series of occupations that took place over a period of some five hundred centuries.

The approach upon which Bordes' ideas are based, the statistical approach, has opened the way for still more extensive and more refined studies in the years ahead. Already some of his conclusions are being challenged as a direct result of work stimulated by his own research. The challenge calls for a major shift of emphasis, a different way of looking at and analyzing Neanderthal tool kits. Instead of interpreting them as the products of different tribes or traditions, they can be interpreted as signs that different sorts of activity were going on.

According to this viewpoint, different tool kits do not represent people with different traditions doing essentially the same things, such as hunting, gathering, preparing foods, making

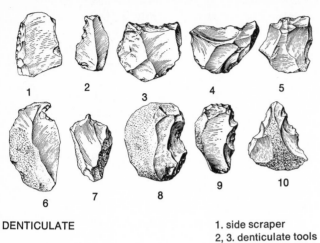

DENTICULATE

1. side scraper
2, 3. denticulate tools
4, 5, 6. notched tools
7. borer
8. notched tool
9, 10. denticulate tools

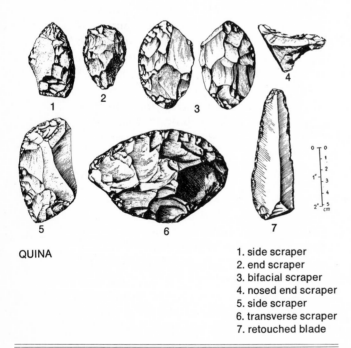

QUINA

1. side scraper
2. end scraper
3. bifacial scraper
4. nosed end scraper
5. side scraper
6. transverse scraper
7. retouched blade

Two Neanderthal tool kits: denticulate (above) and Quina (below).

tools and fires, and so on. They represent people who shared many important cultural characteristics and were simply doing different things at different times and places. For example, the existence of Quina-type and denticulate tool kits might simply indicate that one group was engaged chiefly in scraping hides, while the other group was concentrating on woodworking. In other words, people were using Combe Grenal for different purposes. The focus is less on things that prehistoric people did because their forefathers did them, and more on things they did as part of the practical day-to-day business of staying alive.

The most articulate and influential spokesman for the so-called "functional" point of view is Lewis Binford of the University of New Mexico, who evolved his approach and philosophy during the course of work on American Indian sites. His increasing concern with the more remote prehistory of the Old World is due in large part to his former wife Sally, a graduate of the University of Chicago who has specialized in Neanderthal problems and has worked closely with Bordes. There have been some friendly but heated arguments over the interpretation of Neanderthal data with Bordes and his wife Denise, also an archeologist.

Binford's approach, like Bordes', is a statistical one involving a refinement of the tool-kit concept. Any group of people, prehistoric or primitive or modern, has a large set of tools for carrying out all of its activities. Investigators interested in comparing different cultures may obtain some information from an unsorted collection of items representing the entire assemblage. But the information is likely to be very limited without further analysis. There must be some way of isolating, from the total set, the subsets of tools or specialized tool kits which naturally go together because they are used together in performing specific activities. These subsets and activities must be identified to understand the lives of prehistoric people.

An individual completely ignorant of modern life would confront such a problem in trying to analyze an unsorted collection of the implements we use. The collection might consist of more than a hundred different types of objects, including a mixture of items used in grooming, cooking, writing and sewing: razor blades, pots, paper clips, thimbles, hair curlers, bread knives, ballpoint pens, safety pins, combs, frying pans, letter openers, needles, nail files, funnels, paperweights, and scissors. The task would be to find out which tools were used together and for what tasks.

Analogous problems arise in the study of prehistoric humans. A single collection from a single living place means nothing by itself. The search for subsets of artifacts as clues to repeated practices, living habits, requires a sufficiently large and representative sample of collections—and Binford and his students have introduced a special statistical technique for the analysis of such samples. The technique, known as *factor analysis,* developed out of research conducted during the early 1900's by American psychologists concerned with discovering sets of questions to serve as effective measures of intelligence.

An early application of factor analysis to research on prehistoric tool kits involves evidence obtained from a site in Israel near the Sea of Galilee. The area has been shaped by ancient volcanoes and earthquakes. It marks the northernmost part of the Great Rift Valley system, the huge split in the earth's crust which extends 4,000 miles down through East Africa and past the Olduvai Gorge and ends somewhere in Mozambique. It includes many caves where Neanderthal people lived in times when a now-extinct river flowed through the area to the Dead Sea.

In 1962 Sally Binford excavated one of the caves, a large two-chamber affair located in a steep limestone cliff more than a hundred feet above the floor of a river canyon. The site yielded eight tool collections from as many different deposits in the cave area, collections suitable for analysis, including a total of about 2,000 tools. Sally Binford identified the tools according to Bordes' list of types and under his supervision.

The size of the sample was increased by the addition of eight other tool collections, seven from levels in a shelter near Damascus in Syria and one from a French open-air site near Rouen. The collections were made up of about 2,000 more tools closely related to those found at the Israeli site and presumably manufactured during the same period of prehistory. Moreover, all the tools had been typed by Bordes, which ensured consistency of classification.

Factor analysis calls for a detailed investigation of variations among the items of a sample. In this case the first step was to take one of the tool types, compare it with a second type for each of the sixteen collections, and then evaluate the result. A rating of $+1$ would indicate that the two types varied in exactly the same way—that both types increased by, say, 10 per cent from collection A to collection B, decreased by 25 per cent from B to C, maintained the same proportions in D, and so on. A -1 rating would indicate that the two tool types were exactly out of phase, varying in exactly the opposite way, while 0 would indicate no relationship at all. Intermediate values on the scale from $+1$ to -1 represented different degrees of correlation or association.

The process was repeated over and over again in the Neanderthal study. Each tool type was compared successively to every one of the other thirty-nine tool types (this particular sample including forty of the sixty-odd types listed by Bordes), and every one of the relationships was evaluated. These and many subsequent steps required a prodigious amount of arithmetic. With a high-speed electronic computer, it took about two minutes.

Controversy

Binford verses Bordes, continued.

As the debate over the Mousterian assemblages rages on, Bordes and Binford continue to be the strongest exponents of the traditional and functional positions, respectively. Recent statements by both men have focused on the implications of the length of site occupation for their interpretations. Were these sites occupied year-round or on a seasonal basis?

According to the functional analysis, Neanderthal man relied largely on his mobility as a subsistence strategy. Groups of people sharing the same fundamental cultural orientation engaged in various activities in different places, at different times. If Binford's analysis of the excavated tool kits is correct, then the sites served as temporary camps, occupied on a seasonal basis.

In recent writings, Bordes reaffirms his view that the different assemblages reflect different ethnic groups. He maintains that the various Mousterian traditions existed under a variety of climatic conditions, rarely encountering each other in their sparsely populated world. Bordes points to certain thick layers of deposits which contain a homogeneous distribution of tools as evidence of long term occupation. He disputes the notion that the Mousterians had different winter and summer shelters by restating his belief in the existence of four, and not two, distinct traditions. While the functionalists stress the range of environmental variation in the region, Bordes notes the minimal importance of any but the most extreme differences in environment to the Mousterians. A Mousterian point, he argues, could kill an antelope as readily as a deer.

As further evidence of year-round occupation, Bordes cites a study of reindeer jaws and teeth. Because of the presence of jaws in all stages of tooth eruption, the study concludes that the sites were occupied by the Mousterians year-round. Binford, however, points out a number of serious flaws in the analysis. Essentially, it fails to consider the highly variable patterns of birth and tooth development in reindeer. Binford concludes that a re-analysis of reindeer teeth employing accurate data would demonstrate his own theory, that the sites were occupied on a short-term basis.

Binford also disputes Bordes' claim that different summer and winter sheltering places would require an unlikely agreement between various Mousterian groups as to who used what, when. If there were no ethnically distinctive traditions, as Binford claims, there would be no need for such an agreement. He sees no reason to be surprised that a territory would

be used in the same way over a long period of time, on a seasonal basis. This would explain the existence of thick and homogeneous layers. Furthermore, Binford claims that the different seasonal assemblages do not necessarily correlate with the scrapers and denticulates which Bordes uses to distinguish the different Mousterian cultures.

Binford has also continued his search for evidence to support the functional approach in the study of contemporary Nunamiut Eskimos. He observes that there is a very limited correlation between how tools are actually used and those artifacts which are left to be found by the archeologist. Furthermore, the most expendable artifacts are those which are the least stylistically distinctive, that is, those which show the least ethnic identity. The objects of greatest cultural significance are not likely to be discarded and preserved for the archeological record. These observations lead Binford to question the validity of discriminating ethnic differences on the basis of assemblages such as those which figure prominently in Bordes' analysis. Binford even interpreted Bordes' observation that Mousterian tools were manufactured and utilized in the same area as a strong argument supporting the functionalist position!

F. Clark Howell *(1925–   )
has been an active field archeologist and scholar for the last
25 years. During this time, he has
participated in significant excavations covering almost every major
period of prehistory. In 1953 he
participated in the Neanderthal
excavations at Abri Pataud,
France; in 1963 he directed the
excavations of the Acheulian sites
at Torralba and Ambrona, Spain.
Howell has spent much of the last
ten years searching for early*
Homo *and* Australopithecus
*remains in the Omo basin, in
southern Ethiopia. His innovative
excavation techniques have been
responsible for many of the recent
advances in our knowledge of
prehistory. In addition to field
research and writing, Howell
teaches at the University of
California, Berkeley.*

The final analysis produced five "factors," five sets of tools that varied together as independent clusters with high degrees of correlation. The following is a list of the specialized tool kits together with some suggestions as to how they might have been used:

Tool kit I, 12 tool types including two kinds of borer, a beak-shaped engraver or "bec," and other tools which may have been used to make objects out of wood and bone—perhaps shafts, handles or hafts, tent pegs, and cordage from hides. Maintenance activities.

Tool kit II, 10 tool types including three kinds of spear point as well as many kinds of scraper. Killing and butchering.

Tool kit III, 7 tool types including three kinds of knife for heavy cutting and three kinds of flake for delicate cutting. Food processing, mainly prepared meat.

Tool kit IV, 4 tool types including denticulates for sawing and shredding, and two special types of scraper for fine work. Shredding and cutting, perhaps of wood and other plant materials.

Tool kit V, 6 tool types including points, simple scrapers, and the rabot or push plane. Killing and butchering, but perhaps involving activities more specialized than those requiring tool kit II.

The main tool kits at the Israeli site turn out to be I, II, and III. Tool kit I predominates, which indicates that the cave was used chiefly for maintenance work, for repairing old tools and weapons and making new ones, the sort of tasks most likely to be carried out at a base camp. Tool kit III suggests food processing, another "domestic" activity, while the presence of tool kit II indicates that a small amount of killing and butchering may have been done at the site. The base-camp notion is supported by the fact that the cave is a large one enclosing a naturally lighted area of about 2,700 square feet, representing enough floor space for twenty-five to thirty individuals (on the basis of studies indicating a requirement in such settlements of at least a hundred square feet per person).

The analysis permits further deductions about how the cave was used. Most of the deposits contain tool assemblages that are remarkably alike in the number of tools and tool types and their proportions. This observation fits in with the notion, hinted at by other evidence, that the same group of people used the cave intensively to perform the same general tasks for a relatively short period, say, a few years. Their cooking area may have been located just outside the cave entrance. It is marked by a deposit that includes three small fire layers and an unusually high proportion of tool kit III knives and flakes, tools which could do an effective job of meat carving.

A different living pattern existed at the Syrian site, a shelter containing only about 1,600 square feet of floor space. Tool kits II and V, the killing and butchering factors, tend to predominate here. There is also evidence suggesting that tool kit V may represent the hunting of a type of game which demands that the hunters spend relatively long periods away from the base camp. The general impression is that the site served as a temporary work camp, where hunters stopped to do their butchering and perhaps to make plans for the next day's activities. Only one of its occupation levels contains traces of fire and, as at the Israeli site, this is also the only place where food-processing tool kit III is represented.

After completing the Near Eastern studies the Binfords carried out a more extensive analysis of evidence from Combe Grenal with its fifty-odd Neanderthal layers, 19,000 Neanderthal tools, abundant bone and pollen remains, and a 50,000-year record of Neanderthal occupations. In the Near Eastern study both hunting items (spear points) and scrapers were included in a single one of the five tool kits, II. But in the Combe Grenal analysis this unit breaks into its major components and be-

comes two distinct tool kits. The same effect was noted for maintenance and food processing, each being represented by several different tool kits. In all, the analysis yielded some fourteen different tool kits, believed to be fairly close to a complete listing for the Neanderthals, although future studies may reveal two or three more.

These statistically determined factors or clusters are elements of a most important kind. They can be compared to the small pieces of glass and stone used in making mosaics, and they may be used in re-creating a human pattern, the Neanderthal way of life. Some major features of the pattern have already been discovered.

Combe Grenal has fifty-five Neanderthal occupation layers, forty of them containing enough tools for statistical analysis. Twenty-five of the analyzed layers include one or more of the three kinds of tool kit associated with maintenance activities, and are probably camps—implying that they were either home bases for all members of the groups or else places away from the home site and reserved primarily for intensive activities associated with hunting or food processing. The rest of the layers did not contain maintenance tool kits and are interpreted as stations representing temporary occupations for more specialized activities. A few of these layers do not fit in with this preliminary hypothesis since they include abundant traces of fire, characteristic of intensive settlements rather than temporary stations.

Other associations stimulate new ideas about what was being done and by whom. One of the Binfords' arguments leads from a consideration of the kinds of flint used for different types of tools to new interpretations of some old and puzzling observations. They asked themselves what sort of archeological evidence might help indicate which tasks were done by women, and speculated that since women generally stay near the group's camp or station to care for the children, they might tend to make their tools out of

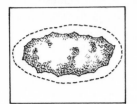

edges of nodule trimmed

top surface trimmed

striking platform made

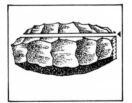

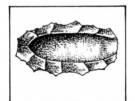

flake struck from nucleus

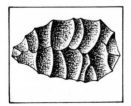

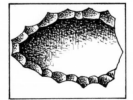

finished tool

*Top and side views of the stages
in making Levallois tools.*

readily available raw material near the site.

This notion immediately raised a simple question which had never been asked before: What sort of tools were made of local materials? The most readily available sources of flint available to the Neanderthals at Combe Grenal were dull grayish or blackish nodules embedded in the walls of their own cave, and the Binfords spent many hours at Bordes' laboratory in Bordeaux going through drawer after drawer jammed with tools, classifying every item by tool type and material and the layer in which it was found. They found that tools made of Combe Grenal flint are likely to be primarily denticulate or notched tools, items commonly associated with the processing of foods—which might well have been predominantly woman's work as it is in primitive hunting tribes today.

Reinforcing and complementing the theory is evidence bearing on man's work. Tools which may be made of any one of several different raw materials, generally from remote sources—for example, opalescent white flint from a site more than a mile away on the plateau above Combe Grenal, or brown flint from Dordogne River gravels—are most often those used in hunting, including spear points and certain types of scraper. One implication is that the variety of materials represents a mark of the hunting life, of men away from their base camp and ready to use whatever suitable material happened to be at hand.

Broader and more complex problems remain to be discovered and solved in the Combe Grenal data, problems involving the further application of factor analysis and the relationship of tool assemblages to other traces of the past. Bordes collected fossil pollens from many layers at the site, and the Binfords have also subjected this material to statistical study, again with the aid of a high-speed computer. The result is eight clusters of pollen types which tend to occur together and tell a story of prevailing climates in the area.

One cluster includes oak, poplar, alder, elm, ivy, ferns and other plants characteristic of low, damp, shaded places such as are found in the upland meadows of the Dordogne region today. Other clusters suggest a typical very dry, very warm forest-margin terrain (blackberry, raspberry, roses, nettles), steppe grasslands (cool-climate grasses and sedges), and cold, seasonally wet conditions (hazel, willow, Queen Anne's lace). As might be expected, a clear-cut relationship exists between climate and activities as indicated by tool kits. In general the pattern of activities under way does not change much as long as the climate remains relatively stable.

There are also six animal clusters. Ibex, wolf and a northern species of horse are typical of cold steppes; deer, Irish elk and an extinct species of rhinoceros indicate open forest; and so on. The greatest variety of animal remains is usually found together with tool kits characteristic of base-camp layers, which suggests that the people chose to settle here precisely because the area contained many kinds of game. On the other hand, the least variety or fewest species are found at more temporary and specialized stations.

Combe Grenal includes three types of so-called shredding station, settlements characterized among other things by a high proportion of denticulates and other notched tools. The animal remains associated with one of the station types consist predominantly of horse and reindeer, and Lewis Binford has a hunch about what was going on. The saw-tooth tools may have been used by the Neanderthals to cut chunks of already butchered meat into little strips that could be hung on racks to dry in the sun or over fires. American Indians used this technique for preserving meat. French traders used to sell them special metal shredders for the cutting operations, tools designed along the same lines as small denticulate flints.

If this technique was practiced by the Neanderthals, one might expect to find clues in appropriate layers, such as the remains of smoke fires, postholes or even pieces of preserved wood from the drying racks. Unless a speculation suggests what excavators could possibly find by way of evidence, unless it suggests specific procedures for its own proof or disproof, it has very little value in stimulating new studies. Some confirmatory evidence exists at Combe Grenal; one of the denticulate layers, for example, contains the posthole as well as traces of fire.

Continuing analysis reveals patterns or fragments of patterns which are beginning to fit together. Small tools such as engravers, borers and endscrapers tend to be found together with the remains of salmon, marmots (a bushy-tailed rodent somewhat resembling a woodchuck), mountain sheep and other rarely killed animals. The association makes sense when you realize that these tools are used for maintenance activities like woodworking and preparing hides, activities generally carried out at base camps occupied for relatively long periods—and the longer the occupation, the greater the chances of finding some rare animals. These and a great many other associations, the output of high-speed computers, are statistical patterns which provide clues to patterns of inferred behavior among prehistoric people.

PREHISTORIC CULTURE: OTHER APPROACHES

Much of what we infer about prehistoric stoneworking techniques comes from the experiments of modern stoneworkers. Among them, one of the acknowledged masters is Don Crabtree, who, for more than forty years, has devoted a major part of his time to this highly specialized work, first as an expert on American Indian artifacts at the Ohio State Museum in Columbus and more recently at the Idaho State

Contemporary flint-workers: Don Crabtree and François Bordes in Crabtree's Idaho workshop.

University Museum. He has made more than 50,000 blades, scrapers, projectile points and other stone tools, and probably broken three or four times that many in the course of his research.

In flintworking, technique is everything, and during recent years Crabtree has become far more interested in techniques and the behavior of materials than in making artifacts. As part of an effort to understand more fully the muscular habits of prehistoric hunters, he may spend hours trying out a single style of removing flakes. When he finds a good source of flint, he may make several hundred pounds of blanks and preformed pieces for future practice sessions. Sometimes he will take pieces worked on both sides and make them thinner and thinner until they break or practically "melt" away, just to develop a mastery of the thinning process.

One of his major projects is a continuing effort to duplicate the work, to learn the "extinct skills," of certain virtuosos among the American Indians. Outstanding examples of stone toolmaking include the laurel-leaf points of the So-lutreans described in the next chapter, Danish daggers and Egyptian bracelets—and, when stone was already on the way out, beautiful flint knives made in Europe and the Near East in a lost-cause attempt to imitate and compete with the new metal blades, even to the point of reproducing in the stone seam lines made during the casting process. Incidentally, to the expert toolmaker many rough and ungainly-looking items represent the work of craftsmen who were fully as skilled as the makers of museum pieces, but who had to cope with inferior material.

Another source of clues to the past is the actual behavior of people who still live primarily by hunting. Primitive people are by no means living in a pristine, untouched state; their world has been changed irrevocably by waves of foreign explorers and settlers. Yet even allowing for all that, certain practices endure, and some striking parallels exist between the present and the remote past. As part of an effort to learn more about what happened at Combe Grenal and elsewhere, Binford is conducting a

Four Folsom points made by Crabtree. At right, an authentic Folsom point found in Illinois.

series of intensive studies among Eskimos living in the Brooks Range region of north-central Alaska, about 250 miles from Fairbanks. In one of his "recent archeology" projects, he excavated the site of a house occupied by Eskimos eighty to ninety years ago.

Among other things, he found caribou lower jawbones, all of which had been cracked open, a practice explained to him by Eskimos who remembered what their fathers and grandfathers had done. The jawbones contained "patik," a fibrous tissue eaten as a starvation food in times of near-famine. The Neanderthal hunters apparently faced similar emergencies, since all but one of several hundred reindeer, horse and ox-cattle jawbones found in Combe Grenal layers were also cracked open. Furthermore, it seems that Eskimos and Neanderthals shared related superstitions. The Alaskan hunters had a taboo against eating material from the jawbones of bears, foxes, wolves and other meat-eating animals—and not a single one of the two

dozen or so bear, wolf, cave lion and hyena jawbones found at Combe Grenal had been shattered.

So observations of contemporary hunters enrich the understanding of prehistory, mainly by suggesting things to look for during archeological excavations, and providing evidence relevant to the question of whether different tool kits represent different traditions or different activities.

The fact remains that we still can only guess at the functions of many tools, but experiments can help us obtain a better picture of prehistoric workers in action. Making a good replica of a specialized tool and then successfully cutting or scraping with it demonstrate only how it could have been used. Further research may be needed to indicate how it was actually used, and one effective approach takes advantage of a kind of built-in evidence, evidence which can be obtained from the original implements themselves, as they are found in excavated sites.

For more than thirty years Sergei Semenov and his associates at the USSR Institute of Archeology in Leningrad have been studying *microwear*, tool marks which cannot be detected by the naked eye. A detailed record can be obtained by treating tool surfaces with metal powders and other chemicals, and then examining them magnified as much as several hundred times under the microscope. This procedure reveals an entirely new "landscape" of wear, a topography of lines and pits, scars, facets, cracks, dull patches and so on.

For example, on the basis of naked-eye inspection, archeologists had tentatively identified one flint tool from Neanderthal times as a knife, since the working edge was polished on both sides as if it had been used repeatedly to cut down through some material. Microscopic examination, however, revealed a system of many fine grooves and indicated a different function. The grooves are not parallel to the edge as they would be if it had been used in a regular back-and-forth cutting action. They run at various angles, often crisscrossing one another, which is precisely the sort of pattern produced with experimental tools serving as scrapers.

The fact that the edge appears rounded under the microscope, as well as the presence of grooves on both sides of the tool, shows that it had been used with a two-way motion, left to right and right to left. Furthermore, the material involved could only have been animal skins, because previous skin-scraping tests had created identical microwear patterns, and different patterns result from the scraping of wood, bone, stone and other materials. A final deduction: the skins were probably fresh and damp, because skins dried in the open gener-

ally contain tiny wind-blown sand grains which produce grooves considerably deeper than those actually observed.

Getting the most out of the microwear approach calls for a three-stage process, as illustrated by the laboratory experiments of Richard Gould, an archeologist at the University of Hawaii. First Gould took two dozen scrapers obtained from Australian aborigines who had been using them to make spear throwers and other wooden objects, and examined them under the microscope. In every case he detected "terminated" fractures on the working edges, characteristic markings produced by the breaking off of tiny irregular chips. Then he made an aboriginal-type scraper out of native stone, and used the tool to trim a mulga-wood shaft the way the aborigines do in preparing a spear. After exactly 1,000 strokes, he examined the tool under the microscope and found fracture markings identical to those on the aborigines' own scrapers.

Finally, Gould located a number of Neanderthal scrapers, Quina-type scrapers which were used by prehistoric people living at the La Quina rock shelter in southern France—and, again, the same markings appeared under the microscope. In other words, he has made a strong case for the notion that the prehistoric tools were used for working wood or some other hard material like bone, and indications are that future microwear research will involve this sort of comparative study on a larger scale.

CONCLUSION

Future studies will have to be extended considerably to arrive at truly scientific theories about the lives of our prehistoric ancestors. A staggering amount of material has already been collected, including skeletal remains of more than 150 Neanderthal individuals from about sev-

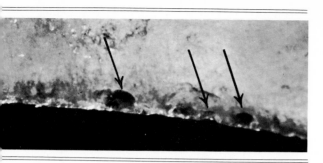

The working edge of a scraper used by Australian aborigines, magnified 25 times. The typical fractures (arrows) compare with those found on the Quina-type scrapers of the Neanderthals.

enty sites throughout the world. An important site is located in northeast China near the Great Wall. Soviet investigators have dug extensively at rich Neanderthal sites along river banks in the Crimea and elsewhere, and have found traces of elaborate burials and semipermanent dwellings. One of the dwelling sites, Molodova in the eastern Soviet Union more than 250 miles from Kiev, includes a large ring of mammoth tusks, perhaps used for supporting posts; inside the ring are bones of horses, rhinoceroses, bison and brown bears and 29,000 pieces of flint and fifteen hearths. There has even been increased activity in Greece and Italy. Other sites have been excavated in Africa, where, in certain regions at least, the pace of evolution seems to have been slower than in Europe.

Evidence for a possible evolutionary lag comes from Isimila, a rich site where thousands of stone tools lie exposed for about three-quarters of a mile along a seasonal stream in the highlands of southern Tanzania. Excavated by Charles Keller of the University of Illinois and Clark Howell, the site includes a typical Acheulian hand-ax-cleaver industry which existed about 75,000 years ago when people at Combe Grenal and elsewhere were using a wider va-

riety of tools. At Desmond Clark's Kalambo Falls site in Zambia, on the other hand, denticulate and notched tools appeared in high proportions not long before the Neanderthals and their tool kits began to disappear .n Europe.

Factor analysis and other statistical techniques will be required increasingly for comparative studies of material from many sites. Bare facts are neither particularly interesting nor particularly informative. They do not speak for themselves in archeology or in any other branch of science. But they will speak if they are treated properly, if they are marshaled and organized. That means using statistics to help get the most out of the evidence, a process which generally requires the aid of a high-speed computer. The relationships involved are too complicated for even the most imaginative investigators to deal with on their own.

Imagination comes into its own most effectively, most powerfully, after the analysis. Computers simply present information organized according to the instructions prepared for them. They indicate that certain types of tools tend to vary together and form statistical clusters, but they say nothing about the uses of individual tools or the activities represented by individual tool kits. It is up to the investigator to frame hypotheses that can be checked. Imagination will have to lead the way in interpreting tendencies involving subtler things than activities, things such as attitudes and beliefs.

Bordes has definite feelings about the men and women whose artifacts he is uncovering. They are still alive for him. As he digs in a rich Quina layer and finds one beautifully worked scraper after another, he is impressed not only with the craftsmanship but also with the fact that the craftsmen were working in an almost automatic fashion, as if they had perfected their techniques and had stopped inventing.

There is another observation about these people. They seem to have done most of the burying of the dead. So one may ask whether a relationship exists between this ordeal and the stereotyped, repetitive aspect of their flint technology—and, if so, what special stresses and fears might have fostered the intensive development of their rituals.

One clue is that they lived chiefly during hard winters when death rates must have been high. The loss of an individual would have had a special impact among people depending directly upon one another for survival, and if the individual was an adult male, his death could have meant the death of the group. Perhaps burial rites developed under the stress of such conditions.

The "feel" of layers related to earlier Acheulian industries hints at an entirely different attitude toward the world. These layers include some hand axes and a relatively high proportion of knives, especially backed knives blunted on one side for a firm and comfortable grip. Bordes believes that Neanderthals using such tools were far more inventive than those using Quina-type tools: "They had some imagination. They made all sorts of backed blades and offbeat tools which you can't classify, including some combination tools, prehistoric versions of today's Swiss pocket knives with scissors and screwdrivers and nail files as well as regular blades. They experimented a great deal, and their experiments worked."

The continuing cooperation between Bordes and Binford shows how productive results can be achieved by investigators whose basic viewpoints differ. The problems at issue demand both the "tribal" or cultural and the functional approaches. Archeologists concerned primarily with cultural factors tend to dig deep, to go back as far as possible into time and obtain a long record of successive changes. Functionally minded archeologists, on the other hand, tend to dig wide, to excavate broad areas at sites which cover more space and can reveal more about the organization of camping places and the variety of activities under way.

Prehistory is sufficiently complex to benefit from both approaches. The best excavations are both deep and wide.

The Effect of Chronic Exposure To Cold on Temperature and Blood Flow of the Hand

G. Malcolm Brown
and John Page

While Binford, Binford, Bordes and other ar-cheologists have been applying modern scientific methods to the study of Neanderthal material remains, physical anthropologists have been employing the modern techniques of the biological sciences to learn what types of physiological adaptations to the cold Neanderthal might have undergone. The following article by two Canadian medical researchers demonstrates just this approach.

Various authors have studied the blood flow of the hand at different ambient temperatures and with the hand at different local temperatures. We know of no published data concerning the effect of chronic exposure to low ambient temperatures on hand blood flow. It is the purpose of this paper to present observation on hand temperature as well as hand blood flow in a group accustomed to low ambient temperatures and to compare these with a control group.

METHOD

The group accustomed to low ambient temperatures consisted of 22 healthy male Eskimos on Southampton Island, Northwest Territories; their ages

Reprinted from the *Journal of Applied Physiology,* **5** (1952).

varied from 18 to 40 years. The observations in this group were carried out in July and August of 1949 and 1950 when the outdoor temperatures ranged from 30° to 67°F. The average room temperature of the Eskimo dwellings during July was found to be about 20°C. The subjects chosen were all men who lived the native life of hunting and fishing during the summer and hunting and trapping during the winter. Their dwellings were the usual tent, shack or igloo.

The control data were collected by repeating the experiments in September and October of 1951 on 37 young, healthy men attending Queen's University, Kingston, Ontario.

All experiments were conducted at a mean room temperature of 20° ± 0.5°C. and a relative humidity from 50 to 60 per cent. The amount of clothing that was comfortable for the Eskimo was worn by both groups, with the exception that the Eskimo wore seal skin muklucks while the control group wore oxfords. This clothing consisted of a woolen shirt and trousers. The subjects were studied in a fasting state.

The experimental method was patterned after the investigation of temperature and blood flow in the forearm by Barcroft and Edholm. Direct hand blood flow measurements were made with a Lewis-Grant type of venous occlusion plethysmograph. Temperatures were measured by means of thermocouples.

Blood pressures were recorded with a sphygmomanometer.

RESULTS/STUDIES CONDUCTED IN ROOM AIR AT 20°C.

The Eskimos were comfortable throughout the 2-hour experiments while the majority of the control group stated that they felt cool. . . . The hand blood flow and temperature of the Eskimo were greater than those of the control group. In both groups, the blood flow and temperature decreased slightly over the 2 hours. A greater degree of fluctuation occurred in the blood flow in the Eskimo subjects. The rectal temperature of the Eskimo remained constant while that of the control group decreased 0.4°C. on the average during the 2-hour period.

STUDIES ON HAND BLOOD FLOW AT DIFFERENT WATER-BATH TEMPERATURES 5-20°C.

Hand blood flows were observed within 45 to 60 seconds following immersion of the hand and forearm. In the 20°C. water-bath, the blood flow of the control group was quickly and markedly reduced while that of the Eskimo fell more slowly. At 5° and 10°C. marked reduction occurred rapidly in both groups. At all bath temperatures in this range the rate of reduction in average hand blood flow was less in the Eskimo. . . .

At any time during the period of observation at these temperatures, the hand blood flow of the Eskimo was greater than that of the control group. The blood flow at 5°C. was greater than that at 10° and 20°C. in both groups, but this effect was more marked in the control group.

30-35°C.

In both groups studied, no appreciable alteration in blood flow occurred upon immersion in the 30° to 35°C. water-baths. A steady state was achieved within 10 minutes in all individuals. The frequency and magnitude of fluctuations in hand blood flow increased as the temperature of the water increased.

The degree of fluctuation was greater in the Eskimo. . . .

38-45°C.

Increased hand blood flow occurred immediately in all control group subjects and the increase was greater at the higher temperatures. A fairly constant pattern was achieved within 30 to 50 minutes. The volume of the blood flow and the frequency and magnitude of fluctuations increased as the temperature increased. . . .

DISCUSSION

Spealman has demonstrated the influence of the general thermal condition of the body on hand blood flow. He observed that the hand blood flow at any given water temperature is greater the warmer the body. The results of the blood flow measurements which we have carried out on the Eskimo at an ambient temperature of 20°C. are similar to those obtained by other workers who have studied the effect of hand temperature on the hand blood flow in man in temperate climates at an ambient temperature of 24° to 27°C. The blood flow and temperature measurements in our control group are in accordance with those made by other workers at similar ambient temperatures on similar subjects. At their usual summer temperature, the Eskimo has a higher hand blood flow at various water-bath temperatures than does the white man used to a temperate climate; and the results of our studies at one ambient temperature, taken with Spealman's results, suggest that at a given water-bath temperature he has also a higher hand blood flow at various ambient temperatures.

It is to be noted that not only is the hand blood flow greater at low temperatures in the Eskimo than in the white man but also that there is a more precipitous drop in the white man to low levels immediately following exposure to cold. This indicates a greater ability on the part of the Eskimo to maintain hand blood flow for short periods of exposure.

Abramson, Zazeela and Marrus in comparing hand blood flow measurements at 32° and 45°C. observed that average hand blood flows showed less difference between subjects at 45° than at 32°C. In addition they found that spontaneous changes in the base line usually observed at 32°C. were practically absent at 45°C. They concluded from these observations that minimal fluctuation occurs in hand blood flow at 45°C. We have found, however, in every individual of both groups studied that the frequency and magnitude of fluctuation in successive observations of blood flow was maximal at 42.5° to 45°C. A similar increase in the frequency and magnitude of fluctuations in forearm blood flow at high bath temperatures has been reported by Barcroft and Edholm, and also noted by ourselves.

We have not been able to find any published data concerning the length of time required for the hand blood flow to equilibrate at various water-bath temperatures. The length of time allowed by different workers for the hand blood flow to adjust to a water-bath has varied from 15 minutes to 120 minutes. In all baths between 5° to 35°C., the hand blood flow of the control group subjects reached a steady state within 10 minutes following immersion whereas 30 to 50 minutes were required at the 38° to 45°C. range. The hand blood flow of the Eskimo was slower in equilibrating in the cold and very warm baths.

The vasodilatation which occurs in the skin in response to extreme local cooling was attributed by Lewis to a local axon reflex. Increased blood flow in response to extreme local cooling has been demonstrated plethysmographically in the fingers and in the hand. The failure of additional and distant noxious stimuli to alter the response in our experiments suggests a local mechanism for this vasodilatation, but tbe observation of Spealman that the volume of hand blood flow was influenced by the general thermal condition of the body even in extremely cold baths, is against this being the only mechanism. Our studies are in accordance with Spealman's observation. We feel that this reaction although it has a local and perhaps chemical basis, as suggested by Lewis, is also influenced by the thermal condition of the body.

It has often been remarked that the Eskimos are better able to work with their bare hands in the cold than are white men. There are certainly many factors concerned in this and perhaps not the least is a remarkable tolerance of discomfort on their part. It seems to us, however, that the increased hand blood flow which we have demonstrated has importance in this regard, and this increased blood flow with the increase in hand temperature may explain the relatively enhanced kinaesthetic sensibility and ability to perform fine movements which have been demonstrated by Mackworth in persons chronically exposed to the cold. Hunter and Whillans have shown that in the cat, exposure of the knee joint to low ambient temperatures is associated with an important increase in the force required to start movement at the joint, and suggested that an increase in the viscosity of synovial fluid and decrease in the flexibility of the joint capsule and tendons are factors which may be responsible. Increased blood flow and temperature would diminish the degree of these changes. There may be other factors such as the difference in the composition of adipose tissue which play a part.

SUMMARY

A comparative study on hand blood flow and temperature has been carried out on Eskimos in the Canadian Eastern Arctic and on medical students living in a temperate climate. One of the effects of chronic exposure of the individual to cold is a reduction in the ambient temperature required for comfort. At this low ambient temperature, the hand blood flow of the Eskimo is twice that of the white man and the skin temperature of his hand is greater. The volume of the hand blood flow of the Eskimo changes more slowly in response to local cold. The degree of spontaneous fluctuation in hand blood flow is greater in the Eskimo and increases in both groups as the local temperature of the hand increases. The alterations which occur in the hand blood flow following chronic exposure to cold would appear to enhance hand function in the cold.

Summary

The scientific analysis of Neanderthal and their culture began in France where the highest concentration of Neanderthal sites is found. Combe Grenal, one cave site excavated by François Bordes, has yielded cultural artifacts—postholes, burial sites and thousands upon thousands of stone tools—covering a period of 85,000 years.

The analysis of some 19,000 Neanderthal tools uncovered at Combe Grenal was based on a statistical approach employing an objective description and classification of each tool. Bordes found that each layer contained different proportions of tools, that is, different tool kits of which there were four basic types. The absence of a regular sequence of development led Bordes to conclude that the four tool kits formed no evolutionary sequence but belonged to coexisting cultural traditions.

An alternative interpretation of the variation in tool kits found at Combe Grenal is that they resulted from different prehistoric activities—hunting, gathering, food preparation, tool making among others—not different cultures. Lewis and Sally Binford, two American archeologists, using computers to carry out a factor analysis of the artifacts, identified fourteen functional tool kits which they believe were used in different combinations at different times in the cave. Despite discrepancies and continued differences of interpretation, the approaches both of Bordes and of Binford and Binford suggest the value of statistics and computers in archeology.

Additional inferences into the lifeways of Neanderthal have come from other sources— the study of present day hunting and gathering societies, the analysis of wear patterns on tools, and the reproduction of prehistoric tool technologies.

Glossary

Denticulate tools   Tools having several notches in a row, usually three or four, forming a set of teeth looking much like saw blades.

Factor analysis   A statistical method of analyzing variations in the degree of association between each item in a sample and all other items in the sample to isolate regularly covariant subgroups.

Microwear analysis   The analysis of prehistoric stone tool wear patterns carried out to determine the function of the tools.

Quina scrapers   Large, quite thick tools, delicately chipped along their curved working edges to produce overlapping 'fish scale' appearance.

Additional Reading

Binford, Sally R. and Lewis R. Binford

1968   New Perspectives in Archeology. Chicago: Aldine.

The classic work on the "new" archeology. Binford and Binford cover the method and theory of archeology as well as specific sites.

Bordes, François

1972   A Tale of Two Caves. New York: Harper and Row.

Bordes' excellent examination of migration patterns of different prehistoric populations based on archeologicial excavations.

McKern, Sharon S. and Thomas W. McKern

1972   Living Prehistory: An introduction to Physical Anthropology and Archaeology. Cummings Publishing Co, California.

A good overall perspective of human prehistory from both the physical and archaeological point of view.

chapter ten

*A brain weight of nine hundred grams is
adequate as an optimum for human behavior.
Anything more is employed in the
commission of misdeeds.*
EARNEST HOOTON

FROM NEANDERTHAL TO CRO-MAGNON

One summer evening several years ago François Bordes played a recording for John Pfeiffer in an old farmhouse not far from Combe Grenal, his home during the excavating season. He called the recording "The Song of the Neanderthals." It was a New Caledonian war chant sung loud and deep and half-shouted to the beating of drums, sung with feeling but strangely without pattern. There was no sustained rhythm, only occasional and random intervals of rhythm which came like interruptions. For a few moments the chanters sang in unison and their voices and the drumbeating seemed to gain in power and purpose, and then the rhythm broke again.

The song, with its flashes of harmony and style, symbolizes the situation of the Neanderthals before they and their works vanished from the archeological record 35,000 to 40,000 years ago. Something new was stirring, another series of changes whose nature investigators are still trying to figure out. But whatever the changes were, they resulted in the shaping of a new breed of human, closely related to the Neanderthals, but nevertheless quite different.

Fossil evidence for the transition is sparse in Europe, but exists at a number of sites in the Near East. For example, there is a cave in Israel, on the slopes of Mount Carmel overlooking the Mediterranean near Haifa, where excavators have found the skeleton of a short, stocky individual with heavy limbs and bony brow ridges, definitely a Neanderthal but not the kind that was living in Western Europe. The brow ridges were less massive, the skull somewhat more rounded. Furthermore, near the cave is a rock shelter which served as a cemetery for people who lived in the region several thousand years later, and who were even closer to modern humans. The ten skeletons recovered there had longer and straighter limbs than the Neanderthals, more prominent chins, and smaller faces.

THE NEAR EAST

Why did such changes occur at that particular time, 40,000 to 50,000 years ago, and why in the Near East? A basic reason, then as throughout the course of human evolution, probably had something to do with obtaining food. The Neanderthals of the Near East were never adapted to extreme cold as were those of glacial Europe. Probably, the early development of herd animals on the growing tundra stimulated cultural and physical changes. Evidence of a concentration on hunting herd animals predates this period, but there are signs of a new, more intensive, continuous and highly organized exploitation of big game.

The general practice during Neanderthal times seems to have been the killing of single animals by single bands, the killing of one animal at a time. The idea was to stalk a herd and go after a particular individual, often an individual weakened by injury or disease or advanced age. To kill herd animals more efficiently, *Homo sapiens* became a herd animal in a new sense. With all the space in the world to live in, he formed more densely settled communities. He invented crowds to become a better predator and a more organized gatherer of the plant food staples.

Conditions were ripe for such developments

in the Near East. More specifically, conditions were ripe within a particular region which includes the cave on Mount Carmel as well as a number of other sites. The full-scale hunting of big game may have originated in lands along the coastline of what is now Israel, Lebanon and Syria—in the corridor formed by the Mediterranean to the west, and to the east by the Lebanon Mountains and other ranges running parallel to the coast and walling the corridor off from the Syrian and Arabian deserts. This is the central idea of a study by Sally Binford, a synthesis of information from many sources, which suggests a new "model" or hypothesis to explain why the Near Eastern corridor became an evolutionary focal area.

Many factors helped bring large groups of people together in this area. Wild cattle, fallow deer and other herd animals grazed in green wooded valleys which rose from the coastal plains and extended into the foothills of the mountains. When leaves and grasses became scarce they moved on, in the spring to pasturelands on the plains and in the fall to highland meadows tucked away in the foothills. Small bands of hunters naturally concentrated where the game was, in the valleys and the narrowest places along seasonal migration routes, and a number of further circumstances encouraged increasing cooperation among them.

For one thing, pollen analysis and other studies indicate that a shift to somewhat drier climates occurred about 40,000 to 45,000 years ago, and that probably helped step up the pace of evolution. It may have intensified the search for food among humans and animals. Herds became larger and their movements through the valleys became more and more mass movements. For the hunters, risks increased as well as opportunities. A single band could go after wild cattle, for example. But it was a dangerous business, more suitable for a number of cooperating bands. These extinct animals should not be pictured as the docile cudchewers of today's farmyards. They were fierce, fast on their feet, big (some of the bulls measuring six and a half feet high at the shoulder), and quite capable of fighting back.

Certain basic observations support the notion that major changes were under way in the Mediterranean corridor. The richest and deepest sites have been found where vegetation and game were most abundant, in the valleys on the western slopes of the coastal ranges. The Mount Carmel cave and rock shelter lie in such a valley, and so do other important sites. For example, farther inland, about fifty miles from Haifa and located not far from Nazareth at the narrowest part of a pass to the mountains of Lebanon, is the enormous Qafzeh Cave where the remains of at least seven individuals were found more than thirty years ago, transitional people resembling those found at the Mount Carmel shelter.

Western valley sites have deposits up to about seventy-five feet deep. There are layers containing Neanderthal tool kits and, in most cases, layers above them containing later tool kits which include high proportions of blades, tool kits characteristic of modern-type people and representing long periods of occupation. There are also signs that wild cattle were hunted intensively. At two sites, the Mount Carmel shelter and a shelter located in a bluff north of Beirut in Lebanon, quantities of cattle bones increase sharply in late Neanderthal levels. One level at the Lebanese shelter contains the bones of only about a dozen individual animals, while the level immediately above it contains more than 500 individuals. These and other observations make a good case for the evolution of a modern-type human in the Near East.

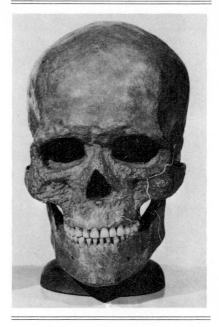

A reconstructed skull of Cro-Magnon man.

CRO-MAGNON

People like ourselves were first recognized at the famous Cro-Magnon shelter located in the limestone cliffs of Les Eyzies. In 1868 workers building a railroad through the Vézère Valley discovered five skeletons deep in the rock at the back of the shelter, the remains of individuals with small faces, high foreheads, protruding chins and other physical features typical of today's populations.

According to the migration theory, one of two theories used to explain the appearance of modern humans in Europe, Cro-Magnon humans came from the Near East and appeared in Europe more than 35,000 years ago during a period of relatively mild, moist climates. They brought a new way of life with them. The change can be observed in their artifacts, among other things. They developed a special technique to obtain the blades or long slender flakes out of which most of the tools were made. The first step was to prepare a roughly cylindrical flint core or nucleus perhaps four to six inches long, rest a bone or antler punch on the

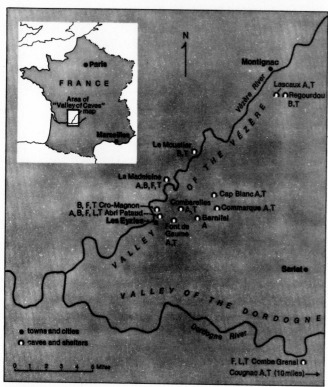

"VALLEY OF CAVES"

Homo sapiens Sites, in Les Eyzies Region, France

Things Found:

A art	L living floors	F fire
B bones of primates	T tools	

worked by earlier methods. Incidentally, full-scale cooperative hunting probably favored the development of this technique, stressing the need for cutting tools which could be manufactured rapidly and in large quantities.

New tools and new varieties of old tools were developed during the period from about 35,000 to 13,000 years ago—large selections of burins to make differently shaped grooves and slots, composite tools consisting of several barbs or other flint elements set into grooved hafts, spear throwers, harpoons, lamps, and so on. The first man-made material was invented, clay mixed with powdered bone as a binder and molded into female figurines and other items. People engaged in such specialized activities as reindeer hunting and mammoth hunting and fishing.

Cro-Magnons brought with them social structures which may have evolved earlier during the course of big-game hunts in valleys of the Near East. They still had bands consisting of several families, from about thirty to as many as a hundred intermarrying persons. But the band was on the way out. We had taken the first major steps toward the full-fledged *tribe*, an association of many bands held together not only by marriage but also by shared traditions and shared problems, including large-scale cooperative hunting and perhaps warfare. We developed rituals and art for coming together and remaining together, accentuating traditions that may have arisen in the remote past, incest taboos and kinship rules which created more intricate and cohesive relationships among larger numbers of individuals.

The Neanderthals of Western Europe had no chance against these people and these institutions. In any competition for the best living places and hunting grounds, and competitions must have occurred on many occasions, they came out second best. Bordes reports signs of cultural decline in some of the upper layers at Combe Grenal, fewer tools made crudely out of

top of the core near the edge, and then strike the punch sharply with a hammerstone. The blow chipped a narrow sliver off the side of the core, and many more slivers were detached by successive blows along the edge in an inward-spiraling path. This "peeling" operation was very efficient. A single flint core weighing some two pounds could yield forty to fifty good blades for an estimated total of up to seventy-five feet of cutting edge, while only six feet would have resulted if the same core had been

The punched blade technique, using a bone punch, as it was probably practiced by the Cro-Magnons.

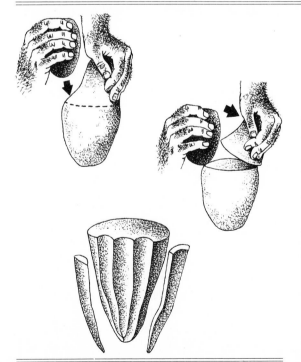

poorly prepared flint nodules, and the end seems to have come with dramatic abruptness at certain sites where layers containing Cro-Magnon tools lie directly above Neanderthal layers.

Impressed by such evidence, a number of investigators have suggested that the Neanderthals were wiped out in a relatively short time, almost as if by plan. It is doubtful that the capacity for systematic mass extermination evolved so early, however, and other evidence suggests a more gradual and complicated process. Conflicts and catastrophes probably took place here and there. Some of the new people may have regarded their less advanced contemporaries as some early American settlers regarded the Indians, as creatures so brutish and inferior that they could be hunted and killed for the fun of it. Nonetheless, this theory is no longer taken seriously.

But things happened somewhat more gradually in other places. One cave in the Les Eyzies area includes a layer that is probably Neanderthal but contains a tool kit with a relatively high proportion of knives, some of them made on long narrow flakes in a manner closely resembling later techniques developed to an advanced stage by Cro-Magnon flint workers. As a matter of fact, the resemblance is so close that at one time the layer was believed to represent a Cro-Magnon rather than a Neanderthal occupation. Perhaps Neanderthal, having already experimented with new toolmaking techniques, learned quickly from the newcomers and joined their tribes in certain localities and eventually became assimilated. All of us probably have some Neanderthal genes. In still other places Neanderthal bands may have retreated and hidden themselves in a last effort to endure. Pockets of Neanderthals may have survived for centuries before the breed died out.

This is the story of what happened, according to the migration theory. Investigators who do not go along with the theory agree that Neanderthal was replaced by Cro-Magnon, but they doubt that Cro-Magnon came from the Near East. Their argument rests on the notion of independent origins, the notion that evolution can proceed along parallel lines in different parts of the world. The transition from Neanderthal to a modern-type human took place in the Near East, to be sure, but not only in the Near East. It may also have taken place in a number of other places during the same general period.

Among other places, it might have happened in Europe. For example, consider the Les Eyzies cave containing the layer made up of Neanderthal as well as Cro-Magnon tools. That can be interpreted as indicating that the Neanderthals learned from and joined the visitors from the Near East. It can also be interpreted as a sign that the Neanderthals were developing on their own, and that in the process of developing they evolved into modern-type humans. Judging by similar evidence, as well as studies of fossil remains, some investigators believe that the same development probably occurred some 4,000 miles away in South Africa.

There are hints that the transition may have occurred independently in the Far East. A mixed tool kit has also been found at the Chinese site mentioned in the last chapter, the one near the Great Wall. The site includes a high proportion of denticulates and other typical Neanderthal tools—but nearly a third of the tools are the sort found predominantly in Cro-Magnon sites. It is clearly a transitional type of tool kit, and may have been used by a transitional type of human.

We do not know enough to choose between the two theories. The migration theory finds strong support in the fact that as far as the fossil record is concerned, the best evidence for people in transition comes from the Near East. Certainly the change might also have taken place elsewhere, but in general, direct fossil evidence is limited. Furthermore, the notion of independent origins sometimes seems to lean too heavily on coincidence, on accepting that people in different places can make the same sort of tools without communicating with one another. On the other hand, considering that people are far more alike than they are different and that they faced very similar problems in the prehistoric past, it should hardly be surprising that they generally arrived at very similar solutions.

In any case, the Neanderthals were definitely on the way out. They had learned to cope with glacial conditions, but from about 35,000 years ago on, all the action, all the new ideas and new inventions would be the work of modern humans. For the next 25,000 years or so we know them best from the record they left in France,

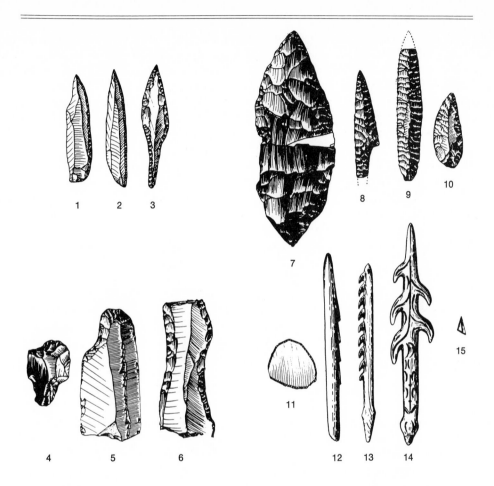

PERIGORDIAN: more than
35,000 to 23,000 years ago

1, 2, 3. typical Perigordian
points

AURIGNACIAN: about 35,000 to
20,000 years ago

4. nosed scraper
5. nosed scraper

6. blade

SOLUTREAN: About 20,000 to
17,000 years ago

7. laurel leaf
8. shouldered point
9. willow leaf
10. unifacial point (worked on
one side only)

MAGDALENIAN: 17,000 to
12,000 years ago

11. scraper
12, 13. harpoon with single
row of barbs
14. harpoon with double row
of barbs
15. triangle

*Major tool kits of modern-type
prehistoric humans in Europe.*

especially in the Les Eyzies area. The record includes four major types of tool kit dated by a
method which, like the potassium-argon clock,
depends on the steady rate of decay of a
radioactive element, in this case a radioactive

form of carbon known as *carbon 14*. The
technique involves chemical analyses of charcoal samples, working best for material less
than 40,000 years old. It has provided the following approximate durations for the following

tool kits which are generally believed to reflect cultural differences and new levels of cultural development:

Perigordian, named after the region which includes Les Eyzies. More than 35,000 to about 23,000 years ago.

Aurignacian, named after the Aurignac site in the Pyrenees. About 35,000 to 20,000 years ago.

Solutrean, named after the extensive open-air site near the village of Solutré in east central France. 20,000 to about 17,000 years ago.

Magdalenian, named after the La Madeleine shelter about three miles from Les Eyzies. 17,000 to 12,000 years ago.

THE PERIGORDIANS

Recent investigations emphasize the complexity that lies behind this deceptively straightforward sequence. An interesting early Perigordian occupation layer has been found in a cave in the village of Arcy-sur-Cure about a hundred miles southeast of Paris, one of the few caves which happens to have been discovered by design rather than by accident. About twenty years ago, André Leroi-Gourhan of the University of Paris was surveying the village for prehistoric camping places and noticed, high on a hillside, a little shelter formed by a peculiarly curved section of rock.

He suspected that the shelter might be the top of a buried cave, a possibility reinforced by two further clues. Badgers in the area are good cave locaters. They seem to sense the location of hidden chambers that will make cozy nests, and, sure enough, there was a badger hole in the hillside with some flint tools in it. Also, a large oak tree was growing in the rich loosened soil near the foot of the hill, another local mark of caved-in places. The first season of digging revealed a thick layer of red earth rich in pre-historic remains, and excavating has been going on at the site, off and on, ever since.

The layer, which lies above Neanderthal layers, contains an early Perigordian tool kit, including characteristic knives with a curved back blunted by the removal of tiny parallel flakes as well as denticulates and other tools commonly found in Neanderthal deposits. A tentlike structure apparently existed inside the cave entrance. There are a dozen postholes arranged in a semicircle around several hearths; the posts were probably mammoth tusks. One of the holes contained an intact tusk with a piece of limestone wedged against it for support. Leroi-Gourhan estimates that a family unit of no more than fifteen persons lived here about 32,000 years ago.

Indications of how their descendants lived some 10,000 years later come from a site just off the main street of Les Eyzies, the Abri Pataud. (*Abri* is French for "shelter" and Pataud is the family name of the farmers who owned the site in the nineteenth century.) The site lies directly against the limestone cliff that dominates the town, a few minutes' walk from a hotel built into the old Cro-Magnon shelter. It has been excavated by Hallam Movius of Harvard University. Bedrock was reached at a depth of more than thirty feet after six seasons of digging which uncovered fourteen occupation layers. In all, more than 50,000 worked pieces of flint have been cataloged.

The third layer from the top contains a tool kit typical of those generally found at more recent sites representing the last stages of the culture, the evolved or final Perigordian of about 23,000 years ago. Its outstanding feature is a row of hearths more than thirty feet long under the rocky overhang of the shelter. Lying around the hearths are smooth river pebbles, most of them broken and colored red or black by the action of heat. These stones were very probably "pot boilers" that had been heated in a fire and then dropped into water to bring it to a

Hallam Movius, Jr.
(1907-   )
an active member of the faculty at Harvard University since 1930, has carried out archeological excavations in Czechoslovakia, Palestine, Ireland, Burma, Java, and most recently, in France. Movius is best known for his theory on the distribution of Oldowan and Acheulian tools in the Old World from 700,000 to 75,000 years ago. While he has been criticized for drawing conclusions on the basis of relatively little evidence, Movius is one of the few archeologists to speculate on worldwide patterns of Homo erectus prehistory. In recent years, he has devoted his energies to the excavation of Abri Pataud, the Cro-Magnon shelter in Les Eyzies, France.

boil for cooking. American Indians used the technique not long ago, and Basque shepherds in the Cantabrian Mountains of northern Spain still use it occasionally to boil milk and water.

The row of hearths is only part of a large complex. In front of the row and also roughly parallel to the rear of the shelter is a row of large limestone blocks, some weighing half a ton or more. They form a solid barrier, except for a gap at one end which may have served as the "doorway" into a long house built for a community of several families. The entire arrangement as well as the tool assemblage found with it suggests that the people who lived here, huddled around their fires during glacial winters, organized themselves into larger groups and engaged in a wider variety of activities than the Perigordians of earlier times.

THE AURIGNACIANS

The Aurignacian tradition is quite distinct from the Perigordian. It includes the first known cave art. There are also special kinds of scrapers and burins, and a variety of elaborate bone tools such as points with split bases for firm hafting, presumably at the ends of spear or javelin shafts. Apparently the Aurignacians came from some area outside Western Europe, and they came with an established way of life, generally involving large all-year-round camps with a number of "satellite" sites nearby for special activities.

The nine deepest Abri Pataud layers, ending at bedrock and covering a period of about 4,000 to 5,000 years, contain Aurignacian tool kits. Signs of change during that period include sharp reductions in the proportions of some bone and flint tools and the appearance of new types, notably new bone points.

Movius found an unusual pattern in one of the early Aurignacian layers, a complex made up of two shallow pits and seven hearths. The

Model of the Aurignacian "pseudomorph" on exhibit at the Smithsonian Institution.

Another noteworthy site is the Morin Cave in northern Spain, which was probably occupied on and off over a span of some 50,000 years and includes, besides the Neanderthal layers mentioned in the preceding chapter, a number of Aurignacian living floors. One of them is of special interest since it has yielded evidence of intensive occupation and a unique burial complex. Freeman's reconstruction of the past begins about 30,000 years ago when a family of about half a dozen members moved in, cleared off and leveled the floor, and proceeded to make themselves at home for ten to twenty-five years.

They dug a roughly rectangular depression about fifteen feet from the cave mouth, built stone walls, and set up a row of posts to support a windbreak or roof. Five postholes were detected because the soil filling them was softer and darker than the surrounding soil, and finer in texture. Also, in two cases the dark circular area included a still darker central area, suggesting that a post had rotted away and been replaced. Careful excavating even uncovered marks made by a digging stick when the posts were being replaced, curved grooves whose shape and location indicate that they were made by a right-handed person kneeling as he dug. The result of this construction was a shelter within a shelter, a semisubterranean hut inside the cave.

The most striking find came from a deeper part of the cave. More than forty feet from the entrance were two burial mounds, and one of them contained a remarkable object—a kind of natural earth-model, a rounded three-dimensional mold of a person and associated grave goods. What had happened over the years was that as the body decomposed, the soft parts were replaced by fine sediments which filled the cavities and ultimately produced a replica of the body, a so-called pseudomorph.

A study of the mold reveals that the buried person was more than six feet tall, and had

pits are located near the front of the shelter, measure four to five feet across, and served some purpose which is still obscure. One possibility is that they may represent the floors of small conical huts made of hides supported by a central pole, something like American Indian tepees.

A Solutrean "laurel-leaf" blade.

the Aurignacian pseudomorph is on exhibit at the Smithsonian Institution in Washington.

The very coexistence of the Perigordians and Aurignacians in France raises some questions that cannot be answered at present. They apparently hunted in the same regions under the same conditions during the same general period, living as contemporaries for thousands of years. Yet they seem not to have influenced one another appreciably, a surprising state of affairs considering the human capacity for minding one's neighbor's business.

A clue may be found in their ways of life. Denise Bordes, who has specialized in studies of the prehistoric cultures of modern *Homo sapiens,* points out that as a rule the Perigordians are represented by relatively thin layers which suggest brief or intermittent occupations. Also, their sites are generally scattered throughout the Les Eyzies region and located in different kinds of terrain. The Aurignacians, on the other hand, tended to concentrate in narrow valleys or against cliff walls which contain clusters of neighboring shelters. Their layers are usually on the thick side, implying more people or longer occupations or both. The difference in the location of Perigordian and Aurignacian sites can also be interpreted as evidence of functional, not cultural variation.

THE SOLUTREANS

been decapitated and laid on his side with arms flexed in front of his face. The mold also shows traces of what may be thongs or rope used to bind the arms, as well as another pseudomorph representing a small animal, perhaps a kid or deer, which had been placed over the dead person's head. Freeman spent more than a month digging in this area and preparing the earth around the burial so that it could be removed, with the aid of winches and a home-built railroad, as a solid two-ton clay block. A model of

The Solutrean tradition, which appeared about 20,000 years ago with the passing of the Perigordian and Aurignacian, arose during a period of intense cold. In fact, conditions were probably colder then than at any previous time during the past million years or more. People living in southern France had to contend with severe climates, with winters which may have lasted nine months and brought average temperatures as low as 10 degrees Fahrenheit below zero.

Philip Smith of the University of Montreal, who has made the most recent extensive study of the Solutreans, suggests that they may have originated in the southeast corner of France—in the lower valley of the Rhone River, not far from the edges of the Alpine glaciers. Occupation layers at a number of sites in this region include tools closely resembling those found in early Solutrean tool kits. The same layers also include Neanderthal tools such as thick Quina-type scrapers which, as far as we know, had disappeared from Europe and from the rest of the Old World some ten thousand years before.

The possibility exists that the ancestors of the Solutreans were Neanderthals living past their time in a kind of "lost world" environment, people who had learned Neanderthal toolmaking techniques, or perhaps people who were doing the same things Neanderthals did. The discovery of skeletal remains in precisely dated deposits might help confirm this possibility. But the terrain would certainly have made a good retreat. The lower Rhone valley is a rugged mountainous land, a backwater with caves and shelters located in remote canyons and ravines. In such a region people might not only have preserved old toolmaking traditions but also have developed unusual techniques.

The Solutreans did not endure for long, only about two or three thousand years. But during that relatively brief span they introduced significant changes, and some of the changes may be inferred from the nature of their flintworking. Along with scrapers and burins and quantities of other ordinary items, their tool kits included some of the most beautifully shaped tools ever made. To cite only one example, they produced so-called *laurel leaf blades,* slender symmetrical pieces flat and tapering to a point, and produced dozens of different kinds, long blades and short blades, thin and thick ones, all variations on the same basic theme. Some sites contained so many laurel leaves and other finely shaped tools that they may have been

Stone arrowhead of a type which may have been used by Solutrean hunters.

special workshops organized for a flourishing export trade.

Many laurel leaves are far too delicate for any practical purpose. The longest one known to date was found in 1873, part of a cache of blades uncovered at a site near the Loire River in southeastern France. It was nearly fourteen inches long, about four inches across at its widest point, and only about a quarter of an inch thick. The blade could never have been applied with any force. It would have snapped in two if someone had tried to cut meat with it or use it as a spear point.

Tools like this one represent a new stage in the development of abstract thinking. Hunters had spent extra time producing finely worked hand axes and other implements long before, 200,000 or more years before, but not with such skill and in such large quantities. As far as the archeological record reveals, the Solutreans were the first people to engage on a regular basis in the making of tools to serve as symbols. They doubtless used the tools for some special function, perhaps in rituals or simply as showpieces, a form of art for art's sake.

The Solutreans introduced other advances. They probably had—and may have invented—the bow and arrow. Not long ago Eduardo Ripoll-Perello of Barcelona University dug in a cave in the mountains of southeast Spain, the Cueva de Ambrosio, and found an assortment of points closely resembling arrowheads found by the thousands at American Indian sites. Indeed, if the same points had been uncovered at one of these sites, they would have been identified without question as arrowheads. Similar points have been found in other Spanish caves, and they provide the earliest indirect evidence for the invention of the bow and arrow. (The earliest direct evidence, from a 10,000-year-old open site in Denmark, consists of two arrow shafts preserved in waterlogged deposits with tanged arrowheads still in place.)

Smith notes that the Solutreans usually lived near streams in foothill country. They may have preferred to do their big-game hunting along trails which avoided mountain regions as well as soggy lowland terrain, in relatively dry country which was sufficiently open to permit the easy spotting and pursuit of large animals, and yet contained enough trees and brush for fuel and cover. They vanished abruptly, "like the puffing-out of a candle flame," according to one investigator. There are many problems awaiting further research, research involving the use of modern techniques at certain well-known but not well-excavated sites (notably at the rich type site of Solutré).

THE MAGDALENIANS

At this point the stage was set for perhaps the most spectacular development of the period, the rise and rapid expansion of the Magdalenian tradition. Part of the record has been found at the site for which the tradition was named. It lies on the banks of the Vézère River,

An artist's conception of camouflaged Magdalenian hunters stalking a herd of reindeer.

The great wooly mammoth (now extinct) which was an important food source for the Magdalenians.

in the hollow of a massive limestone-cliff overhang.

The setting is remote now, hidden in the trees on a hairpin loop of the river with water rushing past and meadows nearby. But things hummed here during prehistoric times, perhaps 13,000 to 14,000 years ago. This was predominantly reindeer country, and there were also herds of bison and wild horses in the valley and salmon in the rapids of the river. Collections from this site feature tools made of bone and antler and ivory and often decorated with engravings of reindeer, horses, bison, mammoths, abstract spiral designs, fish and stylized fish motifs, and, more rarely, crude human figures.

Magdalenian tool kits include shaft straighteners, spear points, "wands" of unknown purpose and, above all, the first harpoons—a rich variety of harpoons, long and short, with single and double rows of differently shaped barbs. There are also bone needles, first seen in Solutrean deposits but now developed and used in quantity, generally containing eyes which must have required piercing with tiny flint awls. The needles imply the wearing on a large scale of fitted clothing made of hides sewn together, presumably with sinews.

Another prominent item is the *spear thrower,* a device designed essentially to amplify muscle power and still used today by the Australian aborigines. In its contemporary form it consists of a thin flat piece of wood about two or three feet long with a barb at one end that hooks into a hole in the end of a spear shaft. Held over the shoulder with shaft in place, the thrower is snapped forward by a sharp twist of the wrist in a motion that propels the spear several times faster and farther than would be possible with the unaided hand. Prehistoric hunters probably also had wooden spear throwers, although the only surviving specimens are made of antler or ivory. These devices disappear toward the end of Magdalenian times in France, perhaps because bows and arrows were beginning to be used on a widespread basis.

Excavations have been resumed at the La Madeleine shelter after years of archeological inactivity. Jean-Marc Bouvier, one of Bordes' associates, has found large numbers of artifacts including narrow little blades which are less than half an inch long and were made as cutting elements to be hafted in composite tools. His main objective is to obtain a clearer picture of the origin and evolution of the toolmakers, and so far he has dug to a depth of more than twelve feet and identified several Magdalenian layers representing different stages of development.

The shelter itself is only part of a larger living complex. It marks the first in a line of prehistoric "row houses," occupied shelters strung out side by side for several hundred feet along the cliff. About twenty miles farther downstream along a two-mile stretch of the Dordogne River is another row of shelters which housed an estimated 400 to 600 persons. This sort of housing pattern is often associated with the Magdalenians, particularly during their later stages. They tended to establish large concentrated settlements along low-lying river banks.

Such settlements were not confined to shelters and cliff edges. Rich and thick occupation layers, as yet unexcavated, extend out to the Vézère River at La Madeleine, and it seems that the people lived and worked in the open here and elsewhere, perhaps using the shelters only in the worst weather. As archeologists became more and more aware of this tendency, they began paying serious attention to reports of extensive open-air sites in areas containing no caves or shelters. Flints kept turning up during the plowing season on highland farms on the plateaus above the cliffs.

Most digging has been done in caves and shelters, which contained deep protected deposits with many occupation layers and offered the opportunity to go far back in time and reconstruct cultural changes. Current interest in sites on the open plains is in line with the renewed emphasis on wide excavations and the search for evidence of what people did, their full range of activities.

For example, extensive traces of the hunters and their prey have been uncovered along the Don River in the southwestern Soviet Union. A cluster of rich sites is located near Kostenki, Russian for "bone village," where mammoth fossils were found in medieval times and regarded as the remains of half-human giants who lived in underground caverns. This area includes a row of eight hearths in which bone was burned, almost certainly because wood was scarce on the plains; the hearths may have been located inside a long house with a gabled wooden roof and clay-supported walls. Similar settlements have also been found in open stretches near the Ural and Caucasus Mountains, in Czechoslovakia, and in northern Germany.

Another interesting site known as Pincevent is a 25-acre Magdalenian settlement about thirty-five miles southeast of Paris, not far from the palace of Fontainebleau. After more than three years and 300,000 man-hours of digging, Leroi-Gourhan and his associates uncovered about five acres of what seems to have been a summer-fall camp for reindeer hunting. One of half a dozen living floors consists of three hearths and three sleeping areas, all of which may have been enclosed by a large tent made of skins. The entire site is in a remarkable state of preservation, and includes considerable pollen and animal remains as well as hearths.

THE FIRST ART MOVEMENT

The post-Neanderthal period, from Aurignacian to Magdalenian times, produced the world's first great art "movement" as well as the most advanced technology. Some of its most spectacular products are found in underground galleries, away from natural light in the passages and chambers and niches of limestone caves, and indicate in a most vivid fashion how completely hunting dominated the attention and imagination of prehistoric *Homo sapiens*. We rarely drew people, and never anything that would be recognized as a landscape, although there are a wide variety of signs which have no obvious meaning to us. Our overwhelming concern was with game animals seen as individuals, clearly defined and detached, and isolated from their natural settings.

The great majority of art caves are located in France and Spain. According to one count, France has sixty-five sites and Spain thirty. About half of all known sites are concentrated in three regions: along a ninety-mile stretch of the northern coast of Spain, in the French Pyrenees fifty miles south of Toulouse, and in the countryside around Les Eyzies.

Controversy

André Leroi-Gourhan: The Interpretation of Cave Art

Anthropologists have argued over the interpretation of Paleolithic cave art since its discovery. Assuming Paleolithic people to be too "primitive" for religious expression, early 19th century archeologists considered the pictures which adorned the ancient cave walls merely decorative. As cultural anthropologists began to report on the totemism of Australian aborigines, cave art was reinterpreted as being functional in rituals of sympathetic magic. Employing ethnographic parallels, anthropologists proposed that we depicted animals in order to gain control over or increase the numbers of prey. Geometric forms were interpreted as symbolizing the same ideas as they do in contemporary primitive cultures.

The classical interpretation of Paleolithic cave art remained essentially unquestioned until challenged by André Leroi-Gourhan. Leroi-Gourhan objected to the application of ethnographic parallels to a few, supposedly representative, examples of cave art. In his own research he examined over 65 caves, conducting an extensive analysis of Paleolithic art in its natural context with reference to nothing but the art itself. Starting with different methodological and interpretive assumptions, he arrived at conclusions radically different from those of previous theorists.

Dividing each cave into seven regions, Leroi-Gourhan observed distinctive patterns in the distribution of animal figures and geometric signs. Horses and bison, for example—species which accounted for well over half the animals represented—were usually found in large chambers and passages while such carnivores as lions and bears tended to appear only in isolated cave recesses. He further observed that bison and bison-associated animals were found almost exclusively in the central part of decorated walls in large galleries. The bison were represented along with horses and horse-associated animals. His study of these patterns led Leroi-Gourhan to consider that the horse and bison groups represented two distinct themes.

Unlike theorists before him, Leroi-Gourhan believed that panels with multiple figures were meant to suggest scenes and that the superpositioning of figures in these scenes was intended by the artists to express meaningful associations. Furthermore, Leroi-Gourhan interpreted the pictured animals not in terms of food or danger, but as sexual symbols. He proposed that the bison and horse groups represent the female and male principles, respectively, and that the lines, dots, ovals, and triangles traditionally interpreted as weapons, traps, and huts were actually associated with one or the other of the sexual groupings. Leroi-Gourhan viewed the cave as an organized sanctuary systematically decorated to express a world-view based on the association and opposition of male and female principles.

As intriguing as this theory may be, there are many flaws in Leroi-Gourhan's approach. Most caves do not lend themselves to a rigid analysis. In many cases, entrances may have changed since Paleolithic times. Moreover, it is not always clear where one picture ends and another begins. Leroi-Gourhan based his thematic associations on physical proximity, but he provided no clear guidelines for establishing the intentional grouping of figures and signs.

Leroi-Gourhan showed surprisingly little concern with size, color, position, or even number of represented animals. Although he carefully counted the panels in which each species appeared, he put no emphasis on the number of individuals pictured. Is one horse and one bison as significant an association as one horse and a dozen bison? In defining his thematic groups, Leroi-Gourhan attached little meaning to the relative size, position, and prominence of figures.

Do bison and horses represent thematic groups, or were they simply the two species most commonly observed in large herds? If, as Leroi-Gourhan suggested, the geometric stylization of human genitalia is a result of Paleolithic prudery, why are some human and animal figures pictured with sex organs? And why would bison, which are clearly represented as male or female, be used to represent the female principle exclusively?

Leroi-Gourhan assumed that superpositioning always implies intentional grouping either by contemporary artists or by subsequent generations. Studies of superpositioning in African and Australian art suggest a less consistent motivation. It is true that superpositioning is often used to express the association of images, but it may also reflect nothing more than a later artist's expression of disinterest in an earlier artist's work. Leroi-Gourhan's off-handed dismissal of ethnographic parallels prevented him from considering this possibility.

There is still much to be learned about the meaning of Paleolithic art. Leroi-Gourhan has contributed enormously to the scientific analysis of cave art, but it is difficult to accept all his conclusions at this point. Perhaps some art served as decoration, some in sympathetic magic, and some as illustrations of mystical beliefs and practices. Until more is understood about the daily life of Paleolithic people and the uses to which they put caves, we can neither prove nor disprove such theories.

The Les Eyzies region includes the largest cluster of art sites as well as the most striking of the lot, the famous Lascaux cave located in the woods on a plateau above the valley of the Vézère. Four boys and a dog discovered it during a walk early one September afternoon in 1940, the dog disappearing down a hole half-concealed by roots and moss and the boys scrambling after.

There is no prelude to the splendor of Lascaux. The entrance leads down a short flight of stairs directly into the main hall. You stand silent in the dark and lights are turned on and images appear as if projected on a screen, in a kind of three-dimensional panorama since the wall curves in front of you and around at the sides. For that moment, almost before the eye has a chance to look and before the ideas and questions start flowing, you take in the scene at once.

Then the experience breaks into parts. The animals become individuals in a frieze along the upper wall of the hall, along an overhanging ledge formed by the scooping-out action of an ancient river. Four bulls in black outline with black curving horns dominate the assemblage; one of them, the largest cave painting yet discovered, measures eighteen feet long. Two of the bulls face one another, and five red stags fill the space between them. The frieze also includes six black horses, a large red horse, three cows, a so-called unicorn which is actually a two-horned creature resembling no known species, and other animals which are difficult to distinguish because they are partly covered by more recently painted figures.

Below the frieze two dark holes mark passages which branch off from the main hall and lead to places underground which have not yet been thoroughly explored. The left-hand passage slopes downhill far into the rock. It contains forty more pictures.

The other passage is even more intriguing. A small chamber, which looks like a rather uninteresting dead end until one comes closer, lies off to the side. One must step carefully at this point because there is a pit here under a domed ceiling covered with a tangle of engraved lines and crisscross patterns and unidentifiable remnants of some red and black paintings. The edge of the hole is worn smooth as if many persons had lowered themselves to the bottom in times past, perhaps by rope. (A fragment of three-ply rope has been found in the cave.)

Today an iron ladder extends into the pit. It leads to a ledge and a work unique in the records of cave art—a buffalo disemboweled by a spear through its hindquarters, a stick-figure man with a bird's head falling backward directly in front of the buffalo, a pole with a bird on it below the man, and to the left behind the man a two-horned rhinoceros. This is known as the Shaft of the Dead Man.

Two major art caves are located some fifteen miles downriver from Lascaux in Les Eyzies—Font-de-Gaume—and another in Spain at Altamira. In 1875 Don Marcelino de Sautuola, a nobleman and amateur archeologist, started investigating the cave called Altamira discovered near his estate in the village of Santillana del Mar on the northern coast of Spain—again, as at Lascaux, after a dog had disappeared down a hole in the earth. He worked on and off for four years, often with his young daughter Maria for company, collecting bones and artifacts not far from the mouth of the cave and not far from a side chamber with a very low ceiling. He had gone into this chamber a number of times on his hands and kneees, always looking down in an unsuccessful search for a place to dig.

One day Maria, who was twelve years old at the time and did not have to crawl, wandered into the chamber and looked up and saw paintings by candlelight. The ceiling looks something like an upside-down relief map of low hilly country, and animals up to seven feet long have been engraved and painted on its bulges and hollows to give an almost sculptured sense of three dimensions.

De Sautuola was convinced of the prehistoric origins of the paintings on the spot. The figures on the ceiling at Altamira were very much like those he had seen the year before at the Paris World's Fair, figures engraved on pieces of bone and antler and already identified as the work of prehistoric people.

Most authorities found this line of reasoning too direct. They were ready to accept engravings on bone, but not engravings or paintings on cave walls. They balked at the notion that people who wore skins and used stone tools went deep into underground places equipped with pigments, brushes, lamps and other artist's supplies—and with the purposes and imagination required to create fine polychrome paintings. A Spanish professor administered the finishing touch by dismissing the paintings as forgeries and revealing the identity of the presumed forger, an artist who had been living at de Sautuola's estate for a number of years.

That dampened official interest in cave art until just before the turn of the century, when resistance began to crumble under the pressure of new evidence. In 1895 a local archeologist reported paintings and engravings in a Les Eyzies cave. Soon reports were coming from many quarters. In 1901 a group of prehistorians guided by a local farmer found pictures at Les Combarelles and, a week later, at Font-de-Gaume. One of the group, the young priest Henri Breuil, was to spend the next six decades reproducing and studying cave art. In 1902, fourteen years following the death of de Sautuola, he visited Altamira and helped establish the authenticity of its paintings. Not long afterward half a dozen further art caves were found within a few miles of Altamira.

Prehistoric art served a number of purposes, perhaps the least complicated being to bring color and form into the home. Most paintings and engravings in living spaces at cave mouths

Abbe Henri Breuil
(1877–1961)
dominated the study of primitive cave art for the entire first half of this century. As a jealous leader, he was often responsible for eliminating dissent among his young followers. Breuil's response to one former student who suggested that he might not be correct about the authenticity of the art in a certain cave, was never to speak to her again. Nevertheless, under his direction and tireless energy, cave art throughout France, Spain and Southern Africa was uncovered and preserved for future generations. At the age of sixty-nine Breuil was still crawling through tunnels to examine specimens, sometimes becoming wedged in place and requiring the aid of pushing and pulling assistants to be freed.

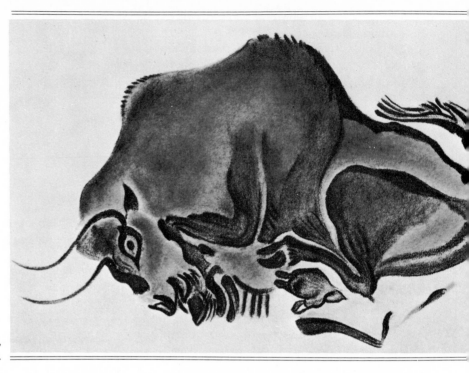

*Painting of a curled female bison,
discovered at Altamira.*

or in rock shelters have disintegrated because they were exposed to the weather. Some complete figures survive, however, and remnants often turn up during excavations.

Other purposes are more elusive and involve a shift from open living quarters to hidden chambers and passages, from light to darkness. Most cave art is located deep underground, and some works are extremely difficult to get at. In Arcy-sur-Cure, Leroi-Gourhan once guided John Pfeiffer through a small cave which extends only about a hundred yards into a cliffside, but it was a long hundred yards.

As Pfeiffer describes: "The entrance was a 'torpedo tube,' a horizontal tunnel just about big enough for a man to squeeze into. He went in headfirst, wriggling along salamander-fashion and pushing a lamp in front of him over the muddy floor, and I followed. Crawling is hard work with solid rock all around and

one's face usually an inch or so above the mud and sometimes in it. At one point the tunnel becomes even more constricted, and I had to hunch my shoulders and inhale deeply to force myself through." Further hazards existed on the way to a chamber with engravings in it, including a place where one had to skirt the slippery edge of a pit leading to still deeper passages.

Even after negotiating such passages, additional problems may be encountered in finding the art. For motives which remain obscure but which certainly involved the deliberate creation and overcoming of obstacles, the artists often chose surfaces difficult of access where they would have to work in cramped and awkward positions—in crawl spaces and alcoves, close to the floor, crammed into corners, above and at the bottom of pits like the Shaft of the Dead Man at Lascaux.

An important clue to the meaning of this

hidden art involves Cro-Magnon's concern with his effectiveness as a provider. Half the battle in hunting and fighting is confidence; and if he was anything like modern people, he used ritual on numerous occasions to help replenish and increase his powers. Perhaps he cast spells on his prey. Certain places in the depths of caves are covered with superimposed figures, figures drawn one on top of the other and overlapping as if the artists paid little attention to the work of their predecessors but considerable attention to where the art was located.

Another possible use of art was in initiation ceremonies. In many primitive tribes coming of age is a time of ordeals and revelations. A hint of prehistoric initiations was discovered more than sixty years ago when a man and his son rowed a boat into the Tuc d'Audoubert cave in the French Pyrenees. A stream, the remnant of a swift river that had originally formed the cave, took them to a gravel beach and a passage leading to a hall with a pond in it and white stalactites. At the end of the hall they climbed a steep slope or "chimney." Breaking through a sheet of stalagmite at the top, they followed a tunnel several hundred yards through chambers and a torpedo-tube section, and found not far from the end of the cave a large circular room with two clay statues of bison propped up against a rock at the center. Near the statues is a clay area with small heelprints in a circle, as if children had danced there, perhaps preparing for a vigil or ordeal.

Several theories involve what may have been meeting rooms. There are several caves where one climbs to the top of a natural platform and looks down on a chamber and practically sees the audience looking up at one.

These theories all have a measure of plausibility and should make one thing clear: no single notion, however ingenious, can account for even a major proportion of the observed facts. People were doing many things with their art and with their caves. The caves represent protoinstitutional sites before the coming of separate specialized institutions; from time to time they probably served as prehistoric archives, shrines, playgrounds, offices, schools, vigil places, theaters. Indeed, for limited periods at least some of them may have been as bustling for those times as downtown business and cultural centers are today. Generally speaking, the more we learn about settled communities in open-air sites like those near Kostenki and Fontainebleau, the more carefully we must reexamine our notions about how people used caves.

POPULATION EXPLOSION

All the evidence tells of a powerful people who could live where they wanted to live, where the big herd animals were. And there is more than that in the record. Life was changing in response to factors beyond the control and knowledge of the people, as the result of a complex chain of events which involved geological forces and caused a major population explosion. Surviving signs of the change are everywhere. The most recent Magdalenians, people who lived 14,000 to 12,000 years ago, occupied three to four times more sites than their predecessors, and occupied a large number of sites that had never been used before.

New studies, particularly those of Lewis Binford, indicate that the population explosion may have been one result of widespread geographical and biological changes accompanying the retreat of the Scandinavian Ice Sheet and other glaciers. The changes depended on the shape of the ocean basins, on the contours of lands beneath the sea. In general the bottom does not dip sharply from the shoreline on out. There is a long gradual slope, amounting to a very gentle downhill grade and forming the so-called continental shelf, which may extend as much as 800 miles (off the Siberian coast in the Arctic Ocean). The shelf ends rather abruptly, with a precipitous drop at the edge to ocean floors more than two miles deep.

If sea levels started dropping today, and dropped at a steady rate of a foot per day, the slope of the continental shelf is such that in ten days the waves of the earth's oceans would recede about a mile on the average, adding that much dry land to national coasts. In a year or so sea levels would fall enough to expose some 11,500,000 square miles of land that had once been submerged, a total area about the size of Africa. Most of the great harbors of the world would become lesser inland cities with a wide coastal plain separating them from the sea. New York City, for example, would lie stranded more than a hundred miles from the Atlantic Ocean.

This is the way things stood about 20,000 years ago during early Solutrean times when the glaciers had completed one of their major advances. Masses of ice more than a mile high covered vast areas and captured enough water from the oceans to lower sea levels by 250 to 500 feet, exposing most of the continental shelf throughout the world.

Other changes affected the course of evolution. The coasts were more turbulent places than they are now and considerably less hospitable to life, human and otherwise. Since the land generally extended to the steep edge of the continental shelf, the waters along the shores were deep and cold. They contained relatively small quantities of plankton and other species, which provide food for schools of larger fish. Furthermore, most major rivers tended to flow swiftly into the seas, often cascading with a roar over the edge of the shelf— and such conditions are not particularly attractive to organisms which prefer quieter environments. According to Binford, only a few species of mollusk, mussel-like organisms, clung in clusters to rocks near the cascades, as compared to more than forty species found in the sluggish flat delta regions of today's rivers.

More abundant times came with the melting and retreat of the glaciers. Ocean levels rose and waters crept back across the plains of the exposed continental shelf, covering them with a wide sunlit and sun-warmed shallow sea, a natural marine farmland where many forms of life flourished. And the cascades vanished, as rivers instead of spilling over the edge of the shelf flowed into the shallows and merged less violently with the seas. The sheer bulk of marine life along the world's seacoasts is estimated to have increased more than a hundred times during the period from 20,000 to 16,000 years ago, and it is no coincidence that people seem to have begun eating seafood on a large scale during this period.

Life changed in the interior as well as along the coasts. Salmon and other fish that migrate upstream to spawn could not negotiate high coastal cascades; but when the cascades disappeared, they began using the rivers increasingly as waterways. And they turned up in southern France, among other places, in the Dordogne River and its tributaries and in the waters rushing past the fields and trees outside the La Madeleine shelter. The region was also a stopping place for flocks of migratory birds on their way to new breeding grounds created by retreating glaciers.

The development of harpoons was part of the new technology created to take advantage of these food sources. The existence of other equipment made of less durable material can only be inferred. American Indians living on the northwest coast of the Pacific camp at salmon runs suspend basket traps in the falls, and remove the heads of the fish on the spot before bringing their catch back to the village for drying. Prehistoric people were capable of developing similar techniques. Sites exist along the Dordogne River, near rapids, where the banks are practically solid with fish scales, and salmon vertebrae are found in many sites occupied by the Magdalenians.

But their population explosion was not simply due to a larger food supply and the development of large-scale food preservation and storage. The chief difference was a more steady and reliable supply. Migratory fish and birds came at a most convenient season, during the spring when food yields from reindeer and other migratory animals declined because herds dispersed to take care of their young. Binford suggests that one result may have been an increased trend toward all-year-round settlements, reducing the need to pack up and move on to new hunting grounds, and permitting an adjustment of primitive birth-control measures. As long as mothers had to keep on the move, they were limited to one child every three or four years, because that was all they could carry. Nomadic tribes have always been forced to rely on abortion, infanticide, and taboos against becoming pregnant during lactation, and these practices could be relaxed in more settled times, with fish and fowl to supplement basic supplies of reindeer meat.

According to this reconstruction of times past, all the conditions favoring expansion and population explosions had existed before, during former glacial retreats—that is, all but one. More ancient times had seen floodings of the great coastal plain and the vanishing of cascades beneath rising waters and migrations of previous generations of fish and birds. The new ingredient this time was a breed of *Homo sapiens* with the technology and capacity for social organization required to exploit the changing environment.

Humans were evolving all over the world, multiplying and expanding into a great many other regions. For example, hunters reached Australia at about the time when Aurignacian families were settling down in the Abri Pataud and Morin Cave, an outstanding achievement

A mass slaughter site in the New World. These fossil bison ribs were discovered in eastern Colorado. Notice the "steps" formed by different levels of excavation.

Stone block containing bison ribs and arrowhead, found in New Mexico.

considering that the crossing required some island-hopping and boats seaworthy enough to negotiate perhaps 50 to more than 100 miles of open water. Finds in Australia include the world's oldest ground stone axes, reliably dated back at least 18,000 years, which is so much earlier than anything comparable found in Europe or the Near East that one British investigator came, saw, and simply refused to accept the evidence.

People entered the New World somewhat later, perhaps 15,000 to 20,000 years ago, and apparently did not have to make a water crossing. The glaciers had begun to melt, but sea levels were still low and people followed mammoths, mastodons, bison and other immigrants over a plain more than a thousand miles wide connecting northern Asia and Alaska. North America has a number of spectacular mass-slaughter sites, generally located in marshy areas or stream beds, and often at sharp bends or meanders which form deep-cut natural walls and keep animals from escaping. The remains of about 200 bison have been found at one such site in Colorado.

Changes were under way at an accelerating rate and on a worldwide basis, social and psychological changes some of which can be inferred from studies of flint artifacts. If assemblages of Neanderthal tools from two widely separated sites in Western Europe were thoroughly mixed, even an expert would find it extremely difficult to sort them out again. But in a similar experiment involving two tool kits from the period that started only a few millennia later, say two Solutrean tool kits, the job of unmixing would be much easier.

The difference represents a change in outlook. Neanderthal groups did not make tools according to strictly controlled and distinctive regional patterns. But later as populations increased and people lived closer to one another geographically, they unconsciously developed ways of increasing what Edwin Wilmsen of the University of Michigan calls their "social distance." They developed a new quality of self-awareness and group-awareness, a way of making themselves distinct from "the others," an enhanced sense of style which is reflected in the making of their artifacts. And with all this came a new breed of human being and modern races and a new brain, essentially the same brain which shapes our activities today.

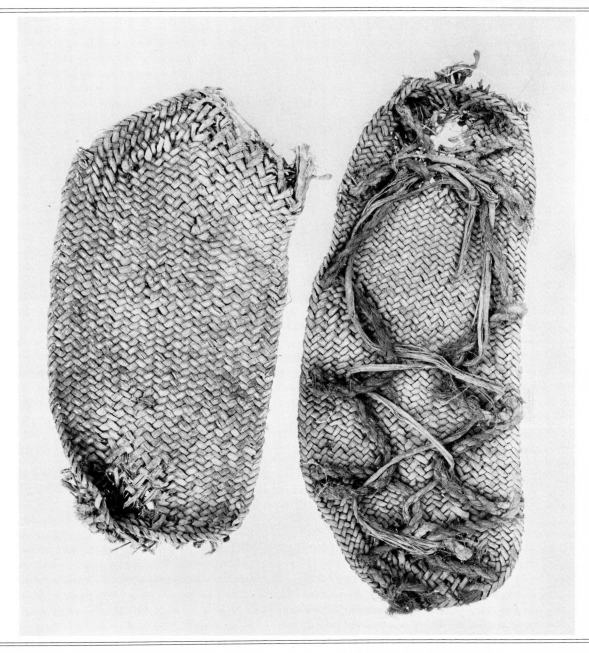

The Humanness of Prehistoric Man

René Dubos

The following piece, from René Dubos Pulitzer Prize-winning book, So Human an Animal, *demonstrates the essential continuity in the humanity of* Homo sapiens *over the last hundred thousand years. Consistent with the discoveries of all four subdisciplines of anthropology, Dubos concludes that our defining characteristic as a species is that we are social beings.*

In a cave of eastern Oregon, near the village of Fort Rock, the American archaeologist L. S. Cressman and his students discovered in 1936 a cache of seventy-five sandals buried in volcanic pumice. Most of these are now on display in the archaeological

Reprinted by permission of Charles Scribner's Sons from *So Human an Animal* by René Dubos. Copyright © 1968 by René Dubos.

museum of Oregon State University at Eugene. The sandals are woven from shredded sagebrush bark twisted into tight ropes thinner than an ordinary pencil, and they exhibit great uniformity in workmanship. They measure from 9 to 12 inches in length and would therefore fit a modern man. Yet archaeological evidence, recently confirmed by carbon 14 dating, proves that they were manufactured by Indians some 9,000 years ago.

Eastern Oregon is now a desert country, but during the Late Paleolithic period there was a large lake in the region where the sandals were discovered. The Indians who then lived around the lake had apparently developed a complex social organization, as is attested by the storage of so many artifacts in a single cave. Human occupation of the area was probably interrupted by the volcanic eruption that deposited the layer of pumice over the floor of the

Fort Rock cave. On first contact, the hot pumice charred the sandals somewhat, but after cooling it acted as a protective layer preventing further deterioration from the inclemencies of the weather and attack by microbes and insects.

The detailed description of the sandals published by Dr. Cressman gives an idea of the workmanship of the Stone Age Indians:

"Five pieces of rope laid lengthwise to the long axis of the foot served as warps and were fastened tightly together by twining weft strands. The toe ends of the warp strands, left untwisted, were folded back over the toes to form a protective pocket and, held slackly together, were fastened to the sides of the sandals by rather loose twining. The tie-string was drawn through a series of loops around the heel and on the sides made by the looped weft strands. All were alike except a few which had cords running tightly and slightly diagonally across the sole. The purpose of this cord is unknown; if it had been serviceable as a non-skid device, it would probably have been more widely used. In some sandals pine needles had been added for padding."

Other types of sandals woven by Indians many thousand years ago have been discovered in several parts of the United States and can be seen in anthropological museums. They differ in workmanship and in style from region to region, indeed from one cave to the other in the same region. Sandals found in Catlow Cave, Oregon, are not as well made as the ones from Fort Rock, even though the two sites are close to each other and were occupied by Indians during approximately the same period.

Sandals discovered in still other caves are made of tule, or more rarely of grass, instead of sagebrush bark. Irrespective of the material of which they are made, some are obviously designed for rough usage while others are more refined in style—some so elegant in design and workmanship that they would not seem out of place in a New York Fifth Avenue shop.

A few of the ancient Indian sandals are child size and have rabbit fur woven into them as if for warmth and softness. Again quoting Dr. Cressman, an

Oregon cave yielded ". . . a pair of small sandals for a five- or six-year-old child, tied together by strings as we might tie a pair of sneakers. Nearby were two toy baskets, and a little farther off was a dart for a 'dart and wheel' game. Because these objects lay close together, we are sure that they were the sandals and playthings of an Indian girl who had lived in that cave several thousand years ago. One day something happened; sandals and toys were left where they were last used, as we might leave shoes and toys on the living room floor."

The prehistoric sandals, large or small, crude or stylish, create a sense of kinship with the human beings who made and used them many thousands of years ago. The variety of workmanship and the design for various types of usage make it apparent, better than words ever could, that Stone Age man had mastered many skills and developed a complex familial and societal organization.

The humanness of prehistoric man is of direct relevance to our own lives, because we have inherited from him most of our physiological and mental characteristics and we share with him the same fundamental needs and urges. Many aspects of modern life are profoundly affected by the forces that shaped *Homo sapiens* and his life as far back as the Late Paleolithic or Old Stone Age, more than 100,000 years ago.

Homo sapiens does not differ from animals so much by his ability to learn as by the kinds of things he learns, in particular by the accumulation of his social experiences in the course of collective enterprises over thousands of generations. In other words, the human species is best characterized by its social history.

Summary

Between 35,000 and 40,000 years ago the Neanderthal subspecies disappeared from Europe and was replaced by a variety of modern *Homo sapiens,* Cro-Magnon man. Evidence of the transition from Neanderthal to Cro-Magnon is found in the Near East.

The emergence of modern varieties of humans in the Near East is associated with the dessication of the region between 45,000 and 40,000 years ago. The drier climate forced large herds of wild cattle into narrow seasonal migration routes. Groups of Neanderthals, following their prey, came together and united for organized, coordinated hunting and more efficient multiple kills. Improved hunting permitted more people to live together, and in some as yet unknown way, is related to the evolution of Cro-Magnon from Neanderthal.

In Europe, Cro-Magnon remains are associated with evidence of increasing social and technological complexity. Large tribes, many with permanent settlements, replaced the smaller bands of Neanderthal society. Tools became highly diverse and specialized—burins to make grooves and slots, composite tools of several flint elements set into grooved hafts, spear throwers, harpoons. Complex symbols associated with artistic forms of expression, cave paintings and clay figurines, made their appearance.

A point of contention among archeologists is the relationship between Cro-Magnon in the Near East and in Europe. Many argue that modern humans developed in the Near East and migrated to Europe, displacing Neanderthal. It is believed that different groups of Neanderthal either merged with Cro-Magnon or retreated to backwaters. The temporal and spatial coexistence of Acheulian and blade tool kits at various sites in Europe is evidence of contact between the two subspecies. Others contend that the coexistence of the two technologies is evidence of the evolution of one from the other, not competition.

Four distinct Cro-Magnon cultures appeared in Europe between 35,000 and 12,000 years ago. The two earliest, the Perigordian and the Aurignacian cultures, coexisted for 10,000 years without significant cross-fertilization. While the former occupied a series of sites, each for a short period of time during the year, the latter maintained permanent settlements. The third Cro-Magnon tradition, the Solutrean culture, appeared from 20,000 to 17,000 years ago during a period of glacial advance. It is characterized by a peculiar combination of Neanderthal tool types and highly developed laurel leaf blades, slender, symmetrical, flat blades, tapered to a point.

The most spectacular and final Cro-Magnon culture of the period, the Magdalenian tradition, is identified by tools of finely engraved bone, antler, and ivory, harpoons, needles and spear throwers. They had large settlements, in cave shelters and on open land, housing upwards of four to six hundred people. During the five thousand years of Magdalenian florescence, the population increased three to four fold. This population explosion is related to the advanced technology of the Magdalenians and the natural abundance that provided stable, dependable resources.

The favorable environment in Europe during Magdalenian times was brought about by the melting of glaciers around the world. The rising ocean levels covered previously dry continental shelves. Since the continental shelf supports most species of mollusks and provides easy access to rivers for fish that spawn upstream, aquatic life along the coast and inland flourished. The Magdalenians exploited these new sources of food. Similar environmental alterations throughout the world stimulated the migration of *Homo sapiens* to the New World and Australia.

Glossary

Aurignacian tradition   A Cro-Magnon culture that existed from 35,000 to 20,000 years ago in Europe.

Blades   Long, slender, stone flakes out of which Cro-Magnons made most of their tools.

Carbon-14 Dating   A technique of dating based on the measurement of the quantity of radioactive carbon-14 in a sample of organic remains.

Magdalenian tradition   A Cro-Magnon culture that existed in Europe from 17,000 to 12,000 years ago.

Perigordian tradition   A Cro-Magnon culture that existed in Europe from 35,000 to 23,000 years ago.

Solutrean tradition   A Cro-Magnon culture that existed in Europe from 20,000 to 17,000 years ago.

Spear thrower   A Magdalenian device designed to amplify muscle power, capable of throwing a spear several times faster and harder than with bare hands.

Tribe   For archeologists, the tribe is an intermarrying group of people, sharing a common tradition and cooperating in large-scale, multiple kill hunting. For cultural anthropologists, who study contemporary tribal societies, the tribe is a more complex type of social structure.

Additional Reading

Binford, Sally R.

1968   Early Upper Pleistocene Adaptations in the Levant. American Anthropologist, volume 70, pp. 707–717.

Excellent discussion of the Neanderthal subsistence patterns for the advanced student.

Brace, C. Loring

1964   The Fate of the 'Classic' Neanderthals: A Consideration of Hominid Catastrophism. Current Anthropology, volume 5, pp. 3–27.

This is an excellent step by step examination of the "Classic" and progressive neanderthals. The reading is intense, but worth the effort.

1967   The stages of Human Evolution: Human and cultural origins. Englewoods Cliffs, N.J., Prentice-Hall, Inc.

An excellent introduction to the stages of evolution. Considers the question of hominid catastrophism as well as various stages in hominid development.

Poirier, Frank E.

1973   Fossil Man. An Evolutionary Journey. The C.V. Mosby Co. Chapter 11.

An excellent discussion of the Neanderthal problem. Considers the environment as well as the physiology of Neanderthals.

Smith, Philip E. L.

1964   The Solutrean Culture. Scientific American, volume 211, no. 2 pp. 86–94.

A fine discussion of the Neanderthal tool kit.

chapter eleven

*How can I tell what I think
till I see what I say?*
EDWARD M. FORSTER

Anthropological Linguistics/ THE EVOLUTION OF LANGUAGE

An abiding activity by humans in all societies is to distinguish themselves from lower animals. All societies have creation myths that tell how the world and the people and animals in it came into being. These myths identify traits unique to humans, traits that separate humans from animals. Understandably, language is frequently included among these traits. It is recognized as special, as fundamentally different from the communication systems of other animals, by every society. Human language is unique. It allows us to communicate about anything, anytime, anyplace, to reflect on ourselves, to be conscious, to maintain and transmit cultural traditions. It is flexible beyond imagination, communicating the exactness of an engineering textbook or the subtlety of any human interaction. Language, perhaps above everything else, has served as the mark of the human condition.

EARLY THEORIES OF LANGUAGE ORIGINS

It is not surprising, then, that an enormous amount of scholarly activity has been devoted to the questions, "When did human language first appear? How did it appear? And why?" In the nineteenth century the popularity of the Darwinian theory of evolution led to endless speculation about the origins and evolution of language. So rife were ideas about how language originated and evolved that the Linguistic Society of Paris imposed a constitutional ban on papers dealing with the topic in 1866. The members of the society were disturbed by the lack of any direct evidence of the evolution of language. Most fossil remains of early humans were yet to be discovered; non-Western languages, erroneously thought to be more primitive than European languages, were unrecorded; the science of *phonetics*, the study of the sounds which make up speech, was new and unsophisticated; and the study of primate communication systems had not yet begun, at least not in an organized, systematic way. In short, the many sources that provide us with information about language today were simply not available. Neither lack of data nor the prohibitions of the Linguistic Society, however, halted the speculations on language origins.

The ideas that were current in the nineteenth century appear fanciful in the light of our present knowledge, and perhaps a trifle absurd. Yet the questions that these nineteenth-century scientists were trying to answer are some of the same ones we address today. In 1877, a German linguist, Max Muller, summarized many of the available theories. According to Muller, the pooh-pooh or interjection theory proposed that spontaneous sounds such as oh!, hey!, ow!, and oops! represent the linguistic forms of early humans. Sounds made in reaction to pain, surprise, anger, happiness, and so on, began to refer to those states. With this "naming" process, prelinguistic humans had begun the change to linguistic humans.

According to the bow-wow or onomatopoeia theory, human speech arose when our ancestors first started imitating natural sounds. The sound of rain, rushing water, thunder, wind,

and animal calls were typical sources of imitation. It is easy to see why some natural sounds might be imitated. Accurate imitations of animal sounds could have been useful in hunting as they still are today. Why, though, would early people have wanted to imitate the sounds of wind or thunder, for instance? Even if we could produce fairly convincing reasons why a large number of sounds would have been imitated, we would have only a very weak statement about the origins of language. We would still have to account for how the imitations became linguistic, that is, how they changed from more or less accurate mimicry of sounds to words. The number of onomatopoetic words in any language is very small compared to the rest of the vocabulary. It is unlikely that this could have been the major source of language.

Despite their limitations, the interjection and the onomatopoeia theories address an important question: How did "naming" develop? Language is fundamentally a relation of sound and meaning. At some point sounds, or vocalizations, came to be associated with definite objects and events. Vocalizations became *referential;* they pointed to or referred to "things" in the environment. They became the names of the "things." They designated aspects of the environment in a regular, recurrent way, such that all members of a society would have access to the same meaning just as an English speaker has sounds like "house" or "rain," that are understood by all other English speakers.

For vocalizations to have meaning, the association between sound and meaning must be consistent and socially shared. But the association itself, the relation between sound and meaning, is also *arbitrary.* The word "dog" bears no necessary relationship to the class of animals named by the term. There is nothing in the sounds making up the utterance "dog" that would lead non-speakers to suspect it referred to *Canis familiaris.* The relationship is arbitrary and has to be learned.

The interjection and onomatopoeia theories tried to locate the "naming" process in a one-to-one relationship between a vocalization and a referent, the object or feeling being named. According to these theories, the relationship might become arbitrary in time, but was not arbitrary at first. The interjection theory located the non-arbitrary base in the involuntary exclamations associated with various emotions, and the onomatopoeia theory located it in sound symbolism. The transition from non-arbitrary vocalizations to arbitrary ones would not, according to these theories, require a profound change all at once.

We do know that some time in the distant past our early hominid ancestors began to acquire referential speech, and in time, the relationship between the majority of the vocalizations and their referents became arbitrary. There is no reason, however, to believe that anything as specific as sound symbolism or sound mimicry was the transitional step between non-arbitrary and arbitrary vocalizations. Theories that locate naming in these processes place too much emphasis on sounds as the units that evolved in language. They leave unanswered the more fundamental questions of language evolution. What were the conditions that led to the naming of environmental features? What were the consequences? What advantages accrued to the hominids who first began to use referential speech?

OPENING THE CALL SYSTEM

Two anthropologists, Charles Hockett and Robert Ascher, recently provided some interesting speculations on how several features of human language, including naming, might have originated. They note that between 3–11 million years ago a prolonged, extensive drought reduced the available habitat for our hominid ancestors. These ancestors were forest dwellers, and as the forest receded, the food supply diminished. Competition for favorable habitat and food must have greatly increased. It is highly likely that the competition produced situations where food and danger were associated time and time again. This could have been the breeding ground for human language.

Assuming that early hominids had *call systems* similar to those of modern primates, Hockett and Ascher suggest that the frequent association of food and danger could have elicited a mixture of calls. Primate call systems contain a small number of distinct calls, each with its own meaning. The call system is *closed,* that is, the calls are not recombinable to form new calls. The mixture of calls, a blend of the sound properties of the food and danger call, could have been the basis of the development of an *open call system,* one in which new vocalizations can be produced to refer to new "things." Following Hockett and Ascher's arguments, suppose that a primate group had a food call with the sound properties ABCD and a danger call consisting of EFGH. These calls would be distinct and normally uttered in different contexts. With the increased association of danger and food, however, it is possible that the calls would be produced simultaneously, producing a blending of the calls. What started as a food call, ABCD, followed by a danger call, EFGH, might have blended to produce ABGH, meaning "food + danger." This would increase the calls from two to three: ABCD for "food," ABGH for "food + danger," EFGH for "danger." It is also logical that if GH meant "danger" when combined with AB, "food," CD could acquire the meaning "no danger."

The change from a simple, closed system to a primitive but open system would be highly significant. Although the structural change is minor, the implications are far-reaching. First, the ability to combine messages means that we

Controversy

Language: When Was It First Used?

When did people first begin to use language? We will probably never know the precise answer to this question, for our knowledge of human linguistic history can only be deduced from the study of the artifacts left behind. New research into this area, however, suggests that human language and culture may be considerably older than was previously suspected.

Unlike stone tools, symbolic artifacts invariably indicate the presence of some sort of cultural tradition. In his efforts to trace the evolution of human communication, archaeologist Alexander Marshack has made an extensive study of Paleolithic art objects. Marshack examined under a microscope a group of animal images carved by Cro-Magnon people nearly 35,000 years ago and observes that the carefully carved details on these artifacts have been worn down by many years of handling. He further notes that many of the objects were made at some later date for a purpose which has yet to be learned. From this evidence, Marshack concludes that these figures were not intended to be merely representational ornaments but, rather, that they were part of a complex symbolic tradition.

In his microscopic examination of Neanderthal artifacts, which predate the Cro-Magnon remains, Marshack discovered forms of symbolic expression similar to that of the Cro-Magnons. Since it is generally assumed that the Neanderthals had few, if any, forms of artistic expression, a reevaluation appeared necessary. The Neanderthal who manufactured a particular tiny pendant, for example, would have to have had excellent two-handed manipulative abilities and keen visual acuity. Moreover, the tools used to make the pendant would have had no adaptive value except in the context of a cultural tradition. The presence of symbolic markings on engraved objects suggests the possibility of some level of linguistic competence.

An especially startling bit of evidence for the early manufacture of symbolic artifacts was the discovery of an engraved ox-bone believed to be some 300,000 years old. Microscopic examination revealed that the images on the bone are remarkably similar to those which later characterized the tradition of the Upper Paleolithic. Marshack speculates that language would have been extremely useful in a culture which created images intended not as abstract representations but rather for symbolic or ritualistic use. Some have argued, however, that there are relatively few Neanderthal objects with symbolic markings. Marshack believes that this may be due to the perishability of the materials used. The need for language is further implied by the need for special tools, materials, and skills in the manufacture of artifacts. The carrying out of subsistence activities can be transmitted fairly easily without recourse to language; hunting and gathering techniques are readily learned through observation and experimentation. The manufacture of symbolic artifacts, on the other hand, cannot be understood in terms of the observable world. According to Marshack, the evolution of a complex cultural tradition as reflected in symbolic artwork would seem to require some degree of linguistic ability.

At what point does the exhibition of symbolic behavior evolve into linguistic sophistication? Marshack turns to a consideration of chimpanzees to answer this question. Like humans, a chimp uses his hands for both practical tasks and for simple communication. Chimps also communicate through vocalization, although efforts to teach them language have been for the most part unsuccessful. Marshack suggests that the development of language among the early hominids came about as subsistence activities became increasingly specialized and cultural in nature. The need for language evolved in response to the increasing complexity of human communicative needs. Cultural complexity, then, is the key factor in the evolution of language.

From his study of prehistoric artifacts, Marshack concludes that the naming of symbolic images began very long ago and evolved slowly over several million years. Although images probably could be named early in the evolutionary record, the evolution of complex linguistic structures seems to have been a more recent development. Marshack stresses that it is to cultural evolution and not abstract linguistic theory at which we must look in seeking the origins of language.

can talk about the possible emergence of a simple *grammar,* a set of rules about how units of meaning are combined. The incipient grammatical rules would not be complicated: AB can be combined with CD to produce one message, with GH to produce another; CD and GH could not be combined, since the message would be meaningless, "no danger + danger." Even such a low level, minimal grammar would require greater sensitivity to the relationship between sound and meaning. Since there would no longer be an immediate, one-to-one relationship between environmental stimuli and sounds, more effort would be necessary to create messages.

A second consequence of the hypothetical change from a closed to an open call system involves the concept of negation. To produce the call "food + no danger" the capacity to conceive of negative circumstances must exist. This is an important design feature of language, one that gives enormous flexibility to language. It's not just that the kinds and numbers of possible utterances would be increased; rather the use of the negative as an attribute (*no* danger) means that it is possible to communicate objectively about things that are not present and perhaps not even "real." This is called *displacement.* Humans can easily think about and talk about objects and activities removed in time and space. This is something that other animals, including non-human primates, almost never do. They are constrained to communicate about the here-and-now, the events and activities that are unfolding at the present. To produce the call "no danger" would require a capacity for displacement exceeding what non-human primates presently appear to have. Information about what constitutes danger would have to be stored in some long-term memory system and processes for retrieving the information would be necessary.

Displacement implies not only more complex cognitive or memory processes, but the pre-

sence of *semanticity,* of categories of meaning. The call "no danger" implies the existence of a category of meaning which includes all animals which are not dangerous. Something like EFGH may have been associated with dangerous animals, such as leopards, prior to the emergence of displacement and semanticity. The new message ABCD, "food + no danger," means that a class or category of those dangerous animals is given a label. The use of the label implies the category. The sounds become a word, pointing or referring to a category of things that are dangerous, just as the word "predator" refers to a class of animals having identifiable and predictable characteristics.

To summarize, opening of the call system necessitates profound changes in the nature of the system. The makeup of the calls changes from individual, isolated units to combined, blended ones, and a grammar to control the combinations emerges. Negation appears, as does the capacity for displacement, and the relationship between vocalization and referent becomes semantic. These changes were all essential for the evolution of human language from early hominid call systems.

Unlike Hockett and Ascher, however, many linguists believe that blending was a factor in these changes, but not the major factor. Blending could have encouraged the opening of the call system by requiring greater attention to the sound properties of calls, but the major changes had to be in other areas. According to many linguists, the fundamental questions are about increases in intelligence. For example, what motivated early hominids to decide when and what to say? If the relationship between calls and their objects became arbitrary and if there was no longer a one-to-one relationship between object and sound, decisions had to be made about how, what, when, and where things were said. An increase in intelligence must underlie the increasingly complicated decision-making processes.

It must also follow that the decision-making be related to the environment in some way. A hominid group with an open call system would have adaptive advantages over groups with closed call systems; they would control more information about the environment and be better able to adapt, to adjust, and even to control it. But the advantages would not necessarily count as the reasons why the individual primates would begin to use an open system. Some more immediate advantages would be needed to motivate a primate to adopt new methods of communication. One motivation might be the ability to obtain more food or to obtain food more easily. Enhanced status is also a possible motivation.

It is clear that decisions about the environment would include the social as well as the physical environment. Social concerns would, in fact, likely be paramount. In other words, language must have originated among highly social hominids. Solitary primates, such as the orangutan, would not have experienced pressure to adopt an open communication system. Highly social animals, on the other hand, would have been far more likely to adopt novel communication patterns. Much of their behavior would have had to be coordinated with other members of the group. Their sociability would have also been conducive to the adoption and spread of innovations.

COMMUNICATION AMONG NON-HUMAN PRIMATES

Much of the recent speculation on the evolution of language, like the work of Hockett and Ascher, is based on the study of communication systems among non-human primates. Charles Darwin recognized this potential over a hundred years ago when he suggested that the clearest precursors of human language would be found among our primate relatives.

Paradoxically, the role of sounds in the communication of apes is not as advanced as in other animal species, such as song birds and some insect species. Sounds are not unimportant among our closest living relatives, but they are simply part of a larger complex of signals. Nothing in the communication systems of contemporary primate species approaches the sounds employed in human speech.

It would be useful at this point to review briefly some results of research on non-human primate sound systems. To begin, what do primates communicate about? Several features are commonly present in one form or another: food (recognition, possession), reproduction (courtship, mating), location, hostility and aggression, fear, bonding, and care of offspring (feeding, protection). Studies of non-human primate call systems have shown that most species have approximately ten to twenty-five discrete calls.

Two points need to be stressed about primate calls. First, they are only part of the signals in an act of communication. Primate communication is multimodal; several methods of communication are employed at the same time. Posture, gesture, facial expression, proximity, eye contact, smell, and touch can all be used to send a message. Each message type—communication about food, danger, and so on—has its own particular combination of features. Sound carries only part of the message. The chief function of the call is to bring attention to the fact that a message is about to be sent. Once the attention of other primates is obtained, communication is non-vocal. Of course this is not true of all messages, but overall it is the dominant pattern. The second point to be emphasized is the emotional nature of the calls. The calls of a monkey or ape vary in pitch, intensity, and duration, and each variation is relative to the emotional state of the animal. A highly excited animal will produce calls quite different from one that is only mildly disturbed. The emotional base of the sound system is ideal for communicating subtle differences in the moods of animals. The calls can be finely tuned to the state of excitement of the animal, whether the source of excitement is fear, anger, hostility, pleasure, or anything else.

While the function of calls may be to attract attention, they are motivated by changes in the emotional state of the animal. These changes are related to environmental factors, such as attack by another animal or the discovery of food. There may even be little justification for saying that primates have food calls or danger calls. Jane Lancaster, an anthropologist, has suggested that the calls should be viewed as indicating levels of excitement, not as food or danger calls. This distinction is not inconsequential. To argue that there is a "food call" is to claim that there is a category of "things" labeled "food." This would imply the beginning of a semantic base, of a categorization of parts of the environment, which is imputing too much content to the calls. Lancaster's position is more tenable: categories of environmental features may elicit identifiable, predictable calls, but the calls are not labels themselves. They do not refer to "things," but to changes in the emotional state of the animal.

The responsive and emotional nature of primate calls compounds the problem of how a closed system became an open one. If closed systems did not contain referential calls initially, how did calls come to refer to things? The excitement call stimulated by food had to become a call eliciting attention to food before it could become a "name" for food. Speculation, therefore, about how categories of meaning and naming developed becomes more and more involved. We are now in a better position, however, to evaluate some of the earlier speculations. We can see that although the concept of blending is useful for thinking about some of the processes that had to occur in the evolution of language, it leaves open the question of how

food calls and danger calls developed in the first place.

To summarize, the picture that emerges of non-human primate communication in natural settings is a multimodal system that relies primarily on vision and only secondarily on the vocal-auditory system. The number of distinct calls is small, ranging from ten to twenty or so; the calls serve to attract attention so that other communication can proceed. What motivates the calls is the emotional state of the animal. The calls tend to be distinct because of the similar reactions of members of a species to some stimulus—food, danger, and so on. The vocal signals are expressive, however, not referential. We assume that our hominid ancestors had a similar communication system.

How did an expressive system evolve into a referential, symbolic one? A considerable amount of speculation has focused on the linguistic machinery that would be involved in this change. The emergence of linguistic form and structure did, indeed, occur, and we have to account for them in evolution. However, it probably is a mistake to speculate, initially, on the form of language, the linguistic makeup of words and phrases. The assumption that a form, a "word" or label, appeared, full-blown, places a heavy burden on an explanation of how and why it appeared as it did. Perhaps we would do well to suspend briefly speculations about linguistic form and turn to consider other features of communication.

GESTURE AND LANGUAGE ORIGINS

The tremendous gap between the expressive vocalizations of non-human primates and the symbolic, referential ones of humans has led to speculation that language did not evolve directly in the vocal-auditory channel. The changes would have been too great, with too many intermediate steps. Instead, it is possible that the origin of human language is rooted in the gestures that early hominids used to communicate. In the close-knit social systems of our closest relatives gestural communication is certainly fundamental. Non-human primates rely heavily on changes in body posture, facial expressions, blinking the eyelids, raising the eyebrows, exposing teeth for example, and directional movement, one animal displacing another from a particular spot or location.

These gestures can be taken as primitive, generalized "pointing," as indicating that attention should be given to a communicative episode. The pointing suggests that some behavioral change should be anticipated—baring the teeth might mean something like "keep your distance or pay the consequences" or more likely "stop what you're doing or something will happen." For the gestural pointing to communicate, other primates must be able to "read" the gestures. They have to follow the gestures visually and "interpret" the meaning—that some behavior is or will be associated with the gesture. The general idea is that the pointing quality of these gestures was the rudimentary form of the "naming" in referential speech.

One proponent of the gestural theory of the origin of language, Gordon Hewes, an anthropologist at the University of Colorado, has proposed that the "reading" capacity must have increased during the period of savannah dwelling by early hominids. Their terrestrial subsistence activity—hunting and scavenging—would have increased the premium on gestural communication. Gestural imitation, then, could have served as a vehicle for several of the developments necessary for the emergence of language. The training of the young could occur without difficulty. Second, the imitation of pointing removes the communication act from its original context, perhaps initiating the development of displacement. Third, the rela-

tionship between sign and object would become more arbitrary, closer to the semantic relationship in human languages.

The gestural theory is also attractive in at least one other respect: it emphasizes the visual channel in the early stages of language development. It is well known that primate vision is highly advanced and critical to primate social behavior. Jane Lancaster observes that a deaf primate would have a much greater chance of survival than a blind one. The gestural theory follows the line of least biological resistance in another way: changes in the anatomy and function of the voice box and throat would not be a prerequisite to early language development, as it would in a vocal-auditory model.

The manual-gestural theory of language origin does, however, have some weaknesses. One concerns the use of hands for signing. Once we move away from the gestures that primates exhibit—eyebrow raising, baring the canines, eye blinking, and so on—and consider the use of the hands in gesturing, the evidence becomes thin. Chimpanzees use their hands in several ways, to groom other members of the troop, to hold and carry objects, to make and use simple tools, and to threaten and display. The importance of the hands for gestural communication is not paramount. Moreover, the hands are not used for direct pointing. A Dutch zoologist, Adrian Kordtland, concluded that chimpanzees do not rely heavily on their hands for signalling and communication. Even in their expressive behavior, chimpanzees do not exploit the potential of their hands.

Did pointing with the hands occur among the early hominids? If they used their hands to point, what were the events that led to that behavior? Were there intermediate phases? It is hard to conceive of gesture-pointing becoming "naming"-pointing without some intermediate phase in which pointing was much more explicit than that of modern primates. This is not to say that something like finger-pointing did not occur, but the whole area needs to be explored much further. Perhaps the transition from hand gestures to hand pointing was based in the use of hands for other activities as well. Pointing may have been the end result of a long series of changes in which the hands became a more important part of the hominid adaptation to the environment. Tool making and tool use in a savannah dwelling population could have been the basis of increased reliance on the hands. Greater hand and eye coordination would have been required, of course, associated with advanced neural development. Pointing with the hands could have arisen in these contexts, leading eventually to referential pointing.

An awareness of environmental complexity is another one of the prerequisites for referential pointing. What information do we have about present-day primates and their awareness of environmental factors? We have seen that their vocalizations do not name environmental factors, but that does not mean that primates do not or cannot recognize them. They easily distinguish some categories of objects and events in the environment. They know which plants are edible and which are preferred foods; they distinguish dangerous animals from those that pose no threat; and they know which animals must be shown deference within their own group. Moreover, members of a troop greet one another, especially if they have been temporarily separated. If the separation has been exceptionally long, the greeting can be quite effusive. It is clear that rather subtle distinctions are made about context and environment. The capacity for recognition and categorization is not lacking; nevertheless, things aren't given names. Thus, present-day primates already have much of the behavioral framework for naming or labeling. We can assume that this is an ancient capacity with a long history in primates.

Language is, as we have been emphasizing, not merely linguistic structure, not the "machinery" that produces the linguistic form, but a social phenomenon on the one hand and a capacity to generate the linguistic form on the other. Linguistic form developed within social contexts. Speculations about the evolution of language are, consequently, best focused on the evolution of various components of the linguistic form within the context of the particular social functions of language.

Many of these components have already been mentioned—the capacity to distinguish and classify parts of the environment, the capacity to "point" or designate, the capacity to categorize objects, the capacity for displacement, the capacity to imitate, the capacity to decide when and where to vocalize. To these we can add the capacity to transfer information from the visual channel to the vocal-auditory channel, the capacity to articulate sounds, and the capacity to generalize. Undoubtedly there are many others; the list is not exhaustive nor is it ordered in terms of importance of the various capacities. Nonetheless, we can see that the investigation into the origin and evolution of language is essentially an investigation of the evolution of human culture and human intelligence. As the various capacities began to unfold, due to the general evolutionary processes of natural selection, behavior came under voluntary control. Information about the environment—about food, reproduction, individuals, groups—formed the nucleus of culture that was passed from generation to generation and that became increasingly important in the evolution of the human species.

Before talking about physical evolution and the evidence it provides for the evolution of language capacity, we need to look more carefully at the capacities noted above. Some rather ingenious experimental work with our closest relatives, chimpanzees, has shown that their capacity for language is far more advanced than was earlier realized.

R. Allen Gardner *teaches psychology at the University of Nevada and has spent the last ten years teaching a chimpanzee, Washoe, to speak with ASL, the American Sign Language. Since the aim of the experiment was to teach a chimpanzee to converse in everyday contexts, Washoe was provided with her own trailer and a compound in which she had complete freedom. During all waking hours at least one person was with her "chattering" in sign language. It was decided that all communication would be limited to ASL and various gestural sounds of which chimpanzees are capable. Washoe was not to be distracted by vocal communication in any language. While it is clear that non-human primates do not have the language abilities of* Homo sapiens, *the limits of their language capacity have yet to be established.*

CHIMPANZEES: SIGN LANGUAGE

Numerous projects studying chimpanzees and language are underway, principally at the University of Oklahoma, the Yerkes Primate Research Center in Georgia, the Delta Regional Primate Research Center in Louisiana, and the University of Pennsylvania. An earlier study was carried out at the University of Nevada by two psychologists, Allen and Beatrice Gardner. The results of their work with a female chimpanzee, Washoe, are particularly relevant for the study of language evolution.

When Washoe was approximately one year old, her trainers began to teach her to communicate using the American Sign Language (ASL) for the deaf. The Gardners' decision to use ASL with Washoe was based on two facts: chimpanzees, even as adults, are very imitative

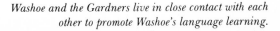

Washoe and the Gardners live in close contact with each other to promote Washoe's language learning.

and gesticulatory animals; and chimpanzees lack the speech apparatus to articulate the sounds of language. Earlier experiments to teach chimpanzees to verbalize human language were not notably successful, the absence of appropriate vocalizing apparatus certainly being a factor. ASL seemed to be a more appropriate language for chimpanzees.

Progress with Washoe was slow at first. The sign "come-gimme" was acquired only after seven months, but once that sign had been acquired others were quick to follow. After twenty-two months, Washoe had a vocabulary of 34 signs; after forty months, she had 92 signs; and after six years she had accumulated over 100 different signs. That far exceeds the accomplishments of chimpanzees raised in human homes who were encouraged to use human language. One of those chimpanzees, Vicki, managed a vocabulary of three words— "mama," "papa," and "cup"—although her comprehension of human speech was far superior to her ability to produce it.

In approximate order, the first signs that Washoe acquired were "come-gimme," "up," "sweet," "go," "hear-listen," "tickle," "open," "toothbrush," "hurry," "funny," "hurt," "drink," "sorry," "please," "food-eat," and "flower." The meanings of the signs, however, were not congruent with the meanings that English speakers intend when they employ words. Washoe used "sweet" only in the sense of dessert. No other meanings, such as pleasing to the taste, pleasing in general, fresh, or not salty were attached to the sign. This is not to belittle Washoe's accomplishments, but simply to demonstrate her limitations. It is quite clear that many of the criteria for meaning were satisfied. For one, the relationship between sign and referent in many cases was arbitrary: Washoe could use symbols. For another, the capacity for classification was clearly present: the name "flower" was produced in response to actual flowers and pictures of flowers, and "hurt" appeared to be the

Beatrice T. Gardner *(1933–   ), a psychologist by training, is famous for her work with Washoe, a chimpanzee. In this century two attempts to raise chimpanzees with human families to teach them to speak failed. Concluding that non-human primates did not have the intelligence to learn a language, many researchers gave up on the idea altogether. Beatrice Gardner, with her husband R. Allen Gardner, decided that chimpanzees might have the capacity for language, but were limited by their vocal apparatus. In place of sounds they substituted ASL, the word-for-sign American Sign Language used by the deaf in North America. Washoe's success with ASL has resulted in a complete reevaluation of our understanding of the evolution of language.*

name of "generalized injury." The sign indicated cuts, bruises on herself and on others, and even red stains on a person. Another important quality was displacement: Washoe used signs independent of immediate stimuli. The sign "sweet" was used when no sweets were actually present.

Washoe's success in sign language acquisition and use has important implications for the evolution of language capacity. Chimpanzees have the capacity for naming objects and activities. This capacity is, therefore, very old. What Washoe tells us is that the prerequisites for naming have been present in the primate line of descent for a long time, perhaps 10–15 million years.

One other point about Washoe's first signs deserves some attention. If we look carefully at what the signs point to for their meaning, we can see that many, in fact most, are labels for

Demonstrating her ability to "talk", Washoe says "drink" to Beatrice Gardner.

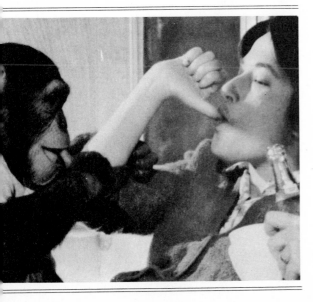

activities. "Funny," for instance, doesn't mean comical or amusing, rather it is used during games between the trainers and Washoe, most likely referring to the activity of playing. Even some words that look like nouns, "toothbrush" for example, are signs for activities more than for objects. "Toothbrush" would be used after meals, implying that the activity to follow was named, not the object. The importance of this—the naming of activities rather than objects—is that it is consistent with what we might expect in the origin of names. Giving something a name implies that it is important, that it is significant. Naming an object implies that the object has some relevance to the user of the name. If we think about this in terms of evolution, it makes sense that names for activities would be among the first "words" to appear. First, the expressive calls and gestures that reflect the emotional state of the users are activity-situated; they occur in the midst of activity. The transition from expressive communication to naming would occur within the contexts of activities. Second, the high degree of social cohesion among hominid groups would also be supportive of activity-naming. What primates communicate about are social relations among individual members. Signals concern dominance, submission, threats, mating, play, in sum, how individuals work out their relations with one another. It seems plausible that those activities would be named before labels would be applied to features of the natural environment such as trees, stones, or even food and water. This suggests that early "words" were more verb-like than they were noun-like, more activity oriented than object oriented.

The Origin of Grammar

Considerable controversy has swirled around the question, "Is Washoe's language human?"

This is actually a false issue: whether Washoe's language is human or not depends on what aspect of language one is talking about. If some of the traits mentioned above are considered, then her language certainly qualifies as human. If we are talking about the complexities of grammar, then Washoe's use of sign language is not at the human level. Comparing Washoe's accomplishments to a list of traits common or universal in human languages, she would score positively on many of the vocabulary components, negatively for almost all traits of grammar, and negatively on the social dimensions of language—speech, status-appropriate speech, formal versus informal speech.

The claim that Washoe has little or no capacity for grammar may appear surprising, since early in her training she began producing sequences of signs. She produced, for instance, strings of signs like "hurry open," "gimme sweet," "tickle Washoe," "hurry please sweet drink," "you me go out." Do these not constitute grammar? The answer has to be that the mere sequencing of signs does not in itself indicate that grammar is present. Grammar is more than strings of words; it is the ordering of strings of words. The telegraphic expression "cat bite" means something different than "bite cat," and the difference is due to the order of the words.

To say that Washoe's strings of signs were grammatical, we would need evidence that order was important. At the present, there is little such evidence. For many of the strings of signs, order seems unimportant to Washoe. "Box open" means nothing different than "open box." Some preference for order in some constructions does exist, however: "you me go" is far more likely to occur than "me you go." This is probably due more to the organization of activities than to grammar. The sign "go" tends to occur in the context of moving in a desired direction. Hand-in-hand with her trainer, or riding the trainer's shoulders, Washoe would

sign "go," usually with some objective in mind such as going outside the mobile home that was her quarters. The meaning, again, can be distorted by how we understand the word "go." A better interpretation of Washoe's use would be something like "take-there" or "allow-go-there." The meaning is more dependent on the situation than the word "go" itself implies. Thus, the preferred order "you me go" could be the result of Washoe's coding of the sequencing of activity—"You take action [open the door] I go out." That sequence would be more consistent with experience than, "I go out, you take action [open the door]."

The serial ordering of experience must have been a factor in the emergence of grammar. Logical sequences and outcomes are likely bases for sequencing linguistic accounts of experience. Supportive evidence can be found from several sources. The majority of the world's human languages have subject-verb-object sentence word order. The agent of an action is the subject of the sentence, the action is the verb, and the object is what is acted upon by the verb or by the subject through the verb. This pattern, agent-action-object, appears to be a strategy used by children acquiring language. It is consistent with much of their experience. Further, individuals who are congenitally deaf have a difficult time understanding and acquiring passive sentence constructions. While sentences like "the cat scratched the dog" do not present any problems, the construction "the dog was scratched by the cat" is difficult. It is likely to be interpreted as "the dog scratched the cat." Young children make exactly the same kinds of mistakes with passives.

While the origin of grammar was embedded in the serial coding of experience, the complex forms of grammar characteristic of human languages probably developed late in the history of the species. When our ancestors began naming, in ways similar to Washoe's, they likely began to use sequences of names randomly ordered.

When sequences are short, two to four words, they are fairly easy to understand, particularly in a context. The expression "bite cat" is as clear as "cat bite" if a cat has just bitten someone. It is only when meaning is ambiguous that word order becomes important. This means that displacement was probably fairly advanced when grammar began to develop.

The emergence of grammar was dependent on the increased complexity of communication and culture. We can assume that acquisition of names or words increased throughout the period of development of culture. As more and more of our ancestors' knowledge of their social and natural environment became more extensive and codified, their vocabulary must also have increased. The capacity for storing words was probably limited at first—Washoe acquired only slightly more than 100 signs in six years—but during evolution it expanded greatly. Most individuals control several thousand words in their language capacity, and the passive recognition capacity of individuals may be up to 100,000. With the increasing number of words and the development of displacement, some higher level organizing device became necessary. This was grammar. As names became more and more specific, as they became more precise, it was possible to use them out of context. The meaning of strings of words became less dependent on the sequencing of behavior. To compensate, the order of words began to carry meaning such that "cat bite" would have one meaning and "bite cat" another.

Grammar is a very powerful device for organizing and expanding meaning. If a language has only 10 words but cannot combine them, then only 10 messages are possible. If constructions of two items are permitted but the order of the items carries no additional meaning, then the number of possible messages is 55 (the original 10, plus word 1 + word 2, word 1 + word 3 . . . word 9 + word 10). If the constructions of two items are permitted and

the order of the items also carries meaning, the total number of messages would increase to 110 (word 1 + word 2 would have one meaning, word 2 + word 1 would have another . . .). If constructions with three items are possible, ignoring order, 91 messages could be constructed. If order is considered, 1,110 three-item messages could be created. If we increase the vocabulary to 100 items and allow five-item constructions, in which order also gives meaning, there are 1,111,100 possible messages. This number far exceeds what is necessary for human language. We might note that Washoe's sign language contained approximately 100 words and some five-word constructions, but the constructions were free of meaningful word order.

We can assume that the earliest strings of names were unordered except for some tendency for the order to match experience. The serial order of experience contributed to the development of word order, to a kind of pregrammar, but grammar, with its power to create an extremely large number of messages with only a few items and rules, probably did not develop until comparatively late in the evolution of language. It was only after a large increase in vocabulary size that the power of grammar would be needed. We can conclude that for grammar to appear, the size of the vocabulary would have to exceed the capacity of present-day chimpanzees. Experimental work with other chimpanzees, using other methods of communication, supports these conclusions.

ANATOMICAL EVIDENCE: THE SPEECH APPARATUS

Anatomical evidence tends to support the hypothesis that language, with all of its human characteristics, appeared late in the prehistoric record. We know that as a consequence of upright stance, the anatomy of the chin, oral cav-

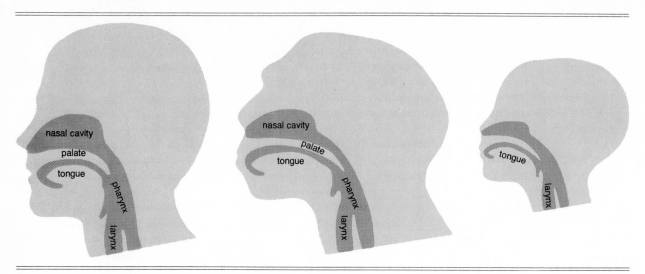

The speech apparatus of Homo sapiens sapiens *(above),* Homo sapiens neanderthalensis *(middle), and the* Homo sapiens sapiens *infant (right) indicates that Neanderthal did not have the ability to form many sounds because of the position of the nasal cavity, mouth, and pharynx.*

ity, tongue, and pharynx changed slightly. These changes had significant effects on the ability of hominids to produce sounds. In humans, the nasal cavity can be closed off, allowing air to be expelled solely through the oral cavity. Articulations can be non-nasal, an anatomical impossibility among other primates. More importantly, the *pharynx,* the tube connecting the oral and nasal cavities with the *larynx* or voice box and the *esophagus,* was increased in length and size. In primates, air expelled from the lungs passes through the voice box to vibrate and resonate in the pharynx. But the human pharynx has more resonance potential than that of other primates because of its length. Humans can produce the three fundamental vowels "i", "a", and "u" necessary for human speech, while apes have more limited articulation capabilities.

Philip Lieberman, a linguist at Brown University, has carried out some interesting research on the evolution of the speech tract. Lieberman and his collaborators constructed a model of the vocal tract from a Neanderthal fossil skull. Using a computer program, they determined what kinds of sounds the vocal tract could have produced. They found that the vocal tract was similar in shape to chimpanzees and present-day human infants, and concluded that none of those tracts could produce the vowels "i", "a", and "u", or the back consonants "k" and "g". Lieberman and his associates also concluded that the rate of speech would be affected, that Neanderthal could speak only fifteen words a minute, about one-tenth the rate of modern human speech.

Examinations of other fossil skulls showed that Australopithecines had a vocal tract similar to that of Neanderthals. Some late *Homo erectus* fossils, however, showed strong evidence of changes toward a modern vocal tract. Lieberman further speculated that Neanderthals were not in the evolutionary line leading to *Homo sapiens,* since there was no evidence of a developed vocal tract. If Lieberman's work is accurate, then spoken language that sounded like human speech appeared fairly recently, in the range of 30,000 to 50,000 years ago. It should be noted, though, that not all of Lieberman's hypotheses are generally accepted. The relative merits of his research are currently under debate in technical journals. One major objection is that the Neanderthal specimen he used is a slightly aberrant form; another objection is that his reconstruction of the Neanderthal vocal tract may not be accurate.

The Brain

The brain has undergone several changes in the course of hominid evolution. It has more than doubled in size, and most of that increase has been in the hemispheres of the brain. There has been an increase in the number and depth of convolutions in the cerebral cortex and in the number of nerve fibers connecting the two hemispheres. The brain has also become *lateralized*, that is, the two hemispheres have become functionally distinct. These developments have implications for the evolution of language.

Two systems of the brain are involved in speech: the *limbic system* which regulates the emotions and the sound communications that are emotion laden, and the *neocortical system* which regulates the information content of speech. The limbic system is the older of the two systems, regulating the expressive vocalizations of non-human primates as well. While the limbic system is bilateral, that is, it employs both hemispheres of the brain equally, the neocortical system, developed only in humans, uses predominantly the left hemisphere of the brain. The neocortical system did not replace the limbic system, or arise from it; it developed as new tissue in the structure of the brain. It is the dominant regulator of the information content and the production of speech and operates independent of emotional factors.

The evolutionary development of brain

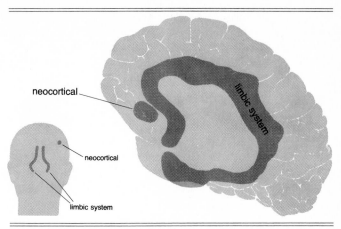

The neocortical system (above), which controls verbal communication, is found in the left hemisphere of the brain only. The limbic system (below), which controls nonverbal communication, is found in both hemispheres of the brain.

structure and function is completely consistent with what we have seen in the evolution of sound communication. Vocalizations were progressively freed from emotions and context. They became more abstract; that is, they carried more information content. The dominance of the left hemisphere, which controls the right side of the body, is also consistent with the idea that right-handedness, associated with stone tool manufacture, was connected to the general increase in cultural complexity and the potential for language. The location of the center for the control of right-handedness and speech in the left hemisphere of the brain probably was part and parcel of the same evolutionary process.

What does the right hemisphere of the brain have to do with language? Interestingly, the right hemisphere can assume the same control of speech as the left hemisphere, but only up to a certain age of an individual. If a child acquiring language prior to approximately three years of age receives an injury to the speech area of the left hemisphere, the right hemisphere can begin to assume the speech functions, and language recovery may be complete. After the age of three, however, recovery is slower. As the age of a child approaches twelve years, the right hemisphere has a much more limited ability to take over functions of speech.

Additional evidence for the role of the right hemisphere comes from recent studies of individuals who have undergone surgery that has severed the *corpus callosum,* the part of the brain linking the left and right hemispheres. These "split-brain" individuals have shown that the right hemisphere can "recognize" objects in the environment, but the individuals cannot supply the speech to name the objects. When asked to point to a given object, they can do so without difficulty or hesitation. This indicates that the right hemisphere has the same potential as the left hemisphere for understanding language, but not for verbalizing it. This provides further evidence for the priority of naming as a first step in language evolution. The expanded frontal lobes of the brain must have been associated with the evolution of intelligence, naming, and culture. The development of speech control in the dominant hemisphere was most likely a later occurrence, which is consistent with our interpretations of primate studies.

THE ACQUISITION OF LANGUAGE BY CHILDREN

Once evolved, the capacity for language has been remarkably uniform among all members of the human species. There are no primitive languages because there is no primitive intelligence. Given adequate exposure to language, any child born into any society can acquire the language of that community with relative ease. He can also acquire the language of any other community, no matter how different the actual structure of the languages may be. Children in all societies go through the same early stages of language acquisition at roughly the same ages. The onset of vocabulary acquisition is approximately 10–14 months and the onset of multi-word utterances is from 18 to 26 months. There is clearly an innate predisposition to acquire language in *Homo sapiens.*

In recent years these facts were taken as evidence that the acquisition of language structure was fixed, almost predetermined. It is more accurate to say that the maturation of the capacity for language acquisition follows a pattern. The pattern is similar for all children from birth to the age of five years or so. Despite these consistencies, the acquisition of language is also highly dependent on a supportive social environment. It is obvious, for instance, that children deprived of contact with speakers of a language will not acquire the language. The meanings of words are acquired through imitation, observation, instruction, explanation, and most importantly, through use. Although children may utter a particular word, they do not necessarily mean the same thing that adults mean. "Doggie," for instance, may refer to any four-legged animal and only later, through use, correction, and increased awareness of the environment, come to refer to *Canis familiaris.*

When we consider children's acquisition of grammar, environmental support is problematic. Adult speakers are not aware of the intricacies of their grammatical systems. They do not "know," in a conscious way, the structure of their language. Yet children learn the important distinctions of grammar, usually during the first few years of life. Without social interaction children could not learn the rules of grammar. They would have no models against which to test the accuracy of their sentences.

The importance of the social environment is being stressed because the basis of language acquisition is experience. A biologically based capacity for language is, of course, necessary, and the acquisition of language is contingent on the maturation of those capacities. However, a child's use of language in social contexts undeniably promotes language acquisition. Children learn through interaction with the people and objects surrounding them. They learn through experience long before they begin to express these experiences in language. Children know what food is and the satisfaction of eating before they are able to indicate verbally what they want or when they want it. Their first vocabulary items are strongly functional—naming caretakers (usually mama and papa), food, drink, and bodily needs like sleeping. As their experiences multiply, the child's ability to name things increases.

The acquisition of two word utterances also follows the path of experience. Roger Brown, a Harvard psychologist, who pioneered much of the research in language acquisition, has shown that the early two-word constructions of children are based on a small number of relationships of meaning—"this doggie, more milk, no sleep"—all based on experience. In each case, word order tends to be fairly regular, but this is due to the child's perception of what occurs around him, not to grammar. As with chimpanzees like Washoe, children appear to see the world in subject-verb-object order. The order is also reinforced by the speech of the surrounding adults, by the presentation of examples of the language in use, not a series of grammatical rules. The increased ability of children to store and process larger units of information about their experiences yields longer utterances. And with these longer constructions, grammar develops to facilitate communication. Exactly how this happens is not yet clear, but we now know enough to reject the claim that children are pre-programmed to acquire language through the application of grammatical rules. Grammar is more of a result than a cause; once grammatical rules are internalized by the child, the potential for communicating complex thoughts increases astronomically.

The course of language acquisition in children has some strong parallels with the sketch of language evolution presented. The two fundamental developments in evolution were naming and grammar, and we have seen that these emerged out of increasing complexity in social behavior and cultural information. Just as our hominid ancestors did, children create and discover finer and more precise ways of relating information about the environment and themselves to other individuals.

There is another intriguing way in which language acquisition parallels the evolution of language. The ability to name things occurred as vocalizations were progressively freed from emotion and affect. Children advance through a similar process. Their first vocalized act is crying, which can vary in volume and rate to signal different emotional states. Older infants, without the use of words, can communicate vocally with what linguists call *prosodic features*—pitch, tone, duration, and volume. They can indicate anger, distress, contentment, glee and a host of other emotions by varying these features. And those actions can produce behavioral reactions, sometimes overreactions, in others. As we have described, non-human primate communication operates in a very similar way.

Vocal communication based on the modulation of prosodic features does not disappear when children begin to acquire words or grammar. They continue to be extremely important in human communication. We rely on changes in pitch, rate of speech, volume, and so on, to express all manner of moods in our speech. We sing or shout for joy, bellow in rage, bubble with enthusiasm, yell or scream in pain, argue heatedly, speak forcefully. The entire meaning of a sentence can change depending on where we place the stress in our pronunciation, and it is often true that how we say something is more important than what we say.

The expressive mode of speech and referential speech are not completely separate systems. To the contrary, they are highly integrated;

many, perhaps most, of our communicative acts rely on both modes. The expressive mode appears to have come first in evolution, develops first in the acquisition of language, and often takes precedence in meaning when the two modes are combined. All this indicates that it is appropriate to view the emergence of non-affective speech as simply one of the kinds of communication that evolved, not the only or the most important kind. It is true, certainly, that one of the profound changes was the freeing of utterances from affect. It is essential that individuals could talk dispassionately about themselves and the environment; that trait is basic to human language. At the same time, though, dispassionate speech is needed only at certain times and in certain instances. The use of dispassionate speech is defined by the social environment. In other words, speakers have to know how and under what circumstances one should speak without feeling or affect. Since almost all the earliest forms of communication were based on affect, it seems reasonable to assume non-affective speech was the product of a long evolutionary process rooted in the ways individuals related to one another. All forms of speech, all modes of communication evolved in a matrix of social relations. It is there, in how hominids related to one another and in how cultural information was used to organize those relations, that the questions about the origin and evolution of language must ultimately be unraveled.

The Voices of Time

Edward T. Hall

One of the remarkable attributes of human language is its ability to communicate distinctive perspectives on many different topics. As Hall demonstrates, the concept of time takes different forms in societies around the world. What is appropriate for one type of society would be inappropriate for another. Obviously, our notion of time as a scheduled, regularly occurring phenomenon is intimately related to the level of technological complexity in our society. It wouldn't work in Afghanistan, just as their conception of time wouldn't work in the United States. What interests us here, however, is that human language has evolved a level of flexibility that allows it to communicate all conceptions of time and, for that matter, all conceptions of space, matter, natural, supernatural, and on and on.

Time talks. It speaks more plainly than words. The message it conveys comes through loud and clear. Because it is manipulated less consciously, it is subject to less distortion than the spoken language. It can shout the truth where words lie.

AMERICAN TIME

People of the Western world, particularly Americans, tend to think of time as something fixed in nature, something around us and from which we cannot escape; an ever-present part of the environment, just like the air we breathe. That it might be experienced in any other way seems unnatural and strange, a feeling which is rarely modified even when we begin to discover how really differently it is handled by some other people. Within the West itself certain cultures rank time much lower in over-all importance than we do. In Latin America, for example, where time is treated rather cavalierly, one commonly hears the expression, "Our time or your time?" *¿"Hora americana, hora mejicana?"*

As a rule, Americans think of time as a road or a ribbon stretching into the future, along which one progresses. The road has segments or compartments which are to be kept discrete ("one thing at a time"). People who cannot schedule time are looked down upon as impractical. In at least some parts of Latin America, the North American (their term for us) finds himself annoyed when he has made an appointment with somebody, only to find a lot of other things going on at the same time. An old friend of mine of Spanish cultural heritage used to run his business according to the "Latino" system. This meant that up to fifteen people were in his office at one time. Business which might have been finished in a quarter of an hour sometimes took a whole day. He realized, of course, that the Anglo-Americans were disturbed by this and used to make some allowance for them, a dispensation which meant that they spent only an hour or so in his office when they had planned on a few minutes. The American concept of the discreteness of time and the necessity for scheduling was at variance with this amiable and seemingly confusing Latin system. However, if my friend had adhered to the American system he would have destroyed a vital part of his prosperity. People who came to do business with him also came to find out things and to visit each other. The ten to fifteen Spanish-Americans and Indians who used to sit around the office (among whom I later found myself after I had learned to relax a little) played their own part in a particular type of communications network.

Not only do we Americans segment and schedule time, but we look ahead and are oriented almost entirely toward the future. We like new things and are preoccupied with change. We want to know how to overcome resistance to change. In fact, scientific theories and even some pseudo-scientific ones, which incorporate a striking theory of change, are often given special attention.

Time with us is handled much like a material; we earn it, spend it, save it, waste it. To us it is somewhat immoral to have two things going on at the same time. In Latin America it is not uncommon for one man to have a number of simultaneous jobs which he either carries on from one desk or which he moves between, spending a small amount of time on each.

While we look to the future, our view of it is limited. The future to us is the foreseeable future, not the future of the South Asian that may involve centuries. Indeed, our perspective is so short as to inhibit the operation of a good many practical projects, such as sixty- and one-hundred-year conservation works requiring public support and public funds. Anyone who has worked in industry or in the government of the United States has heard the following: "Gentlemen, this is for the long term! Five or ten years."

For us a "long time" can be almost anything—ten or twenty years, two or three months, a few weeks, or even a couple of days. The South Asian, however, feels that it is perfectly realistic to think of a "long time" in terms of thousands of years or even an endless period. A colleague once described their conceptualization of time as follows: "Time is like a museum with endless corridors and alcoves. You, the viewer, are walking through the museum in the dark, holding a light to each scene as you pass it. God is the curator of the museum, and only He knows all that is in it. One lifetime represents one alcove."

The American's view of the future is linked to a view of the past, for tradition plays an equally limited part in American culture. As a whole, we push it aside or leave it to a few souls who are interested in the past for very special reasons. There are, of course, a few pockets, such as New England and the South, where tradition is emphasized. But in the realm of business, which is the dominant model of United States life, tradition is equated with *experience,* and experience is thought of as being very close to if not synonymous with know-how. Know-how is one of our prized possessions, so that when we look backward it is rarely to take pleasure in the past itself but usually to calculate the know-how, to assess the prognosis for success in the future.

Promptness is also valued highly in American life. If people are not prompt, it is often taken either as an insult or as an indication that they are not quite responsible. There are those, of a psychological bent, who would say that we are obsessed with time. They can point to individuals in American culture who are literally time-ridden. And even the rest of us feel very strongly about time because we have been taught to take it so seriously. We have stressed this aspect of culture and developed it to a point unequaled anywhere in the world, except, perhaps, in Switzerland and north Germany. Many people criticize our obsessional handling of time. They attribute ulcers and hypertension to the pressure engendered by such a system. Perhaps they are right.

SOME OTHER CONCEPTS OF TIME

Even within the very borders of the United States there are people who handle time in a way which is almost incomprehensible to those who have not made a major effort to understand it. The Pueblo Indians, for example, who live in the Southwest, have a sense of time which is at complete variance with the clock-bound habits of the ordinary American citizen. For the Pueblos events begin when the time is ripe and no sooner.

I can still remember a Christmas dance I attended some twenty-five years ago at one of the pueblos near the Rio Grande. I had to travel over bumpy roads for forty-five miles to get there. At seven thousand feet the ordeal of winter cold at one o'clock in the morning is almost unbearable. Shivering in the still darkness of the pueblo, I kept searching for a clue as to when the dance would begin.

Outside everything was impenetrably quiet. Occa-sionally there was the muffled beat of a deep pueblo drum, the opening of a door, or the piercing of the night's darkness with a shaft of light. In the church where the dance was to take place a few white townsfolk were huddled together on a balcony, groping for some clue which would suggest how much longer they were going to suffer. "Last year I heard they started at ten o'clock." "They can't start until the priest comes." "There is no way of telling when they will start." All this punctuated by chatter-ing teeth and the stamping of feet to keep up circulation.

Suddenly an Indian opened the door, entered, and poked up the fire in the stove. Everyone nudged his neighbor: "Maybe they are going to begin now." Another hour passed. Another Indian came in from outside, walked across the nave of the church, and disappeared through another door. "Certainly now they will begin. After all, it's almost two o'clock." Someone guessed that they were just being ornery in the hope that the white men would go away. Another had a friend in the pueblo and went to his house to ask when the dance would begin. Nobody knew. Suddenly, when the whites were almost exhausted, there burst upon the night the deep sounds of the drums, rattles, and low males voices singing. Without warning the dance had begun.

After years of performances such as this, no white man in his right mind will hazard a guess as to when one of these ceremonial dances will begin. Those of us who have learned now know that the dance doesn't start at a particular time. It is geared to no schedule. It starts when "things" are ready!

Time does not heal on Truk! Past events stack up, placing an ever-increasing burden on the Trukese and weighing heavily on the present. They are, in fact, treated as though they had just occurred. This was borne out by something which happened shortly after the American occupation of the atoll at the end of World War II.

A villager arrived all out of breath at the military government headquarters. He said that a murder had been committed in the village and that the murderer was running around loose. Quite naturally the military government officer became alarmed. He was about to dispatch M.P.s to arrest the culprit when he remembered that someone had warned him about acting precipitously when dealing with "natives." A little inquiry turned up the fact that the victim had been "fooling around" with the murderer's wife. Still more inquiry of a routine type, designed to establish the place and date of the crime, revealed that the murder had not occurred a few hours or even days ago, as one might expect, but seventeen years before. The murderer had been running around loose in the village all this time.

A further example of how time does not heal on Truk is that of a land dispute that started with the German occupation in the 1890s, was carried on down through the Japanese occupation, and was still current and acrimonious when the Americans arrived in 1946.

Prior to Missionary Moses' arrival on Uman in 1867 life on Truk was characterized by violent and bloody warfare. Villages, instead of being built on the shore where life was a little easier, were placed on the sides of mountains where they could be better protected. Attacks would come without notice and often without apparent provocation. Or a fight might start if a man stole a coconut from a tree that was not his or waylaid a woman and took advantage of her. Years later someone would start thinking about the wrong and decide that it still had not been righted. A village would be attacked again in the middle of the night.

When charges were brought against a chief for things he had done to his people, every little slight, every minor graft would be listed; nothing would be forgotten. Damages would be asked for everything. It seemed preposterous to us Americans, particularly when we looked at the lists of charges. "How could a chief be so corrupt?" "How could the people remember so much?"

Though the Truk islanders carry the accumulated burden of time past on their shoulders, they show an almost total inability to grasp the notion that two events can take place at the same time when they are any distance apart. When the Japanese occupied

Truk at the end of World War I they took Artie Moses, chief of the island of Uman, to Tokyo. Artie was made to send a wireless message back to his people as a demonstration of the wizardry of Japanese technology. His family refused to believe that he had sent it, that he had said anything at all, though they knew he was in Tokyo. Places at a distance are very real to them, but people who are away are very much away, and any interaction with them is unthinkable.

An entirely different handling of time is reported by the anthropologist Paul Bohannan for the Tiv, a primitive people who live in Nigeria. Like the Navajo, they point to the sun to indicate a general time of day, and they also observe the movement of the moon as it waxes and wanes. What is different is the way they use and experience time. For the Tiv, time is like a capsule. There is a time for visiting, for cooking, or for working; and when one is in one of these times, one does not shift to another.

The Tiv equivalent of the week lasts five to seven days. It is not tied into periodic natural events, such as the phases of the moon. The day of the week is named after the things which are being sold in the nearest "market." If we had the equivalent, Monday would be "automobiles" in Washington, D.C., "furniture" in Baltimore, and "yard goods" in New York. Each of these might be followed by the days for appliances, liquor, and diamonds in the respective cities. This would mean that as you traveled about the day of the week would keep changing, depending on where you were.

A requisite of our own temporal system is that the components must add up: Sixty seconds have to equal one minute, sixty minutes one hour. The American is perplexed by people who do not do this. The African specialist Henri Alexandre Junod, reporting on the Thonga, tells of a medicine man who had memorized a seventy-year chronology and detail the events of each and every year in sequence. Yet this same man spoke of the period he had memorized as an "era" which he computed at "four months and eight hundred years' duration." The usual reaction to this story and others like it is that the man was primitive, like a child, and did not understand what he was saying, because how could seventy years possibly be the same as eight hundred? As students of culture we can no longer dismiss other conceptualizations of reality by saying that they are childlike. We must go much deeper. In the case of the Thonga it seems that a "chronology" is one thing and an "era" something else quite different, and there is no relation between the two in operational terms.

If these distinctions between European-American time and other conceptions of time seem to draw too heavily on primitive peoples, let me mention two other examples—from cultures which are as civilized, if not as industrialized, as our own. In comparing the United States with Iran and Afghanistan very great differences in the handling of time appear. The American attitude toward appointments is an example. Once while in Tehran I had an opportunity to observe some young Iranians making plans for a party. After plans were made to pick up everyone at appointed times and places everything began to fall apart. People would leave messages that they were unable to take so-and-so or were going somewhere else, knowing full well that the person who had been given the message couldn't possibly deliver it. One girl was left stranded on a street corner, and no one seemed to be concerned about it. One of my informants explained that he himself had had many similar experiences. Once he had made eleven appointments to meet a friend. Each time one of them failed to show up. The twelfth time they swore they would both be there, that nothing would interfere. The friend failed to arrive. After waiting for forty-five minutes my informant phoned his friend and found him still at home. The following conversation is an approximation of what took place:

"Is that you, Abdul?" "Yes." "Why aren't you here? I thought we were to meet for sure." "Oh, but it was raining," said Abdul with a sort of whining intonation that is very common in Parsi.

If present appointments are treated rather cavalierly, the past in Iran takes on a very great importance. People look back on what they feel are the wonders of the past and the great ages of Persian culture. Yet the future seems to have little reality or certainty to it. Businessmen have been known to invest hundreds of thousands of dollars in factories of various sorts without making the slightest plan as to how to use them. A complete woolen mill was bought and shipped to Tehran before the buyer had raised enough money to erect it, to buy supplies, or even to train personnel. When American teams of technicians came to help Iran's economy they constantly had to cope with what seemed to them an almost total lack of planning.

Moving east from Iran to Afghanistan, one gets farther afield from American time concepts. A few years ago in Kabul a man appeared, looking for his brother. He asked all the merchants of the marketplace if they had seen his brother and told them where he was staying in case his brother arrived and wanted to find him. The next year he was back and repeated the performance. By this time one of the members of the American embassy had heard about his inquiries and asked if he had found his brother. The man answered that he and his brother had agreed to meet in Kabul, but neither of them had said what year.

Summary

Speculation on the origins of human language developed in the nineteenth century, shortly after Darwin presented his theory of evolution. Early theories addressed themselves to the problem of the initiation of naming. How did particular sounds come to be associated with particular objects? One theory, the pooh-pooh or interjection theory, proposed that exclamations such as "ow!" and "hey!" came to be names for the related emotions, pain and surprise. Another theory, the bow-wow or onomatopoeia theory, saw the origins of naming in the imitation of natural sounds—animal calls, the rain, the wind. Neither theory, however, explains the development of arbitrary sound-meaning relationships common to all human languages, or the expansion of a limited number of "names" to the thousands found in any language.

Recently, two anthropologists have described a potential process for the development of an open call system from a closed one. Assuming there existed a call for food and a call for danger, the frequent common occurrence of food and danger could have resulted in the combination of the two calls to create a third call, "food and danger." Whereas this change appears minor, it alters the entire structure of communication, opening the call system for the creation of new words, initiating a simple grammar, and developing the capacity for displacement. Additionally, displacement implies the development of semantics, of categories of meaning.

Much of the recent speculation on language origins is based on the study of primate call systems. Non-human primates use a number of different calls to communicate about food, reproduction, aggression, fear, bonding and child care. It appears, however, that the call is just one of the modes of communication used by primates. Many non-verbal modes, such as gesture, smell, touch, and eye contact, are employed at the same time. Additionally, the calls appear to communicate moods and mood changes more than they name "things" in the environment. Primates do not communicate the presence of food, for instance, they communicate a level of excitement which draws the attention of others to the food. It appears, then, that theories of language evolution must consider the development of "naming" before considering the means by which naming systems became opened.

Recent studies indicate that language may have begun with a system of naming based on gesturing rather than vocal communication. Considering the visual and manual abilities of the higher primates, it is not unreasonable to assume that "pointing" was the first form of naming. Non-human primates have a high level of object recognition as well as the habit of imitating the gestures of others. Those who have studied primates in the wild, however, report that the animals do not employ gesturing extensively. The capability for gestural "naming" appears to be underutilized in primates.

Support for the gestural theory of language evolution comes from experiments with chimpanzee language acquisition employing sign language in place of sound. Using the American Sign Language (ASL) for the deaf, one chimpanzee, Washoe, learned over one hundred signs during six years of training. While Washoe did not learn to use these words with the same subtlety as any human speaker of a language, she was capable of classification and displacement. Clearly, the relationship between her signs and the referents was arbitrary. Washoe's success indicates that the capacity for sign language acquisition was present early in the evolution of hominoids.

The nature of Washoe's first signs also provides insight into the origin of language. Her first signs were the names of activities rather than objects. This indicates that naming first developed with respect to activities, probably those of some evolutionary significance. Additionally, it appears that Washoe was not capable of grammar. While her speech did have some order, it was subject-verb-object order, a natural outcome of the chronology of events. Logic, rather than grammar, appears to have been the basis of ordering. It is likely that grammar did not develop until cultural complexity required an efficient mechanism for communicating complex events without relying on the continual creation of new symbols. A language with 100 items in which word order gives meaning up to five-word constructions can produce 1,111,100 messages. One in which order does not communicate meaning is limited to 100 messages.

Anatomical evidence tends to support the notion that speech was a relatively late development. Studies of the relationship of the pharynx, larynx and esophagus in *Australopithecus* indicate that it was incapable of creating certain vowels and consonants. By the time of late *Homo erectus*, however, all the anatomical features necessary for speech were fully evolved.

The brain also provides evidence for the late development of speech. The limbic system, which controls emotions and emotional vocalizations, exists in both lobes. However, the neocortical system, the specialized portion of the brain which controls the informational content of speech, exists in the left hemisphere only. Additionally, it develops later than the limbic system in the maturational process. This indicates that the neocortical system developed late in the evolution of the species, slowly freeing communication from its emotional base.

The study of language acquisition in children also supports these general conclusions about language development. Children have an innate ability to learn language. It requires reinforcement and experience, however, to bring out that ability. In other words, as has been stressed, language is only significant in a complex social and cultural environment. Children begin speaking with single words and multiple-word statements which take subject-verb-object order. As the necessity to communicate more complex thoughts develops, grammar is acquired. Simultaneously, the emotional elements of communication decline and the informational elements increase. Expressive speech never disappears in adults but it is employed in limited circumstances only. It is likely that future developments in the analysis of the evolution of language will stress the social and informational basis of human communication.

Glossary

Arbitrariness The random relationship between sound and meaning in all human languages. Once the sound-meaning connections are established by social convention, people can communicate about almost anything.

Call system The verbal-auditory communication system of non-human primates in which each call has a fixed meaning.

Closed call system One in which calls cannot be recombined to create new messages.

Corpus callosum The nerve tissue that connects the two hemispheres of the brain.

Displacement The ability of human language to communicate about subjects removed in time and space from the immediate context.

Esophagus The tube connecting the pharynx, near the mouth, to the stomach.

Grammar The rules controlling the way units of meaning, "words," are combined in a language to form meaningful statements.

Larynx The voice box.

Lateralization The developmental specialization of a part of the brain in one hemisphere only.

Limbic system The "old" part of the brain which regulates basic responses such as fear, hunger, and aggression and the verbal components of those responses.

Neocortical system   The part of the brain that regulates the information content of speech.

Open call system   One in which calls can be recombined to create new messages.

Phonetics   The study of the sounds employed in a language.

Prosodic features   The elements of verbal communication other than the informational content of the "words," such as pitch, tone, and volume.

Referential speech   Verbal communication that "names" or refers to things in the environment.

Semantics   The relationship between the sounds and the "things" they refer to in a language.

Additional Reading

Altmann, Stuart A., editor
1967   Social Communication Among Primates. Chicago: University of Chicago Press.

A comprehensive series of excellent articles on the social life of non-human primates.

Hall, Edward T.
1959   The Silent Language. Greenwich, Conn.: Fawcett Publications.

A fascinating study of the nonverbal communication that accompanies all social interaction. The author points out that patterns of this "silent language" are culturally determined.

Lieberman, Phillip
1975   On the Origins of Language: An Introduction to the Evolution of Human Speech. New York: Macmillan.

A thoughtful introduction to the origins of language.

1972   The Speech of Primates. The Hague: Mouton.

Lieberman examines language as a product of vocal anatomy, a controversial approach to the evolution of communication.

Stross, Brian
1976   The Origin and Evolution of Language. Dubuque: William Brown Publishing Co.

A good discussion of the evolution of language for the advanced student.

Wescott, Roger, editor
1974   Language Origins, Silver Spring, Maryland: Linstok Press.

Some rather well thought out examinations of the alternative explanations of the origin of language.

chapter twelve

Cultural Anthropology/
CONCEPTS AND THEORIES
OF CULTURE

Since the subject of this section is cultural anthropology, we ought to have a clear idea of what we mean by "culture" at the outset. It is a term everyone uses quite freely, but with only a vague sense of agreement on its meaning. Even social scientists don't always agree on the definition of culture; two anthropologists once collected more than 160 meanings of the term! Sometimes we think of culture as referring to the life style of the upper class. In order to "have culture," one must attend the opera, art museums, and other such events. Other times we might call a person "uncultured," meaning uncouth or rude, although technically, as anthropologists use the word, there is no such thing as an uncultured person since every individual participates in some cultural tradition. And the list of definitions goes on and on. Yet obviously there must be some commonly accepted meaning if cultural anthropologists are to be able to work together and compare their knowledge and understanding of human behavior.

DEFINITION OF CULTURE

Culture is that aspect of our existence which makes us similar to some other people, yet different from the majority of the people in the world. We are all basically the same physically, in that we are members of the same species. And we are all different in that each of us has an individual personality that cannot be duplicated. It is culture that binds us together into a group sharing a certain degree of similarity, overcoming the individual differences among us yet setting us apart from other groups. Thus when we speak of culture we mean a way of life common to a group of people, a collection of beliefs and attitudes, shared understandings and patterns of behavior that allow those people to live together in relative harmony, but set them apart from other peoples. Culture is what makes us "Americans" rather than Germans, Chinese or Bantu.

Perhaps the best definition of culture, as it is used in anthropology, is still the one proposed by Edward B. Tylor more than 100 years ago in his book *Primitive Culture.* Tylor defined culture as *"that complex whole which includes knowledge, belief, art, morals, law, customs, and any other capabilities and habits acquired by man as a member of society."*

That complex whole . . .

Let us take a closer look at this definition to see what some of its implications are. First of all, culture is "that complex whole." It is not just a series of unrelated things that happen to have been picked up and thrown together by a group of people as they wandered around the earth. It is a whole, an integrated unit. The parts of any culture fit together—not just the physical aspects such as tools, houses and clothing, but the nonmaterial aspects of culture such as the patterns of behavior followed by the members of the group. As Tylor's definition indicates, culture includes those intangibles such as knowledge, belief, art, morals, law, customs and other capabilities and habits. They form a context for each other. Law and morals

and customs must be based upon knowledge and belief, and must be reflected in the way people act toward one another.

. . . . acquired by man . . .

Second, Tylor's definition tells us that culture is "acquired by man." This has several implications, among them that culture is not inherited or instinctive, and also that culture is unique to the human species. Many anthropologists no longer believe that culture is a uniquely human characteristic, and we will discuss this problem in more detail. But the fact that culture is *acquired* is important for understanding why people behave the way they do. A person learns a culture from the members of his or her group. If you had been born and raised in Japan, you would speak fluent Japanese and feel perfectly comfortable following Japanese customs and traditions. There is no biological basis for one culture as opposed to another, just as there is no relationship between a person's racial characteristics and his or her culture.

Alfred Kroeber provided an interesting example to illustrate this distinction between the inborn character of most nonhuman behavior and the learned cultural behavior of human beings. Suppose we hatch some ant eggs on a deserted island. The resulting ant colony will be an exact reproduction of the previous generation of ants, including their social behavior. Ants have a set of rules they follow in acting together as a group, but these rules are not learned as a result of interaction with other ants of the previous generation. They are instinctive and part of the heredity of the ants in each new generation. That is why we can be sure that the newly hatched ants will be and act exactly like their parents' generation, even though they will never see any members of that generation.

Suppose we do the same with a group of in-

Since the earliest days of human society, dining together has been an important way by which an individual acquires culture as a member of a group.

fants from our own society (pretending for the sake of argument that it were possible). Certainly we would not expect the same results—a generation of people just like their parents. Rather, the result would be a horde of people essentially without culture. If they were somehow able to survive (which would also be impossible), they might develop their own culture, different from any other way of life on earth. They would not speak a language that was intelligible to anyone else, nor would they dress or eat or do anything else in a way that reflected their parents' culture. Although born of American parents, there is no way that such individuals could acquire American culture without

being taught. Only in science fiction can test-tube babies be programmed for a specific way of life before they are born.

. . . as a member of society.

A third implication of Tylor's definition is that culture is shared and that learning takes place within the confines of a group. Culture is a group phenomenon, not an individual one; it pertains to societies, or people who share a way of life. Of course, ants and bees are organized into what we call societies, as are some higher primates, including baboons and chimpanzees. But we distinguish between the social life of insects, which is instinctive, and the social life of human beings, which is learned or acquired. In the case of nonhuman primates, the distinction is less clear: We used to think that tool using and learned behavior were unique to human beings. Recently, however, we have discovered chimpanzees actually manufacturing tools for themselves, as discussed in Chapter 3. The assumption that animals could not learn and could not transfer learned behavior to other members of the species has also been challenged by studies of Japanese macaques. Japanese investigators have used the feeding grounds of macaques in extended studies of the origin and spread of eating habits, for example the habit of carrying sweet potatoes to the ocean's edge and washing the dirt off. This trick was invented some sixteen years ago by Imo, a highly precocious female macaque only eighteen months old at the time, apparently young enough so that she had not yet learned to share the traditional primate fear of water. Her playmates were soon washing their potatoes, but the rest of the troop continued to use the old and less efficient method of brushing the dirt off with their hands. Five years later, the new method had spread from Imo and her playmates to their mothers and later to their own offspring. Having discarded tool use and invention and the learning and sharing of behavior as ways of distinguishing primate behavior from human behavior, we still held onto the last distinguishing feature—language. But even the use of language can no longer separate human cultural behavior from nonhuman primate behavior, as evidenced by Washoe's success with sign language discussed in Chapter 11.

Of course, there are limitations to the culture of nonhuman primates. As far as we know, no

A definite social hierarchy exists among many primate societies. How does their behavior differ from human cultural behavior?

ape has developed social institutions such as religion, law, ethics, or economics. One way of comprehending the fundamental difference between people and apes is in the quantitative separation between them—the sheer amount of cultural behavior practiced by human beings as opposed to the relatively small proportion found among other primates. Anthropologist George Peter Murdock has compiled a list of what he calls *cultural universals,* basic solutions to the problems of living that are found in one form or another in all cultures. This list gives us an intuitive feeling for the humanness of our species by pointing out how many different kinds of behavior are shared by all human beings no matter where they come from. We may be able to define some nonhuman behavior as "cultural," but this does not mean that other animals have a culture in the same sense that we do, as this list illustrates. In reading over some of these universals. presented below, think about their form in your own culture, and then

THE PARADOXES OF CULTURE

The study of variation brings out one of several paradoxes built into the concept of culture: *although culture is universal, each local or regional manifestation is unique.* Every group of people has a culture and shares a way of life, yet in each region of the world different sets of experiences and particular ecological and historical factors impinge upon the culture, resulting in regional variation. The universals of culture provide a framework within which this variety occurs.

A second paradox of culture is that *while it is stable and predictable for the people who share it and use it as a basis for organizing their lives, it is at the same time undergoing constant and continuous change.* If we look at the process by which children are taught the culture of their parents, we can see this paradox at work. As children learn their culture, they provide stability and continuity over time, and they are able to carry on the traditions of previous generations. This presents us with a static view of culture. However, the process of training a child is never complete, so that no one generation is a mirror image of the previous one. If each succeeding generation is different from the preceding one, the result will obviously be change in the culture over time. This presents an apparent contradiction in the concept of culture, for it is at the same time both static and dynamic, preserving tradition while having a built-in mechanism for continuous change. We can see this in our own lives, as stability and change operate together, sometimes creating problems as they come into conflict. For example, in terms of technology our culture is extremely dynamic. Technological change is not only common in America today, it is expected. We are urged to buy certain products because they are "new," "improved," and different from what they were

Food tastes are culturally prescribed. Here Balinese men prepare a meal to be roasted over coals.

in the past. Our culture places heavy emphasis upon change in the technological realm. But other aspects of our culture have not kept pace with our technology, and this has led to disastrous results. Our inability to limit our use of energy and to foresee the possible crisis of pollution and depletion of resources has led to the present situation where our cities are being smothered and our waterways are unable to support life. This is an example of how we are relatively static in terms of the changes in our values and attitudes about our way of life, and as a result we fall behind the rapid advances in our technology.

A third paradox is found in the fact that *we are to a large extent unconscious of our culture, and unaware of many aspects of it.* This is in part due to the way in which we learn our culture. We internalize our way of life to the point where it becomes so "natural" that we do not pay attention to what we do. We become unconscious of the rules that govern our behavior because we are so used to following the patterns prescribed for us. No individual ever knows his entire culture, for each is acquainted with only a portion, depending upon his position in society. There are many social positions that are mutually exclusive; that is, if we occupy one position we are automatically excluded from another. For example, if a person occupies the role of father he is automatically excluded from the role of mother. A person in the upper class cannot share in the culture of the lower class, and vice versa. Even though the upper and lower classes are both a part of American culture, they have separate cultural contents of their own, and no one can know what it is like to be in both at the same time. This same kind of cultural isolation is true for all kinds of specialized knowledge, such as occupational specialization. Clergy, politicians, police officers, students and farmers all share in American culture, yet all have their own unique aspects of it. The more complex the social organization— the more different kinds of people there are in a society—the smaller proportion of the total culture any one individual can possibly know. Thus both because of the way we learn our culture and because of the nature of culture itself, we are unconscious of and excluded from much of it.

SOCIALIZATION: LEARNING THE CULTURE

Social behavior is based upon mutual expectation. We are able to operate in our normal daily

The process of socialization will teach these children to keep aggressive impulses under control.

routine because we have complete confidence that other people will behave in a predictable and orderly fashion, responding to the same cues in much the same way we do. If this were not so, we could not have the kind of society that we do. Cultural anthropologists are interested in how people learn the proper behavior in each social setting, and the appropriate cues to trigger that behavior. We want to know how people learn the values that they share as members of the same group. And we try to show how all of what we learn and how we learn it fits together into a pattern, or what we call a *configuration.*

Socialization is the term we use to describe the process of learning to be a member of a society, a process that is slightly different in every society. Obviously groups of people vary in terms of how they teach their new members to act in acceptable ways. It is these differences and similarities in the process of teaching and learning the culture that are of interest to the anthropologist. Socialization includes the teaching and learning of all aspects of culture. It is not limited to physical considerations such as table manners or driving a car, but includes values, morals, attitudes, suspicions, literally everything, mental as well as physical. Furthermore, socialization is never really complete, because no individual is an exact social replica of his or her parents, any more than an individual can be an exact physical replica of his or her parents. Each succeeding generation differs slightly from the preceding one, indicating that the socialization process is imperfect at best.

The primary interest of anthropologists is in the aspects of personality shared with all other members of a society, rather than in the deviant nature that makes every person a unique individual. This assumes that there is some pattern or regularity in the way children of a culture are brought up, and in the things they learn. The process of learning the culture begins in infancy and continues throughout life, as a person forms a general outlook toward life and then continues to adapt that outlook to changing social and material conditions. The basic focus of anthropology, in dealing with the subjects of culture and personality and how they are related, is upon the relationship between the way a culture molds its youths' personalities and their psychological makeup in later life. In other words, we look for regularities both in the way children are raised and in the way adults behave, assuming that early childhood experiences have a lot to do with the formation of adult personalities. We study the actual child-rearing techniques practiced by parents and other socializing institutions such as schools, peer groups in which the children interact, and a variety of experiences that most children share. In each case, we try to see how these ex-

Children learn appropriate behavior as part of the socialization process. (Above) *Bushmen children crack roasted Mungongo nuts.* (Below) *Navajo students learn the traditional techniques of sand painting to illustrate modern ecological concepts.*

Team sports provide an acceptable channel for aggressive behavior. This hockey player is the twentieth-century version of a medieval knight in armor, for whom tourneys and warfare served much the same purpose.

periences affect behavior in the adult population, assuming that values learned in infancy have a way of showing up in many adults. If children are encouraged to behave in a certain way, and are positively rewarded for such behavior, they are likely to associate a positive value with that behavior that will carry on throughout their lives.

We can see how the anthropological approach can help us understand personality patterns in our own culture. Adult behavior considered appropriate in American society is reinforced through the way we train our children. Positive values such as individual achievement, competition, and freedom of choice are a strong part of almost every parent's approach to childrearing. Negative feelings are transmitted just as strongly to children through parents, teachers, peers, and even impersonal media

such as television. We cannot underestimate the role of television in the transmission of American culture to the youth of today, particularly its effects in homogenizing the members of the impressionable young age group that is growing up in a TV culture. In our present-day society, experiencing an increasing wave of crime and violence and an apparent loss of realism concerning war and the death and destruction it brings, we are beginning to look at this relationship between television programming and cultural values more closely. In a recent study of television programs aired on Saturday mornings—prime time for young children— the following results were discovered: 89 percent of the time was devoted to entertainment programs, including 70 percent comedy drama, primarily cartoons; 62 percent of all programs were animated; 3 out of 10 dramatic segments were saturated with violence, and 71 percent had at least one instance of human violence with or without the use of weapons. Another interesting conclusion was that although in 52 percent of the segments the violence was directed at humans, in only 4 percent did this result in death or injury. Is it any wonder that our children are growing up with the idea that violence is entertaining, and relatively harmless?

We must qualify the anthropological approach to the study of culture and personality by noting that there is always a tremendous range of personalities within a given society. When we speak of similarities, we do not mean any kind of unanimous personality trait found in all members of the society; rather, we are referring to a personality type that is found most frequently. We must also recognize that these dominant personality types can change rapidly within a culture. For example, during the era when Hitler was in power in Europe, the Jews as a group offered relatively little armed resistance. There were minor uprisings, but the Jewish population of Europe did not band together and stand against Hitler in armed conflict. Yet their descendants who make up a large part of the population of Israel today have developed exactly the opposite personality type. Partly as a result of the Jews' experiences in Europe a generation ago, the Israelis of today defend themselves and their small country in a way that has enabled them to survive in what can only be described as most hostile surroundings.

Before we continue with our discussion of the way culture works, it is necessary to discuss the way in which the concept of culture has developed in anthropology. As we have indicated, the concept of culture is one of the major theoretical statements in anthropology. It is the center of the anthropological view of people. If Tylor's definition of culture is carefully considered, if the list of cultural universals is care-fully examined, it should be clear that it is difficult to consider human beings apart from a culture. A person without the ability to communicate, without family, without ritual would hardly be considered human. Humanness is not simply a physical form; it is the sum of all the qualities found in all cultures in one form or another. To be human is to have a culture, a learned, patterned system of behavior. Since culture is almost synonymous with anthropology, it is of value to understand the different approaches to culture anthropologists have taken over the last hundred years. As you will see, anthropologists have analyzed culture from many different perspectives; moreover, they continue to maintain a number of different approaches to the analysis of culture to this day. While it might be disappointing that anthropologists cannot agree on how to explain culture, it is also true that controversy is the framework within which innovation takes place.

THE RISE OF THE CONCEPT OF CULTURE

Our modern understanding of culture did not spring full-blown from the head of some anthropologist but developed from centuries upon centuries of human curiosity about humans. It wasn't until the nineteenth century, however, that anthropology began to form as a separate discipline. Theories of social evolution grounded in the notion of the progress of the human species came from many different sources. During the Middle Ages the diversity of the world tended to be ordered into a system ranking various plants, animals, and even human societies from lowest to highest. This ordering system was known as the "Chain of Being," and according to the biblical account of Creation, it was a static order created by God. But by the seventeenth century, the "Chain of Being" had become a dynamic concept, conceived as a ladder up which the higher forms had ascended through time, out of a condition represented by the lower forms. As such, it accustomed people to view diversity in a specific arrangement, ranking the elements from the lowest to the highest. Among human societies the highest was considered to be Western civilization and the lowest, the "savages." When the notion of progress was added to this penchant for ranking and ordering, it provided social theorists with the dynamic view of human society. Thus, cultures began to be arranged and ranked, and a theory of cultural evolution was devised to explain the similarities and differences that existed around the world.

CULTURAL EVOLUTIONISM

One of the earliest anthropologists of this period to propose a theory of cultural evolution was Edward B. Tylor, who is frequently called the father of anthropology. Tylor was born in England in 1832. Although he completed the standard schooling, he was not eligible to enter a university in England because of his Quaker religious background. Instead, he entered the family business where he probably would have remained had ill health not forced him to seek a better climate. Tylor then spent a year traveling in the United States, Cuba, and Mexico, part of the time working on an archeological expedition. This experience led him to develop an interest in other societies, thus beginning his long career in anthropology. In 1861, he published his first book, *Anahuac,* based on his archeological and ethnographic experience in Mexico. Four years later came *Researches in the Early History of Mankind,* a book that thrust him into the middle of the controversy raging among nineteenth-century scholars about the course of evolution.

Religious orthodoxy had, for some time, been fighting the idea that civilized societies

Culver Pictures, Inc.

Edward Burnett Tylor *(1832–1917) is frequently called the father of modern anthropology. In 1865 he published* Researches into the Early History of Mankind, *establishing himself as a major figure in the field of anthropology and a proponent of the theory of cultural evolution. Tylor was particularly concerned with refuting the ideas of a group of biblical scholars known as the "degenerationists," who argued that humans were created in God's image—the most perfect form—and that contemporary "savages" must have degenerated from an earlier higher level. He countered this belief with the argument that humans were continually improving and progressing, and that contemporary non-Western peoples simply had not changed as rapidly nor in the same direction.*

had developed gradually from a primitive state comparable to that of the so-called savages. It was felt that the contemporary non-Western peoples, with their practices of marrying more than one wife, going about almost naked, and worshipping pagan gods, were not creatures worthy of God's initial human creation. A countertheory was put forth which claimed that a kind of *degeneration* had occurred; mankind, originally created in a highly civilized state, had degenerated to a savage state in some cases. According to the biblical account of Creation, people were created in the image of God. If God created the first people as savages, then what did this say about God's own image? The theory of degeneration solved this problem. In opposition to degenerationism, Tylor proposed his theory of the evolution of civilization from a lower to a higher state, supporting his argument with studies of contemporary non-Western peoples and the archeological record. Tylor's theory was based upon two assumptions: the basic similarity of the human mind, and the fact that primitive peoples represent an earlier stage of cultural evolution through which civilized societies passed.

Next, Tylor turned to the problem of reconstructing cultural evolution, demonstrating the progression from primitive to civilized peoples. In *Primitive Culture,* published in 1871, he used the *doctrine of survivals,* derived from biology and archeology, to provide evidence of earlier cultural forms. The doctrine of survivals states that some elements of any contemporary culture are the remains of a past condition of that culture. Just as vestigial organs are non-functional survivals of earlier stages of physical evolution and archeological remains are evidence of earlier stages of technological development, cultural survivals were presumed to be non-functional, historical cultural remains. Survivals included adult games, proverbs, linguistic expressions and many other cultural features, according to Tylor. Archery, for example, was clearly a survival from an earlier stage of technological development when the bow and arrow were not toys, but weapons upo which people relied to obtain food.

Of course, the argument for cultural evolu-

tion based on survivals was not very sound. Survivals only prove that evolution has taken place if you accept them as survivals in the first place. In other words, the argument was circular. Unless Tylor could present proof that survivals were actually the cultural remains of a former state of society, which he couldn't, the entire theory was open to question. Logical inconsistencies, however, did not prevent evolutionists from continuing their work.

Another important evolutionist, an American contemporary of Tylor, was Lewis Henry Morgan. Trained as a lawyer, Morgan maintained a keen interest in American Indians, spending much of his time among the Iroquois Indians of upstate New York. In 1851 he published his first ethnography, *The League of the Ho-de-na-sau-nee,* on the Iroquois. Later, Morgan's study of kinship, based on information collected in his travels among the Indians of

To Tylor, the Kalahari Bushman and the white anthropologist would have represented societies at different stages of an upward cultural evolution.

Controversy

Human Nature:
Biology vs. culture

What is a human? This seemingly simple question is the basis of all the social sciences. The eighteenth-century view of *Homo sapiens* was that human nature, like the entire universe, follows certain fixed laws and that cultural variations simply involve the changing of costumes, languages, and other surface manifestations of the universal human principle. Today, however, most anthropologists agree that no person exists who is unmodified by his or her culture. Is each person no more than a reflection of the time and place into which he or she chances to be born?

Traditionally, social science has looked at *Homo sapiens* as an animal with many layers which could be analyzed one at a time. Take away the outer manifestations of culture and one finds the regularities of social organization. Beneath these lie the psychological factors which motivate human behavior. Finally, one comes to the quintessential biological entity that is a person. Anthropologists, sociologists, psychologists, and biologists each had their distinctive role to play in the study of mankind. Anthropology searched for the universals in human culture and tried to distinguish these universals from the cultural traits which were viewed as no more than historical accidents.

Today, some theorists such as Clifford Geertz are disputing this view of people and culture. Are the supposed universals described by traditional anthropologists meaningful categories? When we speak of religion, property, and family as universal elements of human culture, are we merely grouping similar phenomena for the sake of convenient classification? European, Asian, and African cultures all exhibit behavior we call religious, but do the nature-worship rituals of the Eskimo, the pontifications of the Catholic church, and all the teachings of the Taoist really share a common quality which may be meaningfully defined as "religion"? Similarly, efforts to categorize universal human tendencies to mate, claim property, and seek shelter from the elements tend to result in categorizations so general as to be virtually useless in seeking to define the essential nature of humankind. A growing number of anthropologists are beginning to suggest that the way to search for the human essence is not to generalize the similarities among various cultures but to explore the distinctive elements of each.

According to these anthropologists, culture is best viewed not as a complex of customs, traditions, and behavioral patterns but, rather, as a programming mechanism for the governing of behavior. Because people are able to think, their behavioral possibilities are virtually limitless. How people live their lives is far less determined by their genetic make-up and anatomical structure than is the case for animals with simpler brains and nervous systems. Without culture, we would be adrift in a vast sea of behavioral possibilities. According to this view, culture is not an ornament of human life but an essential feature which provides guidance and direction to our otherwise unstructured behavioral repertoire.

Traditionally, biological evolution has been assumed to have pre-dated cultural evolution. That is, *Homo sapiens* was believed to have evolved to the point at which his anatomical structure was sufficiently developed to render him capable of producing and transmitting culture. Thereafter, his evolutionary responses to environmental pressures were predominantly cultural rather than genetic. It now seems clear that the transition of humans into cultural beings actually involved a long chain of complex genetic changes stretched out over a period of millions of years. There is no one point which may be identified as the birthday of cultural humankind.

The slow growth of culture must have played a significant role in human evolution. The use of tools and an increased reliance on symbolic behavior created a new environment to which people were obliged to adapt. Culture, the brain, and the body each shaped the evolution of the other human features. The complex function of the human nervous system is closely linked to the cultural symbols which evolved along with it. In fact, our intellectual, instinctive, and emotional capabilities would be entirely unfocussed if not directed by the symbolic system upon which they rely. In effect, there can be no humans without culture.

According to this theory, *Homo sapiens* is an incomplete animal who completes himself through the information provided by his particular culture. He does not have to learn to eat or to feel sexual desire, but what he eats and how he acts on his desire are factors determined by the culture he is part of. The course of human evolution was such that culture has taken precedence over instincts in determining human behavior.

Ultimately, this view of humanity requires a new direction in the quest for understanding human nature. Rather than examining only those elements which appear to be common to all cultures in order to arrive at a cross-cultural consensus of human nature, the nature of humankind might be found by exploring the full range of cultural diversity. Cultural diversity, not consistency or universality, might be the key to understanding human societies.

Morgan would have classified the Sioux Indians at the level of "upper savagery."

North America and in an eight page questionnaire sent to hundreds of missionaries, colonial officials and Indian agents throughout the world, culminated in his massive book, *Systems*

of Consanguinity and Affinity. His main contribution to evolutionary theory came in *Ancient Society,* published in 1877, in which he traced cultural evolution by studying family, economy, government, language, property, and religion.

Morgan presented an evolutionary scheme of the progress of human society in three stages—savagery, barbarism and civilization. Lower savagery was the condition of the infancy of the human race, in which people lived with essentially no regulation over their moral lives. Middle savagery commenced with the introduction of fishing and the use of fire, and was exemplified by the Australian Aborigines. The level of upper savagery began with the use of the bow and arrow, and included American Indian societies. Similarly, Morgan associated lower, middle and upper barbarism with different technological advances. The final stage, civilization, began with the use of a phonetic alphabet and the production of written records. Morgan saw progressive changes in the advancing moral condition of society as well. He claimed, for example, that in early primitive societies sexual promiscuity was the rule. In such a case, paternity would be uncertain; therefore descent, or membership in a family group, would be transferred from generation to generation through the female line. Later, as promiscuity was replaced by regulated sexual relations, paternity could be established. Morgan also argued that property became more important as societies rose up the ladder of evolution. Since property was strongly associated with males, according to Morgan, this resulted in a male-oriented descent system in the final stages of evolution.

Morgan also tied the notion of human biological evolution to that of cultural evolution. For example, he claimed that as human culture evolved, the brain increased in size. In *Ancient Society* he writes, "With the production of inventions and discoveries, and with the growth of institutions, the human mind necessarily grew and expanded; and we are led to recognize a gradual enlargement of the brain itself, particularly of the cerebral portion."

The writings of Morgan and Tylor are typical in many ways of nineteenth-century cultural evolutionism. Their strong belief that Western society was the highest evolutionary form, their reliance upon the notion of progress, and their use of survivals to prove the existence of past evolutionary stages are all characteristic of early anthropological theory.

THE REACTION TO EVOLUTIONISM

Ultimately it was the lack of scientific rigor in the application of cultural evolutionary theory that led to its downfall. Toward the end of the nineteenth century this approach was challenged, with the attack being led by Franz Boas, a German immigrant who founded the first department of anthropology in the United States at Clark University in 1888. Boas was originally trained as a physicist, then turned to geography, and while on a field trip became interested in anthropology. His scientific background was important, however, for it led him to question the methods of nineteenth-century anthropologists. Perhaps because of his foreign heritage and upbringing, he also reacted strongly against what he felt were strong racist overtones in the theory of cultural evolution.

Thus Boas mounted a two-pronged attack against classical evolutionism, one based upon scientific principles of investigation and the other upon the implicit racism and the lack of an objective view of other cultures. In scientific terms, Boas did not agree with the theory of cultural evolution as it was expressed by nineteenth-century anthropologists, for he felt it ignored the most fundamental and clearly observable source of change—the contact between two cultures. Evolutionists had tended to minimize the role of *diffusion,* the spread of an innovation from its point of origin throughout an area, to neighboring regions. But Boas, who was to become a dominant figure in American anthropology in the early twentieth century, held firmly that rather than looking at the unfolding of the potential for civilization, we must focus upon the effects of contact between two or more groups with different cultures.

Boas' attack on evolutionism led to a new method in cultural anthropology in the United States, with an emphasis upon collecting minute facts rather than constructing grand theories. He was considered the leader of the so-called American historical school of anthropology, because of his emphasis upon the role of history in the reconstruction of cultural evolution. Boas was adamant in his rejection of the type of conjecture used by nineteeth-century evolutionists. Only after we have gathered all the historical evidence, he argued, can we begin to discern laws of cultural change. Most of the early work investigating the diffusion of culture was done in American Indian societies, both because they were a handy subject for American anthropologists and because there was a great deal of concern for recording (if not preserving) the traditions of what seemed to be a disappearing culture. The goal was to reconstruct the past, establishing the origin, development and spread of every aspect of culture—not just material objects such as weapons, tools, ornaments, and the like, but the intangible aspects such as folk tales, dances, magical practices, and religious beliefs. If this seemed rather tedious and at times unproductive (which it certainly does in retrospect), Boas justified such a method by claiming that if anthropology was to become a science, it had to have a firm basis in fact, not just conjecture. By examining the form and geographical distribution of any aspect of a culture, he felt he was on the way to understanding how it came into being, and ultimately how it spread from one culture to another. This understanding was the key to formulating a law of cultural evolution.

Boas never produced any major theory of culture change, for he had embarked upon a never-ending search for detail that would not lead him to any conclusions until it was all gathered. He is an important figure in anthropology, however, for two reasons. First, he led the battle against applying an evolutionary theory to culture as it had been applied to biology, and his criticisms were so effective that he literally laid evolutionism to rest for more than half a century in cultural anthropology. Second, Boas is an influential figure because of the important role he played in training a large number of students who in turn became the leaders of anthropology in the early twentieth century.

Configurationism

Alfred L. Kroeber, a student of Boas and a follower of his historical method, solved the problem of the lack of written records of nonliterate societies by using written, historical materials from Western societies for his studies. Kroeber felt that history exhibited a pattern of change in recurring cycles regardless of the level of development of the society.

In one of his early works, he analyzed dress fashions, noting how the elements of women's formal dresses, such as hemline, neckline, width of skirt, and breadth of shoulders, varied in a predictable cycle over the years. From this realization, he developed the anthropological notion of style as a property of culture. Human beings tend to stylize their behavior and their material culture, forming consistent patterns that change in regular and predictable directions over time. At the outset, a group of people can make an almost unlimited number of choices in the style of a particular object, but

with each choice the successive alternatives become narrower. This is true whether we are discussing dress fashions, automobile designs, or patterns of thought such as might be expressed in religious ideology. Eventually a pattern will be explored to the fullest possible extent, and will become exhausted, leading to a drastic new change that is not simply a variation on an old theme, but the introduction of a totally new theme.

Kroeber maintained that in looking for the cause of fluctuations in patterns, and in the seemingly cyclical nature of stylistic change in dress fashions and other aspects of culture, we must look beyond the individuals actively engaged in creating styles. The time span involved overrules the role of any individual in determining the overall course of change. Rather, Kroeber maintained, we must look to the basic nature of culture itself for an explanation. In other words, Kroeber held that culture is *superorganic*—it exists on a level above the individuals who make up a population. Men and women may contribute to a style, but their contributions are tempered by the overall direction that their culture has taken in the past. This does not deny their free will to do as they like, but suggests rather that their free will is guided by their cultural heritage, over which they have no control. They will act in a certain way because they choose to do so, but they will choose on the basis of their culture, the way they have been taught to behave in their society.

Kroeber attempted to expand his study of the process of history to a broader scale in a larger, all-encompassing work, *Configurations of Culture Growth.* Concerned with the question of creativity as it is affected by culture, Kroeber explored the tendency for great cultural achievements to occur in bursts, such as Greek culture between 500 and 200 B.C. Kroeber claimed that geniuses have appeared in clusters throughout history because of the cyclical nature of the growth of civilizations. His book was

Ruth Fulton Benedict
(1887–1948)
conducted research in various American Indian cultures, and in 1934 she published Patterns of Culture, *a major contribution to the anthropological literature of the period. She had studied under Franz Boas, who was noted as the leading opponent to cultural evolutionism of the nineteenth century, because it implied racist attitudes of white and Western superiority. Benedict's writings showed the influence of Boas, and in* Patterns of Culture *she offered a strong justification for the doctrine of cultural relativism. She argued that one could not judge a culture or rank it against another, for all cultures are unique entities, each with its own separate identity, history, and intrinsic value.*

an attempt to derive a law explaining these cycles, to describe a series of configurations in the pattern of growth of civilizations. Unfortunately for him, the results of his study were inconclusive. He found no regularity in the length of a period of creativity, in the appearance of the peak or climax or in the time between such bursts of creativity.

Ruth Benedict, another student of Boas, shared with Kroeber the Boasian commitment to the integrity of each culture and the need for historical documentation of any generalizations about culture change. But Benedict's work also reflected an interest in combining elements of psychology with the anthropological approach. In *Patterns of Culture,* she emphasized that cultures must be taken as wholes, each integrated on its own principles, each with its own *configuration.* She stressed that a culture is organized around a basic theme, and that all of the various elements of that culture fit together. In applying this approach to cross-cultural studies, Benedict looked at several different societies and described them in terms of their personality configurations, pointing out how these personality types fit in with the overall configuration.

Among the societies Benedict studied were two North American Indian groups, the Zuñi Indians of the southwestern United States, and the Kwakiutl Indians of the northwest coast. She described the basic configuration of Zuñi culture as "Apollonian"—very cooperative, never excessive in any aspect of life, not seeking to express individuality. The typical Zuñi was a person who sought to blend into the group, and who did not wish to stand out as superior or as being above the other members of the tribe. Benedict then went on to point out how this personality type was reinforced in other elements of Zuñi culture, thus forming the overall cultural configuration. Child-training patterns were designed to suppress individuality. Initiation ceremonies were characterized by a lack of ordeal (the Apollonian type is never excessive), and the youths were initiated in a group setting. Marriage was relatively casual. Leadership among the Zuñi was declined whenever possible, and was accepted only with great reluctance. People tended to shun positions of authority. Ceremonial and religious associations likewise reinforced this configuration.

The Kwakiutl Indians presented a cultural configuration much different from that of the Zuñi, a configuration termed "Dionysian" by Benedict. The Kwakiutl were characterized by a frenzied outlook, excess being the rule rather than the exception. They were ambitious and striving, and individualistic. The ideal man among the Kwakiutl was one who had a will to power, who always attempted to prove his superiority. Child-training practices reinforced this pattern, emphasizing the achievement of the individual over cooperation with the group. In the initiation ceremonies, a boy was expected to go out by himself and experience a personal relationship with the supernatural. Marriage entailed a tremendous celebration, not the casual kind of ceremony between two people that it was among the Zuñi. Leadership among the Kwakiutl was sought by any possible means, and Kwakiutl society was characterized by a constant struggle for power. Religious positions included that of the shaman, a priest who wielded enormous personal power.

Benedict's study of cultural configurations illustrates how numerous aspects of life reinforce the basic pattern of culture, whatever it might be. This is not to say that everyone is just like this—there are frenzied Zuñis just as there are passive Kwakiutls—but rather that it is a pattern that describes the typical member of the society, and to which all members conform to some extent. Benedict's approach suggests that, based upon the configuration of the culture, the personality is *more likely* to conform to one type than another.

Culture and Personality

One of the first anthropologists to investigate personality and cultural patterning was Margaret Mead. In the 1920s Mead conducted re-search on Samoa, during which she became interested in comparing the period of adolescence for Samoan girls and American girls. She concluded that the patterns of stress that characterize the American adolescence are absent from Samoan culture, with the result that the adult personality is different in the two cultures. But even beyond the question of personality, the period of adolescence in the two cultures is typical of an overall pattern that emerges for each. Samoan culture does not emphasize the drastic and abrupt change in status during adolescence that American culture does. In general, Mead found that Americans experience a number of abrupt status changes, and as a result there is more stress involved in the American life style than in the Samoan. There is a correlation not only between child rearing and adult personality, but with the majority of the rest of cultural institutions and values as well. They all form a pattern that can be expressed through the personalities of the members of that culture, through the form that each institution takes.

The noted psychoanalyst Sigmund Freud was also an important influence on the *culture and personality* approach in anthropology. Although Freud's attempts to reconstruct an evolutionary theory in his book *Totem and Taboo* had been completely discarded, other aspects of his approach to psychology were valuable additions to anthropology. Principles such as repression, the formation of guilt and anxiety, the relation between frustration and aggression, and the concept of sublimation were all used to illustrate the connection between childhood experiences and adult personality. Whereas Boas had been concerned primarily with the material aspects of a culture, his students were influenced by Freud to include in their analysis not only the physical characteristics of a cultural item, but the meaning of a trait for the people who possessed it.

The problem with the early studies of culture

and personality, such as Benedict's and Mead's, was that they were of necessity highly impressionistic. Moreover, the attribution of a single configuration to a culture was highly subjective. They were conducted in a way that did not allow them to be duplicated, or to be tested. This meant that any contributions they made to anthropological theory had to be accepted on faith—not a very solid foundation for a growing science. Fortunately, the field of culture and personality did not rely solely upon the configurational approach, but branched out into other areas of investigation.

One of the most important theoretical approaches was introduced by the psychiatrist Abram Kardiner, who, during the 1930s along with anthropologists Ralph Linton and Margaret Mead and others, developed the concept

Margaret Mead studied the Samoan culture extensively. Here she is shown with a Samoan girl, during one of her early field trips.

of *basic personality structure*. Taking the notion of patterns of culture as given, Kardiner sought to ground it in some aspect of culture. He focused on what he called *primary institutions,* those concerned with disciplining, gratifying and inhibiting the child during the first years of life. Primary institutions are those responsible for the formation of the personality in the early formative years of a child's life. They will differ from one culture to another, so that there can be no comprehensive list of what might be considered a primary institution, but generally they relate to patterns of child-rearing in a culture.

Kardiner's theory was that as a result of sharing basic childhood experiences, adults in a population share patterns of behavior and personality. This approach has been applied by other anthropologists since it was first developed in the 1930s, with the result that today we understand a great deal about the psychological dimensions of culture, and why personality can vary so greatly from one group to another. The culture and personality approach continues to be popular in contemporary anthropological studies, with new techniques being developed to measure more exactly those psychological factors involved in human behavior. One of the more fruitful areas of study has been with the psychological dimensions of culture change, including the way in which traditional values are adapted to new situations, or the effect of culture contact upon a people's belief system.

Functionalism

In contrast to the American school, British anthropologists turned away from history completely. Claiming that historical reconstruction was not possible for nonliterate societies, they limited their studies to cultures and institutions as they exist today. This was called the synchronic approach, from the Greek roots meaning "together in time," as opposed to a diachronic, "across time," historical approach. The British school acquired the name *functionalism* because of its stress on the functions of social institutions. Two major figures emerged in the early development of functionalism, Bronislaw Malinowski, a native of Poland who studied anthropology in London, and A.R. Radcliffe-Brown. While they viewed culture in strikingly different ways, both were committed to the synchronic approach and to the concept of function.

Malinowski meant by functionalism the explanation of a feature of culture by reference to the biological needs of human beings. Culture, he claimed, is established in response to seven human biological needs: nutrition, reproduction, bodily comfort, safety, relaxation, movement and growth. Cultural institutions are designed to satisfy these needs: marriage and the family satisfy the need for reproduction, shelter and dress help maintain bodily comfort, training and education satisfy growth, and so on. At the same time that culture satisfies these basic biological needs, it creates other "derived" needs of its own. While culture keeps people alive, it must also maintain itself. Economic institutions are necessary to renew cultural apparatus such as tools and weapons; social control institutions are necessary to regulate social behavior; political institutions are required to organize labor and to regulate competition. Malinowski claimed that the symbolic aspects of culture—organized knowledge, institutions of magic and religion, the arts, sports—also function to satisfy these primary and derived needs.

Malinowski's approach to the study of culture examines the universal pattern of a particular act and then the cultural context in which it is carried out. For example, he explained the traditional payments a man makes to his sister's husband among the Trobriand Islanders of the South Pacific by referring first to the universal need for economic exchange. Next, Malinowski noted that the Trobriand Islanders inherit kinship group membership from their mother's group, not their father's group. (As we will discuss in greater detail in Chapter 15, in all societies a person must marry someone outside his own kinship group.) Thus, a man's children are members of his wife's group while his sister's children will be the next generation of members of his own kinship group. Therefore, the gift to the sister's husband is in return for the children provided for the man's group, according to Malinowski. Such a functionalist explanation eliminates the conjecture of the evolutionist approach.

The second direction of functionalism, the work of Radcliffe-Brown, was derived from the approach of Emile Durkheim, the French sociologist. According to Durkheim, the "function" of an institution in a society is similar to the "function" of an organ in the body, and the relations between institutions form a structure just as an organism has structure. Human society retains the same orderliness as the anatomy of a living organism.

For Radcliffe-Brown, the study of human behavior could best be conducted by trying to understand how patterns of behavior fit together in any particular society, at any one point in time. Like Malinowski, he rejected the conjectural approach of evolutionism, but he did not seek to explain culture on the basis of human biological needs. Rather, he looked at the inner dynamics of the structure of a culture, and related the function of a particular pattern of behavior to that structure.

In an article entitled "The Mother's Brother in South Africa," Radcliffe-Brown reacted against the conjectural explanations of nineteenth-century cultural evolutionism. The evolutionists explained the close, informal relationship between a boy and his mother's brother among the Bathonga of Portugese East Africa as a "survival" from a period in which the Bathonga inherited kinship group membership

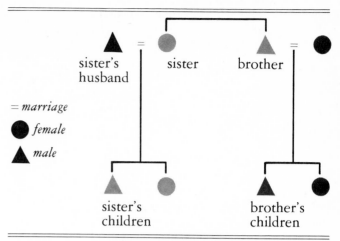

= *marriage*

● *female*

▲ *male*

The dark-shaded and light-shaded shapes mark the members of the two kinship groups.

through the mother, as among the Trobriand Islanders. Today the Bathonga inherit through the male line. In contrast, Radcliffe-Brown was able to demonstrate that the relationship between a boy and his mother's brother was an extension of his relationship with his mother, and that other elements of the culture were consistent with this trait. While this does not provide an explanation of the origin of the custom, it does show how the culture is integrated without resorting to conjectural history.

The functionalist approach in anthropology has been criticized widely for its synchronic view of culture, and its inability to explain change. Additionally, by looking at the way cultural institutions are organized and focusing on social order rather than social change, we tend to develop a conservative bias. If we view a society as existing in harmony, then any change can be likened to disease in an organism, something to be overcome to retain the equilibrium of the social order. Such an equilibrium model of society masks the reality of social life, in which conflict and change occur constantly. It has also been suggested that, contrary to Malinowski's view, not every element in a culture contributes a positive function, and not every element is indispensable.

THE REVIVAL OF EVOLUTIONISM

Despite the attacks on evolutionary theory by the Boasians in the United States and the functionalists in Great Britain, the evolutionist approach was revived, due largely to the efforts of one man, Leslie A. White. Nineteenth-century evolutionists had been criticized for using typically Western patterns of family organization, political organization and the like as a standard of measure for non-Western societies. White tried to avoid this problem by eliminating value-laden terms for the stages of evolution and by using quantitative rather than qualitative measures. He proposed that we could establish a general evolutionary progression for culture by calculating the amount of energy consumed per capita. This figure would be an indication of the level of progress of a culture. This approach has several implications, among them the notion that a society that harnesses and uses more energy per capita is more advanced than a society using less energy. White maintained, however, that his goal was not to rank societies, but to prove that culture as a whole had evolved. Thus, what was important to him was not the fact that the United States uses more energy than India or Egypt or any other country, but that there has been a continual progression over time in the capability of civilized nations to utilize more energy.

Technology, which determines the amount of energy harnessed and the efficiency of its utilization, was the basis of White's theory of cultural evolution. According to him, the technological component of culture determines the ideological and sociological components—kinship, economics, politics, religion, and so on. In a society where little energy was used, White predicted an entirely different political organization, religion, and kinship system than in a society where massive amounts of energy were used. While this appears to be little more than a restatement of common knowledge, that small-scale societies are different from large-scale industrial societies, White was actually adding a theoretical statement about the determining factor in cultural change, technology.

To test White's theory of cultural evolution, Marshall Sahlins analyzed 14 societies in Polynesia. The results of this were published. in his book *Social Stratification in Polynesia*. Sahlins was concerned with the relationship between technology and social stratification, the system of ranking members of a society. After arriving at a complex set of measures of social stratification, Sahlins was able to divide the Polynesian societies into three different categories—one highly stratified, a second only moderately stratified, and a third almost entirely unstratified. Sahlins then applied the principle of technological determinism derived from White's theory: if the amount of energy harnessed per capita varies, then the degree of social stratification should vary accordingly. Thus, there should be some technological explanation for the three different levels of social stratification in Polynesia. Indeed Sahlins found what he was searching for, not in the tools used or the techniques for exploiting the resources of the environment, but in the actual environmental conditions themselves. The groupings of societies according to stratification corresponded directly to the ecological differences among those islands. The most highly stratified societies were all found on large land masses containing a variety of ecological zones, good soil conditions, and a multitude of resources available for human exploitation. Those islands with an intermediate level of social stratification were smaller, with fewer ecological zones, and fewer resources. And the least stratified societies inhabited atolls, low islands on coral reefs, with little soil, little ecological variety, and few resources for exploitation. Since the productivity of the islands was directly related to the social stratification, Sahlins considered this supported the validity of White's theory.

Another refinement of White's evolutionary theory was presented by Julian Steward, in his *Theory of Culture Change*. Steward made the distinction between the nineteenth-century theory of cultural evolution, which he called *unilinear,* and White's theory, which he termed *universal.* In the nineteenth-century formula, all cultures either went through or would eventually pass through the same series of stages; there was only one line of change. Universal evolution, in contrast, concerned a series of stages through which culture as a whole has passed. It is universal, because it is a one-time process, not repeated by each individual culture.

Steward was not happy with either of these approaches. He did not agree that all cultures would pass through the same stages, nor did he see any utility in looking at a sequence of change that pertained to but one example, as White's did. He proposed an alternative evolutionary approach, which he termed *multilinear.* History, he claimed, was full of examples of parallel development of cultures in widely scattered parts of the world. Not all cultures went through exactly the same stages, but in many cases the stages were similar. It was here that he felt evolution could be applied most profitably.

To illustrate the utility of the concept of multilinear evolution, Steward derived a causal explanation for the rise of complex civilizations in Mesopotamia, Egypt, China, Mesoamerica and Peru. In each case, he found the same sequence of development—hunting and gathering, agriculture, then various stages of large-scale political organization. The origin of these regularities, according to Steward, lay in the ecological conditions in which each civilization evolved. In each case, the society existed in a fertile river valley surrounded by an arid hinterland. As hunting and gathering gave way to agriculture, the population expanded and irrigation was required to open new land for cultivation. Eventually, the expansion of irrigation led to the need for a centralized political authority to regulate the system of canals. Once established, political authority expanded and the various stages of large-scale civilization evolved. While Steward's approach cannot explain variations among the different civilizations, such as the different types of expansion, his explanation of the causes of parallel evolution is a major contribution to cultural evolutionary theory.

Evolutionary theory has also given rise to *cultural ecology,* a new approach that is concerned with understanding how humans behave in terms of the environment. The approach developed from the works of Sahlins and of Steward which suggested that environment played a major role in cultural evolution. Cultural ecologists are not environmental determinists, however; they do not believe that culture is defined solely by the environment. Rather, they seek to understand the interaction between culture and environment, the influence of culture on environment as well as the influence of environment on culture.

Cultural ecology emphasizes research design and techniques, calling on such related disciplines as biology, medicine, nutrition, demography and the various agricultural sciences in attempting to construct a picture of interacting life forms and environment. Most studies in this field, however, are unable to designate the causes of change. An ecologist can explain the nutritive or medicinal value of a particular cultural practice, such as abstaining from eating pork, but a statement of causality or origin cannot be derived from that explanation. In this sense, cultural ecological studies are similar to biological evolutionary theory that is able to explain adaptation but not predict or specify the origins or causes of change.

THE NEW ETHNOGRAPHY

More recently, a number of anthropologists in the United States have sought to move away from the grand-scale theorizing of the evolutionary approach to improving fieldwork techniques and reducing the bias of the investigator. The new ethnography or *ethnoscience,* as it is called, attempts to understand a culture from the native's point of view. Most of ethnography has imposed a structure on the data, classifying them according to a single system that would allow for easy cross-cultural comparison. In contrast, the new ethnography is designed to discover what is culturally meaningful to the individuals of a particular group, to recognize what distinctions the natives consider significant in their unique way of looking at the world. It is, in simple terms, an attempt to "get inside the native's head." For example, Harold Conklin found that the Hanunoo of the Philippines order colors in a different way than we do. We tend to organize and categorize colors on the basis of hue, brightness and the saturation of color. The Hanunoo use moisture, surface texture and lightness. Such a classification of color is closely associated with Hanunoo views on plant life and with the consumption of various plants. While it might not make any sense to us to ignore hue in ordering colors, it does fit in with their total culture.

While the new ethnography is successful in overcoming the problem of cultural bias or distortion in anthropological research, it creates new problems of its own. For one, the sheer amount of time required from an informant means that the anthropologist is forced to rely upon a few informants at most to relate the entire body of cultural data. Therefore, it is difficult to check on whether the information is an accurate reflection of the entire group's cultural outlook, or whether it is peculiar to the individual. Also, the content of any culture is so enormous that to conduct this type of research for more than a few narrow topics would be impossible. Imagine a book containing all of the information, all of the unwritten rules that form the basis for cultural behavior! This appears to be the most serious problem of all for the new ethnography, for it means that the approach is of limited utility in cross-cultural studies.

STRUCTURALISM

Another theoretical orientation in anthropology, loosely termed *structuralism* or sometimes "French structuralism," represents an attempt to overcome the problem of cross-cultural comparison while maintaining the natives' view of the world. The leading figure in this school is the French anthropologist, Claude Lévi-Strauss. As clearly as one can state his position in a few short sentences, Lévi-Strauss claims that elements of all cultures are essentially the product of a single mental process common to all humanity. Although the outer appearance of comparable cultural elements may differ, they have a common inner structure that reflects the common structure of human thought. Lévi-Strauss claims that we can indeed infer crucial facts about the human mind from observing its cultural manifestations and that these facts should be equally true for all people.

Myths, for example, portray the contradictions that plague the human mind and present logical ways of avoiding these contradictions, according to Lévi-Strauss. In a book entitled *Structural Anthropology,* he cites a Pueblo Indian myth that contains a threefold distinction between agriculture, hunting, and war. Lévi-Strauss considers that the myth solves the logical contradiction between life and death that plagues all of humanity by introducing a mediating principle. Agriculture represents life, war represents death, and hunting is the mediating category because it requires death in the preservation of human life.

While there is some logic to the assumption that all humans engage in comparable mental processes since we are members of the same species, many anthropologists find Lévi-Strauss's intricate combinations of the elements of myths too idiosyncratic. It is, after all, Lévi-Strauss who selects the myths to be analyzed, who orders and arranges the elements and who "uncovers" the structure hidden deep within. While his work has been a thoughtful stimulus to all anthropologists, it appears to lack one basic attribute of a science: that others should be able to repeat the work and achieve the same results.

CONCLUSION

It is always difficult to perceive one's immediate surroundings in perspective. Historians can piece together the fragments of the past much more carefully and meticulously than they can the present. The same is true for anthropologists discussing anthropological theory. We become more vague when dealing with theoretical approaches of the 1970s than with those of the 1870s. Indeed, it is frequently much easier to be critical of a contemporary approach, to point out its problems, than to be supportive, to point out its benefits and advantages. This has, perhaps, been true of our discussion of the new ethnography and of Lévi-Straussian structuralism.

Yet, there does seem to be something quite different about the last decade of anthropological theorizing. The new approaches appear to be narrower in focus and more specific in methodology (with the obvious exception of French structuralism). The grand scale of cultural evolutionism or the breadth of Boasian historicism seems to be missing. While it is difficult to foresee the future of anthropological theory, it is likely that new theories will stress methodology oriented towards the study of limited aspects of the anthropological universe.

Of course, other trends will have their influence on theory as well. The 1960s and 1970s have seen anthropology move from the study of non-Western peoples to a more introspective look at our own societies. With this change, sometimes forced by the governments of newly independent nations and sometimes brought on by a realization of the need for help in solving our own social problems, anthropologists have had to develop new analytical techniques and new research methods. We have turned to other disciplines for help, often borrowing a great deal from medical science, education, and city planning among many other fields. Possibly the most significant common theme in recent anthropological theory has been the attempt to develop a framework for understanding human behavior in modern, complex societies. Perhaps this merging of disciplines, and their theories and research methodologies, will be the boost that anthropology needs to move into the future as a revitalized science.

Focus

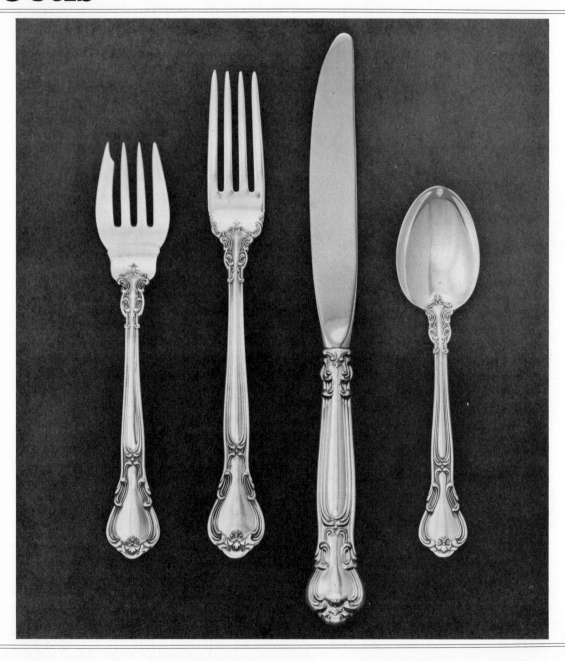

E. A. Hammel

Sexual Symbolism in Flatware

The following article demonstrates a Lévi-Strauss-type analysis of a cultural feature common to Western society. Students will probably find themselves torn between the logic and beauty of the analysis and a feeling of its total irrelevance. Since anthropologists are not above the use of humorous exaggeration to make a point, it will be up to the student to determine the author's attitude towards structuralism. Perhaps this article should be carefully considered over dinner?

Reprinted from the *Kroeber Anthropological Society Papers* **37** (1967).

The methods and theses presented by Professor Lévi-Strauss have opened new vistas in the understanding (indeed, in the *Verstehen*) of cultural phenomena. Professor Lévi-Strauss's analyses have usually been based on exotic data, but one recent article, "The Culinary Triangle," pushes the new attitudes and methods squarely into the breach left by the paucity of consideration of more common materials. If, indeed, these new theories have relevance for our understanding of symbolism in its myriad forms, why should we not apply them to data close at hand? Such applications would have two advantages: the familiarity of the data would facilitate verification of the hypotheses, and the hypotheses, thus confirmed, would provide greater scientific and humanistic understanding of the world and culture in which we ourselves live. It is the intention of this paper, both in method and in empirical subject, to deepen Lévi-Struass's stimulating penetration into the obscurity of the culinary triangle.

One of the commonest lexical domains in the area of material culture in Western civilization is that of "flatware," that is, the metal instruments employed in eating. True, these materials sometimes are of wood or plastic, and there is some overlap with the domain of "cutlery," so that some particular items fall into both domains (steak knives, for instance). Nevertheless, the limits of the domain are sufficiently distinct to allow analysis of its contents. I do not intend here to perpetuate the naturalistic bias evidenced in so many "componential" analyses, by restricting myself only to the elaboration of some code for the designation of immediately observable characteristics of the objects themselves, or of complex manipulation of such codes; rather, I will be concerned with the discussion of the structural relationships *between the objects,* except for a few comments on their particular nature. We are thus concerned not only (or not even principally) with the structure of some referential set of observable characteristics (as in componential analyses), or with the manipulation of these notations of reference for the reduction of redundancy (as in transformational analyses), but rather with componential and transformational theorizing about the direct relationships between the objects of our concern. In this, we hope to stress again the general principles of such relationships so often found in all varieties of symbolism, including behavior ordinarily considered to be purely instrumental.

It is first of all noteworthy that the general set "flatware" consists of three and only three immediately constituent subsets. In asking informants the control question . . . , "How many kinds of flatware are there?", we usually received the answer, "Three." In reply to another question, "What kinds of flatware are there?", we learned, "Knives, forks, and spoons" (in that order). It is only with difficulty that one can persuade informants to expand the number of immediately constituent sets, and informants are often confused about the precise nature and structural position of items so elicited (e.g., the infant's "pusher" in Britain). There is really no difficulty, however, in their identification of the three sets named or in their assignment of individual items of flatware to one or another of the subsets; they almost always show high agreement . . . . We know, of course, that it is no accident that there are three subsets.

The three subsets, however, contrast with one another on a series of binary rather than of trinary, quaternary, or any other kind of dimensions. The structure of three subsets is in fact an epiphenomenon of the multiplicity of binary distinctions . . . these distinctions extend beyond the material to the behavioral sphere and indeed to the structure of opposition and mediation in symbolism.

We should first consider the structure of the oppositions themselves, then pass to examination of mediating principles. I should like to offer one of the principal hypotheses immediately, namely that these utensils are basically sexual symbols. Their differentiation on these principles is thus basically one of male versus female, but the distinctions are not absolute. Rather, they are relative distinctions, and it is most important to stress this, not only from a methodological but also from a theoretical point of view. We can best carry out this portion of the analysis if we distinguish "more male" from "less male," understanding that in any particular opposition, the first of these is "male" and the second "female" in the relative sense noted.

We may first note that knives and forks are sharp, while spoons are rounded, the first displaying male and the second female characteristics. However, forks are possessed of multiple sharp members and knives only of one, so that we may initially judge forks in this instance to be more male than knives. Thus, with respect to knives and spoons, forks are male; with respect to forks, in this illustration, knives are female, but they are male with respect to spoons, and spoons are female with respect to forks and knives. The maleness of forks is also demonstrated by the phonetic similarity between their lexeme and one of the (in several senses) vulgar expressions for sexual intercourse (John Thompson, personal communication, 1964). This interesting homonymy does not occur in other languages with which I am familiar, but statistical proof is not required for essentially mechanical structural models. To go on with these physical characteristics, we observe that knives and forks are elongate while spoons are curved; I do not refer here only to the length of the utensils but to their form. In length, it is also true that knives and forks are longer than spoons in most instances; that is, if the utensils are matched for their rank in length, it will generally be found that, in any set of flatware, the longest knife is longer than the longest spoon, as is the longest fork longer than the longest spoon, etc. The fact that one can find some spoon that is longer than some knife is irrelevant, for the essential initial pairing has not been accomplished. Now, again with respect to length, it is true that knives are longer than forks of equivalent rank in their own subset. It would thus be apparent that knives were more male than forks, and this might refute the evidence of greater (multiple) maleness of forks noted above. However, it seems to me that mere length is only the crudest measure of maleness, and in this instance, I would not accept the detail as refutation. It does, however, raise the issue, and we must reserve for later consideration this problem of ambiguity concerning the degree of maleness of knife and fork. The ambiguity is intensified by the fact that the three-tined fork is a symbol for the sea, which is in many cases itself a female symbol, but also associated with a male deity. Further, we may note that both knives and forks are relatively flat in their form, compared to spoons, but that forks are slightly cupped, with respect to knives. Again, knives and forks appear more male than spoons, but forks are in an intermediate position, as with length.

We may turn now to the nature of culinary action rather than just of form. How do these utensils function in opposition? First, we are obliged to distinguish European (particularly British) custom from American; I would like to draw particular attention to the theoretical significance of this

necessity. We will see here that apparently disparate cultural forms, spatially separated, are in fact only allomorphs of the same structural entity. Both in America and in Europe (including Britain), the fork is used to pierce and in conjunction with the knife to pierce while the knife cuts. Maleness is demonstrated for the fork by its piercing action and for the knife by its penetration; however, the cutting action of the knife suggests some anti-male aggression as well, directed against the fork, a point on which we will comment later. The carnal focus of this opposition should not go unnoticed.

The problem of the ambiguous position of the fork can also be illustrated in consideration of its use with foods other than meat. In America, the fork is used in the same fashion as the spoon for certain kinds of foods which are of a consistency that does not admit of piercing. The knife is not an adjunct to or a substitute in this operation, at least not in sectors of the society in which all utensils are available. In Britain, the fork is also used as a receptacle, but in conjunction with the knife, receiving that which is placed on it by the (male) knife. Even in the joint use of knife and fork with meat, we must note that although the action of the fork with respect to the meat is to pierce, its function with respect to the knife is to hold or grip. Thus the fork grips while the knife penetrates, even if only edgewise. The ambiguity of the situation is precisely what one should expect, and it is the advantage of this nominological method not only to expose but also to explain such ambiguities. We may note further, before proceeding, that at the end of the actions described above, the operation of the knife and fork is to disengage or withdraw, while that of the spoon is to release or pour out. The function of the fork, in its ambiguous role with certain foods not amenable to penetration, is also to release or pour out.

Before proceeding to a discussion of principles of mediation and analysis of these relationships, we should note a few more types of opposition. In any initial use of these utensils, the fork is usually seized with the left hand, and the knife with the right, when the two are used jointly. (This is reversed, of course, by persons who are left-handed.) In Europe, the fork is seized with the left hand even when used alone, while in America it is seized with the right in a more female kind of usage, since the spoon is normally used with the right hand alone in all instances. It is also true that the fork in America is transferred to the right hand after the cutting operation in conjunction with the knife has been completed. Thus, at the conclusion of an ambiguous operation in which the fork pierces yet grips, while the knife penetrates and cuts against it, the American fork is shifted to the female side, that is, to the hand which is otherwise occupied only by an exclusively female utensil, the spoon, or by a utensil functioning as a spoon.

We come now to the problem of mediation. By mediation I do not mean only the intervention of objects or persons but also the intervention of explanatory principles, as in the concept of "intervening variables."

In laying the service, which is itself of some significance, we find that in America the fork is always placed to the left of the plate and the spoon to the right. The knife mediates between these two symbols of maleness and femaleness in its intermediate position. Clearly the fork has the more male position, in extreme opposition to the spoon, while the knife falls between the two. In Britain, the fork is opposed to the knife, with the latter at the right side of the plate, while the female symbol, the spoon, mediates between them in horizontal position across the top of the plate. It should be very clear that the symbolic structure involved here, including its "ambiguities," is not only sexual but rather Oedipal. The intermediate, vacillating, ambiguous position of the fork is thus clarified. We see the reasons why the British spoon mediates between the knife and fork, and why the American knife comes between the fork and spoon. The aggressive symbolism of the knife, cutting against the fork, is elucidated, and the significance of the ancient folk verse " . . . and the fork ran away with the spoon" is made apparent.

We cannot ignore the fact that, historically, the fork is an outgrowth of the knife, of a knife with a bifurcate point which developed into two tines. These two tines then developed into three, and later

into four. The multiplicity of the male symbolism in the fork can be seen as an overcompensation for subordinate status, as a kind of wish-fulfillment through the mechanism known to folklorists as "kenning," or as a recognition of the immanency of lineage fission. We must also observe the early determined opposition to the fork offered by the celibate males of the Church, who occupied the same position in that structure as the fork in flatware.

Thus we see that by this method of successive consideration of types of form and of action, on a series of binary discriminations, we can solve the problems of ambiguity which pervade cultural symbolism. In fact, we should go further and point out that such ambiguity is the very essence of cultural symbolism and is basic to its flexibility, its power, and its capability of subsuming enormous specific domains.

Summary

As anthropologists use the term, *culture* is the way of life shared by a group of people. It is what makes people similar to one another and unites them as a group. Culture is *acquired* behavior; it is learned rather than inherited genetically.

Not too long ago, anthropologists believed that culture was a uniquely human phenomenon, but as more was learned about the behavior of other primates, this notion has been discarded. We have recognized that culture as a dividing line between the human species and other animals is not as clear-cut as we used to believe. If we look at the kinds of behavior that are found in all societies, or what we refer to as *cultural universals,* we recognize many things that are not found in the behavior of any other species.

Culture is transmitted from one generation to the next through the process known as *socialization.* Although the methods of teaching children the appropriate behavior patterns may vary from one society to another, all societies engage in some form of child training. We assume that early childhood experiences will have a lasting effect upon an individual, and insofar as the same basic experiences are shared by most children in a society, a general personality pattern will be shared among most adults in that society.

The study of culture was first formalized in the nineteenth century with the founding of anthropology. Early anthropologists, Edward B. Tylor and Lewis Henry Morgan among others, attempted to prove that cultures had evolved from a primitive to a civilized state. Their evidence consisted of the analysis of *survivals* from earlier stages of cultural development and highly speculative evolutionary schemes.

By the beginning of this century anthropologists such as Franz Boas in the United States reacted against the lack of a factual base in cultural evolutionism. Their work stressed, instead, the collection of available historical evidence of culture change and the recording of disappearing cultures. Boas' student, Alfred L. Kroeber, continued the empirical analysis of culture and cultural change, searching for recurring patterns in recorded history on which to establish laws of culture change. Ruth Benedict, another student of Boas, studied the internal consistencies in cultures, describing cultural *configurations* in terms of personality characteristics and bringing together concepts from anthropology and psychology. Margaret Mead also integrated anthropology and psychology and worked with Abram Kardiner, a noted psychiatrist, and other anthropologists developing the concept of the *basic personality structure.* They focused on the *primary institutions* operating on a child in the first years of life as the crucial elements in the formation of personality in different cultures.

In England, the school of functionalism developed in response to speculative evolutionism. Under the direction of Bronislaw Malinowski, one form of functionalism stressed the role of culture in fulfilling the basic biological needs and the derived cultural needs of humans. Another branch of functionalism, led by A.R. Radcliffe-Brown, defined function by analogy with the organs of the body which contribute to the maintenance of the system as a whole. While Radcliffe-Brown demonstrated the internal consistencies of a cultural organism, Malinowski showed how different cultural elements aided in the fulfillment of basic and derived needs.

Contrary to the trend, one American anthropologist, Leslie White, maintained that cultural evolution should not be ignored, but simply reworked to eliminate conjecture and bias. White maintained that an unbiased measure of progress was to be found in the energy a society consumed per capita. According to his theory, energy consumption should vary from culture to culture with technology. White's theory was tested by Marshall Sahlins who demonstrated that Polynesian societies with greater social stratification consumed more energy per capita. Sahlins found, however, that environment, not technology, was the determinant of energy consumption in this case. Another refinement of White's theory was made by Julian Steward who demonstrated that similar causes could account for the rise of civilization in different places around the world. White's theory of evolution also led to the development of *cultural ecology* which concerns itself with the interaction between culture and environment.

Recently, another approach to culture has developed that stresses improved fieldwork techniques over grand theories. *Ethnoscience,* as it is called, attempts to analyze the native's view of his universe by examining the distinctions made by the culture. Another development in anthropological theory is the growth of French structuralism under the direction of Claude Lévi-Strauss. Structuralism attempts to uncover the universal structure of culture in the analysis of the hidden meanings of cultural elements.

Glossary

basic personality type The features of personality that are shared by most of a society's members and that result from the early childhood experiences the group's members have in common.

configuration The integration of the different traits of a culture into a dominant pattern or central theme. The different institutions of the culture are organized around this central theme.

cultural ecology An approach to the study of culture that stresses the interaction between culture and environment.

cultural universals The basic solutions to the problems of living that are found in one form or another in all cultures.

culture The shared way of life, common to a group and acquired by people as members of society. This way of life is learned through interaction with other people, and includes both material aspects and intangible knowledge (beliefs, attitudes, values, rules of behavior, etc.).

culture and personality The branch of cultural anthropology that studies the relationship between the way the culture molds children's personalities and the psychological makeup of the adults.

degeneration The nineteenth-century, anti-evolutionary theory that humans were created in a highly civilized state and declined to savagery in some cases.

diffusion The spread of a cultural trait to other societies from its place of origin.

doctrine of survivals The nineteenth-century evolutionist theory that all cultures contain the remains of earlier stages of development.

eschatology The philosophy of each culture concerning the nature of death and the afterlife.

ethnoscience An approach to the study of culture that emphasizes the recording and analysis of each culture's view of the world.

instinct The inborn traits that characterize most nonhuman animal behavior.

multilinear evolution Julian Steward's theory stressing the analysis of the evolution of culture along similar lines in different parts of the world.

primary institutions The groups and individuals who play a fundamental role in the process of child rearing (e.g., peers, family, early schooling).

socialization The process of learning to be a member of a society. A child learns the appropriate rules of behavior by interacting with people in the society.

society An organized group of individuals engaging in social interaction and forming a unit bound together by their shared way of life or culture.

superorganic The conceptualization of a culture as existing on a level above that of the individuals who make up a population.

unilinear evolution Nineteenth-century evolutionism which held that all societies had passed through exactly the same stages.

universal evolution Leslie White's concept of evolutionary stages through which human culture passed as a whole.

Additional Reading

Benedict, Ruth
1959 (orig. 1934) Patterns of Culture. Preface by Margaret Mead. Boston: Houghton Mifflin Co.

The classic study of three societies—the Zuñi, Kwakiutl and Dobu—and the patterns of culture in each.

Harris, Marvin
1968 The Rise of Anthropological Theory: A History of Theories of Culture. New York: Thomas Y. Crowell.

One of the most comprehensive reviews of anthropological theory ever written, but best left for the student with a well-developed background in the field.

Kroeber, Alfred L., and Clyde Kluckhohn
1952 Culture: A Critical Review of Concepts and Definitions. Papers of the Peabody Museum of American Archaeology and Ethnology, Harvard University, volume 47.

A collection of definitions of culture, with comments on their utility for anthropology.

LeVine, Robert A.
1973 Culture, Behavior and Personality. Chicago: Aldine.

A review and criticism of previous theories of personality and a discussion of a Darwinian model as the framework for the author's own approach to the study of personality.

Mead, Margaret
1928 Coming of Age in Samoa. New York: William Morrow & Company.

A comparison of the process of growing up among Samoan and American adolescent girls.

Radcliffe-Brown, A. R.
1952 Structure and Function in Primitive Society. New York: The Free Press.

A series of articles containing the classic statements of British functionalism by one of the founders of the approach.

Sahlins, Marshall, and Elman Service (editors)
1960 Evolution and Culture. Ann Arbor: University of Michigan Press.

A review of the new approach to cultural evolution, begun by Leslie White and carried on by his students, Sahlins and Service among them.

chapter thirteen

THE AIMS AND METHODS OF CULTURAL ANTHROPOLOGY

Culture is the way of life shared by a group of people, setting them off from others. Anthropologists who go to live in a foreign culture necessarily leave the familiarity of their own culture and enter a situation in which they do not know all the rules of proper behavior. Eventually they learn a new culture, and are then able to describe it and analyze it. This is the way cultural anthropologists conduct research. As you can see, it can be very exciting, but it can also cause many problems.

CULTURE SHOCK

An anthropologist's experience in living and working in a foreign culture can be lonely and frustrating; we must disregard much of our own cultural background in order to get along in the new world in which we find ourselves. In the process of shedding our cultural preferences, we frequently experience what we call *culture shock*. This is not something limited to anthropologists, for if you have ever spent much time outside your own country, or even in a vastly different subculture within the country, you have probably had a taste of it yourself. Culture shock is a feeling of depression and utter frustration that overcomes persons when they first begin to comprehend the tremendous difference between the way of life they are used to and the way of life in their new setting.

Why does culture shock occur? In the process

319

Nancy Howell made a study of acquaintance networks among the Bushmen of the Kalahari Desert. Fieldwork of this sort is an important aspect of modern anthropology.

of being brought up in a society, every individual is trained to accept the values of the group, and to follow the unwritten code of behavior. As part of the process of learning a culture, we are taught to believe in that culture, to believe that it is the right way, the best way to live. The values are not only seen as the ones that fit in with that particular way of life, they are considered the best ones for all people to follow. Any other way of doing things that does not follow the same value system is wrong, and often even repugnant. Thus when persons leave their own culture and enter another, their old values come into conflict with the new ones they find. The solutions to the problems that we face daily are not the same from one culture to another, and the patterns of behavior, the norms and the morals differ as well. Additionally, there are the overwhelming frustrations of working in a new language. The researcher is cut off from sources of information necessary for his work and isolated from the level of human contact he is accustomed to in his native culture. Sometimes the barriers to communication are insurmountable.

While working in a village in the Swiss Alps, John Friedl was curious about what aspects of their traditional culture the villagers accepted and what they rejected, and why. To understand the effects of modernization in a formerly agricultural village, he asked all kinds of questions about personal identity, morality, self-evaluation, attitudes toward family and friends, goals and ambitions, and so forth. At the same time, Friedl wanted them to get to know him better, and tried to engage them in conversation which would enable him to reciprocate. But somehow, whenever they started talking about his personal experiences, the topic always shifted to what were currently the key issues in their picture of America. They could not have cared less about his values, attitudes, goals, etc. What they wanted to know was why Jackie Kennedy had married Aristotle Onassis. Did she really need the money? And did Lyndon Johnson really have John Kennedy killed, and how did he get away with it? Did they still wear guns in the wild West, and ride horses, and shoot each other in the streets? Did gangsters in Chicago still carry sub-machine guns and rub each other out in gang wars? The more vehemently Friedl protested against this image of his culture that they had apparently picked up from TV, movies and popular magazines, the less they wanted to talk to him about America. Friedl was ruining their fun by telling them things they did not want to hear, and so they avoided him. In all the time he was there he was never able to portray himself to them, and despite his attempts to alter his image he remained a mystery to adults and young people alike in the village.

ETHNOCENTRISM

Culture shock can be an excellent lesson in relative values and in the general understanding of human differences. The reason that culture shock occurs is that we are unprepared for these differences. By the very nature of the way we are taught our culture, we are all what is called *ethnocentric*. The term comes from the Greek root *ethnos*, meaning a people or group. Thus enthnocentric refers to the fact that our outlook or world view is centered around our own way of life to the exclusion of others. Ethnocentrism is the belief that one's own patterns of behavior are the best, most natural, beautiful, right, or important. A corollary to this is the belief that everyone else, to the extent that he lives differently, lives by inhuman, irrational, unnatural or wrong standards.

Ethnocentrism is the point of view that one's own culture is preferred to all others, and as such it is characteristic of how all people feel about themselves as compared to outsiders. There is no one in our society who is not ethnocentric to some degree, no matter how liberal and open-minded he might claim to be. There will always be something he will find re-pugnant in another culture, whether it be a pattern of sexual practices that conflicts with his own moral code, a way of treating friends or relatives, or simply a favorite food that he somehow cannot manage to get down with a smile. It is not something we should be ashamed of, because it is a natural outcome of growing up in our society, or in any society. However, as anthropologists who study other cultures we should be constantly aware of our ethnocentricity, so that when tempted to make value judgments about another way of life, we are able to hold back and look at the situation objectively, recognizing our bias.

Ethnocentrism can be seen in many aspects of the culture—in myths, folk tales, proverbs, and even the language of most peoples. For example, in many languages, particularly among non-Western societies, the word used to refer to one's own tribe or ethnic group literally means "man" or "human." The implication of course is that those who are members of other groups are somewhat less than human. For example, the term "Eskimo," used to designate

The inhabitants of this Alpine village actively resented having their incorrect concepts about America corrected by a visiting anthropologist.

those Indian groups that inhabit the Arctic and sub-Arctic regions, is an Indian word used by neighbors of the Eskimos who observed their strange way of life, but did not share it. The term means literally "eaters of raw flesh," and as such is an ethnocentric observation about cultural peculiarities that were normal to one group and thoroughly repulsive to another. On the other hand, if we look at one term by which a subgroup among the Eskimos called itself (they obviously did not perceive their eating of raw flesh as a significant way of differentiating themselves), we find the term "Inuit," which literally means "real people." Here, then, is a contrast between one's own group, which is real, and the rest of the world, which is not so "real." Both terms, "Eskimo" and "Inuit," are equally ethnocentric—one as an observation about differences, the other as a self-evaluation.

Shifting from language to myths and folk tales, we can see an excellent example of ethnocentrism in the creation myth of the Cherokee Indians. According to this story, the Creator made three clay images of man and baked them in an oven. In his haste to admire his handiwork, he took the first image out of the oven before it was fully baked, and found it was too pale. He waited awhile, then removed the second image, and it was just right, a full golden, reddish-brown hue. He was so pleased with his work that he sat there and admired it, completely forgetting about the third image. Finally he smelled it burning, but by the time he could rescue it from the oven it had already been burnt, and it came out completely black.

Food is perhaps the most common manifestation of ethnocentrism. Every culture has developed special preferences for certain kinds of food and drink, and equally strong negative attitudes toward others. It is interesting to note that much of this ethnocentrism is in our heads, and not in our tongues, for something may taste perfectly delicious until we are told what it is. We have all heard stories about someone being fed a meal of snake or horse meat or something equally objectionable in American culture, and commenting on how tasty it was—until, that is, he was told what he had just eaten, upon which he turned green and hurriedly asked to be excused from the table.

One of the favorite delicacies in China is dog meat; the thought of eating a dog is enough to make most Americans sick to their stomachs. Yet we can see how this is part of a cultural pattern. Americans keep dogs as pets, and develop close relationships with them. Thus we tend to think of a dog as almost human, and would not dream of eating its meat. Horses, too, sometimes become close pets, and horse meat is likewise rejected by most Americans, although

The name by which these Eskimos call themselves means "real people," implying that other humans are inferior. This is a perfect example of ethnocentrism.

certainly not because of its taste. You may have eaten it without even knowing it, and probably you would not recognize it if someone didn't tell you what you were eating. On the other hand, we generally do not develop close relationships with cows or pigs, animals that we eat without any twinge of conscience. In India a cow is treated with the kind of personal care that a horse or even a dog receives in our country, and the thought of eating beef is similar to our feeling about eating dog meat. On the other hand, in China dogs are not treated as kindly as they are in the United States. In the absence of a personal relationship with a dog as a pet, it becomes quite similar to a cow in our culture, and can be eaten easily.

We learn to be ethnocentric as part of growing up in our society. John Friedl happened upon an old geography textbook used in grammar schools in the United States around 1920, entitled *Our Wonder World*, Volume 1: The World and Its Peoples. It begins with a discussion of the heavens, the place of the earth in the heavens, the origin of the earth, the nature of the earth's surface, and the animals that live and have lived here. It then goes into the story of human evolution and the evolution of culture.

Of particular interest to him, as a cultural anthropologist, were the two chapters on human variation and cultural diversity, entitled "The Queer People of the World," and "Other Peoples of the World." In "The Queer People of the World," subtitled "The Black, Brown, Red, and Yellow Races and Their Ways," the reader is taken on a tour of some of the more bizarre customs of other cultures, described in the most ethnocentric terms conceivable. The chapter begins with a rather sophisticated statement of the awareness of cultural differences:

To be queer is to be different from what is ordinary and normal. Each one of us decides from his own experience and surroundings what is natural and

Our society considers a thick, juicy steak to be the ultimate in fine dining. But because of their reverence for sacred cows, these Indians would be revolted at the thought of eating beef.

reasonable. Then we feel that everybody who departs from these ways of ours is a bit queer.

So "queer peoples" are no more strange and odd to us than we are to them. If you visited some of the places and tribes about which you are going to read, you would find yourself such an odd sight that children and grown persons would turn and follow you in the streets, just as you might turn and follow a circus parade if you met one. In the great human family there are many peoples whose ways and habits are unlike ours, and our interest is in these very differences. Some are uncivilized, and so take us back to a kind of life more like that of our ancestors than anything we are acquainted with; others are highly civilized, but their civilization is on another plane from ours.[1]

[1]*Our Wonder World*, Vol. 1. Chicago: Geo. L. Shuman & Co., 1918, p. 308.

Despite this disclaimer, the chapter goes on to make some incredible claims, totally unscientific and unacceptable in light of today's knowledge about other cultures. In the subsection "Peoples of the Negro or Black Division," we read the following:

First, let us take some of the black peoples, who live mostly in the Sudan, South Africa, and Australasia, but have migrated to many other parts of the world. Some of the most interesting of these black-skinned peoples live still in Africa. The true black people are the Negroes, whose home is in the middle part of Africa. They are the people with the black skins, the woolly heads, the thick lips, the flat noses, and the beautiful white teeth. The home of the Bantu race is the great southern section of Africa. They are not so black as the Negroes. Both peoples are brave, intelligent, and able to adapt themselves to new conditions and take on civilization. Smaller tribes are the Pygmies, the Hottentots, and the Bushmen, all far below the Negroes and Bantus in intelligence.[2]

There is no attempt to describe other ways of life in a total cultural context, but only to show how inferior they are when compared to our civilized customs. The other side of the coin is never presented, so that the young, impressionable minds of the readers of this textbook could learn that values are a relative thing. There is a description of the Bushmen, who "eat every creeping, running, and flying thing they can lay their hands on, including snakes and slugs." But nowhere is it mentioned how utterly repulsive it might seem to a Bushman, who shares all of his food with his relatives and friends and everyone in his society, if he were to see a rich fat-cat in our industrial society who gorged himself on food and was 50 pounds overweight, while others in his society went to bed hungry. We are ethnocentric because we are not taught to question our own way of life,

These Bushwomen of the Kalahari Desert are gathering nuts for the evening meal.

but only to evaluate other practices against ours as a standard.

It is necessary to stop right here for a moment, to make a very important point. We have been describing anthropology in such a way that the reader might come to the conclusion that by studying it he or she can avoid being ethnocentric. This is not true. Modern anthropology as a discipline is moving away from ethnocentrism, and is advocating a perspective that allows for the acceptance of all diverse cultural practices without culture-bound evaluations. However, anthropologists, as human beings raised in a cultural setting, are and always will be ethnocentric. We can produce lofty treatises on how one must accept other ways as valid, but that does not mean that we can accept them in our own lives and practice them. Anthropologists, through long hours of training and personal discipline in their fieldwork, can learn to be more tolerant, but they will always

[2]*Ibid.*, p. 308.

be culture-bound to some extent. We can never completely get inside someone else's skin and live our lives according to the rules of another culture. Thus we cannot guarantee that by the time you finish this book you will no longer be ethnocentric, any more than we could say that we have shed all the narrowmindedness that was a part of our upbringing. Ethnocentrism is not something we can will away—it creeps back constantly, as the following story illustrates.

A woman anthropologist was conducting field research in Colombia, and in the course of her work she learned that a particular Indian group there practiced the custom known as bride-price. According to this tradition, when a man took a woman as his wife, he or his family was obliged to offer a payment (in cattle, other goods, or money, or a combination of them all) to the bride's family. Although this is a fairly common practice in many non-Western societies (and elements of it can be seen in our own marriage customs, if you look closely), the anthropologist became upset at it, for she felt that it challenged the dignity of a woman to be bought and sold like any other possession. It never occurred to her that while it might rob a woman of her dignity in Western society, it could have exactly the opposite effect in the culture she was studying. Allowing her own values to come through, she asked one recent bride if it didn't bother her to be purchased like a cow. The woman replied by asking the anthropologist how much her husband had paid for her when they were married. Of course, the anthropologist explained that her husband had not paid anything, that we did not do such things in our society. "Oh, what a horrible thing," replied the Indian woman. "Your husband didn't even give a single cow for you? You must not be worth anything."[3]

---

[3]George M. Foster, *Traditional Societies and Technological Change*, Second Edition. New York: Harper & Row, 1973, p. 87.

CULTURAL RELATIVISM

The widespread reaction against ethnocentrism in anthropology is a relatively recent occurrence. The leading figure in the battle against the beliefs espoused in nineteenth-century anthropology was German-born Franz Boas, a dominant figure in the field of anthropology in the United States from the beginning of this century until his death in 1942. Not only did he influence anthropology through his many writings on all aspects of the field, but he taught a generation of anthropologists his methods and his beliefs, and his legacy has had a profound impact upon the discipline long after his death.

Anthropology in the nineteenth century was riddled with ethnocentrism, as were other social sciences. The theory of Charles Darwin, innocuous enough when applied to the natural world of plants and animals, became a dangerous tool in the hands of social scientists who applied it to cultural differences among human populations. Of course, Darwin himself never meant his theory of evolution to be applied to social change—on this point he is very clear—but others took some of the principles on which he based his theory and used them to explain the course of social evolution, usually in the absence of hard facts to support their claims. It was this "Social Darwinism," which really was not Darwin's theory at all, but a misapplication of it by others, that Franz Boas reacted against so strongly.

When Darwin's evolutionary scheme was transferred to social evolution, the result was a number of ethnocentric doctrines, all of which were based upon a very superior attitude toward Western society, and a condescending attitude toward the so-called primitives who were the subject of investigation by anthropologists and some sociologists. This view of evolution prompted a racist theory that placed non-Western, nonwhite societies on a lower scale of

Controversy

Biological and Cultural Evolution

The application of evolutionary theory to the study of culture has been an ongoing controversy among anthropologists since the idea was first introduced by Tylor in the nineteenth century. Rejected by Boas and subsequently revived by White, cultural evolution has been debated and argued by the most influential social scientists of this century. Is it valid to apply the principles of biological evolution to the analysis of cultural change?

It is clear to any student of anthropology that many sociocultural structures and functions appear to be closely analogous to biological structures and functions. The process by which culture is passed from generation to generation, for example, may be compared to the process by which genetic traits are transmitted. In the case of culture, changes are introduced as innovations in the system. Like genetic mutations, cultural innovations either survive and alter the nature of the social organism or else they become extinct. Analogies such as this have led many anthropologists to assume that something akin to natural selection accounts for the presumed parallel development of human societies.

There are many problems involved in using a biological model to explain cultural phenomena. The most immediate of these is the faulty equation of the mechanisms of genetic change with those of cultural change. Unlike genetic mutations, cultural innovations do not occur at random. An innovation is not likely to arise in a cultural setting in which it is totally inappropriate. People in a tropical climate, for example, are much less likely to develop techniques for making fur coats than people in the Arctic. An animal, on the other hand, is equally likely to grow a heavy coat through genetic mutation whether it lives in a warm or cold environment. In the case of biological evolution, natural selection determines which mutations will endure but does not cause those mutations to occur in the first place.

Biological and cultural evolution also differ in regard to the end results of change. Biological evolution involves the replacement of one form by another. Birds, for example, evolved wings to fly but lost the efficient use of their legs. Cultural evolution, on the other hand, is cumulative. *Homo sapiens* invented the airplane to fly, but he is still able to walk or to employ alternative methods of transportation. Moreover, cultural changes are reversible. An ostrich cannot grow another pair of legs because it finds that its wings are no longer useful. Cultural changes, however, can be reversed if they prove unsatisfactory. Finally, unlike biologically distinct species which cannot interbreed, cultures can share and exchange their innovations.

Perhaps the most profound difference between biological and cultural evolution is the time frame within which changes occur. The biological evolution of modern humans involved countless genetic mutations taking place over the course of many millions of years. Cultural changes, on the other hand, can occur within a single generation. There is no biological parallel to the tremendous technological advances which were achieved in the hundred years between 1865 and 1975.

The rapidity of cultural change, the spread of innovations from one individual to another within a generation, is the main advantage of culture over biology as a mode of adaptation. Unlike other animals, people do not need to depend upon genetic transmission to add innovations to their adaptive repertoire. Of course, variation in the rate of reproduction is, nevertheless, important to cultural evolution: the most successful cultural innovations are usually those which result in greater population size and the maximum production of energy. Ultimately, however, learning proves to be a more efficient device for spreading innovations than reproduction or random mutations.

Considering the vast differences between cultural and biological evolution, is it appropriate for cultural theory to draw on a biological model? Cultural and biological evolution differ, after all, on the source of innovation, the way in which new features are incorporated into the existing structure, the reversibility of change, and the pace of change. Ultimately, it would seem that evolutionary theory may provide an interesting perspective on cultural change, but the biological model cannot be used directly to scientifically predict and explain cultural phenomena. While the biological model has stimulated the development of a cultural model of evolution, the differences between the two systems appear to outweigh the similarities.

A Sepik River tribesman of New Guinea. The culture of his society is a valid and realistic adaptation to the environment in which he lives.

cultural and physical development, simply because they did not have the technological and military capabilities that were found in the Western countries. It was felt that if we, as Westerners, could conquer and subdue other societies through our military superiority, then the rest of our culture—our political system, our religious convictions, our moral code—must also be superior. This in turn led to the belief that if we compared all of the societies around the world to our own, we could set up a scale on which we could rank them; those most like us were higher up the ladder, while those least like us were placed at the bottom.

This view of social evolution tended to justify the policy of colonialism and domination of the non-Western countries. It was felt, for example, that if the forces of evolution were operating on societies, eliminating those that were unfit, then the best thing to do was to let nature take its course. Colonizing a group of people was a way of helping them to survive in the face of impending extinction. Of course, the fact that they would have to be made more like Westerners (in dress, language, religion, and the like) was a necessity that never questioned. Until Boas, no one ever challenged the logical fallacies in such a theory—the fact that there is a clear difference between societies and organisms, and that the mechanisms of change in one are not the same as in the other. No one mentioned that societies struggled for survival in a completely different context than organisms did (it was a physical battle, rather than a question of adaptation). No one pointed out that Social Darwinism was a conservative philosophy designed to maintain the status quo, which happened to be the domination of the world by the Western nations. Also, and perhaps most importantly to Boas, no one questioned the racist implications of this theory.

Nineteenth-century theories of social evolution were inherently racist because they were based upon the assumed superiority of the Western world, which meant the white world; non-Western, nonwhite societies occupied the lower levels of the evolutionary sequence. Anthropology, as a newly developing science in the nineteenth century, had inherited the problem of classifying the different peoples of the world, and had to devise a way to document the obvious racial differences in a more scientific manner. Of course the political and economic situation in America had a strong impact upon the directions that anthropologists took in their research and reporting. Despite the fact that the slaves had been emancipated and attained equal rights in law after the Civil War (or perhaps because of that fact), many Americans sought more scientific verifications of their prejudices, a more acceptable proof of the inferiority of the nonwhite races. Thus anthropology, along with all other branches of science in the nineteenth century, became a way to soothe the troubled conscience of the American middle class.

It was against this background that Boas entered the scene. Perhaps he had an advantage in his opposition to the previous half-century of American anthropology, in that he was German by birth, trained in German universities, without the heritage of American culture and American history to influence his ideas and penetrate his values. He rejected the attempts that had been made to show a correlation between race and level of cultural evolution—that is, the superiority of Western, white cultures. He was particularly vexed by the assumption that nonwhites were less ingelligent. While many claimed that the crudeness of primitive material culture was an indication of their mental inferiority, Boas pointed to the elaborate crafts from all over the world to counter this argument.

In his opposition to the ethnocentrism of nineteenth-century anthropology, Boas arrived at a position best described as *cultural relativism.* By this he meant that the anthropologist must maintain strict neutrality in describing and comparing other cultures, and make no judgments concerning the merits of one culture over another. Cultural relativism for Boas was an ethical position, by which all cultures were taken as equal, each as a separate unit with its own integrity, none of which should be compared to our own culture in terms of how they measure up to our standards. This position dominated anthropology in the early 1900s, and has been an important part of the field ever since.

Cultural relativism was a logical outcome of Boas' work in showing that the history of each group was distinct. Thus, whatever a culture is like today, it became that way as a result of its own development, and therefore cannot be ranked against another culture with a different history. Each culture has changed over time, some more than others in particular areas, and

some as a response to certain pressures that others did not face. The point for Boas was that because each culture had its own independent history, all groups could not be compared on a scale of excellence that conformed to any one particular group. There could be no assumption that there was a model toward which all change had been directed in the past, for change had proceeded in many different directions at the same time.

Boas' position, which he passed on to his stu-

If Western ideas about the necessity for family planning are to be effective in non-Western cultures, they must fit into the context of existing cultural patterns.

dents as perhaps his greatest gift to anthropology, involves both an attempt to maintain neutrality in analyzing cultural differences, and at the same time an awareness of one's own cultural biases, which inevitably creep in. If we are to make judgments about another culture, they should not be based upon our own background, but on the basis of our experience in that other culture—and only on that basis. In short, the anthropologist should put everything else out of mind when describing another people.

Every culture proposes solutions to the problems people face. If the anthropologist is to look at these solutions—for example, looking at a house as a solution to the problem of shelter—then she must consider it from the point of view of those people, in the context of their culture. If a solution seems to her impractical based upon her background and her knowledge of a different way of doing it, she must not overlook the fact that within its own context it may be very practical indeed.

Even one's perception of the physical world is affected by relative cultural interpretations. In the first chapter of this book, it was noted that not every language contains the same number of basic words for colors. We might find a language in which blue and green and red were all called by one term. It is hard for us to comprehend, but that does not make it any less valid a solution to the problem of describing the physical world. To turn the tables slightly, in many societies there are distinct words used to refer to relatives whom we lump together under one term in the English language. We use the word "uncle" to describe several different kinds of relatives: father's brother, mother's brother, father's sister's husband, and mother's sister's husband, as well as occasionally people who are great-uncles, and sometimes even people who are not uncles in any biological relationship, but who are close to us in a social sense. Yet in many societies there are distinct terms for each of these different types of uncle. If we find these societies strange because they call red and green and blue by the same term, think of how strange we must seem to them, when we can't even tell the difference between our mother's brother and our father's brother, or between an uncle by birth and an uncle by marriage. How ignorant we must be of the entire biological process of reproduction!

RELATIVE VALUES

Cultural differences in morals and values are the strongest factors in culture shock and are the most difficult parts of another culture to accept. When the anthropologist goes into the field, he is confronted with a totally new value system that most likely conflicts with his own in many ways. He may find many values totally unacceptable to him personally—a perfectly valid conclusion to come to—yet if he is true to his discipline he will not let this enter into his work. Rather, he must describe and analyze them as they fit into the entire culture of which they are a part. He may not approve, and he most certainly will reject the opportunity to participate, but if he is to translate the total culture he is studying, then he must present the practices he disapproves of in a completely objective fashion, so that the reader can understand what they mean to the people of that culture, without any outside evaluation by the anthropologist.

We may be studying a society where infanticide—the killing of young children—is practiced in order to maintain control over the population, a sort of retroactive birth control. The anthropologist might strongly disapprove. But if he is to present the culture objectively, he must explain this custom as it is perceived by the people who practice it. Among some traditional Eskimo groups, a similar practice existed. A person who became too old to carry his or her share of the workload was left out on the

Suppose this Australian aborigine kills his infant child. Considering that his tribe lives in a harsh land that can support few people, has he committed murder or performed a socially useful service?

is an accepted practice for which people are adequately prepared throughout their lives, and not some kind of treachery sprung upon an individual as a result of a criminal conspiracy. Finally, it should be considered in light of the ecological situation in which the Eskimos live. Making a living in the Arctic is difficult at best, and the necessity of feeding an extra mouth, especially when there is little hope that the individual will again become productive in the food-procurement process, would mean that the whole group would suffer. It is not a question of Eskimos not liking old people, but rather a question of what is best for the entire group. We would not expect—and indeed we do not find—this practice to exist where there was adequate food to support those who were not able to contribute to the hunting efforts.

Morality is not always as clear-cut as it might seem. While we can be firmly convinced of the validity of our own moral standards, we must recognize that they fit only one way of life. The lesson of cultural relativism is that we must always be on guard against applying our values and our moral standards to other ways of doing things. There can be no absolute standards. Anything that is possible is potentially acceptable in a particular cultural context. Every society has a system of morals and values, even if they vary tremendously from one to another. We may make judgments about whether that system is effective in any one society, but we may not make judgments about the specific content of such a system. For example, we might ask whether cultural relativism can be used to justify any sort of practice, such as cannibalism. We can explain it on the basis of conditions affecting the group. We can analyze it and determine whether it is effective, and how it fits in with other related practices. We can compare it to other practices in other societies as long as we maintain the distinctness of each. As anthropologists it is our place to explain why certain cultural practices occur among a given

ice to die. This may seem like an uncivilized way of dealing with one's parents, who raised one and gave one their love and care. Yet to describe it as that, and not to go into how it fits in with the rest of Eskimo culture, would not be acceptable according to anthropological standards. It is important to know, for example, that this is not done against the will of the old person. It is also necessary to recognize that this group and others do not. Any justification we offer is based on our own private opinions, which are determined by our own cultural background. This does not mean that if we feel something is wrong, we do not have the obligation to say so. We cannot sit back in our chairs and explain the extermination of the Jews in Hitler's Germany or the racism in the United States, and claim that our responsibility is over. We must speak out against injustice whenever and wherever we find it. But we must make a distinction between our obligations as objective observers of other cultures, and our responsibilities as human beings.

For the professional anthropologist, cultural relativism is a way of attaining objectivity. It is not a stopping point, but a starting point; it is a basic tool, necessary for carrying out research in foreign cultures. Just as it is necessary for students of anthropology to understand the concept of cultural relativism before attempting to understand other societies objectively, the anthropologist depends directly on the ability to tural relativism before venturing forth into the field. The quality of data collected by an anthropologist depends directly on his ability to view another culture with complete objectivity. With these thoughts in mind, we are now ready to examine the process of fieldwork more closely.

REVOLUTIONIZING FIELDWORK

Throughout the nineteenth century anthropology was frequently taken up as the hobby of well-to-do scholars who had the means and the opportunity to travel to out of the way places and study exotic peoples. A number of anthropologists also engaged in the analysis of the peoples of the world through written accounts put together by others, especially if they could not afford the time and expense of a field expedition on their own. This type of "armchair" anthropology, based upon travel diaries and missionary accounts rather than on intensive field research, led to a particular style of analysis that could not hope to capture the true nature of traditional societies. Even among those who were fortunate enough to engage in field research, there was still no systematic attempt to adhere to a rigorous control of research techniques.

It was not until the twentieth century that anthropologists grew really concerned with the quality of their research, and began to develop a set of standards for the fieldworker. One of the most important figures in leading the way toward a controlled method for cultural anthropology was Bronislaw Malinowski. Born in Poland, Malinowski was first trained in mathematics, but early in life he became interested in anthropology. He studied in London, then went to the Pacific, where he was carrying out research when World War I broke out. He ended up in Australia, where, as a citizen of the German nation with which Australia was at war, he was subject to internment for the duration of the conflict. He was, however, able to persuade the officials to allow him the alternative of internment not in Australia itself, but on a small group of islands to the north, called the Trobriands. There, he argued, he could do no harm, yet would be able to continue his research. Malinowski lived in the islands for several years, sharing the way of life of the natives. Isolated from civilization, he was forced to live in native villages, learn their language, and participate completely in their way of life.

As a result of his lengthy field experience, Malinowski published a series of books and articles on the culture of the Trobriand Islanders, dealing successively with their economics, their forms of social control, kinship and marriage patterns, and religion and magic. In the course of his work he also laid out in great detail his experiences in the field, emphasizing many ways in which they were different from the more traditional anthropological fieldwork, and pointing out the necessity of some of his novel approaches to his research. In *Argonauts of the Western Pacific,* published in 1922, Malinowski offers one of the earliest statements of the problems and requirements of anthropological fieldwork.

First, he said that to be effective and to produce valid results, the anthropologist must *live in the native community.* Until his time researchers had indeed conducted field studies out among the natives, but rarely so intensively. A typical research design would have the anthropologist working out of a mission outpost or a colonial office, perhaps making short trips into the field for more thorough investigations, but never really penetrating the day-to-day life of the natives. Frequently interpreters would be used, adding another filter through which information about native customs must pass, removing the anthropologist yet another step away from the object of the study. Malinowski's experience on the Trobriand Islands convinced him that only by becoming a part of the daily life of the community could the anthropologist hope to be able to put together a valid picture of what the culture means to the members of the group.

Second, Malinowski insisted that the anthropologist must *learn the native language.* If the goal of the cultural anthropologist in a descriptive ethnography is to translate one culture into another without losing accuracy, then first he must be able to comprehend it on its own terms. This requires learning to think in the language of the natives, not just learning to understand their utterances. Only when we are able to see the world as a native does can we begin to translate his culture, and if language determines the way we order our observations, then thinking in another language is essential to sharing another culture. Again, this was a revelation for the anthropological method when

Malinowski first suggested it, for most anthropologists had become accustomed to working with interpreters, especially in areas where the native language was not widely known or was not a part of a literary tradition that could have been incorporated into the anthropologist's formal education.

Finally, Malinowski advocated that the anthropologist adopt the method known as *participant observation.* Observation alone is not enough, he argued, for an observer cannot know the true meaning of the actions of others until he himself has an opportunity to participate in them. Conversely, participation alone is insufficient, for without the ability to step back and observe objectively, we are unable to grasp the meaning of our actions. This is clearly the case in our own culture, where we are frequently unaware of the meaning of many of

Close relationships can develop as a result of fieldwork. This anthropologist poses with his friend, a native New Hebrides islander in the Pacific.

our daily activities or the interrelationships between them, as the rest of this book will point out. Therefore the anthropologist must both participate in and observe the daily routine of life in the native community in order to learn the culture. In addition, he must include in his participant observation the special irregular occurrences which, although not part of the daily routine, are equally important to the overall picture of the culture. Deaths, ceremonials, quarrels and the like are just as important a topic for research as the routine activities of raising a family, making a living, maintaining social relationships and so forth.

But participation and scientific, objective observation are difficult actions to combine, as can be seen in an important controversy between two famous anthropologists who studied the same community. In the 1920s Robert Redfield went to the Mexican village of Tepoztlán, where he conducted field research.[4] Seventeen years later another anthropologist, Oscar Lewis, also went to Tepoztlán to do a restudy of the same community.[5] Lewis had read Redfield's work and was puzzled by it, finding many inconsistencies with what he found to be the case. Redfield's description of life in Tepoztlán is one of an idyllic rural setting where people were happy, healthy, and well-integrated. When Oscar Lewis studied the same community he found exactly the opposite: Tepoztlán was characterized by constant suspicion and tension, there was no cooperation among the villagers, and social relations were typically weak and strife-ridden.

The first question that comes to mind is: How can the village have changed so much in such a short period of time? But a deeper look at the situation reveals that it was not the village

The University of Chicago Press

Robert Redfield *(1897–1957)*
first studied the Mexican village of Tepoztlán in 1926. He concluded that there are basic similarities among peasant societies throughout the world, and led cultural anthropology out of its narrow concentration upon isolated, so-called primitive tribal societies. Redfield also developed what has come to be called the "folk-urban continuum," contrasting the way of life of the city with that of the isolated tribal or "folk" community.

---

[4]Robert Redfield, *Tepoztlán, A Mexican Village.* Chicago: University of Chicago Press, 1930.

[5]Oscar Lewis, *Life in a Mexican Village: Tepoztlán Restudied.* Urbana: University of Illinois Press, 1951.

that changed, but the outlook of the two different observers. Redfield's personal outlook was one which favored the rural life style over that of the city. He considered the city to be the source of cultural decay, a center of disorganization where the "pure" character of the countryman breaks down under the pressures of the fast-paced urban routine. Thus, Redfield had a predetermined preference for rural life, and when he lived and worked in Tepoztlan he was not able to overcome this bias. He saw every-

Arnold Katz

Oscar Lewis *(1914–1970) engaged in a restudy of the village of Tepoztlán in 1943, where Robert Redfield had conducted his research 17 years earlier. Lewis centered upon conflict in the village, and was concerned with the causes of suffering and discomfort for the villagers, whereas Redfield had centered upon harmonious interaction and the source of enjoyment for people. The result, of course, was a completely different picture of life in Tepoztlán, calling into question the objectivity of anthropological research.*

thing good in the life there, and overlooked much of what was bad. Lewis, on the other hand, approached his research from the opposite point of view. He felt that peasant life was one of suffering, that poor people were disadvantaged, and that Redfield's notion about the relative values of country versus city life was backwards. Thus in his work in Tepoztlán he looked for—and found—suspicion and distrust where Redfield had described harmony

and cooperation. We can derive a lesson from the errors of both men. We must be aware not only of our culture and its impact upon our evaluation of another way of life, but also of our own personality and the preferences we hold for certain parts of our culture as opposed to others. We do not have to change in order to be good anthropologists, but we do have to suppress some of our stronger feelings in order to ensure that our observations will be objective.

Initially it may seem that anthropological field research is a romantic escapade into the exotic life of a far-off tribe; however, the following passage describing Napoleon Chagnon's first encounter with the Yanomamö, an Indian society of Venezuela, will cause you to reconsider:

The excitement of meeting my first Indians was almost unbearable as I duck-waddled through the low passage into the village clearing. I looked up and gasped when I saw a dozen burly, naked, filthy, hideous men staring at us down the shafts of their drawn arrows! Immense wads of green tobacco were stuck between their lower teeth and lips making them look even more hideous, and strands of dark-green slime dripped or hung from their noses. We arrived at the village while the men were blowing a hallucinogenic drug up their noses. One of the side effects of the drug is a runny nose. The mucus is always saturated with the green powder and the Indians usually let it run freely from their nostrils. My next discovery was that there were a dozen or so vicious, underfed dogs snapping at my legs, circling me as if I were going to be their next meal. I just stood there holding my notebook, helpless and pathetic. Then the stench of the decaying vegetation and filth struck me and I almost got sick. I was horrified. What sort of a welcome was this for the person who came here to live with you and learn your way of life, to become friends with you?[6]

[6]Napoleon A. Chagnon, *Yanomamö, the Fierce People*. New York: Holt, Rinehart and Winston, 1968, p. 5.

A typical Yanomamö Indian as described by Chagnon.

METHODS OF RESEARCH

So far we have concentrated on the prerequisites for anthropological fieldwork. But once these have been met, how does the anthropologist conduct research? What do we look for when we go to work in a foreign culture? What kinds of questions do we ask, and how do we know whom we should ask? Obviously the anthropologist must structure the research in some way; we cannot simply move into a village and expect the people to flock to our doorstep, presenting a description to us in tightly organized pieces corresponding to the chapters of a book.

Unwritten Rules

One way in which anthropologists seek to understand another culture is to uncover the rules that govern behavior for members of that group. This is not restricted to the written laws covering transgressions of acceptable behavior in a legal sense, but includes the unwritten codes of conduct for all kinds of actions. Every society has these rules, and they are shared by almost all members to an extremely high degree. We are able to interact with other members of our society because we expect that in certain stituations they will respond in a limited number of ways. Without such an expectation all social interaction would be chaotic. Thus, if you meet someone for the first time and extend your hand, you do so with the understanding that he will do likewise and the two of you will shake hands. You do not expect that he will pour hot coffee on your hand, or grab it and give you a judo flip. Indeed, if something like that did happen, you would be justifiably shocked. Thus we have a basic rule that governs behavior in this kind of situation, and when we put together a collection of this kind of rules for all situations we are able to behave as a native in American culture.

When anthropologists go into a foreign culture they are at a disadvantage in that they do not know all of these rules. Furthermore, it is not easy to uncover them. We cannot simply sit down and ask a native to recite all the rules of behavior in his society. Rather, we must learn these rules by observing how other people react in certain situations, and by piecing together what information we have at hand. The trouble is that at the same time we are trying to be a part of this group, to participate as well as to observe, and in our participation we are likely to break many of the rules of conduct unknowingly, making it all the more difficult for the adult members of the society to accept us as one of them and treat us as equals.

The social behavior of these Japanese monks is based on their mutual understanding of what is proper in a given situation.

Let us look at another example from our own culture, to point out how difficult it can be for an outsider to learn these rules. Suppose a foreigner, in the United States for the first time, comes from a culture where it is customary for a person to bargain with the seller over the price of an item he wishes to buy, a practice found in many societies. Our visitor no sooner arrives in the country than he realizes he has forgotten his toothpaste. So he walks into a drug store, picks up a tube of toothpaste marked 69¢, and takes it to the counter, where he offers the pharmacist 50¢ for it. The pharmacist would probably look at this kook in disbelief and think about calling the men in the white coats to come and get him. No doubt the strong reaction would lead our foreigner to conclude rather hurriedly that bargaining over

the price of something is simply not done—he has broken an unwritten rule of behavior in American society, and the reaction over a paltry 19¢ was so strong that he would not likely do it again. But let's put him in a different situation, where instead of buying a tube of toothpaste he is shopping for a used car. He walks onto Honest John's Used Car Lot, where he sets his eyes upon a 1948 Plymouth, priced at only $995. Remembering his escapade in the drug store, and wanting very much to fit in with American culture, he doesn't even think twice, but simply forks over the money. Bargaining, he has concluded, is un-American. Imagine the look on Honest John's face!

Once the fieldworker begins to uncover the rules of behavior, he must put them together into a related system or code. The problem is that they are nowhere consciously formulated or recorded; in contrast to the written legal restrictions on what may not be done, there is no written handbook on the minute details of how one should behave in everyday interactions. Sometimes only a minor variation in style can have a major effect on meaning, changing an ordinary action into the most serious insult, yet nowhere will you find these variations described and accessible to an outsider. We are all aware of the symbolic meaning of various hand gestures, for instance. In our country, for example, holding up the middle finger of the hand conveys a certain meaning to the observer, a meaning sufficiently strong in some cases to prompt arrest, or to invite physical confrontation. In some parts of Europe this gesture is replaced by one in which you hold up both the index and the middle fingers, with the back of the hand facing the observer (and not the front of the hand, as in the noted "V for Victory" sign made famous by Winston Churchill during World War II). One day John Friedl was in a department store in Geneva, Switzerland, asking the saleswoman for two pairs of socks. "How many?" she asked. "Two," he re-

Tourists in an unfamiliar situation can look pretty silly. The anthropologist confronted with an entirely different culture often makes himself look even sillier until he learns appropriate social behavior.

plied, holding up two fingers to emphasize his request. It was, of course, a completely innocent mistake, but embarassing to all concerned.

In trying to uncover these rules of behavior, the anthropologist is limited in the questions he can ask. It is much easier, for example, to construct a hypothetical situation and ask an informant to describe proper behavior than it is to ask about what is correct in the abstract. For example, we might want to know about the philosophy of crime and punishment in a society; we could be interested in what crimes were taken most seriously, and for what reasons. This is not as simple as it sounds, for even if there is a written legal code that defines punishments for various crimes, it does not cap-

ture the variation in everyday occurrences of these crimes, the kinds of things that influence a jury but do not become part of the formal legal code. Thus, in doing research on crime and social control in a village, we might sit down with an informant and ask specific questions in the abstract, such as what he thinks is the most serious crime. The answer will probably parallel the formal legal answer for the society as a whole, but it will not necessarily enable us to understand how that legal code would be carried out in a specific case. It is much like the example of bargaining over the purchase price in our country: We cannot set a hard and fast rule for an outsider to follow, because so many different factors can affect whether we bargain or whether we accept the price as given.

Real vs. Ideal, Back Region, and Impression Management

There are always many aspects of their way of life that informants cannot accurately describe. Most of an individual's daily routine is so much a part of him that he cannot stop to analyze it, but simply acts it out without thinking. Thus to ask a question about it might not bring any response, because the individual does not perceive it either as important or as fitting in with a set of rules governing his behavior. In other words, we are unaware of much of the meaning of our behavior to an objective observer. This raises the distinction between what we call the "real" and the "ideal" behavior in culture. Everyone sees himself as conforming to the ideals, and frequently there is substantial agreement on what those ideals are. But when we observe a group of people in the same activities, we find that there is not as much conformity with those ideals as people would lead us to believe. It is here that the anthropologist must supplement his questions with observations; asking yields the ideal, while observing yields the real. Both are essential to understanding behavior in any society.

For example, if we were to inquire about driving an automobile in the United States, we would most likely be told the basic rules upon which all Americans agree: Stop for stop signs and red lights, do not exceed the speed limit, do not double park, etc. This yields the "ideal." But if we were to observe American driving practices, we would have a picture of the "real" behavior involved in driving a car. The next time you're out in traffic, watch and see how many people roll through a stop sign without coming to a complete halt. Or better still, drive 55 miles per hour on the freeway and count the number of cars that pass you, compared to the number you pass. You'll soon see why participation must go hand in hand with inquiries about a people's way of life.

In addition to the discrepancy between real and ideal behavior, there is always an area which people conceal from some observers, so that their actions appear to correspond to the ideal, even when they themselves know that other times this is not the case. This is what the anthropologist Gerald Berreman has called the

Negotiating heavy traffic requires an understanding of both unwritten rules and the formal code of traffic laws.

"back region."[7] By this term he means an area of behavior concealed by a group of people in order to control the impression an outsider obtains about them. For example, if you are away at school and you go home over Christmas, your parents will probably ask you how much you study. You will most likely exaggerate somewhat, concealing some of your activities that detract from your study time. Students definitely have a back region which they keep hidden from parents (and frequently from their professors as well).

The back region is thus the conscious effort to conceal deviations from the ideal behavior. This feature of social interaction is called *impression management,* for it involves the attempt of the individual to manage the impression that others have of him. If you stop and think for a minute about the different kinds of clothes you wear on different occasions, you can see this as a form of impression management. You probably don't wear a coat and tie or an expensive suit to anthropology class, but if you were going to a bank to ask for a loan, you certainly wouldn't want to go in wearing torn Levi's and a sweatshirt. You would want to create the impression that you were stable and employed, and that you could be counted on to repay the money, and grubby clothes just do not convey that impression. So you "manage" your impression by dressing up, concealing the back region of your life from the bank official. There is nothing dishonest about this, and we really don't feel guilty about doing it. It is just that we all have many facets to our social life, we all fit into society in many different ways, and we control which ways we fit in at any particular time according to the impression we wish to create.

The importance to the anthropologist of the concepts of back region and impression management is obvious. The people we observe, if

---

[7]Gerald D. Berreman, *Behind Many Masks.* Monograph Number 4 of the Society for Applied Anthropology, 1962.

they are aware of our presence, are managing their impression. While we want to get to know their "normal" behavior, they want to conceal certain aspects of it from us.

This leads us to the question of how we can evaluate the information we receive in the process of doing fieldwork. How do we know when we ask an informant a question that he will tell us the truth? How can we evaluate his version of the truth as opposed to someone else's? One way to get around this problem is to obtain as much information about a particular question from as many different people as possible. In this way, we can put together a composite picture that will be more accurate, in much the same way that a jury weighs the conflicting evidence in a trial and tries to come up with a more accurate picture of what happened.

Structuring Behavior

Another important distinction that anthropologists make in doing their research contrasts the structure they assign to behavior they observe with the way it is perceived to be ordered by the people themselves. There is usually a discrepancy between what we call the "folk image" in the minds of the natives of another culture, and the "analytical image" in the mind of the anthropologist. Of course, neither one is right or wrong; both can be completely accurate in entirely different ways.

People perceive their behavior as fitting into a pattern according to what they have learned about their culture. The anthropologist is an outsider who brings with him a knowledge of many different ways of life, not just his own. He may view the behavior in a completely different light, see different meanings in it or a different structure to it than the people themselves see. For example, as a result of the way you were brought up in American culture, you treat your brothers and sisters in a certain way (your folk image of what is proper within the family), but the anthropologist might see your interaction with your siblings as an example of family structure and patterns of authority, tied in with patterns of inheritance, the relative importance of age and sex, the prescribed roles for various family members, and so on (his analytical image of the American family in the abstract sense). This does not mean that the anthropologist ignores the folk image, for it is his job to understand behavior not just as it would be explained to an outsider, but as it has meaning to a member of the culture. But he does tend to look beyond specific events and try to form an overall pattern. People are not always conscious of the implications of what they do. They act in a certain way because it is "natural," or because it is "the right thing to do." By using an analytical image, the anthropologist can obtain a better understanding of these implications, even if the people themselves cannot substantiate his claims. This distinction is explained very well by the anthropologist John Middleton in the following passage from his book about the Lugbara, a society in Uganda, East Africa:

The reader may well wonder why it is necessary for the anthropologist to use these special terms to describe a society whose members do not themselves find it necessary to do so. The anthropologist is sometimes accused of building up a needlessly complex structural model, while the people he is studying seem to manage very well without it. In the case of a people like the Lugbara the reason is simple, but I think it is important to state it. The Lugbara "live" their society; they do not have to describe it or analyze it so as to make sense of it to outsiders. For a Lugbara, the range of everyday social relations, the context of his everyday life, is narrow. He is concerned with at the most about a score of small local groups and lineages. . . . But the anthropologist is in a different position. He is, in a sense, outside and above the society. . . . To describe this pattern, which is found throughout Lugbara, the anthropologist requires special terms which are not needed by the people themselves.[8]

Studying World View

So far we have discussed the way in which the anthropologist studies the structure of society and the rules that govern everyday behavior, both from the perspective of the participant in the culture and from the objective, analytical viewpoint of an outsider. There is a third area of study that can only be approached from the insider's perspective, something we call *world view.* The world view of a culture refers to the basic outlook held in common by most members of a society. It is not something that we can ask about directly in questioning informants; rather we must learn about it through inference, through compiling the various clues about what is in the minds of the people we are observing. Furthermore, we cannot be content to get inside one individual's head, but have to focus on the general attitudes of the entire society. We may be able to ask a person how he feels about a particular question, but we are interested in the thoughts of an individual as he typifies the outlook of the entire society, not as a single person or a unique case.

A common aspect of the world view of people who in a sense live closer to nature than we do in industrial society is that they perceive themselves to be a part of the natural system on earth, whereas we see ourselves as being outside that system. We in industrial society have learned to control the environment, and we see ourselves as dominant over nature. People who live off the land, through hunting and gathering or cultivation or both, do not participate in this technological mastery over the earth. They have a different world view, in that they feel a

Women of the Riff Mountains of Morocco. A male anthropologist would find it very difficult to get a rounded picture of life in their society where women are isolated and must keep their faces covered.

closer affinity to nature. When a Bushman of the Kalahari Desert in South Africa kills a giraffe, he feels a loss, for he recognizes that a living spirit has departed from the world. When a Plains Indian killed a buffalo, it was not a part of his plan to dominate nature, it was a part of his interaction with nature.

Perhaps the anthropological approach to the study of world view is best summed up by Malinowski:

. . . the final goal, of which an Ethnographer should never lose sight . . . is, briefly, to grasp the native's point of view, his relation to life, to realise *his* vision of *his* world. We have to study man, and we must study what concerns him most intimately, that is, the hold which life has on him. In each culture, the values are slightly different; people aspire after different aims, follow different impulses, yearn after a different form of happiness. In each culture, we find different institutions in which man pursues his life-interest, different customs by which he satisfies his aspirations, different codes of law and morality which reward his virtues or punish his defections. To study the institutions, customs, and codes or to study the behaviour

[8]John Middleton, *The Lugbara of Uganda.* New York: Holt, Rinehart and Winston, 1965, p. 36.

American Museum of Natural History

Margaret Mead *(1901 –)*
undertook her doctoral research in
Samoa, designed to study the rela-
tionship between patterns of child-
rearing and adult personalities.
She was particularly interested in
the experiences of adolescent girls
in Samoa as they compared to
American cultural experiences,
and the differences in general
personality types that resulted.
Along with Ruth Benedict, Mar-
garet Mead was an important
early link between psychology and
anthropology. She conducted a
pioneer study of women and chil-
dren in foreign cultures —until
then, male field researchers had
been relatively unsuccessful at
gathering confidential information
on females in other cultures.

and mentality without realising the substance of their happiness—is, in my opinion, to miss the greatest reward which we can hope to obtain from the study of man.[9]

[9]Bronislaw Malinowski, *Argonauts of the Western Pacific.* New York: E.P. Dutton, 1922, p. 25.

CONCLUSION

To conclude our discussion of the method of anthropology, it is important to note just how difficult it is for the anthropologist to fit into the society he is studying. He is coming into a community as a perfect stranger, not knowing the cues and rules for behavior, yet wanting people to accept him and take him into their homes and their private lives and reveal to him the most intimate details of their behavior. Is it any wonder that they reject him, or that they think he is crazy? Colby Hatfield has made an interesting analysis of the role of the anthropologist in the field, separating it into three parts corresponding to the impression the fieldworker frequently makes upon the people he is studying.[10] First of all, he says the anthropologist is seen as a child. He speaks the language poorly and makes many mistakes, both serious and silly. He does not know the rules of behavior, and is often discourteous or insulting. He is incompetent at even the simplest of tasks, because he has not had the opportunity to learn the techniques prevalent in that culture. All of these characteristics are true of children.

A second role the anthropologist slips into in a community, especially if it is a poor rural village such as anthropologists have traditionally sought out, is what Hatfield calls the "Fort Knox" syndrome. The Western anthropologist on even the skimpiest of research grants generally has much more capital at his disposal than the average villager. Thus they view him as a storehouse of wealth. He is willing to pay for the services the villagers render, and to their mind it seems as if he never runs out of money. At the same time, he obviously does not have to work for a living, because all he does is walk

[10]Colby R. Hatfield, Jr., "Fieldwork: Toward a Model of Mutual Exploitation." *Anthropological Quarterly* 46:1:15–29, 1973.

around the village all day asking questions. His money miraculously appears in the mail every month, but it is not clear who is paying him for what, nor is it clear that the source of this interminable wealth is not a money tree that never dries up. So the anthropologist is constantly battling against this image, although frequently it is a losing battle.

Third, the anthropologist is often assigned the role of "Sahib," as Hatfield calls it, the expert in all things, the exalted foreigner who possesses power that the community members could not hope to acquire. After all, the anthropologist is literate, whereas the people anthropologists have traditionally studied have not been. The anthropologist is able to deal with government bureaucracies, which in itself is a kind of power. He knows about people and places in the four corners of the world, and can tell stories that challenge the imagination of even the most cosmopolitan villager. Despite the fact that he comes on like a child in their own culture, there is obviously something there, and so the anthropologist is given the artificial status of village expert.

Try as he might during his fieldwork in the Swiss Alps, John Friedl could not get the farmers to let him help them with their tasks. They felt that a city fellow shouldn't get his hands dirty working in the fields. When Friedl pointed out to them that he had put on his work clothes, and actually wanted to help, they would respond by saying something like, "Oh, what do you have work clothes for?" They would laugh at the silly questions he asked about their farming and livestock-raising practices, much as if he were a naive young boy. And they were amazed at the fact that he bought all his food, and did not even grow his own potatoes. On the other hand, they did respect his ability to deal with aspects of the outside world with which they had had little experience. Friedl was asked to translate for them, to type letters and reports, and to inter-

pret the meaning of various happenings. Perhaps most important of all in their minds was the fact that he could explain American television programs that appeared on their TV screens, appropriately dubbed in German. Hatfield's description of the fieldworker as child-Fort-Knox-Sahib certainly rings true from Friedl's experience, and points out some of the problems the anthropologist faces.

We have said much about these problems, and about the kinds of situations the anthropologist encounters, but little about actual techniques of fieldwork. We have not, for example, gone into great detail describing the proper way to phrase a question or to write up an interview, or the best way to use a tape recorder or a camera. This is perhaps due to the fact that we firmly believe in the individuality of each fieldworker and the need for flexibility according to the situation. The graduate student trained in anthropology generally does not receive this kind of instruction in the narrow detail of the methods he is to use. It is assumed he will adjust to the demands of the community he lives in, and any attempt to arrive at a hard-and-fast rule of how to do research would not be valid. Besides, doing anthropological research calls for a lot of personal qualities that simply cannot be acquired through training— the perseverance to stick it out, the control over one's temper when people laugh at you and kids throw snowballs at you, the ability to eat whatever you are given with a smile and compliment the chef even if you don't like fried lizard, and perhaps above all the ability to cope with the loneliness when you are so far away from home for so long. There is no technique to these aspects of fieldwork, and there is no way to train for them. Not everyone who starts out to become an anthropologist finishes the task, but those who do usually develop their own personal way of doing research that fits both their own personal idiosyncrasies and the unique demands of the research setting.

Focus

Richard Borshay Lee

Eating Christmas
in the Kalahari

In the following article, Richard B. Lee describes a situation in which all of his theory and classroom training could not help him overcome a basic gap in communication across cultural boundaries. The author was making a special effort to share his resources with his hosts, and not only misunderstood their response to his kindness, but was insulted by it. Had the story ended there, it would simply have been another case of cultural limitations preventing people from growing closer together and learning about each other. However, Lee was able to penetrate the cultural patterns of the Bushmen and learn the true meaning of their apparent unfriendliness and ungratefulness.

Reprinted from *Natural History,* **78,** December 1969.

Editor's Note: The !Kung and other Bushmen speak click languages. In the story, three different clicks are used:

1. The dental click (/), as in /ai/ai, /ontah, and /gaugo. The click is sometimes written in English as tsk-tsk.
2. The alveopalatal click (!), as in Ben!a and !Kung.
3. The lateral click (//), as in //gom.

Clicks function as consonants; a word may have more than one, as in /n!au.

The !Kung Bushmen's knowledge of Christmas is thirdhand. The London Missionary Society brought the holiday to the southern Tswana tribes in the early nineteenth century. Later, native catechists spread the idea far and wide among the Bantu-speaking pastoralists, even in the remotest corners of the Kalahari Desert. The Bushmen's idea of the Christmas story, stripped to its essentials, is "praise the birth of white man's god-chief"; what keeps their interest in the holiday high is the Tswana-Herero custom of slaughtering an ox for his Bushmen neighbors as an annual goodwill gesture. Since the 1930s, part of the Bushmen's annual round of activities has included a December congregation at the cattle posts for trading, marriage brokering, and several days of trance-dance feasting at which the local Tswana headman is host.

As a social anthropologist working with !Kung Bushmen, I found that the Christmas ox custom suited my purposes. I had come to the Kalahari to study the hunting and gathering subsistence economy of the !Kung, and to accomplish that it was essential not to provide them with food, share my own food, or interfere in any way with their food-gathering activities. While liberal handouts of tobacco and medical supplies were appreciated, they were scarcely adequate to erase the glaring disparity in wealth between the anthropologist, who maintained a two-month inventory of canned goods, and the Bushmen, who rarely had a day's supply of food on hand. My approach, while paying off in terms of data, left me open to frequent accusations of stinginess and hard-heartedness. By their lights, I was a miser.

The Christmas ox was to be my way of saying thank you for the cooperation of the past year; and since it was to be our last Christmas in the field. I determined to slaughter the largest, meatiest ox that money could buy, insuring that the feast and trance dance would be a success.

Through December I kept my eyes open at the wells as the cattle were brought down for watering. Several animals were offered, but none had quite the grossness that I had in mind. Then, ten days before the holiday, a Herero friend led an ox of astonishing size and mass up to our camp. It was solid black, stood five feet high at the shoulder, had a five-foot span of horns, and must have weighed 1,200 pounds on the hoof. Food consumption calculations are my specialty, and I quickly figured that bones and viscera aside, there was enough meat—at least four pounds—for every man, woman, and child of the 150 Bushmen in the vicinity of /ai/ai who were expected at the feast.

Having found the right animal at last, I paid the Herero L20 ($56) and asked him to keep the beast with his herd until Christmas day. The next morning word spread among the people that the big solid black ond was the ox chosen by /ontah (my Bushman name; it means, roughly, "whitey") for the Christmas feast. That afternoon I received the first delegation. Ben!a, an outspoken sixty-year-old mother of five, came to the point slowly.

"Where were you planning to eat Christmas?"

"Right here at /ai/ai," I replied.

"Alone or with others?"

"I expect to invite all the people to eat Christmas with me."

"Eat what?"

"I have purchased Yehave's black ox, and I am going to slaughter and cook it."

"That's what we were told at the well but refused to believe it until we heard it from yourself."

"Well, it's the black one," I replied expansively, although wondering what she was driving at.

"Oh, no!" Ben!a groaned, turning to her group. "They were right." Turning back to me she asked, "Do you expect us to eat that bag of bones?"

"Bag of bones! It's the biggest ox at /ai/ai."

"Big, yes, but old. And thin, Everybody knows there's no meat on that old ox. What did you expect us to eat off it, the horns?"

Everybody chuckled at Ben!a's one-liner as they walked away, but all I could manage was a weak grin.

That evening it was the turn of the young men. They came to sit at our evening fire.

/gaugo, about my age, spoke to me man-to-man.

"/ontah, you have always been square with us," he lied. "What has happened to change your heart? That sack of guts and bones of Yehave's will hardly feed one camp, let alone all the Bushmen around /ai/ai." And he proceeded to enumerate the seven camps in the /ai/ai vicinity, family by family. "Perhaps you have forgotten that we are not few, but many. Or are you too blind to tell the difference between a proper cow and an old wreck? That ox is thin to the point of death."

"Look, you guys," I retorted, "that is a beautiful animal, and I'm sure you will eat it with pleasure at

Christmas."

"Of course we will eat it; it's food. But it won't fill us up to the point where we will have enough strength to dance. We will eat and go home with stomachs rumbling."

That night as we turned in, I asked my wife, Nancy: "What did you think of the black ox?"

"It looked enormous to me. Why?"

"Well, about eight different people have told me I got gypped; that the ox is nothing but bones."

"What's the angle?" Nancy asked. "Did they have a better one to sell?"

"No, they just said that it was going to be a grim Christmas because there won't be enough meat to go around. Maybe I'll get an independent judge to look at the beast in the morning."

Bright and early, Halingisi, a Tswana cattle owner, appeared at our camp. But before I could ask him to give me his opinion on Yehave's black ox, he gave me the eye signal that indicated a confidential chat. We left the camp and sat down.

"/ontah, I'm surprised at you; you've lived here for three years and still haven't learned anything about cattle."

"But what else can a person do but choose the biggest, strongest animal one can find?" I retorted.

"Look, just because an animal is big doesn't mean that it has plenty of meat on it. The black one was a beauty when it was younger, but now it is thin to the point of death."

"Well I've already bought it. What can I do at this stage?"

"Bought it already? I thought you were just considering it. Well, you'll have to kill it and serve it, I suppose. But don't expect much of a dance to follow."

My spirits dropped rapidly. I could believe that Ben!a and /gaugo just might be putting me on about the black ox, but Halingisi seemed to be an impartial critic. I went around that day feeling as though I had bought a lemon of a used car.

In the afternoon it was Tamazo's turn. Tomazo is a fine hunter, a top trance performer and one of my most reliable informants. He approached the subject of the Christmas cow as part of my continuing Bushmen education.

"My friend, the way it is with us Bushmen," he began, "is that we love meat. And even more than that, we love fat. When we hunt we always search for the fat ones, the ones dripping with layers of white fat: fat that turns into a clear, thick oil in the cooking pot, fat that slides down your gullet, fills your stomach and gives you a roaring diarrhea," he rhapsodized.

"So, feeling as we do," he continued, "it gives us pain to be served such a scrawny thing as Yehave's black ox. It is big, yes, and no doubt its giant bones are good for soup, but fat is what we really crave and so we will eat Christmas this year with a heavy heart."

The prospect of a gloomy Christmas now had me worried, so I asked Tomazo what I could do about it.

"Look for a fat one, a young one . . . smaller, but fat. Fat enough to make us //gom ('evacuate the bowels'), then we will be happy."

My suspicions were aroused when Tomazo said that he happened to know of a young, fat, barren cow that the owner was willing to part with. Was Toma working on commission, I wondered? But I dispelled this unworthy thought when we approached the Herero owner of the cow in question and found that he had decided not to sell.

The scrawny wreck of a Christmas ox now became the talk of the /ai/ai water hole and was the first news told to the outlying groups as they began to come in from the bush for the feast. What finally convinced me that real trouble might be brewing was the visit from u!au, an old conservative with a reputation for fierceness. His nickname meant spear and referred to an incident thirty years ago in which he had speared a man to death. He had an intense manner; fixing me with his eyes, he said in clipped tones:

"I have only just heard about the black ox today, or else I would have come here earlier. /ontah, do you honestly think you can serve meat like that to people and avoid a fight?" He paused, letting the implications sink in. "I don't mean fight you, /ontah; you are a white man. I mean a fight between Bushmen. There are many fierce ones here, and with such a small quantity of meat to distribute, how can you give everybody a fair share? Someone is sure to accuse another of taking too much or hogging all the choice pieces. Then you will see what happens when some go hungry while others eat."

The possibility of at least a serious argument struck me as all too real. I had witnessed the tension that surrounds the distribution of meat from a kudu or gemsbok kill, and had documented many arguments that sprang up from a real or imagined slight in meat distribution. The owners of a kill may spend up to two hours arranging and rearranging the piles of meat under the gaze of a circle of recipients before handing them out. And I also knew that the Christmas feast at /ai/ai would be bringing together groups that had feuded in the past.

Convinced now of the gravity of the situation, I went in earnest to search for a second cow; but all my inquiries failed to turn one up.

The Christmas feast was evidently going to be a disaster, and the incessant complaints about the meagerness of the ox had already taken the fun out of it for me. Moreover, I was getting bored with the wisecracks, and after losing my temper a few times, I resolved to serve the beast anyway. If the meat fell short, the hell with it. In the Bushmen idiom, I announced to all who would listen:

"I am a poor man and blind. If I have chosen one that is too old and too thin, we will eat it anyway and see if there is enough meat there to quiet the rumbling of our stomachs."

On hearing this speech, Ben!a offered me a rare word of comfort. "It's thin," she said philosophically, "but the bones will make a good soup."

At dawn Christmas morning, instinct told me to turn over the butchering and cooking to a friend and take off with Nancy to spend Christmas alone in the bush. But curiosity kept me from retreating. I wanted to see what such a scrawny ox looked like on butchering, and if there was going to be a fight, I wanted to catch every word of it. Anthropologists are incurable that way.

The great beast was driven up to our dancing ground, and a shot in the forehead dropped it in its tracks. Then, freshly cut branches were heaped around the fallen carcass to receive the meat. Ten men volunteered to help with the cutting. I asked /gaugo to make the breast bone cut. This cut, which begins the butchering process for most large game, offers easy access for removal of the viscera. But it also allows the hunter to spot-check the amount of fat on the animal. A fat game animal carries a white layer up to an inch thick on the chest, while in a thin one, the knife will quickly cut to bone. All eyes fixed on his hand as /gaugo, dwarfed by the great carcass, knelt to the breast. The first cut opened a pool of solid white in the black skin. The second and third cut widened and deepened the creamy white. Still no bone. It was pure fat; it must have been two inches thick.

"Hey /gau," I burst out," "that ox is loaded with fat. What's this about the ox being too thin to bother eating? Are you out of your mind?"

"Fat?" /gau shot back, "You call that fat? This wreck is thin, sick, dead!" And he broke out laughing. So did everyone else. They rolled on the ground, paralyzed with laughter. Everybody laughed except me; I was thinking.

I ran back to the tent and burst in just as Nancy was getting up. "Hey, the black ox. It's fat as hell! They were kidding about it being too thin to eat. It was a joke or something. A put-on. Everyone is really delighted with it!"

"Some joke," my wife replied. "It was so funny that you were ready to pack up and leave /ai/ai."

If it had indeed been a joke, it had been an extraordinarily convincing one, and tinged, I thought, with more than a touch of malice as many jokes are. Nevertheless, that it was a joke lifted my spirits considerably, and I returned to the butchering site where the shape of the ox was rapidly disappearing under the axes and knives of the butchers. The atmosphere had become festive. Grinning broadly, their arms covered with blood well past the elbow, men packed chunks of meat into the big cast-iron cooking pots, fifty pounds to the load, and muttered and chuckled all the while about the thinness and worthlessness of the animal and /ontah's poor judgment.

We danced and ate that ox two days and two nights; we cooked and distributed fourteen potfuls of meat and no one went home hungry and no fights broke out.

But the "joke" stayed in my mind. I had a growing feeling that something important had happened in my relationship with the Bushmen and that the clue lay in the meaning of the joke. Several days later, when most of the people had dispersed back to the bush camps, I rasied the question with Hakekgose, a Tswana man who had grown up among the !Kung, married a !Kung girl, and who probably knew their culture better than any other non-Bushman.

"With us whites," I began, "Christmas is supposed to be the day of friendship and brotherly love. What I can't figure out is why the Bushmen went to such lengths to criticize and belittle the ox I had bought for the feast. The animal was perfectly good and their jokes and wisecracks practically ruined the holiday for me."

"So it really did bother you," said Hakekgose. "Well, that's the way they always talk. When I take my rifle and go hunting with them, if I miss, they laugh at me for the rest of the day. But even if I hit and bring one down, it's no better. To them, the kill is always too small or too old or too thin; and as we sit down on the kill site to cook and eat the liver, they keep grumbling, even with their mouths full of meat. They say things like, 'Oh this is awful! What a worthless animal! Whatever made me think that this Tswana rascal could hunt!' "

"Is this the way outsiders are treated?" I asked.

"No, it is their custom; they talk that way to each other too. Go and ask them."

/gaugo had been one of the most enthusiastic in making me feel bad about the merit of the Christmas ox. I sought him out first.

"Why did you tell me the black ox was worthless, when you could see that it was loaded with fat and meat?"

"It is our way," he said smiling. "We always like to fool people about that. Say there is a Bushman who has been hunting. He must not come home and announce like a braggard, 'I have killed a big one in the bush!' He must first sit down in silence until I or someone else comes up to his fire and asks, 'What did you see today?' He replies quietly, 'Ah, I'm no good for hunting. I saw nothing at all [pause] just a little tiny one.' Then I smile to myself," /gaugo continued, "because I know he has killed something big.

"In the morning we make up a party of four or five people to cut up and carry the meat back to the camp. When we arrive at the kill we examine it and cry out, 'You mean to say you have dragged us all the way out here in order to make us cart home your pile of bones? Oh, if I had known it was this thin I wouldn't have come.' Another one pipes up, 'People, to think I gave up a nice day in the shade for this. At home we may be hungry but at least we have nice cool water to drink.' If the horns are big, someone says, 'Did you think that somehow you were going to boil down the horns for soup?'

"To all this you must respond in kind. 'I agree,' you say, 'this one is not worth the effort; let's just cook the liver for strength and leave the rest for the hyenas. It is not too late to hunt today and even a duiker or a steenbok would be better than this mess.'

"Then you set to work nevertheless; butcher the animal, carry the meat back to the camp and everyone eats," /gaugo concluded.

Things were beginning to make sense. Next, I went to Tomazo. He corroborated /gaugo's story of the obligatory insults over a kill and added a few details of his own.

"But," I asked, "why insult a man after he has gone to all that trouble to track and kill an animal and when he is going to share the meat with you so that your children will have something to eat?"

"Arrogance," was his cryptic answer.

"Arrogance?"

-'Yes, when a young man kills much meat he comes to think of himself as a chief or a big man, and he thinks of the rest of us as his servants or inferiors. We can't accept this. We refuse one who boasts, for someday his pride will make him kill somebody. So we always speak of his meat as worthless. This way we cool his heart and make him gentle."

Summary

Our culture establishes a pattern of life for us that is very difficult to live without. When we travel to a foreign country and take on another way of life, we become very uncomfortable. Our values no longer fit the situation, our expectations usually prove to be wrong, and it is difficult for us to fit in with other people and behave as they do. This creates a feeling known as *culture shock,* something that is not limited to anthropologists who conduct fieldwork in another culture, but can be experienced by anyone.

In the process of learning our culture, we also are taught to believe that our way of life is correct, that it is good, indeed the best possible way to live. This attitude is known as *ethnocentrism,* and is a feeling of cultural superiority. It is found in our reactions to foreign customs, in our myths and proverbs, even in our dietary preferences. And ethnocentrism is perpetuated (not always consciously) through our educational system, which tends to put down other people's ways of doing things as bizarre or inferior.

Through our training in anthropology and the study of other customs, we attempt to overcome as much of our ethnocentrism as possible. We try to become more objective about cultural differences, to be tolerant of other people. This attitude is known as *cultural relativism,* and is based on the proposition that all values are relative and that there are no absolute standards that are valid in all cultural settings. Before an anthropologist can undertake fieldwork, it is essential that he or she attain a degree of cultural relativism.

One of the leading figures in the development of objective methods of field research in anthropology is Bronislaw Malinowski, who engaged in what is called *participant observation.* Malinowski recommended that all anthropologists live in the native community, learn the native language, and try to understand the culture from the native's point of view. A major difficulty in conducting research in a foreign culture is maintaining objectivity in the face of massive culture shock. If the anthropologist is reduced to making value judgments about the way of life of the people being studied, then he or she will never be able to describe or analyze that culture without personal prejudices slipping in.

In doing research in a foreign culture, the anthropologist tries to uncover the unwritten rules that govern people's behavior. Frequently it is difficult to do this simply by asking people why they act in a particular way. Therefore the anthropologist must combine several different methods, including actual participation in the culture, questioning informants who share the culture, and standing back and observing as an outsider. One of the problems the anthropologist must overcome is the universal tendency of all people to create an impression of themselves by concealing certain aspects of their lives and emphasizing others, a process we call *impression management.* In uncovering the hidden behavior of people in another culture, the anthropologist must engage in a bit of impression management himself, proving that it is just as natural for us as for anyone else.

The anthropologist's role in another culture is frequently made difficult by the fact that although we are in many ways similar to children, in that we do not know all the rules of behavior and we do not speak the language perfectly, we are nonetheless adults and cannot be treated as children. In addition, anthropologists are frequently in command of more resources—money, an automobile, books and specialized knowledge, etc.—than the people they are studying. This leads people to place all kinds of demands upon the visitor, and makes it difficult for the anthropologist to be completely accepted as "one of the gang."

Glossary

analytic image The manner in which an anthropologist organizes or structures the behavior of a particular culture.

back region A term referring to an area of behavior concealed by a group of people in order to control an outsider's impression of them.

cultural relativism A doctrine that states that judgments should not be made concerning the merits of one culture over another; rather, each culture has its own integrity.

culture shock The trauma experienced by people who enter a new cultural setting.

ethnocentrism The belief that one's own patterns of behavior are preferable to those of all other cultures.

folk image The manner in which the natives of a particular culture organize or structure their own behavior.

ideal behavior Those rules of conduct that are learned and shared by the members of a particular culture.

impression management The attempt of an individual to control the opinions that others have of him.

infanticide The killing of infants, usually practiced in order to maintain control over the population.

participant observation The method employed by the anthropologist in conducting field research, aimed at an equal balance between actual participation in the community and objective observation of that community.

real behavior The actual behavior patterns participated in by members of a particular culture, which do not necessarily conform to the ideal behaviors expressed by the natives themselves.

Social Darwinism A theory based upon the erroneous application of Darwinian principles to social and cultural evolution, and from the ethnocentric standpoint that Western culture is more advanced than "primitive" cultures.

world view The basic outlook held in common by most members of a society.

Additional Readings

Bates, Marston
1967   Gluttons and Libertines: Human Problems of Being Natural. New York: Vintage Books.

A humorous study of eating and sexual practices in cross-cultural perspective. Particularly valuable in light of the preceding discussion of relative values and ethnocentrism regarding foods and morals.

Golde, Peggy (editor)
1970   Women in the Field. Chicago: Aldine.

As the title implies, a collection of papers by 12 women dealing with the specific problems of being a woman engaged in anthropological research.

Pelto, Pertti J.
1970   Anthropological Research: The Structure of Inquiry. New York: Harper & Row.

One of the more detailed books treating the various research techniques and approaches used by anthropologists, this book is especially valuable for its blend of the humanistic and scientific elements of fieldwork.

Powdermaker, Hortense
1966   Stranger and Friend: The Way of an Anthropologist. New York: W. W. Norton.

A personal account of the author's research in four societies, and the different approach adopted in each.

Turnbull, Colin
1972   The Mountain People. New York: Simon and Schuster.

A fascinating, if somewhat grim, account of the Ik, a tribe in Kenya, East Africa, who were displaced and in the process of starving to death when the author made his study.

chapter fourteen

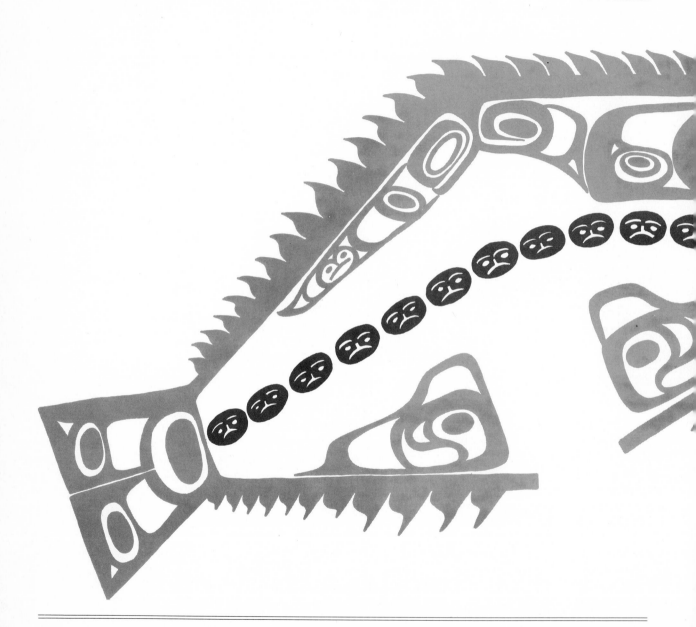

Social Organization

In its simplest sense, a *society* is an organized group of individuals who interact with one another and form a cohesive unit. This definition would include not only human groups, but baboons, bees, ants and any other nonhuman "social" animals. There is no implication of culture in the definition of society, for we can talk of baboon "social organization" without recognizing baboon culture. It is only when we speak of human societies that we refer to the concept of culture, for among people we find that the basic principle around which the group is organized is the way of life that its members share—their culture. The society forms a cohesive unit because its members share the same language, values, knowledge, and beliefs. In short, the society is unified by the similarity of its members in the way of life that they follow; they tend to think of themselves as members of the same group. A society can range from a complex civilization such as "American society" all the way down to a small unit such as an army company or a ship's crew. There need not be political boundaries setting it off from others; although we tend to think in terms of nation-states as viable, independent units, a society can exist below the national level or across national boundaries. We might speak of Jewish society

A market is much more than just a physical structure—it also includes a wide range of culturally patterned behavior.

or Chinese society as extending into many widely separate political units.

DEFINITION OF SOCIETY

The term *society* refers to an association of individuals. When we speak of social relations we are dealing with interaction among members of that group. Further, when we speak of social organization, we are referring to the patterns of that interaction. We assume that there is some sort of structure to the personal interaction within a society, and in analyzing that structure we tend to assign behavior to certain categories we have created. In doing this we divide the people of the society into various groups, many of which cross-cut each other, such as families, clans, states, classes, clubs, and so on. Further, we can analyze behavior in terms of its political, economic or religious components, although the people themselves might not make these distinctions in everyday life.

Society, then, is an artificial construct used by anthropologists to see patterns in other people's behavior. As we group these patterns together, the behavior takes on a structure with separate units that we refer to as *institutions*. An institution is simply a pattern of behavior which focuses upon a central theme. We may speak of a market as an economic institution, but there is more to a market than simply a building where people buy and sell. We also mean the activities involved in production, distribution, sales and consumption. We refer to the patterns of behavior involved in exchanging goods, and the values and preferences and other intangibles associated with that exchange. Thus a market as an economic institution is much more than a simple economic consideration of supply and demand, or a compilation of sales figures—it is a total realm of behavior involved with exchange.

The same is true for religion. When we speak of a religious institution, we are referring to much more than the church and what goes on inside it. We include in our scope of religious institutions all kinds of behavior that might be considered religious, such as the control that religious beliefs exert over individuals in their daily behavior, or the nature of community integration through shared belief systems. When we put all these patterns of behavior together from all of the different institutions we have analyzed, we can begin to see how they are tied together and how they affect one another. This provides us with the basic framework of the social structure.

SOCIAL SOLIDARITY

If a society is a group of people, then there must be something that holds them together, something that provides the group with continuity through time. In part it is a system of values shared by the members of the group which keeps them from splitting off into countless smaller groups. In other words, there is a certain degree of consensus about how people ought to behave, and as long as the members of a society share these beliefs and follow the basic rules, they remain together in a cohesive group. At the same time, it is clear that people cooperating and working together as a group can usually accomplish more than each individual working separately; it is to everyone's advantage to operate as a group, since society can provide more for each individual than he can obtain by himself. Another principle of social cohesion can best be termed "negative" solidarity, in the sense that people are held together by negative rather than positive forces. Although an individual might not think he is receiving positive benefits from the group, there may be no viable alternative—there may be nowhere else to go. The limitations upon moving from one group to another can be geographical, or they can simply be cultural. Language barriers, for example, can be a major stumbling block in moving from one society to another. In some cases people are forced to remain together because no one else wants them. Many minority groups in the United States are held together in part by the fact that there is nowhere else for the members to go in American society. Indians, Blacks, Mexican-Americans, and many other minorities are frequently unwelcome in middle-class American society, and thus they are forced to establish a solidarity group by negative pressures from the outside, in addition to the positive pressures drawing members to the group from within.

The question of social solidarity was the main focus of the French sociologist Emile Durkheim. In *The Division of Labor in Society,* Durkheim offers us an understanding of one of the fundamental differences between traditional societies that anthropologists have studied in non-Western settings, and our own modern industrial society. He points out that social sol-

idarity is directly linked to the division of labor in society, which is another way of referring to the degree of specialization or the extent to which the tasks that people perform are divided among different groups of specialists, rather than everyone doing basically the same work and repeating the efforts of others in the society.

Mechanical Solidarity

Durkheim proposes two contrasting models of society, each with a different kind of social solidarity. The first type he calls *mechanical solidarity,* in which there is very little division of labor—that is, in which everyone does basically the same tasks, and therefore they share the same experiences. It is highly likely that their sharing of culture will go further, then, to incorporate values and beliefs as well. If there is

These baboons are grooming each other, a social act which reinforces the hierarchy and cohesive structure of the group.

Bushmen dancing and singing around a campfire. Their wide range of shared behavior places the Bushmen relatively closer to the model of mechanical solidarity.

The New York Public Library

Emile Durkheim *(1858–1917) a noted French sociologist, is also an important figure in the history of anthropology.* The Division of Labor in Society *(1893), his first major book, was an attempt to solve the problem of alienation. He argued that in a complex civilization where specialization occurred, people must be bound together by their dependence upon one another—but they must not become so specialized that they lose sight of their affinity for each other. In a later book,* Suicide *(1897), he put this theory into practice once again, by explaining the higher rate of suicide in some societies as a result of alienation. In his last great work,* The Elementary Forms of the Religious Life *(1912), Durkheim identified many factors in the relation of religion to the rest of society.*

little variety in experience, there will be little variety in attitudes toward how things should be done, and this similarity will be reflected in other aspects of the social structure as well.

This kind of homogeneity exists not only in communities in foreign societies, but within small groups in our own. For example, if we examine a group such as a labor union we find a greater degree of solidarity than if we look at a typical middle-class neighborhood made up of many different kinds of people from different walks of life, with various occupations, religions, and levels of education. Within a trade union, the members are all at basically the same income level with the same occupation and to a certain extent the same kinds of experiences. And the same situation will hold not only for trade unions, but for any small group of relatively similar individuals—ethnic groups, religious associations, other professional associations, or whatever. As the group gets larger in size and more varied in its membership base, the tendency toward solidarity based upon uniformity will disappear, and the pressures exerted upon members to conform will have less effect, and will be less successful.

Organic Solidarity

Durkheim then turned to the opposite type of solidarity, which he found in what he called *organic society.* He used the term *organic* to refer to the fact that in such a society the situation is similar to the way the parts of an organism operate. The human body, for example, is composed of a number of different organs—heart, lungs, liver, kidneys, brain, etc. Each contributes something different to the operation of the whole organism. If the heart suddenly stopped pumping blood and started digesting food, the organism would not survive. It depends upon each organ performing its own special task, each contributing something different to the whole.

This is how Durkheim viewed organic society, as made up of many different parts, each with a different and specialized contribution to make to the overall operation of society. The farmer would produce food, the manufacturer would produce material goods, the middleman would specialize in the exchange of food and manufactured goods, and others would perform various specialized services. The more specialized people become, the greater the interdependence of the different parts of society.

Durkheim suggested that history has seen a progression from mechanical to organic society, and with it a change in the kind of solidarity that holds people together in societies. We can see how this is directly related to cultural anthropology, for it enables us to understand a

The specialization evident on this auto assembly line is typical of the model of organic solidarity.

basic difference between the nature of the groups that anthropologists have tended to study in the past, and our own society. We are a very specialized country, with a wide variety of people each doing their own thing.

When we examine social structure, we have to take into account that as the society becomes more complex—more like the organic model—the structure becomes more difficult to see clearly. If everyone is a hunter or a cultivator, we have no difficulty figuring out how they relate to each other. But it is not as evident how the various specialized groups are related in our own society. Thus anthropologists have tended to confine their studies to societies with simpler social structures, and when they have gone into complex societies they have zeroed in on a small segment which they can describe as if it were a homogeneous, isolated unit. Anthropologists are more inclined to write about an ethnic neighborhood in a city, than about the entire city itself; they write about specialized groups within American society, but not about the totality of American society. It is much easier to see what members of a trade union have in common than to try to figure out what the nature of social solidarity is among 210 million Americans. And it is much more productive to study small groups where our findings can be applied, than to study a group so large and diverse that even if we did come up with some results we could not use them in a practical manner.

Thus Durkheim's distinction between a society in which people are held together through similarity and one in which they are bound together by virtue of their interdependence can give us a starting point from which to overcome some of our ethnocentric bias in looking at other ways of life. We must realize that our values arise out of experiences that we share with only a small proportion of our fellow Americans, and even fewer of our fellow world citizens. If we are to rely upon other people for providing us with their specialized products and services, we must also recognize their differences and respect them. Our culture is simply too complex for us to be able to comprehend all aspects of it.

STRUCTURE AND FUNCTION

Durkheim's discussion of social solidarity and its relationship to the division of labor is important not only for its explanation of one of the fundamental differences between Western and non-Western societies, but also for its analysis of how the different elements of a society fit together. Anatomy and physiology detail the structure of the different parts of the human body and how each of them functions to contribute to the working of the overall organism. In the same way, the anthropologist seeks to understand the structure of society—how the different institutions fit together, and how each element in that structure functions to maintain the whole. It was Durkheim who contributed the concept of the functional integration of society by showing how the division of labor (a social institution) is related to the legal and moral codes (two other social institutions) and how each contributes something different to the social solidarity (the maintenance of the whole). The concepts of structure and function are intertwined. Society is an integrated unit made up of many different parts, each related to the others, each contributing something different, functioning in its own different way to keep the system intact. As an institution changes, the others will react to that change and will compensate for it, thus changing themselves in the process. All will remain integrated into a single unit.

We can see how this principle of functional integration operates on a number of different levels in our society. For example, on a rather general level we can discuss the relationship between religion, economics, and politics in American society—three different institutions. The political system is basically democratic, offering a relative degree of freedom to each individual to act as he wishes within certain limits. The economic system is one of free enterprise, so that each individual can engage in whatever economic activities he chooses (again within certain limits) in an attempt to maximize his own advantage. Individual achievement is fostered by the political freedom allowed. Finally, the religious ethic of American Protestantism emphasizes hard work and savings and achievement as positive virtues, so that a religious person is not driven to devote all of his time to worship, but instead is encouraged to work hard to support his family and his community. In the process, he is encouraged to take advantage of the economic and political freedom offered him. In this way the political ideology of democracy, coupled with the economic system of free enterprise, and supported by the religious ideology of the Protestant Ethic, all combine to form an integrated unit centered around a basic theme. We could also assume that if one of these basic institutions were to change, it would affect the others. If Americans all of a sudden adopted a religious outlook that stressed withdrawal and prayer to the exclusion of work, or if political freedom were withdrawn, the free enterprise system would no longer be effective, and would most likely be replaced by something else. But in the long run a new means of integrating the parts of the social structure would be found.

We can also look at functional analysis on a more microscopic level, in that we can search for direct links with certain aspects of the social structure and the immediate results that they produce. Government economists do this all the time when they talk about the relationship between the rate of inflation and unemployment, or the cost of living and the balance of trade. Criminologists make the same kinds of functional links between different elements of the social structure when they relate a major drug bust in Marseilles, France, to a rise in street crime in New York City: As the drug supply diminishes, the demand rises, hence the cost rises, hence the crime rate rises because people who need money to support a drug habit must now find a way to get more money.

It is important to point out that we cannot observe social structure any more than we can observe culture. Both are abstractions. What we observe is the behavior of human beings in a social context. As we do so, it becomes obvious that this behavior is predictable and that it is ordered into some sort of pattern. From this point we conclude that there is a structure which guides social relations, even though it is an abstract structure that we apply as observers, rather than as actors. This structure is just as real as the structure we apply to organisms, or to language; it is a generalization about the relationships of the parts. Just as all organisms are unique, all societies are unique, and we can only compare them by making generalizations about the similarities we perceive in their structures. Without concepts such as structure and function, we could not have a science dealing with human behavior, any more than we could have a science of anatomy or physiology.

Manifest and Latent Functions

Another aspect to the concept of function is a distinction made by sociologist Robert Merton between what he calls manifest and latent functions. Merton points out that an activity may have more than one function, and one or more of its functions may be unconscious or at least not obvious to those who practice it. The *manifest function* of a pattern of behavior is the effect or result that is apparent to the members of the society. It is the reason they will tell you why they are doing something, if you inquire. It is the agreed upon value of the action, the ideal as opposed to the real. The *latent function* of the activity is the effect or result that is not apparent to the members of society who engage in it.

Let us look at an example to illustrate this distinction. In American society, when a person dies we frequently follow a pattern of behavior collectively designated as a funeral. This can include a religious service, a meeting of family and friends either before or after the service, and the burial service in which the body is interred in a cemetery. If we were to inquire of Americans who engage in this practice what its functions were, we would probably receive some of the following answers, which we could designate functions of a funeral: (1) The fu-

How many functions of a funeral are evident in this picture?

neral serves to dispose of the body of the deceased, an obvious necessity in any case. (2) The gathering of friends and relatives at the funeral functions to console the family of the deceased, to support them and comfort them in their time of sorrow. (3) The religious service, in which prayers are offered for the deceased, is designed to aid the soul or spirit in its journey to whatever lies beyond in the afterlife. (4) In addition, a part of the funeral service can be designed to commemorate the achievements of the deceased, and thus serve as a memorial to that person, which in turn also comforts the family. All of these are fairly obvious functions of a funeral, functions which Merton would term manifest because they are known to the participants.

But what about some of the less obvious functions of the funeral, which might be apparent to the anthropologist looking at it from the outside but not to the participants? For one thing, the funeral service unwittingly becomes a vehicle for exhibiting wealth. The family may rationalize it in a different way, but their actions are quite clearly part of the pattern commonly called *conspicuous consumption*, which means that the things that we buy (consume) and then openly exhibit (conspicuously) are designed not just for our own enjoyment, but also for the impression they will make upon others who observe us. In the case of a funeral, we can see this pattern of exhibiting wealth in many ways. The size, shape, and material of the casket are important, not because we are concerned about whether the deceased will be comfortable in the grave, and certainly not because we are worried about how long it will last under the ground. Instead, the expense of the casket is important simply because for the few minutes when it will be observed by those who attend the funeral it is a way of indicating wealth and social position. Surely no one would claim that the deceased is more likely to be admitted to heaven in a metal casket than in a pine box!

Another latent function of a funeral is to provide a break in the routine for those who attend, although most people will certainly exclaim that they would rather have the deceased back among the living than use the funeral as an excuse to have a family reunion. In some societies the funeral actually becomes a party event, as in the case of the Irish wake, where liquor flows freely and people gather together into the night. In the process of bringing people together, a funeral serves the latent function of reinforcing the solidarity of the group. Members of the typical middle-class American family of today are frequently spread throughout the city, state, and even the country, making close contact difficult and family gatherings a relatively rare occurrence. However, the funeral offers the family a chance to get together, bringing close and distant relatives to the same place at the same time; weddings and other similar events also serve the same purpose.

A funeral can also serve the latent function of elevating another person into a higher social position. When someone dies, the position he or she held is vacated, and must be filled by someone else. In the family, if the father or breadwinner dies, then someone else—usually the eldest son or perhaps the brother of the deceased—must step into that role. The funeral ceremony and ritual can thus indicate this elevation of another individual into the vacant position through the tasks assigned in the actual ceremony. A son, for example, might be called upon to take an active role in the funeral, or he might at least be mentioned by the clergyman who performs the ceremony, a subtle instruction in his new duties. The same is true for each of the many different social positions that the deceased held during his or her lifetime, all of which have not been left vacant and must be filled anew.

Finally, there is the latent function in the funeral ceremony of alleviating the innate

The wide variety of tombstones here indicates that they not only serve to identify grave sites but also illustrate a type of conspicuous consumption.

human fear of death. Through the religious and social rituals, these fears can be minimized. Those who participate in the ceremony become aware of their concern for the deceased, and in the process they convince themselves that just as they have not forgotten the individual after his death, so too they will not be forgotten by their friends and relatives when they are gone. As they pray for the soul of the deceased, they help to alleviate their fears about the afterlife, for just as they hope to aid the spirit of the deceased and bring him closer to God and to heaven, so they expect that others will do the

A typically non-Western funeral in New Guinea. What obvious functions does it share with the funeral pictured on page 360?

same for them. In short, while people are openly acting out their concern for the deceased—the manifest function of the funeral—at the same time they are in an unconscious way acting out their concern for themselves, exchanging their time and effort now for the time and effort of others on their behalf in the future.

Of course, it might be difficult to get anyone to admit that they had any of these feelings in mind when they attended a funeral, and this is one reason why anthropologists stress the importance of studying the latent functions of social behavior as well as the manifest functions. It is only through a combination of analyzing what the people think they are doing, as well as what it appears to the objective and impartial observer that they are doing, that we obtain a full and clear picture of how the society works. The functions of various institutions cannot be limited to the conscious interpretations the people themselves attribute to them, for as we have seen in the example of a funeral, there are many more functions that are obvious to us as outside observers and social scientists. To ignore these functions would be to ignore a large portion of the structure of society. If our goal as cultural anthropologists is to understand human behavior, then we must investigate it from all points of view, and not limit ourselves to what the members of a particular group want us to see, or to the functions that they feel are important.

STATUS

The concept of social structure in general, or specifically the structure of any particular society, really refers to an abstraction of the typical behavior of members of the society. If every individual behaved differently and every situation were completely new and unexpected, there would be no way for us to know what people would do under certain circumstances, or to predict how they would act. Thus in order for us to arrive at this kind of abstraction, social behavior must be consistent. People must act in pretty much the same way in similar situations, even though technically no two sequences of events are exactly the same in all respects. As participants in society, therefore, we must be able to generalize about social interaction—that is, we must be able to say that even though a personal interaction we are now engaging in is unique, it is similar enough to an activity we experienced in the past that we can also expect others to recognize it as such and to act in a predictable manner. In other words, social interaction must be based upon two factors: *expectation* and *reciprocation*.

The fact that we can predict what others will do in a certain situation is essential to the structuring of social behavior. Without this element of expectation society would be disorderly and chaotic. Just imagine what it would be like if you never knew how anyone would act toward you. You feel perfectly confortable extending your hand to shake hands with someone you meet for the first time, only because you expect them to do the same. If each time you did it you received a different response, ranging from a handshake to a punch in the nose, you would soon grow wary of handshaking. But that

doesn't happen, because in our society, as throughout the world, there is a way of defining every situation so that the expected behavior is immediately clear. Behavior becomes structured and orderly because we send out signals which define situations and place them in categories that we and those we interact with can relate to.

The definition of the situation rests in part upon the assignment of *status* to individuals. The term comes from the Latin word for position, and in general it refers to the social position a person holds relative to a particular situation. A status can be either *ascribed* if a person is born into it, or *achieved* if it requires competition or special effort. "Sister," "male," and "King

Status plays an important role in international relations. Here Queen Elizabeth is greeted by Sultan Abdul Balin.

The Watergate hearings showed that certain political figures were not behaving according to their expected roles. The American public therefore assigned them a new, lower status.

of England" are all ascribed statuses, since you as an individual have nothing to say about occupying such a position. Achieved statuses would include "student," "bricklayer," and "husband." The majority of statuses in all societies are ascribed. Even in our own society, of all the positions we hold, most were determined for us at birth. Besides our age and sex, over which we have no control, we are also restricted by being born into a particular ethnic and social group that largely determines our place in society.

We can arrive at a structure for society by assigning statuses or social positions to all individuals as actors in a social setting. In the example above, when two individuals meet for the first time and are introduced, they immediately assign the position of "newcomer" to themselves and to the other person. The situation then takes on structure, just as if we could calculate it with a mathematical formula: (new-comer + newcomer) × introduction = handshake. This formula applies to all similar situations governed by the same rules, so that even though we have never seen the particular individual before, we are reasonably certain that he will reciprocate and shake our hand. If he does not, we immediately assign him a new status, something like "different kind of newcomer," and make a mental note of all that we know about him so that we can predict the behavior of others more accurately in the future. For example, in recent years the traditional handshake has been replaced among some members of American society (many blacks, most athletes, and many college students, among others) by a slightly different way of holding the hand, with the fingers extending over the other individual's wrist rather than into the palm of his hand.

We are constantly assigning statuses to those individuals with whom we come in contact in our daily lives. Often we have cues about what status to assign new individuals, and then as we get to know them better we change our evaluation of them, and thus their social position. When we meet a policeman in uniform, for example, we immediately know what that individual's social position is in the situation at hand, because the uniform gives us the cue we need. However, if we meet an off-duty policeman socially and he is not introduced as such, we probably will not be able to place him immediately as a policeman (although some people would disagree), and we would put him in a nebulous category of strangers who are as yet undefined.

A status can be defined as a *collection of rights and duties.* In terms of social interaction, if we are to have structure in our behavior it is essential that we are able to expect certain things of others (rights) and in return they must be able to expect certain things of us (duties). Obviously not every status entails the same collection of rights and duties. In the case of a policeman, the definition of appropriate behavior for all individuals engaged in interaction is quite clear. The policeman, by virtue of the authority invested in him by law, is entitled to strict obedience. In return, as private citizens we are entitled to—and the policeman is obliged to give us—fair and impartial enforcement of the law and protection from violations of the law by others. The fact that this ideal situation is not always achieved, and that there are varying interpretations of what is fair and how far the letter of the law extends, does not negate the fact that the status of policeman (and alternately of private citizen, criminal, etc.) does define a situation in which we can predict behavior with reasonable accuracy. Remember, status is a combination of the ideal situation and the real behavior of people who occupy statuses in social interaction. We are always reevaluating people in the light of their behavior and the behavior of others in similar positions, so that the structure we assign to society changes as the statuses of different groups of people change.

ROLE

If a status is a position with certain rights and duties, then we can refer to the behavior appropriate to that position as a *role.* A role refers to the *expected behavior in a particular situation.* Thus the position of professor means that it is my role to act as teacher and scholar. The traditional position of father entails the role of breadwinner, disciplinarian, decision maker, and general head of the household (although such roles are rapidly changing, indicating that the concept of social structure is not at all static). In this sense, role and status are inseparable. Just as statuses combine to form the social struc-

In recent years women have taken over jobs traditionally assigned to men. This situation has been accompanied by a change in the general status of women.

ture, roles combine to form the behavior patterns that we call institutions.

An indication of the dynamic nature of roles occurs when a large number of people do not follow the ideal pattern of behavior we assign to their status. For example, we all recognize the need for a certain amount of compromise in politics, a certain amount of force in law enforcement, or a certain amount of elitism in the world of entertainment. However, when it appears to us that the majority of people who hold a particular status are exceeding the limits we have in mind, then we either change the behavior of those individuals or else we simply redefine the role of these individuals so that we alter our evaluation of what is appropriate behavior for them. The Knapp Commission's investigations into corruption in New York's police force was an attempt to change the behavior of policemen and restore public confidence in their law enforcement agencies; likewise, the Watergate trials and the forced resignations, first of former Vice-President Agnew, then of former President Nixon, were attempts to change the role assigned by the public to politicians. It is interesting to follow these reevaluations in public opinion polls, where people are asked to rank a number of statuses according to their prestige. Because of the widespread corruption among public officials uncovered in recent years, the status of politicians has fallen lower and lower on this ranking scale, now resting somewhere near the bottom along with used car salesmen, well below many positions requiring far less education and responsibility. What this indicates is that although our ideals concerning the behavior of politicians are still the same, we are recognizing that in reality these ideals are less likely to be met. We therefore expect something different, which affects the prestige of those occupying the position of politician in our society.

The concepts of status and role are meaningful only in relation to other statuses and roles, and therefore they cannot exist in isolation. All individuals occupy a number of different statuses, each with its own appropriate role behavior, and usually these positions operate in harmony so that there are no basic contradictions. An individual might occupy the statuses of bank president, churchgoer, country club member, upper-class suburban dweller, husband, father, lodge member, and so on. All of these positions fit together, and we would not be surprised to find an individual who occupied them at the same time. On the other hand, we would be shocked to find a person occupying an unlikely combination of statuses such as bank president, race car driver, ex-convict, ghetto dweller, and suburban country club member. The behavior appropriate to some of these positions would conflict with that appropriate to others, and while it would not be impossible for one person to occupy all of these positions, it certainly would not be very likely.

If this sounds like some obscure, difficult theory concocted to make life confusing, it is not; it is exactly what you yourself do every day, only you do it unconsciously. Every time you interact with other people, you are following the model that you have constructed in your mind for how society is structured, and what your position in that structure is. The reason for pointing this out to you is that while it might not be necessary to know it in order to be a functioning member of American society, it is absolutely essential to understand how any other society works. Just as you learned to speak English long before you studied grammar and learned the formal structure of the language consciously, you have learned the rules of social behavior without being aware of their structure. If, as an anthropologist, you want to learn the rules for another society, it helps to know what their basis is, and how your own society works. Thus anthropology teaches us not only about other people, but most important of all, it teaches us about ourselves.

A typical board of directors meeting—no women!

Change in Status and Role

The concepts of status and role are fairly stable for society as a whole, although they are constantly changing for individuals within the society. The social structure is based upon a certain number of positions filled by various individuals. It is unimportant who fills what positions for the overall structure of the society. Thus although the new army recruit or draftee is likely to spend only a few years in the service, making for a rapid turnover of personnel, nevertheless the army maintains continuity over time. Likewise, although the makeup of Congress changes every two years after each election, with new members replacing old ones, still the present session of Congress is not too different from the last one, nor will the next be too different from the present.

On the other hand, for the individual member of society the concepts of status and role are dynamic, changing frequently and drastically. A person's statuses and roles change throughout his life. They change with his age, from child to adult to senior citizen; they change with his generation, from child to parent to grandparent; and they change as he learns new skills and achieves new social positions. In addition, one's status and role can change with relation to the social situation, in that an individual can retain the same level of skills and the same income, yet his status will change as all of his contemporaries pass him by, elevating their own positions relative to his.

Just as our statuses change, learning new roles is a continuing process throughout our lifetime. We learn our initial roles through the training we receive as children. We are taught what is appropriate in each situation, not based upon any absolute standard, but relative to our particular ascribed characteristics. Thus we are taught one thing if we are male, another if we are female; we learn different limitations based upon what our "appropriate" social position is perceived to be. Later in life we may reject the appropriateness of that position, and seek a different social position, in which case we will have to learn new patterns of behavior to go with our new status.

A role must be validated if we are to achieve a particular status. Once we have in mind what that status is, we set out to gain the appropriate responses from people, to convince them that we are in fact entitled to the status we seek. If we want to achieve the status of student, we dress accordingly, carry books under our arms, attend classes (sometimes), and go through the whole set of behaviors appropriate to students. On the other hand, if we want to achieve the status of "deviant," we simply act in a way that we think will convince people that we are different and that we do not follow the rules. The degree depends upon just how deviant we want to be considered. Curiously enough, even the path to deviance in our society is predictable. Have you ever noticed how the present generation of college students, who are shaking off the codes of behavior taught them by the previous generation, all look quite similar?

This movement from one status to another is called *social mobility*. We usually speak of mobility from a lower to a higher position, such as from the lower to the middle class, or from a working-class blue-collar job to a middle-class white-collar job. As we move from one status to another we again seek to have our new position validated by society. For example, we usually think of membership in the middle class as being mainly a function of income. Yet in recent years many members of the working class, particularly those who belong to strong unions, have experienced a rise in income that places them in the middle class if we stick to that criterion alone. However, if you were to place two individuals on a scale of social standing—one a school teacher earning $10,000 per year, the other a truck driver earning $15,000 per year—you would probably make a distinction between the two based on factors other than income. You might consider, for example, that the teacher has had five years of college, or that he wears a suit and tie to work, while the teamster probably has not attended college and might not have finished high school, and he does not wear dress clothes when working. In fact, the teamster himself most likely would recognize these differences, and would have aspirations for his children which included the college education that the teacher had.

In such a case, social mobility is obviously based upon more than just income. For the teamster to move into the middle class entails many elements of change. Some of these changes can be made simply based upon a rise in income, such as moving into a different neighborhood, buying a more expensive car, or wearing better clothes. Other changes can be made only with great difficulty, and frequently take another generation. Thus the teamster sends his children to better schools, not because education is important to him in making a living, but because in his quest to validate his role as a member of the middle class he finds that education is an important criterion. While he may not be able to return to school himself, he wants at the very least to insure that his children will have their middle-class membership validated. Likewise, the speech patterns that identify one as less educated—the frequent use of double negatives, or words such as "ain't"—cannot always be dropped in a single generation, but at least they can be eliminated in future generations. Again, this is not because the teamster needs to speak "textbook English" in order to communicate effectively in American society, but because he recognizes that his middle-class status will more likely be validated if he speaks in a particular way.

Role Conflict

Sometimes we occupy several different positions in our society, and the behavior appropriate to one is not in harmony with what is appropriate to another. This creates a situation called *role conflict,* when two roles clash with each other in a given situation. This is the kind of theme that makes for great soap operas, where the plot centers on a person torn between two duties, and no matter which one he or she chooses, someone will be hurt or some obligation will be violated. One of the basic problems with role conflict is that others hold conflicting expectations of you and your behavior, and no matter how you act in a given situation, you cannot meet the expectations of all. This problem is described quite well by the anthropologist Lloyd Fallers, who discusses the problems of the chief in Africa after the British colonized the area.[1]

The setting of this study is among the Basoga, a tribal group located in East Africa. Prior to the British colonization of Basoga society, the chief had a clearly defined set of obligations and duties in his interaction with members of his society. The Basoga chiefdom was not a secure position, and constant warfare and threat of revolt checked the ruler's power. Thus if the chief was to remain in office he had to balance the opposing factions in his society, and the lack of a stable leadership attested to the fact that such a balance was difficult to maintain for long periods of time.

When the British took over, they wanted to set up a stable system through which they could operate their colonial administration more efficiently. In order to do this, they made the position of chief more secure, giving him both economic and military support. The chief received a fixed salary from the native administration treasury, and he was granted civil service status complete with a pension. All of these developments strengthened the chief's ties to the British, but at the same time they weakened his ties to his own people. The salary he received lowered his prestige in the eyes of his fellow tribesmen, for it created a dependency upon someone else. The chiefdom became an achieved status based upon education, rather than as ascribed status based upon royal birth, and the entry of non-royal blood into the chiefdom somehow cheapened the office as far as the natives were concerned. Thus the men who held the position of chief were torn between two worlds, as their ties with the British strengthened and they moved farther away from the role of traditional Basoga leader.

Also, the obligations of the two roles of chief came into conflict. As a member of the British

civil service system, the chief had to take on a new set of values, which frequently conflicted with the old values he had held as a Basoga tribesman. As a Basoga, the chief owes loyalty to members of his own family or tribe, and must respond to the requests of his subjects according to how closely they are related, and how obligated he feels to them. However, as a civil servant he must remain impartial and not grant favors to anyone for any reason. The result is that at different times, and depending upon the individual and the situation, both systems of values function. If the chief maintains his impartiality he will alienate his friends and relatives, and go against his own values which he has learned throughout his life. On the other hand, if he gives in to his tribesmen's demands, he will not be faithfully exercising his authority as a civil servant, and stands a good chance of losing his job. One consequence of this role conflict is a high casualty rate among chiefs, and a rapid turnover. Either the chief is caught breaking civil service rules, or else he applies them strictly and is framed by his own family and friends, who resent the violation of traditional obligations.

SOCIAL STRATIFICATION

In addition to holding a particular status within many different social circles, we all have a more generalized position in our society based upon the sum total of all of our statuses. Every society ranks its members according to their overall position. In larger groups, such as the population of the United States, this ranking is relatively inexact, but in small groups where all people know and interact with each other as individuals, the entire population can be ranked, with each individual occupying a separate rung on the social ladder. This ranking of the members of a group according to status is called *social stratification*. It occurs on the basis of both

---

[1]Lloyd A. Fallers, "The Predicament of the Modern African Chief: An Instance from Uganda." *American Anthropologist* 57:2:290–297, 1955.

Controversy

Social Stratification: Conflict or Cohesion

Every known society exhibits some form of stratification. In simple societies, stratification may be based on such biological factors as sex or age. In more complex cultures, however, social stratification may be expressed more subtly in economic status, political power, or social prestige. Is social inequality inevitable? This question has been debated for many years between functionalists and conflict theorists.

Functionalists and conflict theorists represent two opposing theoretical perspectives on the nature of modern society. Functionalism, following Durkheim, views complex society as a system of mutually interdependent parts, each of which serves some necessary function. Accordingly, functionalists tend to stress the common needs and interests of the various segments of society. Conflict theorists, on the other hand, tend to view society as an ongoing struggle between groups with conflicting interests. From this point of view, a society is structured in such a way as to provide maximum benefits to the group which has managed to attain the most power. Obviously, how one views social stratification will depend upon one's overall theoretical perspective on society.

The functionalist theory of stratification was developed largely in response to the conflict theory of the followers of Karl Marx. Essentially, functionalists believe that social inequality is a device which societies have evolved to insure that the most important positions are filled by the most qualified people. A society is made up of many roles that must be continually filled. Not all positions are equally pleasant, equally important, or equally demanding in regard to training or ability. Functionalists argue that a society must offer incentives in order to attract qualified individuals to positions which might otherwise be too demanding or unrewarding. Wealth, power, and prestige are the inducements which are offered and which give rise to social stratification.

In our society, for example, a doctor holds a high-paying and highly prestigious position. The job of the doctor is not, on face value, a very attractive one. Many years of hard training are required, the hours are long and unpredictable, and the work itself can be physically taxing. In order to attract qualified individuals to fill this vital role, society offers the would-be doctor substantial rewards. On the other hand, positions which are considered less important and are easier to fill because they require less skill and commitment are rewarded with considerably less money, power, and prestige. According to the functionalists, a society must be stratified in order to operate efficiently. Why should anyone work hard for the public welfare in a truly egalitarian society?

Conflict theorists take a considerably different position on the inevitability of social stratification. According to this view, all jobs in society are of equal importance. Clerks and bookkeepers are no less important to the operation of a business than executive vice-presidents. If a job were not essential to the functioning of society, it would soon disappear. Conflict theorists believe that selfishness and inequality of ability are not inherent human traits but, rather, the result of cultural conditioning. Properly educated, people could learn to perform whatever tasks are required of them for the good of society. Moreover, they would gladly perform their duties without concern for personal wealth, power, or prestige. The classless society envisioned by the followers of Marx would function smoothly and efficiently without the oppression and exploitation which tend to characterize stratified societies.

Conflict theorists believe that societies tend to be run by force and not by consensus. People in power use their advantages to exploit others in order to further their own interests. As long as there is inequality, the ruling class will continue to do whatever it must to retain its superior position. It is for this reason that conflict theorists accuse functionalists of supporting oppression when the latter suggest that stratification is a socially functional phenomenon.

Today, most conflict theorists concede that the quest for absolute equality is a futile one. Marxist revolutions in Russia, China, and Cuba have demonstrated the seemingly inherent conflicts between social equality and human self-interest. Until a society of altruistic beings comes into existence, the question of whether stratification is inevitable will remain moot. Meanwhile the conflict theorists continue to advocate the minimization of class differences within the social hierarchy.

To some extent, social theorists are becoming less dogmatic in their arguments. It has become clear to many functionalists and conflict theorists alike that neither perspective is fully adequate in explaining the nature of social stratification. The functionalist can explain how to motivate an individual to seek a social position which he might otherwise be reluctant to pursue, while the conflict theorist can predict the tendency of an individual to seek greater rewards than those to which his position should entitle him. A synthesis of the two perspectives might suggest insights into the problem of social stratification which neither alone can provide.

All cultures assign tasks based on a division of labor by sex. (Above) A woman carries wheat. (Below) A man makes a pair of shoes.

ascribed and achieved statuses: people are ranked according to ascribed characteristics such as age, sex, and family affiliation, and according to achieved characteristics such as occupation, wealth, or special talents.

Every society makes a social distinction based upon sex, and almost universally women are accorded a lower status than men. Age is also used as a frequent basis for determining relative position on the social ladder, and when combined with sex it forms a concrete set of criteria by which people are ranked. In China, for example, two principles operate in deter-

mining on the most general level what a person's rank is: maleness is above femaleness, and age is a positive value. Thus the oldest man in the village is usually the highest ranking member of his lineage, even though he might not be recognized for specific skills or for his wisdom and experience. This is not to suggest that in traditional China only age and sex mattered—obviously people were respected for their accomplishments as well. However, in any social setting, age and sex were always taken into account.

The universal distinction between the sexes is usually backed up by a myth to substantiate the social order as somehow divine, correct, or in accord with the order of the universe. It is also a fact that women work as hard or harder than men in most societies, and there is invariably a division of labor by sex in which the women have little authority or control. Each culture has developed its own ideas about the nature of women, independently of one another, and often these ideas are quite different. For example, we traditionally have seen women as ministering angels, the "Florence Nightingale" image. This is certainly nothing like the traditional idea of woman's nature held by the Iroquois Indians, who, when they captured a prisoner in a battle with another tribe, would turn him over the women to torture, since women were considered much more sadistic than men. Only the exceptional opponent who had exhibited extraordinary bravery would be granted mercy and be killed by the men as a reward for his courage.

Because of the image we have of women, we ascribe certain occupations to them as "fitting." This is an important element in the social stratification that exists in our culture, and one against which the women's liberation movement has reacted so strongly. But notice that in reacting against the stratification itself, women have had to change the idealized image that men had about them, which has included, at least among some of the more militant advocates of woman's liberation, an actual change in women's behavior. Thus we have traditionally seen women as suited for various kinds of jobs that required "feminine skills," including things which did not require physical strength, ability to make decisions, or other intrusions upon accepted male roles. Ask any old-line executive how important his (female) secretary is to him, and he will tell you that he could not get along without her. But ask him why there are no woman executives in his corporation and he will tell you that women simply are not suited for such jobs. Women should be librarians, secretaries, and waitresses, but not construction workers, bank presidents, or professors, accord-

ing to the traditional American cultural values. Fortunately these views are changing, and with the change comes a realization of the fact that we, like everyone else in the world, are culture-bound and must work hard to shake off some of the preconceived notions we have about social stratification which have no basis in fact.

In other cultures, too, occupations are similarly ascribed to different sexes based upon the commonly accepted view of what is considered appropriate. Among the Arapesh of New Guinea, for example, women are expected to carry heavier loads than men because their heads, upon which they balance their baskets, are so much harder and stronger. In Tasmania, seal hunting is woman's work. They swim out to the seal rocks, stalk the animals and kill them. They also hunt possums, which requires them to climb large trees. Men would not think of performing these tasks, because it is agreed that they are "woman's work." In Madagascar, when the peasants cultivate rice, men make the seed beds and terraces for planting, and women do the back-breaking work of transplanting the rice. Such division of tasks is typical of most societies, and equally typical is the fact that there is no apparent logic to the way in which jobs are assigned which can explain the practice cross-culturally.

Also, the division of labor by sex can change over time. In the Swiss village studied by John Friedl, there were certain jobs traditionally considered appropriate for men because they required physical strength, while other tasks were reserved mainly for women. Agricultural duties were shared but were clearly divided. After World War II, however, men began to take jobs in factories which kept them from participating in the agricultural operation. At the same time, they wanted to keep their farms going so that they would have something to fall back on in case their new industrial jobs did not prove stable. As the men spent more of their time at work, the women began to take over the agricultural labor, including what were formerly defined as strictly male jobs, such as harvesting and carrying the hay to the barns. The men did help out after work and on weekends, but inevitably women had to bear the brunt of the agricultural labor if the farm operation were to be maintained. As it stands now, the cultural views about what is appropriate for each of the sexes have changed to meet the new economic situation—factory jobs are for men, and household tasks (including agriculture) are for women. Even this pattern is changing, however, as young girls are finding jobs in light industry on assembly lines, working side by side with men.

Stratification by sex is typical of almost all societies. There may be an exception, but we cannot think of one. Scenes such as women wearing veils in public indicate values associated with male superiority that are held almost universally. In a typical peasant society, for example, one rarely sees a woman in a bar or coffee house; these places are reserved for male gatherings. Women congregate in places associated with female tasks, or in the home, itself the domain of the woman much of the time. The point is that most, if not all, societies attach all sex-derived status distinctions to the fundamental biological difference between men and women. We should recognize, however, that just because this biological difference is invoked to justify sex discrimination does not mean that it is a valid basis. In fact, stratification by sex is a cultural practice based upon culturally determined values, not biological factors.

Stratification on the basis of age is another question. There is no denying the validity of at least some of the biological and cultural arguments about inequality in different age groups. There is no substitute for experience as far as certain skills or capabilities are concerned. This does not mean that there is a biological justification for extending all of the privileges of high status to the older members of the population. We would not want *all* 80-year-old Americans to be allowed to drive simply because of the supposed maturity and good judgment they possess, any more than we would want 12-year-olds to drive because their reflexes are quick. We compromise by requiring a minimal attainment of both maturity and quick reflexes, in that we consider both an age limit and the successful completion of a performance test as necessary prerequisites to obtaining a driver's license. Again, not all societies would treat stratification on the basis of age in the same way that we do, indicating that stratification based upon any criterion is primarily a cultural question, not a biological one.

Caste

One of the most extreme forms of social stratification is the organization of society into sharply differentiated groups known as *castes*. A caste can be defined as a group of people jointly assigned a position in the social hierarchy. Furthermore, a person is born into a caste and cannot change his affiliation throughout his life. Caste membership is based upon ascribed characteristics acquired at birth, such as the caste membership of one's parents, which is passed down from one generation to the next. It can also be based upon physical features such as skin color, again an ascribed characteristic that is inherited. The boundaries of a caste are maintained socially through the practice of *endogamy* (marriage within a group—derived from the Greek *endo* = within, and *gamy* = marriage), by which a person may only marry someone from his or her own caste. Thus, if there are genetic factors that identify an individual's caste membership, such as skin color, these tend to be maintained through the proscription against marrying outside the group.

The most commonly recognized caste system

Tasks in an Indian village are divided not only on the basis of age and sex, but also according to the caste of the worker.

is found in traditional India. Vestiges of the system still remain there, especially in rural areas, although it has been formally outlawed since India became independent from Great Britain. In this system, caste affiliation carries with it a total social ranking. Every aspect of an individual's life is limited by his caste. Because of the ascribed nature of caste membership, each local caste group is made up of related individuals, usually a series of families within the same village. In India, caste is linked with occupation, at least ideally. A person has a particular occupation based upon the caste into which he was born. A carpenter's son becomes a carpenter, just as a farmer's son becomes a farmer. Of course, in a small village there will not be a representative of every caste to fill every con-

ceivable occupation, and so where a position is not filled by a member of the appropriate caste someone else will take it up. This will not enable him to change his caste, however, and if he is a member of the carpenter caste he will remain so, even though his duties might now include weaving rather than carpentry.

In India the caste system operates according to the customs established by the Hindu religion. Each caste is ranked in a hierarchy according to the principles of Hindu tradition which place positive values on certain kinds of behavior, especially the avoidance of what are considered to be ritually polluting acts.

Thus, in traditional India a village consists of a number of castes, each with many members. Each caste fulfills a certain function; occupations are linked to castes and limited to their members. With each caste performing a special function all are able to survive, but they become dependent upon one another. The ranking system that places castes in a social hierarchy insures that this system will operate in a stable manner by forcing some individuals into occupations they might not otherwise choose for themselves. And the entire system is supported by the Hindu teachings, which emphasize the fact that different behavior is appropriate for each social level, and that to avoid doing what is prescribed for one's particular station in life is wrong.

The term *caste* is not limited to India, and can be applied to any similarly stratified group within a social hierarchy, in which membership is hereditary and permanent. For example, consider the racial situation in the southern United States. The relationship between the higher castes and the untouchables in India is similar to that between blacks and whites in the South, since they form separate social groups that are arranged in a hierarchy, maintained through endogamy or in-marriage, and membership in either group is both hereditary and permanent. Furthermore, in India caste also includes an occupational specialization to some degree, or at least the prohibition from engaging in certain occupations. The same situation applies in the South, where certain occupations are restricted to blacks and others are considered suitable only for whites.

In both India and the American South, there are rigid rules of avoidance between castes, and certain types of contact are considered contaminating. These taboos against inter-caste contact are symbolically rather than literally in-

The type of racial segregation once practiced in the American South was similar to the caste system in traditional India.

jurious, as evidenced by the inconsistency with which they are applied. For example, sexual contact is supposedly injurious, but in the traditional South the double standard applied, just as it did in India. Upper-caste men were permitted to have contact with lower-caste women (either high-caste Indians or white slave masters), while contact of the opposite sort (low-caste men with high-caste women, or black men with white women) was prohibited. In both cases, the high and low castes are economically interdependent, and the restrictions governing contact between them do not cut into the upper caste's need for lower-caste products and services. In other words, the distinction between the two social levels in the South, and between the higher castes and lower castes in India, was made strong enough to maintain clear social boundaries, but not so strong as to impose total isolation and thus negate the economic and social advantages to be gained by the higher castes from the exploitation of the lower. The high caste stood to gain not only in economic terms, through the exploitation of low-caste labor, but in social terms, such as the acquisition of prestige and a higher position in the social hierarchy.

In pointing out the parallels between India and some aspects of our own society, we can see one of the most positive values of cross-cultural studies in anthropology. Most Americans who have had little experience in the study of a foreign culture are limited in the perspectives they can have on their own way of life. For middle-class Americans who have grown up in suburban areas of the United States, the tendency is to look at all aspects of American culture as a variation upon the theme of middle-class culture with which they are familiar. It is by bringing in outside models such as the caste system of India—models which present us with a more clear-cut illustration of a social situation than we can find in our own society—that anthropology can contribute this added perspective. The study of other cultures enables us to look for similarities in our own society, rather than viewing everything as purely "American." Indeed, the parallels between caste in India and the racial situation in the South are striking, whether we accept them or not.

Class

Another form of social stratification is the division of society into groups that we call *classes*. A person is a member of a class based upon a number of factors such as wealth, education, and occupation. Unlike a caste system, a class system of stratification is a ranking of different kinds of people which is based upon their achieved as well as their ascribed characteristics. Class membership is a subjective evaluation. Almost everyone in the lower classes tends to place himself slightly higher, while those in the higher classes tend to look down upon those below them and rank them lower than they would rank themselves. Outsiders' evaluations are equally subjective, based as they are upon specified criteria which seem important to the outsider but might not be important to the people themselves. There is no absolute way of defining a person's class, because it is a combination of factors, any one of which can take on greater or lesser importance in light of the others. For example, the "upper crust" in American society might be considerably less wealthy than some of the *nouveau riche*, those business tycoons who have made a fortune in recent years, but who still lack the grace and sophistication of the older, more established wealthy families.

Classes tend to be endogamous, but the restrictions against marrying outside one's class are by no means rigid. We tend to seek out partners from the same class, not because there are overt rules that guide us in that direction, but because the factors of income, education,

The only hunting permitted in Ohio on Sundays is the typically upper-class activity of foxhunting. The law tends to reinforce the class system in many ways.

and general similarity in life style create similar tastes and preferences among members of the same class. In fact, in our own society there are many pressures, some of them not very subtle, that dictate whom we may choose as potential mates, and these pressures are mainly based upon a combination of class and caste characteristics—race and general social position. Of course, the system is not entirely rigid, as evidenced by the occasional rise of a young man or woman out of the lower class and into the limelight, whereby he or she eventually is able to move into a higher class and seek out its members as friends and associates, even as potential mates. But the fact that these kinds of stories are considered newsworthy illustrates that they are exceptional, and that they happen in spite of the obstacles they must overcome. We are far less surprised—indeed we are not surprised at all—when we read of Richard Nixon's daughter marrying Dwight Eisenhower's grandson, because it conforms to our expectations of class endogamy.

Although a caste system is a more rigid system of social stratification, it is no more completely closed than a class system is completely open. Although ideally in a caste system there is no mobility, the rules governing the interaction of members of different castes are frequently bent. At the same time, ideally in a class system mobility is freely possible from a lower to a higher class, but in reality class mobility frequently does not exist, and there are often unwritten rules that keep people from advancing out of a lower class ranking and into a higher one. The businessman who rose from the ghetto to become a millionaire can send his children to exclusive schools, drive a fancy car and live in an expensive house, but that will not get him an invitation to join the upper-class elite, who reject him because of his social background.

In contrast to a caste, a class is not joined together in an organized manner. People are not fully conscious of their class affiliation, and are therefore not held together by a mutual feeling of membership in a group. In a caste system, the members of a particular caste are united in a corporate group, with distinct boundaries and close personal ties. Considering the relationship between caste affiliation and occupation as it exists in India, it is difficult for a person *not* to be aware of his caste as he performs his daily tasks and adheres to the ritual behavior demanded of him in his station in life. Likewise, a black in America must constantly live with the fact that he is a different color, just as a sweeper in an Indian village is continually reminded of his untouchable status.

Another contrast between caste and class is the fact that a caste is based upon kinship, whereas a class is a collection of people who are similar in many ways, but are not assumed to be related biologically. Strict caste endogamy maintains the kinship basis for caste membership, while looser marriage restrictions in a class system and the possibility of mobility prevent classes from developing a kinship base. If in fact classes seem to be basically endogamous, it is for different reasons than those used to enforce and justify caste endogamy.

Finally, caste is often viewed as if it were acceptable to all in the system, in the sense that they accept the justification of the system through religious or other doctrines. However, both in India and the United States this is not the case, especially among the lower castes who must bear the brunt of the "dirty work" while receiving only a small share of the social and economic rewards. Neither lower-caste people nor lower-class people accept the justification for their being where they are. In a society such as our own, the social philosophy explains a person's being in the lower social levels through personal inadequacy. The argument goes that if there is unlimited mobility and anyone who has the ability and ambition can get ahead (the Great American Myth), the only explanation for those who are at the bottom is that they either don't have the talent or else they lack the ambition. As we have seen, however, the Great American Myth must be exposed as false. Unlimited mobility does not exist, and our open class system is superimposed upon a closed caste system that keeps people at the bottom of the social hierarchy by virtue of their ascribed characteristics despite their personal abilities. To suggest that all people accept the social or religious philosophy used to justify this situation, either in American society or in Indian society, is a naive attempt on the part of those in the higher social levels to avoid feeling guilty for their disproportionate share of society's economic wealth and social rewards.

What It Would Be Like If Women Win

Gloria Steinem

Gloria Steinem is the founder and editor of Ms. *magazine, and has been a leader in the women's liberation movement since its inception. In the following article, which first appeared in* Time *magazine, Ms. Steinem describes "What It Would Be Like If Women Win." Toward the end of her article Steinem states that "the most radical goal of the movement is egalitarianism." Egalitarianism has become a fashionable word; it simply means a society where people are not judged on the basis of color, age, sex, etc. Decide for yourself what its consequences would be.*

Any change is fearful, especially one affecting both politics and sex roles, so let me begin these utopian speculations with a fact. To break the ice.

Women don't want to exchange places with men. Male chauvinists, science-fiction writers and comedians may favor that idea for its shock value, but psychologists say it is a fantasy based on ruling-class ego and guilt. Men assume that women want to imitate them, which is just what white people assumed about blacks. An assumption so strong that it may convince the second-class group of the need to imitate, but for both women and blacks that stage has passed. Guilt produces the question: What if they

Reprinted from *Time,* August 31, 1970, with permission from the author.

could treat us as we have treated them?

That is not our goal. But we do want to change the economic system to one more based on merit. In Women's Lib Utopia, there will be free access to good jobs—and decent pay for the bad ones women have been performing all along, including housework. Increased skilled labor might lead to a four-hour workday, and higher wages would encourage further mechanization of repetitive jobs now kept alive by cheap labor.

With women as half the country's elected representatives, and a woman President once in a while, the country's *machismo* problems would be greatly reduced. The old-fashioned idea that manhood depends on violence and victory is, after all, an important part of our troubles in the streets, and in Viet Nam. I'm not saying that women leaders would eliminate violence. We are not more moral than men; we are only uncorrupted by power so far. When we do acquire power, we might turn out to have an equal impulse toward aggression. Even now, Margaret Mead believes that women fight less often but more fiercely than men, because women are not taught the rules of the war game and fight only when cornered. But for the next 50 years or so, women in politics will be very valuable by tempering the idea of manhood into something less aggressive and better suited to this crowded, post-atomic planet. . . .

Men will have to give up ruling-class privileges, but

in return they will no longer be the only ones to support the family, get drafted, bear the strain of power and responsibility. . . . In England, more men type and run switchboards. In India and Israel, a woman rules. In Sweden, both parents take care of the children. In this country, come Utopia, men and women won't reverse roles: they will be free to choose according to individual talents and preferences.

If role reform sounds sexually unsettling, think how it will change the sexual hypocrisy we have now. No more sex arranged on the barter system, with women pretending interest, and men never sure whether they are loved for themselves or for the security few women can get any other way. . . . No more men who are encouraged to spend a lifetime living with inferiors: with housekeepers, or dependent creatures who are still children. No more domineering wives, emasculating women, and "Jewish mothers," all of whom are simply human beings with all their normal ambition and drive confined to the home. No more unequal partnerships that eventually doom love and sex.

In order to produce that kind of confidence and individuality, child rearing will train according to talent. Little girls will no longer be surrounded by air-tight, self-fulfilling prophecies of natural passivity, lack of ambition and objectivity, inability to exercise power, and dexterity. . . .

Schools and universities will help to break traditional sex roles, even when parents will not. Half the teachers will be men, a rarity now at preschool and elementary levels: girls will not necessarily serve cookies or boys hoist up the flag. Athletic teams will be picked only by strength and skill. Sexually segregated courses like auto mechanics and home economics will be taken by boys and girls together. New courses in sexual politics will explore female subjugation as the model for political oppression, and women's history will be an academic staple, along with black history, at least until the white-male-oriented textbooks are integrated and rewritten.

As for the American child's classic problem—too much mother, too little father—that would be cured

by an equalization of parental responsibility. Free nurseries, school lunches, family cafeterias built into every housing complex, service companies that will do household cleaning chores in a regular, businesslike way, and more responsibility by the entire community for the children: all these will make it possible for both mother and father to work, and to have equal leisure time with the children at home.

The revolution would not take away the option of being a housewife. A woman who prefers to be her husband's housekeeper and/or hostess would receive a percentage of his pay determined by the domestic relations courts. If divorced, she might be eligible for a pension fund, and for a job-training allowance. Or a divorce could be treated the same way that the dissolution of a business partnership is now.

If these proposals seem farfetched, consider Sweden, where most of them are already in effect. Sweden is not yet a working Women's Lib model; most of the role-reform programs began less than a decade ago, and are just beginning to take hold. But that country is so far ahead of us in recognizing the problem that Swedish statements on sex and equality sound like bulletins from the moon.

Our marriage laws, for instance, are so reactionary that Women's Lib groups want couples to take a compulsory written exam on the law, as for a driver's license, before going through with the wedding. A man has alimony and wifely debts to worry about, but a woman may lose so many of her civil rights that in the U.S. now, in important legal ways, she becomes a child again. In some states, she cannot sign credit agreements, use her maiden name, incorporate a business, or establish a legal residence of her own. Being a wife, according to most social and legal definitions, is still a 19th century thing.

Assuming, however, that these blatantly sexist laws are abolished or reformed, that job discrimination is forbidden, that parents share financial responsibility for each other and the children, and that sexual relationships become partnerships of equal adults (some pretty big assumptions), then marriage will probably go right on. Men and women are, after all, physically complementary. . . .

What will exist is a variety of alternative life-styles. Since the population explosion dictates that childbearing be kept to a minimum, parents-and-children will be only one of many "families": couples, age groups, working groups, mixed communes, blood-related clans, class groups, creative groups. Single women will have the right to stay single without ridicule, without the attitudes now betrayed by "spinster" and "bachelor." Lesbians or homosexuals will no longer be denied legally binding marriages, complete with mutual-support agreements and inheritance rights. Paradoxically, the number of homosexuals may get smaller. With fewer overpossessive mothers and fewer fathers who hold up an impossibly cruel or perfectionist idea of manhood, boys will be less likely to be denied or reject their identity as males.

Changes that now seem small may get bigger:

Men's Lib. Men now suffer from more diseases due to stress, heart attacks, ulcers, a higher suicide rate, greater difficulty living alone, less adaptability to change and, in general, a shorter life span than women. There is some scientific evidence that what produces physical problems is not work itself, but the inability to choose which work, and how much. With women bearing half the financial responsibility, and with the idea of "masculine" jobs gone, men might well feel freer and live longer.

Religion. Protestant women are already becoming ordained ministers: radical nuns are carrying out liturgical functions that were once the exclusive property of priests: Jewish women are rewriting prayers—particularly those that Orthodox Jews recite every morning thanking God they are not female. In the future, the church will become an area of equal participation by women. This means, of course, that organized religion will have to give up one of its great historical weapons: sexual repression. . . .

Literary Problems. Revised sex roles will outdate more children's books than civil rights ever did. Only a few children had the problem of a *Little Black Sambo,* but most have the male-female stereotypes of "Dick and Jane." A boomlet of children's books about mothers who work has already begun, and liberated parents and editors are beginning to pressure for change in the textbook industry. Fiction writing will change more gradually, but romantic novels with wilting heroines and swashbuckling heroes will be reduced to historical value. Or perhaps to the sado-masochist trade. . . . As for the literary plots that turn on forced marriages or horrific abortions, they will seem as dated as Prohibition stories. Free legal abortions and free birth control will force writers to give up pregnancy as the *deus ex machina.*

Manners and Fashion. Dress will be more androgynous, with class symbols becoming more important than sexual ones. Pro- or anti-Establishment styles may already be more vital than who is wearing them. Hardhats are just as likely to rough up antiwar girls as antiwar men in the street, and police understand that women are just as likely to be pushers or bombers. Dances haven't required that one partner lead the other for years, anyway. Chivalry will transfer itself to those who need it, or deserve respect: old people, admired people, anyone with an armload of packages. . . .

For those with nostalgia for a simpler past, here is a word of comfort. Anthropologist Geoffrey Gorer studied the few peaceful human tribes and discovered one common characteristic: sex roles were not polarized. Differences of dress and occupation were at a minimum. Society, in other words, was not using sexual blackmail as a way of getting women to do cheap labor, or men to be aggressive.

Thus Women's Lib may achieve a more peaceful society on the way toward its other goals. That is why the Swedish government considers reform to bring about greater equality in the sex roles one of its most important concerns. As Prime Minister Olof Palme explained in a widely ignored speech delivered in Washington this spring: "It is *human beings* we shall emancipate. In Sweden today, if a politician should declare that the woman ought to have a different role from man's, he would be regarded as something from the Stone Age." In other words, the most radical goal of the movement is egalitarianism.

If Women's Lib wins, perhaps we all do.

Summary

A *society* is an organized group of people who interact with one another and share a common way of life or a culture. We think of the interaction between members of a society as being structured, and we can organize it into categories, or what we call *institutions*. For example, we may speak of economic institutions such as a marketplace, or legal institutions such as a courtroom.

People in a society are held together by virtue of the shared values and the way of life common to them. Emile Durkheim, the French sociologist, summarized two types of solidarity found in different societies. One he called *mechanical solidarity,* because everyone was pretty much like everyone else, there was little specialization and people shared the same values, thus behaving almost "mechanically." The other he called *organic solidarity,* because, like an organism, it was made up of different parts that performed different functions. Just as the human body is made up of different organs, such as the heart, lungs, liver and brain, so is an organic society made up of many different specialized groups, each of which makes a different contribution to the overall society. In mechanical societies, solidarity is based upon the similarity of the members, and the fact that people tend to agree upon things. In organic societies, it is derived from the dependence that people feel toward one another because of their differences.

Because behavior follows predictable patterns, we may speak of a *social structure,* or the relationship between these different patterns. For example, we may consider the relationship between religion and law in American society, noting the basis for our laws in our religious teachings. We may then speak of the *function* that an institution has in relation to this structure, such as the function of religion in providing the basis for our legal system. Not all functions of our behavior are evident to us. Those aspects that are obvious to us are called *manifest* functions, while those that are not so obvious are called *latent* functions.

We can get along with other people because we know what to expect from them in certain social situations, and likewise they can rely upon us to act in a predictable manner. In other words, social interaction is based upon *expectation* and *reciprocation.* Part of the way we decide how to behave is determined by the status we assign people in a given situation. A status can be *ascribed,* based on characteristics that a person is born with or has no control over, such as age or sex or race, or it can be *achieved,* based upon personal actions or abilities. For each status there is an appropriate pattern of behavior, which we call a *role.*

In the course of a lifetime an individual's social position may change, through the process known as *social mobility.* Movement from a lower to a higher social position may be associated with such changes as an increase in income or education, advance in age, development of new skills, or any other aspect of a person's life that causes others to reassess their evaluation of that person.

Every individual occupies a number of different statuses, each with its own appropriate form of behavior. Occasionally a situation arises where the different expectations are incompatible, a situation known as *role conflict.*

Every society ranks its members according to their overall position, or what we call *social stratification.* This can occur on the basis of both ascribed and achieved characteristics, including such factors as age, sex, occupation, wealth, or special abilities or talents. All societies recognize a social distinction based upon sex, the women usually being accorded a lower status. Age is also a universal factor in social stratification, although not always in the same way. The justification for using age and sex as the basis for stratification is usually culturally derived.

Some societies have a system of stratification known as *caste*. A caste is a group of people jointly assigned a position in the social hierarchy, and it is usually a permanent grouping which an individual cannot change. Caste membership is based upon ascribed characteristics: you inherit membership in a caste based upon the caste affiliation of one or both parents. Caste boundaries are maintained through restricted marriage patterns, or *endogamy*. The most apparent form of the caste system is found in India, and although it has been officially outlawed, some aspects of it still persist in many areas of that country.

In contrast to the caste system is a type of stratification known as *class*. A class is a more open grouping, less clearly defined than a caste. It is often based upon such factors as wealth, education and occupation. People can move in and out of a class, unlike a caste. Although marriage tends to occur within the limits of a class, there is no absolute rule that it must. Although a person's class affiliation is initially based upon that of his or her parents, it ultimately becomes more of an achieved position. Aspects of both caste and class can be found in American society.

Glossary

achieved status   A social position that a person holds by virtue of individual effort or competition.

ascribed status   A social position that a person holds by virtue of inherited characteristics, rather than through individual effort or competition.

caste   A group of people jointly assigned a position in the social hierarchy based upon inherited characteristics.

class   A group of people assigned a position in society based upon a combination of inherited characteristics and those traits earned through individual effort and competition.

conspicuous consumption   The buying of goods and services as a means of demonstrating one's wealth and social position.

division of labor   The degree of differentiation of tasks in society and their performance by different groups of specialists, rather than everyone doing the same work.

egalitarianism   The doctrine advocating social equality for all members of a society, regardless of social and biological position at birth.

endogamy   The practice that confines marriage to another member of an individual's group, or a proscription against marrying outside the group.

expectation and reciprocation   Two factors of social behavior referring to the predictability and consistency of social interaction, and making the structuring of social behavior possible.

institution   A pattern of behavior that focuses upon a central theme (e.g., economy: marketplace).

latent function   The effect or result of a pattern of behavior that is not apparent to the members of society who are engaging in it.

manifest function   The effect or result of a pattern of behavior that is apparent to the members of a society.

mechanical solidarity   Durkheim's description of the binding force which holds a small-scale society together on the basis of the members' shared, uniform experience, and their consensus on values, attitudes and beliefs.

negative solidarity   A force that holds people together because they are unable to leave the group due to geographical or language barriers, or cultural limitations upon mobility.

organic solidarity   Durkheim's description of the binding force that holds a group together on the basis of their dependence upon each other. This applies to societies with a maximum division of labor.

role   The appropriate and expected behavior attached to a social position in a particular situation.

role conflict   The condition of an individual occupying several different positions in society, in which the appropriate behaviors do not coincide.

2

2

social mobility   The process of moving from one position to another in society, and adopting the appropriate behaviors attached to the new social position.

social solidarity   The way a group is bound together through a shared system of values and the manner in which the group's members depend upon one another for each other's goods and services.

social stratification   The ranking of the members of a group according to the sum total of an individual's inherited characteristics and those traits earned through individual effort and competition.

social structure   The way groups are organized in a society, and the way the relationships between these groups are defined.

society   An organized group of individuals engaging in social interaction and forming a unit bound together by their shared way of life or culture.

status   The social position a person holds relative to a particular situation, and which is associated with a particular collection of rights and duties.

taboo   (also tabu) A ritual prohibition against a specific behavior or contact with an object or person, usually punishable by supernatural sanctions.

Additional Reading

Dollard, John
1957   Caste and Class in a Southern Town. Third Edition. Garden City, N.Y.: Doubleday & Company.

An analysis of social stratification in the American South, applying the concepts of caste and class.

Farber, Jerry
1959   The Student as Nigger. North Hollywood, Calif.: Contact Books.

An interesting look at the nature of student status in American culture, in the context of social stratification both within the university and in the wider society.

Lundberg, Ferdinand
1968   The Rich and the Super-Rich. New York: Bantam Books.

Biographical sketches and histories of some of the leading families in the United States, documenting their acquisition of great wealth and power.

Mandelbaum, David G.
1970   Society in India. Volume 1, Continuity and Change. Berkeley: University of California Press.

A thorough study of the nature of social organization in traditional India.

Montagu, Ashley
1968   The Natural Superiority of Women. Revised Edition. New York: Collier Books.

A noted anthropologist debunks the myth of male superiority by drawing upon cross-cultural examples to present contradictions to the misconceptions about women.

chapter fifteen

Marriage: the state of a community consisting of a master, a mistress and two slaves, making in all two.

AMBROSE BIERCE

KINSHIP, MARRIAGE, AND THE FAMILY

In the previous chapters we have surveyed the discipline of anthropology and some basic concepts used by cultural anthropologists in their work. We are now ready to begin looking at some of the specific elements of culture that anthropologists concentrate upon, so that we can see how the anthropologist is able to piece together the puzzle of life and better understand the incredible differences and surprising similarities found throughout the world.

KINSHIP SYSTEMS

We begin our discussion of the elements of social organization with kinship, for a number of very good reasons. *Kinship* is another word for the system of defining and organizing one's relatives. It provides the basis for social structure in all societies, and particularly in the traditional, non-Western societies that have been the focus of anthropological investigation for so long, kinship is the overriding principle upon which social relations rest. In our own modern industrial society this is less the case, for efficiency demands that a person fill a particular position not because of who he is, but based upon what he can do. But we should recognize that this is the exception rather than the rule, and that in most societies a person occupies a social position primarily as a result of his relationships to others in the group.

388 / CULTURAL ANTHROPOLOGY

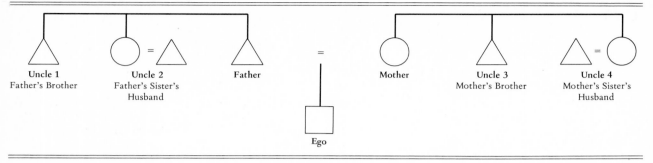

15-1

Every culture provides its own system of relationships for dealing with the human biological necessities of reproduction, training, and passage from one generation to another. There are two fundamental types of relationships, those between people who are related biologically or genetically, whom we call "blood relatives" in our language, and those who are related by marriage. Of course, anthropologists have adopted the appropriate jargon terms for these two types of relationships (it seems we never pass up an opportunity to create a new scientific term, and kinship offers many such opportunities). We call blood relatives *consanguineal* relations, while those who are related by marriage we call *affinal* relations. People who are related to us by blood can trace their relationship back to a common ancestor, whether or not they are the same number of generations removed from that ancestor. Thus according to the American system of calculating biological relationships, we would include anyone who was descended from a common ancestor on any generational level, such as brother or sister, aunt or uncle, cousin, etc. Relatives by marriage usually cannot trace a relationship through a common ancestor, but have "married into" the family—for example, husband or wife, "in-laws," or an aunt or uncle who married a "blood" uncle or aunt, respectively.

When we speak of kinship in any society, we generally refer to it as a *system*. This implies that the set of relationships recognized as significant among the members of the group are ordered and arranged systematically so that they are regular and predictable. To the degree that a particular society is kinship-oriented, this system of relations can serve as the basis for economic interaction such as the distribution of food and assignment of labor tasks, political interaction such as the distribution of power and authority over other individuals in the society, and many other aspects of life for members of the group. In addition, kinship can define the relationships between a group of people and the land they occupy, or the way in which land and other commodities are transferred from one member to another. It can determine who is to marry whom, as well as who may not marry whom. It provides the context within which new members of the society are trained in the culture they are to bear throughout their lives. In short, kinship organization can and does permeate every aspect of social behavior among some societies, and even in our own society which deemphasizes the importance of blood relations in most social contexts, our kinship system is crucial to our way of life.

KINSHIP TERMINOLOGY

By virtue of the fact that most people marry and most married couples have more than one child, we are related to a very large number of people, both living and dead. If, for example, your great-great-grandfather had two children, each of whom had two children, and so on down to your generation, you would have one brother or sister, two first cousins, four second cousins, and eight third cousins, all in your generation, not to mention the aunts and uncles, first and second cousins once removed, and so on. And remember, you have had eight great-great-grandfathers! As you can see, the number of relatives accumulates rapidly with each new generation.

In every culture there is a set of terms used to describe relatives. But it is important to note that not every society uses the same categories to group relatives, or makes the same distinctions between different kinds of relationships. What is significant in one culture, and is therefore noted in the distinction of categories of re-latives, could very well be completely insig-nificant in another culture, and therefore merged into a single category. Let us look at a specific example, In American culture we have a category described by the term "uncle." This group of people includes relatives of four kinds: (1) the brother of our father, (2) the hus-band of our father's sister, (3) the brother of our mother, and (4) the husband of our mother's sister. We can indicate this in Figure 15-1, which is a shorthand way of illustrating kinship relationships. In this diagram we use the following symbols: a triangle signifies a male, a circle a female, and a square an indi-vidual of either sex. In addition, an equal sign designates a marriage, a vertical line means de-scent, and a horizontal line indicates a brother-sister or sibling relationship. We use these sym-bols to designate the individuals as they are re-lated to one central reference point, which we call "Ego." All relationships are calculated from that one individual's point of view. It helps if you put yourself in Ego's place when looking at the diagram, and it does not matter in this case whether you are male or female.

In our culture the term "uncle" can have a variety of meanings, not all of them related to kinship.

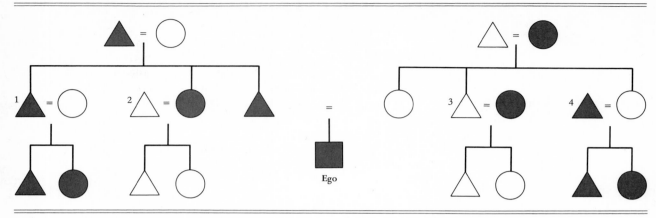

15-3

Now we may ask why it is that we put these four different types of relationship into the same category and call them by the same term. Does this happen in all cultures? The answer, of course, is that it does not, for as we shall see shortly, whereas for Americans the distinction between different kinds of uncles is relatively unimportant, for members of another culture this distinction can be crucial to the way the people organize their lives and their social interaction.

The reason that kinship terms vary from one culture to another (beyond the obvious differences in language) is that the system of organizing relations differs. The terms that people use are simply a handy device for putting that system into operation in everyday interaction with other people. A further reason for the variation in terms is that each category is based upon certain patterns of behavior expected from the individuals within that category. In other words, *kin terms are role terms,* that is, they designate not only a biological relationship but a *social relationship* as well. They vary from one culture to another because the behavior expected from individuals varies with each different culture.

Let us return to our example of the category "uncle" to see how this can be so. In American culture we generally expect the same treatment from all four kinds of uncles. For one thing, we do not make a legal distinction between our mother's brother and our father's brother. They are both expected to act toward us in the same way. While the husbands of our parents' sisters are not related by blood, they are married to people who are, and thus they are expected to adopt the behavior patterns of their spouses. This is not to say that every uncle will treat us exactly alike—obviously we all have favorites—but only that as our system operates, we would *expect* the same treatment from all.

In another society the situation might be quite different, however. Suppose, for example, that instead of tracing our line of descent through both parents equally, we tend to favor one over the other. This is not as farfetched as it might sound, for after all, in our society we do take our father's name and not our mother's in most cases. In some societies inheritance is even more one-sided than this, and when a child is born it inherits membership in a kinship group only through one side of the family—either the

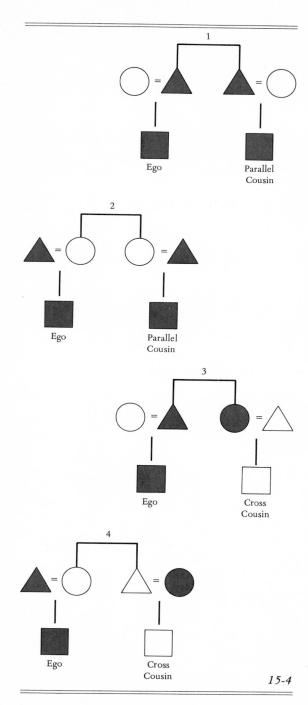

15-4

mother's side (called *matrilineal*) or the father's side (*patrilineal*). Let us assume, for the sake of simplicity, that there are two groups in a society, the Smiths and the Joneses. Furthermore, it is forbidden for a Smith to marry another Smith, and likewise for a Jones to marry another Jones. Finally, let us assume that the child inherits not only its surname, but also its kin group membership from its father. We can see why there might be a tendency to differentiate between types of uncles in such a society, for the distinction would become significant given the new set of rules for figuring relationships. This point is illustrated more clearly in Figure 15-3, where the dark figures designate Smiths, the light figures Joneses.

We can see what distinguishes between different kinds of uncles in this diagram. Uncle 1 is a Smith, the same as Ego; his children will be Smiths likewise. Uncle 2 is a Jones, a different kin group from Ego, and his children will also be members of a different kin group; thus he is significantly different from Uncle 1, both because of his own kin group affiliation and because his children belong to a pool of potential marriage partners for Ego, while the children of Uncle 1 do not. Uncle 3 is likewise a Jones, and in terms of kin group affiliation he is in the same category as Uncle 2. Note, however, that while 3 is a blood relative because he is the brother of Ego's mother, 2 is not a blood relative, but is related to Ego by marriage. Finally, Uncle 4 is a Smith, and in terms of kin group membership is of the same type as Uncle 1. Again, however, note that while Uncle 1 is a blood relative, Uncle 4 is not.

Now, how does this application of kinship terminology operate in real life? The Yanomamö, a tribe located along the Orinoco River in Venezuela, are a patrilineal society, that is, a child inherits its kin group membership from its father, and not from its mother. The different types of uncles are significant in that not all are related to Ego to the same degree, and this difference is reflected in the kinship terminology. Ego calls his father by the term *Hayä;* he uses the same term for his father's brother, who belongs to the same clan, having inherited his membership from Ego's father's father. But Ego calls his mother's brother by a different term, *Shoaiyä,* indicating that he is in some way different from Ego's father and father's brother.

According to the terminology used among the Yanomamö there is no difference between father and father's brother. This does not mean that people don't really recognize any difference—only that the kin term reflects an emphasis on group membership rather than biological parentage.

There is an important lesson to learn from this principle of ordering various people into categories. We tend to assume that because we organize relatives in a certain way in our own society, there is some fundamental principle of kinship organization that we follow, and that in cultures where our practices are not found the people are backward. However, this is clearly not the case. A kinship system can be ordered around any set of principles, and there is no right or wrong way to do it.

Whereas in our society it is generally not the custom to marry our cousin, in some societies this is not only allowed, but also it is the ideal. If we look back to Figure 15-1, once again, we can see why this is so. If Ego is a member of his father's kin group, but not his mother's, then he will have two types of cousins (in our sense of the term): those who belong to his own group and those who belong to another. Which cousins will belong to which group (in this example) can be determined by a simple rule: *parallel cousins* are members of the same group while *cross cousins* are not. By parallel cousins we mean those cousins who are related to Ego through relatives of the same (parallel) sex, namely mother and *mother's sister* or father and *father's brother.* Cross cousins, conversely, are

those who are related to Ego through relatives of the opposite sex: mother and *mother's brother,* or father and *father's sister.* This distinction is illustrated in Figure 15-4.

Now in our society with so many millions of people and so many different kinship groups, we have no trouble finding suitable marriage partners who are not related to us. But in many smaller societies, where the number of potential marriage partners is extremely limited, there can be complications involved in finding a husband or wife. Accordingly, a rule that designates that the ideal marriage partner is a cross-cousin insures that every individual will marry someone from a different kin group. Of course, such a system never works exactly, because nowhere does every married couple produce exactly two children, one of each sex, who grow up to marry and continue this process. But if the ideal is there in the minds of the people, then it instills in them a strong value associated with marrying outside the kin group.

THE BASIS OF KIN TERMS

In American culture we rely upon four criteria in assigning kinship terms to individuals. First, we sometimes make a distinction based on the *sex* of the individual, so that we call a male sibling a brother and a female sibling a sister. Note that this is not true in all cases, since we have only one term for cousin regardless of sex. But in many categories we do have this distinction (for instance, mother/father, aunt/uncle, nephew/niece).

Second, we make a distinction based upon *generation.* Thus we have a distinct term for members of different generations, such as daughter, mother, grandmother, etc. Technically this distinction also exists for cousins, although it is not as rigidly used in everyday conversation. We tend to lump cousins of different

The New York Public Library

Lewis Henry Morgan *(1818–1881) is perhaps the best known American anthropologist of the nineteenth century. Trained as a lawyer, Morgan developed an interest in anthropology through his experiences with the Iroquois Indians near his home in upstate New York. He began studying other Indian tribes, and in* Systems of Consanguinity and Affinity *(1871), he compared kinship systems and terminologies. As an outgrowth of his kinship studies, Morgan began to contemplate these differences in terms of an evolutionary sequence—he believed that the differences in kin terminologies could be explained by the fact that some societies represented an earlier stage of cultural evolution, and therefore their kinship systems were older.*

generations together, especially as they grow more distant, although theoretically we could make a distinction between "first cousin," "first cousin once removed," "second cousin," and so on.

Third, we make a distinction in kin terms based upon the differences between a relative who is related to us in a direct line of *descent* from a common ancestor, and one who is not. Thus we distinguish between our father and our father's brother, or uncle. Other such distinctions include mother and aunt, son and nephew, grandfather and great-uncle, etc. This distinction is one between *lineal* relatives (because they are on the direct line of descent) and *collateral* relatives (because they are lateral branches of Ego's family tree, not part of the main trunk or line).

Finally, we make a distinction in some cases between relatives who are related by blood (*consanguineal*) and those related by marriage (*affinal*). This distinction includes the different categories such as brother and brother-in-law, mother and mother-in-law, etc. But note that it is not valid for all categories in that we use the same term for consanguineal and affinal uncles or aunts.

Additional factors are sometimes used in other cultures in determining kinship terms applied to individuals, although they do not come into play in the American system. One such consideration can be the sex of the linking relative. Using such a means of distinguishing kinship relationships, called *bifurcation,* we would make a distinction between a relative related through a female and the same general type of relative related through a male. For example, we would have one term for mother's brother and another for father's brother, or we might have separate terms for brother's children and sister's children. We do not make these distinctions in our society (in the first case all are uncles, in the second either nephews or nieces), but in many non-Western societies they are important in determining kinship system categories.

Another potentially important factor which

A Zulu family in East Transvaal, South Africa.

we do not use in American society is the *sex of the speaker*. Many kinship terminologies have a different structure and a different set of categories depending upon whether the person speaking (Ego) is a male or a female. Such a distinction could reflect a fundamental principle of social inequality between the sexes. If a girl calls her uncle a different term from that used by a boy, it might indicate that the relationship between the uncle and the boy is expected to be completely different—with a different set of rights and obligations on the part of each— from the relationship between the uncle and

the girl. Thus, within its own cultural context this practice makes sense.

Another factor used in distinguishing between kinship terms is the *relative age of the speaker,* that is, relative to the person designated by the term. Thus, a boy might use one kin term to refer to his older brother, and a second term to refer to his younger brother. Again, while this would not make much sense in American culture, in a society where age was of crucial importance in determining social relationships, it would be meaningful to recognize the importance of relative age in the kin terms used.

At this point you might ask, why is it necessary to know about all of these different factors in assigning kinship terms to various people in different societies around the world? We have stressed throughout this book that one of the best ways to learn to understand your own culture is to look outside it. If we accept the fact that there is a structure to our way of life, the task of uncovering that structure is made much easier by knowing what we are looking for.

Also, it is valuable to know just how important kinship can be in ordering the lives of people in other cultures. In American society we tend to minimize the importance of kinship because so many of its primary functions have been taken over by other institutions—the work group, the church group, the schools, etc. But in many non-Western societies kinship still operates as the major ordering force in the lives of the people, and for them almost everything is seen in the context of their kinship system.

Finally, terms carry social meanings as well as biological meanings, and as such they designate particular patterns of behavior that are appropriate to a particular situation. Frequently a kin term can be used as a cue to what is expected of an individual. The anthropologist Paul Bohannan gives an example from his fieldwork among the Tiv in Africa. He reports that if an informant wanted to give him a gift, he would call him "my father," because one bestowed gifts upon people whom one respected and honored. But if the informant wanted to correct Bohannan's grammar or etiquette, he called him "my child," since it was expected that children would not know all the rules of proper social conduct, and were still in the process of learning the language. Thus, even though Bohannan was clearly an adult, his role in the Tiv society sometimes coincided with that of a child. Other terms of address were also used that functioned not only to inform Bohannan of the expectations of the speaker, but in more general terms to define the situation for all involved.

AMERICAN KINSHIP TERMINOLOGY

We have already mentioned some aspects of the American system of kinship and the terms for relatives in the standard usage of the English language. But it remains to look at it in more detail, and to demonstrate that American kinship is in fact a system, and that it is only one of many possibilities found in the world today.

In the American kinship system we trace our relationships equally through both sides of the family, rather than leaning heavily or entirely upon the mother's side or the father's side. This means that we tend to treat people related through our mother and through our father in the same manner, and we use the same kinship terms to designate relatives no matter which side of the family they are on. The formal system of terms used by Americans is similar to the general type known to anthropologists as the "Eskimo" kinship terminology.

But American kinship is more than a set of formal terms, for there are a variety of informal words used to address or refer to individuals in a variety of situations. For example, although we have the formal term "mother," we may use any one of a number of alternate terms, such as "mom," "mommy," "ma," or we may use a first name, a nickname, a diminutive, or some other descriptive or joking term such as "old woman" or "old lady." The same holds true for the term "father," which can be replaced by a less authoritarian term such as "pop" or "daddy," or by "old man." These latter terms tend to be used in reference rather than in address—that is, we might refer to our father as "old man" when talking about him to someone else out of his earshot, but we would be less likely to use that term to address him personally. This points to a distinction between different kinds of terms used depending upon whether that individual is being addressed, referred to in his or her presence, or referred to in his or her absence. Then we might use the term "mother" when referring to her in a discussion with our father, the term "ma" or "mom" when speaking to her personally, the term "my mother" when speaking to a member of our peer group about her when she is not there. These forms of reference and address vary considerably with the situation.

From this variation in the use of terms to designate an individual, we can see that each term has two basic functions: to organize relatives into categories or classify them, and to define or describe a role. Thus when we use the term "uncle" in standard American kinship terminology we are both categorizing an individual in terms of his relationship to us and at the same time we are defining a general set of behavior that it is understood that individual follows in interacting with us. It is important to note that these alternate terms are therefore not synonyms, that is, they do not have exactly the same meaning. It does not mean the same thing to say "father" and "daddy." One has a ring of formality and authority, while the other implies a closer and more informal relationship.

This use of kin terms to designate behavior rather than actual biological relationships points out another aspect of the flexibility of kinship systems, as well as their importance in the overall structure of society. In many situations in social interaction, we behave toward others in a way that corresponds to kinship behavior, even though we are not related. Sometimes people formalize that behavior through the creation of artificial, or *fictive,* kinship ties. For example, the anthropologist Elliot Liebow, in his book *Tally's Corner* about a black ghetto in Washington, D.C., describes a relationship called "going for cousins." This is a way for two people of the opposite sex to establish a close personal relationship with no sexual overtones. By invoking the cousin relationship, which in American culture implies a taboo against sex, the two people can avoid suspicion by the rest of the community. The important aspect of this action from the anthropologist's point of view is that it is done within the context of kinship, indicating how crucial it is to the overall pattern of social relationships.

DESCENT

Having discussed the various relationships between individuals in a society and the meaning of those relationships, it remains to be seen how the members of a society determine who their relatives are. In every culture there are rules that establish how one defines one's kin, and who is to be included or excluded. The categories of relatives are arbitrarily limited according to these rules. One feature of the kinship system that serves to define the various categories of kinsmen is what we call *descent,* which represents the way in which two blood relatives trace their relationship to a common ancestor. This is not a biological consideration but a social one, for if the culture does not recognize the biological link between two individuals as significant, then according to the rules of that culture they are not related. It is not a question of how many physical characteristics they share as a result of having a common genetic heritage. It is simply a social fact.

Descent relationships can be reckoned through one line (either male or female) or through both. If descent is figured only through the mother's line, it is *matrilineal;* if only through the father's line, it is *patrilineal;* if through both, it is *bilateral.* As we noted earlier in this chapter, by excluding people related through one parent we divide our biologically related relatives into two groups, only one of which is recognized as part of our kin group. Frequently people related to a common ancestor will have a name, and will be considered as a corporate group with certain common rights and privileges. Perhaps the group will hold land in common for its members, or it might also be associated with a common religious shrine, or the possession of a common fund of knowledge such as a family ritual or myth. A *clan* is such a descent group, as is a *lineage,* the major difference being that a lineage consists of members who can trace their relationship to an actual common ancestor, while the members of a clan assume that they are related but cannot actually trace their links back far enough to reach that common ancestor.

In many cases there is a logical explanation among the people themselves, as well as for the anthropologist, for the particular type of descent. For example, the prevailing theory of conception might have something to do with whether descent is traced through the male or the female line, or both. Of course, in American culture we recognize the role of each parent in the process of conception, and biologically speaking we consider a child to be equally close to both parents. Thus it seems logical to us that descent in American culture is traced equally through both the male and female lines.

Among the Ashanti in West Africa, people believe that the blood of the child is contributed only by the mother, while the spiritual makeup of the child comes from the father. Since the Ashanti distinguish between two aspects of the self—the physical being and the spiritual being—the descent of each part of the individual is traced according to different principles. Biological descent among the Ashanti is therefore matrilineal, since it is the mother who contributes the physical essence to the infant, while spiritual descent is patrilineal, and the child becomes a member of his father's spiritual kin group.

Most societies in the world reckon descent through the male line, a fact that proves the importance of social considerations over biological factors. For even though it is obvious that

For these Sepik River tribesmen of New Guinea, some festivities are occasions for the whole family.

the child is a part of its mother in a biological sense, in male-dominated societies (which include the vast majority) it is the male prerogative that wins out. Where men own property and hold power, they seek to retain that property and power as an exclusive right unto themselves. They can do this only if they are able to exclude women from positions of power, and it is through the descent system that they make sure that male children will carry on the tradition and female children will follow in the footsteps of their mothers.

Besides the prevailing theory of conception or the predominance of the male prerogative, there might be obvious economic reasons for one kind of descent existing in a particular society. Residence patterns are sometimes tied in with descent. In a matrilineal society the husband often comes to live in his wife's home village, thus reinforcing the pattern of descent, and conversely for a patrilineal society. If property is owned and distributed by men then patriliny is likely, whereas if it is owned and distributed by women (as is the case in some societies) then matriliny is more likely to be found. On the other hand, if a male skill such as hunting is based upon close knowledge of the area and experience in hunting it, then patrilineal descent is probable, because in that way men would retain rights over the hunting territory and be more likely to keep their place of residence over generations. This in effect maximizes the benefits of the experience of elders, who can pass along their specialized knowledge of the region and their skills in hunting the local game in the most efficient manner.

MARRIAGE AND FAMILY

If kinship is the basis for social organization in all societies in the world, then marriage is the basis for kinship. Of course, strictly speaking marriage is not an absolute necessity for human society. People could reproduce and train new members of society without the institution of marriage and without organizing society into family units to carry out these functions. Yet in no society in the world is this completely the case; marriage and the family are cultural universals, found in some form everywhere. Marriage functions to control sexual activity within the society, following the rules upon which members of the group are organized. The family functions as a primary group in the socialization of the young, and it also defines the channels by which membership in a kinship group is transferred (descent) and by which material and nonmaterial possessions are passed down through the generations (inheritance).

Actually, marriage has several possible func-

This Bolivian bride and groom are just leaving the church in which they were married. Every human culture has some version of marriage as the basis of family structure.

tions it can perform in different societies. Where society is concerned over the legitimacy of its new members, marriage establishes a set of legal parents. Where society is concerned about the restriction of sexual activity among its members, marriage provides guidelines for such activity. In some societies, marriage can be used to establish control over an individual's labor power, usually in the case of a woman who comes to live with her husband and his family. In many societies marriage carries with it a transfer of property, thus giving over the rights to that property—land, money, material goods, or whatever—to the family of one of the spouses.

An important element in any marriage, and one that should not be overlooked even in our own society, is the relationship that is established between two groups. A marriage is not simply an agreement between two people that they are in love and want to live together (although in modern society this is becoming more common); rather, a marriage in most societies is a contract that binds two families or even larger groups together socially, and sometimes economically. Among the nobility in traditional Europe, marriages were often arranged by heads of state in a way that would tie two countries together. The marriage of Phillip II

The status of the King of the Yoruba tribe in West Nigeria is enhanced by his 156 wives, several of whom are shown here.

of Spain and Mary Tudor, daughter of King Henry VIII and Catherine of Aragon, was a way of solidifying the relationship between Spain and England, forming a social, economic, and military bond between the two countries. Often inbreeding among the nobility was designed to prevent the division of royal estates as well, since by keeping the wealth within a small group there was less danger of spreading the royal fortunes and power too thinly.

Likewise in non-Western societies, marriage can be more of an economic contract than a bond between two individuals. Among the Tiwi in northern Australia, a man acquires a wife by promising his first-born daughter to his future father-in-law, or to the latter's close relatives. The more wives he can obtain, the more daughters he can promise, and thus the stronger his ties with other groups in his society. As he grows older, he begins to reap the rewards of his shrewd economic transactions, by acquiring more younger wives who will produce more daughters he can trade off for promises of future wives—a kind of male-oriented primitive social security system.

This list of possible functions of marriage in different societies may be extended, and merely serves to indicate some of the basic ways in which marriage can be viewed: sexual access, parentage, labor, property and alliance.

THE FAMILY: VARIATIONS ON A THEME

Every society recognizes the family as an important unit, but each places a different emphasis upon which members are most important and how that family unit should be structured. Thus the makeup of the family differs from one culture to another. In the United States, as in most industrial countries in the world, the family has grown smaller in response to the challenges of the industrial economy. Mobility,

An extended Minnesota farm family, effective in a rural setting but cumbersome in the city.

both social and geographical, has trimmed the family down to a small unit that can move about easily and does not present an economic burden to the breadwinner. Whereas on the farm a number of extra hands might be helpful, in the city the presence of uncles and aunts, grandparents and cousins, all under one roof, is most inefficient. As a result, the typical family in our culture has become what we call the *nuclear* family, formed around the nucleus of parents and children with few, if any, others.

In contrast to the American family composed typically of one married couple and their offspring, many societies recognize the family as a residential unit which includes a wider circle of relatives. When more than two generations are represented, and particularly when collateral as well as lineal relatives reside in the household (e.g., aunts and uncles, or cousins), we speak of an *extended* family. This family type is more fre-

quently found in agricultural peasant or tribal societies, and tends to disappear as the country becomes more urbanized. A variant of the extended family is what is called the *joint* family (or joint extended family), which consists of a married couple, their unmarried sons and daughters, and the nuclear families of their married sons.

Usually we think of the family not only in terms of biological and marital relationships, but also as an economic unit, a unit for socializing the young, and in general related to a number of different functions simultaneously. However, this is not always the case, and in some societies the biological family is not the equivalent of the social unit—that is, the satisfaction of sexual needs is separated from other functions of the family. Such was the case among the Nayar, a people of southern India, where the institution of marriage existed in a

very different form from what we would consider normal. Around the time of puberty, each Nayar girl was ritually married according to the proper religious ceremony to a boy selected from a lineage linked to that of the girl by ties of mutual exchange. Following the ceremony the couple were secluded for a few days whereupon sexual activity might take place, but was not necessary. The couple then separated, with the boy returning to his home village and the girl to hers. Once they were separated, the girl had no further obligations to her husband until he died, when she and her children (by whatever man) had to observe a death ritual on his behalf.

After the ritual marriage and separation each party went his or her own way. The woman was free to engage in affairs with whomever she chose (provided the man was of the proper social position in Nayar society), and the man was

Every culture has its own set of prescribed behaviors connected with marriage. This Zulu bride must keep her face covered for two days before the wedding ceremony.

likewise unhindered from entering into such relationships. Satisfaction of sexual desires and reproduction were thus fulfilled through a series of informal love affairs that established no permanent bond between a woman and her lover. A woman could have as many lovers as she wished at any one time, or she could restrict her attention to one man. They could be fleeting affairs, or they could be long-term relationships. The lover would visit after supper and leave early the next morning, leaving his weapons outside her door as a sign to others. Anyone who arrived and found another's weapons there was free to sleep on the woman's porch.

The children of such unions called their mother's lovers by the term meaning "lord" or "leader," and such a term did not carry with it the implication of either biological or legal paternity. Even when paternity could definitely be established, the man had no obligations to his children other than paying for the expense of their birth. The children became the sole responsibility of the mother's kinship unit, or her *matrilineage*. This female-centered kinship unit included men, such as the brothers of the woman or her mother's brothers, and these men were obliged to contribute to the care and raising of the children born into the group, just as they were relieved of their obligations toward their own "biological" children born into another woman's matrilineage.

The explanation for this type of marriage—surely one of the most curious forms of that institution found anywhere in the world—lies in the general pattern of social organization among the Nayar. Traditional Indian society was divided into a number of distinct social groups, called *castes*. Each caste was ritually linked with a specific occupation, and along with it went a whole set of rules and a way of life appropriate only to that caste. The Nayars were traditionally a warrior caste, and it is thought that the lack of paternal responsibility and household obligations was functional in that it left the men free to follow their occupation. Of course the men were responsible for the children in their own matrilineage, but the matrilineage as a whole took care of the children and could take over the obligations in the man's absence. At the same time, the pattern of courtship and sexual activity seemed to fit in with the life style of the warrior caste, enabling men who were away from home (and women whose husbands might be away much of the time) to engage in a normal sex life with the approval of their society. As the need for warriors diminished and the caste system was finally abolished, this pattern also disappeared.

It has also been suggested that the Nayar marriage pattern had a function in maintaining the unity of the matrilineage. If a man became permanently devoted to one wife, his ties to his sisters and their children would diminish. By separating the marriage ritual from the actual performance of the biological functions of sexual activity and reproduction, the biological father is legally removed from playing an important role in his children's matrilineage.

Thus, while procreation is necessary for the continuance of the matrilineage, husbands are not. The Nayar marriage institution is one way of seeing that this distinction is maintained.

Nayar society shows the extreme range of variability of the family and marriage as social institutions, and as such it is of interest to the anthropologist. The Nayars represent a woman-centered family in a male-centered society, for while the matrilineage is the basic feature of social organization, the male-dominated warrior caste is the central focus of the group. Another variant on the family is the case of a woman-centered family in a woman-centered society. Bronislaw Malinowski's work in the Trobriand Islands in the Western Pacific describes this type of society.

In the Trobriands, descent is reckoned only through the mother's line. This fits in with the prevailing theory of conception and procreation found in the Trobriand Islands. It is thought that the mother alone contributes to the makeup of the child, and the father is only a passive agent. Therefore, the child is closer to all members of its mother's kinship group, or matriline, and is not considered to be of the same group as its father, who belongs to another matriline. This pattern results in a different set of statuses and rules, with correspondingly different kinds of behavior between members of the family. For example, the term for "father" means, literally, "husband of my mother." The father is considered an outsider with regard to family affairs, and where male activity within the family is concerned, it is the mother's brother who bears the responsibility.

Nevertheless, the father is a close companion to his children, and the relationship between them is one of great warmth. However, the authoritarian role of father as head of the household and disciplinarian, which is so common in Western society, is not filled by the father in Trobriand society. Instead, it is the mother's brother who becomes the authority figure, due

to his membership in the family group. He grants his sister's son permission to do things which would normally come from the father in other societies. A boy inherits property from his mother's brother, not from his father.

THE INCEST TABOO

Malinowski's description of the structure of the family in the Trobriands raises another interesting question regarding the institution known as the *incest taboo.* In every society there are rules which prohibit incest, i.e., sexual relations between certain relatives. The same rules are not found everywhere—what is important is that some rules exist in all societies. A number of theories have been proposed to explain why this should be the case, but as yet anthropologists have not arrived at a conclusive answer to this problem.

The reason for Malinowski's interest in the question of the incest taboo can be traced back to the work of Sigmund Freud, the noted founder of psychoanalysis. In *Totem and Taboo,* Freud suggested that the incest taboo originated when early man, in a fit of jealousy and rage over being denied access to the women of his group by a domineering father, banded together with his brothers and killed the father, ate him in cannibalistic style, and then engaged in sexual relations with his mother and sisters. But guilt caught up with him, and once he realized how horrible his crime had been, he renounced his sexual rights to the women of his family, thus creating the incest taboo. Freud argued that this was the first truly cultural act of mankind, for it represented an increased level of conscience and the thoughtful structuring of social (in this case sexual) relations as a result of that conscience.

Malinowski reacted strongly against Freud's discussion of the incest taboo, based upon his field experience in the Trobriands. Freud had

Controversy

Incest: Why Not?

Anthropologists have long been fascinated by the universal taboo against incest. A wide variety of theories have been proposed to explain the origins of the taboo, but none has yet achieved universal acceptance. In recent years, a number of interesting alternatives to the traditional theories have been raised.

Two of the oldest theories explaining the incest taboo have been concerned with the destructive effects of sexual competition among family members and the dangers of genetic inbreeding. The inbreeding theory has been repeatedly criticized on the grounds that, first, inbreeding is not necessarily harmful and, second, primitive people could not have had a sufficient understanding of genetic biology to fashion their culture accordingly. The sexual competition theory has been criticized as being ethnocentric; other societies are not as possessive about sexual access as are Americans. One study, however, suggests that these two elements may provide the answer to the puzzle of the incest taboo.

Current tic evidence indicates that inbreeding among humans is, indeed, highly undesirable. Inbreeding between parents and offspring or between siblings greatly increases the percentage of individuals with recessive traits, traits requiring a matched pair of genes to develop in the individual. Recessive traits can be harmful or advantageous to the organism. Because mutation is a random process, however, the ratio of harmful to advantageous recessive genes is very high. Inbreeding can produce a superior strain in a species by eliminating all disadvantageous recessives; but, genetic experimentation with animals has demonstrated that close inbreeding becomes increasingly undesirable as the age of reproductive maturity becomes greater and the number of offspring fewer. Humans reach puberty at a late age and our offspring are widely spaced and few in number. Close inbreeding would soon decrease the breeding population to a point at which survival would be seriously threatened.

Obviously, primitive cultures were unaware of the biological dangers of inbreeding. Some groups, however, may have institutionalized incest and exogamy in order to prevent sexual competition within the family. Those groups which adopted a taboo against incest would then benefit from the advantages of preventing inbreeding. Groups which continued to inbreed would be gradually eliminated through the process of natural selection. Later, exogamy may have proved to offer the additional adaptive value of broadening the base of cultural cooperation between families.

Other theorists have proposed that exogamy in early humans was the result of biological necessity. According to this theory, the short life span and reproductive cycle of primitive people made inbreeding between parents and their offspring pracitcally impossible and between siblings highly improbable. Early humans are believed to have begun child-bearing at a relatively late point in their lives and to have died at an early age. An extended weaning period, common among hunters and gatherers and known to interfere with fertility, further decreased the length of early humans' already brief breeding period. Of the children who were born, at least half were likely to die within a few months. Many more probably never reached adulthood.

What are the implications of this pattern for incestuous behavior? Inbreeding between mother and son was extremely unlikely. If the first-born child were a son, his mother would probably be well past child-bearing age or even dead by the time he was old enough to mate. At most, a first-born son might impregnate his mother once before her death. He would have to look for younger women, however, in order to create an enduring child-rearing unit. The sexual division of labor requires active male and female partners for successful survival. Although unions between father and daughter could occur with greater frequency, the early death of the father again makes this relationship unsatisfactory as far as child-rearing is concerned.

What about inbreeding between brothers and sisters? If offspring happen to be male and female, and if both live to maturity, and if there are not too many years between them, then there is a chance that inbreeding will occur. However, if the boy is older, he will probably be committed to providing for another woman by the time his sister is sexually mature. If, on the other hand, the sister is the elder of the two, she will probably be suckling a child by the time her brother reaches puberty. The sexual division of labor among people with a short life span makes a few years difference in age highly significant.

According to this argument, then, early humans mated out because it was the only way they could mate at all. Even today, the Comanche regard incest not as a moral wrong but as a practical impossibility. Under primitive conditions, the rule of exogamy was enforced because inbreeding was not conducive to the creation of stable family units. Survival required the mating of individuals of similar age as soon as each was physically able. Only later were the other adaptive advantages of exogamy recognized. If this ecological theory is correct, the universal incest taboo originated not out of psychological or sociological considerations but out of basic biological needs.

suggested that the incest taboo that prohibited sexual relations between parents and children or between siblings was a result of this early struggle between father and sons—ultimately a question of power and authority.

Instead, Malinowski argued that the incest taboo was a way by which society could prevent a host of destructive tensions from arising between members of the family and the wider kinship unit. By prohibiting sexual relations between members of the nuclear family, the incest taboo insures that the jealousies and internal conflicts that could lead to the breakup of the family will be avoided. It has nothing to do with the history of the human race in the sense that Freud was referring to some long-forgotten act of early men, but instead can be seen in purely functional terms as a way of enabling society to continue to operate effectively.

A number of other theories have been proposed to account for the incest taboo, but each is equally unconvincing as a total explanation. According to some theorists, the incest taboo is a way of avoiding the harmful effects of inbreeding. But this argument does not explain why the incest taboo exists in nonliterate, non-Western societies where the science of genetics is unknown. Early human beings were surely not sophisticated enough in the knowledge of reproduction and transmission of genetic characteristics from one generation to the next to establish a law such as the incest taboo on a purely scientific basis. The explanation must lie elsewhere.

More recently, the theory has been proposed that the incest taboo is really a way in which human beings are able to form a society. The argument is that if men and women who are related by blood ties also form the family unit (through marriage and reproduction with each other), then the result is a self-sufficient group very small in size. The only way for that group to grow and become allied with others is to exchange marriage partners with another group

and thus form a bond with them. But in order to do this, there must be a renunciation of sexual rights among the members of a group that forces them to exchange mates with others—otherwise this contract would not be necessary.

It is further suggested that this basic feature of reciprocity is a part of human nature, that is, that the human species is essentially sociable and has a built-in need to give and to receive. Where early men were able to exchange women with other groups nearby, the social bonds that arose between the two groups proved to be a strong advantage. As this practice spread, the success was so overwhelming that the rules preventing intercourse between members of the same family were made stronger. Thus, we can view the incest taboo, according to this theory, as the result of cultural evolution, whereby a cultural practice conferred a strong advantage upon those who adopted it. This theory of incest does seem more plausible than the others, but the trouble is we have no way of proving it conclusively. And it does not explain to our complete satisfaction why the incest taboo includes different sets of relatives in different societies (or even different degrees of relationships in our own society, as evidenced by the variety of laws found in different states in the United States).

MARRIAGE

The question of incest prohibitions brings us to another major focus, the institution of marriage. Just as there are a number of different possibilities within a wide range of family structures, there is a great deal of variation in the structure of marriage and the rules that govern whom one may or may not marry. But we ought not confuse rules about marriage with rules prohibiting incest. The former deal with the establishment of a conjugal unit, whereas the latter deal strictly with sexual relations. A prohibition against marrying someone is not the same thing as a prohibition against having intercourse with them, although certainly both could be applied to the same individual. However, in many cases restrictions against marrying a certain type of individual go along with cultural expectations that one is entitled to, or at least allowed to, have intercourse with that type of individual. In India, for example, one is prohibited from marrying an individual who belongs to a caste on a lower social level than one's own. Thus a member of the farmer caste is not allowed to marry a member of the sweeper caste, and to do so would mean expulsion from the caste and probably from the village as well. Yet it is commonly expected that some men from the higher farmer caste will engage in sexual intercourse with some women of lower castes such as the sweeper caste (the opposite—men from a lower caste having intercourse with women from the higher caste—is not tolerated). Obviously, the similarity with other societies, ours included, is not remote. Consider, for instance, the recent sexual scandals of certain British politicians and prostitutes.

Marriage is a difficult institution to define so as to allow for all the possibilities and varieties found in the world. The example of the Nayar cited earlier points out one extreme of marriage, where the couple remains together for only a few days and sex is not a necessary part of the relationship. There are a number of factors that can vary in any marriage, and each society has its own set of rules to govern what form these factors will take.

Number of Mates

A marriage can be between any number of people of either sex. One man can be married to one woman, as is the case in our society. This variant is known as *monogamy,* derived from two

Serial monogamy is often seen among prominent people. Here Zsa Zsa Gabor obtains a quickie Mexican divorce before proceeding to her next marriage.

Greek words, *mono-* (one) and *-gamy* (marriage). Lately, we have seen the onset of a new variant of monogamy, in which an individual of either sex takes a succession of spouses—an increasingly common practice as the divorce rate climbs. This pattern has been termed "serial monogamy," and except for the legal ceremony of marriage, it resembles the Nayar pattern described earlier.

The alternative to monogamy is the practice whereby an individual has more than one spouse at the same time, termed *polygamy,* again from the Greek, *poly-* (many). A man can have more than one wife (*polygyny*—*gyn-* is the Greek stem for "woman"), or a woman can have more than one husband (*polyandry*—*andr-* is related to *anthro-,* the Greek stem for "man"). Cases of polygyny are more frequent in the anthropological literature. Especially where the family is an economic unit and the women are called upon to contribute much of the labor, the addition of a wife can be seen as a contribution to the well-being of the entire family. The added wives are not looked upon simply for their sexual attributes or their child-bearing capability, but for their labor potential as well.

In traditional pre-revolution China we find an interesting example of polygyny. In some areas of China it was an acceptable practice for a man to bring into his household a second wife, usually with the first wife's permission, and only after the man had become wealthy enough to be able to support two wives. The second wife was a welcome addition to the family from the point of view of both the husband and the first wife. The husband was glad to have her as a sexual partner—the first marriage was arranged by the families, and the couple had no choice in their mate. Their sex life was supposed to come second to the woman's role in the man's household and in his lineage, and there was no guarantee that the couple ever would be personally compatible, nor was that of crucial importance. Thus, if the husband chose a second wife, it would be a woman who appealed to him in different ways and for different reasons. At the same time, the first wife would be glad to have another person around to share the household chores, and since the second wife was usually much younger than the first, the patterns of authority would be clearly defined. By bringing in a second wife, a couple could provide for themselves, each in his or her own way, for the future.

Authority

Since a marriage establishes ties between two or more individuals and sets up new roles, there must be new patterns of authority to go along with these new roles. In the Chinese example noted above, the society is male-dominated to the extreme. Men make all the important decisions and are the focus of attention. A woman can be divorced and returned to her family if she does not produce a male heir for her husband. (Ironically, we know now that it is the sperm cell contributed by the male that determines the sex of the infant.) The woman in Chinese society is the head of her internal household and exercises authority over her

In its simplest form, the American marriage ceremony requires only the presence of the couple and a presiding official.

children, but outwardly the marriage is based upon the principle of male dominance and authority.

One of the clearest cases of authority resting with the woman is found in the so-called "matrifocal" family typical of lower-class ghetto life in the United States and in other industrializing countries. In this situation, because of the economic and social strains upon the family, the role of the father is minimized. The marriage bond becomes weak or nonexistent, and as a result the woman is not in a secure position as the wife of a single man, but rather she must form alliances with a succession of men for varying lengths of time. The result is that where the father is frequently absent, the only continuity in the family is that between the mother and her children, and the family life becomes centered around the mother rather than the father.

Residence

Where a couple live after they are married is subject to variation from one culture to another. In American society the newlyweds are usually expected to go out and find a place of their own, rather than move in with the parents of either one. This pattern is called *neolocal* residence (*neo* = new), and it is typical of most industrial nations in the world. It fits in closely with the economic system that demands mobility, so that the family is not tied to one place or a larger group of people. It also fits in well with the prevalence of the nuclear family, although it should be pointed out that while the ideal of nuclear families and neolocal residence might exist in Western nations, they cannot be realized in many countries which are experiencing an acute housing shortage. In the nations of Eastern Europe, such as Czechoslovakia, Poland, and even Russia, the movement from the country to the city has been so rapid that housing facilities are simply inadequate to take care

Garlanded with flowers, an Indian bride and groom perform a prescribed marriage ritual before a company of guests.

of all the people who want to move to the city. As a result, people are forced to double up with relatives in small apartments, while they sit patiently on a long waiting list for a place of their own.

Another possibility is to reside with the family of either the bride or the groom, a practice prescribed in some societies. If the new family is established in the household of the groom's father it is called *patrilocal,* and this practice is frequently found in patrilineal societies where descent is traced through the male line as well.

If the new family is set up in the household of the bride's mother, it is called *matrilocal,* and while it is less common, it is usually found in conjunction with a matrilineal society.

Choice of Mate

In no society do people have an absolutely free rein when choosing a mate. Even in our own society, where the restrictions are almost nonexistent, there are clearly defined laws prohibiting a person from marrying a close relative. In addition, there are social rules that do not carry the weight of laws but operate just as effectively in limiting marriage choices. Thus, in spite of increasingly common mixed marriages, for most Americans the notion of interracial marriage is unacceptable, and to a lesser extent the idea of a marriage between two people of different religions is equally unpopular for some. Whether we recognize it or not, we are extremely likely to marry someone of the same social class, the same race, the same basic religious conviction—in short, someone like us in almost all ways. We may think we are exercising our right of free choice, but we are really acting within the limitations imposed upon us by our culture, which we have had drummed into our heads time and again as we grew up and learned what the appropriate patterns of behavior were in our culture.

Not every culture allows for any freedom in the choice of a mate. The rules restricting potential marriage partners can exclude or include a variety of different people, which immediately poses limits to the choice an individual can make. Usually there are rules that force an individual to marry outside the limits of a certain group (at least the nuclear family), while other rules define a different set of limits for a group *within* which that individual should seek a partner. When marriage is *prohibited* within a group (however that group is defined)

we call it *exogamy* (*exo* = outside; *gamy* = marriage). Conversely, when marriage is *confined* to a specific group, we have *endogamy* (*endo* = within). Sometimes these two principles can operate together to restrict marriage choices, while other times only one of the two will be in force. For example, in American culture we really don't have strict rules of exogamy—that is, that we must marry outside of a particular group—except for the laws that govern what is defined as incest. However, in our society we do have very strong social prohibitions against interracial marriages. Thus we could say that America practices race endogamy.

Economic Exchange and Marriage

Not every society expects an exchange at the time of marriage. In the United States a couple may marry without any economic transaction at all. However, in many societies there is an exchange that accompanies the actual marriage ceremony, indicating that for most people marriage is much more than a social ceremony uniting two people. Two patterns emerge in the exchange, payments from the groom's family to the bride's, called *bride-price,* and payments from the bride's family to the groom's, called *dowry.* A marriage can be accompanied by one or both, and the exchanges can be equal or unequal.

The payment of bride-price seems to imply that a woman is viewed as a commodity; however, this is not always true. In general, where the woman comes to live with her husband in his father's household or at least in the same village, her labor potential is transferred from the household where she was born and raised to the one where she will live henceforth. Thus the bride-price can be seen as a way of compensating the girl's family for the loss of her services. In addition, the new role of the woman in her marriage is to produce heirs for her husband's kin group, and the girl's own family has no legal claim to her children.

The idea behind the opposite type of payment, dowry, is that the man brings into the marriage what wealth he has inherited, plus his labor and earning capacity. The woman, on the ......, will probably not inherit much if anything from her parents, and her potential earning power is greatly reduced by the fact that she will be expected to bear and raise children and take care of the household chores. In some societies dowry is used as a means to acquire a more prestigious or higher-class husband for a girl.

A third alternative is the equal exchange between both families, so that the dowry and bride-price match each other in value. One might think that this would be unnecessary, except that it is once again a reaffirmation of the fact that marriage is an economic arrangement, not just a social ceremony. Also, by demanding equal exchange, a family can assure their son or daughter of a spouse of at least equal social standing, for by putting up a dowry or bride-price of a certain value they eliminate as future mates for their daughter or son anyone whose family cannot match that value. Equal exchange is thus another way of restricting the choice of mates in a subtle manner according to unwritten rules.

The dress and jewelry of these pretty Nigerian girls proclaim that they have reached marriageable age.

Age at Marriage

The age at which individuals of either sex are expected to marry is subject to great variation from one culture to another. For men, marriage is usually not appropriate until they are self-supporting, although here we must make a distinction between the actual marriage ceremony and the establishment of a household. In some areas of India, for example, a boy is married even before he reaches puberty, but his young bride then returns to her parents' home and the couple do not take up residence together for several years thereafter. At the other extreme is the case of the male in traditional Irish peasant society. A man was not supposed to marry until he had taken over the proprietorship of his father's farm. This meant that until his father died or retired, the boy was under his authority and did not have the means to support his own family. In many cases this situation extended until the son was well into his forties, and his position in the family was emphasized by the fact that other men in the community continued to refer to him as "boy," although he was in all other respects a fully grown man.

On the other hand, marriage for women is more closely related to the biological function of childbearing. Obviously any society that forced all of its women to wait until their forties to marry would soon die out. However, it is not unknown for women to postpone marriage (or for society to exert pressure upon women to marry later) in order to exert some measure of population control, especially where there are no artificial means of birth control available. Since a woman's fertile period usually lasts from her early teens until her forties, by postponing marriage until the late twenties or thirties a woman can effectively limit the number of children she bears.

Divorce and Remarriage

Some marriages can be dissolved rather easily, while others cannot be terminated except by the death of one of the spouses. In Hollywood, it seems as if marriages have all but lost their meaning, while in Italy until a few years ago the thought of divorce was out of the question. Even today, under the "liberalized" divorce law in Italy, the couple must be separated for five years before a divorce can be granted. In some cases the practice of divorce and the strength of the marriage bond have to do with the economic exchange involved in the marriage. If the dowry or bride-price must be returned, the bond is stronger because the families are reluctant to give up what they have received.

In other cases, the strength of the bond is a one-sided affair, depending upon who has the power and authority in the society. A tradition in Islamic culture allows a man to divorce his wife simply by stating before a witness "I di-

vorce you, I divorce you, I divorce you!" (If it were that easy in the United States, a lot of lawyers would be out of a job!) Usually the termination of a marriage is a part of the male prerogative that exists in most societies, although in our divorce courts the majority of cases are filed by women, apparently reflecting the different economic roles of men and women in that divorce frequently entails the payment of alimony by the man.

Whether a marriage is terminated by divorce or by the death of one of the spouses, the question of remarriage for one or both partners is another variable in the institution of marriage as it is found in different cultures. At one extreme is the case where no remarriage is possible. In India among the high castes a custom known as *suttee* dictated that when a man died, his wife was supposed to throw herself upon his funeral pyre and burn to death as he was being cremated. This practice, of course, is most effective in eliminating any possibility of remarriage for a woman, although there is (not surprisingly) no similar custom binding a man when his wife dies. In other cultures, when a woman's husband dies, it is considered the duty of the man's brother or brothers to provide for her, and she is married to one of them. It can also happen that when a woman dies, her husband obtains marital rights to an unmarried sister, if she has one. In both cases, the custom reflects once again the economic interest in the marriage, for the payment of a bride-price or dowry entitles the family to the services of the man or woman, and a premature death does not relieve the family of the deceased from that obligation.

Rights and Duties

The rights and duties of each marriage partner differ widely from one culture to another. Henry VIII used as a justification for at least one of his divorces the fact that his wife did not provide him with a male heir. In traditional China, providing a child was not enough. It had to be a male heir, to carry on the tradition and name of the patrilineage. In our own society the traditional rights and duties of each spouse have been changing quite rapidly, and what were legitimate expectations a generation ago are no longer agreed upon by all. For example, a man can no longer expect that his wife will assume the traditional role of "housewife," which includes cooking, cleaning and raising a family. With the introduction of birth control and equal rights and employment opportunities for women, the traditional female roles are no longer so clearly defined; women have choices they did not have a few years ago. What this means for the institution of marriage in the United States is that the rights and duties of each partner will have to be redefined according to the wishes and preferences of both. Many more people are choosing not to have children today than a generation ago, and working wives are making it necessary for their husbands to assume a greater responsibility for the household maintenance. Also, with the traditional role of sexual consort no longer limited to a marriage partner (the pill had a lot to do with this), many people are preferring to assume much of the nature of married life without actually going through the official ceremony, which makes for a much more flexible, if somewhat less "stable," living arrangement.

Actually, recent statistics indicate that more people are getting married than ever. More couples may be living together before (or without) marriage, but eventually most do get married, though not necessarily to each other. What is really changing is the open acceptance of premarital sex, which in turn changes the nature of marriage as an institution and the expectations of a couple entering into it.

Not long ago John Friedl was interviewed by a local radio station concerning his thoughts on whether the institution of marriage was breaking down in the United States. His answer was that it was not breaking down, but going through a period of rapid adjustment to the many changes that we have experienced in the last generation in our society. It may be that if fewer people choose the formality of a marriage ceremony as a prerequisite to a married life style, we will have to redefine what we mean by marriage. But as long as there is a need for men and women to interact in order to reproduce, and as long as men and women seek out each other's company in any kind of permanent or even semipermanent relationship, there will be something that we can call marriage.

THE
Tragicall Hiſtorie of
HAMLET
Prince of Denmarke

By William Shake-ſpeare.

As it hath beene diuerſe times acted by his Highneſſe ſer-
uants in the Cittie of London : as alſo in the two V-
niuerſities of Cambridge and Oxford, and elſe-where

At London printed for N.L. and Iohn Trundell.
1603.

Laura Bohannan

Shakespeare in the Bush

In the article that follows, Laura Bohannan describes her difficulty in trying to tell the Tiv, with whom she was working at the time, the story of Hamlet. *The problem that Bohannan encountered is directly related to the concepts of kinship and marriage and the family. It is easy to see how if one does not start out with the same expectations, one is likely to react very differently to the behavior one observes.*

Just before I left Oxford for the Tiv in West Africa, conversation turned to the season at Stratford. "You Americans," said a friend, "often have difficulty with Shakespeare. He was, after all, a very English poet, and one can easily misinterpret the universal by misunderstanding the particular."

I protested that human nature is pretty much the same the whole world over; at least the general plot and motivation of the greater tragedies would always be clear—everywhere—although some details of custom might have to be explained and difficulties of translation might produce other slight changes. To end an argument we could not conclude, my friend gave me a copy of *Hamlet* to study in the African bush. . . .

It was my second field trip to the African tribe, and I thought myself ready to live in one of its remote sections—an area difficult to cross even on foot. I eventually settled on the hillock of a very knowledgeable old man. Like the other elders of the vicinity, the old man spent most of his time performing ceremonies seldom seen these days in the more accessible

Reprinted from *Natural History,* 75 (1966), by permission of the author.

parts of the tribe. I was delighted. Soon there would be three months of enforced isolation and leisure. Then, I thought, they would have even more time to perform ceremonies and explain them to me.

I was quite mistaken. Most of the ceremonies demanded the presence of elders from several homesteads. As the swamps rose, the old men found it too difficult to walk from one homestead to the next, and the ceremonies gradually ceased. As the swamps rose even higher, all activities but one came to an end. The women brewed beer from maize and millet. Men, women, and children sat on their hillocks and drank it.

People began to drink at dawn. By midmorning the whole homestead was singing, dancing, and drumming. By noon or before, I either had to join the party or retire to my own hut and my books. . . . Since I lacked their capacity for the thick native beer, I spent more and more time with *Hamlet.* Before the end of the second month, grace descended on me. I was quite sure that *Hamlet* had only one possible interpretation, and that one universally obvious.

Early every morning, in the hope of having some serious talk before the beer party, I used to call on the old man at his reception hut. One day I crawled through the low doorway and found most of the men of the homestead sitting huddled in their ragged cloths. . . . In the center were three pots of beer. The party had started.

The old man greeted me cordially. "Sit down and drink." I accepted a large calabash full of beer, poured some into a small drinking gourd, and tossed it down.

"It is better like this," the old man said, looking at me approvingly and plucking at the thatch that had caught in my hair. "You should sit and drink with us more often. Your servants tell me that when you are not with us, you sit inside your hut looking at a paper."

The old man was acquainted with four kinds of "papers": tax receipts, bride price receipts, court fee receipts, and letters. . . . I did not wish them to think me silly enough to look at any such papers for days on end, and I hastily explained that my "paper" was one of the "things of long ago" of my country.

"Ah," said the old man. "Tell us."

I protested that I was not a storyteller. Storytelling is a skilled art among them; their standards are high, and the audiences critical—and vocal in their criticism. I protested in vain. This morning they wanted to hear a story while they drank. They threatened to tell me no more stories until I told them one of mine. Finally, the old man promised that no one would criticize my style "for we know you are struggling with our language." "But," put in one of the elders, "you must explain what we do not understand, as we do when we tell you our stories." Realizing that here was my chance to prove *Hamlet* universally intelligible, I agreed.

The old man handed me some more beer to help me on with my storytelling. . . . I began in the proper style,

"Not yesterday, not yesterday, but long ago, a thing occurred. One night three men were keeping watch outside the homestead of the great chief, when suddenly they saw the former chief approach them."

"Why was he no longer their chief?"

"He was dead," I explained. "That is why they were troubled and afraid when they saw him."

"Impossible," began one of the elders, handing his pipe on to his neighbor, who interrupted, "Of course it wasn't the dead chief. It was an omen sent by a witch. Go on."

Slightly shaken, I continued. "One of these three was a man who knew things"—the closest translation for scholar, but unfortunately it also meant witch. The second elder looked triumphantly at the first. "So he spoke to the dead chief saying, 'Tell us what we must do so you may rest in your grave,' but the

dead chief did not answer. He vanished, and they could see him no more. Then the man who knew things—his name was Horatio—said this event was the affair of the dead chief's son, Hamlet."

There was a general shaking of heads round the circle. "Had the dead chief no living brothers? Or was this son the chief?"

"No," I replied. "That is, he had one living brother who became the chief when the elder brother died."

The old man muttered: such omens were matters for chiefs and elders, not for youngsters; no good could come of going behind a chief's back; clearly Horatio was not a man who knew things.

"Yes, he was," I insisted, shooing a chicken away from my beer. "In our country the son is next to the father. The dead chief's younger brother had become the great chief. He had also married his elder brother's widow only about a month after the funeral."

"He did well," the old man beamed and announced to the others, "I told you that if we knew more about Europeans, we would find they really were very like us. In our country also," he added to me, "the younger brother marries the elder brother's widow and becomes the father of his children. Now, if your uncle, who married your widowed mother, is your father's full brother, then he will be a real father to you. Did Hamlet's father and uncle have one mother?"

His question barely penetrated my mind; I was too upset and thrown too far off balance by having one of the most important elements of *Hamlet* knocked straight out of the picture. Rather uncertainly I said that I thought they had the same mother, but I wasn't sure—the story didn't say. The old man told me severely that these genealogical details made all the difference and that when I got home I must ask the elders about it. He shouted out the door to one of his younger wives to bring his goatskin bag.

Determined to save what I could of the mother motif, I took a deep breath and began again. "The son Hamlet was very sad because his mother had married again so quickly. There was no need for her to do so, and it is our custom for a widow not to go to her next husband until she has mourned for two years."

"Two years is too long," objected the wife, who had appeared with the old man's battered goatskin bag. "Who will hoe your farms for you while you have no husband?"

"Hamlet," I retorted without thinking, "was old enough to hoe his mother's farms himself. There was no need for her to remarry." No one looked convinced. I gave up. "His mother and the great chief told Hamlet not to be sad, for the great chief himself would be a father to Hamlet. Furthermore, Hamlet would be the next chief: therefore he must stay to learn the things of a chief. Hamlet agreed to remain, and all the rest went off to drink beer."

While I paused, perplexed at how to render Hamlet's disgusted soliloquy to an audience convinced that Claudius and Gertrude had behaved in the best possible manner, one of the young men asked me who had married the other wives of the dead chief.

"He had no other wives," I told him.

"But a chief must have many wives! How else can he brew beer and prepare food for all his guests?"

I said firmly that in our country even chiefs had only one wife, that they had servants to do their work, and that they paid them from tax money.

It was better, they returned, for a chief to have many wives and sons who would help him hoe his farms and feed his people; then everyone loved the chief who gave much and took nothing—taxes were a bad thing.

I agreed with the last comment, but for the rest fell back on their favorite way of fobbing off my questions:

"That is the way it is done, so that is how we do it."

I decided to skip the soliloquy. Even if Claudius was here thought quite right to marry his brother's widow, there remained the poison motif, and I knew they would disapprove of fratricide. More hopefully I resumed, "That night Hamlet kept watch with the three who had seen his dead father. The dead chief again appeared, and although the others were afraid, Hamlet followed his dead father off to one side.

When they were alone, Hamlet's dead father spoke."

"Omens can't talk!" The old man was emphatic.

"Hamlet's dead father wasn't an omen. Seeing him might have been an omen, but he was not." My audience looked as confused as I sounded. "It was Hamlet's dead father. It was a thing we call a 'ghost.' " I had to use the English word, for unlike many of the neighboring tribes, these people didn't believe in the survival after death of any individuating part of the personality.

"What is a 'ghost?' An omen?"

"No, a 'ghost' is someone who is dead but who walks around and can talk, and people can hear him and see him but not touch him."

They objected. "One can touch zombis."

"No, no! It was not a dead body the witches had animated to sacrifice and eat. No one else made Hamlet's dead father walk. He did it himself."

"Dead men can't walk" protested my audience as one man.

I was quite willing to compromise. "A 'ghost' is the dead man's shadow."

But again they objected. "Dead men cast no shadows."

"They do in my country," I snapped.

The old man quelled the babble of disbelief that arose immediately and told me with that insincere, but courteous, agreement one extends to the fancies of the young, ignorant, and superstitious, "No doubt in your country the dead can also walk without being zombis." From the depths of his bag he produced a withered fragment of kola nut, bit off one end to show it wasn't poisoned, and handed me the rest as a peace offering.

"Anyhow," I resumed, "Hamlet's dead father said that his own brother, the one who became chief, had poisoned him. He wanted Hamlet to avenge him. Hamlet believed this in his heart, for he did not like his father's brother." I took another swallow of beer. "In the country of the great chief, living in the same homestead, for it was a very large one, was an important elder who was often with the chief to advise and help him. His name was Polonius. Hamlet was courting his daughter, but her father and her brother . . . [I cast hastily about for some tribal analogy] warned her not to let Hamlet visit her when she was alone on her farm, for he would be a great chief and so could not marry her."

"Why not?" asked the wife. . . . He frowned at her for asking stupid questions and growled, "They lived in the same homestead."

"That was not the reason'" I informed them. "Polonius was a stranger who lived in the homestead because he helped the chief, not because he was a relative."

"Then why couldn't Hamlet marry her?"

"He could have," I explained, "but Polonius didn't think he would. After all, Hamlet was a man of great importance who ought to marry a chief's daughter, for in his country a man could have only one wife. Polonius was afraid that if Hamlet made love to his daughter, then no one else would give a high price for her."

"That might be true," remarked one of the shrewder elders, "but a chief's son would give his mistress's father enough presents and patronage to more than make up the difference. Polonius sounds like a fool to me."

"Many people think he was," I agreed. "Meanwhile Polonius sent his son Laertes off to Paris to learn the things of that country, for it was the homestead of a very great chief indeed. Because he was afraid that Laertes might waste a lot of money on beer and women and gambling, or get into trouble by fighting, he sent one of his servants to Paris secretly, to spy out what Laertes was doing. One day Hamlet came upon Polonius's daughter Ophelia. He behaved so oddly he frightened her. Indeed"—I was fumbling for words to express the dubious quality of Hamlet's madness—"the chief and many others had also noticed that when Hamlet talked one could understand the words but not what they meant. Many people thought that he had become mad." My audience suddenly became much more attentive. "The great chief wanted to know what was wrong with Hamlet, so he sent for two of Hamlet's age mates [school friends would have taken long explanation] to talk to Hamlet and find out what troubled

his heart. Hamlet, seeing that they had been bribed by the chief to betray him, told them nothing. Polonius, however, insisted that Hamlet was mad because he had been forbidden to see Ophelia, whom he loved."

"Why," inquired a bewildered voice, "should anyone bewitch Hamlet on that account?"

"Bewitch him?"

"Yes, only witchcraft can make anyone mad, unless, of course, one sees the beings that lurk in the forest."

I stopped being a storyteller, took out my notebook and demanded to be told more about these two causes of madness. Even while they spoke and I jotted notes, I tried to calculate the effect of this new factor on the plot. Hamlet had not been exposed to the beings that lurk in the forests. Only his relatives in the male line could bewitch him. Barring relatives not mentioned by Shakespeare, it had to be Claudius who was attempting to harm him. And, of course, it was.

For the moment I staved off questions by saying that the great chief also refused to believe that Hamlet was mad for the love of Ophelia and nothing else. "He was sure that something much more important was troubling Hamlet's heart."

"Now Hamlet's age mates," I continued, "had brought with them a famous storyteller. Hamlet decided to have this man tell the chief and all his homestead a story about a man who had poisoned his brother because he desired his brother's wife and wished to be chief himself. Hamlet was sure the great chief could not hear the story without making a sign if he was indeed guilty, and then he would discover whether his dead father had told him the truth."

The old man interrupted, with deep cunning, "Why should a father lie to his son?" he asked.

I hedged: "Hamlet wasn't sure that it really was his dead father." It was impossible to say anything, in that language, about devil-inspired visions.

"You mean," he said "it actually was an omen, and he knew witches sometimes send false ones. Hamlet was a fool not to go to one skilled in reading omens and divining the truth in the first place. A man-who-sees-the-truth could have told him how his father died, if he really had been poisoned, and if there was witchcraft in it; then Hamlet could have called the elders to settle the matter."

The shrewd elder ventured to disagree. "Because his father's brother was a great chief, one-who-sees-the-truth might therefore have been afraid to tell it. I think it was for that reason that a friend of Hamlet's father—a witch and an elder—sent an omen so his friend's son would know. Was the omen true?"

"Yes," I said, abandoning ghosts and the devil; a witch-sent omen it would have to be. "It was true, for when the storyteller was telling his tale before all the homestead, the great chief rose in fear. Afraid that Hamlet knew his secret he planned to have him killed."

The stage set of the next bit presented some difficulties of translation. I began cautiously. "The great chief told Hamlet's mother to find out from her son what he knew. But because a woman's children are always first in her heart, he had the important elder Polonius hide behind a cloth that hung against the wall of Hamlet's mother's sleeping hut. Hamlet started to scold his mother for what she had done."

There was a shocked murmur from everyone. A man should never scold his mother.

"She called out in fear, and Polonius moved behind the cloth. Shouting, 'A rat!' Hamlet took his machete and slashed through the cloth." I paused for dramatic effect. "He had killed Polonius!"

The old men looked at each other in supreme disgust. "That Polonius truly was a fool and a man who knew nothing! What child would not know enough to shout, 'It's me!' " With a pang, I remembered that these people are ardent hunters, always armed with bow, arrow, and machete; at the first rustle in the grass an arrow ia aimed and ready, and the hunter shouts "Game!" If no human voice answers immediately, the arrow speeds on its way. Like a good hunter Hamlet had shouted, "A rat!"

I rushed in to save Polonius's reputation. "Polonius did speak. Hamlet heard him. But he thought it was the chief and wished to kill him to avenge his father. He had meant to kill him earlier that evening. . . ." I broke down, unable to describe to these pagans, who

had no belief in individual afterlife, the difference between dying at one's prayers and dying "unhousell'd, disappointed, unaneled."

This time I had shocked my audience seriously.

"For a man to raise his hand against his father's brother and the one who has become his father— that is a terrible thing. The elders ought to let such a man be bewitched."

I nibbled at my kola nut in some perplexity, then pointed out that the man had killed Hamlet's father.

"No," pronounced the old man, speaking less to me than to the young men sitting behind the elders. "If your father's brother has killed your father, you must appeal to your father's age mates; *they* may avenge him. No man may use violence against his senior relatives." Another thought struck him. "But if his father's brother had indeed been wicked enough to bewitch Hamlet and make him mad that would be a good story indeed, for it would be his fault that Hamlet, being mad, no longer had any sense and thus was ready to kill his father's brother."

There was a murmur of applause. *Hamlet* was again a good story to them, but it no longer seemed quite the same story to me. As I thought over the coming complications of plot and motive, I lost courage and decided to skim over dangerous ground quickly.

"The great chief," I went on, "was not sorry that Hamlet had killed Polonius. It gave him a reason to send Hamlet away, with his two treacherous age mates, with letters to a chief of a far country, saying that Hamlet should be killed. But Hamlet changed the writing on their papers, so that the chief killed his age mates instead." I encountered a reproachful glare from one of the men whom I had told undetectable forgery was not merely immoral but beyond human skill. I looked the other way.

"Before Hamlet could return, Laertes came back for his father's funeral. The great chief told him Hamlet had killed Polonius. Laertes swore to kill Hamlet because of this, and because his sister Ophelia, hearing her father had been killed by the man she loved, went mad and drowned in the river."

"Have you already forgotten what we told you?"

The old man was reproachful. "One cannot take vengeance on a madman. Hamlet killed Polonius in his madness. As for the girl, she not only went mad, she was drowned. Only witches can make people drown. Water itself can't hurt anything. It is merely something one drinks and bathes in."

I began to get cross. "If you don't like the story, I'll stop."

The old man made soothing noises and himself poured me some more beer. "You tell the story well, and we are listening. But it is clear that the elders of your country have never told you what the story really means. No, don't interrupt! We believe you when you say your marriage customs are different, or your clothes and weapons. But people are the same everywhere; therefore, there are always witches and it is we, the elders, who know how witches work. We told you it was the great chief who wished to kill Hamlet, and now your own words have proved us right. Who were Ophelia's male relatives?"

"There were only her father and her brother." Hamlet was clearly out of my hands.

"There must have been many more; this also you must ask of your elders when you get back to your country. From what you tell us, since Polonius was dead, it must have been Laertes who killed Ophelia, although I do not see the reason for it."

We had emptied one pot of beer, and the old men argued the point with slightly tipsy interest. Finally one of them demanded of me, "What did the servant of Polonius say on his return?"

With difficulty I recollected Reynaldo and his mission. "I don't think he did return before Polonius was killed."

"Listen," said the elder, "and I will tell you how it was and how your story will go, then you may tell me if I am right. Polonius knew his son would get into trouble, and so he did. He had many fines to pay for fighting, and debts from gambling. But he had only two ways of getting money quickly. One was to marry off his sister at once, but it is difficult to find a man who will marry a woman desired by the son of a chief. For if the chief's heir commits adultery with your wife, what can you do? Only a fool calls a case

against a man who will someday be his judge. Therefore Laertes had to take the second way: he killed his sister by witchcraft, drowning her so he could secretly sell her body to the witches."

I raised an objection. "They found her body and buried it. Indeed Laertes jumped into the grave to see his sister once more—so, you see, the body was truly there. Hamlet, who had just come back, jumped in after him."

"What did I tell you?" The elder appealed to the others. "Laertes was up to no good with his sister's body. Hamlet prevented him, because the chief's heir, like a chief, does not wish any other man to grow rich and powerful. Laertes would be angry, because he would have killed his sister without benefit to himself. In our country he would try to kill Hamlet for that reason. Is this not what happened?"

"More or less," I admitted. "when the great chief found Hamlet was still alive, he encouraged Laertes to try to kill Hamlet and arranged a fight with machetes between them. In the fight both the young men were wounded to death. Hamlet's mother drank the poisoned beer that the chief meant for Hamlet in case he won the fight. When he saw his mother die of poison, Hamlet, dying, managed to kill his father's brother with his machete."

"You see, I was right!" exclaimed the elder.

"That was a very good story," added the old man, "and you told it with very few mistakes. There was just one more error, at the very end. The poison Hamlet's mother drank was obviously meant for the survivor of the fight, whichever it was. If Laertes had won, the great chief would have poisoned him, for no one would know that he arranged Hamlet's death. Then, too, he need not fear Laertes' witchcraft; it takes a strong heart to kill one's only sister by witchcraft.

"Sometime," concluded the old man, gathering his ragged toga about him, "you must tell us some more stories of your country. We, who are elders, will instruct you in their true meaning, so that when you return to your own land your elders will see that you have not been sitting in the bush, but among those who know things and who have taught you wisdom."

Summary

Kinship is the system of defining relationships and organizing relatives into different categories. Although in American society it is relatively unimportant as a determinant of how we organize the rest of our life, for most people in the world kinship provides the basis for all other social relations. By studying kinship in other societies we are better able to understand our own system, and the role it plays in our lives.

Kinship terms are a way of categorizing relatives. Such terms are based not only upon biological relationships between individuals, but upon social relationships as well—that is, kinship terms designate certain patterns of behavior expected from individuals. Who a culture places in any particular category can vary, depending upon what the members of that culture consider to be significant factors in determining relationships.

Marriage and the family are institutions that exist in every human society, although the form they take can differ greatly. Within the limits of what we consider to be a family, there can be anything from a nuclear family (parents and children) to a residential group, called an extended family, that includes many additional relatives. Marriage differs from one society to another in a number of ways. A man or woman can have more than one spouse. Authority can be equal or it can be vested on the male or (less frequently) on the female side. Residence after marriage can be with the husband's family, the wife's family, or in a new place independent of either. Mates can be selected by the parents in an arranged marriage, or there can be varying degrees of free choice. Economic exchange can accompany the marriage, in the form of dowry, bride-price, or both. Age at marriage can range from infancy to delayed marriages in one's thirties or forties. The marriage bond can be strong, or it can be broken relatively easily; remarriage may be allowed (and in fact required), or it can be forbidden. And the rights and duties of each spouse can differ as the roles are defined by society.

Glossary

affinal   The term referring to the relationship between people through marriage.

bifurcation   A term referring to the means of distinguishing kinship relationships on the basis of the sex of the linking relative.

bilateral descent   The system of tracing descent (inheriting kin group membership) through both parents equally, i.e., through both the male and female line.

bride-price   A payment made by the groom's family to the bride's as a part of the marriage contract.

clan   A descent group in which the members assume that they are related but cannot actually trace their links back far enough to reach a common ancestor.

collateral   A term referring to individuals who are related to Ego, but are not on the direct line of descent.

consanguineal   The term referring to the biological or genetic relationship between people.

cross cousins   A term referring to those cousins who are related to Ego through relatives of the opposite sex.

descent   The rules by which kin group membership is defined, and the way in which two blood relatives trace their relationship to a common ancestor.

dowry   A payment made by the bride's family to the groom's as a part of the marriage contract.

Ego   The central reference point from which all relationships can be calculated on a kinship diagram.

endogamy   The practice that confines marriage to another member of an individual's group, or a practice against marrying outside the group.

Eskimo kinship terminology   A general type of kinship terminology and the formal system of terms employed in American kinship.

exogamy   The prohibition against marriage within a group, however that group is defined.

extended family   The family unit in which more than two generations are represented, and particularly when collateral as well as lineal relatives reside in the household (e.g., aunts, uncles, cousins).

fictive kinship ties   An artificial category of relationships that have been formalized in a kinship system between individuals who are not biologically related.

incest taboo   A set of rules found in some form in every society, which prohibit sexual relations between certain relatives.

inheritance   The means by which material and nonmaterial possessions are transferred from one generation to the next.

joint family (joint extended family)   A variant of the extended family unit which consists of a married couple, their unmarried sons and daughters, and the nuclear families of their married sons.

kinship   The system of defining and organizing one's relatives.

kinship terminology   The set of terms people use to distinguish between different categories of relatives.

lineage   A descent group in which the members can trace their relationship to an actual common ancestor.

lineal   A term referring to individuals who are related to Ego through the direct line of descent.

matrifocal family   The family unit in which the strongest bonds are those between the mother and her children.

matrilineal descent   The system of tracing descent through the female line.

matrilocal residence   The residence pattern in which the couple resides in the bride's mother's household after marriage.

monogamy   The marriage of one man and one woman.

neolocal residence   The residence pattern in which the couple, after marriage, establish a household of their own, rather than moving in with the parents of either the bride or the groom.

nuclear family   The family unit composed of a married couple and their offspring.

parallel cousins   A term referring to those cousins who are related to Ego through relatives of the same (parallel) sex, such as father's brother's children or mother's sister's children.

patrilineal descent   The system of tracing descent through the male line—through the father's side.

patrilocal residence   The residence pattern in which the couple reside in the groom's father's household after marriage.

polyandry   A marriage in which a woman has more than one husband at the same time.

polygamy   The marriage practice whereby an individual has more than one spouse at the same time.

polygyny   The marriage practice whereby a man has more than one wife at the same time.

serial monogamy   A variant of monogamy, in which an individual of either sex takes a succession of spouses, one at a time, divorcing in between.

suttee   A custom formerly found among the high castes in India, in which a woman would throw herself upon her husband's funeral pyre and burn to death as he was being cremated.

Additional Readings

Bohannan, Paul
1963   Social Anthropology. New York: Holt, Rinehart and Winston.

A basic introductory textbook, this volume contains an excellent section on kinship and marriage.

Elkin, A. P.
1964   The Australian Aborigines. Garden City, N.Y.: Doubleday & Company.

The classic study of a people who have perhaps the most complex kinship system known.

Fox, Robin
1967   Kinship and Marriage. An Anthropological Perspective. Baltimore: Pelican Books.

A more detailed analysis, dealing in greater depth with the major facets of kinship and marriage.

Schneider, David M.
1968 American Kinship: A Cultural Account. Englewood Cliffs, N.J.: Prentice-Hall.

An interesting account of American kinship. The reader will be rewarded with many new insights into American culture, as well as some interesting and humorous perspectives about our kinship system.

Schusky, Ernest L.
1972 Manual for Kinship Analysis. Second Edition. New York: Holt, Rinehart and Winston.

A short but thorough handbook for understanding kinship systems and terminologies. The author explains kinship in simple language.

chapter sixteen

Children know such a lot now.
Soon they don't believe in fairies,
and every time a child says "I don't
believe in fairies" there is a fairy
somewhere that falls down dead.

JAMES M. BARRIE: *Peter Pan*

RELIGION, MAGIC AND WITCHCRAFT

To the newcomer to anthropology, it appears that most anthropological studies include at least a chapter on the religion of the people being studied, and often an entire book may be devoted to the subject. Why should this be the case? Are non-Western people innately more religious than we are? The answer lies in the fact that religious institutions in non-Western societies are more closely interrelated with the rest of the lives of those people than they are in our own society, making it difficult, if not impossible, to study any aspect of their life without touching upon their religious behavior. By virtue of our advanced technology, we have removed ourselves from the daily problems involved in wresting a living from the land; we

have gained some degree of control over the natural environment. In other words, we are further removed from nature than our contemporaries in non-Western societies, and our religious institutions reflect this distance by becoming more secularized. The effect that religion has upon molding economic, political, legal and other social institutions is therefore minimized.

As we will see, religion is not an easy phenomenon to study cross-culturally. It is especially difficult to understand the "why" of religious beliefs and practices in other societies. Compare the study of religion, for example, to the study of agricultural practices in another culture—an equally interesting and valuable topic for the anthropologist. The variety of agricultural practices and the reasons behind them cannot vary too much from one culture to another, due to the ecological limitations imposed by the environment. In contrast, with religion the variation is almost unlimited. Anything within the realm of the human imagination is possible. And, whereas we have scientific answers for the "why" of agriculture, we have no such answers for the "why" of religion.

Religion was first defined by Sir Edward Tylor over a hundred years ago as the belief in spiritual beings. In our discussion of the anthropological approach to the study of religion we will not limit our attention to such beliefs, however, for we also wish to include the basic assumptions that people make about other forces in the universe and the place of man in nature, and the practices that people carry out in an attempt to control their environment.

First, let us consider the relationship among religion, magic and science. Although these three categories seem to be quite distinct in our own culture, we find that for many non-Western peoples they tend to be fused together, and it is difficult for the observer to separate them. *Religion* is basically a belief system, which includes myths that explain the social and religious order and rituals through which the members of the religious community carry out their beliefs and act out the myths to explain the unknown. *Magic* is the attempt to manipulate the forces of nature to derive certain desired results. As such magic can be religious activity in some contexts, since it is part of a belief system dealing with forces of power and relating man to nature. The main difference is that magic assumes human power over the forces of the universe, whereas religion generally does not. *Science,* on the other hand, is different from both religion and magic in that it is based upon observed relationships in the knowable universe; its attempt to manipulate natural forces is based upon experiment and is not designed to call upon supernatural powers, as does magic.

Magic, science and religion exist together in all societies. American culture is characterized by the predominance of science and our ability to control the environment by resorting to natural (as opposed to supernatural) forces. The American farmer, for example, uses fertilizers to increase his yield, irrigation to overcome the natural lack of rainfall, pesticides to kill off insects, and a host of scientific methods to insure his success. He probably also resorts to magic, but in our science-oriented culture he calls it "superstition." "Don't plant on Friday the 13th," for example, would be a superstitious dictum not unlike the magical practices of many non-Western peoples. The main difference is that although we bend to such superstitions, it is usually not with the same degree of conviction that one applies to magical practices.

In a society where people do not have this technological ability to control the environment, they must resort to magic and religion. They perform a rain dance to bring on the rain that is so vital to survival, whereas our knowledge of meteorology would never lead us to perform a rain dance, because we "know" that rain is a natural phenomenon and not subject to supernatural control. In a technologically less advanced society, people might also employ magic to insure a good yield, such as not planting under a full moon or not allowing a woman to help with the harvest while she is menstruating. Such practices are ways of manipulating or appeasing the spirits or the supernatural forces that are seen as governing success in agriculture. But despite the predominance of religion, magic, or science, there will be elements of each in all cultures. There usually is some element of "science" in practices that appear magical to us. People probably would not perform a rain dance when rain was not normally expected, indicating that a certain amount of observation and "scientific" prediction is prerequisite for expecting success from magical practices.

In this chapter we will first discuss religion as a cultural universal. We will be concerned especially with the relationship between religion and other aspects of the social order. We will then go on to discuss magic and witchcraft, illustrating how they too are related to the wider social context in which they exist.

COMPARATIVE STUDIES OF RELIGION

People tend to take their religious beliefs for granted. They learn them as they grow up, and they develop understandings about them as a part of their culture. Recall our earlier discussion of the definition of culture, in which we pointed out that much of what we learn is on an unconscious level, and that we never really analyze our behavior. Thus if we call upon someone to articulate his religious beliefs, the results would probably be surprisingly unrewarding. Imagine a non-Western anthropologist asking an American Christian informant to explain how God couls be one and three at the same time, or to describe to him what God looks like. We would find the same problem if we tried to investigate religion in another society. We are always bound by our own beliefs and concepts about religion, and even the questions we ask are necessarily limited to our own culturally determined religious framework.

The French sociologist, Emile Durkheim, emphasized three aspects of religion: (1) the social context of religious systems; (2) the sacred aspect of religion; and (3) the moral basis of religion in society.[1] Let us discuss each of these in order.

[1] Emile Durkheim, *The Elementary Forms of the Religious Life.* London: George Allen & Unwin, Ltd. 1915.

The real purpose of religion, according to Durkheim, is to express people's beliefs about the universe. Religion structures the universe, puts things in order, relates what is unknown to what is known. Other anthropologists have stated this same principle in different ways. Such an example might be more difficult to see in our own society because of strict separation of church and state, but elsewhere it is quite clear. In traditional China, for example, the Emperor was the incarnation of God, and the Imperial City was conceived as being an earthly duplication of the Heavenly City. In ancient Egypt, the Pharaoh was not only the head of

The temple of Ramses II, Egyptian Pharaoh around 1250 B.C. Egyptian law and the Paraoh authority were divinely ordained, thus making any crime a sin against both the State and Divine Authority.

state, but was descended from God. As Bronislaw Malinowski pointed out, the nature of the social order is justified in the myths that people create and in which they believe.[2] Thus myths not only explain things that cannot be otherwise understood, they explain why the world is the way it is and why it should remain that way. They serve, in Malinowski's words, as a charter for the social system.

Secondly, Durkheim divided things into the two categories of "sacred" and "profane." Some things in every society are set apart, and are considered special—either dangerous, or powerful, or imbued with a certain mystical aura. These things are sacred, in contrast with the rest of the world, which is ordinary, or profane. Every society considers different things sacred according to the religious beliefs of the group, but the setting apart of sacred things is a cultural universal.

The third point made by Durkheim is that religion imposes a moral compulsion upon people to act in a certain way. As part of the system of beliefs about the nature of the universe, religion offers a guide to behavior among people, including a system of rules they must follow. Furthermore, because the religious beliefs are so deeply ingrained in the individual through his cultural training, religion offers a pattern of social control. When an individual violates a religious rule governing his behavior he feels guilty, whether or not he is actually caught and punished. At the same time, when he follows the rules he feels good about it and his beliefs are reinforced. We are all familiar with this notion in Western religions, in which a belief in salvation and an afterlife is directly linked to the proper adherence to a code of behavior during one's earthly life.

Thus we can say that religion fulfills basic, universal human needs, by enabling people to

The congregation prepares to enter a Protestant church for Sunday services. Churches in the United States tend to have both religious and secular functions.

cope with the unknown and uncontrollable. It is difficult for us to comprehend the extent of many of these functions of religion, for in American culture we are used to exercising more control over our environment, and there is little that happens in our everyday life that science has not provided an explanation for. In the United States, religion has therefore become more secular in recent years. It still performs the same functions, but only to a limited extent. For example, Western religions have become more preoccupied with the path to salvation, and less with the control of supernatural power. We have no scientific knowledge about the concepts of the soul and afterlife, and these have become primary concerns of religion, replacing more mundane (to us) problems, such as climate, illness and the like.

It is also interesting to note that in recent years we have heard much about a "crisis" in religion in the United States, referring to the

[2]Bronislaw Malinowski, *Myth in Primitive Psychology*. London: Routledge & Kegan Paul, 1926.

drastic changes in the function of religion in our society. At the same time there has been a revival of religious fervor in the past decade in certain social circles. One explanation for this religious resurgence can be found in the rapidly changing morality of American society, for with it has come a strong plea for returning to a stronger moral order. Religion is thus attempting to provide some stability in an era of otherwise uncontrollable change. As we have pointed out earlier, social life must be based upon rules of behavior. Religion can provide those rules so that human interaction can be based upon predictable responses and the expectation of certain patterns of behavior. Thus the religious response to the contemporary scene in American culture is basically a conservative one: seeking a return to an old morality rather than creating an adjustment to the new one.

In studying religion from a comparative perspective, it is helpful to keep this threefold definition in mind, both to guide our investigations and to avoid falling into our own cultural trap and becoming subjective in our analysis of non-Western religious behavior. We should concentrate on the integration of religion with the rest of the social order, the particular elements of the culture that are set off from the rest and treated as sacred, and the cohesion of the religious community based upon their shared set of values and rules of behavior as part of their religious tradition.

Religious groups sometimes dramatize their beliefs by a symbolic separation from the rest of society. These members of the Hare Krishna cult demonstrate the growing acceptance of certain non-Western religious practices by Western society.

RELIGIOUS BELIEFS

The most basic religious belief is the attribution of a spirit or soul to all living things, a belief which Edward Tylor called *animism.* Tylor found this type of belief to be universal, and it is easy to see why all peoples would arrive at basically the same kind of belief in an attempt to deal with the unknown or inexplicable. A belief in spirits or souls arises out of experiences such as dreaming or hallucinogenic trances, where despite the seemingly normal outward appearance of the individual, some inner "thing" leaves the body and engages in its own activities. What better way to explain the fact that a person can awake from a deep sleep, without having moved, and recount an adventure that occurred in a dream? How else can you explain the unconscious and unremembered actions of a person in a trance? And likewise in death the body remains, yet obviously something within the body has gone—that same "inner spirit." Sometimes the spirit is thought to dwell in the shadow of a person during the day, but to leave and wander about at night while he sleeps.

With the notion of two separate beings—one tangible and earthly and the other intangible and spiritual—such experiences make sense. Tylor thought this to be the most basic of all religious beliefs and set it forth as his minimal definition of religion. Animism, and its extension to inanimate objects, is religious in that the spirits are worshipped, and they are thought to have some kind of supernatural power. The attribution of a spirit and a supernatural power to animate and inanimate objects alike is a way of explaining the unknown and relating humankind to the universe.

Inherent in the notion of animism is the concept of power. Furthermore, it is a special kind of power that cannot be controlled, because it is supernatural in origin. It can only be observed and in some cases manipulated, but not created or destroyed. Belief in such power is characteristic of many different religious systems, and anthropologists have used the term *mana* to denote it in its various forms. Mana is a supernatural force which in itself is neither good nor bad, but simply exists in nature. It can be manipulated to good or bad ends, but at the same time it is frequently capricious, seeming to act in different ways at different times without any logical explanation. It is the nature of mana to be unpredictable and uncontrollable.

Closely associated with the concept of mana is *taboo* (also spelled *tabu*), a restriction on the behavior of humans to avoid contact with such power. (The words *mana* and *taboo* are derived from a Melanesian language where such beliefs are common and where they were first described by anthropologists.) Taboo is based upon the notion that power can be dangerous and that people need to follow a set of rules defining their behavior with respect to sacred beings and objects.

The concept of a special power such as mana can have many functions in a society. It can explain why some people are different than others—better hunters, better farmers, more

Many religions have stressed the handling of snakes, as a symbolic means of demonstrating the presence of a divine protective power.

successful lovers, or talented artists. The power can lie within the individual, or in some physical object he has at his disposal. A brave and successful warrior can excel because he himself is endowed with mana, or because he possesses objects which transfer their power to him, such as a magic charm worn around the neck, or a specially powerful bow or spear.

A taboo is a prohibition against certain kinds of behavior. The authority behind this prohibition is often found in supernatural power, and in the danger inherent in the behavior itself. The prohibition can be completely arbitrary, with no "logical" explanation to back it up, or it can be directly based upon commonly understood and accepted principles. For example, in the Garden of Eden there was no reason given why the fruit could not be eaten. It was an arbitrary dictum set forth by the Lord, which was to be followed unquestioningly. Other taboos may have a clearer explanation behind them. In native Hawaiian culture, and also in ancient Egypt, it was the custom for people of royal blood (kings or pharaohs) to marry only with relatives, preferably sisters. Furthermore, it was taboo for king or pharaoh to have sexual intercourse with a commoner. The reason for this taboo was that these individuals were of divine origin, and as such they were embodied with a great deal of mana. While another member of the royal family also inherited this divine power, a commoner did not. Thus to produce offspring with a commoner would defile the power. Only by producing children within the royal line could the purity of the divine ruler be guaranteed. However, since there was no need to worry about the purity of the divine lineage among commoners, the prescribed pattern of incest among the royal family was not found in the rest of society; instead there were strong prohibitions against incestual relations. A taboo is thus a kind of sacred law that replaces secular law in maintaining some form of social control.

In analyzing these various types of religious

Snake-handling, although legally forbidden, is still practiced by some fundamentalist Christian sects as a demonstration of faith.

beliefs, we might ask what creates and sustains them in a society. The answer can be found in the study of *myth*. Like animism and the belief in supernatural power, myth is a cultural universal. Myths are the vehicles through which a society expresses its beliefs about things it holds sacred. They are sacred stories that contain explanations of how things came to be the way they are, and how they should be maintained.

Earlier we discussed the caste system of India as a form of social organization with a rigid hierarchy of stratified social groupings, known as castes. This system finds its justification in the mythology embodied in Hindu theology, the basis for the religious belief of most Indian people. According to the Hindu teachings, when a person dies he or she goes on to another life through the process of reincarnation. Since a person is born into a particular caste and remains in it throughout his life, the only changes that occur in one's status come about through *reincarnation*—being born into a higher or lower caste in the next life. Furthermore, the way to achieve a higher status in the next life is not by emulating a high-caste life style in the present life, but by following exactly the rules of behavior for the station in which one is born. Any attempt to leave one's caste and achieve higher status within one's lifetime is a violation of this rule, and will result in returning in a lower caste (or possibly in a sub-human form) in the next life.

We can see how the myth of caste and reincarnation serves as a charter for the system of social stratification in India. In effect, it justifies the way things are and seeks to perpetuate them in the future. And the same is true for every culture. In America, for example, we have (to select but one from a vast array of myths) the series of stories told by Horatio Alger, in which the pattern of unlimited individual achievement is described. Alger's stories tell of a young boy (or girl) from humble origins who, through individual effort and initia-

tive, "makes it" in the outside world. This has grown into a common system of beliefs in American culture, with the notion that anyone can achieve success up to the limits of his or her own capabilities. Yet, as we all are aware, equality is not universal in our society, for there is discrimination practiced on the basis of race, sex, religion, and many other factors. The "equality of opportunity" myth serves as a justification for our system of free enterprise, but it does not describe reality.

Baptism is a Christian ritual marking passage from one stage of religious life to another.

RELIGIOUS PRACTICES

If myth presents society with the "why" of religious life, then *ritual* can be said to be the "how" by which those concepts are put into practice. A ritual is a prescribed way of carrying out a religious activity, such as a prayer, an act of worship, or a sacrifice. Rituals can be held in conjunction with regular events, such as the seasons in the agricultural cycle, or they can occur irregularly at birth, marriage, illness, or any unique or unplanned event. Rituals are important not only for their spiritual value, but for their symbolic meaning for the group. They signify that the proper actions have been performed so that the deities or spirits will be satisfied, but at the same time they have a deeper meaning to the members of the group, for they help to establish group boundaries by setting off those who have performed the necessary rituals, and who are therefore part of the select group, from those who have not. In examining several different types of rituals we can see how they reinforce the belief system of a society, and how a wide variety of rituals can perform the same basic functions for the group.

A typical collection of rituals with which we are all familiar are those surrounding the different stages of life: birth, entry into a religious community, adulthood, marriage, and so on until death. At each stage there is a particular ritual to signify the change in the individual (as much for society's benefit as for the individual's). Thus a typical progression of such rituals in American culture might be baptism, communion, confirmation, betrothal and marriage, and so on until the last rites or the funeral. Note that in our society the formal status of adulthood is conferred primarily through a secular rather than a religious ritual, and it is not as clearly defined as others. One might include in the process of achieving adulthood a number of significant events, such as obtaining a driver's

The Bar Mitzvah is an example of a life crisis rite in the Jewish tradition.

Controversy

Is Science Our Religion?

The religious beliefs held by people all over the world are so varied and numerous that it is almost impossible to make any general statement about them. The one element that all have in common, however, is the belief that their viewpoint provides a reliable insight into the true nature of reality, that their perspective is in some sense an accurate one. We sometimes find fault with the myths and theologies of alien cultures by alluding to what we call "proven scientific facts." We know, for example, that the earth is not flat because scientists have proved it to be otherwise. Are these facts of ours any more intrinsically valid than the facts of the religions they rebuff? Is there any real difference between religious faith and our faith in science?

Anthropologists have never fully agreed on a satisfactory definition of religion. In their efforts to incorporate the many various practices and beliefs which people associate with the supernatural plane of existence, social scientists have become increasingly general in their definitions. Some definitions have been phrased in such general terms as to encompass nearly every aspect of a culture. Clifford Geertz, for example defined religion as:

. . . a system of symbols which acts to establish powerful, peruasive and long-lasting moods and motivations in men by formulating conceptions of a general order of existence and clothing these conceptions with such an aura of factuality that the moods and motivations seem uniquely realistic.†

†Geertz, Clifford, "Religion as a Cultural System," in W.A. Lessa and E.Z. Vogt, eds., *Reader in Comparative Religion*, New York: Harper & Row, 1965, p. 206.

Clearly, this definition takes in a great deal more than a culture's notions concerning God, morality, and the afterlife. Most anthropologists would agree that all social, political, and economic institutions are affected by and, in turn, effect religious beliefs. There are clearly religious overtones to such seemingly irreligious phenomena as the ideological conflict between the capitalist and the communist powers. The concern of the anthropologist is not to specify which cultural traits are religious in nature and which are not, but rather to understand why one trait occurs in culture A while a different trait is displayed by culture B.

According to Geertz's definition, however, any system of beliefs may be characterized as religion. The attitude which is engendered by such a perspective can be very valuable to the anthropologists in their efforts to resist the temptations of ethnocentrism. In studying the world's cultures, it is important to remember that no system of values is inherently more correct than any other. What are we to do, then, with our unyielding faith in the scientific method?

Certainly, science has no greater claim to the truth than any religion. The ever-changing body of scientific knowledge illustrates the fact that people continue to change their minds about what is true in the universe. The fact that change has been so prevalent in the history of science, however, suggests a fundamental difference between science and religion. Religion involves an unchanging and unchallengeable body of beliefs which are held to be the truth. Scientific knowledge is a body of hypotheses, theories, and laws which are subject to constant re-evaluation. Science is always open to change

because it is essentially a method of seeking truth and not a statement of dogma.

Science is unique among all symbolic systems of belief in that it invites the disproof of its own methods and principles. Unlike the priest, the scientist is prepared to discard his current beliefs if they are proved wrong. Those who challenge scientific beliefs are praised as innovative experimenters while those who challenge religious beliefs are condemned as heretics. Science deals in assumptions and not conclusions. Obviously, this spirit of free and open-ended inquiry is descriptive only of pure science and not necessarily of science as it is practiced by human beings under political and financial pressures. There are corrupt scientists just as there are corrupt priests.

Unlike religious tenets, scientific beliefs are subject to constant testing. The scientific method involves the formulation of hypotheses which are systematically examined and provisionally accepted only until more satisfactory explanations can be found. The scientist is forever doubting his own beliefs. Religious beliefs, on the other hand, are untested and, in many cases, untestable. Questions of the spirit are not subject to empirical analysis. A soul cannot be measured and analyzed. Where religion is founded on faith, science is rooted in skepticism. Often, religion serves to offer answers which science is unable to provide. It is largely for this reason that science and religion continue to coexist in our own culture today. Science, for instance, cannot say that there is no God. On the other hand, neither can it prove unequivocally that there is a God. It can only report that sufficient evidence has not yet been found to support the hypothesis of his existence.

license, registering for voting (or attaining the age of 18), the twenty-first birthday and graduation from high school or college. In some cases even the wedding ceremony can be a confirmation of adult status.

Rituals of this type, which confer a new status upon an individual, are called *rites of passage,* referring to the fact that they involve the passage from one stage to another in the life cycle. Although every culture defines the limits of these stages somewhat differently, all cultures celebrate these changes through rites of passage. It is interesting also to note that in some cultures, such as our own, the passage from one stage to the next is a relatively informal, gradual process without much pressure or ceremony.

In contrast to the American pattern of achieving adulthood, in some societies this transition is much more abrupt, and is marked by a single important ceremony. Among many tribal societies, a boy's passage from childhood to adulthood is marked by ritual circumcision at puberty. As a child the boy is taught to fear this ritual, and the closer he comes to it the more intense his anxiety becomes. Yet at the same time, he is taught that only as an adult male can he participate in the meaningful religious activities of his tribe, so there is no alternative to the rite of passage. In the actual ceremony itself, the boy's fears are intensified even further by the older men who perform the circumcision. They may dance and sing of the "killing" they are about to do, or offer their condolences to the mothers of the initiates. The young boys are built up to a feverish pitch, and are often forced to fast and go without sleep for some time prior to the ceremony. During the circumcision they are removed from their families and from the rest of the group, and taken to an isolated place where the sacred operation will take place.

In many ways this type of circumcision ceremony is comparable to the old-fashioned fraternity initiation, with its hazing and its method of building up anxiety in the initiates.

Only young men who have undergone rites initiating them into adulthood may gather in this fortified longhouse in New Guinea.

A "pledge" spends a year or more seeking admission to the chosen group, during which time he is taught the basics of fraternity life, but never allowed to share the "sacred" secrets of the group. The act of initiation itself is built up by the members, so that at the same time that the pledge increases his desire to gain this new status, he is instilled with fear, or at least discomfort, about what will be involved in the initiation ceremony itself. Rumors of corporal punishment, personal embarrassment and other forms of hazing merely add to his concern. When the time finally arrives for him to undergo initiation, he does so with a mixture of pride and anxiety, eagerness and hesitancy. And once the ceremony is over and he is accepted as a member of the group, he usually guards the secrets and the sacred knowledge he has obtained as jealously as his predecessors did before him.

Another type of rite of passage is known as a *vision quest.* In some Plains Indian tribes a boy could only become a man by acquiring spiritual power through a hallucinatory vision. Throughout his childhood a Crow Indian boy constantly heard from his peers and his elders that the only way he could acquire power in his society was through a vision. As he grew older, his desire for the good things in life—many horses, an important wife, and social recognition from his fellow tribesmen—ultimately drove him to seek a vision. First, he would go off alone, perhaps deep into the woods or to the top of a mountain. There he would beseech the spirits to bestow a vision upon him, a power for his own use. He might fast for many days, induce exhaustion, or inflict pain upon himself in order to gain the sympathy of the gods. When this finally happened, he would have a vision in which valuable information was obtained to be used for success upon returning to the tribe. The benefits of the vision were of many kinds; they might include supernatural power as a curer or medicine man, or economic power, or perhaps some special ability as a warrior, or as a tribal leader.

Whereas the vision quest is an individual act performed in isolation, away from the rest of the group, other rituals involving the transmission of supernatural power through a human agent can occur in a group situation. One such religious practice is *spirit possession,* in which a person becomes possessed by a supernatural spirit, usually in a state of trance. The individual then acts as a medium through which the spirit communicates to the people. The trance can be induced by ingesting drugs or other substances, or by dancing or some other physical activity. Messages can be transmitted concerning future events, the nature or cure of an illness, the cause of some evil event, or almost any question for which a supernatural answer would be suitable. Possession frequently spreads throughout the group, for the high-pitched excitement and frenzied activities are often contagious. The recent popularity of the best-selling book and movie *The Exorcist* has revived interest in spirit possession in our society, once again illustrating the parallels between Western and non-Western cultures.

The examples given here are by no means an exhaustive list of the types of religious activities found throughout the world. They do, however, point out a few ways in which ritual is important to the religious life of a society as a whole, as well as to the individuals who practice it. In the following section we will attempt to draw together the elements of religion that we have discussed so far, to show how a particular belief system, coupled with a mythology and a collection of ritual activities, can act as an organizing principle around which people live their lives together and interact as members of a social group. For this we turn to a discussion of the religious system known as *totemism.*

TOTEMISM

The term *totem,* derived from the Chippewa Indian language spoken in the Great Lakes area, refers to a natural item, either animate or inanimate, with which an individual or a group identifies. Although such identification is found among American Indian tribes, the most complete examples of religions based upon the relationship between a group of people and a totem are found in Australia.

A totem can be an animal, a plant, or a natural inanimate object such as a rock, which is used as the symbol signifying the unity of the

Totemism is most common among American Indian and Australian aboriginal cultures. These Indian totem poles stand near Lake Tahoe, Nevada.

group. A society may be divided into many totemic groups, each identifying with a different totem. In its most extreme form, such as is found among Australian Aborigines, the totem is not merely a symbol of unity shared by a group of people; it is one with them. The identification is complete, not symbolic, and when a person says "I am a wallaby," he does not mean he is a member of the wallaby totemic group, or clan, but rather that he is of the same species as the wallaby, that there is a blood tie between him and all of the members of his group and the wallaby.

Totemism can be seen as a form of nature worship, where the spirit of the human and the spirit of the animal or plant that serves as the totem for the group are merged. Usually there are a number of taboos, or avoidances as-

sociated with totemism. It is common, for example, that a person will be strictly forbidden to eat any member of the totemic species, or to kill the totemic animal or plant, except on special ritual occasions when the unity of the group is celebrated in a special ceremony.

We are all familiar with symbolic elements of totemism in our own culture. While we might not attach religious significance to the identification of a group with a particular animal, plant, or other natural object, we do recognize it as a principle of organization. Our sports teams, for example, are not simply referred to in terms of their locations or home towns, which would certainly be sufficient to distinguish among them, but also are identified with a mascot of some sort. The mascot can be human (San Francisco 49ers, Kansas City

Chiefs, Cleveland Indians); it can be animal (Boston Bruins, Baltimore Orioles, Detroit Lions); it can be a plant (Ohio State Buckeyes, Toronto Maple Leafs); or it can be some kind of inanimate object that serves as a unifying symbol (Chicago White Sox, Detroit Pistons, New York Jets). Ralph Linton documented the development of totemic groups in the United States Army during World War I, showing that although the religious significance does not exist, the apparent universal tendency to organize and categorize the universe extends to all societies, and is not just a phenomenon attributable to the so-called primitive mentality.

Linton described the "Rainbow Division," the 42nd Division of the U.S. Army during World War I. Shortly after the name was assigned to the division in 1918, members began to use the term "Rainbow" to refer to themselves, rather than the formal name of 42nd Division. Furthermore, the members of the Rainbow Division developed the idea that the actual appearance of a rainbow in the sky was a particularly good omen for them (but not necessarily for anyone else). This notion gained popularity until it became so strong that members of the division actually claimed seeing rainbows in the sky just before going into battle or after a victory, even though the weather conditions would have ruled out such an occurrence. The men in the division began to use the rainbow increasingly as their symbol, painting it on their equipment and even using it as a personal insignia worn on the shoulder—despite official regulations forbidding such actions. Eventually the idea spread to other divisions, which adopted different "totems" for themselves.

RELIGIOUS SPECIALISTS

While religious beliefs and practices might differ tremendously from one society to another, all are similar in that they include individuals who occupy positions as *religious specialists.* Such positions are based on the premise that there will always be an unequal distribution of knowledge and of personal ability, and that individuals with more than their share of these are in a better position to relate to the supernatural. They can be primarily religious in the sense that they seek help from the divine or spiritual world, or they can be more magical, in that they attempt to manipulate the spirits or the supernatural forces.

In our society, we have religious specialists who have undergone a training program to qualify them for their positions. A clergyman is a person who holds authority based upon his religious office. There is nothing inherent in his personality that attracts and maintains this authority. On the other hand, we also have lay preachers in some religious movements who hold their authority based upon their personal innate abilities, and not simply on their education. Thus we have two kinds of specialization—one where the power is in the office, and another where the power is in the individual. This same distinction holds true for religious specialists in other societies as well.

In contrast to the position of priest, who learns his religious knowledge through a formal training period, in many societies there is a religious specialist whose powers come directly from the supernatural forces, spirits, or gods. Of course, both types of specialists can exist together in the same society. This latter type, who serves as a vehicle for communication from the supernatural, is called a *shaman,* a Siberian term derived from a group of Eskimo societies where such specialists are found. The Plains Indians also had such specialists, and there an individual aspiring to become a shaman had to seek the necessary power through a vision. In other societies, however, a shaman can be anyone who comes into direct contact with a spirit.

Becoming a shaman can be the result of a mystical experience, such as a vision, or a period of special training, or both. It is interesting to note that many anthropologists have cast a skeptical eye toward shamans, noting how they use such tricks as ventriloquism, sleight of hand, and the creation of various optical illusions to achieve their results. Thus in a practical sense a shaman requires a certain kind of training, not in the religious doctrines which he interprets as a priest would, but in the methods he uses in his normal religious activities. Shamans are known in many societies as witch doctors or curers who are able to help their clients by using various supernatural powers to suck out the poison that is harming them, pull out the foreign matter in the "soul" of the client, or advise the person on rituals to perform in order to rid himself of the evil infesting his body or his spirit. But the important distinction between a shaman and another religious specialist such as a priest is that the shaman is not himself the actor, but is merely the medium for the supernatural spirit that performs the act.

Shamans can also act as diviners, individuals who are able to foresee future events or un-

Every culture has its religious specialists. Here a Zulu shaman sucks the foreign spirit out through the ear of a patient.

cover the causes of past events. A diviner may attempt to discern the will of the gods, which enables the group to gain control over future events or to plan around them. A diviner can also discover the mysterious supernatural cause of an illness, when no other cause is readily apparent. Divination thus takes many different forms, but in most societies it can be considered a religious activity in the sense that it deals with the supernatural and involves an attempt to control the forces of the universe.

Priests, shamans and diviners are but a few of the many types of religious specialists found throughout the world. The important feature to note is not so much the tremendous variety of specialists that exists, but rather that in most cases specialists perform many of the same functions for society.

MAGIC AND WITCHCRAFT

As we have noted, all people seek to control their environment. They do this through manipulating the supernatural, through the practice of *magic;* through the explanation of how or why things happened the way they did, which is related to *witchcraft;* and through the prediction of future events, which is *divination.* We have discussed divination in the previous section, and we turn now to witchcraft and magic.

Magic is manipulative; it is like science in the sense that it seeks control over the forces of the universe, but it is unlike science in that it uses supernatural means to gain that control. Magic can be good or bad; it can be directed against an individual or an entire group; and it can be practiced by an individual or a group of people. When it succeeds, that is proof the magic is effective, that the spirits exist and that they can be manipulated. When it fails, however, that is not proof of the opposite. Rather, it is an indication that the proper rituals were not performed cor-

This Bushman healer has entered a trance in preparation for a laying on of hands in the effort to heal a patient.

rectly, or that an important rule was broken, or that someone else also used magic to counteract the force. It is never the supernatural power that is at fault, but always the human practitioner.

In an early discussion of magic, Sir James Frazer isolated two basic principles: (1) Like produces like, which he called the *law of similarity,* or *imitative magic.* (2) Things that have been in contact with each other continue to exert an effect upon one another after they have become separated, which he called the *law of contact,* or *contagious magic.*[3] A person who practices magic is likely to use one of these two laws as the basis for the actual manipulations he per-

[3]James G. Frazer, *The Golden Bough.* Abridged edition. New York: The Macmillan Co., 1922. Chapter 3.

The New York Public Library

Sir James Frazer (1854–1941) *was one of the most influential anthropologists of his time, due primarily to his monumental work* The Golden Bough. *In this work, Frazer traced the evolution of human culture through the successive stages of reliance upon magic, religion, and science. It is one of the most detailed and complete accounts of various practices among human cultures, as well as one of the last truly classic evolutionary works of the period. One of Frazer's many important contributions to anthropology concerned the distinction between different types of magic—imitative magic, such as the use of a doll to imitate a desired result upon a person, and contagious magic, where a severed portion of a person (nail, hair, or clothing) is used to practice magic on that person.*

forms; and frequently these two principles are found together.

One of the best-known examples of the law of similarity in magical practices is found in *voo-doo*. A person first makes a doll in the image of the intended victim, then injures the doll image, such as by sticking a pin in it, or destroys it. By applying the principle of like producing like, the magic is supposed to be carried from the doll to the victim, producing the same result of injury or death. Voodoo has been shown to be very successful in some cases, and there are documented examples of people actually dying after they had been the victims of voodoo magic. Walter Cannon has shown that this results from the strength of beliefs about the effectiveness of voodoo.[4] Where the belief is deeply ingrained, the fear of voodoo is enough to cause death. He traces the physiological consequences of the reaction: the body becomes stimulated because of the initial fear; when this condition is prolonged, a subsequent state of shock can set in, which may result in reduced blood pressure, deterioration of the heart and other similar effects. The lack of food and water compounds the problem, and if it continues for more than a few days, the result can be fatal.

The law of similarity in magical practices can also be used for benevolent purposes. Eskimos of the Bering Strait region fashion dolls in the image of young babies, and give them to barren women to increase their ability to conceive. This law can also serve as a prevention or cure for illness, such as the use of a yellow substance to prevent jaundice, or something red to prevent bleeding. In medieval Germany, ashes were rubbed on the forehead of a person with a high fever, in the hope that just as the ashes had cooled, so would the patient's fever.

There are also negative practices or taboos based upon the law of similarity in magic. These taboos tell us what not to do in order for a desired effect to occur, or to avoid an unfavorable result. For example, among the Es-

[4]Walter B. Cannon, " 'Voodoo' Death." *American Anthropologist* 44:169–181, 1942.

A houngan, or voodoo priest, possessed by a voodoo spirit during a cermony. In his mouth he holds the severed head of a sacrificed rooster.

kimos of Baffin Land, boys are forbidden to play the game of cat's cradle, because their fingers might later become entangled in the harpoon lines. This practice is taboo, despite the fact that it is a popular game among the girls. In our own society we have what we call superstitions, which are in many ways similar to taboos based upon the law of similarity, and although we might not be as convinced of their effectiveness, we follow them nevertheless. For example, one of the best ways I know to insure a sunny day is to carry an umbrella to work; on the other hand, if I want it to rain, all I have to do is wash my car and leave it parked in the driveway—it never fails!

Regarding the second principle of magic, contagion, the most common practice is the belief that magic worked upon a severed portion of an individual will also affect the person himself. For example, the Navajo have a custom of burying their hair and nail clippings far away from the settlement, for they fear that these items could be used against them. In some tribes in Australia there is the belief that one can cause a man to become lame by placing a sharp piece of glass or bone in his footprint, which is considered to be part of him.

Turning to witchcraft, we generally make a distinction between two different practices: witchcraft, which is an inherent trait, and sorcery, which can be learned. Witchcraft has many potential functions in society: it provides an outlet for aggression and hostility, a way of resolving tensions and conflicts, and it provides a convenient scapegoat for society. It can regulate the antagonisms that inevitably arise in any social situation. And it can explain otherwise inexplicable events, such as failure, disease, or misfortune. It has been pointed out frequently how witchcraft can act as a mechanism for social control, by regulating the behavior of certain members of the group. People can be forced to follow certain desired patterns of behavior, either because they are afraid of becoming the victims of a witch, or because they are afraid of being accused of being witches themselves. Thus if we are to study the social effects of witchcraft, we must also study the patterns of opposition to witchcraft, the way witches are dealt with in a society.

E. E. Evans-Pritchard, an anthropologist well-known for his studies of African societies, discusses the ways in which witchcraft explains unfortunate events among the Azande, an Af-

Because men use harpoon lines to hunt seals, Eskimo boys do not play cat's cradle lest they become entangled in the lines. This is an example of the law of similarity in magic.

rican group living near the Congo River.[5] At the same time, witchcraft is an important aspect of other elements in the social life of the Azande, such as the way in which accusations prevent an individual from striving for success at the expense of others. A man who is too successful is likely to be accused of being a witch, and because men fear such accusations they tend to remain at a relatively even level with others in the group. Evans-Pritchard points out that most of the Azande take witchcraft for granted. They expect to find it in their daily lives, and are not surprised when it does occur, for it is a natural outgrowth of living together with other people in a social setting.

In what is perhaps the most thorough study of the relationship between witchcraft beliefs and practices and other aspects of the social order, S.F. Nadel compares witchcraft among four African societies.[6] He groups them into two pairs, the Nupe and Gwari in northern Nigeria and the Korongo and Mesakin in the Nuba Mountains of the central Sudan. Within each pair there is a great deal of cultural similarity, but a different pattern of witchcraft beliefs.

In comparing Nupe and Gwari witchcraft, Nadel points out that while the beliefs about the nature of witchcraft are similar (i.e., it is evil and destroys life), Nupe witches are always women, while in Gwari there is no sex distinction and witches and their victims can be of either sex. This can be explained by the strong sex antagonism in Nupe society, and by the fact that only women are accused of witchcraft, and only men have the power to defeat witchcraft. Among the Gwari no such sex antagonism exists. Digging deeper in the social factors involved, Nadel points to the economic and social independence of women in Nupe society. Women generally work as traders, and their agriculturalist husbands are frequently in debt to them. Women also are known to refuse to have children, thus freeing themselves for their jobs. This creates a role reversal so strong that it is reflected in the patterns of witchcraft.

In comparing witchcraft in Korongo and Mesakin societies, Nadel points out again how similar they are in so many ways, such as envi-

---

[5]E. E. Evans-Pritchard, *Witchcraft, Oracles and Magic Among the Azande.* Oxford: Clarendon Press, 1937.

[6]S. F. Nadel, "Witchcraft in Four African Societies: An Essay in Comparison." *American Anthropologist* 54:18–29, 1952.

ronment, language, economics, political organization, religious beliefs and kinship system. However, to understand witchcraft, he says, we must understand the system of age grading that occurs in both societies. Male adolescence revolves around a formal division into age groups, which in turn are centered around the exhibition of virility through athletic activities. At puberty this exhibition of virility is formalized in a ceremony and at the celebration, each boy receives as a present an animal from the herd of his mother's brother. Since the boy will eventually inherit the entire herd of the mother's brother, this pattern of gift giving is normal in both societies.

Regarding witchcraft in these groups, Nadel notes that the Korongo have no witchcraft beliefs at all, while the Mesakin are obsessed by fears of witchcraft and accusations of being a witch. These accusations frequently entail violent quarrels, and lead to physical attacks. Among the Mesakin, witchcraft operates most often between a boy and his mother's brother. Since witchcraft is seen as occurring only if there is some reason for resentment or anger, it is usually caused by an argument over the anticipated inheritance, that is, the gift at the initiation ceremony.

The distinction between these two societies seems to lie in the fact that while among the Korongo the duty of the mother's brother to give his sister's son an animal is never refused, the Mesakin mother's brother always refuses at first, and often the animal must be taken by force. Thus quarrels over the gift are frequent, and if by chance something should happen to the Mesakin youth while such a quarrel is in progress, the mother's brother is usually accused of witchcraft.

Nadel assigns the difference between these two groups to cultural differences in adult attitudes toward life, and especially toward growing old. In both groups there is a hatred toward aging. Yet the Korongo men accept it, whereas the Mesakin attempt to avoid it, even to the point of concealing and denying sexual intercourse, believed to be the major cause of aging. Now in both societies the mother's brother sees in the demand for a gift the reminder that he is growing old. The gift anticipates the death of the donor, since upon his death the entire herd will be turned over to his heir, the sister's son. In Korongo society the men are prepared for a gradual decline and thus it is more acceptable, while for the Mesakin there is no gradual transition from youth to old age, and it is more difficult to accept when it arrives.

Clearly, then, there is more hostility toward the sister's son and toward the whole process of the gift-giving in Mesakin society, which helps to explain their beliefs about witchcraft. Every man projects his frustrations into the allegations that others are guilty of witchcraft, and in punishing them he eliminates his own guilt feelings. Nadel also points out that the Korongo, who have no witchcraft, have a full mythology which explains the important things in the world in another way, whereas the Mesakin do not have such a well-developed mythology.

In conclusion, Nadel suggests that witchcraft beliefs are related to specific anxieties and stresses in social life. These anxieties can arise from childhood experiences, but they can also be the result of adult experiences, as in the Mesakin. Secondly, he suggests that witchcraft accusations tend to uphold the desired state of society by identifying the witch as the one who transgresses the values of the expected behavior. And finally, while it may be true that witchcraft beliefs serve to deflect hostilities in society, they may also create even greater tensions. The hostility may only be deflected in the sense that it is redirected toward a few convenient scapegoats.

Focus

Horace Miner

Body Ritual Among the Nacirema

In the following article by Horace Miner, "Body Ritual Among the Nacirema," we are introduced to religious beliefs and a series of magical practices that are as different from our own way of life as night is from day. Perhaps this obsession of the Nacirema is at least a partial explanation of why they were never able to attain civilization, for with the domination of ritual they had to endure, they probably had little time to devote to technological advancement.

Reprinted from *American Anthropologist,* **58** (1956).

The anthropologist has become so familiar with the diversity of ways in which different peoples behave in similar situations that he is not apt to be surprised by even the most exotic customs. In fact, if all of the logically possible combinations of behavior have not been found somewhere in the world, he is apt to suspect that they must be present in some yet undescribed tribe. This point has, in fact, been expressed with respect to clan organization by Murdock. In this light, the magical beliefs and practices of the Nacirema present such unusual aspects that it seems desirable to describe them as an example of the extremes to which human behavior can go.

Professor Linton first brought the ritual of the

Nacirema to the attention of anthropologists twenty years ago, but the culture of this people is still very poorly understood. They are a North American group living in the territory between the Canadian Cree, the Yaqui and Tarahumare of Mexico, and the Carib and Arawak of the Antilles. Little is known of their origin, although tradition states that they came from the east. According to Nacirema mythology, their nation was originated by a culture hero, Notgnihsaw, who is otherwise known for two great feats of strength—the throwing of a piece of wampum across the river Pa-To-Mac and the chopping down of a cherry tree in which the Spirit of Truth resided.

Nacirema culture is characterized by a highly developed market economy which has evolved in a rich natural habitat. While much of the people's time is devoted to economic pursuits, a large part of the fruits of these labors and a considerable portion of the day are spent in ritual activity. The focus of this activity is the human body, the appearance and health of which loom as a dominant concern in the ethos of the people. While such a concern is certainly not unusual, its ceremonial aspects and associated philosophy are unique.

The fundamental belief underlying the whole system appears to be that the human body is ugly and that its natural tendency is to debility and disease. Incarcerated in such a body, man's only hope is to avert these characteristics through the use of the powerful influences of ritual and ceremony. Every household has one or more shrines devoted to this purpose. The more powerful individuals in the society have several shrines in their houses and, in fact, the opulence of a house is often referred to in terms of the number of such ritual centers it possesses. Most houses are of wattle and daub construction, but the shrine rooms of the more wealthy are walled with stone. Poorer families imitate the rich by applying pottery plaques to their shrine walls.

While each family has at least one such shrine, the rituals associated with it are not family ceremonies but are private and secret. The rites are normally only discussed with children, and then only during the period when they are being initiated into these mysteries. I was able, however, to establish sufficient rapport with the natives to examine these shrines and to have the rituals described to me.

The focal point of the shrine is a box or chest which is built into the wall. In this chest are kept the many charms and magical potions without which no native believes he could live. These preparations are secured from a variety of specialized practitioners. The most powerful of these are medicine men, whose assistance must be rewarded with substantial gifts. However, the medicine men do not provide the curative potions for their clients, but decide what the ingredients should be and then write them down in an ancient and secret language. This writing is understood only by the medicine men and by the herbalists who, for another gift, provide the required charm.

The charm is not disposed of after it has served its purpose, but is placed in the charm-box of the household shrine. As these magical materials are specific for certain ills, and the real or imagined maladies of the people are many, the charm-box is usually full to overflowing. The magical packets are so numerous that people forget what their purposes were and fear to use them again. While the natives are very vague on this point, we can only assume that the idea in returning all the old magical materials is that their presence in the charm-box, before which the body rituals are conducted, will in some way protect the worshipper.

Beneath the charm-box is a small font. Each day every member of the family, in succession, enters the shrine room, bows his head before the charm box, mingles different sorts of holy water in the font, and proceeds with a brief rite of ablution. The holy waters are secured from the Water Temple of the community, where the priests conduct elaborate ceremonies to make the liquid ritually pure.

In the hierarchy of magical practitioners, and below the medicine men in prestige, are specialists whose designation is best translated "holy-mouth-men." The Nacirema have an almost pathological horror of and fascination with the mouth, the condition of which is believed to have a supernatural influence on all social relationships. Were it not for the rituals of the mouth, they believe that their teeth would fall out, their gums bleed, their jaws shrink, their friends desert them, and their lovers reject them. They also believe that a strong relationship exists between oral and moral characteristics. For example, there is a ritual ablution of the mouth for children which is supposed to improve their moral fiber.

The daily body ritual performed by everyone includes a mouth-rite. Despite the fact that these people are so punctilious about care of the mouth, this rite involves a practice which strikes the uninitiated stranger as revolting. It was reported to me that the ritual consists of inserting a small bundle of hog hairs into the mouth, along with certain magical powders, and then moving the bundle in a highly formalized series of gestures.

In addition to the private mouth-rite, the people seek out a holy-mouth-man once or twice a year. These practitioners have an impressive set of paraphernalia, consisting of a variety of augers, awls, probes, and prods. The use of these objects in the exorcism of the evils of the mouth involves almost unbelievable ritual torture of the client. The holy-mouth-man opens the client's mouth and, using the above mentioned tools, enlarges any holes which decay may have created in the teeth. Magical materials are put into these holes. If there are no naturally occurring holes in the teeth, large sections of one or more teeth are gouged out so that the supernatural substance can be applied. In the client's view, the purpose of these ministrations is to arrest decay and to draw friends. The extremely sacred and traditional character of the rite is evident in the fact that the natives return to the holy-mouth-man year after year, despite the fact that their teeth continue to decay.

It is to be hoped that, when a thorough study of the Nacirema is made there will be careful inquiry into the personality structure of these people. One has but to watch the gleam in the eye of a holy-mouth-man, as he jabs an awl into an exposed nerve, to suspect that a certain amount of sadism is involved. If this can be established, a very interesting pattern emerges, for most of the population shows definite masochistic tendencies. It was to these that Professor Linton referred in discussing a distinctive part of the daily body ritual which is performed only by men. This part of the rite involves scraping and lacerating the surface of the face with a sharp instrument. Special women's rites are perfomed only four times during each lunar month, but what they lack in frequency is made up in barbarity. As part of this ceremony, women bake their heads in small ovens for about an hour. The theoretically interesting point is that what seems to be a preponderantly masochistic people have developed sadistic specialists.

The medicine men have an imposing temple, or *latipso*, in every community of any size. The more elaborate ceremonies required to treat very sick patients, can only be performed at this temple. These ceremonies involve not only the thaumaturge but a permanent group of vestal maidens who move sedately about the temple chambers in distinctive costume and headdress.

The *latipso* ceremonies are so harsh that it is phenomenal that a fair proportion of the really sick natives who enter the temple ever recover. Small children whose indoctrination is still incomplete have been known to resist attempts to take them to the temple because "that is where you go to die." Despite this fact, sick adults are not only willing but eager to undergo the protracted ritual purification, if they can afford to do so. No matter how ill the supplicant or how grave the emergency, the guardians of many temples will not admit a client if he cannot give a rich gift to the custodian. Even after one has gained admission and survived the ceremonies, the guardians will not permit the neophyte to leave until he makes still another gift.

The supplicant entering the temple is first stripped of all his or her clothes. In every-day life the Nacirema avoids exposure of his body and its natural functions. Bathing and excretory acts are performed only in the secrecy of the household shrine, where they are ritualized as part of the body-rites. Psychological shock results from the fact that body secrecy is suddenly lost upon entry into the *latipso*. A man, whose wife has never seen him in an excretory act, suddenly finds himself naked and assisted by a vestal maiden while he performs natural functions into a sacred vessel. This sort of ceremonial treatment is necessitated by the fact that the excreta are used by a diviner to ascertain the course and nature of the client's sickness. Female clients, on the other hand, find their naked bodies are subjected to the scrutiny, manipulation and prodding of the medicine men.

Few supplicants in the temple are well enough to do anything but lie on their hard beds. The daily ceremonies, like the rites of the holy-mouth-men, involve discomfort and torture. With ritual precision, the vestals awaken their miserable charges each dawn and roll them about on their beds of pain while performing ablutions, in the formal movements of which the maidens are highly trained. At other times they insert magic wands in the supplicant's mouth or force him to eat substances which are supposed to be healing. From time to time the medicine men come to their clients and jab magically treated needles into their flesh. The fact that these temple ceremonies may not cure and may even kill the neophyte, in no way decreases the people's faith in the medicine men.

There remains one other kind of practitioner, known as a "listener." This witch-doctor has the power to exorcise the devils that lodge in the heads of people who have been bewitched. The Nacirema believe that parents bewitch their own children. Mothers are particularly suspected of putting a curse on children while teaching them the secret body rituals. The counter-magic of the witch-doctor is unusual in its lack of ritual. The patient simply tells the "listener" all his troubles and fears, beginning with the earliest difficulties he can remember. The memory displayed by the Nacirema in these exorcism sessions is truly remarkable. It is not uncommon for the patient to bemoan the rejection he felt being weaned as a babe, and a few individuals even see

their troubles going back to the traumatic effects of their own birth.

In conclusion, mention must be made of certain practices which have their base in native esthetics but which depend upon the pervasive aversion to the natural body and its functions. These are ritual fasts to make fat people thin and ceremonial feasts to make thin people fat. Still other rites are used to make women's breasts larger if they are small, and smaller if they are large. General dissatisfaction with breast shape is symbolized in the fact that the ideal form is virtually outside the range of human variation. A few women afflicted with almost inhuman hypermammary developments are so idolized that they make a handsome living by simply going from village to village and permitting the natives to stare at them for a fee.

Reference has already been made to the fact that excretory functions are ritualized, routinized, and relegated to secrecy. Natural reproductive functions are similarly distorted. Intercourse is taboo as a topic and scheduled as an act. Efforts are made to avoid pregnancy by the use of magical material or by limiting intercourse to certain phases of the moon. Conception is actually very infrequent. When pregnant, women dress so as to hide their condition. Parturition takes place in secret, without friends or relatives to assist, and the majority of women do not nurse their infants.

Our review of the ritual life of the Nacirema has certainly shown them to be a magic-ridden people. It is hard to understand how they have managed to exist so long under the burdens which they have imposed upon themselves. But even such exotic customs as these take on real meaning when they are viewed with the insight provided by Malinowski when he wrote:

"Looking from far and above, from our high places of safety in the developed civilization, it is easy to see all the crudity and irrelevance of magic. But without its power and guidance early man could not have mastered his practical difficulties as he has done, nor could men have advanced to the higher stages of civilization."

SUMMARY

Religion has been one of the most studied aspects of non-Western societies, not because other people are more religious than we are, but rather because their religious behavior is not clearly divided from other aspects of their social life. We usually distinguish between *religion,* which is a belief system that explains the social and spiritual order, *magic,* an attempt to manipulate the forces of nature, and *science,* which is based upon experiment and does not call upon supernatural power. Religion, magic and science exist together in all societies.

Religion exists in a social context, that is, religious beliefs are an expression of the way people order their lives. It is also a way of dividing up the universe into things *sacred* and things *profane,* and thereby setting apart those elements that are considered special. Religion also imposes a moral pressure upon people to act in accordance with what is believed to be right or proper.

One of the most basic religious beliefs is the attribution of a spirit or soul to all living things, called *animism.* Usually this takes the form of a belief in two separate beings, one tangible and earthly, the other intangible and spiritual. Another common belief is in the concept of supernatural power, frequently uncontrollable, which we call *mana.* Associated with this concept is that of *taboo,* a restriction on behavior to avoid contact with such power or to avoid certain actions that would cause the power to work against oneself. Religious beliefs are created and sustained by *myths,* or sacred stories that contain explanations of how things came to be the way they are and how they should be maintained. Myths are accepted on faith, and need not be verified in order to be considered valid.

A *ritual* is a prescribed way of carrying out a religious activity, such as a prayer, an act of worship, or a sacrifice. Rituals surrounding the different stages of life, such as birth, marriage or death, are called *rites of passage.* In some societies an individual could gain entry into adult status only by acquiring spiritual power through a hallucinatory vision, a ritual known as a *vision quest.*

Totemism is a religious system found among many peoples through the world. A *totem* is a natural item with which an individual or a group identifies. A society may be divided into many different totemic groups, each with its own totem. Totemism can form the basis for a moral code for the society by prescribing rules concerning eligible marriage partners, guidelines for interaction among members of the society, and even rules involving the interaction between people and their natural environment.

All societies include individuals who occupy positions as *religious specialists.* In some cases these are people who have undergone specialized training for their position, while in others a person occupies such a position as a result of innate personal qualities. A *priest* is an example of a religious specialist who must undertake a period of formal training. In contrast, a *shaman* is a religious specialist whose powers come directly from the supernatural forces; while there may be a training period involved in becoming a shaman, that in itself is not sufficient. A third type of religious specialist is a *diviner,* an individual who can foresee future events or uncover the causes of past events.

Magic is a practice designed to manipulate the supernatural forces, whereas *witchcraft* is used as an explanation of how or why things happened as they did. Magic can be good or bad, designed to benefit or harm a person or group of people. Sir James Frazer discussed two principles of magic: *the law of similarity,* which states that an action will produce a similar effect; and the *law of contact,* which states that things that have been in contact with each other continue to exert an effect upon one another after they have become separated.

Witchcraft can be used to explain unfortunate events. If an accident occurs in an otherwise normal activity, it can be explained by witchcraft. Also, witchcraft can function as a way of relieving tensions that arise in a society.

Glossary

age grading The organization of groups in some societies based upon the association of individuals of similar age.

animism A religious belief in which a spirit or soul is attributed to all living things, and sometimes is extended to inanimate objects.

diviner A religious specialist who is able to foresee future events or uncover the causes of past events. Divination reflects an attempt to control the forces of the universe through the prediction of future events.

law of contact A principle in the use of magic stating that things that have been in contact with each other continue to exert an effect upon one another after they have become separated.

law of similarity A principle in the use of magic that involves manipulation of symbolic objects to produce the same effect upon an actual person or activity.

magic An attempt to manipulate the forces of nature to derive certain desired results.

mana A concept found in many religious systems, which refers to a supernatural force or power in nature.

myth A sacred story that serves as an explanation for the natural environment, a group's relationship to the supernatural or spirit world, and their cultural customs and rituals.

profane Those aspects of society that are considered ordinary, having no special religious significance.

reincarnation A concept found in the Hindu religion that refers to the rebirth of an individual into a higher or lower social position in the next life.

religion A belief system, which includes myths that explain the social and spiritual order, and rituals through which the members of the religious community carry out their beliefs and act out the myths.

religious specialist A position held in society by the individual considered most able to relate to the supernatural.

rite of passage (also called **life crisis rite**) A ceremony marking the change from one period or stage of life into another (e.g., baptism, bar mitzvah, marriage, funeral).

ritual A prescribed way of carrying out a religious activity, such as a prayer, an act of worship, or a sacrifice.

sacred Those aspects of society that are considered special (such as dangerous or powerful) and are thought of as having a certain mystical quality.

science A system of beliefs based upon observed relationships in the knowable universe, and an attempt to manipulate natural forces based upon experiment.

secularization The process by which a society becomes more reliant upon civil attitudes and explanations, rather than religious attitudes and explanations.

shaman A religious specialist considered to have contact with spirits, and whose powers come directly from the supernatural forces.

spirit possession A religious practice involving the transmission of supernatural power through a human agent.

superstition A belief system lending support to certain activities, which is based upon supernatural explanations.

taboo (also **tabu**) A ritual prohibition against a specific behavior pattern, punishable by supernatural sanctions.

totemism A religious system based upon the concept of totem, which may be an animal, a plant or a natural inanimate object signifying the symbolic unity of a group. A society may be divided into several totemic groups, each identifying with a particular totem, and in the extreme form, claiming a blood tie with the totem.

witchcraft   An explanation of how or why certain events occurred. Witchcraft functions as an outlet for aggression and hostility, resolves tensions and conflicts, explains otherwise inexplicable events, and acts as a mechanism of social control by regulating behavior of certain members of the group.

Additional Reading

Elkin, A. P.
1954   Australian Aborigines. Third Edition. Garden City, N.Y.: Anchor Books.

A thorough analysis of totemism is included in this study of the cultures of native Australians.

LaBarre, Weston
1962   They Shall Take Up Serpents: Psychology of the Southern Snake-Handling Cult. New York: Schocken Books.

A study of a snake-handling Pentecostal church in the American South.

Lessa, William A., and Evon Z. Vogt (editors)
1972   Reader in Comparative Religion. Third Edition. New York: Harper & Row.

An excellent collection of articles on the anthropology of religion.

Malinowski, Bronislaw
1948   Magic, Science and Religion, and Other Essays. Glencoe: The Free Press.

A collection of papers, including the famous article distinguishing magic, science and religion.

Wallace, Anthony F. C.
1966   Religion: An Anthropological View. New York: Random House.

One of many modern-day texts dealing with the anthropological approach to the study of religion.

Weller, Jack E.
1966   Yesterday's People. Lexington: University of Kentucky Press.

The author, himself a minister in Kentucky, portrays traditional Appalachian religious beliefs and practices.

chapter seventeen

A peasant father throws his hat upon the ground. "What did I do?" he asks one of his sons. "You threw your hat upon the ground," the son answers, whereupon the father strikes him. He picks up his hat and asks another son, "What did I do?" "You picked up your hat," the son replies and gets a blow in his turn. "What did I do?" the father asks the third son. "I don't know," the smart one replies. "Remember, sons," the father concludes, "if someone asks you how many goats your father has, the answer is, you don't know."

EDWARD C. BANFIELD

ECONOMICS, POLITICS, AND SOCIAL CONTROL

The anthropological approach to economics raises entirely different questions from the traditional approach of the economist. In this chapter we will face the problem of determining exactly what falls under the heading of economic behavior, political behavior and legal behavior. In our own society we usually have little difficulty differentiating among economic, political and legal behaviors, but this is not the case among non-Western peoples. Instead, we find that in these societies there are no clear distinctions among the various areas of social life. Institutions that in our society are neatly divided into different categories are so intricately

tied together in some other societies that they cannot be separated. What may seem like a religious ceremony can also be a setting for economic exchange from another perspective, or a reaffirmation of the distribution of power and authority from a third. In this section we will review a number of different types of economic systems found in non-Western societies, demonstrating how they are fused with other types of behavior. Because of this fusion, the societies in question can be be studied only in the context of the total social system.

The anthropological approach to economics attempts to show that if economic theory is to

Agricultural practices in India are typical of a peasant economy, relying heavily on human and animal power.

be considered valid, it must apply not only to Western industrial society, but to all societies. In the discussion that follows, we will first make a distinction among *primitive, peasant* and *industrial* economies. Then we will go on to consider three different modes of exchange—*reciprocity, redistribution,* and *market exchange* based upon supply and demand. Finally, we will indicate how the study of these different economic types and modes of exchange can lead us to a better understanding of the nature of social organization and the integration of culture.

PRIMITIVE, PEASANT AND INDUSTRIAL ECONOMIC SYSTEMS

Western economic theory is based on the premise that in a cash economy, people in a competitive situation will try to make as much money as they can. However, the anthropological approach to economics around the world cannot accept this as the guiding force in economic activity. In many non-Western societies other values influence the way people act. Prestige, or the obligations of kinship, or any of a number of outside factors might lead a person to disregard monetary gain and to make an economic decision that to us would seem "irrational." This is possible because not everyone is able to separate economic activity from other aspects of life to the extent that we do. For example, the American business ethic would have us believe that there is no place for favoritism in a competitive business situation. The boss's son has to earn his promotion like anyone else. (In reality, of course, we can easily cite instances where the boss's son or daughter received special considerations.) Yet in many societies a statement that denies such favoritism would be regarded as ridiculous. The son is entitled to special favors, and it would be foolish not to expect him to be treated differently.

The blending of economics with other aspects of social life, such as religion, marriage, or kinship, is typical of traditional societies in contrast to our own industrial society. What we call "primitive" economies are found in many non-Western societies studied by anthropologists, including not only hunters and gatherers, but some agricultural and horticultural groups as well. These are small-scale

Irrigation of rice crops in Madras uses a simple system which has remained unchanged over thousands of years.

Grain is threshed near a village outside of Cairo, Egypt. Many traditional societies such as this one are undergoing a change from subsistence to a market-oriented culture.

economies, found among relatively isolated, self-sufficient groups. There is little division of labor within the society, which means that virtually everyone is engaged in the same economic activity. What little surplus the people are able to produce goes to their own fund to be used for ceremonies and special occasions; no surplus is produced to be exported or marketed. In sum, the primitive economy is one that is controlled exclusively by the local community. It is based upon a relatively simple

technology using primarily human and animal power.

In contrast to the primitive system of production and limited pattern of consumption and exchange stands the modern industrial economy, with its advanced technology. Production in the industrial economy is almost exclusively for exchange, which means that there is no self-sufficiency on the community level. The division of labor is extremely high, with specialists taking over almost every aspect of the society. The economy is controlled on the national or even the international level, and the individual producer is subject to pressures from the outside in his economic activity. Typical of the industrial economic system is our concept of the farmer as an agricultural businessman, a cultivator who is totally integrated into the market system and who produces crops for sale in a market system in return for a cash profit.

Midway between these two economic types is the peasant economy. Peasants are partly self-sufficient, and while they resemble producers in a primitive economic system in many ways, they also share characteristics with the modern farmer. There is no great division of labor in a peasant community, with almost every individual engaged in the production of food for consumption. Peasants rely upon a simple technology, with traditional tools made from locally available materials, and animal power yielding the major source of energy. But unlike the primitive economy, peasant producers are tied to a wider market system and are not completely autonomous in their production. The means and the results of production are controlled to some extent by an outside elite group, be it the state or a local sovereign or whatever, and they are forced to rely upon a politically

This elderly Swiss farmer uses the traditional hand scythe to mow his hay.

and economically dominant town or city for their subsistence. They are taxed or in some other way do not have complete control over their land and labor. At the same time, peasants are distinguished from modern farmers in an industrial society by the fact that for the peasant cultivator, agriculture is a way of life and not simply an occupation. The peasant tills the soil because it is a part of his tradition, while the farmer does so because it is a way to make a living.

With this brief distinction between three different economic systems in mind, let us turn to a discussion of the types of exchange to see how economic activity can be viewed in different societies. Note that most anthropological investigations have been concerned with societies characterized by primitive and peasant economic systems; only recently have anthropologists devoted any interest to modern industrial economies, and even then it has been with the idea of pointing out how on a microscopic level we can see elements of primitive and peasant economics in our own society.

The economic historian Karl Polanyi, in his book *The Great Transformation,* has defined three patterns of exchange which can be considered the basis for any economic system: *reciprocity, redistribution* and *market exchange.* Whereas Western economists tend to rely most heavily upon the nature of market exchange for an understanding of economics, anthropologists have found the other two types equally important in their studies of non-Western societies. Market exchange implies the law of supply and demand dictating who exchanges what with whom. Redistribution entails the collection of goods by a central authority, and then the reallocation of those goods according to some principle to members of the society. Reciprocity exists where people exchange goods without a market system and a law of supply and demand, and without an outside authority intervening.

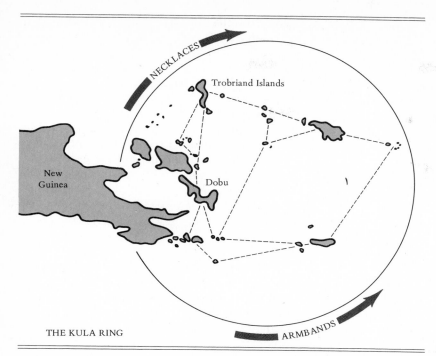

NECKLACES

Trobriand Islands

New
Guinea

Dobu

THE KULA RING

ARMBANDS

Kula Ring.

Reciprocity

Whereas redistribution implies stratification, reciprocity can occur in both highly stratified and basically egalitarian societies. It can be concerned with the exchange of goods such as agricultural products and handicrafts, or it can involve other items, such as the exchange of women between two groups. Frequently there are reciprocal arrangements among members of the same family or wider kinship group, and these arrangements are inherent in the kin obligations of the society. Among the Bushmen of the Kalahari Desert of South Africa, each individual does his or her part in hunting game or gathering roots, berries and other vegetable food during the day. When a hunter or a group of hunters succeed in making a big kill, the meat they bring home is divided among their kinsmen, with the expectation that when someone else makes the kill the next time the debt will be repaid. It is not important that an exact balance ever be struck, so long as the obligations of reciprocation are maintained.

Bronislaw Malinowski, in his work on the Trobriand Islanders, describes a complex set of reciprocal relationships among the different island groups with whom the Trobrianders trade. One aspect of this economic system is called the *Kula Ring,* in which a series of island groups forming a ring engage in the exchange of shell ornaments and other ritually significant items. The trading ring is organized so that different items travel in different directions. For example, the Trobrianders trade arm bands for necklaces with the people from Dobu. This sequence would never be reversed, that is, the

Bronislaw Malinowski *(1884–1942) spent six years studying the peoples of the Australian territories during World War I. His contribution to the field of anthropology rests not only with his emphasis upon field research and the method of participant observation (see Chapter 4); in his work in the Pacific, he produced many valuable accounts of the economic, religious and sexual lives of the people he studied. His analysis of the Kula Ring as an economic institution among the Trobriand Islanders offers a valuable insight into the function of trading expeditions for the people within the island ring. He also offered the view of a people's mythology as an explanation and justification for their social order—in his words, myth serves as a charter for society.*

Dobuans would never give the Trobrianders arm bands, and the Trobrianders would never give the Dobuans necklaces. In addition, each Kula trader has a number of formally estab-lished trading partnerships with whom he may exchange these ritually important items.

The necklaces and arm bands and other treasures to be exchanged are held in very high esteem. They are used only on special ceremonial occasions, and each piece is well known to all traders, having its own name and history. Furthermore, these items cannot be used to buy anything other than ritual trade items. In other words, a Kula trader could not use a necklace to buy food, but only to buy an arm band. The value of each piece is established according to its qualities, and is generally agreed upon by all members of the trade ring. It has been suggested that the Kula Ring operates on the basis of a primitive form of currency, for these ritual items are used in much the same way that we use money.

On the surface it would seem that there is no rational explanation for this form of ritual exchange among members of the Kula Ring. The canoe trips required for trading expeditions cover long stretches of the open seas and entail a great deal of danger for the traders. We can see why certain items might be assigned ritual value, particularly when they are made of material, not locally available, that can only be acquired through trading with other island groups. But it is difficult to understand why these expeditions continue once a sufficient supply of these items has been secured. It would almost seem as if the Trobrianders and the others in the ring are inveterate traders who would go to any lengths to get together for an exchange.

Upon deeper analysis, however, the reason for the trade expeditions becomes clear. The Trobriand Islanders make a distinction between trade of ritual items such as arm bands and necklaces, and the trade of practical items such as food and tools. When they set off on a trading excursion, it is with the expressed purpose of exchanging only ritual items. Yet this most emphasized activity, which possesses the most significance in terms of the motivation for trade, is actually the least significant in practical terms. The canoes used for Kula trade are laden with trade items of practical importance as well, and these items are exchanged as a preliminary to the Kula trade. The practical items do not have a ritual value attached to them, and they are the subject of much haggling back and forth among the traders. As long as all of the participants recognize that the mission really revolves around Kula trade, this kind of haggling can occur, although it is expressly forbidden to argue over the value of a Kula item. Trading partners who have a firmly established Kula relationship may not trade practical subsistence items with each other, which also prevents them from haggling with each other over any items at all.

In other words, although the Trobrianders don't admit it, the Kula trade is really important for two reasons: not only does it bring about the exchange of ritually valuable items, but it also brings people together for the "incidental" exchange of more important subsistence items. Thus we can see two types of exchange operating at the same time, the Kula system which is basically a type of reciprocity, and the incidental trading which is a type of market exchange with fluctuating values depending upon supply and demand.

Both the Bushmen and the Trobriand patterns of reciprocity are examples of a primitive economic system, in which small-scale, relatively isolated societies control their own local economies and are basically self-sufficient. To illustrate the reciprocal type of exchange among a peasant society, we turn to the example of the *jajmani* system found in many peasant villages in India.

In a highly stratified society such as India, reciprocation is generally more carefully calculated. In the *jajmani* system, traditional payments are made for services. This is not a market system of exchange, however, because the

Farm hands in Punjab, India, build a thatched shed for the wheat harvest.

values of the services are not based on supply and demand, but are fixed according to tradition. The *jajmani* system presents a means of reciprocation in the Indian village based upon the caste system and its implied occupational specialization.

Although most peasant villages in India are dependent primarily upon subsistence agriculture for their survival, not all families in these villages till the soil. Because of the complex system of stratification, only certain members of the community are landowners and farmers. Others who belong to different castes have various occupations according to their caste membership and its appropriate behavior. Some

Controversy

The True Leisure Society: Where Is It?

There is an assumption among those of us who live in modern industrial societies that we have come a very long way from the primitive people for whom life is a never-ending struggle to survive. In our society, we boast, labor-saving machinery and sophisticated technology have eliminated much of the drudgery of daily living. The implication of such a claim is that industrial humans can spend less time at work and more time at play. Is this a valid assumption? Where is the true leisure society?

In order to compare the utilization of energy among various peoples, a society must be viewed as an ecosystem which is characterized by a measurable pattern of energy flow. There must be some qualitative method of evaluating the amount of energy that people put into the system compared to the amount that comes out. In preindustrial societies, the most important factor in the energy flow is the

manner in which food energy is obtained from plant and animal sources. Marvin Harris expresses the relationship between food production and energy output in a simple equation: food energy (E) expressed in calories produced annually is equal to the number of food producers (m) times the hours of work per food producer (t) times the calories used per food producer each hour (r) times the average number of calories produced for each calorie used (e)—in short, $E = m \times t \times r \times e$. The larger the value of e, the greater the efficiency of the food producing system, and, consequently, the less time that must be spent on subsistence activities.

What does this formula reveal when applied to the various ecosystems in which people participate? Harris began by computing the efficiency of the hunting and gathering system of the Bushmen of the Kalahari Desert. According to Richard Lee, an anthropologist who spent much time among the Bushmen, the average daily production of food energy in a Bushman camp was 64,200 calories. To produce this energy, 7.4 workers worked 6 hours each. Assuming that the Bushmen worked at a comfortable rate, they would have expended some 150 calories per hour above the energy expended at rest. Multiplying 7.4 workers by 6 hours per worker by 150 calories per hour, we arrive at a daily investment of roughly 6600 calories. Dividing the 64,200 calories which were produced by the 6600 invested yields a figure of 9.6. This figure represents e, the efficiency factor in the energy formula.

To arrive at E, the annual calorie output, we multiply 64,200 calories by 365 days to get 23,433,000 calories per year. An average of 20 different adults were engaged in food production over a period of several weeks. Substituting 20 for *m* and solving for *t*, we arrive at the rough equation: 23,000,000 (annual calories) = 20 (food producers) × 805 (hours per food producer) × 150 (calories expended per hour) × 9.6 (efficiency factor).

What does this equation tell us about the ecosystem of the Bushmen? To find out, Harris proceeded to compute the energy formulas for several different energy utilization systems. For one village of West African hoe agriculturalists, the following formula was derived: 460,000,000 (annual calories) = 334 (food producers) × 820 (hours per food producer) × 150 (calories expended per hour) × 11.2 (efficiency factor). Although the population and labor force are much larger, the efficiency of this system was found to be roughly the same as that of the Bushmen. In contrast, the efficiency factor of a Chinese village practicing advanced techniques of irrigation agriculture was computed at 53.5.

It is difficult to evaluate accurately the efficiency of an industrial agricultural society. When the energy formula is applied directly to the American farmer, we find that the worker who puts in 9 hours of work per acre is rewarded with an astounding 6000 calories for every calorie he expends. However, there are several factors which render these figures highly misleading. First, some three-quarters of all American crop lands are used to produce animal feeds. Second, a great deal of labor is used in making machinery, fuel, and chemicals which the farmer needs.

In order to compare the efficiency of labor in preindustrial and postindustrial systems, we might consider how many hours people must work to obtain their annual ration of calories. Based on an average hourly income of $3.42 and a per capita food bill of $600, the American blue collar worker must work about 180 hours per year compared to 122 hours for the Chinese irrigation farmer.

These statistics suggest some surprising conclusions about the relationship between technological society and leisure time. Despite popular assumptions to the contrary, higher productivity in our society is generally paid for by an increased amount of time spent on subsistence-related activities. In hunting and gathering societies, slash and burn agricultural systems, and irrigation farming societies, increasing work time can lead to depletion of resources and, therefore, is recognized as being counter-productive. The Bushmen, for example, do not gather more food than they can use before it begins to spoil. In modern industry, on the other hand, increased work time yields increased production. Technology allows us to produce and store goods almost without limitations. We do not face starvation from day to day, but we pay for our security with our leisure.

How, then, does leisure time in societies such as our own compare to that in less technologically advanced societies? Although there are not much data to indicate how much time is devoted to non-food producing labor in various societies, it has been estimated that most hunters and gatherers spend 6 or fewer hours in subsistence activities. Their annual labors are roughly the same as those of the American worker with a 40-hour week and a three-week vacation. Our technology has been used to increase output, not to increase leisure.

families practice specialized crafts, such as carpenters who make the farmers' tools or water carriers who provide water from the village wells for the rest of the residents. In return, each villager receives payments for his or her services in the form of agricultural produce from the farmer caste, and equivalent services or products from members of the other castes. Thus the landowner commands the services of a wide group of lower caste specialists. The *jajmani* system is the means which enables each specialist, including the cultivator, to obtain the goods and services of others in order to have the variety necessary for his existence. As such it is an institutionalized form of reciprocity among the villagers.

It is impossible, however, to separate the *jajmani* system as an economic institution from other institutions in Indian society. The Hindu religion forms the basis for the *jajmani* system by providing the religious philosophy upon which the caste system is based. Clearly without the social stratification that the caste system implies, and the religious prohibition against people in certain levels of the social hierarchy performing various tasks, the *jajmani* system could not operate, since everyone in the village could cultivate his own land and provide his own products and specialized services. Thus the *jajmani* system is fused with religious practices, and is not simply economic. Likewise, the religion provides clear prescriptions for behavior for each caste, and thus forms the basis for the institutions of social control on the village level. Political and legal power and authority are delegated partly on the basis of religious tenets, and partly on the basis of economic power, both of which are supported by the *jajmani* system. Although it is in one sense an economic institution, we also define the *jajmani* primarily in social terms as a network of alliances between groups of individuals who practice different occupations. It enables them to exchange their goods and services, but not without bringing into play the entire context of Indian society.

Money is rarely important in the *jajmani* system. It is the exchange of goods and services with values defined according to tradition that has enabled the system to be maintained in the villages. Hereditary customs keep this system closed, unlike our open-market system with its free competition. In fact, where local village economies have become more dependent upon cash, the *jajmani* system has begun to break down. Consider, for example, what would be the result of translating a carpenter's payment of grain to a payment in cash. According to the traditional system, in return for his manufacture and repair of a farmer's tools, a carpenter would receive a payment of a certain amount of grain, which in terms of feeding his family has a fixed value over time. The grain payment will feed the same number of people today that it would have a hundred years ago. If we translate that to a cash payment, again with a fixed amount being recorded according to the tradition, the carpenter's actual payments in terms of how many mouths he can feed now fluctuates, as the value of the cash varies. And if the payment in cash is designed to rise and fall with the value of the currency so that a carpenter's payment maintains a steady relative value, then the traditional system of payments no longer holds.

Redistribution

Redistribution generally refers to some sort of enforced organization that replaces reciprocity, and at the same time increases output by requiring a surplus product to support a group of nonagriculturalists. In a redistributive system of exchange, products are collected and reallocated among the entire population. Obviously the reallocation changes the original distribution of goods in some way, otherwise there would be no need to collect them in the first

This market scene in an Indian village demonstrates that market exchange exists along with the reciprocity of the jajmani system.

place. Usually this change is in the form of support for a nonproducing elite, which retains the lion's share for itself, thus entrenching its power. Karl Wittfogel, in his book *Oriental Despotism,* has argued that this classic model of a redistributive form of exchange was characteristic of irrigation societies such as that of ancient Egypt. According to his theory, societies grew up around the riverbeds in otherwise arid regions of the world. The rivers afforded the people the necessary water and fertile soil to produce agricultural crops to support a relatively dense population. Eventually, however, the population outgrew the land, and in order to support greater numbers of people irrigation was necessary. As the irrigation system grew more complex, more intricate regulation and a greater concentration of power to enforce these regulations were required. The ultimate result was the organization of an elite group at the head of society, which solidified its power through laws and religious edicts.

Such was the case among the Pharaohs of ancient Egypt. Originally their power was based upon the regulation of irrigation along the Nile River, but the Pharaohs of ancient Egypt eventually spread out their base of power and justified it through the religious doctrines adopted by the common people. They forced the agricultural population to produce a surplus, which was turned over to them, and then redistributed to nonagricultural workers and elites. In this way they were able to support the tremendous population of workers responsible for the construction of the pyramids.

As in the case of reciprocity, redistribution is frequently imbedded in a complex set of kinship relationships with other members of society. In some cases the central figure who collects and redistributes goods might be the head of a large extended household, or he might have only a fictive relationship to the producers, which he calls upon in his demand for surplus production. The Pharaoh was believed to be the divine incarnation on earth and thus related to all men symbolically. Likewise, a tribal chieftain, representing the spirit of all the ancestors of the tribe, could invoke his position as head of the tribe and symbolic leader of the people in collecting and reallocating the tribe's resources. Since all members of the tribe are considered to be related to one another through descent from a common ancestor, their leader would be empowered to represent the group in such a way.

Redistribution as a form of exchange need not always involve the head of state collecting and reallocating goods from all members of society. Rather, we can find many examples of a combination of both redistribution and reciprocity operating together, in the sense that one individual might collect and then give away goods, with the expectation that those to whom he has given something will reciprocate in some fashion. Such is the case among the Kwakiutl Indians, in an institution known as the *potlatch*.

During the winter when little productive activity could be carried out, the Kwakiutl turned to ceremonial activities, in which redistribution was cloaked in the form of festivals and ritual gift-giving. Vast feasts were held, sometimes accompanied by a potlatch, in which a man would give away his material possessions. A potlatch

Kwakiutl Indians of the Pacific Northwest display objects to be given away at a potlatch as a means of achieving status.

was an important ceremonial occasion used to validate a life crisis ceremony. A man would give a potlatch following his initiation into a secret society, or his marriage, or on any of a number of important ceremonial occasions. In the course of the potlatch he would seek to prove his worthiness of the position he claimed to hold, and to increase his prestige. The actual redistribution of his worldly possessions was quite ostentatious, and was designed to shame his guests and flaunt his own status. A man would spend months or even years preparing for this one occasion, borrowing and saving all he could, in order to have enough to give away. The principle of the potlatch was for a man to be able to give away more than his guests could reciprocate. By doing this he proved his importance and validated a higher status for himself. As a result, the guests at the potlatch now felt obligated to reciprocate with an even greater gift-giving festival.

Even more degrading to the guests than giving away wealth was the act of destroying it. A man giving a potlatch might end with a grand finale in which he literally burned blankets, canoes, valuable copper items and even food. Then, having achieved the ultimate in status, he would pay off the debts he had incurred in storing up all of this wealth, certain of the fact that he would be invited to the potlatches of others and receive payments from them. At the same time, he would begin amassing a new fortune for his next potlatch, for having achieved a particular status, he could never rest on his laurels. The higher the status he could achieve, the better off he would be at the potlatches of others; one did not gain any status at all by simply inviting a bunch of people to a potlatch, secure in the knowledge that they could be easily shamed.

Situations similar to the potlatch are not unknown in our own society. There is the case of a man who builds up an enormous estate and gives much of it away to charity in return for prestige, elevated social status, and perhaps even a prestigious and secure position in government or business—consider what it takes to become an ambassador! A debutante ball in our society is in some ways similar to a potlatch. First, it is something only for the wealthy, used to maintain or elevate their high status in society. Not everyone can have a coming-out party—it takes social position, not just money. In throwing such a party, an individual is actually redistributing some of his wealth to other members of the society. Also like the potlatch, he is doing this with the expectation that others will reciprocate. If they don't, he will make a note of it and not invite them to his next party. The point is that although cloaked in "strange" behavior, economic activity in other societies is not much different from our own.

We might also look at redistribution, as found in the potlatch, as a form of savings institution. A man acquires prestige through distributing a surplus. The prestige is shared by his clan or his family. Then if he or his family should have a bad year, or a river should run dry or a herd disappear, he can rely upon others who are indebted to him. In this sense, distributing a surplus, by whatever means, serves the same purpose as putting money in the bank.

Market Exchange

We are all familiar with the typical American market system, ruled by the balance of supply and demand. In our economic behavior we tend to think in terms of calculated exchange in an impersonal setting. Each individual attempts to maximize his profit by calculating or estimating the return for labor and products. In other market systems, however, this is not always the case. Within the context of the Haitian market, for example, trade is bound up with a special personal relationship of intermediaries. This relationship is called *pratik*, and refers to the personal ties between an intermediary and those with whom she deals.

A *pratik* relationship is established between a woman trader and her customer. On the one side are the producers who use her as an intermediary in getting their goods to market, and on the other side are the retailers in the market who get their products from her. Bonds are established between the woman and her clients in various ways, but are always based upon a personalized relation, such as granting a "baker's dozen," extending credit, or lowering prices. This bond of *pratik* sets up obligations on the part of all participants, and in effect tends to lower profits while providing greater security. The reason for *pratik* existing can be seen in the nature of the rural economy of Haiti. Production is relatively high, yet comparatively few people are actually engaged in agriculture. As a result there are literally thousands of women who make a small living through trading. Admittedly this could be a high risk occupation, since the competition is so keen and the profit margin is so low. As a way of lowering the risk and increasing security, women establish personal bonds with both producers and retailers. For example, if you give a person a lower price consistently, you reduce your profit, but at the same time when the supply is such that he can go elsewhere for an even lower price, you still have a hold on him. Or, for example, as a trader you pay the producer slightly more than is necessary when the supply is high and the demand is low, with the result that when supply grows scarce, your *pratik* relationship means that he will hold some back for you, and you will not be shut out of the market.

Thus *pratik* relationships tend to stabilize what would otherwise be a highly fluctuating market situation due to the unstable nature of the Haitian agricultural economy. *Pratik* modifies pure competition by giving certain individuals priority in the market. As such, it appears on closer examination to be a highly practical, rational arrangement based upon the economic context in which it is found.

ECONOMIC AND SOCIAL ORGANIZATION

So far we have surveyed briefly several basic economic types and three modes of exchange that can occur within these economic systems. We have also seen that to characterize the economy of any society as based solely on reciprocity, redistribution or market exchange is incorrect. Any economy is a combination of all of these types of exchange, with one perhaps appearing as the dominant pattern. We must also be aware of the relationship between economics and other aspects of the social organization, that is, other basic institutions within the society. We pointed this out to a limited degree in the discussion of the *jajmani* system, indicating how it is reinforced through the religious doctrines found in India, and how it fits together with the system of social stratification that permeates all social relations in Indian villages.

We must also recognize that what appear to us as basic principles of economic activity in Western society are not followed by every society, and in fact are not even fundamental values associated with every culture. Our notion of maximizing individual profit, for example, is foreign to many people, who would prefer to engage in transactions which promoted solidarity (such as *pratik* relationships), calculating their profit in social as well as monetary terms.

In a band of Bushmen, leadership is normally informal and unstructured, based on group consensus. Here a group of Bushwomen are shown in camp.

In previous chapters we have seen how marriage can be viewed as an economic exchange rather than a social activity, and in fact in most rural areas of non-Western societies the notion of a love object as the basis for a marriage runs counter to many basic values of the community. Also, we are accustomed to viewing our economic transactions in terms of calculating and weighing the alternatives. However, we must be aware of the fact that many values cannot be calculated, and many objects cannot have a value assigned to them. In a small, isolated community where everyone knows everyone else and all people interact with one another on a close, personal basis, getting ahead is rarely as important as fitting in with the group. Prestige and social approval of one's actions can be much more important than a higher material standard of living, and these factors will enter into any calculations made by a resident of the community. Coming from another culture, we tend to look at such economic activities as irrational because they violate our views on what is "rational" according to our system of values. But we must take into account the nonmaterial, intangible values that the people themselves assign to things. When we do this, their actions almost always turn out to be just as "rational" in their own context as ours are for us.

COMPARATIVE POLITICAL INSTITUTIONS

Just as with economics, we tend to look at politics as a separate aspect of life. If you were asked to describe politics in American society, you would probably begin by mentioning the structure of our system of government, the nature of political parties, the democratic system of free elections, and so forth. It is quite unlikely that you would bring in such nonpolitical institutions as the family, the church, or the school system. Yet just as we learned in looking at economics cross-culturally, in most societies political behavior is fused with many other aspects of social organization, and does not exist as a separate and distinguishable arena for social interaction.

We can define politics in a most elementary sense as the legitimate use of force or authority within a society. Thus we all engage in some sort of political behavior, for an essential ingredient in living together with other people is a recognized delegation of authority based on special capabilities, greater wisdom and experience, physical superiority, or whatever other criteria we choose. Politics is the way by which people maintain peace within a group and define their group relative to the outside world. Usually we define such a group by associating it with a geographical unit, as with a nation or a state, but this need not always be the case.

Band Organization

The form of political organization known as a *band* is found primarily among people who depend upon hunting and gathering. We can better understand how band organization works if we consider it in the context of the problems that a hunting and gathering society must face and the environment in which they live. People who live from the land without practicing agriculture, raising livestock, or in some other way increasing the amount of food available, may require a great deal of land to support them. This is because they may quickly exhaust the available food supply in a given area, and are forced to move on to a new source of food. Sometimes they follow migratory animals (which in turn are merely following the abundance of food and water for themselves), but more often the movement of a hunting and gathering band is based upon a combination of animal and plant food. Various trees ripen in different seasons, and the rainy season lasts

Dinka tribesmen of Sudan meet at a tribal council.

longer or comes later in one area than another. All of these factors make for a unique life style, to which the band seems suited.

Hunting and gathering bands tend to be rather small throughout most of the year, with groups of perhaps 25 to 40 individuals forming the basic residential unit. Of course, the size of the group fluctuates, so that when food is plentiful several bands might join together for a feast, and when food is scarce a number of splinter groups will spread out over a larger area seeking water, animals and edible vegetation. Each band will consider a general area as its own, and while there are not specific boundaries that limit the movement of the group, members rarely go beyond what they consider to be their own territory in the normal course of events. Boundaries may overlap slightly, so that two groups might come into contact when each is on the fringe of its territory, but for the most part a band is isolated from its neighbors and goes about its daily activities alone.

Two elements of political organization operate in maintaining the band—the internal organization of the small group, and the external set of regulations governing the overall organization of a large number of neighboring groups in situations when they come into contact. On the level of the individual group, we can see how the combination of the environment and the way of life would lead to a loose-knit organization. Little in this way of life is permanent. Groups are frequently splitting up, with families going off to join another group, or larger factions forming their own band. Sometimes the group becomes too large to derive sufficient support from the surrounding area, and new land must be used. At other times, internal disputes may be solved by a division of a band into two or more groups. Moreover, a necessary aspect of life as a hunter/gatherer is that each person contribute something to the overall support of the group. There is no room for the nonproductive old or weak individuals when the food supply is so limited. As a result, each family tends to be self-sufficient, and does not rely as heavily upon the rest of the society for its existence as we are accustomed to doing. (Consider where you would be today if you had to grow your own food, make your own clothes and even manufacture your own automobile.)

The ties that bind people together in a band are necessarily of a different nature from the ties that bind people together in a modern industrial society. If a disagreement occurs, each party will feel free to leave the group if he cannot abide by the solution that is reached. To compare it to our own way of life, it is almost like membership in a club. One is free to drop out and join another such group if one does not get along or if one disagrees with changes that are made. But very few of us would go so far as to drop out of American society just because we disagreed with some of its laws, or because the candidate we voted for lost the election. We have become so specialized that we rely upon others in our society to keep us alive, whereas the typical Bushman, or Australian Aborigine, or Eskimo—all members of societies with band organization—is much better able to get along by himself or with only his family, despite the more hostile environment in which he lives.

Within such a group, the established form of governance tends to be based upon the principle of equality. This is not to say that there are no differences among members of the group, for every individual will be ranked and evaluated according to his or her own particular skill, as a hunter, a storyteller, a successful curer, or whatever. But when decisions are made that affect the group as a whole, they are made on the basis of consensus, and are not imposed by one dominant king or chief. Cooperation in all endeavors is the best insurance for survival. If a hunter is successful, he shares his kill with the rest of the group, for he knows that the time will come when his luck will be down and someone else will share with him. This form of cooperation extends not just to the distribution of food, but to the very concept of ownership itself. The resources of the band belong to everyone equally, and are to be shared by all. If there is a leader in such a society, he achieves this status based upon his personal qualities and the respect of his fellow band members. He has no authority to impose his own desires upon the rest of the group against their will, and should he attempt to do so, he will probably lose his position as leader.

A second type of political relationship regulates interaction among two or more small bands. Occasionally two groups will come into contact in areas where their territory overlaps. At other times several groups will gather to celebrate a special event, usually coinciding with a time of year when the food supply is abundant, such as the return of the migratory animals, the ripening of wild grains or other vegetation, the onset of the rainy season, or some other seasonal change in the environment. In such a setting, the bonds which hold these groups together in a political alliance can be most important, for they not only guard against warfare, but they help to integrate the groups and give them a common basis of interaction.

Although they are self-sufficient in the sense that they can obtain enough food to support themselves, bands cannot exist in total isolation from one another. A group of fewer than 40 or 50 people contains only a few families, and thus the number of potential mates for an individual is extremely limited. As we saw in the earlier chapter on kinship, every society has some form of incest taboo, restricting marriage to someone outside the immediate family. Over the years the inbreeding among a few families in a group of this size would mean that there would be no one left as an eligible marriage partner, and if a group remained isolated and continued to obey the incest taboo, it would soon die out. On the other hand, the incest taboo, which forces people to look beyond their own group, at the same time creates a combination of cooperation and dependency upon neighboring groups. It is an interesting question whether the incest taboo originated in the process of cultural evolution as a means of forcing potentially hostile neighbors to cooperate and overcome their differences in order to find marriage partners. Surely it is one of the most effective means of preventing warfare at the band level, for each individual has ties with many other groups through the marriages of his or her relatives, and who would want to engage in a battle with his relatives?

Tribes and Chiefdoms

There are very few hunting and gathering societies in the world today, and much of our information about band organizations is based upon reports of early contact with such groups in the past. Most non-Western peoples live in larger groups and obtain their living by other means, which creates an entirely different set of problems requiring political solutions. One such form is *tribal organization.*

A tribe may contain hundreds or even thousands of people, making the delegation of authority and maintenance of order a much more complex process than in a band. Yet even at the tribal level, politics is not a separate institution, but is closely involved with the rest of the social organization. A family might exercise economic control over land, and thus engage in behavior that we would call "economic." It might also be engaged in an alliance with other families, to which we would apply the term "politics." Or it might be the center of a religious activity, such as ancestor worship. Thus when we consider political organization on the tribal level, as on the band level, we are really looking at political behavior of people in a wider social context, and not specifically political institutions that stand apart from the rest of society (as a political party is set apart in our own society).

A tribe can be generally defined as a confederation of groups who recognize a relationship with one another, usually in the form of common ethnic origin, common language, or a strong pattern of interaction based on intermarriage or presumed kinship. On a lower level of organization, a tribe is divided into smaller segments such as villages or regional groups, which in turn are divided into clans or lineages, and on the lowest level, families and households. The tribe is considered political in the sense that it is the broadest base upon which joint activities can be organized and carried out by the group and in the name of the group.

Tribal political organization can be important in controlling behavior within the tribe, and in organizing activity in opposition to other outside groups. Of course, it can also operate to coordinate economic activity such as trading networks, or religious activity as in the pattern of worshipping a tribal deity—but this is part of the political process as well. Within the tribe, any dispute or opposition among smaller groups can be settled on the next higher level. If two families argue, the settlement can be reached by appealing to the clan dignitaries, whose authority is derived from and backed by the tribe itself. If two clans should engage in a feud, the ultimate solution may be handed down by the village headman. On the other hand, if there is opposition from some group outside the tribe, then it is the entire tribe that acts together in unison. This form of political organization is called *segmentary opposition,* and it is not unique to tribal societies. We have it in our own political system. For example, the southern Democrats and the northern Democrats might disagree over whom to nominate for the presidency, but once a nominee is chosen, both will support that candidate. On a higher level, both the Republicans and the Democrats will support the American President, regardless of party, in opposition to the leader of another country. And if we should be invaded by creatures from outer space, we would probably overcome our differences with the Russians and join forces against what would be our common enemy. Segmentary opposition is merely a way of defining allegiance on different levels of organization, according to the scope of the problem.

The tribal form of segmentary political organization is perhaps the simplest type of politi-

In some cultures even the rules for warfare are carefully laid out to keep fatalities at a minimum. Dugum Dani tribesmen of New Guinea are engaged here in a ritual battle with their neighbors.

cal system, next to the egalitarian band. It offers an opportunity to organize behavior on different levels, but because it is so decentralized there is little power to enforce cooperation unless people themselves seek it out. As power becomes more concentrated in the hands of one or a few leaders, the political organization of the group becomes more complex. Such a system is frequently referred to as a *chiefdom,* where regional or tribal groups are organized under the authority of a single official. The chief can call upon the members of the group not just for political purposes, but usually he can organize economic activity or religious events as well. Thus the chief tends to be a strong force in bringing together the segments of the tribe, uniting them in a single group, while retaining a greater degree of authority over the activity of each member.

The chiefdom is a significant case of tribal

political organization, for it is the beginning of centralized power which is so important in the ultimate evolution of the state-based society we are familiar with in the Western world. Also with the chiefdom comes the establishment of a system of ranking, or social stratification. In a band, all people are inherently equal, and while one man's greater skill as a hunter might give him more say in the organization of the hunt, it does not give him the right to more than his share of the kill. In a small tribal society the same holds true. A person might be recognized for some achievement or skill and obtain a certain amount of power or influence for it, but such power can change with the fortunes of the individual.

In a chiefdom, the headman is entitled to special treatment because of his position, and his family, lineage and village all the way down the line are able to share in his prestige and high position. The chief may be in a position to tax the population and allocate the goods in a program of redistribution. Such power can easily lead to an increase in the ranking differences within the society, for the reallocation of goods will entrench the chief and other higher ranking members in their elevated positions. It can also lead to an increase in the size of the society held together under one central authority. Traditional Hawaii was a chiefdom, with a population of over 100,000. As the chiefdom becomes more centralized, concentrating more power in the hands of a single individual, the society grows more like a state.

State Organization

A *state* is essentially a territorially based government with strong power to organize and carry out activity for the achievement of group goals. It is the most common form of political organization in Western societies, although as we have seen, it is by no means the only type of political system that can exist. There is no sharp distinction between a chiefdom and a state, just as there is no clear line dividing a chiefdom from a tribe. Indeed, there can be elementary forms of state organization headed by someone whom we might call a chief, in that his position is not as a secular leader (such as a president or prime minister), but is a religious and perhaps even a kinship position as well.

The state is distinguished from other forms of political organization in the degree to which it can force people to act in certain ways. Its authority can be defined on religious grounds or it can be a secular authority, such as that in our own society where the coercive power of government rests with "the will of the people." The main feature setting the state apart from a chiefdom is the fact that the state is backed by the threat of force to coerce individuals. Along with this power goes a division into classes and, with more developed state governmental organizations, a bureaucracy as well, which distinguishes the political institutions from the rest of society.

LAW AND SOCIAL CONTROL

Politics, as the legitimate use of force or authority in a society, is closely related to law and social control. The anthropologist who studies this area of social behavior is interested not only in the formal definitions of rules, but in the way people actually act, whether they conform to the rules or not. We assume that the rules people follow reflect their basic values, but at the same time we have to assume that the formal rules that they recognize are not always a true indicator of the way they behave. Since laws are a guide to what is appropriate behavior in a particular society, we can learn from them what kinds of actions people consider to be contrary to their values, and the degree of punishment can also indicate the extent of the transgression. In our own society we can get a clear picture of American values by looking at various actions that are defined as illegal, and comparing punishment generally associated with each crime. A minor traffic offense calls for a small fine, while petty theft might land the culprit in jail for a short time. In contrast, armed robbery would probably meet with a stiffer sentence than the white collar crime of embezzlement, even though the armed robber might net only a few dollars while the embezzler could get away with millions. Right away this tells us something about American values related to violence.

The same kinds of insights can help the anthropologist understand something about the values shared by people in other societies. We also recognize that not all legal sanctions are formal or written down in a code of laws. There are many rules that people are expected to follow, and for which they are punished in some sense if they do not. Social control can work in very subtle ways to mold the behavior of the members of a group, by such practices as exclusion from group activities, gossip, or even open criticism. The offense can be as simple as failure to observe proper table manners—by no means breaking the law, but nonetheless a transgression against the shared values of the rest of society. We are all subject to such pressure, as you will recognize immediately in looking at the clothes you wear, the way you speak, the places you go and the people with whom you associate.

An example of how a legal system operates in a society different from our own will illustrate the basic assumptions that anthropologists make about the role of laws in the process of social control. Among Eskimos there are no specialized legal institutions such as we have in our courts, our police departments and the like. The prevailing principle in Eskimo law is that when someone violates your rights, you must take the law into your own hands and seek to correct the situation yourself. No matter who has the right on his side, the ultimate outcome usually depends upon who has the power and strength. This does not mean that the biggest and toughest individual can bully everyone else around, however, because if the offense is too blatant or repeated too often, he will find that his opponent's relatives step in against him, while his own kinsmen quietly turn the other way.

If a member of an Eskimo community is considered undesirable by the rest of the group, he may be removed either by exile or by execution. But even here, there is no strictly legal institution to deal with the situation; instead, an injured party can gather enough support for his cause, and then the offender's family will be asked to impose the sentence. In this way, no feuds can develop, an important factor to consider in an environment where people must cooperate in order to survive. Thus if we look closely at legal behavior in Eskimo society, we can see how the basic values of ruggedness, individuality and the struggle for survival are reinforced in the way people deal with behavior that violates the rules of conduct.

As with Eskimo society, in the Trobriand Islands most minor infractions are counteracted by self-help, that is, it is the individual's obligation to right any wrong that has been done to him. If a feud should start, there are recognized ways to end the disagreement without a great deal of bloodshed. The community can enforce a solution by first ending the fighting, and then mediating between the parties involved. One possibility is a "bloodwealth" to be paid by the offender—and the community may have to force the victim to accept such payment if he is unwilling. Another option is to resort to some kind of harmless contest, in which the disputants can settle their grievance without bloodshed. The Eskimos have a tradition known as a "song duel," in which each combatant tries to outdo the other in inventing songs that shame and ridicule the opponent. The group sits around and listens to the "duel," and eventually offers its judgment as to the victorious songster. Similar solutions can be reached through wrestling matches or other contests of strength in which no lasting damage is done. The alternative if the feud is allowed to continue is a situation in which the entire society is torn apart into warring camps, as in the famous legend of the Hatfields and McCoys.

An interesting aspect of the anthropological study of law occurs when two cultures come into contact and the legal system of one does not fit in with that of the other. Such a case was described by the columnist Anthony Lewis in a story reported in the International *Herald Tribune* several years ago. In this case, a man from a rural village in what used to be British East Africa (now Tanzania) was charged with murdering an old woman. He pleaded self-defense, claiming that she was a witch and had threatened to kill him through her use of magic. The man related to the court how one of his children became ill and eventually died. The old woman, who was a relative of the man, had been assigned the task of preparing the boy's funeral, but she had refused to do so, claiming she had cast a spell on the child. Instead, she had threatened to kill the man and his entire family. Shortly thereafter another child died, but when the man demanded that the woman cease her witchcraft, she had simply laughed at him and told him he was next. He left, and returned with an axe, which he used to kill her. Then he turned himself in.

The question for the anthropologist, or for any student of comparative law, is how to reconcile the interaction of two legal systems based upon two sets of values and moral codes. From the one standpoint, the man was clearly justified in killing the old woman, for his belief in witchcraft was genuine, and his fear was seemingly supported by the death of two of his child-

ren. However, from another point of view, there is a significant difference between the violent act of killing someone with an axe and the comparatively passive, and to some minds unsubstantiated, act of killing someone with witchcraft. Before reading on to see how the judges decided the case, you might stop and think what you would do if asked to sit on the jury.

Initially the man was convicted and sentenced to death. The case was then appealed to a panel of three judges, each of whom offered a different opinion. The first judge claimed that while the man's beliefs were unquestionably sincere, the law of the land had to be based upon reason, and a belief in witchcraft was simply unreasonable. If the newly developing country were to advance beyond its primitive background, such beliefs would have to be discouraged. The new law of the land was English common law, and witchcraft was unacceptable in that context. The second judge held that what was important was not the technicality of English law, but the motivation that drove the defendant to commit the murder. In this case, the man's motives were justifiable, and he should be judged not guilty. The third judge pulled the whole case together, rejecting the interpretations of the first two. While traditional beliefs were sincere, he argued that the country could not move ahead on that basis. And while English traditions were in many ways more "rational," they could not be strictly applied outside the cultural context in which they arose. Instead, the solution should be a compromise between the two systems: The man should be judged guilty, to emphasize the wrong he had committed, but he should be given a lighter sentence, in recognition of the basis for his crime. The important lesson for students of anthropology is that law and social control are culture-bound, and reflect the system of which they are a part. There are no absolute truths that can form the basis for any legal system, and there are no rights or wrongs which can be argued in all cultural contexts.

We can also learn much about the inequities in our own legal system from studying law in other cultures. If we recognize that American society is made up of many segments with vast cultural differences, we must be willing to apply this understanding to the way our own laws are interpreted. The values and moral codes of Americans are different according to the various life styles that we follow. The resident of an inner-city ghetto faces different problems from the suburban middle-class individual or the rural farmer, and thus must find different solutions to those problems. Yet many of our laws are rigidly structured and do not take into account these cultural differences.

Let us consider, for example, the different ways of expressing disagreement or hostility in American culture—a linguistic question, but one that reflects cultural differences. If a middle-class white businessman were to say, "I do not agree with the policies of the President," we would probably think nothing of it. However, if a militant Black Nationalist were to say something like "Off the pig President," he might run the risk of being arrested for threatening the life of the President, even though in his cultural context the meaning of his words was the same. To prove that it is the culturally determined set of values and not the individual himself that is affected by the rigidity of the law, consider the typical ballgame taunt, "Kill the umpire!" Surely no one was ever arrested for threatening the life of another person with such a cheer. Literally speaking, it is every bit as threatening as "Off the pig!" but the cultural context is different, in that a sports event is an acceptable vehicle for expressing hostility and a public rally against a political figure sometimes is not.

Finally, if we are to study social control and understand the nature of law cross-culturally, we must recognize that there is a positive side to

Civil disobedience and public protest are long-standing traditions in American culture.

conflict. Opposition to an outside force can bind a group together by strengthening the group consciousness and promoting identity. Conflict can preserve the group by offering a safety valve for aggression and hostility. In fact, the absence of conflict does not necessarily imply stability, because there may be the potential for tremendous upheaval (as in a society ruled by a strong military dictatorship that allows no dissent). Moreover, conflict can serve to unite people who might otherwise never have come together in a joint venture. Every four years people find themselves working in support of a political candidate, side by side with others who are quite unlike themselves. An even stronger example occurs in time of war, when men and women from all walks of life are brought together in the armed services and forced to share a common life style and depend upon each other for their survival. The solidarity promoted by conflict in such an instance is perhaps the strongest possible bond.

Focus

Elliot Liebow   ## Men and Jobs

In the following article, Elliot Liebow points out how in one segment of our society economic decisions are based upon a set of values quite different from what we normally assume to be the "American way." More important, he shows how these decisions are rational, given the conditions affecting the people who make them. In addition, he points out how middle-class Americans are culture-bound in expecting all others to act as they do, and in critcizing them for acting differently, without bothering to go to the trouble of investigating and evaluating the different circumstances in which other people live.

Reprinted from Elliot Liebow, *Tally's Corner*. Boston: Little, Brown and Company, Inc. (1967). Abridged with permission.

A pickup truck drives slowly down the street. The truck stops as it comes abreast of a man sitting on a cast-iron porch and the white driver calls out, asking if the man wants a day's work. The man shakes his head and the truck moves on up the block, stopping again whenever idling men come within calling distance of the driver. At the Carry-out corner, five men debate the question briefly and shake their heads no to the truck. The truck turns the corner and repeats the same performance up the next street. In the distance, one can see one man, then another, climb into the back of the truck and sit down. In starts and stops, the truck finally disappears.

What is it we have witnessed here? A labor scavenger rebuffed by his would-be prey? Lazy, irresponsible men turning down an honest day's pay for an honest day's work? Or a more complex phenomenon marking the intersection of economic forces, social values and individual states of mind and body?

Let us look again at the driver of the truck. He has been able to recruit only two or three men from each twenty or fifty he contacts. To him, it is clear that the others simply do not choose to work. Singly or in groups, belly-empty or belly-full, sullen or gregarious, drunk or sober, they confirm what he has read, heard and knows from his own experience: these men wouldn't take a job if it were handed to them on a platter.

Quite apart from the question of whether or not this is true of some of the men he sees on the street, it is clearly not true of all of them. If it were, he would not have come here in the first place; or having come, he would have left with an empty truck. It is not even true of most of them, for most of the men he sees on the street this weekday morning do, in fact, have jobs. But since, at the moment, they are neither working nor sleeping, and since they hate the depressing room or apartment they live in, or because there is nothing to do there, or because they want to get away from their wives or anyone else living there, they are out on the street, indistinguishable from those who do not have jobs or do not want them. Some, like Boley, a member of a trash-collection crew in a suburban housing development, work Saturdays and are off on this weekday. Some, like Sweets, work nights cleaning up middle-class trash, dirt, dishes and garbage, and mopping the floors of the office buildings, hotels, restaurants, toilets and other public places dirtied during the day. Some men work for retail businesses such as liquor stores which do not begin the day until ten o'clock. Some laborers, like Tally, have already come back from the job because the ground was too wet for pick and shovel or because the weather was too cold for pouring concrete. Other employed men stayed off the job today for personal reasons: Clarence to go to a funeral at eleven this morning and Sea Cat to answer a subpoena as a witness in a criminal proceeding.

Also on the street, unwitting contributors to the impression taken away by the truck driver, are the halt and the lame. The man on the cast-iron steps strokes one gnarled arthritic hand with the other and says he doesn't know whether or not he'll live long enough to be eligible for Social Security. He pauses, then adds matter-of-factly, "Most times, I don't care whether I do or don't." Stoopy's left leg was polio-withered in childhood. Raymond, who looks as if he could tear out a fire hydrant, coughs up blood if he bends or moves suddenly. The quiet man who hangs out in front of the Saratoga apartments has a steel hook strapped onto his left elbow. And had the man in the truck been able to look into the wine-clouded eyes of the man in the green cap, he would have realized that the man did not even understand he was being offered a day's work.

Others, having had jobs and been laid off, are drawing unemployment compensation (up to $44 per week) and have nothing to gain by accepting work which pays little more than this and frequently less.

Still others, like Bumdoodle the numbers man, are working hard at illegal ways of making money, hustlers who are on the street to turn a dollar any way they can buying and selling sex, liquor, narcotics, stolen goods, or anything else that turns up.

Only a handful remains unaccounted for. There is Tonk, who cannot bring himself to take a job away from the corner, because, according to the other men, he suspects his wife will be unfaithful if given the opportunity. There is Stanton, who has not reported to work for four days now, not since Bernice disappeared. He bought a brand new knife against her return. She had done this twice before, he said, but not for so long and not without warning, and he had forgiven her. But this time, "I ain't got it in me to forgive her again." His rage and shame are there for all to see as he paces the Carry-out and the corner, day and night, hoping to catch a glimpse of her.

And finally, there are those like Arthur, able-bodied men who have no visible means of support, legal or illegal, who neither have jobs nor want them.

The truck driver, among others, believes the Arthurs to be representative of all the men he sees idling on the street during his own working hours. They are not, but they cannot be dismissed simply because they are a small minority. It is not enough to explain them away as being lazy or irresponsible or both because an able-bodied man with responsibilities who refuses work is, by the truck driver's definition, lazy and irresponsible. Such an answer begs the question. It is descriptive of the facts; it does not explain them.

Putting aside, for the moment, what the men say and feel, and looking at what they actually do and the choices they make, getting a job, keeping a job, and doing well at it is clearly of low priority. Arthur will not take a job at all. Leroy is supposed to be on his job at 4:00 P.M. but it is already 4:10 and he still cannot bring himself to leave the free games he has accumulated on the pinball machine in the Carry-out. Tonk started a construction job on Wednesday, worked Thursday and Friday, then didn't go back again. On the same kind of job, Sea Cat quit in the second week. Sweets had been working three months as a busboy in a restaurant, then quit without notice, not sure himself why he did so. A real estate agent, saying he was more interested in getting the job done than in the cost, asked Richard to give him an estimate on repairing and painting the inside of a house, but Richard, after looking over the job, somehow never got around to submitting an estimate. During one period, Tonk would not leave the corner to take a job because his wife might prove unfaithful; Stanton would not take a job because his woman had been unfaithful.

Thus, the man-job relationship is a tenuous one. At any given moment, a job may occupy a relatively low position on the streetcorner scale of real values. Getting a job may be subordinated to relations with women or to other non-job considerations; the commitment to a job one already has is frequently shallow and tentative.

Objective economic considerations are frequently a controlling factor in a man's refusal to take a job. How much the job pays is a crucial question but seldom asked. He knows how much it pays. Working as a stock clerk, a delivery boy, or even behind the counter of liquor stores, drug stores and other retail businesses pays one dollar an hour. So, too, do most busboy, car-wash, janitorial and other jobs available to him. Some jobs, such as dishwasher, may dip as low as eighty cents an hour and others, such as elevator operator or work in a junk yard, may offer $1.15 or $1.25. Take-home pay for jobs such as these ranges from $35 to $50 a week, but a take-home pay of over $45 for a five-day week is the exception rather than the rule.

One of the principal advantages of these kinds of jobs is that they offer fairly regular work. Most of them involve essential services and are therefore somewhat less responsive to business conditions than are some higher paying, less menial jobs. Most of them are also inside jobs not dependent on the weather, as are construction jobs and other higher-paying outside work.

Another seemingly important advantage of working in hotels, restaurants, office and apartment buildings and retail establishments is that they frequently offer an opportunity for stealing on the job. But stealing can be a two-edged sword. Apart from increasing the cost of the goods or services to the general public, a less obvious result is that the practice usually acts as a depressant on the employee's own wage level. Owners of small retail establishments and other employers frequently anticipate employee stealing and adjust the wage rate accordingly. Tonk's employer explained why he was paying Tonk $35 for a 55–60-hour workweek. These men will all steal, he said. Although he keeps close watch on Tonk, he estimates that Tonk steals from $35 to $40 a week. What he steals, when added to his regular earnings, brings his take-home pay to $70 or $75 per week. The employer said he did not mind this because Tonk is worth that much to the business. But if he were to pay Tonk outright the full value of his labor, Tonk would still be stealing $35–$40 per week and this, he said, the business simply would not support.

This wage arrangement, with stealing built-in, was satisfactory to both parties, with each one independently expressing his satisfaction. Such a wage-theft system, however, is not as balanced and equitable as it appears. Since the wage level rests on the premise that the employee will steal the unpaid value of his labor, the man who does not steal on the job is penalized. And furthermore, even if he does not steal, no one would believe him; the employer and others believe he steals because the system presumes it.

Nor is the man who steals, as he is expected to, as well off as he believes himself to be. The employer may occasionally close his eyes to the worker's stealing but not often and not for long. He is, after all, a businessman and cannot always find it within himself to let a man steal from him, even if the man is stealing his own wages. Moreover, it is only by keeping close watch on the worker that the employer can control how much is stolen and thereby protect himself against the employee's stealing more than he is worth. From this viewpoint, then, the employer is not in wage-theft collusion with the employee. In the case of Tonk, for instance, the employer was not actively abetting the theft. His estimate of how much Tonk was stealing was based on what he thought Tonk was able to steal despite his own best efforts to prevent him from stealing anything at all. Were he to have caught Tonk in the act of stealing, he would, of course, have fired him from the job and perhaps called the police as well. Thus, in an actual if not in a legal sense, all the elements of entrapment are present. The employer knowingly provides the conditions which entice (force) the employee to steal the unpaid value of his labor, but at the same time he punishes him for theft if he catches him doing so.

Other consequences of the wage-theft system are even more damaging to the employee. Let us, for argument's sake, say that Tonk is in no danger of entrapment; that his employer is willing to wink at the stealing and that Tonk, for his part, is perfectly willing to earn a little, steal a little. Let us say, too, that he is paid $35 a week and allowed to steal $35. His money income—as measured by the goods and services he can purchase with it—is, of course, $70. But not all of his income is available to him for all purposes. He cannot draw on what he steals to build his self-respect or to measure his self-worth. For this, he can draw only on his earnings—the amount given him publicly and voluntarily in exchange for his labor. His "respect" and "self-worth" income remains at $35—only half that of the man who also receives $70 but all of it in the form of wages. His earnings publicly measure the worth of his labor to his employer, and they are important to others and to himself in taking the measure of his worth as a man.

With or without stealing, and quite apart from any interior processes going on in the man who refuses such a job or quits it casually and without apparent reason, the objective fact is that menial jobs in retailing or in the service trades simply do not pay enough to support a man and his family. This is not to say that the worker is underpaid; this may or may not be true. Whether he is or not, the plain fact is that, in such a job, he cannot make a living. Nor can he take much comfort in the fact that these jobs tend to offer more regular, steadier work. If he cannot live on the $45 or $50 he makes in one week, the longer he works, the longer he cannot live on what he makes.

Construction work, even for unskilled laborers, usually pays better, with the hourly rate ranging from $1.50 to $2.60 an hour. Importantly, too, good references, a good driving record, a tenth grade (or any high school) education, previous experience, the ability to "bring police clearance with you" are not normally required of laborers as they frequently are for some of the jobs in retailing or in the service trades.

Construction work, however, has its own objective disadvantages. It is, first of all, seasonal work for the great bulk of the laborers, beginning early in the spring and tapering off as winter weather sets in. And even during the season the work is frequently irregular. Early or late in the season, snow or temperatures too low for concrete frequently sends the laborers back home, and during late spring or summer, a heavy rain on Tuesday or Wednesday, leaving a lot of water and mud behind it, can mean a two- or three-day workweek for the pick-and-shovel men and other unskilled laborers.

The elements are not the only hazard. As the project moves from one construction stage to another, laborers—usually without warning—are laid off, sometimes permanently or sometimes for weeks at a time. The more fortunate or the better workers are told periodically to "take a walk for two, three days."

Both getting the construction job and getting to it are also relatively more difficult than is the case for the menial jobs in retailing and the service trades. Job competition is always fierce. In the city, the large construction projects are unionized. One has to have ready cash to get into the union to become eligible to work on these projects and, being eligible, one has to find an opening. Unless one "knows somebody," say a foreman or a laborer who knows the day before that they are going to take on new men in the morning, this can be a difficult and disheartening search.

Many of the nonunion jobs are in suburban Maryland or Virginia. The newspaper ads say, "Report ready to work to the trailer at the intersection of Rte. 11 and Old Bridge Rd., Bunston, Virginia (or Maryland)," but this location may be ten, fifteen, or even twenty-five miles from the Carry-out.

Heavy, backbreaking labor of the kind that used to be regularly associated with bull gangs or concrete gangs is no longer characteristic of laboring jobs, especially those with the larger, well-equipped construction companies. Brute strength is still required from time to time, as on smaller jobs where it is not economical to bring in heavy equipment or where the small, undercapitalized contractor has none to bring in. In many cases, however, the conveyor belt has replaced the wheelbarrow or the Georgia buggy, mechanized forklifts have eliminated heavy, manual lifting, and a variety of digging machines have replaced the pick and shovel. The result is fewer jobs for unskilled laborers and, in many cases, a work speed-up for those who do have jobs. Machines now set the pace formerly set by men. Formerly, a laborer pushed a wheelbarrow of wet cement to a particular spot, dumped it, and returned for another load. Another laborer, in hip boots, pushed the wet concrete around with a shovel or a hoe, getting it

roughly level in preparation for the skilled finishers. He had relatively small loads to contend with and had only to keep up with the men pushing the wheelbarrows. Now, the job for the man pushing the wheelbarrow is gone and the wet concrete comes rushing down a chute at the man in the hip boots who must "spread it quick or drown."

Men who have been running an elevator, washing dishes, or "pulling trash" cannot easily move into laboring jobs. They lack the basic skills for "unskilled" construction labor, familiarity with tools and materials, and tricks of the trade without which hard jobs are made harder. Previously unused or untrained muscles rebel in pain against the new and insistent demands made upon them, seriously compromising the man's performance and testing his willingness to see the job through.

In summary of objective job considerations, then, the most important fact is that a man who is able and willing to work cannot earn enough money to support himself, his wife, and one or more children. A man's chances for working regularly are good only if he is willing to work for less than he can live on, and sometimes not even then. On some jobs, the wage rate is deceptively higher than on others, but the higher the wage rate, the more difficult it is to get the job, and the less the job security. Higher-paying construction work tends to be seasonal and, during the season, the amount of work available is highly sensitive to business and weather conditions and to the changing requirements of individual projects. Moreover, high-paying construction jobs are frequently beyond the physical capacity of some of the men, and some of the low-paying jobs are scaled down even lower in accordance with the self-fulfilling assumption that the man will steal part of his wages on the job.

When we look at what the men bring to the job rather than at what the job offers the men, it is essential to keep in mind that we are not looking at men who come to the job fresh, just out of school perhaps, and newly prepared to undertake the task of making a living, or from another job where they earned a living and are prepared to do the same on this job. Each man comes to the job with a long job history characterized by his not being able to support himself and his family. Each man carries this knowledge, born of his experience, with him. He comes to the job flat and stale, wearied by the sameness of it all, convinced of his own incompetence, terrified of responsibility—of being tested still again and found wanting. Possible exceptions are the younger men not yet, or just, married. They suspect all this but have yet to have it confirmed by repeated personal experience over time. But those who are or have been married know it well. It is the experience of the individual and the group; of their fathers and probably their sons. Convinced of their inadequacies, not only do they not seek out those few better-paying jobs which test their resources, but they actively avoid them, gravitating in a mass to the menial, routine jobs which offer no challenge—and therefore pose no threat—to the already diminished images they have of themselves.

Thus Richard does not follow through on the real estate agent's offer. He is afraid to do on his own—minor plastering, replacing broken windows, other minor repairs and painting—exactly what he had been doing for months on a piecework basis under someone else (and which provided him with a solid base from which to derive a cost estimate).

A crucial factor in the streetcorner man's lack of job commitment is the overall value he places on the job. *For his part, the streetcorner man puts no lower value on the job than does the larger society around him.* He knows the social value of the job by the amount of money the employer is willing to pay him for doing it. In a real sense, every pay day, he counts in dollars and cents the value placed on the job by society at large. He is no more (and frequently less) ready to quit and look for another job than his employer is ready to fire him and look for another man. Neither the streetcorner man who performs these jobs nor the society which requires him to perform them assesses the job as one "worth doing and worth doing well." Both employee and employer are contemptuous of the job. The employee shows his contempt by his reluctance to accept it or keep it, the employer by

paying less than is required to support a family. Nor does the low-wage job offer prestige, respect, interesting work, opportunity for learning or advancement, or any other compensation. With few exceptions, jobs filled by the streetcorner men are at the bottom of the employment ladder in every respect, from wage level to prestige. Typically, they are hard, dirty, uninteresting and underpaid. The rest of society (whatever its ideal values regarding the dignity of labor) holds the job of the dishwasher or janitor or unskilled laborer in low esteem if not outright contempt. So does the streetcorner man. He cannot do otherwise. He cannot draw from a job those social values which other people do not put into it.

What lies behind the response to the driver of the pickup truck, then, is a complex combination of attitudes and assessments. The streetcorner man is under continuous assault by his job experiences and job fears. His experiences and fears feed on one another. The kind of job he can get—and frequently only after fighting for it, if then—steadily confirms his fears, depresses his self-confidence and self-esteem until finally, terrified of an opportunity even if one presents itself, he stands defeated by his experiences, his belief in his own self-worth destroyed and his fears a confirmed reality.

Summary

The three topics of this chapter, economics, politics and social control, are not unrelated institutions, but are closely tied together. While in complex industrial states the political, economic and legal institutions are separate, in many societies economics, politics and law are three different types of behavior within the same institutional framework. People do not conceive of their actions in terms of whether they are political, as separate from economic.

In studying economic behavior, the anthropologist recognizes that different principles govern the decisions people make in other societies. While we consider maximization of profit to be the driving force in our own society, in another cultural context other factors might be more important—the obligations of kinship, the feelings one has about the environment, or the sentimental attachment one develops to the land or to cultural traditions.

The same is true of the anthropological approach to politics. Through studying political organization in other societies we recognize the operation of principles that are in many ways foreign to our ideas about how to run a complex state organization. The band is made up of equals; decisions are derived from a consensus of the members, and feuding is avoided. The tribe contains more people, but still we find politics closely integrated with the rest of the social structure, not set off as a separate institution. In a chiefdom we begin to see the division of society into stratified groups and the centralization of power. But it is not until the state that we have a separate group whose task is to rule the society, vested with the authority to do so and backed up by the power to coerce people to behave in a certain way, even if it is against their will. It is only with the state that we have a truly separate political institution, distinguishable (at least to some degree) from religion, economics, the family and other social institutions.

Law and politics can be distinguished in that law is a way of organizing society to deal with internal matters, whereas politics organizes the society to deal with outside groups. The anthropologist who studies law is concerned both with formal rules defining appropriate behavior and with informal or unwritten rules, which can be just as powerful and effective in regulating the way people act. We recognize that while all societies have some form of law, there are no absolute laws that exist in every society throughout the world. A law is a statement about culturally determined values. In our own society, where there is a great deal of cultural diversity, we find many problems in our written legal system, which ignores cultural differences. The cross-cultural perspective of the anthropologist offers us a better understanding of these problems, and the hope of finding a workable solution.

Glossary

band A form of political organization found primarily among hunting and gathering peoples. These groups, usually composed of between 25 and 40 individuals, are loosely organized and tend to be based on a principle of equality.

bloodwealth A social sanction found in Trobriand society to settle disputes and avoid feuding between individuals or groups. The bloodwealth is a payment made by an offender to a victim.

chiefdom A political system in which regional or tribal groups are organized under a centralized position of authority. The chiefdom is associated with a system of ranking or social stratification.

headman The leader of a group in which the authority is based upon the personal qualities of the individual, rather than in a formal position of authority.

industrial economy An economy based upon an advanced technology in a society where tasks are specialized and people perform different jobs. Production is almost exclusively for exchange.

jajmani system An economic system found in many peasant villages in India, based upon the caste system and its implied occupational specialization. In this highly stratified society, it is an institutionalized form of reciprocity.

Kula Ring A pattern of exchange found in some of the islands of Melanesia. The pattern combines an exchange of both ritual trade items and practical items in a yearly cycle between the islands.

law A formal system of rules that are a guide to the appropriate behavior in a particular society, backed by the threat of force.

market exchange A pattern of exchange based upon the law of supply and demand in which each individual attempts to maximize his profits by placing a value on labor and products.

peasant economy An economy in which there is a certain degree of self-sufficiency, and almost every individual is engaged in the production of food for consumption. Peasant producers, however, are tied into a wider market system and are not completely independent in their production.

politics The legitimate use of force or authority within a society. It is also the way by which people maintain peace within a group and define their group relative to the outside world.

potlatch A form of exchange combining redistribution and reciprocity, found among the aboriginal populations of the Pacific Northwest Coast of North America.

pratik The special personal relationship between a woman trader and her customers in the rural market system of Haiti.

primitive economy Small-scale economies, found among relatively isolated, self-sufficient groups in which the members share uniform experiences.

reciprocity A form of exchange involving an arrangement between groups in which items are given and expected in return.

redistribution A pattern of exchange in a stratified society in which there is a collection of goods by a central authority and then a reallocation of those goods to members of the society.

segmentary opposition A form of political organization in which a society is divided into groups, each subdivided into hierarchical units. Alliances are formed within each unit and they provide a mechanism for settling disputes either within the group or between groups.

social control The legal sanctions of a particular society that ensure conformity to the values of that society.

song duel A contest found among Eskimos that is designed to settle disputes without actual fighting.

state A territorially-based government, characterized by a centralization of authority in which people may be directed to follow certain rules by threat of force. There is a specialization of economic tasks and an associated stratification of society.

subsistence agriculture The production of food for one's own consumption.

tribe A confederation of groups who recognize a relationship to one another, usually in the form of common ethnic origin, common language, or a strong pattern of interaction based on intermarriage or presumed kinship.

Additional Reading

Bohannan, Paul (editor)
1967 Law and Warfare: Studies in the Anthropology of Conflict. Garden City, N.Y.: Natural History Press, Doubleday.

A collection of articles on law and warfare in non-Western societies.

Fried, Morton H.
1967 The Evolution of Political Society: An Essay in Political Anthropology. New York: Random House.

A textbook dealing with the anthropological

study of political organization in non-Western societies.

Heider, Karl
1970   The Dugum Dani. Chicago: Aldine.

A study of a tribal society in highland New Guinea, particularly interesting in contrast to the Kalahari Bushmen described by Thomas (see below). The Dugum Dani are perhaps best known for their ritualized warfare, which is depicted in the excellent ethnographic movie, *Dead Birds*.

LeClair, Edward E., Jr., and Harold K. Schneider (editors)
1968   Economic Anthropology. New York: Holt, Rinehart and Winston.

A collection of articles dealing with the major issues in economic anthropology, including the major theoretical division between the substantivist and formalist approaches.

Liebow, Elliot
1967   Tally's Corner. Boston: Little, Brown.

A study of the black ghetto of Washington, D.C., with a valuable perspective on the economics of ghetto life from an insider's point of view.

Nader, Laura (editor)
1968   Law in Culture and Society. Chicago: Aldine.

A collection of articles by anthropologists dealing with law and social control in cross-cultural perspective.

Thomas, Elizabeth Marshall
1959   The Harmless People. New York: Alfred A. Knopf.

A study of the Kalahari Bushmen, a hunting and gathering band.

chapter eighteen

I was born in the middle of human history. . . . Almost as much has happened since I was born as happened before.

KENNETH BOULDING

SOCIAL AND CULTURAL CHANGE IN ANTHROPOLOGY

If we were to compress the entire span of human life on the earth into a single day, agriculture would be invented around 11:56 P.M., people would begin to settle in towns and cities at 11:57, and the industrial revolution would begin shortly after 11:59:30. More change has occurred during the last 30 seconds of this "human day" than in all the time leading up to it.

The increased pace of change throughout the world has affected all contemporary cultures, and anthropologists study change just as they study religion, kinship or economics, to provide a complete picture of human societies.

Anthropologists also participate in projects that actively pursue improvements in the life of members of a society, applying anthropological concepts to practical ends. In this chapter, we will first look at the study of change from an anthropological perspective and then at the various ways anthropology can be useful in programs of social change.

People have been interested in change at least as far back as we have written records. The ancient Greeks compared their own society to that of the barbarians surrounding them and postulated an evolutionary scheme whereby they had emerged from a similar lower stage

489

themselves. Ever since then, as Western societies have come into contact with other peoples who were perhaps not as advanced technologically or who were different in some other way, writers have tried to explain the causes of these differences, that is, why Western society has advanced (or why non-Western society has declined).

Perhaps the most dominant intellectual tradition in the nineteenth century was evolution. Charles Darwin's earth-shaking work *The Origin of Species* (published in 1859), while recognized by many as the first major step toward the development of an evolutionary theory, was really the culmination of a long period of interest in evolution, the processes by which it worked, and the proof of its effect upon life. It is not surprising, then, that a similar trend should develop in anthropology, parallel to Darwin's work in biology, to describe social and cultural change in evolutionary terms. Differences between Western and non-Western cultures were explained as being the result of varying rates of change, or climbing up the evolutionary ladder toward civilization at different speeds.

ACCULTURATION

The challenge to nineteenth-century evolutionism was led by Franz Boas in the United States. Although Boas was an effective spokesman against evolutionism, his own work on the careful documentation of diffusion led to no alternative theory of social change. Boas was influential in the study of change, however, through the students he trained. Where Boas had been concerned with documenting the fact that an innovation had diffused, his followers in the next generation of anthropological investigations became aware of the importance of contact between two or more groups for the diffusion of culture. The result was that between about 1920 and 1950, a major school of an-

thropology arose, based upon the study of social and cultural change through culture contact, a process known as *acculturation*.

Acculturation can be defined as change that occurs when groups of individuals having different cultures come into continuous first-hand contact. This is a rather broad definition, taking into account many different kinds of change and situations of contact. It may help to examine acculturation studies in more detail, with specific examples, to see how anthropologists have viewed change arising out of contact between different groups.

One factor that can affect the exchange of elements of culture is the type of contact between two or more groups. For example, in some situations the contact is between two entire societies, or at least a representative cross-section of each. Thus, where two nonhostile Indian tribes moved into the same region we might expect a blending of culture as members of the two tribes interacted, perhaps intermarried, and in general shared their ways of life. On the other hand, many other situations involve only a selected segment of one society in contact with another. The contact between the Spanish conquerors and the Mexican Indians involved only a small portion of Spanish society, surely not representative of the entire culture. Similarly, American contact with the peoples of the Pacific Islands during World War II was also limited to a small part of American culture, the military. Other examples might affect the cultural exchange differently, as in the case of contact between missionaries from one culture and an entire group in another area, or between traders, miners, or other equally marginal members of a society.

Other interests in acculturation studies have to do with the process of change. What traits were ultimately borrowed by one culture, in what order, and with what resistance? Was a new innovation adopted exactly as it existed in the original culture, or was it changed to fit in

Contact between the Jaluo tribe of Kenya and Western cultures has resulted in the mixture of native and Western dress worn by these dancing women.

better with the borrowers' culture? Was there an element of prestige involved in borrowing? Answers to these and other questions were sought in an attempt to understand the process of cultural and social change, not only for interpreting events in the past, but to predict future change as well.

Plains Indian Culture: The Decline of Tradition

One early study of acculturation was carried out by Margaret Mead, who described the changing culture of a Plains Indian people who had been in contact with white society. At the time of her study in the early 1930s, the contact had been so recent and cataclysmic that adjustment had not been possible, and therefore her study concentrated on the problems of disorganization that resulted from the contact.

The Indians' initial contact with white culture was through fur traders, who introduced guns and steel traps to Indian culture. The second phase of contact was marked by white settlers in the region, the establishment of an Indian agency, a Presbyterian mission, and the disappearance of the buffalo. Finally, in the third phase, the Indians were pressured to abandon their traditional way of life (e.g., living in tipis, hunting, trapping, and fishing) and were encouraged to adopt the way of life of the typical rural white American. Mead points out that even with all these changes, the Indians might have been able to get by, but after a period of about 25 years they had to face the problem of increased white settlement which took their land away from them. The white settlers did not mingle with the Indians, but maintained separate cultures which kept them from getting along with one another. While the Indians were encouraged to adopt the white people's ways, at the same time they were prevented by white prejudice from participating in joint cultural ventures.

As Mead shows in her study of this culture contact, Indian religion broke down almost entirely under the pressure from white contact. Initially all the Indians converted to Presbyterianism as a result of the efforts of the white missionaries. But the new religion failed to provide them with the rewards it preached, and they soon turned to peyote cults for their religious needs. Peyotism also provided an outlet for their traditional ritual ceremonies which did not fit into the Presbyterian service. At the time Mead wrote of this situation, the peyote religion was still the predominant form among the tribe, and very little of either the original re-

Eugene Ray

Melville Jean Herskovits *(1895–1963) is known widely as the first American anthropologist to specialize in African studies, particularly Afro-American cultures in the New World. At a time when American anthropology was concerned primarily with native American cultures, Herskovits applied the same principles of analysis to Africa. After conducting fieldwork in Africa, he turned his attention to Afro-American cultures, particularly in the Caribbean, pointing out how African traditions are reworked into the way of life forced upon them in the New World. Herskovits' study of Afro-American culture led him to an interest in culture change, and he was a leading figure in the development of a school of anthropology concerned with the process of acculturation, or culture change through contact.*

ligious beliefs or the recently adopted white people's religion had been retained. Thus she describes a situation of cultural breakdown,

where contact between two cultures leads not to the sharing of elements of the cultures but to the disorganization and disintegration of a traditional way of life, and at the same time a rejection of much of the new way that is offered.

Caribbean Culture: The Blending of Traditions

In a study of acculturation in the Caribbean, Melville Herskovits describes the process of *syncretism,* the reinterpretation of new cultural elements to fit them in with the already existing traditions. Herskovits studied the introduction of Christian ideas into the religion of blacks in the New World, particularly the relationship between African gods and Catholic saints. He emphasizes that non-European people do not easily abandon their native religious beliefs and practices when confronted with Christianity. Rather, they usually react in one of two ways: they either try to perpetuate the old way and reject anything new; or else they take over the external form of the new elements but reinterpret them to fit into the old way, keeping the old values and meanings alive.

Herskovits cites examples of New World blacks in Cuba, Brazil and Haiti to illustrate this process. He says that while they profess nominal Catholicism, they still belong to cults that are under the direction of priests whose functions are essentially African and whose training follows traditional patterns of instruction and initiation. He also points to specific identifications between African gods and Catholic saints, showing how the content of the old religion is carried over into the form of the new.

Brought over to the New World as slaves, the Africans were baptized into the Catholic church in these countries. The whites tried to eliminate the traditional cults of the blacks, which they feared would serve as a focus for organizing revolutionary activities. Although the groups

Contact between their own culture and white missionaries and teachers resulted in the first formal "schools" for African children such as these.

were broken up to a certain extent, they did manage to continue on local levels. However, since they were officially banned, they were forced to take on a new appearance to hide their real nature. Thus in many of these cults, although the Catholic practices were adopted to placate the whites, they were only a mask for the continuation of traditional rituals.

Herskovits points to some examples of traditional African deities which have been reinterpreted in terms of the Catholic hierarchy of saints. *Legba* is a god in Dahomey who guards the crossroads and entrances to temples, residence compounds and villages. He is also widely worshipped in Haiti, where he must open the path for the supernatural powers. *Legba* is believed by most people from Dahomey who live in Haiti to be the same deity as St. Anthony. The reason for this identification is that the pictures commonly used to depict St. Anthony show him to be an old man, poorly dressed, carrying a cane to support him as he walks. The use of such a cane or wand is frequently attributed to *Legba* as well, who uses it to enforce his watch of the path, and to open the path to supernatural powers.

In a like manner, many other traditional deities are worked into the newly imposed Catholic tradition. Sometimes the saints are even equated with natural phenomena, such as the sun, moon and stars, rather than simply personified. St. John the Baptist, for example, is in some areas of the Caribbean worshipped as the deity who controls thunder and lightning. This is because in pictures of him he is frequently seen holding a lamb, and in traditional Dahomean mythology the ram is the emblem of the god of thunder. In the same vein, saints are added to the Catholic tradition to cover certain areas of the Old World tradition which are otherwise omitted in the Christian scriptures. For example, many blacks in the Caribbean worship such deities as *St. Soleil* (St. Sun), *Ste. la Lune* (St. Moon), *Sts. Etoiles* (Sts. Stars), and *Ste.*

la Terre (St. Earth). Herskovits' study of the contact between traditional African and white cultures in the Caribbean illustrates how flexible people can be in adopting new ways.

REVITALIZATION MOVEMENTS

As an offshoot of acculturation studies, anthropologists in the 1940s and 1950s turned their attention to a particular result of culture contact. As Western culture intruded more and more into the far corners of the world, bringing with it immense wealth and impressive technological mastery, many isolated and relatively unknown peoples saw their old way of life eroded. Helpless in the face of the pressure exerted by the new masters, formerly free and proud people found their traditions no longer effective. Frustration became a widespread social problem. One response was to give up the old ways and try to be like the white man, in the hope of gaining the desired elements of Western culture. Another alternative, practiced by many in response to their powerlessness, was to reject everything new and to preach a return to the "pure" culture of the good old days. Such efforts have been called "revitalization" movements in reference to their attempt to revitalize, or breathe new life into the old cultural patterns and traditions.

Early interest in revitalization movements among anthropologists began with the study of such phenomena as the Ghost Dance of the North American Indians in the late nineteenth century and the Cargo Cults of Melanesia in the twentieth century. Both types of movements arose primarily in response to the disintegration of the former way of life due to contact with white culture. One of the earliest discussions of these movements, as a particular type of response to similar conditions in different parts of the world and at different times, was offered by Anthony Wallace, who actually

These Indians are listening to a recorded address by President Woodrow Wilson.

coined the term "revitalization." He attempted to bring together a variety of movements and describe them in similar structural terms, demonstrating that such widely different occurrences as the rise of Christianity, the Ghost Dance of 1890, the Taiping Rebellion in China, and the Russian Revolution were all variations of the same process of social change.

The process of revitalization is based on dissatisfaction with the present system, and is an attempt by people to create more satisfactory conditions in which to live. What is so special about revitalization is that it is a conscious process designed to produce change, thus making it different from diffusion or acculturation as a type of cultural change. Wallace views revitalization as a reaction to stress: When an individual is faced with a problem, he must either change himself to be able to tolerate it, or else change the stress at its source. But when a group of people experience the same stress, and they choose to do something about it, they are in effect seeking to revitalize their way of life, their culture. They can accomplish this either by changing the physical reality or by altering the psychological reality (that is, their perception of the problem, rather than the root of the problem itself). In this way we can see basic similarities in such seemingly different responses as a passive religious movement that offers a new doctrine (thus changing the psychological reality of the problem) and a revolution, which seeks to change the actual physical cause of the stress through violent means.

The Ghost Dance

Revitalization movements can be classified into a number of different subtypes, which enables us to see even greater similarities, as well as to understand the different causes and reactions on the part of the people affected. First, there are what have been called "nativistic" movements, which place a strong emphasis on the elimination of alien persons, customs, values and materials from the culture. The term *nativism* refers to the attempt to return to the traditional or native cultural patterns and expel anything that is foreign from the culture. In such a movement, frequently certain aspects of the traditional culture are selected as being especially important, and are given symbolic value; rarely is the rejection of *all* new elements accomplished.

The Ghost Dance of the North American Indians is an excellent example of a nativistic movement. It arose out of the frustration experienced by many Indian tribes as a result of contact with the westward-moving whites. Forced to give up their traditional way of life, and stunned by the drastic change in the environment caused by the intrusion of white cul-

Blending ancient tradition with new materials, this Kenyan native wears a feathered headdress and a tin can bracelet as he smokes a Western cigarette.

ture (such as the virtual extermination of the buffalo, which had been so important to Indian culture), the Indians did not know where to turn. Many were forced onto reservations, and began to adopt white culture. They soon found that this was not the answer, for they shared more of the negative aspects of that new way of life than the benefits. They inherited alcoholism, racial discrimination, poverty and illiteracy, but no wealth, power or freedom. In short, the time was ripe for a new solution, one that did not require acquiescence to the authority of the white man.

An Indian prophet named Wovoka provided the answer. He experienced a religious vision, in which he saw into the future. The answer he conveyed to his people, which ultimately spread throughout the Great Plains to a number of Indian tribes, was for the Indian to reject the ways of the white man, return to the old traditions, and practice the new ritual of the Ghost Dance. When this task had been accomplished, that is, when Indian culture had once again become purified of the evil ways of the white man, the buffalo would return, and the dead ancestors of the Indians would ride out of heaven into battle to help them drive the whites from the earth. In some more radical versions of this prophecy it was claimed that those who adhered to the faith would be immune to the bullets of the white man's gun, and could ride into battle without fear of injury or death. It must have been a tragic sight to see a band of Indians riding up to a cavalry troop, armed only with bows and arrows yet secure in their belief that they would not be harmed.

Cargo Cults

A second type of revitalization movement is what has been called a "cargo cult," a term derived from a series of cults found in the Pacific Islands during and after World Wars I and II. Natives on many of these islands saw huge amounts of cargo being delivered to military and mission installations established by Western nations; but at the same time they realized that they were not sharing in the new wealth. They came to believe that if they adopted the ways of the foreigners, they too would be able to receive the cargo. Obviously they did not correctly perceive the relationship between the foreign customs and the delivery of the cargo, and the re-

sult was that they adopted Western dress patterns, built imitation air strips and boat docks, and waited for the planes and ships to deliver their reward.

Cargo cults are thus different from nativistic movements in that they seek to adopt new cultural patterns in order to revitalize their culture, rather than return to traditional ways of life. The earliest anthropological interest in cargo cults was Francis Williams' report in 1923 of such a movement among the native people in New Guinea. The movement was called the *Vailala Madness,* named after a town on the southern coast of New Guinea where it began in 1919. Faced with the technological and military superiority of the white culture, the people sought to adopt many of the alien ways. They destroyed many sacred objects and discontinued earlier ritual practices, substituting Christian elements for them. The actual "mad-

The traditional structure of many aboriginal tribes in Australia was destroyed by their first contact with white culture.

ness" was a dance involving frenzied, uncontrolled excitement, along with the destruction of religious and art treasures.

The doctrine of the Vailala Madness centered around two main themes. First, there was the expectation of the imminent return of the dead, primarily through the vehicle of a cargo ship similar to the steamers which were seen bringing goods to the whites. Second, probably as a result of their perception of the superiority of white culture, the natives adopted the belief that their ancestors were themselves white, and that the deceased who would return on cargo ships would thus be white. There were also many Christian elements in the doctrine of the movement, and many prominent leaders claimed they were Jesus Christ, and that the heavenly state they were expecting would be Jehovah's Land, as described in the Christian teachings.

A common element among all cargo cults is that they occurred in areas where there had been considerable contact with Western culture. In addition, they have occurred where people have not been able to participate in the higher standard of living that they have witnessed in the white community. Thus in the port towns, where the standard of living is higher, such movements have not arisen. Nor have they occurred in the more isolated areas of the Pacific, such as the interior of New Guinea, where European influence has not spread. Cyril Belshaw, an anthropologist who has investigated these movements throughout Melanesia (an area in the Pacific Islands), has concluded that the cults are caused by a change to a position halfway between the old and the new, coupled with the inability to change further. In other words, the people experience enough of the benefits of Western culture to want more, but just as their expectations rise ever higher, they are cut off. One result is that they imitate the ways of the white man, either out of respect or out of jealousy or hatred. It is interesting to compare this type of movement with the concept of nativism, to see how opposite responses to the same basic problem can arise, both generated by culture contact and the prospects of rapid change.

Millenarian Movements

A third type of revitalization movement is a *millenarian movement,* which emphasizes a transformation of the world designed and carried out by a supernatural power. Such a movement is based upon the belief in the coming of the millennium, when all wrongs will be set right. Frequently the millenarian movement takes on a messianic quality, inspired by a charismatic leader who generates a great deal of emotional involvement on the part of the followers. Most radical millenarian movements occur among oppressed peoples, indicating a correlation between social and economic conditions and this type of revitalization attempt.

The functions of these movements, as pointed out by the Italian anthropologist Vittorio Lanternari, tend to be quite varied. They serve as potent agents of change, creating a bridge between the future and the past. They connect religion and politics, for they often can serve as a prototype of a modern revolutionary movement. Revolutions, much like millenarian movements, are brought about by a combination of deprivation and frustration on the part of a large number of people who have seen their culture disintegrate. In many cases what started out as a local and small-scale millenarian movement mushroomed into a full-scale revolution.

The idea of a millennium is most often associated with the period of one thousand years found in the Judeo-Christian tradition, referring to the second coming of Christ. In a wider sense, however, it can be applied to any conception of a perfect age to come, or a perfect place

The Amish are known as the "plain people" because of their attempt to retain their traditional cultural values in the midst of a rapidly changing society.

to be attained. In addition, these movements usually demand of their followers some ordeal which will make them worthy, such as a difficult journey or pilgrimage, a ritual purification, or an act of violence. The idea of a millennium which will bring with it a Golden Age is espe-cially popular in situations of culture contact, but it can be the basis for a movement in a crisis situation which was not necessarily caused by the intrusion of a foreign culture. Famines, plagues, or other natural disasters can lead to a religion-based movement seeking to revitalize the culture, as can a major political upheaval.

Millenarian movements frequently anticipate the coming of a new age in the near future, and although they are vague about the actual mechanisms by which it will become a reality, they offer a plan for bringing it about. We can see an element of millenarianism in many of the major political movements in recent history. Communism, with its utopian view of the future, fits this model, and the Communist movement can be seen as the active force for such a change. Likewise, Nazism advocated a ritual purification that ultimately would lead to a new Golden Age. In these and other cases there are a number of similarities: the importance of charismatic leaders (e.g., Lenin, Hitler); the reliance upon magical properties, or symbolically important beliefs (the assumed invincibility of the German army in World War II closely parallels the notion of the immunity of the Indians to the white man's bullets); the elimination of foreign or unwanted elements from the culture, particularly symbolically important groups (the Russian aristocracy, the German Jews).

It is interesting to reflect on the causes of millenarian movements, and revitalization movements in general. What must happen to a group of people, or to their way of life, before they will actively seek to change things? How severely must their traditions be challenged and their values be negated before they are moved to act? One of the most plausible explanations has been presented by David Aberle, who suggests that the phenomenon of revitalization movements can be understood through the concept of what he calls "relative deprivation." He defines this as "a negative discrepancy be-

tween legitimate expectation and actuality"—
that is, a change over time that leads a group of
people to feel deprived relative to some other
standard. We can measure relative deprivation
by comparing the past to the present circumstances of a single group of people, such as the
impact that the disappearance of the buffalo
had upon the Indian. Thus the Indians of the
late nineteenth century felt deprived relative to
the conditions in which they themselves lived
not so many years earlier. Or we can compare
the present situation of one group to that of
another contemporary group, noting a difference which causes the disadvantaged group to
feel relatively deprived.

It is important to stress the notion of relativity, for as Aberle notes, it is not so much the
discomfort as the dissatisfaction that is a cause
of revitalization movements. For a hunting and
gathering society with an expectation (based on
experience) of going hungry one out of four
days, the failure to find game is not a relative
deprivation. However, for a middle-class American not to be able to afford meat every day is a
relative deprivation, not when compared to the
hunters and gatherers, but when compared to
the past circumstances in American society.

It is important to stress, too, that relative deprivation must exist on a group level for it to be
a significant force in bringing about a revitalization movement. If all of us as individuals feel
we are not accorded a high enough status or
that we are denied our fair share of the things
we strive for, while we might feel deprived on
an individual level, this is not a solid basis for a
social movement. But when conditions promoting dissatisfaction are widespread enough that
the feeling is common among a large proportion of the population, the potential exists for a
strong movement advocating social change.
The concept of relative deprivation thus has a
great deal of relevance for understanding
many of our own social problems today, and we
should be able to apply it, along with other con-

*Poverty is a relative condition. By American standards this
Kentucky family lives at the poverty level. By the standards of most
developing nations, however, they are well-clothed, well-housed,
and well-fed.*

cepts derived from the study of culture, to the solution of those problems.

MODERNIZATION

Modernization is the major theme in recent history, encompassing the social and cultural changes resulting from the Agricultural Revolution, the Industrial Revolution, and more recently the Atomic Revolution. It is a process that has occurred first in Western societies, but which has spread throughout the world, both by design and by chance. Although many of the earlier factors that contributed to modernization were not in fact of Western origin, the culmination of the various processes that have produced the industrial societies of the twentieth century has taken place primarily in Europe and the United States, and only very recently in non-Western countries such as Japan.

Anthropology has an important stake in the study of modernization. Since it is a process occurring in every country in some way or another, there is an urgent need for comparative studies to give us a cross-cultural perspective on the problems encountered in various parts of the world. Moreover, in most societies traditionally studied by anthropologists (tribal and peasant peoples), cultural patterns are changed through contact with the West. Changes ultimately influence the technology, economic order, patterns of social relationships, ideologies, every aspect of traditional life. However, we also recognize that whereas industrial technology grew up in Western countries, and thus was molded to fit the cultural patterns peculiar to those countries, when it is transplanted to the Third World it does not always fit in with the existing patterns in those cultures. As a result, anthropologists who have studied the traditional way of life of these peoples are now interested in how it is being changed

through contact with the West. Frequently they find that the changes in non-Western countries do not follow the pattern of industrialization in Europe and the United States, as the new technology must be modified to fit in with the existing values and traditions.

Modernization is a broad term covering a number of separate processes. It is usually assumed that these processes occur together, and that they are necessarily interrelated. By modernization we usually mean at least the following: economic growth, or *industrialization; urbanization;* and *Westernization.* In this section we shall look at each of these processes separately, comparing the original changes that took place in the West with examples of contemporary changes in the so-called developing nations of the Third World.

Industrialization

The growth of industry in any society cannot occur without related changes in agriculture. By the very fact that industry requires a large number of people to work in factories rather than on farms, there must be a transformation of agriculture so that fewer people can produce more food in order to supply the nonagricultural work force. Thus along with the *industrialization* of a country must come a commercialization of agriculture, so that surplus products can be transported to markets.

The significance of this process for the anthropologist who studies rural people in non-Western countries is obvious. Traditionally such people were *subsistence agriculturalists,* that is, they produced food primarily for their own consumption, with only a little surplus to take care of a few basic needs. They were not integrated into a national or international market system, and many of them even got along without cash, by trading their surplus directly for other products they needed. Industrialization

Urban living at its worst. Drawn to the cities in search of work, many people from simple rural cultures end up in squatter settlements such as this slum on the outskirts of Rio de Janeiro.

also meant a major change in the structure of the rural population, because at least in its early stages it required a larger work force than was available in the cities. Mass migration from rural areas to towns and cities has thus been a trend in industrializing countries. But more than that, it has been selective migration of people in a narrow age group, usually about 15 to 35 years of age, which has left the countryside with a rather uneven proportion of old people. Here the implications for rural life are evident, for without the input of new ideas and the pressure for change from the young, traditions become solidified and the relatively conservative rural communities take on an even more conservative character.

Another important change resulting from industrialization has affected the nature of the family. In a rural farm community the typical family is a large unit made up of several generations, not limited to parents and children. The farm is an ideal place for such a family unit, where there are a variety of tasks for persons of both sexes and all ages, and in a subsistence operation designed merely to produce food for the members of the group, all members of an extended family can carry their weight on the farm. But when the family moves to the city and enters into the industrial work force this is no longer the case. Here the crucial factor affecting the family becomes *mobility*: both geographical (or physical) mobility and social mobility, the ability to rise in the system of social stratification. The urban industrial family is frequently on the move, and the members on the fringe merely hold it back. In addition, the work situation in the city does not offer opportunities for extra members to contribute their share to the family economy, as they could on the farm, and they become a liability to the nuclear family unit that must support them. As a result, the process of modernization has caused a clear shift from the extended family pattern toward the norm of a nuclear family made up of parents and their unmarried offspring.

Urbanization

Urbanization includes not only the growth in the actual size of cities, but the growth in the number of cities and in the proportion of the population living in urban locations. It is generally considered closely related to industrialization because industry is usually located in cities, and people who work in industry must live nearby. In addition to the demographic (population) factors involved in the growth of cities, we generally mean something more by the term *urbanization,* a change not only in the physical nature of the city but in the psychological and cultural makeup of the people who move to the city. Of course, with the growth of cities there must be parallel growth in networks of communication and transportation, market systems, new technological advances, and a growing specialization of labor.

Anthropologists who study urbanization, however, are not only concerned with these broad-scale changes in the city, but also with the effects of city life upon formerly rural people. For example, in rural areas the identification of an individual is generally seen in terms of his family first, then his community. Rarely does an

isolated rural resident think in terms of nationalistic goals, or identify with the nation as a whole. Yet when he moves to the city he finds that his local orientation is no longer useful, and he must change his entire outlook toward the country of which he is a part, rather than the village or even the city. This change from localism to nationalism is connected with a major transformation of the values of the rural migrant, and can be seen as one of the most sweeping effects of urbanization.

Another difference between life in a small village and in the city is the nature of personal interaction. In a rural community everyone knows everyone else personally. People know about each other's pasts, about their interests, their peculiarities; it is hard to keep anything secret in a small village. On the other hand, the city is an anonymous place where a person can literally disappear. People are thrust into situations where they must interact with others whom they have never met. Personalism can no longer serve as the basis for such interaction, and instead people develop ways of dealing with each other in a formal manner according to prescribed rules of behavior. For the new migrant to the city this can be very difficult to adjust to, and can be a source of great frustration. To some extent it can be avoided by the creation of stronger neighborhood ties in areas where there is a high concentration of migrants. Thus we frequently find sections of large cities that are solidly ethnic, where a different language is spoken from the rest of the city, and where people still seem to have the kind of personal relationships that we might expect to find in a village. Such ethnic neighborhoods are adaptations to the city, attempts to maintain some of the old traditions and offer some sense of comfort and security to newcomers who are turned off by the impersonal nature of the rest of the city.

In moving from the country to the city, the migrant experiences a change from what an-

Many ethnic communities in large cities manage to retain a significant portion of their traditional culture.

share the same specialized interests. Of course, this does not all happen overnight. In many cases studied by anthropologists it has been found that even second-generation immigrants still cling to many of the traditions found in the rural areas from which their parents came. In his classic study, Oscar Lewis followed Mexican migrants from a small village to Mexico City, in an attempt to see how the pressures of city life affected their rural "folk" culture. In fact, he found that there was very little breakdown of traditional culture among first-generation migrants. Family ties remained strong, and the people formed what might be called an "urban village," an attempt to create an artificial folk culture in the midst of the city.

In other studies similar trends have been observed. Even in the United States today, rural migrants to cities have been known to resist the pressures of urbanization and maintain many folk traditions. For example, in the past two decades there has been a massive migration of Appalachians to urban areas in the Midwest, prompted by the decline in the two basic economic activities of the region, subsistence agriculture and coal mining. In countless studies of Appalachian migrants to the city it has been found that they maintain very strong ties with their families "back home." The migrants tend to live in parts of the city known as "Little Appalachia," such as the section known as "Uptown" Chicago, where an estimated 50,000 Appalachian migrants reside. They work together in the same factories, worship at the same churches, and in general resist the intrusion of urban culture into their lives wherever possible. Many migrants still communicate regularly with their families in Appalachia; on any Friday evening you can see an almost endless stream of cars heading south across the Ohio River at Cincinnati, Portsmouth or any other city along the river.

What do these two apparently contradictory trends—the simultaneous breakdown and

thropologists call the "folk" culture to the "urban" culture. He moves from a small, relatively isolated, homogeneous village to a large, impersonal, individualistic community. His family becomes less important as he is integrated into the industrial economy, and he turns instead to secular institutions and groups of people who maintenance of folk culture among urban migrants—tell us about the process of urbanization? For one thing, we can see how the traditional way of life that is functional in a small community setting can be a disadvantage to a person living in the city. Thus there will be pressure for the migrant to give up his old ways if he is to succeed in his new home. But at the same time, we can learn a valuable lesson about the nature of culture itself. Culture is basically conservative. We learn patterns of behavior easily in our childhood, but we give them up only with great difficulty as adults. This is why it takes at least one generation, usually more, to see a complete change from folk to urban culture. The migrants themselves tend to hold steadfastly to their traditions, fighting off any newfangled, "citified" ideas. Their children grow up in a kind of dualistic environment: Their parents teach them the old values, and their peers and others with whom they come in contact in the city teach them a new and different set of values. Sometimes they make the transition to urbanites smoothly in one generation, but, depending upon the strength of the urban village in which they are raised and the conservatism of their own cultural heritage, it can take much longer.

Westernization

Of all the aspects of modernization, the concept of *Westernization* is the most difficult to define. By this term we generally refer to the adoption of cultural patterns characteristic of Western society. Many of these changes have already been discussed, such as the predominance of the nuclear family, the rising status of women, and the growth of a market economy and an accompanying market mentality. But Westernization can occur without movement to the city, or without taking a job in industry, and at least as used here the term refers to changes in the values, attitudes, beliefs—the whole psycholog-

Rapid Westernization of developing nations results in some obvious incongruities. Here a Masai chief in traditional dress chats with a Western-dressed Kenyan at Royal College in Nairobi.

ical makeup of individuals in non-Western societies.

One of the most important influences in this process is the mass media. Through communication with the outside world, people in formerly isolated areas become aware of a new prestigious model. New products and materials are made available to people, and high prestige is attached to them. At the same time, although people are unaware of it, it is impossible to adopt a new material culture, including the products and increased standard of living of a newly industrialized and urbanized society, without some of the values associated with industrialization and urbanization rubbing off. For example, a man who used to work on his family farm cannot take a job in a factory without adopting some of the values that go with industrial labor. He will develop a new conception of time and efficiency, something that never had to be exact on the farm. He will begin to calculate the cash value of his labor, whereas on a subsistence-oriented farm his labor had no cash value. Punctuality and precision are basically Western values that were not found in most agricultural societies prior to the spread of Western culture and the beginning of modernization. This is not necessarily because Westerners are so different from people in the rest of the world, but rather because there are certain requirements (we might call them constraints) imposed by the conditions of industrial labor that bring about these values. And the same might be said for city life, with its anonymity and specialization: It is not that these cultural patterns are something innate in the nature of the people who live in Western countries, but rather that the urban industrial centers where these values and patterns were functional were initially located in the West.

We should recognize that Westernization is not an absolute necessity in industrialization. There is no single model of an industrial society that must be followed by all countries. Each culture has its own traditions and its own particular history and direction, and these differences will affect the form that modernization takes in any society. For example, it is generally assumed that part of the process of Westernization is the change from ascribed to achieved status—the introduction of the "merit system" and the elimination of personalism in an impersonal industrial setting. In our own society the idea of nepotism is unacceptable, for it is considered inefficient to promote someone on any basis other than merit. However, in Japanese society, where industrialization has been every bit as successful, this is not the case. A Japanese factory is conceived of as a family, and people are brought into it on that basis.

The factory management is very paternalistic in the way it treats the workers, a far cry from our own system where benefits have been won only through sometimes bitter battles between management and labor unions. The Japanese example proves that industry can operate without a total transformation of the native value system to conform to a Western model. While it is true that Western values usually make for more efficient production in industry, and thus are commonly adopted by the people of newly industrializing nations (although sometimes unknowingly), it is important to recognize the flexibility of any culture, and its ability to accept change without undergoing a total transformation.

MODERNIZATION: A CASE STUDY

The village of Kippel is nestled in a cul-de-sac valley high in the Swiss Alps, surrounded on four sides by mountains. Until recently traffic in and out of the valley was almost nonexistent, and the way of life of its few hundred residents was much the same as when the valley was first settled in the Middle Ages. Almost everyone practiced a mixed economy of agriculture and livestock raising, growing enough grain and potatoes to provide for their needs, and relying mainly upon dairy cattle for the remainder of their diet. Marriage was generally with someone from one of the four villages in the valley, for it was necessary to combine the inheritance of two individuals to provide enough land to support a family, and in addition the limited experience of young people with the outside world almost forced them to look for a spouse at home. Village life was marked by a great deal of cooperation in tasks which required more labor than one household could supply, and there were many such tasks due to the difficulties of farming steep slopes and transporting

The summer pastures around Kippel now serve also as winter ski slopes for tourists, representing a major change in the village economy.

crops or building materials vertically. Also typical of the traditional era of the valley was the dominance of the church (Roman Catholic) over every aspect of life, with many festivals and a great deal of ceremony surrounding daily activities.

Following World War II the Swiss government undertook a program of industrialization in the mountainous regions of the country. Railroad lines were extended into more isolated areas, water power projects required a large labor force to construct and then maintain dams, and many factories were built in mountain regions to promote industry there. A number of men from Kippel left agriculture during these years to take jobs in industry, at first constructing railroad lines, dams and factories, later working there. In 1961 a large aluminum factory was built less than an hour's drive from Kippel, and today more than twenty men from the village work in the factory. Most other men between 35 and 55 work as unskilled or semi-skilled laborers at similar jobs, and commute to work daily, or sometimes weekly, from their homes in Kippel.

The shift from agriculture to industry shortly after World War II led to many drastic changes in Kippel. The younger generation all at once became free to advance and get away from agriculture. Whereas formerly it was expected that when a boy finished primary school he would go to work on his father's farm, he was now expected to continue on in school and learn a trade, or in rare cases obtain even more training and take up a white collar job. Agriculture became something of a hobby for the old men, who were the only full-time farmers left in the village. But the new working class did not give up farming altogether, for there was still a strong feeling of insecurity in the new industrial jobs, and an attachment to the land and to the values of subsistence agriculture. As a result, these men became what is known as *worker-peasants,* that is, people who have gone to work in factories but who have maintained a small agricultural operation on the side. In Kippel, most of the work that was done in the small-scale farming operations is performed by women and young girls, relatives of the male head of the household. The man will help out on weekends and during his vacation, but the main responsibility for farming has definitely shifted. Younger men who have completed school and have better paying employment than their parents now have completely given up the idea of farming, and do not even maintain a small agricultural operation to qualify them as worker-peasants. Thus within one generation Kippel has gone from an agricultural village to a working-class suburb.

Other major economic changes have affected the village life style as well. About ten years ago

The traditional dress of the women of Kippel is now worn only occasionally, as a tourist attraction more than for the sake of tradition.

a group of investors purchased a large tract of land above the neighboring village and began plans to develop a ski resort. In all over $1 million was paid to the owners of this land,

many of them from Kippel. Within a few short years the tourist industry in Kippel and throughout the valley has mushroomed. Villagers now obtain low-interest, government subsidized loans to build new houses, and the typical house includes one flat for the owner's family and at least one or two additional flats to be rented to tourists. A man with such a house can earn as much from the rent he collects as he does from his unskilled job. Several new tourist-oriented projects have sprung up in the villages below the planned ski resort, including a new hotel in Kippel. And of course all of these projects create jobs for local residents, thus transforming the village economic scene once again from a working-class community to a tourist center whose main source of income is rapidly becoming the provision of services.

These economic changes have spelled the end of many traditional aspects of village culture. The communal labor that used to be such an important part of village life, promoting solidarity among the members of the community, now is almost nonexistent. Since there is no labor force engaged in agriculture, there is no interest in maintaining community projects, and when someone needs help today he usually has to pay for it. There is a new emphasis upon inheritance. Whereas formerly everyone sought to put together a complete agricultural unit including land in various parts of the valley and at various altitudes, today the heirs vie for land near the village that can be used as house sites. Formerly valuable agricultural land outside the village limits now has little value.

Marriage patterns have changed in recent years as a result of the economic transformation of the village. Improved transportation facilities and increased experience outside the village have led to a greater proportion of marriage with outsiders. People tend to marry younger today than they did a generation ago, for they are able to gain financial security much earlier than they could when they were planning to be-

Masks such as this one were once worn during a pre-Lenten festival similar to Mardi Gras. Now they are carved primarily for sale to tourists.

learned without going to the city. Finally, there has been a steady decline in the authority and influence of the church upon many younger people, as they broaden their outlook on life through their experiences away from the village.

What has happened in Kippel in the past 30 years is typical of the effects of modernization on small communities throughout the world. Industrialization reaches out and draws these communities into the mainstream of national culture, overcoming the differences that were such an important source of identity for the villagers. Some are pulled into the city, attracted by the promise of fame and fortune. Others, such as the people of Kippel, remain in their village, only to find that it, too, is becoming urbanized, if not in size then at least in its culture. What we are seeing in Europe, and to a lesser extent in the Third World, is the spread of a mass culture, a unifying influence that affects rural people as well as city dwellers. As the world becomes smaller, media intrude into even the most isolated village, farmers are uprooted and drawn into factories or forced to become rural businessmen, and the process of modernization continues to obliterate the traditional cultures that for so long have been the subject of anthropological investigations.

As do many people who have contact with cultures throughout the world, anthropologists often have an instinctual response against modernization. Many of us have felt that we would like to isolate a village or a community from the rest of the universe, to preserve and maintain the traditions that cannot survive in the modern world. Others have felt that they could not stand against the forces of change, but that they might be able to contribute to an easier transition to modernity for the people with whom they worked. When anthropologists attempt to use what they have learned, to apply their knowledge to some practical end, they are practicing applied anthropology. This is the ul-

come farmers and had to wait for their share of the inheritance. There is a growing trend toward emigration, with young people finding that they cannot practice the skills they have timate test of a science. Can we take what has been learned and use it to alleviate some problem? Can we make knowledge work for us? The rest of this chapter will be devoted to exploring this issue and its many ramifications.

APPLIED ANTHROPOLOGY AND CULTURE CHANGE

Anthropology has been called the most humanistic social science, and for many years there was a debate among members of the profession concerning whether anthropology was not in fact an art, rather than a science. Perhaps this difference of opinion derives from the very beginnings of anthropology as an academic discipline, when anthropologists were just as often interested in expanding their knowledge of the exotic as in applying that knowledge to the betterment of their own society or of the people they studied. It was not until the late nineteenth century, however, that anthropology was considered useful as a science, and government officials began to inquire into the application of anthropological investigations. In Europe, anthropology became the tool of colonial governments, for it was recognized that by gaining greater knowledge and understanding of the native peoples and their cultures, a more efficient colonial policy could be created. Colonial administrators and officials in Africa, Asia and the Pacific applied anthropological insights to local policies (although rarely did they think of themselves as anthropologists), working within the structure of the native culture to achieve their government's aims.

If the people had a strong tradition of hereditary chiefdoms, the colonial government would try to set up an administrative system that maintained the continuity of the line of chiefs, incorporating them into the new administrative order. Where a large migrant labor force was required to support the economic en-terprises of the colonial government (as in the diamond and copper mines in South Africa and the plantations of Latin America), migration was encouraged and even forced in each region in a different manner, depending upon the particular traditions of the native people.

In the United States the early application of anthropological investigations was tied in with the so-called Indian problem toward the end of the nineteenth century. There were various views on how to deal with the Indians—whether to help them assimilate into white society, or force them to maintain their own independent culture and actively prevent them from coming into contact with white society. Given the history of violence in the westward movement, and the frequent and often fanatic hatred of the Indians by some whites, it was not likely that the Indians would be left alone to do as they wished. Nor was it widely proposed that they be forced to maintain their own separate culture and identity, for such independence was feared by many whites. The dominant opinion, and the ultimate policy of the American government, was to facilitate the cultural assimilation of Indians into white society. This was a difficult policy to carry out, however, for it had to be combined with a policy of racial segregation. The task for the government officials, therefore, was to find a way to make the Indians conform to white standards while keeping them from intruding upon white society. Anthropologists employed by the Bureau of Indian Affairs and other government agencies were assigned to study Indian culture and find out how it could be altered most efficiently to speed the process of assimilation.

The American concern with the "Indian problem" continued into the twentieth century, until it was overtaken by the "immigrant problem." Large numbers of Europeans, Latin Americans and Asians poured into the United States, settling mainly in the major cities on the east and west coasts and around the Great

The crowds of immigrants who entered American cities during the early twentieth century were faced with enormous problems in maintaining their own independent cultural values.

Lakes. While immigration was nothing new, the problems that arose in the cities, and especially in the ethnic communities within those cities, were alarming. One need only recall the turbulent situation among warring ethnic groups in Chicago during the Prohibition Era to comprehend the dramatic effect of immigration upon American culture. As specialists in foreign cultures, anthropologists were called upon once again to contribute their insights and knowledge to the solution of the "immigrant problem." In fact, however, very little concrete use was made of the contributions of anthropology to the social problems in America

because of the public officials who distrusted social science and social scientists.

During World War II anthropologists contributed their knowledge of foreign cultures to the war effort. Both Allies and enemies were subjected to the scrutiny of students of culture in the hope of learning more about them, and thus about how to deal with them. Where actual fieldwork was impossible, studies were made through the available literary sources. Ultimately some benefits were derived from this effort; our study of Japanese culture helped in the formulation of a surrender policy for the Japanese in the Pacific that took into account the role of the Emperor, and the strong feelings of loyalty and respect for authority among the soldiers, who identified directly with him. The decision to allow the Emperor to remain in that capacity (though stripped of all his power), and to have him give the order of surrender directly to his soldiers, probably saved countless lives. Had the American army attempted to force a surrender without the order of the Emperor, no doubt many Japanese soldiers who did surrender would have fought to their deaths, ignoring any command of a foreign leader whose authority they did not recognize.

Following World War II the focus of applied anthropology changed once again. Two very important tasks were undertaken by the United States and the Western world in general: the reconstruction of those countries whose losses in the war had been devastating, and the attempts to raise the standard of living in the so-called developing countries of the Third World, where the level of poverty and suffering grow even faster than the already overflowing populations. In both cases, but especially in the latter, anthropologists had valuable information to contribute, and in the years immediately following the war a number of professionally trained anthropologists occupied government positions. The primary concern of the programs instituted in this era was how best to plan and carry out the social and cultural change that was required to build or rebuild the economies and societies of the Third World and war-torn countries. It should not be forgotten that the period following the war was one of political tension and conflict between the capitalist countries of the West and the socialist countries of the East, and Western development programs, especially in the heavily populated Third World, were carried out in a situation of intense competition with similar attempts financed by the Soviet Union. Even today, the foreign aid program of the United States is frequently prompted at least as much by political purposes as by humanitarian goals, which means that what the anthropologist can contribute is usually tempered by the political conditions under which the program is to be carried out.

PLANNED CHANGE

The study of applied anthropology is frequently the study of problems in planned change. The applied anthropologist must start out with some basic assumptions about the people he is working with and the changes he is proposing. First of all, he must assume that something which originates in one culture and is molded to fit the ideals and patterns of that culture will not necessarily be acceptable to people who have a different way of life. Instead, people tend to accept innovations from another culture in bits and pieces, reworking

Planned change concentrates heavily on public health programs. The West African Cancer Research Institute in Senegal specializes in diagnosis and treatment of cancer and thyroid disorders.

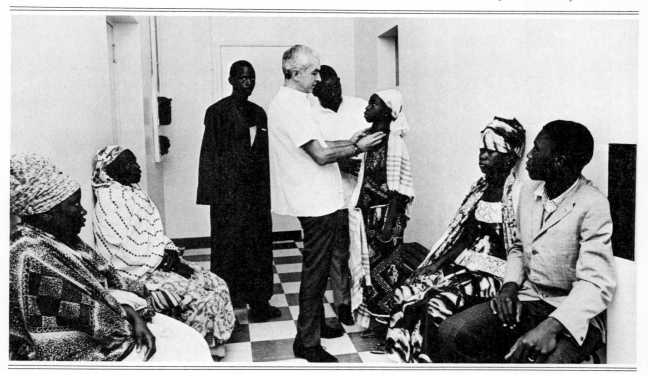

them to fit into their own way of life, discarding aspects of a program that they find objectionable. The result might be that the most important aspect of the program is not accepted, while the more trivial or unnecessary elements are adopted enthusiastically and wholeheartedly. For example, one of the most prominent changes to take place in the early period of self-government of many countries in the Third World is the institution of a national airline. If we examined the way these airlines function in the context of Western society, we would probably conclude that they are "irrational" and "unnecessary." For us, an airline is a means of transportation; in a country with no need for mass air transportation and relatively little wealth to support such a system, it would seem superfluous. Yet we must recognize that the newly emerging countries have borrowed only part of a Western innovation. They perceive the airline as an important symbol of their entry into the modern world, and they have discounted the transportation factor. In this new context we can better understand other functions of a national airline.

Armed with this assumption that innovations must fit a new context, it is the task of the applied anthropologist to see that the program is reworked before it is presented to the people, so that it can be organized in a manner acceptable to them, while at the same time accomplishing the goals of the original plan. There is obviously an ethical question involved in the position of an applied anthropologist. To whom does he owe his allegiance? To the government who pays him to do a job? To the set of values that he holds about what is best for the people he is working with? Or to the people's own values? In a sense, many an applied anthropologist is placed in the role of a counselor whose job it is to convince people to accept something they might otherwise reject. He is required to use his knowledge of their way of life to get them to accept it, by hook or by crook, even if he has to engage in a small-scale con game to accomplish his goal. Yet at the same time the applied anthropologist is placed in such a position because he can operate between two cultures. He is not only aware of how people live in a small community halfway around the world; he is also familiar with the technological advances in the United States and elsewhere. By virtue of his education and knowledge he has a certain responsibility to help those who are less educated and less knowledgable. Certainly there is an ethical question involved in the use of power vested in the anthropologist in such a situation, but if we accept the assumption that there are some basic values we must adhere to in carrying out such programs, then their benefits outweigh accusations of intrusion upon another people and unduly influencing their way of life. Such values include the preference of health over sickness, or the belief that a full stomach is better than an empty stomach, or the right of every individual to an education.

A second assumption made by applied anthropologists is that all change operates within a cultural context. Earlier we defined culture as an integrated system, so that a change in one aspect would have an effect upon others. Consider, for example, what the invention of the automobile has meant to American culture. It has not only facilitated transportation; it has become the focal point of the American economy. People have moved from the cities to suburbs, changing the whole pattern of residence in America from what it was a century ago. With upwards of 40,000 people dying in traffic accidents on our highways each year, most of them still at the age of active reproduction, the population structure of our country has been changed. Farming has become more commercialized, and different crops can be grown and transported to markets more quickly. Recreation patterns have responded to the new method of transportation. And, of course, the automobile has extracted a heavy toll from our environment, polluting the air in our cities and depleting the resources of our land. It is amusing to ask, "What if Henry Ford had known what was going to come of his great invention? Would he still have carried it through?"

But this is precisely the question that the applied anthropologist must ask of himself when placed in a position of evaluating a proposed program of planned change. He knows that there is no such thing as "simple" change—that any change will produce other changes, and that many of those secondary changes will be unanticipated. His job is to try to anticipate as many of them as possible, and to evaluate the overall results of the program, not just the immediate goals. Perhaps after weighing all the relevant factors he can suggest adjustments to head off an undesired consequence, but his responsibility and his ethical duty are always to consider the project in terms of its overall effect upon other people—to reject a program no matter how noble and defensible its goal might be, if the means to achieving that goal cannot be justified. It is especially important in the sense that an anthropologist almost always works with other specialists in programs of planned change, specialists who are not trained to consider the native culture and to plan around it. Someone trained in the mechanics of administration can easily lose sight of the consequences of the program in his striving to complete it most efficiently. It is the anthropologist's responsibility to counsel those who carry out such a program on the price that will be paid in reaching the desired goals, and on alternatives that would avoid such problems while not seriously compromising the overall achievements of the program.

Some programs with which you are probably familiar have taken this approach with great success. The Peace Corps, for example, has adopted a policy of working with the people of

The Peace Corps has been successful largely because it uses many anthropological insights in its work. Here a child is examined at a Peace Corps station in rural Colombia.

Third World countries to solve the problems that they themselves consider serious. Peace Corps volunteers follow closely the basic requirements laid out by Malinowski for anthropological fieldwork that were discussed in Chapter 13. As part of their training and preparation they learn the language of the people with whom they are to work; they live among the people, preferably in the same village or community; they observe the customs of those people and try to fit in with their way of life as much as possible. In short, they do not force their ways upon others, so much as they try to determine what the people want for themselves. While I do not mean to imply that the Peace Corps is totally without its problems, clearly these methods (which have also been adopted by other agencies with similar goals,

Controversy

Anthropological Ethics and the Thai Controversy

In many respects, the ethical questions facing the anthropologist are more complex than those which are faced by other social scientists. As a scientist, the anthropologist is obliged to be as objective and impartial as possible in the cause of his search for truth. As a scientist who studies his fellow human beings, however, he has to make moral decisions. This does not occur regularly among scientists who study stars or molecules. To what extent is the anthropologist accountable for his methods of research and the uses to which his findings are put?

Many anthropologists believe that their job is only to observe and report. In reality, the anthropologist affects the culture he is studying merely by being in it, and his reports may initiate changes which further alter the cultural pattern. Often the anthropologist is torn between his effort to be an objective observer and his temptation to interject his own values. It

might be difficult, for example, for an anthropologist to quietly take notes while culturally accepted infanticide was being carried out. The effort to remain neutral has become increasingly difficult as American and European anthropologists have begun to turn their attention from distant and unfamiliar cultures to the behavioral institutions of their own societies.

Is the goal of anthropology to observe human life on earth as it is or to try to help make it better? In recent years, the American Anthropolgoical Association has been increasingly vocal in its expression of moral positions. The Association has spoken out against the abuse of atomic energy, discrimination based on sex or race, genocide, and chemical warfare. Although some anthropologists argue that the taking of sides on political issues is beyond the scope of their science, the majority maintain that those who study humankind are most qualified and obligated to express their views and to oppose destructive and inhumane social policies. They point out that to say nothing is as significant an act as to say something; to be silent is to contribute to the continuation of the status quo.

The anthropologist is responsible not only to his discipline and to the general public but to the people he is studying as well. He should not deceive them about his aims, exploit them for his personal gain, or betray their confidences. The desire to protect the interests of his subjects often puts the anthropologist in conflict with his sponsors. Almost all research in the social sciences is funded by the government, private business interests, or other institutions which may not share the social scientist's purely objective interest in his work. Should the anthropologist refuse to undertake potentially valuable research if he suspects that his sponsor may apply his findings in a manner not in the best interests of his subjects?

The use of anthropologists in the creation of American military and political strategy has become an especially controversial issue in recent years. The conflict between politics and science is by no means a new problem, however. Franz Boas was chastized by his colleagues in 1919 when he publicly accused several anthropologists of serving as government agents while supposedly conducting scientific research in foreign countries. The ethical issues raised by Boas were raised once again in 1970 when the Student Mobilization Committee to End the War in Vietnam accused American anthropologists sponsored by the United States government of participating in counter–insurgency activities in Thailand. Ultimately, the chairman and another member of the Ethics Committee of the American Anthropological Association resigned when the Association insisted that the investigation of these charges was not the role or function of the Ethics Committee.

According to documentation submitted by the Student Mobilization Committee, the U.S. government hired anthropolgoists and other social scientists to help devise programs to prevent popular rebellion against the oppressive U.S.-backed Thai government. Much of the research conducted by these scientists involved the formation of policies of highly dubious morality. For example, the government observed that food could often be traded for services or information. Anthropologists were asked to discover whether the government's interests would be best served by helping the Thai people to increase their agricultural output or by burning their crops. Anthropologists were also asked to assist in the collection of such data as the location of villages, the ethnic background of the villagers, the names of tribal leaders, the nature of their weaponry, and so forth. As a paid informant, the anthropologist would not only violate his ethical obligation to protect the privacy and anonymity of his subjects but, in effect, he would be serving as a spy for the United States government. Anthropologists were seduced into this role not only by the promise of high salaries and professional prestige but by the suggestion that their work in Southeast Asia could somehow be applied to the solution of social problems in the United States.

During the Vietnam War, the government increasingly relied on social science to achieve its military ambitions. As one American specialist in Thailand observed, "The old formula for successful counter-insurgency used to be ten troops for every guerrilla. Now the formula is ten anthropologists for each guerrilla" (Peter Braestrup, *The New York Times,* March 20, 1967). The anthropologist who chooses not to participate in the deception of his subjects and the collection of data which may be used to harm them may jeopardize his own career and the future funding of the research institution with which he is affiliated. As long as social scientists are dependent upon sponsors, they will be subject to serving the interests of those sponsors. Even the most idealistic social scientist cannot ignore financial and political pressures. How ethical procedures can be followed in the face of such pressures is one of the greatest challenges facing the modern anthropologist.

such as ACTION and VISTA, to name but two) are preferable to those of many earlier planned change programs that operated in complete ignorance of local culture.

BARRIERS AND STIMULANTS TO CHANGE

Books on applied anthropology frequently contain story after story of how a planned change program failed, and how in the analysis of the failure it was discovered that a minor adjustment in the program would have led to improved results, if not total success. George Foster, in *Traditional Cultures and the Impact of Technological Change,* discusses applied anthropology programs in terms of two factors: barriers to change that exist within the traditional cultures, which must be overcome if the program is to succeed; and stimulants to change that can be injected into the program.

In describing the situation in which many applied anthropologists find themselves, Foster cites an ancient Oriental fable:

Once upon a time a monkey and a fish were caught up in a great flood. The monkey, agile and experienced, had the good fortune to scramble up a tree to safety. As he looked down into the raging waters, he saw a fish struggling against the swift current. Filled with a humanitarian desire to help his less fortunate fellow, he reached down and scooped the fish from the water. To the monkey's surprise, the fish was not very grateful for this aid.[1]

The anthropologist who is not aware of the cultural differences to be overcome in instituting a program of planned change might feel very much hurt and surprised, much like the monkey in the fable.

---

[1]George M. Foster, *Traditional Cultures and the Impact of Technological Change.* New York: Harper & Row, 1962, rev. 1973, p. 1.

Barry Evans

George M. Foster
(1913–   ) is active in the field of applied anthropology, and has served in that capacity throughout the world. Traditional Cultures and the Impact of Technological Change *(1962, revised 1973) is a detailed analysis of the barriers and stimulants to planned change encountered by the applied anthropologist in the field. He is also the author of* Applied Anthropology *(1969), and has been instrumental in the development of a program of medical anthropology.*
Foster is also recognized as a leading figure in the rapidly growing field of peasant studies in anthropology. In "What is Folk Culture?" (1953) he raised some important issues concerning the definition of peasants as a valid topic of anthropological investigation.

The anthropologist must recognize that the changes he sees as good and beneficial might not be interpreted as such by the people with whom he is working. If the program is to be a

Leslie A. White *(1900–1975)*
is an important figure in the study
of culture change, and is generally
known as the leader in the revival
of the doctrine of cultural
evolutionism. Although originally
trained in the anti-evolutionist
approach common throughout
American anthropology in the
early part of this century, White
turned to evolutionism after re-
reading the works of Lewis Henry
Morgan. White suggests that ad-
vancement along an evolutionary
scale can be measured according to
the amount of energy a society
harnesses and utilizes, allowing us
to quantify the difference between a
society with a stone-age technology
and a modern industrial society.

success, he must overcome a number of barriers to the change, and this usually means altering the program rather than forcing the
people to alter their way of life. Sometimes this
requires only a minor adjustment to avoid a relatively easily solved problem. For example, in
instituting a rural health program the planners
might begin by offering the services and
medicines free of charge to rural people who
are known to be extremely poor. However, in
many countries, especially among rural peasants who have had a history of exploitation at
the hands of landlords, police and various government officials known collectively as "outsiders," such free assistance is likely to be viewed as
some kind of trick. Why would the government, which has only taken from them in the
past, suddenly develop a humanitarian interest
in the peasants and decide to give them something for nothing? An easy way around this
problem, requiring very little change in the
original plan, is to institute a small charge for
services and medicines dispensed at the rural
health clinic. The fee should be enough to dispel any suspicion that the government might
have something up its sleeve in offering such
services, but it should not be so high as to discourage those people who can least afford it.

Other times the planned change program
might require a drastic reorganization to overcome a barrier to change, and while such major
alterations are certainly not popular with administrators, they are nonetheless necessary if
the program is to have a chance of success. To
continue with our example of a rural health
clinic, in many countries there is a severe shortage of trained medical personnel, but especially of female doctors. At the same time, cultural values of rural peasant women are generally quite conservative. Thus a woman might
not submit to an intimate physical examination
by a male doctor (or her husband might not
permit such an examination, even if his wife
were willing). Given the shortage of female
physicians and the norms of the potential patients, obviously a drastic reorganization of the
program is necessary if it is to reach the majority of the people for whom it is intended. It
might mean that before the program starts
there should be a preliminary effort to train
more women doctors.

Prenatal examinations are often difficult to promote among rural peasant women. Here an expectant mother is being examined by a student nurse from a public health project in Argentina.

Cultural values can act as very strong barriers to change, and it is frequently the task of the applied anthropologist to find a way to present the program of planned change so that it is not perceived as being in conflict with those values. For example, in the United States we tend to place a positive value upon change— any change—for its own sake. We are constantly subjected to advertisements for "new, improved" detergents, foods and almost any other kind of product. Our cars look different every year, as do our clothing styles. One major American company has as its slogan "progress is our most important product." Indeed, it seems we are more willing to accept change than anyone else in the world. And that is exactly the point. In most societies, and especially in nonindustrial areas of the world, people tend to rely just as heavily upon tradition as we do upon change. They feel a strong attachment to the ways of their ancestors, and any attempt to replace their traditions with some newfangled

contraption will be rejected without any consideration for its merit. Thus if he is to be successful in having a program accepted, the applied anthropologist must find some way of introducing it to people so that it will be perceived as compatible with a part of their tradition. Christian missionaries found this out when they learned to work their Christian teachings gradually into the existing system of beliefs of the people, rather than abruptly replacing an entire religious tradition with a new one. The same principle can be applied by anthropologists to other kinds of change.

Other cultural values, such as pride and dignity, can enter into the success of such a program. For example, a program to sell improved seed to farmers in a village in India failed because, although the poorer villagers participated, the wealthier and more influential farmers in the village would have nothing to do with it. The reason, it turned out, was that the best farmers were able to raise enough seed by themselves to feed their families and provide for next year's crop. To buy or borrow seed was a sign that one could not raise a sufficient crop, and for the most successful farmers in the village this would mean a loss of face.[2] Had someone in the program realized this in advance, an alternative could have been worked out, perhaps by trading some of the new, improved seed for some of the old seed from the farmers' last crop. But the assumption that everyone would immediately recognize the value of the new seed ignored the cultural barriers to change in this village. Besides the problems encountered in introducing changes that conflict with basic cultural values, norms, tastes, and the like, there is also a potential series of barriers on what we might term the "social" level—that is, in the area of group relations within a commu-

[2]Morris E. Opler and R. D. Singh, "Economic, Political and Social Change in Villages of North Central India." *Human Organization* 11:2:5–12, 1952.

nity. For example, in many small, tightly knit communities the traditional tasks are carried out in groups so that people interact closely and form strong bonds associated with their work. In a village where there is no running water and no bakery, women will gather together to do their washing at the central fountain or the stream, and they will bake their bread at the communal oven. Facilities such as the fountain and the oven thereby become important not only for their obvious function in these tasks, but also for the opportunity they afford for women to gather together, talk and gossip, and pass the time while doing their work. It might seem to an outsider that an innovation such as piping running water into the home or supplying ovens for each household would improve the standard of living, but for these women it would not improve the *quality* of living. Indeed, it would have the opposite effect, for it would break up an important peer group from which they receive much satisfaction.

Authority is another aspect of the social structure of a community that can serve as a barrier to change. An innovation, if it is to be accepted, must be introduced to those in authority within the community, and their leadership must be seen as an important factor in its overall acceptance. In a village in Peru, several wells were dug to supply water to the villagers. However, the project failed and the villagers did not take advantage of the wells because they were drilled on private land owned by people who were not leaders in the community, and those who did hold high positions of authority were not consulted. As a result, they used their influence to reject the plan.[3]

A third kind of barrier, in addition to cultural and social aspects of the people who are to participate in the program, is what Foster calls a

Mexican mourners light candles in remembrance of their dead relatives.

"psychological" barrier to change. Such problems can frequently be seen as a failure in communication. In an attempt to communicate the nature of the planned change and the proposed benefits, the anthropologist must realize that the message the people receive is not the same as the message he intended to convey. Or, there might be other elements of the program that convey a message to the people without the project administrators ever realizing it. For example, it has been said that Mexican Indians are reluctant to call the priest for the last rites of the Church when a relative is gravely ill, despite the fact that they are devout Catholics.[4] How-

[3]Allan R. Holmberg, "The Wells That Failed." In Edward H. Spicer, ed., *Human Problems in Technological Change.* New York: The Russell Sage Foundation, 1952.

[4]Georgetta Soustelle, cited in Foster, *op. cit.* 1962, rev. 1973, p. 130.

ever, when seen from their point of view, their reluctance makes perfect sense: They have observed from past experience that almost every time the priest is called, the patient dies shortly thereafter. Thus the message conveyed by the Church, which seeks to have all its members receive the last rites before dying, is not the message understood by the Indians.

A similar but more relevant problem for the applied anthropologist deals with the role of the hospital as perceived by the residents of a rural community (or an urban community, for that matter). Usually when people are relatively isolated and hospital care is far away and too expensive for them, they are taken to a hospital only in the most serious cases. As a result, fewer people who enter a hospital survive, for they do not make more casual use of the facilities as do most city dwellers. It is easy to see how such conditions could lead to the belief that a hospital is where someone goes to die, and that confinement (like the last rites of the Church, noted above) should be avoided.

So far it appears as if any attempt to introduce change will automatically be rejected in the face of so many barriers. In part the problem of rejection can be tempered by a thorough study of the subject culture with an eye toward uncovering potential barriers and taking them into account in the planning stage. Yet even the most observant anthropologist will come up against unanticipated barriers, for there will always be unforeseen consequences, new problems that arise after an innovation is introduced. To counter the effects of such barriers, the anthropologist can advocate the use of a number of elements in the program that will stimulate the acceptance of the change, regardless of the potential problems that might be encountered.

We have already mentioned a few such stimulants in other contexts. In some societies, particularly where industrialization has already begun and where consequently Western culture

Women of rural India attend a family planning course conducted by a social worker. Often it is necessary to do more than simply explain how birth control works, as other cultural considerations must be taken into account.

has become a prestige model, many innovations are accepted simply because they are identified with the West, which is synonymous with progress, wealth, and power. Even though people do not perceive a need for latrines or smallpox vaccinations or any similar Western item, they can sometimes be induced to accept them simply because they are a symbol of advancement. While the reasons for the success of the program might not be as valid in the eyes of the administrators, the results are every bit as effective.

Economic gain and competition can serve as stimulants for change. If it can be shown that an innovation will mean more money or a higher standard of living, it is more likely to be accepted. Likewise, promoting competition between individuals, between factions in a community, or even between communities in a region, can often spur people on to accept innovations that they might otherwise have rejected. The competitive instinct can thus be used to overcome the strong tendency on the part of many people throughout the world to cling to their time-tested traditions.

Religious appeal may help to stimulate an innovation, for by appealing to the authority and the tradition of religion one can arouse interest and concern where it might not otherwise exist. If an innovation can be justified by reference to sacred scriptures it has a better chance of being adopted. In one case in India an area of otherwise deserted land was planted with a grove of trees. In an attempt to get the villagers to water the trees and care for them, the grove was dedicated to Krishna, whereby the villagers felt obligated to take care of it.[5] Religion can also be used effectively in promoting education, with the goal of teaching people to read the holy scriptures of their faith.

Finally, it is important to point out that any innovation will have a better chance of success if it can be shown to fit in with already existing cultural patterns. It is important to maintain traditional values, and to adjust the roles of people engaged in the program so that they fit in with the local conditions. It must be recognized that every innovation introduced into a new cultural setting will have to exist in a new context, and no matter how well it might have fit in the culture where it originated, it must be reworked to fit somewhere else. To demonstrate how well it fits can act as a stimulant for its adoption, by overcoming the universal tendency to stick with what is familiar and accept what is new only after a very cautious trial.

---

[5] Albert Mayer and Associates, *Pilot Project India*. Berkeley: University of California Press, 1958.

THE PITFALLS OF PLANNED CHANGE

Throughout the discussion of applied anthropology and the problems that programs of planned change must face, we have stressed the point that by introducing an innovation into another culture we unleash a whole series of changes, not all of which we can predict in advance. Knowing that there will be unanticipated consequences of such actions, the applied anthropologist takes on the additional responsibility of evaluating the program as it progresses, and determining whether its ultimate success will not be at a price that he considers to be too high. If he is lucky he may even anticipate some secondary consequences, and if he is experienced he will apply the results of other similar programs to predict some secondary changes and call them to the attention of those who are running the program.

Anthropologists and others engaged in public health programs have long been aware of the hazards of programs involving dietary change. For example, in an area supported almost entirely by a diet of raw fish, it is known that many people suffer from tapeworms. Thus at first sight it might seem a logical conclusion to introduce a program (including education and the necessary materials) so the people will begin to cook their fish, thus killing the tapeworms before they are consumed. But what about the secondary consequences of cooking fish? We have also learned that where people eat mainly fish and have few additional sources of vitamins, cooking fish can have negative consequences, for cooking lowers the food value of the fish. Thus we might simply be trading the problem of tapeworms for the problem of vitamin deficiency or even malnutrition.

Public health officials in India found that in many villages where cooking was done inside the hut with no chimney and poor ventilation,

These Sudanese children are learning to read in a formal education system.

there was a high incidence of respiratory and eye ailments. They set out to solve this problem, assuming that it would be a simple matter to introduce chimneys and windows and a new kind of stove that would eliminate the smoke from the house. But they did not take into account the secondary consequences of such a change. The huts in many of these villages were made with thatched roofs, and the roofs were infested with wood-boring ants. The high level of smoke, although it caused eye and lung ailments, also kept the ants under control. When a new, low-cost smokeless stove was introduced, the ants began to multiply and ate up the roofs more rapidly. Now this in itself might not seem

serious, except that the cost of a new roof for an Indian peasant is a considerable portion of his income—income that he would otherwise spend to maintain his already meager standard of living. By causing him to replace his roof more frequently, the innovation had the unanticipated consequence of lowering his standard of living in other ways. In effect, he traded respiratory and eye diseases for a poorer diet and fewer clothes, which ultimately also affected his health. Again, the unanticipated consequence was to trade one problem for another. The lesson we can learn from such experiences is not to abandon all hope of helping people, but rather to try to anticipate the consequences of any program of planned change that we intend to introduce, and to look to the experiences of other similar programs in other parts of the world to avoid making the same mistakes over again.

Most applied anthropology has dealt with planned change in the Third World countries, and this is perhaps as it should be. Attempts to spread the wealth and knowledge of the Western world and put them to use in raising the standard of living in other less wealthy countries, helping less fortunate people, have been all too few and infrequent. Thus it is a tragedy when the attempts fail because of the lack of knowledge of foreign cultures, knowledge that anthropologists are better equipped to provide than perhaps anyone else. If anthropology as a discipline is to be criticized, it is not for the role it has played in planned change—the benefits have far outweighed the abuses that have occurred—but rather for its failure to take a stronger stand and to force itself upon programs where no use was made of basic anthropological insights. This is a problem that continues today, and anthropology is still a misunderstood and relatively little-known field, making its use by government and private agencies far less frequent and efficient than it should be.

One Hundred Percent American

Ralph Linton

This short article by Ralph Linton, "One Hundred Percent American," demonstrates the movement of cultural traits and people over the earth's surface during the last few thousand years. We tend to think of change as a recent phenomenon and as having only one direction, from traditional to Western characteristics. We also assume that everything American is a recent invention or discovery. None of these assumptions about culture change or about the origins of our culture are valid.

There can be no question about the average American's Americanism or his desire to preserve this precious heritage at all costs. Nevertheless, some insidious foreign ideas have already wormed their way into his civilization without his realizing what was going on. Thus dawn finds the unsuspecting patriot garbed in pajamas, a garment of East Indian origin, and lying in a bed built on a pattern which originated in either Persia or Asia Minor. He is muffled to the

Reprinted from *The American Mercury*, 40, (1937), pages 427–429. Reprinted by permission of *The American Mercury*, P.O. Box 1306, Torrance, Calif., 90505.

ears in un-American materials: cotton, first domesticated in India; linen, domesticated in the Near East; wool from an animal native to Asia Minor; or silk whose uses were first discovered by the Chinese. All these substances have been transformed into cloth by methods invented in Southwestern Asia. If the weather is cold enough he may even be sleeping under an eiderdown quilt invented in Scandinavia.

On awakening he glances at the clock, a medieval European invention, uses one potent Latin word in abbreviated form, rises in haste, and goes to the bathroom. Here, if he stops to think about it, he must feel himself in the presence of a great American institution; he will have heard stories of both the quality and frequency of foreign plumbing and will know that in no other country does the average man perform his ablutions in the midst of such splendor. But the insidious foreign influence pursues him even here. Glass was invented by the ancient Egyptians, the use of glazed tiles for floors and walls in the Near East, porcelain in China, and the art of enameling on metal by Mediterranean artisans of the Bronze Age. Even his bathtub and toilet are but slightly modified copies of Roman originals. The only purely American contribution to the ensemble is the steam radiator, against which our patriot very briefly and unintentionally places his posterior.

In his bathroom the American washes with soap invented by the ancient Gauls. Next he cleans his teeth, a subversive European practice which did not invade America until the latter part of the eighteenth century. He then shaves, a masochistic rite first developed by the heathen priests of ancient Egypt and Sumer. The process is made less of a penance by the fact that his razor is of steel, an iron-carbon alloy discovered in either India or Turkestan. Lastly, he dries himself on a Turkish towel.

Returning to the bedroom, the unconscious victim of un-American practices removes his clothes from a chair, invented in the Near East, and proceeds to dress. He puts on close-fitting tailored garments whose form derives from the skin clothing of the ancient nomads of the Asiatic steppes and fastens them with buttons whose prototypes appeared in Europe at the close of the Stone Age. This costume is appropriate enough for outdoor exercise in a cold climate, but is quite unsuited to American summers, steam-heated houses, and Pullmans. Nevertheless, foreign ideas and habits hold the unfortunate man in thrall even when common sense tells him that the authentically American costume of gee string and moccasins would be far more comfortable. He puts on his feet stiff coverings made from hide prepared by a process invented in ancient Egypt and cut to a pattern which can be traced back to ancient Greece, and makes sure that they are properly polished, also a Greek idea. Lastly, he ties about his neck a strip of bright-colored cloth which is a vestigial survival of the shoulder shawls worn by seventeenth-century Greeks. He gives himself a final appraisal in the mirror, an old Mediterranean invention, and goes downstairs to breakfast.

Here a whole new series of foreign things confronts him. His food and drink are placed before him in pottery vessels, the popular name of which—china—is sufficient evidence of their origin. His fork is a medieval Italian invention and his spoon a copy of a Roman original. He will usually begin the meal with coffee, an Abyssinian plant first discovered by the Arabs. The American is quite likely to need it to dispel the morning-after effects of over-indulgence in fermented drinks, invented in the Near East; or distilled ones, invented by the alchemists of medieval Europe. Whereas the Arabs took their coffee straight, he will probably sweeten it with sugar, discovered in India; and dilute it with cream, both the domestication of cattle and the technique of milking having originated in Asia Minor.

If our patriot is old-fashioned enough to adhere to the so-called American breakfast, his coffee will be accompanied by an orange, domesticated in the Mediterranean region, a cantaloupe domesticated in Persia, or grapes domesticated in Asia Minor. He will follow this with a bowl of cereal made from grain domesticated in the Near East and prepared by methods also invented there. From this he will go on to waffles, a Scandinavian invention, with plenty of butter, originally a Near-Eastern cosmetic. As a side dish he may have the egg of a bird domesticated in Southeastern Asia or strips of the flesh of an animal domesticated in the same region, which have been salted and smoked by a process invented in Northern Europe.

Summary

Anthropologists of the nineteenth and early twentieth centuries first became interested in culture change as a result of contact with peoples who were different from the Western cultures with which they were familiar. They sought an explanation for these differences, and arrived at an evolutionary theory to account for the apparent change that led to cultural diversity. Then, as anthropology concentrated upon the study of so-called primitive peoples who changed as a result of contact with Western society, they narrowed their field of investigation to the actual processes by which non-Western cultures were transformed through such contact, a process called *acculturation*. Later, they began to see similarities in certain kinds of social movements that arose in contact situations, and focused upon a study of revitalization movements brought about in part by the creation of expectations that could not be met.

More recently, interest has centered upon the process of modernization that has been occurring in Third World countries, where the introduction of industrial economies, the movement of people to cities, and the adoption of Western patterns of behavior have led to major cultural changes. Although these processes frequently occur together, they can also occur independently of one another. The rate of social change throughout the world has also given rise to programs of planned change, in which anthropologists have participated.

Applied anthropology uses the insights gained in the study of other cultures to promote programs of change throughout the world. In the United States, applied anthropology grew out of the concern with cultural differences between whites and Indians, and later became concerned with problems surrounding cultural differences among various immigrant groups.

More recently, anthropologists have contributed to the programs of planned change following World War II.

In any attempt to introduce new cultural elements to people, there will be barriers to change. Values such as modesty, conservatism, pride and even taste, can spell the doom of a program of planned change if they are not taken into account. Authority patterns must be considered, and factions or group dynamics cannot be overlooked in the administration of such a program. Psychological factors such as people's perception of the changes and of their traditional way of life may also serve as barriers to change.

To overcome the barriers to change, the applied anthropologist can call upon stimulants to achieve the aims of the program. Occasionally the changes can be made to appear prestigious in order to get people to adopt them. Economic gain can be a strong motivation for change, as can religious appeal. In every case of change, there will be secondary consequences, many of them unanticipated. It is the role of the applied anthropologist to try to predict these secondary changes, and to plan for them in advance.

Glossary

acculturation A process of culture change that occurs when groups of individuals having different cultures come into continuous first-hand contact.

applied anthropology The use of the knowledge gained in studying other cultures toward the solution of practical problems.

assimilation The process by which a group becomes culturally incorporated into a larger society through contact and the adoption of the larger society's cultural traits.

cargo cult An attempt to adopt new cultural patterns in order for a group to renew their culture, rather than return to traditional ways of life.

folk culture A society characterized by its personalism, smallness, homogeneity and relative isolation.

millenarian movement A revitalization movement in which an oppressed and frustrated people believe in the coming of a new age.

modernization A broad term covering at least economic growth, or industrialization; urbanization; and Westernization.

nativistic movement An attempt to return to the traditional or native cultural patterns and to eliminate alien persons, customs, values, and materials from the culture.

relative deprivation A change over time that leads a group of people to feel deprived relative to some other standard (relative to another group, or to their own past situation).

revitalization movement A conscious process on the part of a people designed to produce change through the renewal of their old cultural patterns and traditions, which have disintegrated due to contact with Western culture.

social mobility The process of moving from one position to another in society, and adopting the appropriate role behaviors attached to the new social position.

syncretism The process of reinterpreting new cultural elements to fit them in with the already existing traditions in a culture.

urbanism The development of cities along with a growth in population size and density. There is usually a specialization of tasks and the division of the work among people trained for special jobs.

urbanization The growth in the size of cities, the number of cities, and the proportion of the population living in urban locations. Urbanization has frequently been associated with the characterization of heterogeneity, impersonalization, and individualism.

Westernization The adoption of cultural patterns characteristic of Western society.

worker-peasants People who have gone to work in factories, but have retained a small agricultural operation on the side.

Additional Reading

Clifton, James A. (editor)

1970 Applied Anthropology: Readings in the Uses of the Science of Man. Boston: Houghton Mifflin.

An excellent collection of articles dealing with applied anthropology, discussing many of the problems and ethical issues raised in this chapter.

Foster, George M.

1969 Applied Anthropology. Boston: Little, Brown.

An expanded analysis of applied anthropology, its methods and goals, which grew out of the original 1962 version of *Traditional Cultures and the Impact of Technological Change*.

Friedl, John

1974 Kippel: A Changing Village in the Alps. New York: Holt, Rinehart and Winston.

A case study of modernization and its effects upon a small village in the Swiss Alps.

Toffler, Alvin

1970 Future Shock. New York: Bantam Books.

The fascinating best-seller dealing with our runaway technology and the failure of the rest of our culture to keep up with it.

Worsley, Peter

1968 The Trumpet Shall Sound: A Study of Cargo Cults in Melanesia. Second Edition. New York: Schocken Books.

The most thorough analysis of Cargo Cults as a response to culture contact. The author traces the history of these movements, and places them in the context of the changing political and economic scene in the Pacific Islands.

chapter nineteen

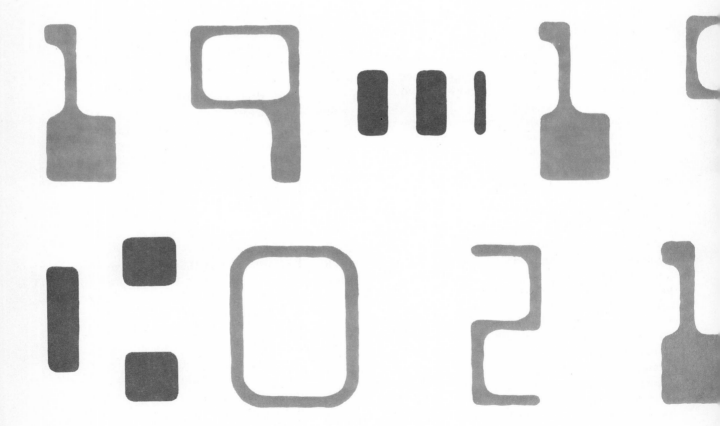

Conclusions/ ANTHROPOLOGY IN THE MODERN WORLD

The challenge for anthropology in the future lies not only in the Third World, but here at home with the problems that beset us today. It is time to abolish the distinction between anthropologists who study foreign cultures and other social scientists who study their own society. We are all students of culture, and if our discipline is to have any validity, it must be applicable to our own culture as well. If we have learned from our study of others, we ought to be able to apply that knowledge to ourselves. We ought to be able to provide some insight into our evolutionary future, to provide an understanding of the complex array of new technologies and new environments with which we are presented daily. We also look forward to anthropology becoming increasingly important in dealing with the cultural differences behind many of the more severe problems in our society, including race relations, sexism, drug addiction, alcoholism and crime. To do this, it is not necessary that every government employee be a trained anthropologist, or that every poverty program be administered by someone with a Ph.D. But it is important that anthropology contribute to our knowledge of the Western world and that anthropologists participate in programs of planned change in the United

Poverty still exists in many parts of the United States.
Welfare payments allow this woman to feed her six children,
but her house has neither water nor electricity.

States as well as other countries. This goal for the discipline of anthropology is the subject of the final chapter of this book.

THE FUTURE: PEOPLE AND TECHNOLOGY

From the time *Australopithecus* first manufactured tools, much of our life style has been in-fluenced by the technology available to us. Over the last hundred years, the vast expansion of our scientific capabilities has been a major force in social change. This trend shows every promise of continuing to stimulate the reorganization of our society. Of all recent inventions the one that hints most strongly at the spirit of things to come is the large-scale electronic computer. This machine has the feel of the future about it, marking an area where evolutionary forces are active and change seems to be particularly intense. It represents a taking-off point, a new direction in the human journey, and its effects promise to be as far-reaching and unpredictable as those of fire.

As a matter of fact, it is the fire story all over again, the sort of story that opens uneventfully, almost in a humdrum manner—and then, slowly at first and later at an accelerating pace, takes on the aspect of a major evolutionary adventure. The first electronic computer was not intended to blaze any trails, and was not regarded as a bold experiment. A development of World War II, it was designed primarily to do something that had been done ever since the invention of guns, to prepare ballistics tables indicating the trajectories of shells for different elevations, wind directions, and so on. Under peacetime conditions such tables had generally been produced by groups of mathematicians working at hand-operated desk calculators, but the war brought a serious shortage of mathematicians and the only alternative was to turn to automatic methods.

Today the computer has become far more than a device for the solution of routine problems. It permits investigators in all fields to deal with problems which would not even have been considered or conceived of in precomputer times, because they would have taken centuries to solve. It permits the doing of things that could never have been done, and thus helps promote basic changes in the nature of research and planning. A new human-machine

Hunting and gathering societies have experienced little technological change, but this does not mean that their cultures are static.

relationship is in the process of being formed, a relationship amounting to a kind of organic union. Computers are strong where we are weak, and weak where we are strong.

The hunting-gathering life did not foster an ability to do arithmetic efficiently. People are sloppy and inaccurate when it comes to working with large numbers and cannot even carry out a moderately difficult series of calculations without making a dozen or more errors. A large electronic computer, on the other hand, may operate for a month and perform billions of calculations before a defective part results in an error. Furthermore, humans work slowly. It would take a mathematician two years to do what a computer does in a minute or so, or a millennium to do what a computer does in an eight-hour day. On the other hand, no machine can yet think creatively in the sense of dealing with novelty, recognizing and discovering and exploring new problems.

The symbiosis between human being and computer takes on a special significance from an evolutionary perspective. The computer serves as an accessory to the brain, a thinking aid built specifically to carry out operations which the brain cannot carry out by itself, logical as well as arithmetical operations. Humans are inclined to view the world in terms of chains of events, to see things as cause-and-effect sequences, a phenomenon reflected in written sentences. Sentences, as formal items each starting with a capital letter and ending with a period, are symbols or models of "linear" approach.

This tendency is another example of living partly in the past. The world of modern *Homo sapiens* is by no means linear, but the world of their prehistoric ancestors was. Most tasks were one-person, one-material tasks like making scrapers, which involved four broad activities in a fixed order: finding a flattish flint nodule, trimming the edges, striking off flakes, and retouching the flakes. Setting a blade in a handle or a spear point in a shaft was somewhat more elaborate, involving more materials and more activities. But any hunter could readily carry out the entire task on his own.

Today's tasks reflect enormously more complicated lives. They require hundreds of materials, thousands of people and activities, hundreds of thousands of parts to be assembled. Furthermore, the essential relationships are not straightforward sequences where one activity leads to another in a simple way; there are lattices and networks and nests of intricately related activities. Activities A and B and C and D may be carried out simultaneously, activity E cannot be started until A and C are completed, F depends on the completion of B and D, G depends on F and A, and so on. Producing a new-model automobile or airplane, a space vehicle or a housing development may require tens of thousands of interdependent activities all of which must be coordinated in flow charts and master plans.

Such problems, problems featuring the interaction of a great many variables, are a sign of the times. They may be found everywhere, not only in factories and on production lines but also in projects involving urban renewal, medical care, crime control and the administration of justice, economic opportunity, and education. The brain alone cannot handle them, but the combination of brain and computer can. The computer, programmed or instructed to apply special mathematical techniques to the analysis of complex systems, enables things to be seen whole. It happens that so far these techniques have been used widely to deal with business and military projects, and not so widely to deal with matters of public welfare. More attention seems to have been devoted to the mathematics of competition and warfare than to the mathematics of cooperative endeavors.

Computers have been developed to serve people, and their duties have been amply publicized. The most impressive are general-purpose machines which do anything they are "told" to do. At any time any one of them may be calculating payrolls or insurance premiums or the orbit of an artificial satellite, checking income-tax returns, simulating a flood or the evolution of a star, predicting election returns, or playing a tournament-level game of chess—depending on the set of instructions, the program, which investigators have prepared for it.

But the computer has already exceeded its role as servant. Upon occasion it may function as an electronic goad, a helpful and necessary and at the same time an upsetting thing which often seems to acquire an impetus of its own. It is not capable of creative thinking. But it forces people to think creatively, perhaps more creatively and precisely than they would if computers did not exist.

The history of the Japan Broadcasting Corporation provides one of the best examples of this effect. The corporation "let a computer into the house" a number of years ago, and the net effect has been a widespread reorganization. The first computer served as an aid to program planners, helping them to schedule shows and allocate studio space well ahead of time. Later, communications were speeded up when it was hooked to half a dozen terminals, including television-type screens on which schedules were displayed for immediate information or revisions. Success along these lines created a demand for still more ambitious plans to coordinate the activities of some 5,000 directors, engineers, and technicians concerned with producing shows—and these plans, in turn, demanded a special control center and other basic changes.

The company now has an entire system of computers, including some 200 terminals, and handles more than 1,800 programs on two television and three radio networks. The system is involved in everything from scheduling programs months in advance to putting programs on the air automatically a fraction of a second before broadcasting time. Among other things, this is the way to cut down on paper work and endless conferences and red tape of all sorts. The use of visual displays has eliminated more than 90 per cent of the 1,800 daily telephone calls and meetings and the 5,000 daily memoranda and reports formerly required to run the business.

This, the first company-wide computer system of its kind, provides a model for research and development in many areas. Organizations in the United States, the Soviet Union and other countries are at work on similar systems to handle their own routines, and it is only a matter of time until larger organizations, including entire industries and government agencies, will proceed along the same course. Computers will bring about radical structural and management changes at these levels as they have already done at the company level in Japan.

They will also bring about a widespread amplification of intelligence. A person at a computer terminal is in effect many times more intelligent than those without a computer at their service. In colleges freshmen sitting at terminals located in classrooms, laboratories and dormitories are already solving easily problems far too difficult for seniors to solve in the days before computers, and the same increase in brain power will continue throughout life. The computer, one of the latest and most remarkable products of human evolution, permits individuals and groups to cope with new complexities of their own making. It is thus actively speeding the process of evolution.

Finally, and this could turn out to be the most significant effect of all, the computer may be used to increase the effectiveness of human adaptation. The brain evolved in times of great physical danger and little social change, but must now cope with times of little physical danger and great social change. Once it was appropriate that ideas and ways of doing things should endure for millennia. But the pace of contemporary developments suggests that the ability to unlearn swiftly is becoming at least as important as the ability to learn swiftly.

In such a context computers may serve as powerful weapons against the persistence of habit, the tendency of people to stay the same as the world changes. Electronic memories are erasable. They can be wiped clean at the flick of a switch and prepared for a fresh start. Computers do not become more and more biased as they age, a distinct advantage in solving new problems.

THE FUTURE: PEOPLE AND THE ENVIRONMENT

While technology has been at the forefront of change in the modern world, humans have yet to develop artificial environments as appropriate for contemporary populations as natural wilderness environments were for prehistoric hunters and gatherers. But that is the job, and a renewed search for such environments is under way. It is characterized by increasing efforts to understand people in groups, grownups as well as children, and to base the design of living and working places on observations of what they do and prefer.

A number of studies indicate the existence of biases that seem to hold for people in many cultures. For example, Dutch investigators find that visitors to parks and other public recreation areas tend to concentrate in transition zones where two different kinds of terrain merge, along seacoasts and the banks of rivers and the edges of forests. At the same time they naturally seek out locations providing some cover at their backs, a cliffside or a sand dune or a dense growth of trees, and in front of them expanses of open space.

Kikuyu women still cultivate their fields with the traditional wooden hoe.

This tendency is made up of many things. There is a feeling for freedom and privacy, a preference for shady spots, and a strong attraction to panoramas and unobstructed views of distant horizons. One thinks immediately of forest-dwelling hominids or prehominids venturing into the plains and ready to dash back into the trees—and later of bands of early hunters living in shelters and caves high on rocky ledges, relatively safe from predators and with a wide view of valleys and grazing animals. Such places offered beauty and security in a world where people were few and bands rarely came across one another.

Today beauty and security must be sought in human-made settings, practically all developed with other things than beauty and security in mind. Humans move about in environments which often promote tension and anxiety and conflict as effectively as if they had been designed for that very purpose. Not long ago a special conference was held in Washington, D.C., to consider "the office building as a current-day artifact in our society . . . not only what an office building is but what it could be—what it should be."

One discussion concerned the headquarters of the Central Intelligence Agency, about as unattractively and unimaginatively designed as most government buildings, only a bit more so, being dominated by gray, narrow tunnel-like corridors 400 feet long and a generally dismal décor to match. In such a "wasteland environment" people tended to dress drably and be suspicious of one another, and on at least one occasion fighting broke out in a corridor. The simple expedient of painting walls and doors with brighter colors produced a notable effect. Employees, female employees in particular, soon began wearing more cheerful and colorful clothing, and there was a marked improvement in morale.

Another case cited at the conference concerned an unplanned experiment in violence, a situation involving two school buildings built at the same site for the same group of high-school students. One building was designed according to the notion that young people naturally tend to rip things apart. It incorporated so-called maintenance-free construction consisting of "hard" spaces enclosed in massive bare walls which are easy to keep clean and difficult to destroy. Vandalism was common in this building; extensive repairs were required. The setting, like most institutional settings, was alien to the student and represented an invitation to trouble.

The other building was based on an entirely different notion of human behavior, the notion that people respond positively to places which they feel belong to them and which incorporate some of the elements of a home setting. The building was designed from the beginning with the needs of the students in mind. There were carpets on the floor, as much for warmth as for appearance, large windows and plenty of light and informal comfortable spaces. Students have done very little damage here.

These examples come as no surprise to architects, who have long been sensitive to the impact of environment on behavior and of behavior on environment. They know how often people have painted walls brighter colors, put in large picture windows, and added extra wings in an effort to undo what has already been done, to humanize the inhumanity built into structures. They also know how much a creatively designed setting, a house or a housing development or a city, can help reduce tensions and contribute to a fulfilling life.

In fact, one of the most original preliminary designs for an urban environment grows directly out of a consideration of human needs and the causes of human anxiety. Christopher Alexander of the University of California at Berkeley starts from scratch with the notion of cities as meeting places and with the most elementary human need of all, the need for intimate contacts with other individuals. He defines an intimate contact as one in which people see one another very often, almost every day, not in offices or public places but under informal and private conditions.

Contacts of this sort were commoner in prehistoric times and in times not long past. Small farms and villages were commoner, and homesteads with large families made up of representatives of three or more generations. Contacts were closer then, although we should guard against becoming overnostalgic because in many cases the contacts were too close and people tended to be ingrown and conservative and to regard all outsiders and outside ideas as alien. But the modern city, for all the oppor-

Extremely conscious of their traditional culture and the environment they live in, these Indians hope to establish a cultural center on land declared surplus by the federal government.

tunities and variety it may offer, produces another form of alienation. Although people may accept or tolerate one another more readily, their contact is often distant and impersonal.

Alexander approaches the problem directly with a plan for a new kind of made-to-order city, including, within densely populated areas, zones designed to encourage certain living features once provided by village-farm settings. He cites psychiatric studies suggesting that mental illness is extra-likely to develop among persons with few intimate contacts or none at all, and that an individual needs at least three or four such contacts. The environment must be organized so that close friends can drop in on one another on the spur of the moment, which means that they should live no more than ten minutes apart. (In today's cities friends or, rather, potential friends usually live half an hour to an hour apart, enough to prevent casual dropping in.)

This general requirement leads to certain design requirements. Each house must be located on a through street for automobile traffic, the street being a thousand feet long at the most and connected with a major traffic artery at both ends. Each house must lie within a hundred yards of twenty-seven other houses, and have private bed-living rooms as well as a transparent communal room which opens on a private garden and can be looked into from the street. Also, the entire residential area must consist of uncluttered countryside and rolling hills.

In all, there are twelve requirements or "geometric considerations," and a residential area that meets them all consists of an artificial landscape, including hills constructed so that the highest and steepest may be nearest the theater-shopping-commercial center of the city, and the lowest and flattest hills furthest from the center. All roads and houses in the area are underground, providing unbroken expanses of countryside. Each house is located so that while its street-side entrance is buried, its garden-side entrance lies on a hill slope and is wide enough to let in daylight for communal and other rooms.

According to Alexander, planners starting with his objective, namely, to create an urban environment fulfilling our need for one another, will arrive at a design that may differ from this one in details but not in any fundamental way. He is also stressing something even more important, a principle that holds, independent of this or that particular plan. Design is no cure-all; it cannot by itself solve problems of mental illness and violence. But it is not arbitrary either. It depends on and is determined to a large extent by human needs.

The fundamental concepts of urban design are bound up with what is known about those needs and will change as more is learned. For example, there are no carefully controlled studies to support the notion that every individual needs three or four intimate contacts or, as a matter of fact, to support most notions about the negative and positive aspects of living in large groups. Most knowledge about the effects of living and working spaces consists of impressions and anecdotes like those discussed at the Washington conference on office buildings.

Solid evidence can be obtained from research on behavior. Cities and communities designed today must take account of tendencies and biases shaped during the course of prehistory, a period representing more than 99 per cent of our time on earth. Until recently this approach has received little more than lip service, partly because architects were preoccupied with other matters and partly because computers and other tools for the analysis of complexity were not widely available. The work of Alexander and others, however, indicates that the approach will play a larger role in planning and building of the future.

THE FUTURE: THE ANTHROPOLOGIST AS ADVISOR

While anthropology has much to contribute to solving the problems of modern society, it is not clear that it will be permitted to do so. In a sense, social science is caught in a paradoxical situation in the 1970s. In this age of specialists, the average person wouldn't dream of pulling his own teeth—he automatically goes to a dentist. We certainly wouldn't think of cutting ourselves open to remove an appendix—we would go to a surgeon. Even for the minor task of unstopping a clogged drain we call a plumber. If our car breaks down, we call a mechanic, and if we get busted, we call a lawyer for legal assistance.

Yet society and its problems are at least as complex as any of these others. Still, if you stop a man on the street, he will almost invariably feel competent to offer his solution to all the social problems that confront us. Every Jane or Joe is an expert on drugs, crime, racial policies, the economy, and our country's military and political foreign policy. How many people call a sociologist when their kids get busted? How many call an anthropologist when a black wants to move into their white neighborhood? More likely they call a real estate agent, who in some neighborhoods doubles as an expert on the racial inferiority of blacks due to his or her long and hard training in the field of not selling them houses.

On a national level, although social scientists are indeed consulted, they are consulted with the foregone conclusion that their findings will fit in with present policies. Scientists are requested to give opinions on scientific matters, not moral questions. On occasion, when their findings do not jibe with official policies, they are summarily rejected. Consider, for example, the commission on pornography established by the late President Lyndon Johnson. It presented him (and later his successor, former President Richard Nixon) with a report concluding that our pornography laws (or better said, our anti-pornography laws) should be relaxed, revised and even eliminated in some cases. Of course, this was an answer based upon the analysis of data subjected to scrutiny by trained social scientists. But it could not be defended when it did not fall in line with the Nixon administration's moral views on the so-called pornography problem. As a result, the report was swept under the rug and no official action was taken. One wonders what the results would have been had the report concluded the opposite!

In case after case, the recommendations of social scientists are rejected because they are found to be politically unacceptable. What are the reasons for this callous treatment of science? As it appears to us, it is rooted in the notion of science as being "value-free." Scholars in this country do research, but are not supposed to make moral decisions. Such decisions are left up to the moralists who "represent" the people. Thus, when scientists come up with conclusions, the moralists still retain the power of veto, which they frequently exercise. And to some degree that is indeed as it should be. Science should not be allowed to impose its findings upon the people without being checked by the people.

But the situation is rarely reversed. No one questioned the moral leaders of the country regarding whether it would be proper to drop an atom bomb. Scientists working on the Manhattan Project, which ultimately produced the bomb in the early 1940s, were asked only to contribute their scientific expertise. They were requested to provide the formula to create an atomic explosion. But when later some of them criticized the way in which this formula was being used, they were branded as incompetent to deal with moral judgments. In those days, the critics were called Communists. No one asked them how to use the bomb—that was a question for another kind of specialist, a military expert.

The notion of a value-free science applies to anthropology as well. It does not mean that the anthropologist has no values, for as we have pointed out throughout this book, all people by virtue of their culture have a set of values that they share to a greater or lesser degree with the remainder of the citizenry. What it does mean is that anthropology as a discipline is not supposed to be oriented toward a particular set of values, but only toward objectivity—truth, if you will. Of course, it is impossible for anthropologists to avoid injecting their own views into their work, and this is why their training is so important, for it teaches them to recognize this cultural bias and to work around it whenever possible. But the reason that science has not played a stronger role in molding society is that anthropologists, along with scientists in other fields, have used the excuse of a value-free science to avoid taking a stand on major social issues, even where their training and experience make them the most likely and most qualified people to do so. We have failed to make a distinction between our scientific investigations and educated opinions, and have hidden behind the wall of objectivity. It is, indeed, as Gerald Berreman has said:

... science has no responsibility, but scientists do. Scientists are people. They cannot escape values in the choices they make or in the effects of their acts.

If we choose to collect our data and make our analyses without regard to their use—leaving that choice to others—we may believe that we are adhering to the most rigorous scientific canons (and hence the most highly *valued* canons) by not intervening in society. But to say nothing is not to be neutral. To say *nothing* is as much a significant act as to say *something*. . . . To be uncommitted is not to be neutral, but to be committed—consciously or not—to the *status quo*. . . .[1]

A Case for Applied Social Science: IQ Tests

Let us offer an example of the use and continued misuse of social science to perpetuate a wrong and harmful myth. Early notions concerning race and intelligence in this country assumed that intelligence was fixed at birth, and could not be affected by an individual's life experience and culture. This notion fit in well with the existing racist theories, for races exhibited different intelligence levels in terms of academic achievement and IQ testing. Moreover, IQ tests were obviously geared to perpetuate this situation, by testing for adherence to middle-class values and standards.

Massive IQ testing began early in the twentieth century. During World War I a large number of draftees were given these tests to determine their aptitudes for various assignments, and in general to rank them according to intelligence, as measured by the standard IQ test. After the war people began to analyze the test results, and especially to sort them out according to race. They found that there was a significant difference between whites and blacks, with whites scoring much higher on the average. These findings were then used to perpetuate the myth of racial inferiority.

Fortunately, more recently these results have been analyzed once again, and we have drawn a different set of conclusions. Until social scientists were willing and able to stand up against the racist onslaught, however, American blacks suffered from the misapplication of so-called scientific findings in an attempt to perpetuate

[1]Gerald D. Berreman, "Is Anthropology Alive? Social Responsibility in Social Anthropology." In *Readings in Anthropology*, Volume 2, Second Edition. Morton H. Fried, ed. New York: T.Y. Crowell, 1968.

the popular notions of white superiority. It has now been demonstrated that IQ tests are not in fact an accurate measure of intelligence, for they ignore many contributing factors affecting the performance of the individual—cultural factors such as home environment, school environment and level of education of parents. Also, it has been shown that the questions on such tests are specifically designed to elicit answers that conform to the standards of middle-class white culture. A black person from a lower-class background would not have the experience necessary to perform well, despite the fact that he or she might have a superior intelligence. For example, a question found on some IQ tests for young children asked them to select from a list of colors the appropriate color for milk. If the child selected the answer "white," he got the question right. Any other answer was marked wrong. However, designers of the test completely ignored class distinctions in grading the examinations. During the Depression, many poor families had to purchase an inferior quality of milk that had a bluish tint. Thus, many ghetto children grew up drinking milk that was not really white, and although their answer "blue" on the test was both accurate and intelligent, they were marked down for it.

In addition to discoveries of the bias of IQ testing and the application of the inaccurate results to racist ideologies, subsequent studies of the results of tests upon World War I GIs indicated that if the scores were looked at from a different perspective, the results could be interpreted in a very different manner. For example, if we compare the scores of Northern blacks and Southern blacks in these tests, we find that the northerners score much higher, indicating a definite environmental factor influencing the test score. Likewise, the longer blacks had been in the North, the higher their scores. Blacks from New York City scored higher in direct proportion to the length of time they had been living there. Thus it could

When the quality of education becomes truly equal for all children, the concept of racial inequality will be eradicated.

not be claimed that Northern blacks scored higher because they were not a representative sample (i.e., the smarter ones migrated north originally). The arguments clearly indicated that there was no genetic factor involved in racial differences in IQ, but rather that it was simply an environmental factor. In fact, when scores were compared even further it was found that New York City blacks scored higher than Alabama whites on the whole, a conclusion that definitely negates racist theories of intelligence that deny the influence of culture upon IQ scores.

One positive result of this approach to the problem of intelligence and race has been the realization that there can be no single standard for measuring intelligence. Rather, it is something that must be seen in its cultural context, for the only true measure of intelligence is one that measures the ability cf the individual to act in a familiar environment. New testing patterns are being developed to get around some of the problems that plagued the old tests. How do you administer such tests to children who have not learned to read quickly or accurately, for example? Is the intelligence test to be a reading test, or should it be more? If it is to be more, then obviously it must not mark the pupil down on his score for poor reading ability. Likewise, language problems can come into play. If we write all tests in a standard white, middle-class vocabulary, surely we must recognize that this puts pupils at a disadvantage who have not learned that form of the English language.

The Tasaday are a completely self-sufficient "Stone Age" tribe recently discovered in the Philippines. What can contact with Western culture offer them? What might they lose through such contact?

CONTEMPORARY USES OF ANTHROPOLOGY

Throughout this book we have pointed out that while society does place constraints upon individuals, it does not prevent them from acting out their individuality within certain limits. And we have also seen that the more diversified and heterogeneous a society becomes, the broader the limits of individuality. Thus, in our own society, with its constitutionally guaranteed freedom of expression, we would expect the greatest amount of individuality—and indeed we find this to be the case. Why, then, are we still plagued with the problem of the selective use and misuse of social science? Why do people disregard so much of the findings of so-cial science in making their decisions about public policies? And why do social scientists, of all people, feel so constrained to keep quiet and watch their findings go unused, or worse yet, misused?

As Peter Berger has pointed out, society provides us with a warm, reasonably comfortable cave in which we can huddle with our fellows.[2] The study of society makes us better able to step out of that cave and act responsibly. An understanding of society is not an alibi for irresponsibility. Understanding racial problems is not an excuse for not doing anything about them—if anything, it is an excuse to do more. At the Nuremburg trials following World War

[2]Peter L. Berger, *Invitation to Sociology: A Humanistic Perspective*. Garden City: Anchor Books, Doubleday, 1963.

Burg-Wartenstein

**Gerald D.
Berreman** *(1930–   )
has conducted fieldwork in the
Aleutian Islands and India, and
has studied social stratification in
India and the United States. He
has published numerous papers
concerning the social responsibilities of anthropology and anthropologists, including "Is Anthropology Alive? Social Responsibility in Social Anthropology"
(1968), "The Peace Corps: A
Dream Betrayed" (1968),
"Academic Colonialism" (1969),
and "Bringing It All Back Home:
Malaise in Anthropology" (1974).
He has been active in the Ethics
Committee of the American Anthropological Association, in an
attempt to provide guidelines for
the profession, particularly in light
of the use of anthropologists by
government agencies in counterin-
surgency research in Southeast
Asia and Latin America.*

II we held Nazi war criminals responsible for
following orders without challenging them, for
not speaking out against injustice. Should we

not charge ourselves with the same responsibility to speak out? In opposing any of the evils
that we see in our own society or anywhere else
in the world, we are exercising our free will.
Only when we refuse to use our free will are we
in danger of losing it.

It is important to point out, in these days
when students are rightly demanding relevance
in their education, some examples of how social
science has been made relevant in the past, and
how it can continue to be applied to present
and future problems. It should also be emphasized that it does not take a Ph.D. to make a
valid point, or to claim the right to apply an
understanding of how society works to the solution of its problems. We have already demonstrated how with the proper approach to the
understanding of racial differences and associated economic and environmental differences, social science has been able to prove the
myth of racial inferiority totally false. The
exploitation of this myth still continues, unfortunately, but at least it is becoming recognized
for what it is, a totally unscientific and un-
documented proposition based on fear rather
than fact.

Social science has, in recent years, also dealt
with deviance, ranging from such mundane
things as divorce to more hotly contested issues
such as homosexuality. The effect has been to
show that deviance is not, as the moralist sees it,
a vice among a handful of degenerates, but a
fairly common phenomenon among all strata
of the population. When Kinsey published his
famous statement that 10 per cent of all males
in the United States had engaged in some type
of homosexual activity sometime during their
life, we were forced to take a more realistic view
of homosexuality in our society. Despite the fact
that such "deviant" behavior was apparently
quite common, until Kinsey's report there was
no attempt to seek legitimation from the rest of
society on the part of homosexuals, for the prevailing attitudes in our country would not have

allowed them to have their say. However, with the growing awareness of homosexuality has come a growing acceptance of it—slow, to be sure, but increasing nonetheless. Major changes in our legislation, for example, are a testimony to the changing attitudes of the American people toward homosexuality. And it is refreshing to note that anthropology has made important contributions to the growing understanding of deviant forms of behavior. Studies by anthropologists have pointed to some of the most bizarre practices known to us, and for many years these descriptions were valued more for their curiosity than for their scientific contribution to the understanding of human behavior. But as we become more aware of what is acceptable in different cultures around the world, we become more tolerant of what was formerly unacceptable in our own society. We become less demanding about the absolute validity of our own way of life and the exclusion of any other way that does not follow our moral code exactly.

In recent years social scientists have been able to demonstrate that many of the moral judgments that we, the people, make about our way of life are based not upon fact, but upon fiction. One of the clearest examples of this is in the argument over the value of capital punishment as a deterrent to crime. Study upon study has indicated that capital punishment does not in fact act as a deterrent to the crimes for which it can be enacted, yet the popular misconception continues. It has been argued over and over again that a person who knows that he or she faces death for committing murder will stop short of killing someone. Yet the facts do not bear out this argument. A recent article in *The New York Times* reported:

The abolition of the death penalty in Canada on December 29, 1967, failed to bring any major increase in the number of murders, according to Government statistics. The figures instead show fairly even increases in years since 1961, in the years both before and after the death penalty was abolished.[3]

By bringing such evidence to public attention, social scientists may be able to turn the energies of the judicial system and the legislatures away from the argument over capital punishment, which in the long run is not productive, and toward the question of how to reform our courts and penal system so that they are more effective in dealing with crime.

These are but a few examples of the potential of social science in understanding current problems. We hope that in reading this book you have learned the values of the comparative approach that anthropology contributed to the social sciences. You have seen that behavior in your own society is just as conventional as anywhere else, and that in the eyes of a person from another culture it can be just as bizarre. It is right or wrong because we define it as such, but there are no absolute standards. All behavior exists in a cultural context. Thus if we can learn to be tolerant of people in other cultures, we should also learn to be tolerant of different kinds of people in our own culture.

It is also the task of the social scientist to point out the causes of contemporary problems, and to set about solving them. From what you have learned about your own society and others, you are better able to identify the causes of these problems. But with that knowledge goes a responsibility to take action. In the words of the late sociologist C. Wright Mills:

If human reason is to play a larger and more explicit role in the making of history, social scientists must surely be among its major carriers. For in their work they represent the use of reason in the understanding of human affairs; that is what they are about.[4]

[3]*The New York Times.* January 21, 1973, p. 16.
[4]C. Wright Mills, *The Sociological Imagination.* New York: Oxford University Press, 1959, p. 179.

One final word. The beauty of our society is that it allows freedom of expression. Dissent could not exist in a totalitarian state, and whether we agree with what a person says, we all believe in his or her right to say it. By that fact alone we must strive all the harder to identify and correct the sources of contemporary problems, even though the cause might lie in the very democratic institutions that form the backbone of our society. A phrase we often hear, or read on bumper stickers or bathroom walls, is: "America—Love It Or Leave It." It is indeed a hollow phrase. It is like a child who has been caught misbehaving saying to his parent, "If you love me you will not spank me." When did love ever preclude striving to make things better? Patriotism and acquiescence cannot possibly be equated today. In fact, silence or blind adherence are perversions of patriotism. The task of the social sciences in this sense becomes very clear. For it is as Edmund Burke said: "The only thing necessary for the triumph of evil is for good men to do nothing."

Additional Reading

Berger, Peter L.
1963   Invitation to Sociology: A Humanistic Perspective. Garden City, N.Y.: Anchor Books, Doubleday & Company.

A sensitive and insightful look at sociology, and social science in general, from the point of view of how it can be meaningful in the context of modern social conditions.

Berreman, Gerald D.
1968   Is Anthropology Alive? In Morton Fried (editor), Readings in Anthropology, volume 2, pp. 845–857. New York: T.Y. Crowell.

The author raises some important questions about the role of anthropology and the anthropologist in the wider society.

Hymes, Dell (editor)
1972   Reinventing Anthropology. New York: Random House.

A stimulating and controversial collection of papers dealing with some of the most hotly debated issues in anthropology today.

Weaver, Thomas (editor)
1973   To See Ourselves: Anthropology and Modern Social Issues. Glenview, Ill.: Scott, Foresman.

A collection of articles dealing with the problems of anthropology in the modern world, especially the way the discipline relates to major social and political issues of the day.

CREDITS

108/Courtesy of The American Museum of Natural History
109/Courtesy of The American Museum of Natural History
112/Henry De Lumley
113/From Pfeiffer, *ibid.*
114/Stuart A. Altmann
116/From Pfeiffer, *ibid.*
118/Irven DeVore
119/F. C. Howell
121/Courtesy of The American Museum of Natural History

Chapter 6
129/Zdenek Burian
130/George Schaller
132/F. C. Howell
136/Irven DeVore
137/J. A. Ambrose
139*B*/Irven DeVore
139*T*/National Geographic Society
141/Courtesy of The American Museum of Natural History
143/John Nance, Panamin/Magnum
145/Irven DeVore
146/Timothy Ransom, Woodfin Camp

Chapter Seven
156/Revil Mason
157/Courtesy of The American Museum of Natural History
159/Courtesy of The American Museum of Natural History
160/Courtesy of The American Museum of Natural History
161*R*/Wide World Photos
161*L*/F. C. Howell
163/Henry De Lumley
164*T*/From Pfeiffer, *ibid.*
164*B*/Richard Gould
169*T*/From Pfeiffer, *ibid.*
169*B*/From Pfeiffer, *ibid.*
171/Courtesy of The American Museum of Natural History

Chapter Eight
179/Zbigniew Rajchel & Wanda Steslicka-Mydlarska, Warsaw University, Poland
180/Courtesy of The American Museum of Natural History
181/Courtesy of The American Museum of Natural History
182/Prof. Henry De Lumley
183/Courtesy of The American Museum of Natural History
184/Zdenek Burian
185/Zdenek Burian
188/Courtesy of The American Museum of Natural History
189/Zdenek Burian
190/Smithsonian Institution
191/Smithsonian Institution
192/*Science* magazine; Clay P. Butler, U.S. Naval Radiological Defense Laboratory, San Francisco

Chapter Nine
200/Courtesy of The American Museum of Natural History
202/François Bordes
204/François Bordes
208/Vic Cox, LSBL Foundation
210/From Pfeiffer, *ibid.*
212/Don E. Crabtree
213*L*/Don E. Crabtree
213*R*/Courtesy of The American Museum of Natural History
215/Richard Gould
217/Courtesy of The American Museum of Natural History

Chapter Ten
225/Courtesy of The American Museum of Natural History
226/From Pfeiffer, *ibid.*
227*TL*/Don E. Crabtree
227*BL*/Don E. Crabtree
227*TR*/Zdenek Burian
229/From Pfeiffer, *ibid.*

231/Harvard University
232/Leslie Freeman
233/Courtesy of The American Museum of Natural History
234/Courtesy of The American Museum of Natural History
235/Zdenek Burian
236/Courtesy of The American Museum of Natural History
241/Wide World Photos
242/Courtesy of The American Museum of Natural History
245/Joe Ben Wheat
246/Courtesy of The American Museum of Natural History
247/Courtesy of The American Museum of Natural History

Chapter Eleven
263/R. A. and B. T. Gardner
264/R. A. and B. T. Gardner
265/R. A. and B. T. Gardner
273/Science Museum, London

Chapter Twelve
285/Cornell Capa, Magnum
286/Irven DeVore
287/Leo Vjals, Frederick Lewis, Marc & Evelyne Bernheim, Woodfin Camp
288*T*/United Nations, Jerry Frank DPI
288*B*/Richard Gould
289/George Rodger, Magnum
290/Nicholas Blurton Jones
291*T*/Irven DeVore, Anthro-Photo
291*B*/Dennis Stock, Magnum
292/From John Friedl, *Cultural Anthropology.*
N.Y., Harper & Row, 1976.
294/Culver Pictures Inc.
295/Irven DeVore, Anthro-Photo
298/Courtesy of The American Museum of Natural History
301/Culver Pictures Inc.
303/Margaret Mead, *Blackberry Winter*

Chapter Thirteen
320/Lee, Anthro-Photo
321/John Friedl
322/Wide World Photos
323/Nat Norman, Frederic Lewis
324/Shostak, Anthro-Photo
328/Elliott Erwitt, Magnum
329/Hubertus Kanus, Rapho/Photo Researchers
331/Courtesy of The American Museum of Natural History
333/Kal Muller, Woodfin Camp
334/The University of Chicago Press
335/Arnold Katz
336/Napoleon A. Chagnon
337/Rene Burri, Magnum
338/Thomas Hopker, Woodfin Camp
339/Wide World Photos
341/Eugene Gordon, Taurus
342/Courtesy of The American Museum of Natural History
344/Courtesy of The American Museum of Natural History

Chapter Fourteen
354/United Nations
355/Tierpark Hellabrunn, Photo Researchers
356*L*/Wide World Photos
356*R*/The New York Public Library
357/General Motors
360/Wide World Photos
361/Bill Powers DPI
362/Magnum
363/Wide World Photos
364/Wide World Photos
365/Wide World Photos
367/Maxwell Coplan, DPI
372*L*/Fujihira, Monkmeyer
372*R*/Eugene Gordon, Taurus
375/Harriet Arnold, DPI
376/Wide World Photos
377/Leonard Lee Rue III, Monkmeyer
379/Ms. Magazine

Chapter Fifteen
388/From Friedl, *ibid.*

389/Culver Pictures
390/From Friedl, *ibid.*
391/From Friedl, *ibid.*
393/New York Public Library
394/Thea Detschek, DPI
397/Elliott Erwitt, Magnum
398/Rothstein, United Nations
399/Marc & Evelyne Bernheim, Woodfin Camp
400-401/The Bettmann Archive
402/Photographic Collection, Univ. Museum, Phila.
407/Wide World Photos
408/Anna Kaufman Moon, Frederic Lewis
409/Bernard Pierre Wolff, Photo Researchers
411/Marilyn Silverstone, Magnum
414/Bettman Archive

Chapter Sixteen
427/George Holton, Photo Researchers
428/George Roos, DPI
429/Rhoda Galyn, Photo Researchers
430/Abbott, Frederic Lewis
431/Wide World Photos
432/Bruce Roberts, Rapho/Photo Researchers
433/Jan Lukas, Rapho/Photo Researchers
436/Barbara Kirk, Peter Arnold
438/American Stock Photos, Frederic Lewis
440/Ewing Galloway
441/Irven DeVore
442/The New York Public Library
443/Odette Mennesson—Rigaud, Photo Researchers
444/Ted Grant, DPI
446/Courtesy of The American Museum of Natural History

Chapter Seventeen
456/Raghubir Singh, Woodfin Camp
457/United Nations
458/John Friedl
459/From Friedl, *ibid.*
460/Courtesy Harcourt Brace Jovanovich, Inc.
461/R. W. Young, DPI
465/United Nations

466/Courtesy of The American Museum of Natural History
468/Hubertus Kanus, Rapho/Photo Researchers
470/George Rodger, Magnum
473/Karl Heider
477/UPI
478/Beryl Goldberg

Chapter Eighteen
491/R. S. Virdee, Frederic Lewis
492/Eugene Ray
493/George Rodger, Magnum
494/Courtesy of The American Museum of Natural History
495/Marc & Evelyne Bernheim, Woodfin Camp
496/Richard Gould
498/Mark Chester, Monkmeyer
499/David Campbell, Photo Researchers
501/Paul Conklin, Monkmeyer
503/Sam Falk, Monkmeyer
504/Marc & Evelyne Bernheim, Woodfin Camp
506/John Friedl
507/John Friedl
508/John Friedl
510/J. Jay Hirz, Frederic Lewis
511/United Nations
513/Francis Laping, DPI
516/Barry Evans
517/Phillip C. Davis
518/United Nations
519/Mexican National Tourist Council
520/United Nations
522/George Rodger, Magnum
523/Beryl Goldberg

Chapter Nineteen
530/Arthur Tress, Photo Researchers
531/Africa Pix, Peter Arnold
534/Marc & Evelyne Bernheim, Woodfin Camp
535/Wide World Photos
539/Jan Lukas, Rapho/Photo Researchers
540/John Nance, Panamin/Magnum
541/Burg-Wartenstein

INDEX

A

Abattoir, 160-62, 175
Aberle, David, 498-99
Abri Pataud (site), 230, 231
Abstract thinking, new stage in
    development of, 234
Acculturation, 490-94
    and Caribbean culture, 492-94
    defined, 490, 526
    and Plains Indian culture, 491-92
Achieved status, 363, 369, 372, 384
ACTION (organization), 513
Adaptation, 22
Adornment, bodily, 287-88
Aegyptopithecus, 40, 71; *see also*
    Apes
Affinal relations, 388, 393, 421
Age
    age grading, 452
    of lineage of *Homo sapiens,* 90-91
    at marriage, 411-12
    stratification by, 376
Agnew, Spiro, 366
Alexander, Christopher, 535, 536
Altamira (site), 240-41
Ambrona (site), 163, 165, 168, 170
Ambrose, Anthony, 137
American Anthropological Associa-
    tion, 514, 515
"American historical school," 299
American Indians
    concern with problems of, 509
    studies of, 295, 298
    and studies on diffusion of cul-
        ture, 299
    tool-making skills of, 212
    See also Plains Indians; *and*
        specific tribes
American Sign Language (ASL),
    263-65, 279
Amiens (site), 182
Analytic image, 340, 351

Animism, 429-30, 452
Anthropological genetics, defined, 8
Anthropological linguistics, defined,
    13-15, 23; *see also* Language
Anthropology
    anthropologists as advisors, 537-
        40
    contemporary uses of, 540-43
    defined, 3-6, 22
    future for, 529-43
    See also Applied anthropology;
        Cultural anthropology
Antigens, defined, 31, 46
Apes
    defined, 46
    first, 40-42
    focus on, 68-71
    See also specific species of apes;
        for example: Baboons; Chim-
        panzees
"Apollonian" culture, 301
Applied anthropology
    and barriers and stimulants to
        change, 516-21
    cultural change and, 509-11
    controversy over, 514-15
    defined, 508-9, 526
    and pitfalls of planned change,
        521-22
    planned change and, 511-13, 516
Arapesh (people), 373
Arbitrariness in sound and
    meaning, 280
Archeological sites
    excavating, 157-65
    location of, 156-57
Archeology (prehistory)
    defined, 9-13, 23
    focus on relationship between
        other fields and, 172-74
Arey-sur-Cure (site), 230, 242
Art movement, first, 237-43
Ascher, Robert, 255, 258, 259

Ascribed status, 363, 364, 369, 372-
    73, 384
Assimilation, defined, 526; *see also*
    Modernization; Westernization
Aurignacians
    tool kit, 230
    tools and shelters of, 231-33
    tradition, defined, 251
Australopithecus, 57, 77-103, 105,
    106, 125, 161
    controversy over species of, 82-83
    culture of, 155
    diet of, 118-20
    estrus among, 141
    evolution of, 116
    hunting by, 132; *see also* Hunting
        and gathering
    life of, 87-89
    migration of, 115
    outside Africa, 112
    predation and, 122-24
    reinterpreted, 89-91
    scavenging by, 129
    sexual dimorphism in, 111
    vocal tract of, 268
Australopithecus africanus, 79,
    80-83, 89, 99-101, 122, 188
    cranial capacity of, 115, 116
Australopithecus boisei, 86, 89-90
Australopithecus robustus, 82, 84,
    86, 89, 100, 101, 123, 188
Authority, marriage and, 408-9
Axes, oldest ground stone, 246;
    see also Hand axes; Tools
Azande (people), 444

B

Baboons, 41
    behavior of, 93-97
    canine display by, 55, 58
    defined, 46

549